The Best Test Preparation and Review Course for the

FE/EIT

Fundamentals of Engineering : AM Exam

Edited by
Moisey Gutman, Ph.D.
Former Senior Research Engineer, Central Scientific and Research Institute Gidropribor
St. Petersburg, Russia

Nesar U. Ahmed, Ph.D.
Assistant Professor of Civil Engineering
Alabama Agricultural & Mechanical University
Normal, AL

Amir Al-Khafaji, Ph.D.
Chairperson & Professor of Civil Engineering
Bradley University, Peoria, IL

S. Balachandran, Ph.D.
Chairperson & Professor of Industrial Engineering
University of Wisconsin–Platteville, Platteville, WI

John M. Cimbala, Ph.D.
Assistant Professor of Mechanical Engineering
Pennsylvania State University, University Park, PA

Leroy Friel, Ph.D., P.E.
Professor of Engineering Science
Montana College of Mineral Science & Technology
Butte, MT

Victor Gerez, Ph.D., P.E.
Chairperson & Professor of Electrical Engineering
Montana State University, Bozeman, MT

Ted Huddleston, Ph.D., P.E.
Chairperson & Professor of Chemical Engineering
University of South Alabama, Mobile, AL

Raouf A. Ibrahim, Ph.D., P.E.
Professor of Mechanical Engineering
Wayne State University, Detroit, MI

Autar K. Kaw, Ph.D.
Assistant Professor of Mechanical Engineering
University of South Florida, Tampa, FL

Siripong Malasri, Ph.D, P.E.
Associate Professor of Civil Engineering
Christian Brothers University, Memphis, TN

Michael R. Muller, Ph.D.
Associate Professor of Mechanical & Aerospace
Engineering
Rutgers University, Piscataway, NJ

Enuma Ozokwelu, Ph.D., P.E.
Advanced Research Chemical Engineer
Eastman Kodak Chemicals Company, Kingsport, TN

Ralph Pike, Ph.D., P.E.
Professor of Chemical Engineering
Louisiana State University, Baton Rouge, LA

Yeshant K. Purandare, Ph.D.
Chairperson & Professor of Chemistry
State University of New York–College of Technology
Farmingdale, NY

Gautam Ray, Ph.D.
Associate Dean of the College of
Engineering & Design
Florida International University, Miami, FL

Nasser-Eddine Rikli, Ph.D.
Professor of Electrical Engineering
Polytechnic University, Brooklyn, NY

Jerry W. Samples, Ph.D., P.E.
Associate Professor of Civil & Mechanical Engineering
United States Military Academy, West Point, NY

Larry Simonson, Ph.D.
Associate Professor of Electrical Engineering
South Dakota School of Mines & Technology
Rapid City, SD

Marcia Sullivan
Electrical Engineer
Willow Software, Inc., Selden, NY

A. Lamont Taylor, Ph.D.
Chairperson & Professor of Chemical Engineering
University of Utah, Salt Lake City, UT

Dev Venugopalan, Ph.D.
Associate Professor of Materials
University of Wisconsin–Milwaukee, Milwaukee, WI

Nikolay G. Zubatov, Ph.D.
Professor of Mechanical Engineering
Purdue University–Calumet, Hammond, IN

Research & Education Association
61 Ethel Road West
Piscataway, New Jersey 08854

The Best Test Preparation & Review Course for the Fundamentals of Engineering/Engineer-in-Training AM Exam

Printed in the United States of America

Library of Congress Control Number 2003101627

International Standard Book Number 0-87891-077-8

REA® is a registered trademark of Research & Education Association, Inc. Piscataway, New Jersey 08854.

ABOUT RESEARCH & EDUCATION ASSOCIATION

Founded in 1959, Research & Education Association is dedicated to publishing the finest and most effective educational materials—including software, study guides, and test preps—for students in middle school, high school, college, graduate school, and beyond.

REA's Test Preparation series includes study guides for all academic levels in almost all disciplines. Research & Education Association publishes test preps for students who have not yet completed high school, as well as high school students preparing to enter college. Students from countries around the world seeking to attend college in the United States will find the assistance they need in REA's publications. For college students seeking advanced degrees, REA publishes test preps for many major graduate school admission examinations in a wide variety of disciplines, including engineering, law, and medicine. Students at every level, in every field, with every ambition can find what they are looking for among REA's publications.

Unlike most test preparation books—which present only a few practice tests that bear little resemblance to the actual exams—REA's series presents tests that accurately depict the official exams in both degree of difficulty and types of questions. REA's practice tests are always based upon the most recently administered exams, and include every type of question that can be expected on the actual exams.

REA's publications and educational materials are highly regarded and continually receive an unprecedented amount of praise from professionals, instructors, librarians, parents, and students. Our authors are as diverse as the subject matter represented in the books we publish. They are well-known in their respective disciplines and serve on the faculties of prestigious high schools, colleges, and universities throughout the United States and Canada.

ACKNOWLEDGMENTS

In addition to our authors, we would like to thank the following: Larry B. Kling, Manager, Editorial Services, for his overall guidance, which brought this revised edition to completion; Catherine Battos for coordinating editorial development of this edition; Nicole Mimnaugh for directing production of the first edition; Gary J. Albert for coordinating development of the first edition; Mark Zipkin for his editorial contributions; and Wende Solano and Network Typesetting, Inc., for typesetting the original manuscript and this revised edition, respectively.

We would like to extend special gratitude to Moisey Gutman, Ph.D., former Senior Research Engineer, Central Scientific and Research Institute Gidropribor, St. Petersburg, Russia, for his extensive editorial contributions to ensure technical accuracy and conformance with NCEES exam guidelines.

Christine Saul, Senior Graphic Designer, designed the cover.

Pam Weston, Production Manager, ensured the book's fitness for production.

CONTENTS

FE/EIT

Fundamentals of Engineering: AM Exam

Independent Study Schedule

STUDY SCHEDULE

The following is a suggested eight-week study schedule for the Fundamentals of Engineering: AM Exam. You may wish to condense or expand the schedule depending on the amount of time remaining before the test. Set aside some time each week, and work straight through the activity without rushing. By following a structured schedule, you will be able to complete an adequate amount of studying, and be more confident and prepared on the day of the exam.

Week 1	Acquaint yourself with this FE: AM Test Preparation book by reading the first two chapters: "You Can Succeed on the FE: AM Exam" and "How to Study for the FE: AM Exam." Take Practice Test 1. When you score the test, be sure to look for areas where you missed many questions. Pay special attention to these areas when you read the review chapters.
Week 2	Begin reviewing chapters 3 and 4. As you read the "Mathematics" and "Electrical Circuits" chapters, try to solve the examples without aid of the solutions. Use the solutions to guide you through any questions you missed. Use the review problems at the end of the chapter to reinforce the concepts you just studied. You may want to leave the last two or three review problems for an overall review at a later date.
Week 3	Study and review chapters 5 and 6. Take notes as you read the chapters; you may even want to write concepts on index cards and thumb through them during the day. As you read the "Statics" and "Dynamics" chapters, try to solve the examples without the aid of the solutions. Use the solutions to guide you through any questions you missed. Leave the last two or three review problems for your final review.
Week 4	Review any notes you have taken over the last few weeks. Study chapters 7 and 8. As you read the "Mechanics of Materials" and "Chemistry" chapters, try to solve the examples without the aid of the solutions. Use the solutions to guide you through any questions you missed. Save some review problems for a final review.

Week 5	Study chapters 9 and 10 while continuing to review your notes. As you read the "Computers" and "Thermodynamics" chapters, try to solve the examples without the aid of the solutions. Use the solutions to guide you through any questions you missed. Continue to leave a few review problems for your final review.
Week 6	Study chapters 11 and 12. As you read the "Fluids" and "Material Science/Structure of Matter" chapters, try to solve the examples without the aid of the solutions. Use the solutions to guide you through any questions you missed. Remember to save a few review problems for your final review.
Week 7	Study chapters 13 and 14. As you read the "Engineering Economics" and "Ethics" chapters, try to solve the examples without the aid of the solutions. Use the solutions to guide you through any questions you missed. Remember to leave a few review problems for your final review.
Week 8	Take Practice Test 2. When you score the test, be sure to look for any improvement in the areas that you missed in Practice Test 1. If you missed many questions in any particular area, go back and review that area. Take Practice Test 3 and record your improvements. Again, return to the review chapters of any areas in which you are weak. Be patient and deliberate as you review; with careful study you can only improve.

FE/EIT

Fundamentals of Engineering: AM Exam

CHAPTER 1

You Can Succeed on
the FE: AM Exam

CHAPTER 1

YOU CAN SUCCEED ON THE FE: AM EXAM

By reviewing and studying this book, you can succeed on the Fundamentals of Engineering Examination Morning Session. The entire FE Exam is an eight-hour, supplied-reference exam split into AM and PM sessions lasting four hours apiece; the morning session is common to all engineering disciplines, while the afternoon session is offered in five disciplines. Because the FE was formerly known as the EIT (Engineer-in-Training) Exam, many aspiring engineers know it today as the "FE/EIT."

The purpose of REA's *The Best Test Preparation & Review Course for the FE: AM Exam* is to prepare you sufficiently for the morning portion of the FE Exam. Our book does this by providing you with 12 review chapters—each of which includes sample problems—and three full-length practice tests. Our review chapters and practice tests have been crafted by experts on the FE to reflect the scope and difficulty level of the actual FE: AM Exam. In accordance with the move by the National Council of Examiners for Engineering and Surveying (NCEES) to all-metric AM exams, we have gone all-metric (with the necessary exception of a few problems). You'll find that our topical reviews are rich in examples that feature thorough, step-by-step solutions. REA's practice tests enable you to completely simulate the FE test-taking experience while providing the added value of detailed explanations for every answer. While availing yourself of either the reviews or the practice tests alone would surely be helpful, we strongly recommend using the two approaches in tandem.

ABOUT OUR AUTHORS

In order to provide review material for you that properly captures all subjects and subtopics covered on the actual FE: AM Exam, every chapter in this book has been carefully prepared by text experts in various fields of engineering. Our authors and editorial review board have thoroughly examined and researched the mechanics of the FE: AM Exam to ensure that our book is accurate, calibrated to the correct difficulty level, and relevant to the FE—from start to finish. Our experts, most of whom are P.E.'s and Ph.D.'s, have been widely published and are highly regarded both within and outside academia, holding positions at leading U.S. colleges and universities and in private industry.

ABOUT THE TEST

The Fundamentals of Engineering Exam is one part in the four-step process toward becoming a professional engineer (P.E.). It is administered by NCEES and is offered twice a year, on Saturdays in April and October. Graduating from an approved four-year engineering program and passing the FE qualifies you for certification as an Engineer-in-Training or an Engineer Intern. The final two steps towards licensing as a P.E. involve completion of four years of additional engineering experience and passing the Principles and Practices of Engineering (PE) Examination, which NCEES also administers. Registration as a professional engineer is deemed both highly rewarding and beneficial in the engineering community.

To register for the FE, contact your state's Board of Examiners for Professional Engineers and Land Surveyors. To find the licensing board in your state and to get information on the exams, contact NCEES:

> National Council of Examiners for Engineering and Surveying
> P.O. Box 1686
> Clemson, SC 29633-1686
> Phone: (800) 250-3196
> Website: http://www.ncees.org

TEST FORMAT

The FE features two distinct sections. One section, the FE: AM, is given in the morning while the other, the FE: PM, is administered in the afternoon. This book will prepare you for the FE: AM Exam[†].

---

† The FE: AM exam is overwhelmingly metric and ultimately will be completely so. This book follows suit.

The FE: AM is a *supplied-reference* exam, so candidates are not permitted to bring reference material into the test center. Instead, you will be mailed a reference guide when you register for the exam. You can also view, at no charge, the entire up-to-date *FE Supplied-Reference Handbook* at the NCEES Website. (Each FE Exam will be administered using the latest edition of the handbook. You can count on your FE handbook review being considerably enhanced by study of our subject reviews and completion of our model tests.) You can also be assured that the NCEES guide will provide all the charts, graphs, tables, and formulae you will need. The same book will be given to you when you sit for the test.

You will have four hours to complete the AM portion of the exam. It consists of 120 questions spanning 12 engineering subjects. The subjects and their approximate corresponding numbers of questions are shown here.

FE: AM SUBJECT DISTRIBUTION

Subject	No. of Problems
Mathematics	24
Electrical Circuits	12
Statics	12
Chemistry	10
Dynamics	10
Thermodynamics	10
Fluid Mechanics	9
Material Science/Structure of Matter	9
Mechanics of Materials	8
Computers	6
Engineering Economics	5
Ethics	5

While thoroughly detailed, our topical reviews lay out the facts for you clearly and cogently. Each chapter begins with a short introduction and then progresses to the specifics of the topics. Each topic is completely explained, using example problems, diagrams, charts, and formulae.

You may wish to take some of the practice exams at various stages in your studying to gauge your strengths and weaknesses. This will help you determine which topics you need to study more. Take one practice test when you finish studying so that you can see how much you have improved. For studying suggestions that will help you to make the best use of your time, see the Study Schedule presented on page xii.

TEST SECTIONS

For studying purposes, the FE: AM can be broken down further into engineering topics. Your registration booklet will explain the breakdown and list the subtopics included under each major heading. The question categories are described briefly in each section that follows.

The topics on the morning portion of the exam appear as distinct questions. They will not be specified or labeled as separate sections or subtests.

Overall, there will be 12 different topics on the FE: AM Exam. The following is a comprehensive summary of the topics included on the exam, along with the types of related questions.

Chemistry (10 questions)

The questions in this section involve the following concepts:

Organic Chemistry	Acids and Bases
Nomenclature	Oxidation and Reduction
Kinetics	Periodicity
Equilibrium	Stoichiometry
Equations	States of Matter
Electrochemistry	Solutions
Inorganic Chemistry	Metals and Nonmetals

Dynamics (10 questions)

These questions will test your knowledge of these concepts:

Kinematics	Work and Energy
Vibrations	Impulse and Momentum
Friction	Force, Mass, and Acceleration

Electrical Circuits (12 questions)

The questions may address the following areas:

AC and DC Circuits	Capacitance and Inductance

Electrical Fields   Fourier and Laplace Transforms

Magnetic Fields   Operational Amplifiers

Ideal Transforms   Diodes

Engineering Economics (5 questions)

The questions may test your knowledge of any of the following topics:

Time Value of Money   Annual Cost

Present and Future Worth   Capitalized Cost

Break-Even Analysis   Valuation and Depreciation

Fluid Mechanics (9 questions)

The questions may deal with any of the following concepts:

Fluid Properties   Fluid Statics

Impulse and Momentum   Similitude

Flow Measurement   Pipe Flow

Compressible Flow

Material Science/Structure of Matter (9 questions)

Concepts which may be included are:

Physical Properties   Materials

Atomic Structure   Crystallography

Phase Diagrams   Processing and Testing

Diffusion   Corrosion

Mathematics (24 questions)

This section will test your knowledge in the following areas:

Integral and Differential Calculus   Laplace Transforms

Probability and Statistics   Differential Equations

Analytical Geometry   Linear Algebra

Vector Analysis

Mechanics of Materials (8 questions)

The questions may test your knowledge of any of the following concepts:

Stress and Strain   Tension and Compression

Shear	Combined Stress
Beams	Columns
Torsion	Bending

Statics (12 questions)

The questions may deal with any of the following:

Vector Forces	2- and 3-Dimensional Equilibrium
Concurrent Force Systems	Centroid Area
Moment of Inertia	Friction

Thermodynamics (10 questions)

The questions may test your knowledge of the following topics:

Properties	Phase Changes
First Law of Thermodynamics	Second Law of Thermodynamics
Energy, Heat, and Work	Mixture of Gases
Availability/Reversibility	Thermodynamic Processes
Ideal Gases	Cycles

Ethics (5 questions)

The questions may test your knowledge of the following topics:

| Relations with Clients | Relations with Peers |
| Relations with the Public | |

Computers (6 questions)

The questions may test your knowledge of the following topics:

| Algorithm Flowcharts | Spreadsheets |
| Psuedocode | Data Transmission and Storage |

SCORING THE EXAM

Your FE: AM score is based upon the number of correct answers you choose. Each of the 120 questions is worth 1 point, and no points are subtracted for incorrect answers. A single score between 0 and 100 is given for the entire test (both AM and PM sections), and both sections are weighted equally. The grade given is on a pass/fail basis. The breakpoint between passing and failing varies from state to state, although 70 is a general reference point for passing. Thus, the general reference point for passing the FE: AM section alone would be 35.

The pass/fail margin is not a percentage of correct answers or a percentage of students who scored lower than you. This number fluctuates from year to year and is reestablished with every test administration. It is based on previous exam administrations and relates your score to those of previous FE examinees.

Because this grading system is so variable, there is no way for you to know exactly what you got on the test. For the purpose of grading the practice tests in this book, however, REA has provided the following formula to calculate your score on the FE: AM practice tests:

$$\left[\frac{\text{No. of questions answered correctly on the FE: AM}}{240}\right] \times 100 = \text{your score}$$

Remember, this formula is meant for the computation of your score on the practice tests in this book and only accounts for the morning half of the exam. It does not compute your score for the actual FE Examination.

TEST-TAKING STRATEGIES

How to Beat the Clock

Every second counts, and you will want to use the available test time in the most efficient manner. Here's how:

1. **Bring a wristwatch!** This will allow you to monitor your time.

2. **Become familiar with the test directions.** You will save valuable time if you already understand the directions on the day of the test.

3. **Pace yourself.** Work steadily and quickly. Do not spend too much time on any one question. Remember, you can always return to the problems that gave you the most difficulty. Try to answer the easiest questions first, then return to the ones you missed.

4. **Begin with the subject areas you know best.** This will give you more time and will also build your confidence. If you use

this strategy, pay strict attention to your answer sheet; you do not want to mismatch the ovals and answers. It may be a good idea to check the problem number and oval number *each time* you mark down an answer.

Guessing Strategy

1. **When all else fails, guess!** The score you achieve depends on the number of correct answers. There is no penalty for wrong answers, so it is a good idea to choose an answer for all of the questions.

2. **When you guess, try to eliminate choices you know to be wrong.** This will allow you to make an educated guess. Here are some examples of what to look for when eliminating answer choices:

   Thermodynamics—check for signs of heat transfer and work.

   Fluid Mechanics—check for signs of pressure reading.

   Statics—check for direction of forces and compression/tension units.

3. **Break each problem down into its simplest components.** Approach each part *one step* at a time. Use diagrams and drawings whenever possible, and do not wait until you get a final answer to assign units. If you decide to move on to another problem, this method will allow you to resume your work without too much difficulty.

A word on calculators... Certain calculators are strictly prohibited from exam sites for all NCEES engineering and land surveying exams. For details, visit the official NCEES Web site at http://www.ncees.org.

FE/EIT

Fundamentals of Engineering: AM Exam

CHAPTER 2

How to Study for the FE: AM Exam

CHAPTER 2

HOW TO STUDY FOR THE FE: AM EXAM

Two groups of people take the FE Exam: college seniors in undergraduate programs and graduate engineers who decide that professional registration is necessary for future growth. Both groups begin their Professional Engineer career with a comprehensive exam covering the entirety of their engineering curriculum. How does one prepare for an exam of such magnitude and importance?

Time is the most important factor when preparing for the FE: AM. Time management is necessary to ensure that each section is reviewed prior to the exam. Once the decision to test has been made, determine how much time you have to study. Divide this time amongst your topics, and make up a schedule which outlines the beginning and ending dates for study of each exam topic; also include time for a final practice test followed by a brief review. Set aside extra time for the more difficult subjects, and include a buffer for unexpected events such as college exams or business trips. There is never enough time to prepare, so make the most of the time that you have.

You can determine which subject areas will require the most time in several ways. Look at your college grades: those courses with the lowest grades probably need the most study. Those subjects outside your major are generally the least used and most easily forgotten. These will require a good deal of review to bring you up to speed. Some of the subjects may not be familiar to you at all because you were not required to study them in college. These subjects may be impossible to learn before the examination, although some can be self-taught. One such subject is engineering economics; the mathematics may not be exceptionally difficult to you and most of the concepts are common sense.

Another way to determine your weaker areas is to take one of the practice tests provided in this book. Our simulated exams will help you assess your strengths and weaknesses. By determining which type of questions you answered incorrectly on the practice tests, you will find the areas that need the most work. Be careful not to neglect the other subjects in your review; do not rule out any subject area until you have reviewed it to some degree.

You may also find that a negative attitude is your biggest stumbling block. Many students do not realize the volume of material they have covered in four years of college. Some begin to study and are immediately overwhelmed because they do not have a plan. It is important that you get a good start and that you are positive as you review and study the material.

You will need some way to measure your preparedness, either with problems from books or with a review book that has sample test questions similar to one on the FE: AM. This book contains sample problems in each section which can be used before, during, or after you review the material to measure your understanding of the subject matter. If you are a wizard in thermodynamics, for example, and are confident in your ability to solve problems, select a few and see what happens. You may want to perform at least a cursory review of the material before jumping into problem solving, since there is always something to learn. If you do well on these initial problems, then momentum has been established. If you do poorly, you might develop a negative attitude as mentioned above. Being positive is essential as you move through the subject areas.

The question that comes to mind at this point is: "How do I review the material?" Before we get into the material itself, let us establish rules that lead to **good study habits**. Time was previously mentioned as the most important issue. When you decide to study you will need blocks of uninterrupted time so that you can get something accomplished. Two hours should be the minimum time block allotted, while four hours should be the maximum. Schedule five-minute breaks into your study period and stay with your schedule. Cramming for the FE can give you poor results, including short-term memory and confusion when synthesis is required.

Next, you need to work in a quiet place, on a flat surface that is not cluttered with other papers or work that needs to be completed before the next day. **Eliminate distractions**—they will rob you of time if you let them. **Do not eat while you study**—few of us can do two things at once and do them both well. Eating does require a lot of attention and disrupts study. Eating a sensible meal before you study resolves the "eating while you work" problem. We encourage you to have a large glass of water available since water quenches your thirst and fills the void which makes you want to get up and find something to eat. In addition, **you should be well rested when you study**. Late nights and early mornings are good for some, especially if you have a family, but the best results are associated with adequate rest.

Lastly, **study on weekend mornings while most people are still asleep**. This allows for a quiet environment and gives you the remainder of the day to do other things. If you must study at night, we suggest two-hour blocks ending before 11 p.m.

Do not spend time memorizing charts, graphs, and formulae; as we said, the FE is a supplied-reference exam, and you will be provided a booklet of equations and other essential information during the test. This reference material will be sent to you prior to your examination date. You can use the supplied-reference book as a guide while studying, since it will give you an indication of the depth of study you will need to pursue. Furthermore, familiarity with the book will alleviate some test anxiety inasmuch as you will be given the same book to use during the exam.

While you review for the test, use the review book supplied by the NCEES, paper, pencil, and a calculator. Texts can be used, but reliance on them should be avoided. The object of the review is to identify what you already know and what requires more work. As you review, move past those equations and concepts that you understand and annotate on your scrap paper those concepts that require more work. Using this method you can review a large quantity of material in a short time and reduce the apparent workload to a manageable amount. Now go back to your study schedule and allocate the remaining time according to the needs of the subject under consideration. Return to the material that requires work and review it or study it until your are satisfied that you can solve problems covering this material. When you have finished the review, you are ready to solve problems.

Solving problems requires practice. To use the problems in this book effectively, you should cover the solution and try to solve the problem on your own. If this is not possible, map out a strategy to answer the problem and then check to see if you have the correct procedure. Remember that most problems that are not solved correctly were never started correctly.

Merely reviewing the solution will not help you to start the problem when you see it again at a later date. Read the problems carefully and in parts. Many people teach that reading the whole problem gives the best overview of what is to come; however, solutions are developed from small clues that are in parts of a sentence. For example, "An engine operates on an Otto cycle," tells a great deal about the thermodynamic processes, the maximum temperature, the compression ratio, and the theoretical thermal efficiency. **Read the problem and break it into manageable parts**. Next, **try to avoid numbers until the problem is well formulated**. Too often, Numbers are often substituted into equations too early and become show stoppers. You will surely need numbers; just use them after the algebra has been completed. **Be methodical**: list the knowns, the requirements of the problem, and check off those bits of knowledge you have as they appear. Checking off the intermediate answers and information you know is a positive attitude builder. Continue to solve problems until you are confident or until you exceed the time allowed in your schedule for that subject area.

As soon as you complete one subject, move to the next. Keep all of your notes as you complete each section. You will need them for your final overall review right before the exam. After you have completed the entire review, you may want to take a practice test. Taking practice exams will test your understanding of all the engineering subject areas and will help you identify sections that need additional study. With the test and the notes that you kept from the subject reviews, you can determine weak areas that require some extra attention.

You should be ready for the exam if you follow these guidelines:

• Program your time wisely.

• Maintain a positive attitude.

• Develop good study habits.

• Review the material smartly and maximize the learning process.

• Do practice problems and practice tests.

• Review again to finalize your preparation.

Good luck on the FE: AM Exam!

FE/EIT

Fundamentals of Engineering: AM Exam

CHAPTER 3

Mathematics

CHAPTER 3

MATHEMATICS

When reviewing for the mathematics portion of the exam, it is strongly recommended that you use the mathematics section of your engineering handbook in addition to this chapter. Your handbook has formulas for areas, surfaces, and volumes. It has tables for derivatives, integrals, statistical functions, and Laplace Transforms. It has definitions and applications. This chapter reviews the fundamental concepts that are emphasized on the exam. Use this chapter along with your handbook to reinforce your mathematical skills.

The supplied reference handbook you will be given for use during the exam contains limited mathematical tables and formulas. Be sure you understand how to use all entries in the handbook, but do not be concerned with memorizing longer tables or additional formulas. The exam seeks to determine how well you understand and can apply the concept of integration, for example, rather than how quickly you can find the correct entry in a Table of Integrals.

ALGEBRA

Algebra defines the rules to allow us to rearrange, expand, and simplify mathematical relationships.

Commutative law for addition and multiplication:

$$a + b = b + a \qquad a \cdot b = b \cdot a$$

Associative law for addition and multiplication:

$$a + (b + c) = (a + b) + c \qquad a \cdot (b \cdot c) = (a \cdot b) \cdot c$$

Distributive law:

$$a \cdot (b + c) = a \cdot b + a \cdot c$$

Partial Fraction Expansion

A ratio of polynomials

$$f(x) = \frac{g(x)}{h(x)}$$

can be written as a sum of terms each of which has a root of $h(x)$ in the denominator.

- Each single real root of $h(x)$ will generate a term of the form:

$$\frac{A}{x - r}$$

- A real root appearing n times will generate a set of terms:

$$\frac{A_1}{(x - r)} + \frac{A_2}{(x - r)^2} + \frac{A_3}{(x - r)^3} + \ldots + \frac{A_n}{(x - r)^n}$$

- A single pair of complex conjugate roots will generate a term of the form:

$$\frac{Ax + B}{x^2 + rx + s}$$

Terms for complex conjugate roots $a + bi$ and $a - bi$ can also be written as

$$\frac{C_1}{x - (a + bi)} + \frac{C_2}{x - (a - bi)}$$

where the constants C_1 and C_2 are a pair of complex conjugates.

- Pairs of complex conjugate roots appearing n times will generate a set of terms:

$$\frac{A_1 x + B_1}{x^2 + rx + s} + \frac{A_2 x + B_2}{\left(x^2 + rx + s\right)^2} + \ldots + \frac{A_n x + B_n}{\left(x^2 + rx + s\right)^n}$$

The function

$$f(x) = \frac{x^2 + 2x - 2}{x^3(x+2)(x^2+x+9)^2}$$

can be expanded as

$$\frac{A_1}{x} + \frac{A_2}{x^2} + \frac{A_3}{x^3} + \frac{B}{x+2} + \frac{C_1 x + D_1}{x^2+x+9} + \frac{C_2 x + D_2}{(x^2+x+9)^2}.$$

EXAMPLE

Expand the following function into partial fractions and solve for the constants.

$$f(x) = \frac{x^2 + 1}{(x-2)(x-1)(2x+1)} = \frac{A}{x-2} + \frac{B}{x-1} + \frac{C}{2x+1}$$

SOLUTION

To solve for the unknown constants A, B, and C, multiply the equation by $(x-2)(x-1)(2x+1)$.

$$x^2 + 1 = A(x-1)(2x+1) + B(x-2)(2x+1) + C(x-2)(x-1)$$

Set $x = 2$ $5 = A(1)(5) + 0 + 0$ $A = 1$

Set $x = 1$ $2 = 0 + B(-1)(3) + 0$ $B = -\dfrac{2}{3}$

Set $x = -\dfrac{1}{2}$ $\dfrac{5}{4} = 0 + 0 + C\left(-\dfrac{5}{2}\right)\left(-\dfrac{3}{2}\right)$ $C = \dfrac{1}{3}$

TRIGONOMETRY

A right triangle, as shown in Figure 1, contains one 90° angle.

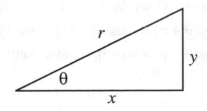

Figure 1. A right triangle

The following definitions and relations apply:

$$x^2 + y^2 = r^2$$

$$\sin\theta = \frac{y}{r} \qquad s = \frac{opp}{hyp}$$

$$\cos\theta = \frac{x}{r} \qquad c = \frac{adj}{hyp}$$

$$\tan\theta = \frac{y}{x} \qquad t = \frac{opp}{adj}$$

$$\csc\theta = \frac{r}{y} = \frac{1}{\sin\theta}$$

$$\sec\theta = \frac{r}{x} = \frac{1}{\cos\theta}$$

$$\cot\theta = \frac{x}{y} = \frac{1}{\tan\theta}$$

$$\sin^2\theta + \cos^2\theta = 1$$

$$1 + \tan^2\theta = \sec^2\theta$$

$$1 + \cot^2\theta = \csc^2\theta$$

$$\sin 2\theta = 2(\sin\theta)(\cos\theta)$$

$$\cos 2\theta = \cos^2\theta - \sin^2\theta$$

$$= 1 - 2\sin^2\theta$$

$$\sin\theta = 2\left[\sin\left(\frac{1}{2}\theta\right)\cos\left(\frac{1}{2}\theta\right)\right]$$

$$\sin\left(\frac{1}{2}\theta\right) = \pm\sqrt{\frac{1}{2}(1 - \cos\theta)}$$

$$\sin(\theta + \phi) = [\sin\theta][\cos\phi] + [\cos\theta][\sin\phi]$$

$$\sin(\theta - \phi) = [\sin\theta][\cos\phi] - [\cos\theta][\sin\phi]$$

$$\cos(\theta + \phi) = [\cos\theta][\cos\phi] - [\sin\theta][\sin\phi]$$

$$\cos(\theta - \phi) = [\cos\theta][\cos\phi] + [\sin\theta][\sin\phi]$$

Laws for a General Triangle

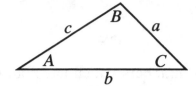

Figure 2. A general triangle

The following laws apply to general triangles, like the one shown in Figure 2,

Law of Sines: $\dfrac{\sin A}{a} = \dfrac{\sin B}{b} = \dfrac{\sin C}{c}$

Law of Cosines: $a^2 = b^2 + c^2 - 2bc(\cos A)$

Area $= \dfrac{1}{2}ab(\sin C)$

Angles, Quadrants, and Signs

Angles are measured from the positive horizontal axis, and the positive direction is counterclockwise.

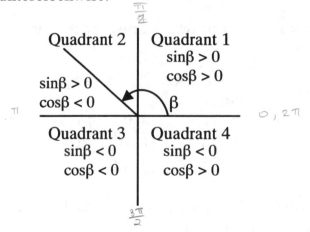

One complete circle is 360° or 2π radians. A right angle of 90° is equivalent to $\dfrac{\pi}{2}$ radians. One radian is equivalent to 57.3°.

LINEAR ALGEBRA

Finding the solution of a set of *n* linear algebraic equations in *n* unknowns is a primary application of matrix manipulation. Before this application is illustrated, some definitions are reviewed.

A **scalar** is a single number which has magnitude only and requires no subscript.

$$C = 4$$

A **vector** is a set of numbers which have both magnitude and direction. They are written with one subscript.

$$\mathbf{a} = \begin{bmatrix} A_1 \\ \cdot \\ \cdot \\ \cdot \\ A_n \end{bmatrix}$$

A **matrix** is an array of vectors requiring two subscripts. The first subscript identifies the **row** position; the second identifies the **column**.

$$\mathbf{A} = \begin{bmatrix} A_{11} \ A_{12} \ .... \ A_{1n} \\ A_{21} \ A_{22} \ .... \ A_{2n} \\ \cdot \\ \cdot \\ A_{m1} \ A_{m2} \ .... A_{mn} \end{bmatrix}$$

To add two vectors or two matrices of the same size, add the corresponding terms.

$$\mathbf{A} + \mathbf{B} = \mathbf{C} \qquad A_{ij} + B_{ij} = C_{ij}$$

$$\begin{bmatrix} 1 & 4 \\ 3 & 9 \\ 2 & 0 \end{bmatrix} + \begin{bmatrix} 4 & 0 \\ 1 & 0 \\ 2 & 3 \end{bmatrix} = \begin{bmatrix} 5 & 4 \\ 4 & 9 \\ 4 & 3 \end{bmatrix}$$

The transpose of a matrix $\mathbf{A}$ is denoted by $\mathbf{A}^T$ and is formed by interchanging rows and columns.

$$\mathbf{A} = \begin{bmatrix} 1 & 2 & 3 \\ 4 & 5 & 6 \end{bmatrix}$$

$$\mathbf{A}^T = \begin{bmatrix} 1 & 4 \\ 2 & 5 \\ 3 & 6 \end{bmatrix}$$

Multiplication of Matrices

$$\mathbf{AB} = \mathbf{C}$$

Each element of **C** is given by $C_{ij} = \displaystyle\sum_{k=1}^{n} A_{ik} B_{kj}$.

Note that multiplication is valid only if the *number of rows in* **A** *is the same as the number of columns in* **B**. Matrix multiplication is not commutative; **AB** is not necessarily the same as **BA**.

Let $\quad \mathbf{A} = \begin{bmatrix} 1 & 2 & 3 \\ 4 & 1 & 2 \end{bmatrix} \quad \mathbf{B} = \begin{bmatrix} 1 & 2 \\ 4 & 1 \\ 3 & 2 \end{bmatrix}$ $\qquad A_{23} B_{32} = C_{22}$

$$\mathbf{AB} = \begin{bmatrix} 1 & 2 & 3 \\ 4 & 1 & 2 \end{bmatrix}\begin{bmatrix} 1 & 2 \\ 4 & 1 \\ 3 & 2 \end{bmatrix}$$

$$= \begin{bmatrix} 1+8+9 & 2+2+6 \\ 4+4+6 & 8+1+4 \end{bmatrix}$$

Thus,

$$\mathbf{AB} = \begin{bmatrix} 18 & 10 \\ 14 & 13 \end{bmatrix}$$

Determinant

The **determinant** |A| is a scalar quantity associated with matrix **A**. The determinant of a two-by-two matrix is

$$|\mathbf{A}| = \begin{vmatrix} A_{11} & A_{12} \\ A_{21} & A_{22} \end{vmatrix} = A_{11}A_{22} - A_{12}A_{21}$$

The determinant of a three-by-three matrix is

$$|\mathbf{B}| = \begin{vmatrix} B_{11} & B_{12} & B_{13} \\ B_{21} & B_{22} & B_{23} \\ B_{31} & B_{32} & B_{33} \end{vmatrix}$$
$$= B_{11}B_{22}B_{33} + B_{12}B_{23}B_{31} + B_{13}B_{21}B_{32}$$
$$- B_{13}B_{22}B_{31} - B_{12}B_{21}B_{33} - B_{11}B_{23}B_{32}$$

EXAMPLE

Find the determinant of an arbitrary three-by-three matrix, $|A|$ where:

$$\mathbf{A} = \begin{bmatrix} -5 & 0 & 2 \\ 6 & 1 & 2 \\ 2 & 3 & 1 \end{bmatrix}$$

SOLUTION

Let

$$\mathbf{A} = \begin{bmatrix} b_{11} & b_{12} & b_{13} \\ b_{21} & b_{22} & b_{23} \\ b_{31} & b_{32} & b_{33} \end{bmatrix}$$

The two-by-two matrix inside the dotted box (- - -) is called a minor.

Expand the above determinant by minors, using the first column.

$$|\mathbf{A}| = +b_{11}\begin{vmatrix} b_{22} & b_{23} \\ b_{32} & b_{33} \end{vmatrix} - b_{21}\begin{vmatrix} b_{12} & b_{13} \\ b_{32} & b_{33} \end{vmatrix} + b_{31}\begin{vmatrix} b_{12} & b_{13} \\ b_{22} & b_{23} \end{vmatrix}$$

$$|\mathbf{A}| = b_{11}(b_{22}b_{33} - b_{32}b_{23}) - b_{21}(b_{12}b_{33} - b_{32}b_{13}) + b_{31}(b_{12}b_{23} - b_{22}b_{13})$$

$$|\mathbf{A}| = -b_{21}(b_{12}b_{33} - b_{32}b_{13}) + b_{22}(b_{11}b_{33} - b_{31}b_{13}) - b_{23}(b_{11}b_{32} - b_{31}b_{12})$$

$$= b_{22}b_{11}b_{33} - b_{22}b_{31}b_{13} - b_{23}b_{11}b_{32} + b_{23}b_{31}b_{12} - b_{21}(b_{12}b_{33} - b_{32}b_{13})$$

$$= b_{11}(b_{22}b_{33} - b_{32}b_{23}) - b_{21}(b_{12}b_{33} - b_{32}b_{13}) + b_{31}(b_{12}b_{23} - b_{22}b_{13})$$

Clearly, this is the same as the first answer. Note, also, that $|\mathbf{A}|$ can be rearranged algebraically until it can be written as:

$$|\mathbf{A}| = b_{11}b_{22}b_{33} + b_{12}b_{23}b_{31} + b_{13}b_{32}b_{21}$$
$$- (b_{13}b_{22}b_{31} + b_{23}b_{32}b_{11} + b_{33}b_{21}b_{12})$$

Expand the determinant by minors, using the first column.

$$|\mathbf{A}| = -5\begin{vmatrix} 1 & 2 \\ 3 & 1 \end{vmatrix} - 6\begin{vmatrix} 0 & 2 \\ 3 & 1 \end{vmatrix} + 2\begin{vmatrix} 0 & 2 \\ 1 & 2 \end{vmatrix}$$

$$= -5(1-6) - 6(0-6) + 2(0-2) = 25 + 36 - 4 = 57$$

Now expand the determinant by minors, using the second row.

$$|\mathbf{A}| = -b_{21}\begin{vmatrix} b_{12} & b_{13} \\ b_{32} & b_{33} \end{vmatrix} + b_{22}\begin{vmatrix} b_{11} & b_{13} \\ b_{31} & b_{33} \end{vmatrix}$$
$$- b_{23}\begin{vmatrix} b_{11} & b_{12} \\ b_{31} & b_{32} \end{vmatrix}$$

Inverse

A **nonsingular** matrix $\mathbf{A}$ possesses a unique **inverse** $\mathbf{A}^{-1}$ such that

$$\mathbf{A}^{-1}\mathbf{A} = \mathbf{A}\,\mathbf{A}^{-1} = \mathbf{I}$$

where $\mathbf{I}$ is the **unit** matrix, which has 1's on the diagonal and 0's in all other positions.

$$I = \begin{bmatrix} 1 & 0 & 0 \dots \\ 0 & 1 & 0 \dots \\ & \dots & \end{bmatrix}$$

If $\mathbf{A}$ is a two-by-two matrix

$$\mathbf{A} = \begin{bmatrix} A_{11} & A_{12} \\ A_{21} & A_{22} \end{bmatrix},$$

its inverse is $\mathbf{A}^{-1} = \dfrac{1}{|\mathbf{A}|}\begin{bmatrix} A_{22} & -A_{12} \\ -A_{21} & A_{11} \end{bmatrix}$

If $\mathbf{A}$ is a general nonsingular square matrix, its inverse is

$$\mathbf{A}^{-1} = \frac{\mathrm{Adj}\ \mathbf{A}}{|\mathbf{A}|}$$

where Adj $\mathbf{A}$ is the **adjoint of A**, which is formed by replacing each element by its **cofactor** and then interchanging rows and columns.

A **singular** matrix has a determinant of 0.

The **rank** of a matrix is the order of the largest square array in that matrix (formed by deleting rows and columns) whose determinant does not vanish. The rank indicates the number of independent relations.

Let
$$\mathbf{A} = \begin{bmatrix} 3 & -1 & -2 \\ 0 & 2 & -1 \\ 4 & -10 & 2 \end{bmatrix}$$

The **minor** M_{12} is found by deleting the first row and second column

$$\begin{bmatrix} 3 & -1 & -2 \\ 0 & 2 & -1 \\ 4 & -10 & 2 \end{bmatrix}$$

and calculating the determinant of the resulting two-by-two matrix

$$M_{12} = \begin{vmatrix} 0 & -1 \\ 4 & 2 \end{vmatrix} = 0 - (-4) = 4.$$

The **cofactor of A_{12}** is

$$C_{12} = (-1)^{1+2} M_{12} = -4.$$

One way to find $|\mathbf{A}|$ is to add the products of the elements of the top row with their cofactors.

$$\begin{aligned} |\mathbf{A}| &= A_{11} C_{11} + A_{12} C_{12} + A_{13} C_{13} \\ &= 3(-1)^{1+1}(4-10) + (-1)(-1)^{1+2}(0+4) + (-2)(-1)^{1+3}(0-8) \\ &= -18 + 4 + 16 = 2 \end{aligned}$$

A Set of Linear Equations

The equations

$$\begin{aligned} A_{11}x_1 + A_{12}x_2 + A_{13}x_3 + \ldots\ldots + A_{1n}x_n &= b_1 \\ A_{21}x_1 + A_{22}x_2 + A_{23}x_3 + \ldots\ldots + A_{2n}x_n &= b_2 \\ A_{31}x_1 + A_{32}x_2 + A_{33}x_3 + \ldots\ldots + A_{3n}x_n &= b_3 \\ \ldots\ldots\ldots\ldots\ldots\ldots\ldots\ldots \\ A_{n1}x_1 + A_{n2}x_2 + A_{n3}x_3 + \ldots\ldots + A_{nn}x_n &= b_n \end{aligned}$$

can be written as $\mathbf{Ax} = \mathbf{b}$

where   **A** is the coefficient matrix

x is the vector of unknowns

b is the vector of constants

$$\mathbf{A} = \begin{bmatrix} A_{11}\, A_{12}\, A_{13}\, A_{14}......A_{1n} \\ A_{21}\, A_{22}\, A_{23}\, A_{24}......A_{2n} \\ A_{31}\, A_{32}\, A_{33}\, A_{34}......A_{3n} \\ ...... \\ A_{n1}\, A_{n2}\, A_{n3}\, A_{n4}......A_{nn} \end{bmatrix}$$

$$\mathbf{x} = \begin{bmatrix} x_1 \\ x_2 \\ x_3 \\ .. \\ x_n \end{bmatrix} \qquad \mathbf{b} = \begin{bmatrix} b_1 \\ b_2 \\ b_3 \\ .. \\ b_n \end{bmatrix}$$

Solution via the Inverse of A

One solution technique is to multiply the equation by $\mathbf{A}^{-1}$.

$$\mathbf{Ax} = \mathbf{b}$$
$$\mathbf{A}^{-1}\mathbf{Ax} = \mathbf{A}^{-1}\mathbf{b}$$
$$\mathbf{Ix} = \mathbf{x} = \mathbf{A}^{-1}\mathbf{b}$$

Solution via Cramer's Rule

Each unknown x_i can be found by

$$x_i = \frac{|\Delta_i|}{|\mathbf{A}|}$$

where $|\mathbf{A}|$ is the determinant of the coefficient matrix, and

$|\Delta_i|$ is the determinant of a matrix formed by replacing the ith column of the coefficient matrix **A** by the vector of constants **b**.

Eigenvalues

Eigenvalues, characteristic values or **latent roots** are scalars and are roots of

$$|\mathbf{A} - \lambda\mathbf{I}| = 0$$

$$\mathbf{A} = \begin{bmatrix} 5 & 4 \\ 1 & 2 \end{bmatrix}$$

$$\mathbf{A} - \lambda\mathbf{I} = \begin{bmatrix} 5 & 4 \\ 1 & 2 \end{bmatrix} - \lambda\begin{bmatrix} 1 & 0 \\ 0 & 1 \end{bmatrix}$$

$$= \begin{bmatrix} 5 - \lambda & 4 \\ 1 & 2 - \lambda \end{bmatrix}$$

$$\begin{vmatrix} 5 - \lambda & 4 \\ 1 & 2 - \lambda \end{vmatrix} = (5 - \lambda)(2 - \lambda) - 4 = 0$$

$$\lambda^2 - 7\lambda + 6 = (\lambda - 6)(\lambda - 1) = 0$$

The Eigenvalues are 1, 6.

VECTOR ANALYSIS

A vector has a direction and a magnitude. In three-dimensional space, vectors can be written as

$$\mathbf{A} = a_x\boldsymbol{i} + a_y\boldsymbol{j} + a_z\boldsymbol{k} \qquad \mathbf{B} = b_x\boldsymbol{i} + b_y\boldsymbol{j} + b_z\boldsymbol{k}$$

where $\boldsymbol{i}$, $\boldsymbol{j}$, and $\boldsymbol{k}$ are unit vectors pointing in the positive x, y, and z directions, respectively.

The magnitude of $\mathbf{A} = \sqrt{a_x^2 + a_y^2 + a_z^2}$.

The **scalar product**, or **dot product**, is a scalar defined by

$$\mathbf{A} \cdot \mathbf{B} = |\mathbf{A}|\,|\mathbf{B}|\cos\beta$$

where $|\mathbf{A}|$ and $|\mathbf{B}|$ are the magnitudes of $\mathbf{A}$ and $\mathbf{B}$, and β is the angle between them. Written in terms of the three components of each vector, the dot product is

$$\mathbf{A} \cdot \mathbf{B} = a_xb_x + a_yb_y + a_zb_z$$

The dot product of perpendicular vectors is 0. The dot product is used to define the projection of vector $\mathbf{A}$ in the direction of $\mathbf{B}$.

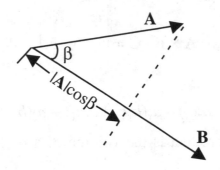

Figure 3. Projection of vector A in the direction of B

The unit vector that points in the direction of **B** is $\dfrac{\mathbf{B}}{|\mathbf{B}|}$. Figure 3 shows that the magnitude of the projection of vector **A** in the direction of **B** is |**A**| cos β.

Proj of **A** on **B** = $|\mathbf{A}| \cos\beta \, \dfrac{\mathbf{B}}{|\mathbf{B}|}$.

The **vector product**, or **cross product**, is written as **C = A × B**. The magnitude of **C** is

$$|\mathbf{C}| = |\mathbf{A}|\,|\mathbf{B}|\sin\beta.$$

The magnitude of **C** is the area of the parallelogram with sides **A** and **B**. The direction of **C** is perpendicular to the plane of **A** and **B** and follows the right-hand rule. If the curled fingers of the right hand are wrapped in the direction from vector **A** to vector **B**, the thumb then points in the direction of **C**. Written in terms of the three components of each vector, the cross product is

$$\mathbf{A} \times \mathbf{B} = (a_y b_z - a_z b_y)i + (a_z b_x - a_x b_z)j + (a_x b_y - a_y b_x)k.$$

This is the determinant of

$$\mathbf{A} \times \mathbf{B} = \begin{vmatrix} a_x & a_y & a_z \\ b_x & b_y & b_z \\ i & j & k \end{vmatrix}$$

The **scalar triple product** is defined as

$$\mathbf{A} \times \mathbf{B} \cdot \mathbf{C} = \begin{vmatrix} a_x & a_y & a_z \\ b_x & b_y & b_z \\ c_x & c_y & c_z \end{vmatrix}$$

$$= a_x(b_y c_z - b_z c_y) - a_y(b_x c_z - b_z c_x) + a_z(b_x c_y - b_y c_x)$$

The scalar triple product is the volume of a parallelepiped with side **A**, **B**, and **C**.

It is convenient to define ∇, a **vector differential operator**, as

$$\nabla = \frac{\partial}{\partial x} i + \frac{\partial}{\partial y} j + \frac{\partial}{\partial z} k.$$

The **gradient** of a scalar function $F(x, y, z)$ is a vector

$$\nabla F = \frac{\partial F}{\partial x} i + \frac{\partial F}{\partial y} j + \frac{\partial F}{\partial z} k.$$

The direction of the gradient vector is perpendicular to the surface $F(x, y, z) = $ constant.

The **divergence** of a vector function **A** is a scalar, which is the dot product of the differential operator and **A**.

$$\nabla \cdot \mathbf{A} = \frac{\partial A_x}{\partial x} + \frac{\partial A_y}{\partial y} + \frac{\partial A_z}{\partial z}$$

The **curl** of a vector function **V** is a vector, which is the cross product of the differential operator and **V**.

$$\nabla \times \mathbf{V} = \left(\frac{\partial v_z}{\partial y} - \frac{\partial v_y}{\partial z} \right) i + \left(\frac{\partial v_x}{\partial z} - \frac{\partial v_z}{\partial x} \right) j + \left(\frac{\partial v_y}{\partial x} - \frac{\partial v_x}{\partial y} \right) k$$

A vector function **V** is conservative or irrotational if it is the gradient of a scalar function $F(x, y, z)$. The curl of a conservative vector function is 0.

Let $\mathbf{A} = 3i + 2j + k$ and $\mathbf{B} = i - 4j + 3k$.

The magnitude of **A** is $|\mathbf{A}| = \sqrt{3^2 + 2^2 + 1^2} = \sqrt{14}$.

The magnitude of $\mathbf{B}$ is $|\mathbf{B}| = \sqrt{1^2 + (-4)^2 + 3^2} = \sqrt{26}$.

The dot product of $\mathbf{A}$ and $\mathbf{B}$ is

$$\mathbf{A} \cdot \mathbf{B} = 3(1) + 2(-4) + 1(3) = -2.$$

The angle between $\mathbf{A}$ and $\mathbf{B}$ is given by

$$\cos\beta = \frac{\mathbf{A} \cdot \mathbf{B}}{|\mathbf{A}||\mathbf{B}|} = \frac{-2}{\sqrt{14 \cdot 26}} = -0.10483 \qquad \beta = 96°$$

The cross product between $\mathbf{A}$ and $\mathbf{B}$ is

$$\mathbf{A} \times \mathbf{B} = (2(3) - 1(-4))\mathbf{i} + (1(1) - 3(3))\mathbf{j} + (3(-4) - 2(1))\mathbf{k}$$
$$= 10\mathbf{i} - 8\mathbf{j} - 14\mathbf{k}$$

The projection of $\mathbf{A}$ in the direction of $\mathbf{B}$ is

$$|\mathbf{A}|\cos\beta \frac{\mathbf{B}}{|\mathbf{B}|} = -0.0769(i - 4j + 3k)$$
$$= -0.0769i + 0.3077j - 0.2308k$$

EXAMPLE

Let $F(x, y, z) = x^2 + 5xy - 8xyz^3 - 5$.

SOLUTION

The gradient of this function is

$$\nabla F = (2x + 5y - 8yz^3)\mathbf{i} + (5x - 8xz^3)\mathbf{j} + (-24xyz^2)\mathbf{k}.$$

Let $\mathbf{V} = \nabla F$ and find the curl of $\mathbf{V}$.

$$\nabla \times \mathbf{V} = (-24xz^2 - (-24xz^2))\mathbf{i} + (-24yz^2 - (-24yz^2))\mathbf{j}$$
$$+ ((5 - 8z^3) - (5 - 8z^3))\mathbf{k} = 0$$

The curl is 0 as expected because $\mathbf{V}$ is the gradient of $F(x, y, z)$.

Complex Numbers

A **complex number** z has a real part and an imaginary part, as illustrated in Figure 4 on the next page.

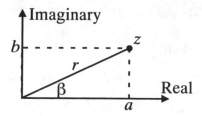

Figure 4. Components of a complex number

From the diagram, $r = \sqrt{a^2 + b^2}$ and $\beta = \arctan\left(\dfrac{b}{a}\right)$.

$$a = r\cos\beta \text{ and } b = r\sin\beta$$

The number z can be expressed in rectangular form,

$$z = a + ib \text{ where } i = \sqrt{-1},$$

or polar form,

$$z = re^{i\beta}.$$

These forms are completely equivalent because of **Euler's Equations**:

$$e^{i\beta} = \cos\beta + i\sin\beta$$

$$e^{-i\beta} = \cos\beta - i\sin\beta$$

$$\sin\beta = \frac{e^{i\beta} - e^{-i\beta}}{2i}$$

$$\cos\beta = \frac{e^{i\beta} + e^{-i\beta}}{2}$$

Complex conjugates in the rectangular form have imaginary parts of opposite signs. The complex conjugate of $7 + 2i$ is $7 - 2i$. Complex conjugates in the polar form are symmetrical with respect to the horizontal axis. When adding and subtracting, it is convenient to use the rectangular form. For finding powers and roots, the polar form is preferred.

Let $z_1 = 3 + 4i$ and $z_2 = 1 - i$.

The sum of z_1 and z_2 is

$$z_1 + z_2 = 3 + 4i + 1 - i = 4 - 3i.$$

The product of z_1 and z_2 is

$$z_1 z_2 = (3 + 4i)(1 - i) = 3 - 3i + 4i - 4i^2 = 3 + i - 4(-1) = 7 + i.$$

To divide z_1 by z_2, multiply the numerator and denominator by the conjugate of z_2.

$$\frac{z_1}{z_2} = \frac{3+4i}{1-i}\frac{1+i}{1+i} = \frac{3+3i+4i+4i^2}{1-i^2} = \frac{3+7i+4(-1)}{1-(-1)} = \frac{-1+7i}{2}$$

To find the cube of z_1, convert to the polar form

$$z_1 = 3 + 4i = 5e^{i0.927}.$$

Note that the angle is expressed as 0.927 radians.

$$z_1^3 = (5e^{i0.927})^3 = 125e^{i2.781}$$

The angle $\beta = 2.781$ radians is in the second quadrant.

To convert to rectangular form

$$a = r\cos\beta = 125\cos(2.781) = 125(-0.936) = -117.0$$
$$b = r\sin\beta = 125\sin(2.781) = 125(0.3528) = 44.1$$

Thus, the cube of $3 + 4i$ is $-116.0 + 44.1i$.

ANALYTICAL GEOMETRY

Straight Lines

The equation of a straight line is $y = mx + b$, where m is the slope and b is the intercept. If two straight lines are perpendicular, their slopes are negative reciprocals.

Conic Sections

The general second degree equation has the form

$$Ax^2 + Bxy + Cy^2 + Dx + Ey + F = 0$$

and describes one of three conic sections:

If $B^2 - 4AC < 0$,   the equation describes an **ellipse**.
                      If $B = 0$ and if $A = C$, this is a **circle**.
If $B^2 - 4AC = 0$,   the equation describes a **parabola**.
If $B^2 - 4AC > 0$,   the equation describes a **hyperbola**.

Circle

The general form for a circle is

$$(x - a)^2 + (y - b)^2 = r^2,$$

where a and b are coordinates of the center, and r is the radius.

Similarly, the general form of a sphere is

$$(x - a)^2 + (y - b)^2 + (z - c)^2 = r^2.$$

Ellipse

The sum of the distances from the two foci F to any point on an ellipse is a constant. For an ellipse centered at the origin, as in Figure 5,

$$\frac{x^2}{a^2} + \frac{y^2}{b^2} = 1$$

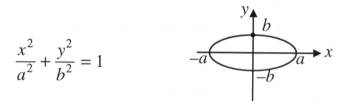

Figure 5. Ellipse at origin

where a and b are the semimajor and semiminor axes. The foci are at $+c$, 0 and $-c$, 0 where $c^2 = a^2 - b^2$.

Parabola

All points on a parabola are equidistant from the focus F and a line called the **directrix**. If the **vertex** is at the origin and the parabola opens to the right, as in Figure 6, the equation is

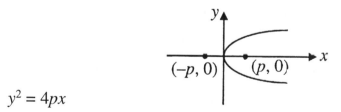

$$y^2 = 4px$$

Figure 6. Parabola

where the **focus** is at $(p, 0)$ and the **directrix** is at $x = -p$.

Hyperbola

The difference of the distances from the foci F to any point on the curve is a constant. If the hyperbola is centered at the origin and opens left and right, as in Figure 7, the standard form is

$$\frac{x^2}{a^2} + \frac{y^2}{b^2} = 1$$

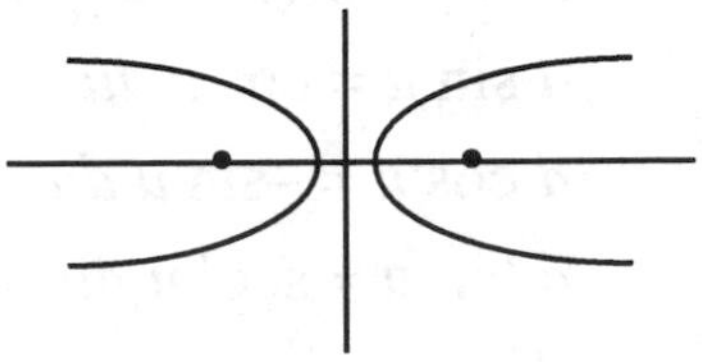

Figure 7. Hyperbola

DIFFERENTIAL CALCULUS

Derivatives

The **derivative** of a function $y(x)$ with respect to the independent variable x is defined as

$$\frac{dy}{dx} = y' = \lim_{\Delta x \to 0} \frac{y(x + \Delta x) - y(x)}{\Delta x}$$

and represents the slope, or how much y changes for a very small change in x. Differentials of standard forms are given in Table 1.

TABLE 1 **DIFFERENTIALS**
$d(au) = a\,du$
$d(u + v - w) = du + dv - dw$
$d(uv) = u\,dv + v\,du$
$d\left(\dfrac{u}{v}\right) = \dfrac{v\,du - u\,dv}{v^2}$
$d(u^n) = nu^{n-1}\,du$
$d(u^v) = vu^{v-1}\,du + u^v(\log_e u)\,dv$
$d(e^u) = e^u\,du$
$d(e^{au}) = ae^{au}\,du$

$$d(a^u) = a^u(\log_e a)\, du$$
$$d(\log_e u) = u^{-1} du$$
$$d(\log_a u) = u^{-1}(\log_a e)\, du$$
$$d(u^u) = u^u(1 + \log_e u)\, du$$
$$d \sin u = \cos u\, du$$
$$d \cos u = -\sin u\, du$$
$$d \tan u = \sec^2 u\, du$$
$$d \cot u = -\csc^2 u\, du$$
$$d \sec u = \tan u \sec u\, du$$
$$d \csc u = -\cot u \csc u\, du$$

Maxima and Minima

For a function $y(x)$, it is necessary that $\dfrac{dy}{dx} = 0$ at points of **maximum** and **minimum** values of y. Such points of 0 slope are called **critical points**.

At a critical point,

if $\dfrac{d^2 y}{dx^2} < 0$, the point is a **local maximum**;

if $\dfrac{d^2 y}{dx^2} > 0$, the point is a **local minimum**; and

if $\dfrac{d^2 y}{dx^2} = 0$, the test fails, no conclusion can be made, and additional analysis is necessary.

Consider the function

$$y = x(x - 1)^3.$$

The first derivative is

$$\frac{dy}{dx} = 3x(x - 1)^2 + (x - 1)^3(1) = (x - 1)^2(4x - 1)$$

and the second derivative is

$$\begin{aligned}
\frac{d^2y}{dx^2} &= (x-1)^2 4 + (4x-1)2(x-1) \\
&= (x-1)(4x-4+8x-2) \\
&= (x-1)(12x-6) \\
&= 6(x-1)(2x-1)
\end{aligned}$$

Critical points exist where

$$\frac{dy}{dx} = 0 \text{ or } x = 1 \text{ and } x = \frac{1}{4}.$$

For $x = 1$, $\frac{d^2y}{dx^2} = 0$. This point could be a local maximum, a local minimum, or neither.

For $x = \frac{1}{4}$, $\frac{d^2y}{dx^2} = 6\left(-\frac{3}{4}\right)\left(-\frac{1}{2}\right) > 0$ and the point is a local minimum.

Test for Increasing or Decreasing Functions

Let y be a function that is differentiable on the interval (a, b).

1. If $\frac{dy}{dx} > 0$ for all x in (a, b), then y is increasing on (a, b).

2. If $\frac{dy}{dx} < 0$ for all x in (a, b), then y is decreasing on (a, b).

3. If $\frac{dy}{dx} = 0$ for all x in (a, b), then y is constant on (a, b).

Test for Concavity

Let y be a function whose second derivative exists on an open interval I.

1. If $\frac{d^2y}{dx^2} > 0$ for all x in I, then the graph of y is concave upward.

2. If $\frac{d^2y}{dx^2} < 0$ for all x in I, then the graph of y is concave downward.

Points of Inflection

If $(c, y(c))$ is a point of inflection of the graph of y, then either $\frac{d^2 y(c)}{dx^2} = 0$ or $\frac{d^2 y}{dx^2}$ is undefined at $x = c$.

Second Derivative Test

Let y be a function such that $\frac{dy(c)}{dx} = 0$ and the second derivative of y exists on an open interval containing c.

1. If $\frac{d^2 y(c)}{dx^2} > 0$, then $y(c)$ is a relative minimum.

2. If $\frac{d^2 y(c)}{dx^2} < 0$, then $y(c)$ is a relative maximum.

3. If $\frac{d^2 y(c)}{dx^2} = 0$, then the test fails.

EXAMPLE

Determine the relative maxima, relative minima, and points of inflection of the function:

$$f(x) = \frac{1}{4} x^4 - \frac{3}{2} x^2.$$

SOLUTION

The derivatives are

$$f'(x) = x^3 - 3x \quad \text{and} \quad f''(x) = 3x^2 - 3.$$

The critical points are solutions of $x^3 - 3x = 0$. We obtain $x = 0$, $\sqrt{3}, -\sqrt{3}$. The Second Derivative Test tells us that

$$x = 0 \text{ is a relative maximum; and}$$
$$x = \sqrt{3}, -\sqrt{3} \text{ are relative minima.}$$

The possible points of inflection are solutions of $3x^2 - 3 = 0$; that is, $x = +1, -1$.

Partial Derivatives

The **partial derivative** of a function $F(x, y, z)$ with respect to x is written as $\dfrac{\partial F}{\partial x}$ and is obtained by considering y and z to be held constant.

The **total differential** of $F(x, y, z)$ is

$$dF = \frac{\partial F}{\partial x}\,dx + \frac{\partial F}{\partial y}\,dy + \frac{\partial F}{\partial z}\,dz.$$

To define the derivative $\dfrac{dy}{dx}$ for an equation in the implicit form

$$F(x, y) = 0,$$

first write the total differential, which has a value of 0, because F has a constant value of 0.

$$dF = \frac{\partial F}{\partial x}\,dx + \frac{\partial F}{\partial y}\,dy = 0$$

Solve for the desired derivative

$$\frac{dy}{dx} = -\frac{\dfrac{\partial F}{\partial x}}{\dfrac{\partial F}{\partial y}}$$

Let $F(x, y) = x^3 + y^2 - 2xy = 0$, then $\dfrac{\partial F}{\partial x} = 3x^2 - 2y$ and $\dfrac{\partial F}{\partial y} = 2y - 2x$.

The total differential is

$$dF = (3x^2 - 2y)dx + (2y - 2x)dy = 0,$$

and the derivative of y with respect to x in this implicit function is

$$\frac{dy}{dx} = \frac{3x^2 - 2y}{2y - 2x}.$$

Limits and L'Hopital's Rule

When seeking a limit, an indeterminate form sometimes results

$$\lim_{x \to a} y(x) = \frac{0}{0} \quad \text{or} \quad \lim_{x \to a} y(x) = \frac{\infty}{\infty}$$

in which case the limit might be found by

$$\lim_{x \to a} \frac{F(x)}{G(x)} = \lim_{x \to a} \frac{F'(x)}{G'(x)}$$

where $F'(x) = \dfrac{dF}{dx}$ and $G'(x) = \dfrac{dG}{dx}$.

L'Hopital's Rule is valid only if the right-hand side exists. The rule can be applied several times in succession if necessary.

INTEGRATION

The **indefinite integral** of $f(x)$ generates a function, which, when differentiated, results in the original $f(x)$. The indefinite integral contains an arbitrary constant of integration.

$$\int \left(x^2 + \frac{1}{x} \right) dx = \frac{x^3}{3} + \ln x + c$$

Table 2 contains integrals of common functions. For simplicity the constant of integration has not been printed, but is understood to be present in every integral.

The **definite integral** of $f(x)$ between $x = a$ and $x = b$ defines the change in the value of the integral as x changes from a to b.

$$\int_a^b \left(1 - x^2 \right) dx = \left[x - \frac{x^3}{3} \right]_a^b$$

$$= b - \frac{b^3}{3} - \left(a - \frac{a^3}{3} \right)$$

TABLE 2
INTEGRALS

$$\int a \, dx = ax$$

$$\int a \bullet f(x)dx = a \int f(x)dx$$

$$\int (u + v)dx = \int u \, dx + \int v \, dx$$

$$\int x^n dx = \frac{x^{n+1}}{n+1}, \; n \neq -1$$

$$\int \frac{dx}{x} = \ln x$$

$$\int \frac{dx}{a+bx} = \frac{1}{b}\ln(a+bx)$$

$$\int \frac{dx}{(a+bx)^2} = -\frac{1}{b(a+bx)}$$

$$\int \frac{dx}{(a+bx)^3} = -\frac{1}{2b(a+bx)^2}$$

$$\int \sin x \, dx = -\cos x$$

$$\int \cos x \, dx = \sin x$$

$$\int \tan x \, dx = -\ln \cos x$$

$$\int \cot x \, dx = \ln \sin x$$

$$\int \sec x \, dx = \ln(\sec x + \tan x) = \ln \tan\left(\frac{\pi}{4} + \frac{x}{2}\right)$$

$$\int \csc x \, dx = \ln(\csc x - \cot x) = \ln \tan \frac{x}{2}$$

$$\int \sin^2 x \, dx = -\frac{1}{2}\cos x \sin x + \frac{1}{2}x = \frac{1}{2}x - \frac{1}{4}\sin 2x$$

$$\int \sin^3 x \, dx = -\frac{1}{3}\cos x \left(\sin^2 x + 2\right)$$

$$\int \sin^n x \, dx = -\frac{\sin^{n-1} x \cos x}{n} + \frac{n-1}{n}\int \sin^{n-2} x \, dx$$

$$\int e^x dx = e^x$$

$$\int e^{ax} dx = \frac{e^{ax}}{a}$$

$$\int b^{ax} dx = \frac{b^{ax}}{a \ln b}$$

$$\int \ln x \, dx = x \ln x - x$$

$$\int a^x \ln a \, dx = a^x$$

Integration by Parts

Integrate the formula for the derivative of a product

$$d(uv) = u\,dv + v\,du$$

to obtain

$$\int d(uv) = \int u\,dv + \int v\,du$$

Rearrange to obtain the formula for integration by parts.

$$\int u\,dv = uv - \int v\,du$$

EXAMPLE

Find $\int x \sin 2x\,dx$.

SOLUTION

Let $u = x\ dv = \sin 2x\,dx$

$$du = dx \qquad\qquad v = \int \sin 2x\,dx = -\frac{1}{2}\cos 2x$$

With these definitions for u and v,

$$\int x \sin 2x\,dx = -\frac{1}{2}x\cos 2x + \frac{1}{2}\int \cos 2x$$

$$= -\frac{1}{2}x\cos 2x + \frac{1}{4}\sin 2x + C$$

Integration and Area

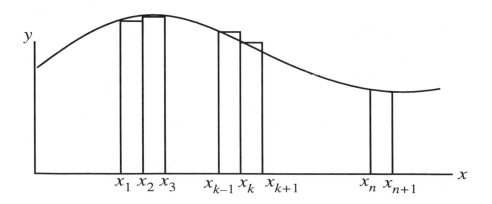

Figure 8. Integration of area under a curve

Using Figure 8 as an example, let $a = x_1$ and $b = x_{n+1}$. The area bounded vertically by the horizontal axis and the continuous function $y(x)$, and bounded horizontally by the ordinates $x = a$ and $x = b$, can be approximated by the sum of the areas of n rectangles. The approximation improves as the number of rectangles increases.

$$\text{Area} = \lim_{\max \Delta x_k \to 0} \sum_{k=1}^{n} f(x_k) \Delta x_k = \int_a^b f(x) dx$$

This is the Fundamental Theorem of Integral Calculus and demonstrates that the definite integral of a continuous function corresponds geometrically to an area.

The computation of areas is easily viewed geometrically by defining a rectangle with an infinitesimal thickness within the region and then performing the integration.

Find the area above the horizontal axis bounded by the parabola $y^2 = 4x$, the x-axis, and the line $x = 4$.

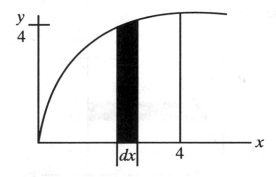

Figure 9. Area under a parabola with respect to x

The area of the vertical rectangle is $y\, dx$, shown in Figure 9, which can be integrated between $x = 0$ and $x = 4$.

$$\int_0^4 y\, dx = \int_0^4 2x^{\frac{1}{2}} dx = \left[2\left(\frac{2}{3}\right) x^{\frac{3}{2}} \right]_0^4 = \frac{32}{3}$$

A horizontal differential rectangle could also be used, as shown in Figure 10. Rectangle area $= (4 - x)\, dy$.

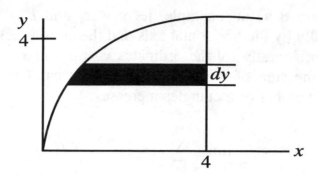

Figure 10. Area under a parabola with respect to y

$$\int_0^4 (4-x)\,dy = \int_0^4 \left(4 - \frac{y^2}{4}\right) dy$$

$$= \left[4y - \frac{y^3}{12}\right]_0^4 = 16 - \frac{16}{3} = \frac{32}{3}$$

Revolve the same area around the line $x = a$, as shown in Figure 11, and find the volume generated.

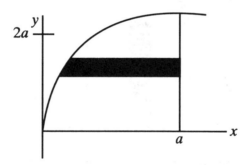

Figure 11. Volume generated by revolving curve about x = a

$$\text{Volume} = \pi \int_0^{2a} (a-x)^2\,dy$$

$$= \pi \int_0^{2a} \left(a - \frac{y^2}{4a}\right)^2 dy$$

$$= \pi \int\limits_{0}^{2a} \left(a^2 - \frac{y^2}{2} + \frac{y^4}{16a^2} \right) dy$$

$$= \pi \left[a^2 y - \frac{y^3}{2 \cdot 3} + \frac{y^5}{5 \cdot 16a^2} \right]_{0}^{2a}$$

$$= \frac{16}{15} \pi a^3$$

Length of a Curve

To find the length of the arc of a plane curve between two given points, we begin by drawing a very short segment of the curve, as in Figure 12.

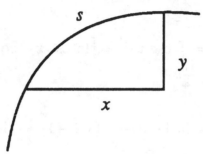

Figure 12. Length of a curve

$$\Delta s = \sqrt{\Delta x^2 + \Delta y^2} = \sqrt{1 + \left(\frac{\Delta y}{\Delta x} \right)^2} \, \Delta x$$

In the limit as Δx becomes infinitesimally small, Δs will follow the curvature of the function, and the total **arc length** is an integral.

$$\text{length} = \int\limits_{a}^{b} \sqrt{1 + \left(\frac{dy}{dx} \right)^2} \, dx$$

If it is more convenient to integrate with respect to y, the integral can be written as

$$\text{length} = \int\limits_{c}^{d} \sqrt{\left(\frac{dx}{dy} \right)^2 + 1} \, dy .$$

If x and y are given in terms of a parameter t, the integral is

$$\text{length} = \int_{t_1}^{t_2} \sqrt{\left(\frac{dx}{dt}\right)^2 + \left(\frac{dy}{dt}\right)^2}\, dt.$$

Find the length of the curve $y = \ln \sin x$ from $x = \frac{\pi}{4}$ to $\frac{\pi}{2}$.

$$\frac{dy}{dx} = \frac{\cos x}{\sin x} = \cot x$$

$$\text{length} = \int_{\frac{1}{4}\pi}^{\frac{1}{2}\pi} \sqrt{1 + \cot^2 x}\, dx$$

$$= \int_{\frac{1}{4}\pi}^{\frac{1}{2}\pi} \csc x\, dx = \Big[\ln(\csc x - \cot x)\Big]_{\frac{1}{4}\pi}^{\frac{1}{2}\pi}$$

$$= \ln(1 - 0) - \ln\left(\sqrt{2} - 1\right) = -\ln\left(\sqrt{2} - 1\right)$$

$$\text{length} = -\ln \frac{2 - 1}{\sqrt{2} + 1} = \ln\left(1 + \sqrt{2}\right)$$

Solids of Revolution

If a given curve is revolved around an axis, it generates a **surface of revolution**. The area of the surface of revolution may be found from a summation of small (infinitesimal) cylinders. The cylinder has a radius x, and hence a circumference of $2\pi x$. The height ds of the cylinder is defined from

$$ds = \sqrt{dy^2 + dx^2} = \sqrt{1 + \left(\frac{dy}{dx}\right)^2}\, dx.$$

The surface of revolution, therefore, has an area equal to $\int 2\pi x\, ds$, or

$$2\pi \int_a^b x \sqrt{1 + \left(\frac{dy}{dx}\right)^2}\, dx$$

where the limits a and b are the values of x at the beginning and end of the portion of the curve to be considered.

EXAMPLE

Find the volume of $y = f(x) = 2x$, when rotated about the x-axis and bounded by $x = 2$.

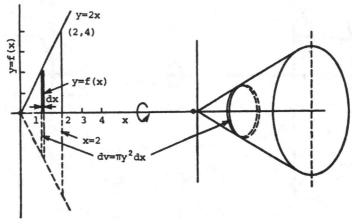

(a) Two-dimensional representation of f(x)

(b) Schematic of disk volume generated by rotating f(x) about the x-axis

Figure 13. Volume of a curve

SOLUTION

Solution #1, Disk Method.

The shaded strip, as shown in Figure 13(a), when rotated about the x-axis, sweeps a volume expressed by the disk as in Figure 13(b). The radius of this disk is y. Hence, its volume is $\pi y^2 \, dx$, where dx is the thickness of the disk. The sum of the volumes of all such disks for $0 \le x \le 2$ and passing to the limit gives:

$$V = \int_0^2 \left(\pi y^2 \right) dx = \pi \int_0^2 (2x)^2 \, dx$$

$$= 4\pi \int_0^2 x^2 \, dx = 4\pi \frac{x^3}{3} \Big|_0^2 = \frac{32\pi}{3}$$

Since an increment of the volume is a disk, this is called the **disk method**.

Solution #2, Shell Method

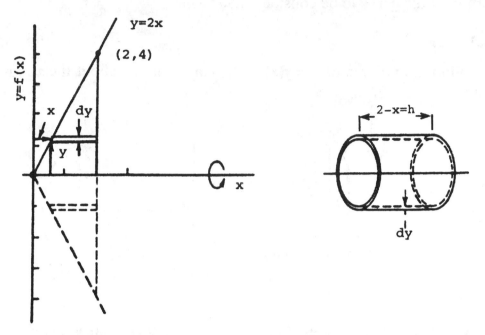

(a) Two-dimensional representation of *f*(*x*)   (b) Element of volume is shell

Figure 14. Shell Method

This volume might be conceived of as a constantly expanding cylindrical shell, the radius *y* of which increases from 0 to 4, Figure 14 (a). The height (*x* value) varies from 2 down to 0. The element of volume is obtained by multiplying circumference by height and by differential of thickness:

$$dV = 2\pi r\,h\,dy$$
$$= 2\pi y(2 - x)dy$$

The height of the element is really the length on the coordinate axis between the outer boundary and the equation of the line $y = 2x$, Figure 14(b). Since *x* is the distance to the function, $2 - x$ equals the height of the shell. All the unknowns in the dV expression must be in terms of *y*, since the differential term is dy. Therefore, we subsititute $\dfrac{y}{2}$ for *x* (from the original equation):

$$dV = 2\pi y\left(2 - \frac{y}{2}\right)dy$$

$$\int dV = 2\pi \int_{0}^{4}\left(2y - \frac{y^2}{2}\right)dy$$

$$V = 2\pi\left(y^2 - \frac{y^3}{6}\right)_0^4 = \frac{32\pi}{3}$$

Integration by Partial Fractions

When a function to be integrated is given in the form of a ratio in which the denominator can be factored, the best approach is to break up the single given ratio into a number of simpler ratios which may be integrated more easily.

In this approach, each factor of the denominator of the given ratio becomes the denominator of a separate fraction, so that the resulting number of separate fractions is equal to the number of factors of the given ratio. The numerators of the separate fractions are then solved from a set of simultaneous equations, which impose the condition that the sum of the separate fractions is equal to the value of the given function.

Double Integral

The **double integral** or **iterated integral** is an integral of an integral

$$\int_a^b \int_{y_1}^{y_2} f(x,y)\,dy\,dx$$

The limits of the inner integral y_1 and y_2 are usually functions of x, while the limits of the outer integral a and b are constants.

EXAMPLE

For Figure 15, use double integration to find the area enclosed by $y = x^2$ and $x + y - 2 = 0$.

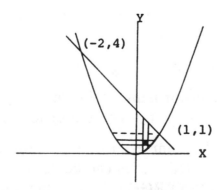

Figure 15. Area of a parabola

SOLUTION

The formula for area in Cartesian coordinates, using double integrals, is:

$$A = \iint dy\,dx \qquad dx = \int_a^b dx \int_{f(x)}^{F(x)} dy.$$

The limits a and b of the integral with respect to x are the x-coordinates of the points of intersection of the two curves. To find the points of intersection, we set $y = x^2$ equal to $y = 2 - x$ and solve for x.

$$x^2 = 2 - x \qquad (x + 2)(x - 1) = 0$$
$$x = -2 \quad x = 1$$

The limits of the integral with respect to y are the two functions. The lower limit is the lower function, the parabola $y = x^2$. The upper limit is the upper function, the line $y = 2 - x$. Therefore,

$$A = \int_{-2}^{1} dx \int_{x^2}^{2-x} dy$$

$$= \int_{-2}^{1} dx \left[y \right]_{x^2}^{2-x}$$

$$= \int_{-2}^{1} \left[2 - x - x^2 \right] dx = \left[2x - \frac{x^2}{2} - \frac{x^3}{3} \right]_{-2}^{1}$$

$$= \frac{7}{6} + \frac{10}{3} = \frac{27}{6}$$

$$= \frac{9}{2} \text{ sq. units}$$

Computations with Series

Series are very useful for numerical computations of such constants as c, π, etc., and for the computations of terms such as $\log x$, $\sin x$, etc.

Hence, if, by one of a number of possible procedures, we can find a series for a function, then that series can be used for computational purposes, but only IF IT CONVERGES. That is, the only kind of series that can be used for computation is a convergent series. The reason for this is that, if a series were not convergent but divergent—more and more terms are added—a continually different result would be obtained. With a convergent series, however, the series approaches a limit and gives an ever more accurate result, the more terms we add. Adding more terms does not change the result substantially after the first several terms, it only makes the result more accurate.

Assuming, then, that a series converges, it can be differentiated, integrated, added to other series, subtracted from other series, and multiplied by a constant, for example. A series, therefore, has a great deal of utility. If, for example, we know the series for sin x, we can find the series for cos x by differentiating that series term by term, since we know that $(d/dx)(\sin x)$ = cos$x$.

In a computation, once convergence is established, the number of terms to be used in the computation depends only on the accuracy desired.

Series

The sum of the first n numbers:

$$\sum(n) = 1 + 2 + 3 + 4 + 5.... + n = \frac{n(n+1)}{2}$$

The sum of the squares of the first n numbers:

$$\sum\left(n^2\right) = 1^2 + 2^2 + 3^2 + 4^2 + 5^2.... + n^2 = \frac{n(n+1)(2n+1)}{6}$$

The sum of the cubes of the first n numbers:

$$\sum\left(n^3\right) = 1^3 + 2^3 + 3^3 + 4^3 + 5^3.... + n^3 = \frac{n^2(n+1)^2}{4}$$

Arithmetic Series

Let C_1 be the first term and C_i be the ith term. Each term differs from the previous term by a constant, d.

$$C_{i+1} = C_i + d$$

The nth term is $C_1 + (n-1)d$, and the sum of n terms is $\frac{n}{2}(2a + (n-1)d)$.

An **arithmetic series** with an infinite number of terms always diverges. The sum of its terms is not defined.

Geometric Series

Let C_1 be the first term and C_i be the ith term. Each term is defined by multiplying the previous term by a constant, r.

$$C_{i+1} = rC_i$$

The nth term is $C_1 r^{n-1}$.

The sum of a **geometric series** with a finite number of terms, n, is

$$S_n = \frac{C_1(1-r^n)}{1-r}.$$

The sum of a series with an infinite number of terms is

$$S_\infty = \frac{C_1}{1-r}.$$

The infinite geometric series converges for $-1 < r < 1$ and diverges otherwise.

Harmonic Series

The general term of this series is

$$C_n = \frac{1}{a + (n-1)d}$$

where a and d are constants.

The sum of n terms where n is finite is

$$S_n = \frac{2}{n(2a + (n-1)d)}.$$

The infinite series always diverges.

The *p*-Series

The general term is $C_n = \dfrac{1}{n^p}$.

The sum of n terms is

$$\sum_{i=1}^{n} = \frac{1}{1^p} + \frac{1}{2^p} + \frac{1}{3^p} + \ldots + \frac{1}{i^p} + \ldots + \frac{1}{n^p}.$$

The infinite series converges if $p > 1$ and diverges otherwise.

Convergence of Infinite Series

If $\lim\limits_{n \to \infty} S_n$ exists, then the series converges. S_n is the sum of n terms.

If $\lim\limits_{n \to \infty} C_n \neq 0$, then the series diverges.

If $\lim\limits_{n \to \infty} C_n = 0$, no conclusions can be made. Additional tests are necessary.

Ratio Test for Convergence

Calculate $\lim\limits_{n \to \infty} \dfrac{C_{n+1}}{C_n} = h$.

The series converges if $h < 1$.

The series diverges if $h > 1$.

The ratio test fails if $h = 1$.

The ratio test will determine convergence for series with terms of alternating signs if the absolute value of the ratio is used.

Definition of Power Series

If x is a variable, then an infinite series of the form

$$\sum_{n=0}^{\infty} a_n x^n = a_0 + a_1 x + a_2 x^2 + a_3 x^3 + \ldots + a_n x^n + \ldots$$

is called a **power series**. More generally, we call a series of the form

$$\sum_{n=0}^{\infty} a_n (x - c)^n = a_0 + a_1 (x - c) + a_2 (x - c)^2 + \ldots + a_n (x - c)^n + \ldots$$

a **power series centered at** c, where c is a constant.

Definition of Taylor and Maclaurin Series

If a function f has derivatives of all orders at $x = c$, then the series

$$\sum_{n=0}^{\infty} \frac{f^{(n)}(c)}{n!} (x - c)^n = f(c) + f'(c)(x - c) + \ldots + \frac{f^{(n)}(c)}{n!} (x - c)^n + \ldots$$

is called the **Taylor series for** $f(x)$ **at** c. Moreover, if $c = 0$, then this series is called the **Maclaurin series for** f.

Comparison Test for Convergence

If G_n and H_n are both series and $g_i < h_i$ for all i, then H_n diverges if G_n diverges, and G_n converges if H_n converges.

Does the following infinite series converge?

$$1 - \frac{1}{2} + \frac{2}{2^2} - \frac{3}{2^3} + \dots + \frac{(-1)^n(-n)}{2^n} + \frac{(-1)^{n+1}(n+1)}{2^{n+1}} + \dots$$

Use the ratio test. Because this is an alternating sign series, we will use the absolute value of the ratio.

$$\lim_{n \to \infty} \left| \frac{Cn+1}{Cn} \right| = \lim_{n \to \infty} \frac{\frac{n+1}{2^{n+1}}}{\frac{n}{2^n}} = \lim_{n \to \infty} \frac{n+1}{2n}$$

$$= \lim_{n \to \infty} \left(\frac{1}{2} + \frac{1}{2n} \right) = \frac{1}{2} < 1$$

Thus, the series converges.

DIFFERENTIAL EQUATIONS

A differential equation displays the relationship among derivatives of a dependent variable

$$a_2 \frac{d^2 y}{dx^2} + a_1 \frac{dy}{dx} + a_0 y = f(x)$$

where x is the **independent variable** and y is the **dependent variable**.

A differential equation is linear if no term contains the dependent variable or any of its derivatives to other than the first power. The example equation is linear if coefficients a_0, a_1, and a_2 are constants or functions of x.

The equation is **homogeneous** if all terms contain the dependent variable or its derivatives. The example would be homogeneous if $f(x) = 0$.

The order of the equation is the order of its highest derivative. The example is second order. The general solution includes a number of arbitrary constants equal to the order. Numerical value of these constants are determined from initial and/or boundary conditions.

First Order

A linear, first order equation can be manipulated into the form

$$\frac{dy}{dx} + h(x)y = g(x).$$

We multiply the equation by an integrating factor

$$u(x) = e^{\int h(x)dx}.$$

The left-hand side forms the derivative of a product.

$$d(y \bullet u(x)) = u(x) \bullet g(x)dx$$

After integration and rearrangement, we get the solution

$$y(x) = \frac{1}{u(x)}\int u(x) \bullet g(x)dx + \frac{C}{u(x)}.$$

EXAMPLE

Find the solution of

$$\frac{dy}{dx} - \frac{1}{x}y = x^2 + 3x - 2.$$

SOLUTION

The integrating factor $u(x) = e^{-\int \frac{dx}{x}} = e^{-\ln x} = \frac{1}{x}.$

Multiply the entire equation by the integrating factor.

$$\frac{1}{x}dy - \frac{y}{x^2}dx = \left(x + 3 - \frac{2}{x}\right)dx$$

$$d\left(\frac{y}{x}\right) = \left(x + 3 - \frac{2}{x}\right)dx$$

Integrate both sides.

$$\frac{y}{x} = \frac{1}{2}x^2 + 3x - 2\ln x + C$$

Finally, solve for y.

$$y = \frac{1}{2}x^3 + 3x^2 - 2x\ln x + Cx$$

Linear Differential Equations with Constant Coefficients

$$a_n\frac{d^n y}{dx^n} + a_{n-1}\frac{d^{n-1}y}{dx^{n-1}} + a_{n-2}\frac{d^{n-2}y}{dx^{n-2}} + \ldots + a_2\frac{d^2 y}{dx^2} + a_1\frac{dy}{dx} + a_0 y = f(x)$$

$a_n, a_{n-1}, a_{n-2}, \ldots, a_2, a_1, a_0$ are constant.

The **general solution** is $y = y_h + y_p$, where y_h is the solution to the homogeneous equation corresponding to $f(x) = 0$ and y_p is the particular solution.

Homogeneous solution y_h:

The characteristic equation corresponding to the homogeneous form of the differential equation is found by replacing the kth derivative with m^k:

$$a_n m^n + a_{n-1}m^{n-1} + a_{n-2}m^{n-2} + \ldots + a_2 m^2 + a_1 m + a_0 = 0$$

Each root of this equation, r_k, appears in y_h in the form $e^{r_k x}$.

- Each distinct real root, r_1, will generate $C_j e^{r_1 x}$.

- Repeated real roots, r_2, will generate

$$C_2 e^{r_2 x} + C_3 x e^{r_2 x}.$$

- Complex roots $r_5 = a + ib$ and $r_6 = a - ib$ can be written in the standard form

$$C_5 e^{r_5 x} + C_6 e^{r_6 x}$$

where the constant coefficients C_5 and C_6 are complex conjugates.

It is convenient to write solution terms corresponding to complex roots with trigonometric functions.

$$e^{ax}(C_7 \sin bx + C_8 \cos bx)$$

Here C_7 and C_8 are real constants. Note that the real part of the complex root, a, appears in the exponent, and the coefficient of the imaginary part, b, appears in the sin and cos arguments.

If the **deferential** equation is m^{th} order, there will be m terms in the homogeneous solution with m constants, the numerical values of which must be determined from m specified data values.

Particular Solution y_p

The particular solution is formed from the sum of $f(x)$ and its derivatives, each term of which has an unknown constant coefficient to be determined by substituting the particular solution into the differential equation. Table 3 displays forms of particular solutions.

TABLE 3 **PARTICULAR SOLUTIONS**	
$f(x)$	y_p
a	A
$ax + b$	$Ax + B$
$ax^n + bx^{n-1} + cx^{n-2} + ...$	$Ax^n + Bx^{n-1} + Cx^{n-2} + ... + Cx + H$
$a \sin cx, \; a \cos cx,$ or $a \sin cx + b \cos cx$	$A \sin cx + B \cos cx$
e^{ax}	Ae^{ax}

Note: If $f(x) = e^{ax}$, and the term e^{ax} also appears in the homogeneous solution, the particular solution has the form Axe^{ax}.

If $f(x) = a \sin cx$ or $a \cos cx$, and these terms also appear in the homogeneous solution, the particular solution has the form $A \, x \sin cx + B \, x \cos cx$.

EXAMPLE

Solve

$$2\frac{dy}{dx} + y = \sin 5x$$

where $y = 10$ at $x = 0$.

SOLUTION

To find the homogeneous solution, write the characteristic equation

$$2m + 1 = 0 \text{ which has a root } m = -\frac{1}{2}.$$

The homogeneous solution is $y_h = Ae^{-\frac{x}{2}}$, where A is a constant to be determined later.

To find the particular solution, we use Table 3 to determine the form is

$$y_p = C \sin 5x + D \cos 5x.$$

To determine the constants C and D, substitute y_p into the differential equation.

$$2(5C \cos 5x - 5D \sin 5x) + (C \sin 5x + D \cos 5x) = \sin 5x$$

Equate coefficients of the sin and cos terms.

$$-10D + C = 1 \qquad 10C + D = 0$$

Solving for C and D gives $C = \frac{1}{101}$ and $D = -\frac{10}{101}$.

The total solution is $y = y_h + y_p$.

$$y = Ae^{-\frac{x}{2}} + \frac{1}{101} \sin 5x - \frac{10}{101} \cos 5x$$

To find A, use $y = 10$ when $x = 0$.

$$10 = A(1) + 0 - \frac{10}{101}(1)$$

Thus, $A = 10 + \frac{10}{101} = 10.099$ and the solution is

$$y = 10.099e^{-\frac{x}{2}} + \frac{1}{101} \sin 5x - \frac{10}{101} \cos 5x.$$

Linear, Second Order with Constant Coefficients

$$a\frac{d^2y}{dx^2} + b\frac{dy}{dx} + cy = f(x)$$

(This equation, with $b > 0$ and $c > 0$, plays an important role in dynamics.)

The homogeneous part of the solution is based on the characteristic equation

$$am^2 + bm + c = 0.$$

This is a quadratic equation and the roots are given by

$$r_1, r_2 = \frac{-b \pm \sqrt{b^2 - 4ac}}{2a}.$$

If $b^2 - 4ac > 0$, there are two distinct real roots, the solution is overdamped, and the homogeneous solution has the form

$$C_1 e^{r_1 x} + C_2 e^{r_2 x}.$$

If $b^2 - 4ac = 0$, there are two repeated roots, the solution is critically damped, and the homogeneous solution has the form

$$C_1 e^{r_1 x} + C_2 x e^{r_1 x}.$$

If $b^2 - 4ac < 0$, the roots are complex conjugates

$$r_1 = \lambda + i\mu \quad r_2 = \lambda - i\mu.$$

The solution is underdamped, and the homogeneous solution has the form

$$e^{\lambda x}(C_1 \cos \mu x + C_2 \sin \mu x).$$

EXAMPLE

Find the solution to

$$\frac{d^2y}{dx^2} + 3\frac{dy}{dx} + 2x = 1 \quad \text{at } x = 0, y = 0, \text{ and } \frac{dy}{dx} = 0.$$

SOLUTION

To find the homogeneous part, write and factor the characteristic equation.

$$m^2 + 3m + 2 = (m + 2)(m + 1) = 0$$

There are two distinct real roots, -2 and -1, and the system is overdamped.

$$y_h = C_1 e^{-2x} + C_2 e^{-x}$$

To find the particular solution, note that the nonhomogeneous term is a constant, and from Table 3, the form of the particular solution is a constant.

$$y_p = A$$

Substitute this particular solution into the original differential equation.

$$0 + 0 + 2A = 1 \quad \text{Thus, } A = \frac{1}{2}$$

The general solution is

$$y = y_h + y_p = C_1 e^{-2x} + C_2 e^{-x} + \frac{1}{2}.$$

Differences

If y is a function of x, and y is given at discrete values of x, this yields a table of values.

The first difference of $f(x)$ is obtained when we subtract $f(x_{i+1}) - f(x_i) i = 0, ..., n$ and is written as

$$f(x_{i+1}) - f(x_i) = \Delta f(x_i) \quad \text{or}$$
$$y_{i+1} - y_i = \Delta y_i$$

which is more commonly used.

The second difference is the difference of the first differences, indicated as

$$\Delta^2 y_i = \Delta y_{i+1} - \Delta y_i.$$

The nth differences are obtained in a similar manner. So we have for any n, an integer, the nth difference of $y = f(x)$ is given by

$$\Delta^n y_i = \Delta^{n-1} y_{i+1} - \Delta^{n-1} y_i.$$

Another way of obtaining the nth difference is by continuously substituting function values. For example,

$$\Delta^2 y_0 = \Delta y_1 - \Delta y_0 = (y_2 - y_1) - (y_1 - y_0) = y_2 - 2y_1 + y_0$$
$$\Delta^2 y_1 = \Delta y_2 - \Delta y_1 = (y_3 - y_2) - (y_2 - y_1) = y_3 - 2y_2 + y_1$$
$$\Delta^3 y_0 = \Delta^2 y_1 - \Delta^2 y_0 = (y_3 - 2y_2 + y_1) - (y_2 - 2y_1 + y_0)$$
$$= y_3 - 3y_2 + 3y_1 - y_0$$

We then have a general formula given by

$$\Delta^k y_0 = y_k - \binom{k}{1} y_{k-1} + \binom{k}{2} y_{k-2} - \dots + (-1)^k \left\{ \begin{matrix} k \\ k \end{matrix} \right\} y_0 = \sum_{i=0}^{k} (-1)^i \binom{k}{i} y_{k-1}$$

where $\binom{k}{i}$ is the binomial coefficient.

Considering the reverse, we may express a value of y in terms of the preceding values of y and the differences. We had

$$y_{i+1} - y_i = \Delta y_i$$

so

$$y_1 = y_0 + \Delta y_0$$

and

$$\Delta^n y_i = \Delta^{n-1} y_{i+1} - \Delta^{n-1} y_i$$

therefore

$$\Delta^3 y_0 = y_3 - 3y_2 + 3y_1 - y_0$$

$$y_3 = y_0 - 3y_1 + 3y_2 + \Delta^3 y_0$$
$$= y_0 + 3(y_2 - y_1) + \Delta^3 y_0$$
$$= y_0 + 3\Delta y_1 + \Delta^3 y_0$$
$$= y_0 + 3(\Delta^2 y_0 + \Delta y_0) + \Delta^3 y_0$$
$$= y_0 + 3\Delta y_0 + 3\Delta^2 y_0 + \Delta^3 y_0$$

So it appears that y_k can be expressed by the general formula

$$y_k = y_0 + \begin{bmatrix} k \\ 1 \end{bmatrix} \Delta y_0 + \begin{bmatrix} k \\ 2 \end{bmatrix} \Delta^2 y_0 + \ldots + \Delta^k y_0$$

$$= \sum_{i=0}^{k} \begin{bmatrix} k \\ i \end{bmatrix} \Delta^i y_0$$

where $\begin{pmatrix} k \\ i \end{pmatrix}$ is the binomial coefficient.

LAPLACE TRANSFORMS

The **Laplace Transform** is an integral transform. A function $f(t)$ can be transformed to $F(s)$ by the following:

$$F(s) = \mathbf{L}(f(t)) = \int_0^\infty f(t)e^{-st}dt$$

Given $F(s)$, the corresponding function $f(t)$ can be found by

$$f(t) = \frac{1}{2\pi i} \int_{a-i\infty}^{a+i\infty} F(s)e^{st}ds$$

In practice a table of transforms such as Table 4 is used. It is important to note that the Laplace Transform is linear.

$$\mathbf{L}(cf(t)) = c\mathbf{L}(f(t))$$
$$\mathbf{L}(f_1(t) + f_2(t)) = \mathbf{L}(f_1(t)) + \mathbf{L}(f_2(t))$$

Also note that the Laplace Transform of a derivative is s multiplied into the transform of the function being differentiated. These transforms are used primarily to solve linear differential equations with constant coefficients.

TABLE 4	
LAPLACE TRANSFORMS	

$f(t)$	$F(s)$
1	$\dfrac{1}{s}$
e^{-at}	$\dfrac{1}{s+a}$
t	$\dfrac{1}{s^2}$
$\sin at$	$\dfrac{a}{s^2+a^2}$
$\cos at$	$\dfrac{s}{s^2+a^2}$
$\dfrac{d\,f(t)}{dt}$	$s\,F(s)-f(0)$
$\dfrac{d^2 f(t)}{dt^2}$	$s^2 F(s)-sf(0)-\dfrac{df}{dt}(0)$
$\displaystyle\int_0^t f(t)dt$	$\dfrac{F(s)}{s}$

Find the transform of $f(t) = e^{-at}$.

$$\mathbf{L}\left(e^{-at}\right) = \int_0^\infty e^{-at}e^{-st}dt = \int_0^\infty e^{-(a+s)t}dt$$

$$= -\left.\frac{e^{-(a+s)t}}{a+s}\right]_0^\infty = 0-\left(-\frac{1}{s+a}\right) = \frac{1}{s+a}$$

Laplace Transform Properties

The Step Function

The transform of the step function is given by

$$\mathbf{L}[f(t)] = \int_0^x e^{-st}dt = \frac{1}{s}$$

Thus,

$$f(t) \leftrightarrow \frac{1}{s}.$$

The Ramp Function

The ramp is $tf(t)$. Hence,

$$\mathbf{L}[tf(t)] = \int_0^\infty te^{-st}dt = \frac{1}{s^2}$$

and

$$tf(t) \leftrightarrow \frac{1}{s^2}.$$

The Impulse Function

The Laplace Transform of an impulse existing at $t = 0$ is

$$\mathbf{L}[\delta(t)] = \int_0^\infty \delta(t)e^{-st}dt = 1.$$

The Exponential Function

For a causal exponential function

$$\mathbf{L}\left[e^{-\alpha t}f(t)\right] = \int_0^\infty e^{-\alpha t}e^{-st}dt = \frac{1}{s+\alpha}.$$

This transform exists even if α is negative—that is, the exponential is a growing one—because s can always be chosen so that $e^{-(\alpha+s)t} \to 0$ as $t \to \infty$.

Linearity

If
$$f_1(t) \leftrightarrow F_1(s) \text{ and } f_2(t) \leftrightarrow F_2(s),$$

then
$$a_1 f_1(t) + a_2 f_2(t) \leftrightarrow a_1 F_1(s) + a_2 F_2(s).$$

Scaling

A change in the time scale can bring about time expansion or compression of a signal depending on the magnitude of the scale change. In the following result, time reflection is disallowed.

If
$$f(t) \leftrightarrow F(s),$$

then
$$f(at) \leftrightarrow \frac{1}{a} F\left(\frac{s}{a}\right), \ a > 0.$$

Integration

If
$$f(t) \leftrightarrow F(s),$$

$$g(t) = \int_{-\infty}^{t} f(\tau)d\tau,$$

then
$$\mathbf{L}[g(t)] = G(s) = \frac{1}{s} F(s) + \frac{1}{s} \int_{-\infty}^{0} f(\tau)d\tau.$$

This can also be written

$$G(s) = \frac{1}{s} F(s) + \frac{g(0)}{s}$$

because
$$g(0) \equiv \int_{-\infty}^{0} f(\tau)d\tau.$$

Differentiation

The differentiation theorem will be most important in the solution of differential equations using the Laplace Transform. It is analogous to the time-advance theorem of the *z*-transform.

If $\qquad f(t) \leftrightarrow F(s)$,

then $\qquad pf(t) \leftrightarrow sF(s) - f(0)$,

$$p^2 f(t) \leftrightarrow s^2 F(s) - sf(0) - pf(0),$$

$$\vdots$$

$$p^n f(t) \leftrightarrow s^n F(s) - s^{n-1} f(0) - s^{n-2} pf(0) - \ldots - p^{n-1} f(0)$$

Periodic Functions

Consider a causal function that is periodic for $t > 0$. We denote the part of $f(t)$ in the first period as $f_T(t)$. That is,

$$f_T(t) = \begin{cases} f(t), & 0 \leq t < T, \\ 0, & \text{elsewhere} \end{cases}$$

Then, if

$$f_T(t) \leftrightarrow F_T(s),$$

$$f(t) \leftrightarrow F_T(s) \frac{1}{1 + e^{-Ts}}.$$

STATISTICS

For a set of n values, x_i, $i = 1, 2, 3, \ldots, n$

- the **mean** or **average** is $\dfrac{\displaystyle\sum_{i=1}^{n} x_i}{n}$.

- the **mode** is the value that occurs most often.

- the **median** is the middle value. The set must be ordered in increasing or decreasing order. If there are an odd number of values, the median is the middle value. If there are an even number of values, the median is the mean of the two values in the middle.

- the **range** is the maximum value–the minimum value.

- the **variance** for a sample is

$$\text{sample variance} = \frac{\sum_{i=1}^{n}(x_i - \text{mean})^2}{n-1}$$

- the **standard deviation** for a sample is the square root of the variance.

The numerical values that are computed from the complete population of numbers are called population parameters. The numerical values that are computed from a random sample and are used to infer information about the complete population are called sample statistics. The equation for the sample variance is given above. The variance computed from complete population data has the formula

$$\text{population variance} = \frac{\sum_{i=1}^{n}(x_i - \text{mean})^2}{n}$$

EXAMPLE

The following 10 values represent a random sample:

$$1, 3, 4, 6, 7, 9, 9, 9, 14, 18$$

Find the mean, mode, median, range, and variance.

SOLUTION

The mean is $\dfrac{1 + 3 + 4 + 6 + 7 + (3 \bullet 9) + 14 + 18}{10} = 8.$

The mode is 9.

There are an even number of values and the median is

$$\frac{7+9}{2} = 8.$$

The range is $18 - 1 = 17$.

The variance is

$$\frac{(1-8)^2 + (3-8)^2 + (4-8)^2 + (6-8)^2 + (7-8)^2 + 3(9-8)^2 + (14-8)^2 + (18-8)^2}{10-1}$$

$$= \frac{234}{9} = 26$$

The sample standard deviation is $\sqrt{26} = 5.10$

Combinations and Permutations

The number of **combinations** of n things taken x at a time is

$$\binom{n}{x} = C(n, x) = \frac{n!}{x!(n-x)!}.$$

The number of **permutations** of n things taken x at a time is

$$P(n, x) = \frac{n!}{(n-x)!}.$$

In a permutation each order or arrangement of the x items is counted. There are more permutations than combinations.

Consider the set of four letters a, b, c, and d. For this set $n = 4$. We wish to consider pairs of letters from this set; $x = 2$. The number of combinations is

$$C(4, 2) = \frac{4!}{2!\,2!} = \frac{4 \cdot 3 \cdot 2 \cdot 1}{2 \cdot 1 \cdot 2 \cdot 1} = 6.$$

These six combinations are *ab, ac, ad, bc, bd,* and *cd.*

The number of permutations is

$$P(n, x) = \frac{4!}{2!} = \frac{4 \cdot 3 \cdot 2 \cdot 1}{2 \cdot 1} = 12.$$

These 12 permutations are *ab, ba, ac, ca, ad, da, bc, cb, bd, db, cd,* and *dc.*

Rules of Probability

Let A and B represent independent events.

The **probability** of A occurring is

$$0 \le p(A) \le 1.$$

If $p(A) = 1$, then the occurrence is a certainty. If $p(A) = 0$, then it will certainly not occur. The probability of A not occurring is

$$p(\text{not } A) = 1 - p(A).$$

The probability of either *A* or *B* or both occurring is

$$p(A + B) = p(A) + p(B) - p(A)p(B).$$

The probability of either *A* or *B* but not both occurring is

$$p(A \text{ or } B) = p(A) + p(B) - 2\,p(A)p(B).$$

The probability of both *A* and *B* occurring is

$$p(A \text{ and } B) = p(A)p(B).$$

Consider a pair of standard six-sided dice.

We roll one die. The probability of rolling a 4 is $\dfrac{1}{6}$.

The probability of not rolling a 4 is $1 - \dfrac{1}{6} = \dfrac{5}{6}$.

The probability of rolling at least a 4 means the probability of rolling a 4, a 5, or a 6, which is

$$p(4) + p(5) + p(6) = \frac{1}{6} + \frac{1}{6} + \frac{1}{6} = \frac{1}{2}.$$

We roll both dice. The probability of rolling a 4 two times is

$$\left(\frac{1}{6}\right)\left(\frac{1}{6}\right) = \frac{1}{36}.$$

We roll both dice. The probability of rolling a 4 on one or the other die, or on both dice is

$$\left(\frac{1}{6}\right) + \left(\frac{1}{6}\right) - \left(\frac{1}{6}\right)\left(\frac{1}{6}\right) = \frac{11}{36}.$$

We roll both dice. The probability of rolling a 4 on one or the other die, but not on both dice (exclusive or), is

$$\left(\frac{1}{6}\right) + \left(\frac{1}{6}\right) - 2\left(\frac{1}{6}\right)\left(\frac{1}{6}\right) = \frac{10}{36}.$$

Normal Distribution

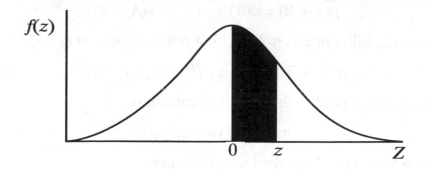

Figure 16. Normal distribution

The **normal** (Figure 16), **gaussian**, or **bell-shaped** distribution is described by its **probability density function**

$$f(Z) = \frac{1}{\sqrt{2\pi}} e^{-\frac{z^2}{2}}$$

where
$$Z = \frac{X - \text{mean}}{\text{standard deviation}}.$$

The probability of finding values between Z_1 and Z_2 is obtained by integrating the density function between these limits.

$$\int_{Z_1}^{Z_2} f(Z)\,dZ$$

In practice, these probabilities are read from the Appendix (at the back of this book), which displays the integral from $Z = 0$ to $Z = z$. Note that the density function is symmetric. Probabilities are indicated by areas under the density function curve.

Probability Density Functions for Continuous Random Variables

In the case of X being a continuous random variable, its probability density function obeys the following conditions:

1) $f(x) \geq 0$ for all x

2) $\int_{-\infty}^{\infty} f(x)dx = 1$

3) $P(a \leq X \leq b) = \int_a^b f(x)dx$

Here $P(a < X < b)$ is the probability of X having a value greater than a and less than b. (Notice "greater than" and "greater than or equal to" give the same value since X is a continuous random variable.)

Consider the function given by

$$f(x) = \begin{cases} \dfrac{1}{x^2} & \text{for } x \geq 1 \\ 0 & \text{otherwise} \end{cases}$$

We show this is a density function. Since $f(x) > 0$ for all x, 1) is satisfied. We see that 2) is satisfied since

$$\int_{-\infty}^{\infty} f(x)dx = \int_1^{\infty} \frac{1}{x^2}dx = -\frac{1}{x}\Big|_1^{\infty} = 1.$$

The probability function is given by

$$P(a \leq X \leq b) = \int_a^b f(x)dx = \int_a^b \frac{1}{x^2}dx.$$

(Here we assume that a and b are greater than 1.)

For example,

$$P(3 \leq X \leq 5) = \int_3^5 \frac{1}{x^2}dx = -\frac{1}{x}\Big|_3^5 = \frac{1}{3} - \frac{1}{5} = \frac{2}{15}.$$

EXAMPLE

Find the constant C that makes $f(x)$ given by

$$f(x) = \begin{cases} \dfrac{C}{x^4} & \text{for } x \geq 1 \\ 0 & \text{otherwise} \end{cases}$$

a density function.

SOLUTION

In order for $f(x)$ to be a probability density, it must satisfy 2). Integrating we have

$$\int_{-\infty}^{\infty} f(x)dx = \int_{1}^{\infty} \frac{C}{x^4}dx$$

$$= \frac{Cx^{-3}}{-3}\Big|_{1}^{\infty} = \frac{C}{3}.$$

Hence,

$$\frac{C}{3} = 1$$

$$C = 3$$

Probability Density Functions for Discrete Random Variables

A probability density function tells how a distribution is weighted from $-\infty$ to ∞. In the case of X being a discrete random variable which has outcomes x_i with probability $p(x_i)$ for $i = 1, 2, 3, ...$ The probability density function $p(x)$ obeys the following conditions:

1) $p(x_i) \geq 0$ for all x

2) $\sum p(x_i) = 1$

3) $P(a \leq X \leq b) = \sum_{i} p(x_i), x_i \in [a,b]$

where here $P(a \leq X \leq b)$ is the probability of X having an outcome within the interval $[a, b]$.

Binomial Distributions

Let X be a binomial random variable with n repetitions. The probability distribution is given by

$$P(X = k) = \binom{n}{k} p^k (1-p)^{n-k} \quad k = 0, 1, 2, ..., n \text{ and } 0 < p < 1$$

$$0 \qquad\qquad \text{otherwise}$$

Note that this is a discrete distribution where the sum of the weights adds up to 1, i.e.,

$$\sum_{k=0}^{n} P(X = k) = \sum_{k=0}^{n} \binom{h}{k} p^k (1-p)^{h-k}$$
$$= \left[p + (1-p) \right]^n$$
$$= 1^n$$
$$= 1$$

Taking $p = \dfrac{1}{2}$ we see that $P(X = k)$ gives the probability of obtaining k heads when flipping a fair coin n times.

Poisson Distribution

Let X be a Poisson random variable. The probability distribution is given by

$$P(X = k) = \frac{e^{-\lambda} \lambda^k}{k!} \qquad k = 0, 1, 2, 3, \ldots$$

Here λ is called the parameter of the Poisson distribution.

As with the binomial distribution, this is a discrete distribution where the sum of the weights add up to 1, i.e.,

$$\sum_{k=0}^{\infty} P(X = k) = \sum_{k=0}^{\infty} \frac{e^{-\lambda} \lambda^k}{k!}$$
$$= e^{-\lambda} e^{\lambda}$$
$$= 1$$

The Poisson distribution is applied in many instances to physical phenomena.

Exponential Distribution

Let x be an exponential random variable. The probability density function is given by

$$f(x) = \begin{cases} \lambda e^{-\lambda x} & \text{for } x \geq 0 \\ 0 & \text{otherwise} \end{cases}$$

Integrating we obtain the probability distribution given by (here $x \geq 0$)

$$P(X \leq x) = \int_0^x \lambda e^{-\lambda x} dx = -e^{-\lambda x}\Big|_0^x = 1 - e^{-\lambda x}.$$

An interesting property of the exponential distribution is the fact that it has "no memory," i.e.,

$$P(X > s + t | X > s) = P(X > t).$$

This distribution is used in many instances to model the failure rate of electrical components.

EXAMPLE

Let T denote the lifetime of a component. Define the reliability of a component by

$$R(t) = P(T > t) = 1 - P(t \leq T)$$
$$= e^{-\lambda T}$$

SOLUTION

Assume $\lambda = 2$. We calculate the number of operating hours given the reliability is specified at 80%. From the equation above, we have

$$R(t) = 0.8 = e^{-2t}$$

hence
$$t = 0.112.$$

This can be interpreted as follows: if 100 components are operating for 0.112 hours, then about 80 of them will not fail during that time.

Hypothesis Testing

The purpose of hypothesis testing is to choose between competing hypotheses about the value of a population parameter. The two competing mutually exclusive hypotheses are usually called the null hypothesis and the alternative hypothesis. For example, suppose the computer industry claims the price of computers has increased by $100 over last year. You believe that the price has increased by more than $100. Letting μ be the parameter which measures the price increase, we establish the null and alternative hypothesis by

$$H_0 : \mu = \$100 \text{ (null hypothesis)}$$
$$H_\mu : \mu > \$100 \text{ (alternative hypothesis)}$$

The above is called a "one-sided" test due to the fact that the alternative hypothesis specifies as completely above the value of 100. If one believes that the price of computers has either increased by more than $100 or increased by less than $100, we have a "two-sided" test where the null and alternative hypothesis are given by

$$H_0 : \mu = \$100 \text{ (null hypothesis)}$$
$$H_a : \mu \neq \$100 \text{ (alternative hypothesis)}$$

There are four possibilities that can occur when a decision is made in the tests above:

1) accepting H_0 when H_0 is true,
2) rejecting H_0 when H_0 is false,
3) rejecting H_0 when H_0 is true,
4) accepting H_0 when H_0 is false.

Note that 3) and 4) are incorrect conclusions. These are labeled Type 1 error and Type 2 error, respectively. We denote by the probability of Type 1 error. The confidence level is then defined by

$$\text{Confidence level} = 1 - P(\text{Type 1 error})$$
$$= 1 - \alpha$$
$$= P(\text{accept } H \mid H \text{ is true})$$

α is also called the level of significance.

In a similiar way we denote by β the probability of Type 2 error. The power is then defined by

$$\text{Power} = 1 - \beta = P(\text{reject } H \mid H \text{ is false}).$$

Note that α and β need not add up to 1.

EXAMPLE

A firm producing light bulbs wants to know if it can claim that its light bulbs last 1,000 burning hours. To answer this question, the firm takes a random sample of 100 bulbs from those it has produced and finds that the average lifetime for this sample is 970 burning hours. The firm knows that the standard deviation of the lifetime of the bulbs it produces is 80 hours. Can the firm claim that the average lifetime of its bulbs is 1,000 hours at the 5% level of significance?

SOLUTION

Since the firm is claiming that the average lifetime of its bulbs is 1,000 hours, we have

$$H_0 : \mu = 1,000; \ H_1 : \mu \neq 1,000.$$

Figure 17 depicts the data from this problem.

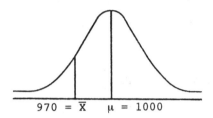

970 = $\overline{X}$ μ = 1000

Figure 17. Normal distribution

The statistic $\dfrac{(\overline{X} - \mu)}{\sigma}$ has a standard normal distribution with a mean of 0 and a standard deviation of 1. We calculate this value, which is called z,

$$z = \frac{\overline{X} - \mu}{\sigma_{\overline{X}}}, \ \text{where} \ \sigma_{\overline{X}} = \frac{\sigma}{\sqrt{n}}$$

and compare the value of z to a critical value. If z lies beyond this critical value, we will reject H_0. For this problem, where we have $\alpha = 5\%$ and a two-tailed test, our critical value is 1.96, since for the standard normal distribution, 2.5% of scores will have a z-value above 1.96 and 2.5% of scores will have a value below −1.96. Therefore, we use the following decision rule: reject H_0 if $z > 1.96$ or $z < -1.96$. Accept H_0 if $-1.96 < z \leq 1.96$.

For the data of this problem

$$\sigma_{\overline{X}} = \frac{80}{\sqrt{100}} = 8 \ \text{and} \ z = \frac{970 - 1,000}{8} = \frac{-30}{8} = -3.75.$$

Since $-3.75 < -1.96$, we reject H_0 and conclude that the average lifetime of the firm's bulbs is not 1,000 hours.

REVIEW PROBLEMS

PROBLEM 1

Find the inverse of

$$\mathbf{A} = \begin{bmatrix} 3 & -1 & -2 \\ 0 & 2 & -1 \\ 4 & -10 & 2 \end{bmatrix}$$

SOLUTION

In the example on p. 28, the determinant was found to be $|\mathbf{A}| = 2$. In order to find the adjoint of A the cofactor of each of the nine elements is needed.

$$\begin{aligned}
C_{11} &= (+1)(4 - 10) & C_{12} &= (-1)(0 + 4) & C_{13} &= (+1)(0 - 8) \\
C_{21} &= (-1)(-2 - 20) & C_{22} &= (+1)(6 + 8) & C_{23} &= (-1)(-30 + 4) \\
C_{31} &= (+1)(1 + 4) & C_{32} &= (-1)(-3 + 0) & C_{33} &= (+1)(6 - 0)
\end{aligned}$$

$$\text{Adj } \mathbf{A} = \begin{bmatrix} -6 & -4 & -8 \\ 22 & 14 & 26 \\ 5 & 3 & 6 \end{bmatrix}^T$$

$$= \begin{bmatrix} -6 & 22 & 5 \\ -4 & 14 & 3 \\ -8 & 26 & 6 \end{bmatrix}$$

The inverse of $\mathbf{A}$ is

$$\mathbf{A}^{-1} = \frac{\text{Adj } \mathbf{A}}{|\mathbf{A}|} = \frac{\text{Adj } \mathbf{A}}{2}$$

$$= \begin{bmatrix} -3 & 11 & 2.5 \\ -2 & 7 & 1.5 \\ -4 & 13 & 3 \end{bmatrix}$$

We can verify the inverse $\mathbf{A}^{-1}$ by multiplying it by A.

$$A^{-1}A = \begin{bmatrix} -3 & 11 & 2.5 \\ -2 & 7 & 1.5 \\ -4 & 13 & 3 \end{bmatrix} \begin{bmatrix} 3 & -1 & -2 \\ 0 & 2 & -1 \\ 4 & -10 & 2 \end{bmatrix}$$

$$= \begin{bmatrix} -9+0+10 & 3+22-25 & 6-11+5 \\ -6+0+6 & 2+14-15 & 4-7+3 \\ -12+0+12 & 4+26-30 & 8-13+6 \end{bmatrix}$$

$$= \begin{bmatrix} 1 & 0 & 0 \\ 0 & 1 & 0 \\ 0 & 0 & 1 \end{bmatrix} = I$$

PROBLEM 2

Solve the following set of equations by a) using the inverse of the coefficient matrix and b) using Cramer's Rule.

$$3x_1 - x_2 - 2x_3 = 4$$
$$2x_2 - x_3 = 2$$
$$4x_1 - 10x_2 + 2x_3 = 1$$

SOLUTION

These equations can be written as $\mathbf{Ax} = \mathbf{b}$, where

$$A = \begin{bmatrix} 3 & -1 & -2 \\ 0 & 2 & -1 \\ 4 & -10 & 2 \end{bmatrix} \quad x = \begin{bmatrix} x_1 \\ x_2 \\ x_3 \end{bmatrix} \quad b = \begin{bmatrix} 4 \\ 2 \\ 1 \end{bmatrix}$$

a) Solution via the inverse of $\mathbf{A}$. The coefficient matrix $\mathbf{A}$ is the same as the matrix in Practice Problem 1 used to illustrate the inverse of a general non-singular matrix. From that problem, the inverse is

$$A^{-1} = \begin{bmatrix} -3 & 11 & 2.5 \\ -2 & 7 & 1.5 \\ -4 & 13 & 3 \end{bmatrix}$$

The $\mathbf{x}$ vector is found by

$$\mathbf{x} = \mathbf{A}^{-1}\mathbf{b} = \begin{bmatrix} -3 & 11 & 2.5 \\ -2 & 7 & 1.5 \\ -4 & 13 & 3 \end{bmatrix} \begin{bmatrix} 4 \\ 2 \\ 1 \end{bmatrix}$$

$$= \begin{bmatrix} -12 & + & 22 & + & 2.5 \\ -8 & + & 14 & + & 1.5 \\ -16 & + & 26 & + & 3 \end{bmatrix} = \begin{bmatrix} 12.5 \\ 7.5 \\ 13 \end{bmatrix}$$

The solution is

$$x_1 = 12.5$$
$$x_2 = 7.5$$
$$x_3 = 13$$

b) Solution via Cramer's Rule.

The determinant of the coefficient matrix **A** is

$$|\mathbf{A}| = \begin{vmatrix} 3 & -1 & -2 \\ 0 & 2 & -1 \\ 4 & -10 & 2 \end{vmatrix} = 2$$

The three determinants $|\Delta_1|$, $|\Delta_2|$, and $|\Delta_3|$ are from matrices formed by replacing the first, second, and third columns, respectively, of the **A** matrix by the *b* vector.

$$|\Delta_1| = \begin{vmatrix} 4 & -1 & -2 \\ 2 & 2 & -1 \\ 1 & -10 & 2 \end{vmatrix} = 25$$

$$|\Delta_2| = \begin{vmatrix} 3 & 4 & -2 \\ 0 & 2 & -1 \\ 4 & 1 & 2 \end{vmatrix} = 15$$

$$|\Delta_3| = \begin{vmatrix} 3 & -1 & 4 \\ 0 & 2 & 2 \\ 4 & -10 & 1 \end{vmatrix} = 26$$

The elements of the **x** vector are given by

$$x_1 = \frac{|\Delta_1|}{|A|} = \frac{25}{2} = 12.5$$

$$x_2 = \frac{|\Delta_2|}{|A|} = \frac{15}{2} = 7.5$$

$$x_3 = \frac{|\Delta_3|}{|A|} = \frac{26}{2} = 13$$

PROBLEM 3

Find the equation of a plane perpendicular to the vector $\mathbf{B} = \mathbf{i} - 4\mathbf{j} + 3\mathbf{k}$.

SOLUTION

Let $\mathbf{G} = x\mathbf{i} + y\mathbf{j} + z\mathbf{k}$ be a vector in the plane. The vectors $\mathbf{G}$ and $\mathbf{B}$ should be perpendicular. Their dot product is zero,

$$\mathbf{G} \bullet \mathbf{B} = 0 = x(1) + y(-4) + z(3)$$

This is the equation of a plane that is perpendicular to $\mathbf{B}$. But an infinite number of parallel planes are perpendicular to $\mathbf{B}$. An additive arbitrary constant can be included.

$$x - 4y + 3z = \text{constant}$$

PROBLEM 4

Let $F(x, y) = x^3 + y^2 - 2xy = 0$, find $\dfrac{dy}{dx}$.

SOLUTION

$$\frac{\partial F}{\partial x} = 3x^2 - 2y \text{ and } \frac{\partial F}{\partial y} = 2y - 2x.$$

The total differential is

$$dF = (3x^2 - 2y)dx + (2y - 2x)dy = 0$$

and the derivative of y with respect to x in this implicit function is

$$\frac{dy}{dx} = \frac{3x^2 - 2y}{2y - 2x}.$$

PROBLEM 5

Integrate the expression: $\int \dfrac{x}{\left(4 - x^2\right)}dx.$

SOLUTION

Let $u = 4 - x^2$ from which $du = -2xdx$.

Using the rule $\int \dfrac{du}{u} = \ln|u| + C$, we obtain

$$\int \frac{(-2x)}{4 - x^2}dx = \ln\left|4 - x^2\right| + C.$$

But, to make this result applicable to the original problem, we require a (-2) in the numerator to obtain the form $\dfrac{du}{u}$. Because this is a constant, it is permissible to multiply the numerator under the integral sign by (-2), as long as we multiply the integral by $\left(-\dfrac{1}{2}\right)$ outside of the integral sign, in order to leave the resultant value unchanged.

Hence,

$$\int \frac{x}{4 - x^2}\,dx = -\frac{1}{2}\int \frac{(-2x)}{4 - x^2}dx.$$

Now we can use

$$-\frac{1}{2}\int \frac{du}{u} = -\frac{1}{2}\ln|u| + C$$

$$\int \frac{xdx}{4 - x^2} = -\frac{1}{2}\ln\left|4 - x^2\right| + C$$

PROBLEM 6

Find the volume of the solid generated by revolving about the Y-axis the region bounded by the parabola: $y = -x^2 + 6x - 8$, and the X-axis.

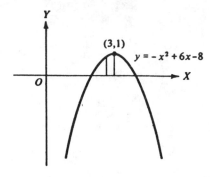
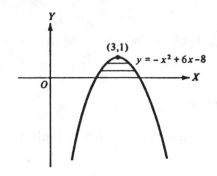

a) Shell method   **b) Disk method**

Figure 18. Volume of a solid with repect to Y

SOLUTION

Method 1. We use the method of cylindrical shells. The curve

$$y = -x^2 + 6x - 8$$

cuts the *X*-axis at $x = 2$ and $x = 4$.

The cylindrical shells are generated by the strip formed by the two lines parallel to the *Y*-axis, at distances x and $x + \Delta x$ from the *Y*-axis, $2 \le x \le 4$, as shown in Figure 18 (a). When this strip is revolved about the *Y*-axis, it generates a cylindrical shell of average height y^*, $y \le y^* \le y + \Delta y$, thickness Δx, and average radius x^*, $x \le x^* \le x + \Delta x$. The volume of this element is

$$\Delta V = 2\pi x * y * \Delta x,$$

where $2\pi x^* y^*$ is the surface area. Expressing y in terms of x and passing to the limits, the sum of the volumes of all such cylindrical shells is the integral:

$$V = 2\pi \int_2^4 x \left(-x^2 + 6x - 8\right) dx$$

$$= 2\pi \int_2^4 \left(-x^3 + 6x^2 - 8x\right) dx$$

$$= 2\pi\left(-\frac{x^4}{4} + 2x^3 - 4x^2\right)\Big|_2^4$$

$$= 2\pi\big((-64 + 128 - 64) - (-4 + 16 - 16)\big)$$

$$= 8\pi$$

Method 2. This can also be thought of as the volume comprising a series of concentric disks with variable outer and inner radii, as sectionally shown in Figure 18(b). The variable radii are as follows:

Since

$$y = -x^2 + 6x - 8,$$

we solve for x.

To complete the square, we require a 9, so that

$$x^2 - 6x + 9$$

constitutes a perfect square. Rewriting the equation,

$$x^2 - 6x + 9 - 9 + 8 = -y$$
$$x^2 - 6x + 9 = 1 - y$$
$$(x - 3)^2 = 1 - y$$

Therefore,

$$x = 3 \pm \sqrt{1 - y}$$

which shows the disks, y units from the x-axis, have an

inner radius $x_{in} = 3 - \sqrt{1 - y}$ and an

outer radius $x_o = 3 + \sqrt{1 - y}$

(The particular one on the x-axis has $x_{in} = 2$ and $x_o = 4$.)

The volume of this disk with thickness dy is:

$$dV = \pi\left(x_o^2 - x_{in}^2\right)dy,$$

or $$dV = \pi\left[(x_0 + x_{in})(x_0 - x_{in})\right]dy.$$

Substituting the values for x_o and x_{in},

$$dV = \left(\left(\left(3 + \sqrt{1-y}\right) + \left(3 - \sqrt{1-y}\right)\right) \cdot \left(\left(3 + \sqrt{1-y}\right)\left(3 + \sqrt{1-y}\right)\right)\right)dy$$
$$= \pi\left(12\sqrt{1-y}\right)dy$$

Since y varies from 0 to 1, the desired volume is:

$$V = 12\pi\int_0^1 (1-y)^{\frac{1}{2}}dy$$
$$= 12\pi\left(-\frac{2}{3}(1-y)^{\frac{3}{2}}\Big|_0^1\right) = 8\pi$$

PROBLEM 7

Integrate: $\int\dfrac{2-x}{x^2+x}dx$.

SOLUTION

To integrate this expression, we use partial fractions. We first find the factors of the denominator. They are (x) and $(x + 1)$. Now we find two numbers, A and B, such that

$$\frac{2-x}{x^2+x} = \frac{A}{x} + \frac{B}{x+1}.$$

Multiplying both sides of this equation by the common denominator, $x(x + 1)$, we obtain: $2 - x = A(x + 1) + B(x)$. When $x(x + 1) = 0$, $x = 0$ or $x = -1$. When $x = 0$, $2 - 0 = A(0 + 1) + B(0)$, and $A = 2$. When $x = -1$, $2 - (-1) = A(0) + B(-1)$ and $B = -3$. We can now write the integral as follows:

$$\int\frac{2-x}{x^2+x}dx = \int\left[\frac{2}{x} - \frac{3}{x+1}\right]dx$$
$$= 2\int\frac{1}{x}dx - 3\int\frac{1}{x+1}dx$$
$$= 2\ln x - 3\ln(x+1) + C.$$

PROBLEM 8

Solve the differential equation

$$\frac{d^2x}{dt^2} + 3\frac{dx}{dt} + 2x = 1 \quad \text{when } t = 0, x = 0, \text{ and } \frac{dx}{dt} = 0.$$

SOLUTION

We use Table 4 to find the transform of each term.

$$\left(s^2X(s) - s0 - 0\right) + 3\left(sX(s) - 0\right) + 2X(s) = \frac{1}{s}$$

$$\left(s^2 + 3s + 2\right)X(s) = \frac{1}{s}$$

Solve for $X(s)$.

$$X(s) = \frac{1}{s\left(s^2 + 3s + 2\right)} = \frac{1}{s(s+1)(s+2)}$$

Expand into partial fractions and solve.

$$X(s) = \frac{\dfrac{1}{2}}{s} + \frac{\dfrac{1}{2}}{s+2} - \frac{1}{s+1}$$

Use Table 4 to transform to time functions.

$$x(t) = \frac{1}{2} + \frac{1}{2}e^{-2t} - e^{-t}$$

PROBLEM 9

The tensile strength of pins produced with a new process is distributed normally with a mean of 35 and a standard deviation of 2.20.

What fraction of pins have a strength exceeding 37?

$$Z = \frac{37 - 35}{2.20} = 0.91$$

SOLUTION

From the Appendix, the probability of finding a strength between $Z = 0$ and $Z = 0.91$ is 0.3186. The probability of finding a strength for $Z > 0$ is 0.5; thus the probability of finding a strength corresponding to $Z > 0.91$ is

$$0.5 - 0.3186 = 0.1814.$$

The probability of finding a strength less than 37 or $Z < 0.91$ is

$$0.5 + 0.3186 = 0.8186.$$

What is the probability of the strength of a pin being between 32 and 36?

$$Z_1 = \frac{32 - 35}{2.20} = -1.36$$

$$Z_2 = \frac{36 - 35}{2.20} = 0.45$$

From the Appendix, the probability is $0.1736 + 0.4131 = 0.5867$.

PROBLEM 10

Consider a fair coin tossed three times. If the random variable x denotes the total number of heads attained in the three tosses, and the density function is given by:

$$p(x) \begin{cases} \dfrac{1}{8} & \text{for } x = 0 \\[2mm] \dfrac{3}{8} & \text{for } x = 1 \\[2mm] \dfrac{3}{8} & \text{for } x = 2 \\[2mm] \dfrac{1}{8} & \text{for } x = 3 \end{cases}$$

What is the probability of getting two or more heads?

SOLUTION

$$P(X \geq 2) = \sum_{x_i e[2,3]} p(x_i)$$
$$= p(2) + p(3)$$
$$= \frac{3}{8} + \frac{1}{8}$$
$$= \frac{1}{2}$$

FE/EIT

Fundamentals of Engineering: AM Exam

CHAPTER 4

Electrical Circuits

CHAPTER 4

ELECTRICAL CIRCUITS

DC CIRCUITS

Current and Voltage

Current i is the net charge crossing a cross section of a conductor per unit time. If a net charge q crosses in a t time interval then:

$$i = \frac{q}{t}.$$

current $= \frac{net\ change}{time}$ $[=]$ Amp $[=]$ $\frac{coulomb}{sec}$

Unit of current = ampere (A), 1A = 1 coulomb of net charge crossing in 1 second

Instantaneous current (i) = time rate of change of charge = $\dfrac{dq}{dt}$

CURRENT FLOW

In metallic conductors, the net movement of charge is due to the displacement of electrons. The flow of current is opposite to the direction of the movement of electrons by convention.

flow of current is opposite the movement of electrons !

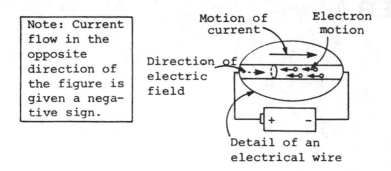

Figure 1. Current flow convention (Note: Current flow in the opposite direction of the figure is given a negative sign.)

Direct current (DC) is defined as a current which is constant due to a steady, unchanging, unidirectional flow of charge.

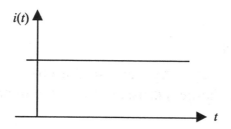

Figure 2. Direct current (DC)

The **voltage** (V or v), or the potential difference between two points, is the measure of the work required to move a unit charge from one point to another. The unit of voltage is the volt (V or v), and is equal to one joule per coulomb. The voltage sign convention is illustrated in Figure 3, where it is assumed that a positive current is supplied by an external source entering terminal 1.

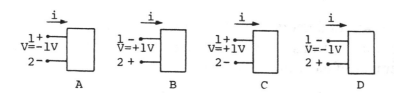

Figure 3. Voltage sign convention

In *C* and *D* of Figure 3, terminal 1 is 1 volt positive with respect to terminal 2. In *A* and *B* of Figure 3, terminal 2 is 1 volt positive with respect to terminal 1.

In Figures *C* and *D* the current enters the positive terminal of the circuit in the box. This means that electrical energy is being transformed (absorbed by the circuit) into another form of energy. In a resistor the electric energy is transformed into heat, in an electric motor into mechanical energy.

Resistor → electrical energy to heat

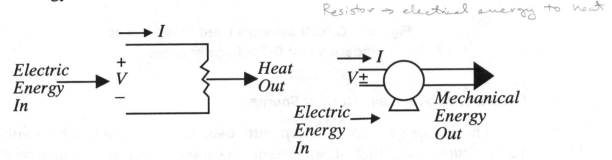

Figure 4. Examples of electric energy being supplied to a circuit element

If the current flows out of the positive terminal, then electric energy is generated in the circuit, as in Figure 5.

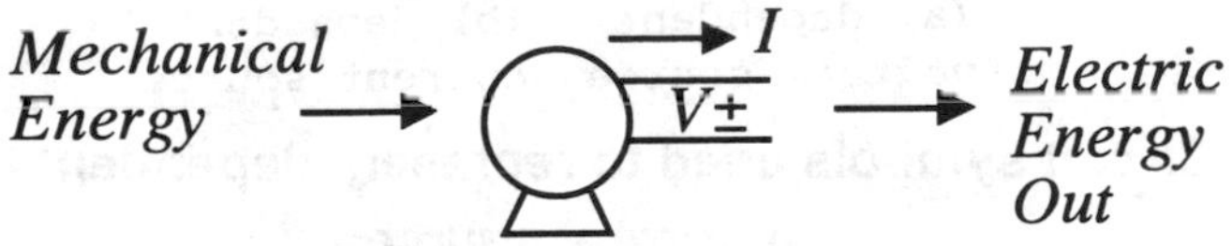

Mechanical Energy → V± → *Electric Energy Out*

Figure 5. Example of electric energy generation

Circuit Elements Found in DC Circuits

Independent Voltage Source

As shown in Figure 6, the same amount of voltage output is supplied continuously by an **independent DC voltage source** regardless of the amount of current drawn from it. The circuit symbols used to represent independent DC voltage sources are shown in Figure 7.

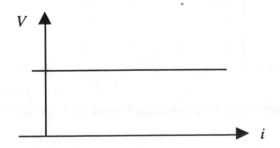

Figure 6. Voltage-current relationship for independent DC voltage sources

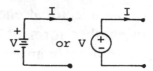

**Figure 7. Circuit symbols used to represent
independent DC voltage sources**

Dependent Voltage and Current Sources

The source quantity of a **dependent source** is determined by a voltage or current existing at some other location in the electrical system under consideration. The circuit symbols used to represent dependent voltage and current sources are shown in Figure 8.

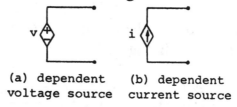

```
(a) dependent        (b) dependent
voltage source    current source
```

**Figure 8. Circuit symbols used to represent dependent DC voltage
and current sources**

Independent Current Source

The current supplied by an **independent DC current source** is constant, as shown in Figure 9, and is completely independent of the voltage across it. The circuit symbol used to represent an independent DC current source is shown in Figure 10.

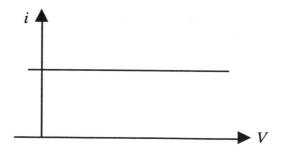

Figure 9. Voltage-current relationship for independent DC current sources

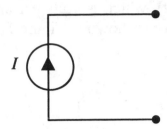

**Figure 10. Circuit symbol used to represent
independent DC current sources**

Both independent current and voltage sources are approximations for a physical element.

Resistance and Conductance

Ohm's Law

The voltage across a conducting material is directly proportional to the current through the material, i.e., v = R*i*, where R (resistance) is the proportionality constant. This is **Ohm's Law** as illustrated in Figure 11.

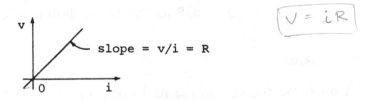

Figure 11. Ohm's Law v = R*i*

Hence, absorbed power in a resistor is given by:

$$p = vi = i^2R = \frac{v^2}{R}.$$

This power is in the form of heat because a resistor is a passive element; it neither delivers power nor stores energy.

Resistance

Resistance (R) is the measure of the tendency of a material to impede the flow of electric charges through it. Resistance is therefore low in good conductors but high in poor conductors (insulators). The unit of resistance is the ohm (Ω), which is volts per ampere. The circuit symbol used to represent a resistor is shown in Figure 12.

$$R \gtrless \begin{array}{c} + \\ v \\ - \end{array}$$

Figure 12. Circuit symbol used to represent a resistor

Two particular cases of resistance are the open and short circuit, shown in Figure 13. If the resistance between two points of a circuit is zero, it is said that a short circuit exists between the two points. If the resistance between two points is infinite, an open circuit is said to exist between these two points.

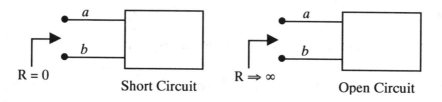

$R = 0$ Short Circuit $R \Rightarrow \infty$ Open Circuit

Figure 13. Short circuit and open circuit

Conductance

Conductance (G) is the reciprocal of resistance, or the ratio of current to voltage:

$$G = \frac{1}{R} = \frac{i}{v}.$$

The unit of conductance is the mho ($\mho$), or siemens (S).

EXAMPLE

With reference to Figure 14, find v if:

(a) $G = 10^{-2} \ \mho$ and $i = 2.5\text{A}$,

(b) $R = 40\Omega$ and the resistor absorbs 250W,

(c) $i = 2.5\text{A}$ and the resistor absorbs 500W.

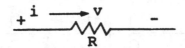

Figure 14. Resistor

SOLUTION

(a) Apply Ohm's Law.

$$v = iR = \frac{i}{G}$$

$$v = \frac{-2.5}{10^{-2}} = -250V$$

(b) We know that $p = vi$ since $v = iR$;

$$p = i^2R = \frac{v^2}{R} \qquad (1)$$

Solving for v,

$$v = \sqrt{pR}$$
$$v = \sqrt{250(40)} = \pm 100V. \text{ Since R absorbs power, } v = +100V.$$

(c) Solving for R in equation (1),

$$R = \frac{p}{i^2} = \frac{500}{(2.5)^2} = 80\,\Omega.$$

Using Ohm's Law:

$$v = iR = 2.5(80) = 200V.$$

Resistor and Conductor Combinations

For a series combination of n resistors:

$R_1 \quad R_2 \quad R_3 \quad R_4 \quad R_n$

Figure 15. Series combination of *n* resistors

$$R_{eq} = R_1 + R_2 + ... + R_n$$

and
$$\frac{1}{G_{eq}} = \frac{1}{G_1} + \frac{1}{G_2} + ... + \frac{1}{G_n}$$

For a parallel combination of *n* resistors:

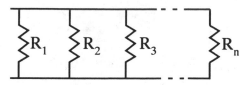

Figure 16. Parallel combination of *n* resistors

$$\frac{1}{R_{eq}} = \frac{1}{R_1} + \frac{1}{R_2} + ... + \frac{1}{R_n}$$

and
$$G_{eq} = G_1 + G_2 + ... + G_n.$$

Wheatstone Bridge

The **Wheatstone Bridge** is used to determine an unknown resistance. Referring to Figure 17, the bridge is balanced by adjusting a variable resistor until no current flows through the ammeter. When the current flow through the ammeter is zero, the current through R_1 will equal the current through R_3, and the current through R_2 will equal the current through R_4. The following equation can then be used to solve for the unknown resistance:

$$\frac{R_1}{R_2} = \frac{R_3}{R_4}.$$

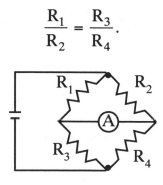

Figure 17. Wheatstone Bridge

Kirchhoff's Laws

Kirchhoff's Current Law (KCL) states that the algebraic sum of all currents entering a node equals the algebraic sum of all currents leaving it, i.e., for a given node Σ currents entering = Σ currents leaving, or

$$\sum_{n=1}^{N} i_n = 0.$$

Kirchhoff's Voltage Law (KVL) states that the algebraic sum of all voltages around a closed loop (or path) is zero, i.e., for a closed loop, Σ potential rises = Σ potential drops.

EXAMPLE

Analyze the circuit in Figure 18 using Kirchhoff's Laws. Find the magnitude and direction of I_2, the current in the upper 2Ω resistor.

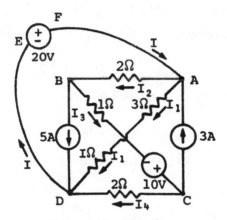

Figure 18. Circuit

SOLUTION

The circuit contains two constant voltage sources and two constant current sources. It has four junctions where three or more wires join, labelled A, B, C, and D, as shown. To begin, we label the unknown currents, I, I_1, I_2, I_3, and I_4, as indicated in Figure 18.

This problem has five unknowns (the five unknown currents) and, therefore, requires five independent equations. Three independent equations are obtained by applying Kirchhoff's Current Sum rule at any three of the four junctions. For convenience, we ignore units and choose junctions A, B, and C:

$$\text{at A, } I + 3 = I_2 + 5; \tag{1}$$

$$\text{at B, } I_2 = I_3 + 5; \tag{2}$$

$$\text{at C, } I_3 = I_4 + 3. \tag{3}$$

The two additional independent equations required for the solution are obtained by applying Kirchhoff's Voltage Sum rule about closed loops in the circuit. As it is difficult to represent the potential drops across the constant current sources, we choose the loops ADEF and ABCDEF:

$$\text{loop ADEF, } 20 = 3I_1 + I_1, \tag{4}$$

$$\text{loop ABCDEF, } 20 = 2I_2 + I_3 - 10 + 2I_4. \tag{5}$$

From (4), by inspection, $I_1 = 5$ amperes. Multiplying (2) by -2 gives

$$-2I_2 + 2I_3 = -10,$$

and, rewriting (5),

$$2I_2 + I_3 + 2I_4 = 30.$$

The sum of these two equations is

$$3I_3 + 2I_4 = 20. \tag{6}$$

Multiplying (3) by two gives

$$2I_3 - 2I_4 = 6$$

which, when summed with (6), results in

$$5I_3 = 26$$

or $I_3 = \dfrac{26}{5}$ amperes. Substituting this result back into (6) gives

$$3\left(\frac{26}{5}\right) + 2I_4 = 20,$$

or $I_4 - \dfrac{11}{5}$ amperes.

The remaining two currents are found by substituting these results, first into (2) and then into (1):

$$I_2 = \left(\frac{26}{5}\right) + 5,$$

$$I = I_2 + 2.$$

Therefore, the current in the upper 2Ω resistor has the magnitude $I_2 = 10\frac{1}{5}$ amperes, and flows in the direction of the arrow shown in the figure. The total current flowing in the circuit is $I = 12\frac{1}{5}$ amperes.

DC Circuit Analysis Techniques

Two common **DC circuit analysis techniques** are mesh analysis and nodal analysis. The general approach to these techniques is listed below. It should be noted that mesh analysis (sometimes called loop analysis) is only applicable to a planar network. By definition, a planar network is a circuit whose diagram can be drawn on a plane surface so that no branch passes over or under any other branch.

Nodal Analysis—General Approach

(1) Convert all voltage sources to current sources.

(2) In each network, determine the number of nodes.

(3) Choose a reference node and assign voltages to the remaining node.

(4) Apply KCL at each node, except at the reference node.

(5) Solve the unknown equations for nodal voltages.

Mesh Analysis — General Approach

(1) Assign closed loops of current called mesh currents, clockwise, to each loop of the circuit.

(2) Apply KVL around each closed loop.

(3) Solve resulting equations for the assumed loop currents.

Thevenin and Norton Equivalent Circuits

A **Thevenin equivalent circuit** consists of a voltage source in series with a resistor, as shown in Figure 19. This equivalent circuit is used to represent a linear, two-terminal network, which may contain both independent and dependent current and voltage sources. The voltage and current sources are set to zero by shorting the voltage sources and treating current sources as open circuits. The Thevenin equivalent resistance, R_{TH}, is the resistance across terminals denoted A and B in the figure, and the open circuit voltage, V_{TH} (also called V_{0C}), is the Thevenin equivalent voltage.

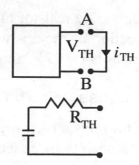

Figure 19. The Thevenin equivalent circuit

ELECTRIC AND MAGNETIC FIELDS

Coulomb's Law

By definition, the force between two point charges of arbitrary positive or negative strengths is given by **Coulomb's Law** as follows:

$$F = k \frac{Q_1 Q_2}{d^2}$$

where Q_1 and Q_2 = Positive or negative charges on either object in coulombs (C)

d = Distance separating the two point charges

k = The constant of proportionality

= $(4\pi\varepsilon_0)^{-1}$ = 8.987×10^9 newton-meter^2/coulomb^2 (Nm^2/C^2)

ε_0 = Permittivity in free space = 8.854×10^{-12} Farad/meter (F/m)

Note that $\varepsilon = \varepsilon_0 \varepsilon_r$ is used for media other than free space, where ε_r is the relative permittivity of the media.

These equations are expressed for free space, where permittivity (ε) is equal to the permittivity in free space (ε_0).

The force F can be expressed in a vector form to indicate its direction as follows:

$$F = \frac{Q_1 Q_2}{4\pi\varepsilon_0 d^2} a_d$$

where unit vector a_d is in the direction of d and $a_d = \dfrac{d}{|d|} = \dfrac{d}{d}$.

EXAMPLE

A negative point charge of 10^{-6} coulomb is situated in air at the origin of a rectangular coordinate system. A second negative point charge of 10^{-4} coulomb is situated on the positive x axis at a distance of 50 cm from the origin. What is the force on the second charge?

SOLUTION

By Coulomb's Law the force

$$F = i \frac{\left(-10^{-6}\right)\left(-10^{-4}\right)}{4\pi \times 0.5^2 \times \dfrac{10^{-9}}{36\pi}}$$

$$= +i3.6 \text{ newtons}$$

That is, there is a force of 3.6 newtons (0.8 lb) in the positive x direction on the second charge.

Electric Field Intensity

Assuming a fixed position point charge Q, then by Coulomb's Law, the force on a test charge Q_t due to Q is:

$$F_t = \frac{QQ_t}{4\pi\varepsilon_0 d_t^2} a_{d_t}.$$

Now, by definition, the **electric field intensity** E due to Q equals the force per unit charge in V/m or N/C.

Hence,

$$E = \frac{F_t}{Q_t} = \frac{Q}{4\pi\varepsilon_0 d_t^2} a_{d_t}.$$

Thus, in general, the electric field intensity E is:

$$E = \frac{Q}{4\pi\varepsilon_0 d^2} a_d,$$

where d is the magnitude of the vector **d**.

In general, if Q is located at $\mathbf{d'} = a\mathbf{a}_x + b\mathbf{a}_y + c\mathbf{a}_z$ and the field is at $\mathbf{d} = x\mathbf{a}_x + y\mathbf{a}_y + z\mathbf{a}_z$, then:

$$E = \frac{Q(d - d')}{4\pi\varepsilon_0 |d - d'|^3}.$$

EXAMPLE

The figure shows eight point charges situated at the corners of a cube. Find the electric field intensity at each point charge, due to the remaining seven point charges.

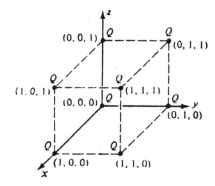

Figure 20. A cubical arrangement of point charges

SOLUTION

First note that the electric field intensity at a point $B(x_2, y_2, z_2)$ due to a point charge Q at point $A\,(x_1, y_1, z_1)$ is given by

$$E_B = \frac{Q}{4\pi\varepsilon_0 (AB)^2} i_{AB} = \frac{Q}{4\pi\varepsilon_0 (AB)^2} \frac{AB}{(AB)} = \frac{Q(AB)}{4\pi\varepsilon_0 (AB)^3}$$

$$= \frac{Q}{4\pi\varepsilon_0} \frac{(x_2 - x_1)i_x + (y_2 - y_1)i_y + (z_2 - z_1)i_z}{\left[(x_2 - x_1)^2 + (y_2 - y_1)^2 + (z_2 - z_1)^2\right]^{3/2}} \tag{1}$$

Now consider the point (1,1,1). Applying (1) to each of the charges at the seven other points and using superposition, the electric field intensity at the point (1,1,1) is

$$E_{(1,1,1)} = \frac{Q}{4\pi\varepsilon_0}\left[\frac{i_x}{(1)^{3/2}} + \frac{i_y}{(1)^{3/2}} + \frac{i_z}{(1)^{3/2}}\right.$$

$$\left. + \frac{i_y + i_z}{(2)^{3/2}} + \frac{i_z + i_x}{(2)^{3/2}} + \frac{i_x + i_y}{(2)^{3/2}} + \frac{i_x + i_y + i_z}{(3)^{3/2}}\right]$$

$$= \frac{Q}{4\pi\varepsilon_0}\left(1 + \frac{1}{\sqrt{2}} + \frac{1}{3\sqrt{3}}\right)\left(i_x + i_y + i_z\right)$$

$$= \frac{3.29Q}{4\pi\varepsilon_0}\left(\frac{i_x + i_y + i_z}{\sqrt{3}}\right)$$

Noting that $\dfrac{i_x + i_y + i_z}{\sqrt{3}}$ is the unit vector directed from $(0,0,0)$ to $(1,1,1)$, the electric field intensity at $(1,1,1)$ is directed diagonally away from $(0,0,0)$ with a magnitude equal to $\dfrac{3.29Q}{4\pi\varepsilon_0}$ N/C. From symmetry considerations, it then follows that the electric field intensity at each point charge, due to the remaining seven point charges, has a magnitude $\dfrac{3.29Q}{4\pi\varepsilon_0}$ N/C, and it is directed away from the corner opposite to that charge.

Electric Field Intensity Due to Point Charges, Volume Charge Distribution, Line of Charge, and Sheet of Charge

The electric field intensity due to two **point charges** as illustrated in Figure 21 is:

$$E = E_1 + E_2 = \frac{Q_1}{4\pi\varepsilon_0 d_1{}^2}\,a_{d_1} + \frac{Q_2}{4\pi\varepsilon_0 d_2{}^2}\,a_{d_2}.$$

Thus, the differential electric field dE due to dQ in Figure 22 is:

$$dE = \frac{dQ}{4\pi\varepsilon_0 d^2}\,a_d = \frac{\rho_v dV}{4\pi\varepsilon_0 d^2}\,a_d,$$

and

$$E = \int_V \frac{\rho_v dV}{4\pi\varepsilon_0 d^2}\,a_d = \text{total electric field at point } P \text{ in the figure.}$$

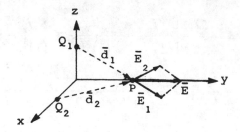

Figure 21. Electric fields produced by point charges

In general, for *k* point charges, the electric field intensity is:

$$E = \sum_{j=1}^{k} \frac{Q_j}{4\pi\varepsilon_0 d_j^{\,2}} a_{d_j}.$$

The field due to a **volume charge distribution** is determined by Gauss's Law. Gauss's law for electric fields in free space is defined as:

$$\oint_s (\varepsilon_0 E) \cdot ds = \int_v \rho_v du \equiv Q$$

where Q is the total charge within a finite volume:

$$Q = \int_V \rho_V dV = \int_V dQ,$$

and ρ_V is the volume charge density:

$$\rho_V = \frac{dQ}{dV} \text{ in C/m}^3.$$

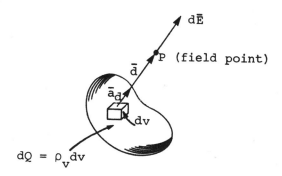

Figure 22. Volume charge

The electric field intensity due to a **line of charge** is determined as follows, using Figure 23. The line charge density is denoted by ρ_ℓ.

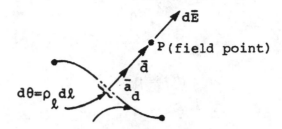

Figure 23. Line of charge

The differential electric field dE due to the line of charge is:

$$dE = \frac{dQ}{4\pi\varepsilon_0 d^2}\, \boldsymbol{a}_d.$$

Hence,

$$dE = \frac{\rho_\ell d\ell}{4\pi\varepsilon_0 d^2}\, \boldsymbol{a}_d,$$

$$E = \int_\ell \frac{\rho_\ell}{4\pi\varepsilon_0 d^2}\, \boldsymbol{a}_d d\ell.$$

For an infinitely long straight wire, the electric field intensity at a distance d from the line of charge is:

$$E = \frac{\rho_\ell}{2\pi\varepsilon_0 d}.$$

The electric field intensity due to a **sheet of charge** is determined using Figure 24, where ρ_s is the surface charge density.

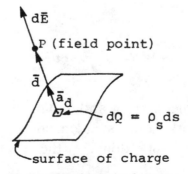

Figure 24. Sheet of charge

The differential electric field dE due to the sheet of charge is:

$$dE = \frac{\rho_s ds}{4\pi\varepsilon_0 d^2} a_d,$$

where

$$dQ = \rho_s ds.$$

Hence,

$$E = \int_s \frac{\rho_s ds}{4\pi\varepsilon_0 d^2} a_d.$$

Work in an Electric Field

In Figure 25 shown below, a small test charge Q is presented in an electric field E.

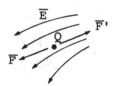

Figure 25. Forces on test charge in electric field *E*

The work done, dW, or the energy needed to move a point charge through a distance dL, is expressed as

$$dW = F' \bullet dL$$
$$= QE \bullet dL$$

where dW is the differential work done by moving the point charge through a differential distance dL.

Or

$$W = -Q\int_A^B E \bullet dL$$

where A and B specify the starting and ending positions of the travelling point charge. Hence, work done is independent of the path taken. Also note, by convention, the work done by the electric field is a negative quantity.

The following table gives the equation for dL in different coordinate systems:

Coordinate systems	dL
Cartesian	$\boldsymbol{a}_x dx + \boldsymbol{a}_y dy + \boldsymbol{a}_z dz$
Cylindrical	$\boldsymbol{a}_r dr + \boldsymbol{a}_\phi r d\phi + \boldsymbol{a}_z dz$
Spherical	$\boldsymbol{a}_r dr + \boldsymbol{a}_\theta r d\theta + \boldsymbol{a}_\phi r \sin\theta d\phi$

Biot-Savart Law

The **Biot-Savart Law** states that the differential magnetic field strength $d\boldsymbol{H}$ at any point P, produced by a differential element dl carrying the current I, is proportional to Idl $Id\ell \times \boldsymbol{a}_R$, where $\boldsymbol{a}_R$ is a unit vector leading from dl to the point P, as shown in Figure 26. The differential magnetic field strength $d\boldsymbol{H}$ is also inversely proportional to the square of the distance from the differential element to the point P.

In mathematical form:

$$dH = \frac{Idl \times \boldsymbol{a}_R}{4\pi R^2} \quad \text{(Ampere/meter, i.e., A/m)}.$$

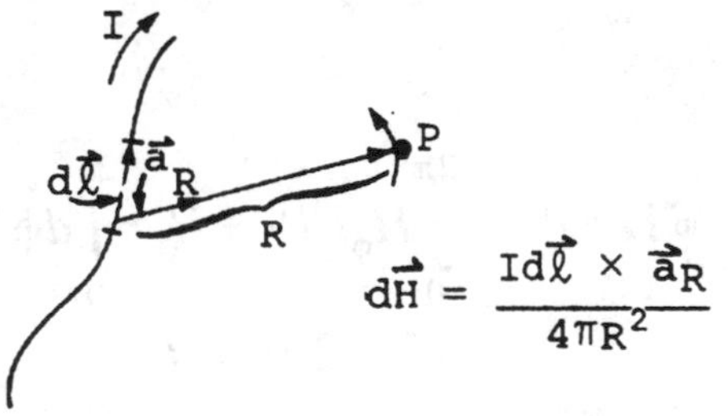

Figure 26. Illustration of Biot-Savart Law

The integral form of the Biot-Savart Law is:

$$H = \int_S \frac{\boldsymbol{K} \times \boldsymbol{a}_R}{4\pi R^2} ds,$$

where $\boldsymbol{K}$ is the surface current density.

Other forms of the Biot-Savart Law include:

$$H = \oint \frac{Idl \times a_R}{4\pi R^2},$$

and

$$H = \int_V \frac{\mathbf{J} \times \mathbf{a_R}}{4\pi R^2} dV$$

where J is the current density.

The Poynting vector, S, is defined as:

$$S = E \times H,$$

and is the instantaneous power density of an electromagnetic wave, with units of webers per square meter (W/m²).

Ampere's Circuital Law

Ampere's Circuital Law states that the line integral of the tangential component of H about any closed path is exactly equal to the current enclosed by that path:

$$\oint H \cdot dl = I.$$

For an application such as in Figure 27, the path is a circle of radius *r*. Using Ampere's Circuital Law, the magnetic field strength is determined as follows:

$$\oint H \cdot dl = \int_0^{2\pi} H_\phi r d\phi = H_\phi r \int_0^{2\pi} d\phi$$

$$= H_\phi \cdot 2\pi r = I$$

$$H = \frac{I}{2\pi r} a_\phi.$$

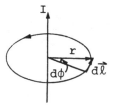

Figure 27. An infinitely long straight filament carrying a direct current *I*

Magnetic Flux and Magnetic Flux Density

Magnetic flux density, *B*, is defined as:

$$B = \mu_o H$$

where μ_o is the permeability of free space:

$$\mu_o = 4\pi \times 10^{-7} \text{ Henry/meter (H/m)}.$$

The use of μ_o assumes free space, for other media:

$$\mu = \mu_o \mu_r$$

where μ_r is the relative permeability of the media. The unit of magnetic flux density is the tesla (T), or webers per square meter (Wb/m^2).

Magnetic flux, ϕ, has units of weber, and is defined in terms of magnetic flux density as follows:

$$B = \frac{\phi}{A},$$

where *A* is the area perpendicular to the flux.

The following example illustrates the use of Ampere's Circuital Law to determine magnetic flux and magnetic flux density.

EXAMPLE

Find the flux between the conductors of the coaxial line shown in the figure. The conductor extends a length *L*.

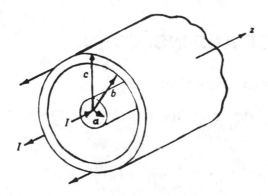

Figure 28. Cross section of a coaxial cable

SOLUTION

By applying Ampere's Law to the region between the conductors,

$$\oint H \cdot d\ell = I_{\text{enclosed}}$$

In the region between the conductors, the current enclosed is I, therefore

$$2\pi r H = I$$

$$H = \frac{I}{2\pi r} \quad (a < r < b)$$

and therefore

$$B = \mu_0 H = \frac{\mu_0 I}{2\pi r} a_\phi$$

The magnetic flux contained between the conductors in a length L is the flux crossing any radial plane extending from $r = a$ to $r = b$ and from, say, $z = 0$ to $z = L$

$$\phi = \int_s B \cdot dS = \int_0^L \int_a^b \frac{\mu_0 I}{2\pi r} a_\phi \cdot dr \, dz a_\phi$$

or

$$\phi = \frac{\mu_0 I L}{2\pi} \ln \frac{b}{a}.$$

CAPACITANCE AND INDUCTANCE

The Parallel Plate Capacitor

A **parallel plate capacitor** is shown in Figure 29. **Capacitance** (C) is defined as:

$$C = K \varepsilon_0 \frac{A}{d}$$

$$= \frac{Q}{v}$$

ε_0 is equal to 8.854 pF/m, and K, the relative dielectric constant, is:

$$K = \frac{\varepsilon}{\varepsilon_0}.$$

For the time variant case:

$$C = \frac{Q(t)}{v(t)}$$

Note that for direct current, the capacitor acts as an open circuit. The unit of capacitance is the farad (F), which is coulombs per volt. The circuit symbols used to represent capacitance are shown in Figure 30.

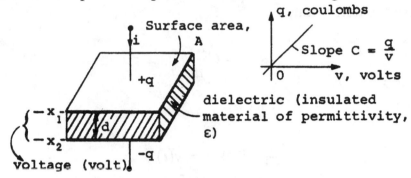

Figure 29. Parallel plate capacitor

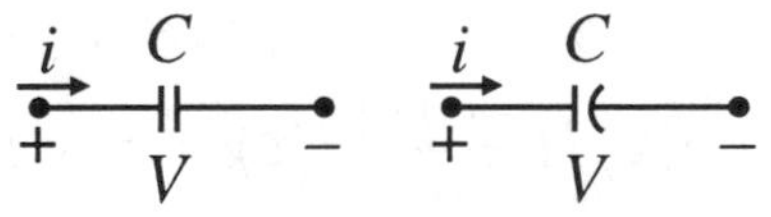

Figure 30. Circuit symbols used to represent capacitors

$$v(t) = \frac{1}{C} \int_{-\infty}^{t} i(\tau) d(\tau)$$

$$i(t) = \frac{dQ(t)}{dt} = C \frac{dv(t)}{dt}$$

$$p = Cv\left(\frac{dv}{dt}\right)$$

and

$$W = \frac{1}{2} Cv^2 = \text{stored energy [joules]}$$

or
$$W = \frac{Q^2}{2C}.$$

EXAMPLE

Consider a capacitor with capacitance $C = 10^{-6}$ farad. Assume that initial voltage across this capacitor is $v_c(0) = 1$ volt. Find the voltage $v_c(t)$ at time $t \geq 0$ on this capacitor if the current through it is $i_c(t) = \cos(10^6 t)$.

SOLUTION

We use the definition,

$$i = C\frac{dv}{dt}$$

solving for v

$$\frac{1}{C}\int_{-\infty}^{t} i(\tau)d\tau = v(t).$$

If we have an initial voltage at time t_o, $-\infty < t_o < t$, we may state that

$$\frac{1}{C}\int_{-\infty}^{t_o} i(\tau)d\tau + \frac{1}{C}\int_{t_o}^{t} i(\tau)d\tau = v(t)$$

$$v(t_o) + \frac{1}{C}\int_{t_o}^{t} i(\tau)d\tau = v(t). \qquad (1)$$

In this problem we are given $v(t_o) = v_c(o) = 1$ volt, $C = 10^{-6}$ farad, and $i_c(t) = \cos(10^6 t)$. We are asked to find $v_c(t)$ at time $t \geq 0$.

Substituting the above conditions into equation (1)

$$v_c(t) = 1 + \frac{1}{10^{-6}}\int_{o}^{t} \cos(10^6 \tau)d\tau$$

$$v_c(t) = 1 + \frac{1}{10^6 \cdot 10^{-6}}\left[\sin(10^6 \tau)\right]_{o}^{t}$$

$$v_c(t) = 1 + \sin(10^6 t)$$

The Iron-Core Inductor

An **iron-core inductor** is shown in Figure 31. Inductance (L) is defined as:

$$L = \frac{\mu N^2 A}{\ell};$$

where

N = Number of turns of coil
μ = Permeability of the core
A = Cross-sectional area of core
ℓ = Mean length of core.

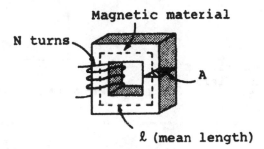

Figure 31. Iron-core inductor

The magnetic flux (ϕ), magnetic field intensity (H), and magnetic flux density (B) relationships of an inductor are:

$$\phi(t) = \left(\frac{\mu N^2 A}{\ell}\right) i(t)$$

$$= L i(t)$$

$$H = \frac{N^2 i}{\ell}$$

$$B = \mu H$$

$$= \frac{\phi}{A}$$

The B-H curve is used to relate magnetic field intensity and magnetic flux density, and is shown in Figure 32 for the iron-core inductor.

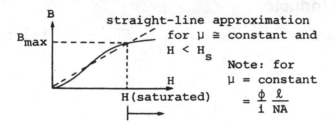

Figure 32. *B-H* curve

The concept of self-inductance is illustrated in Figure 33, which shows the production of magnetic flux by a current. Note that the slope of the graph relating magnetic flux and current is equal to *L*, the inductance. Figure 33 includes the circuit symbol used to represent inductors.

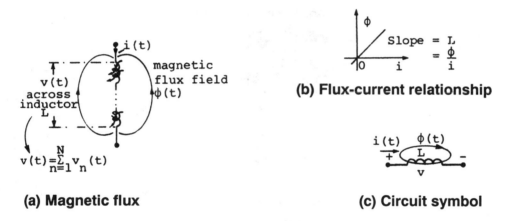

(a) Magnetic flux

(b) Flux-current relationship

(c) Circuit symbol

Figure 33. The concept of self-inductance

Inductance can also be expressed as:

$$L = \frac{Nd\phi(i)}{di}.$$

Voltage, current, energy, and power relationships for inductors are:

$$\oint 1\ell \qquad \oint 2\ell$$

$$\text{Inductance } (L) = \frac{Nd\phi(i)}{di} \text{ [henry (H) or volt-second/ampere]}$$

$$\text{Voltage } v(t) = N(\text{no. of turns of coil}) \times \frac{d\phi(t)}{dt}$$

(rate of change of ϕ with respect to time), or

$$v(t) = \frac{Nd\phi(t)}{dt} \qquad v(t) = L\frac{di(t)}{dt}$$

$$i(t) = \frac{1}{L}\int_{-\infty}^{t} v\, dt$$

$$W = \frac{1}{2}Li^2$$

$$p = vi = Li\frac{di}{dt}[W]$$

In direct current circuits, an inductor acts as a short circuit.

Mutual Inductance

If the magnetic flux produced by the current in due coils links with a second coil, and if this flux changes due to changes in the current, then the change in the current in one coil induces a back voltage in the second. It is said that a mutual inductance exists between the two coils.

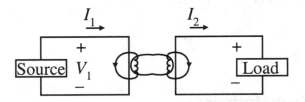

Figure 34. Mutual inductance

The following equations and definitions refer to the circuit in Figure 34:

$\phi_{1\ell}$ = Flux linking only coil 1 $\qquad$ ϕ_m = Mutual flux (linking both coils)

$\phi_{2\ell}$ = Flux linking only coil 2 $\qquad$ $\phi_1 = \phi_{1\ell} + \phi_m$

$\phi_2 = \phi_{2\ell} + \phi_m$ $\qquad\qquad$ ϕ_1 = Total flux linking coil 1

ϕ_2 = Total flux linking coil 2

In linear magnetic materials

$\phi_1 = L_{1\ell}i_1$ $\qquad\qquad\qquad$ $\phi_{2\ell} = L_{2\ell}i_2$

$\phi_m = L_{m1}(i_1) + L_{m2}(i_2)$

The voltage across L_1 in Figure 34 is:

$$\vartheta_1 = L_1 \frac{di_1}{dt} + M_{12} \frac{di_2}{dt},$$

where M_{12} denotes that a voltage response is produced at L_1 due to a current source at L_2, and the voltage across L_2 is:

$$\vartheta_2 = L_2 \frac{di_2}{dt} + M_{21} \frac{di_1}{dt},$$

where M_{21} denotes a voltage responsed at L_2 due to a current source at L_1. It is not necessary to use these subscripts for the mutual inductance, however, as:

$$M_{12} = M_{21} = M,$$

where M is the proportionality constant between two coils (units of henry):

$$M = K\sqrt{L_1 L_2},$$

where the coupling coefficient K is:

$$K = \frac{\phi_m}{\phi_1}.$$

The Iron-Core Transformer

An **iron-core transformer** is shown in Figure 35.

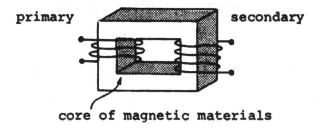

Figure 35. Iron-core transformer

The ratio of primary to secondary windings is the turns ratio:

$$\text{Turns ratio} = \frac{\text{no. of turns on the primary}(N_p)}{\text{no. of turns on the secondary}(N_s)},$$

or

$$\frac{V_p}{V_s} = \frac{N_p}{N_s} \text{ and } \frac{I_p}{I_s} = \frac{N_s}{N_p},$$

where V_p is the voltage across the primary coil and V_s is the voltage across the secondary coil of the transformer. The same notation is used for the current. The number of turns on the primary and secondary coils are used to differentiate between step-up and step-down transformers, as shown in Figure 36.

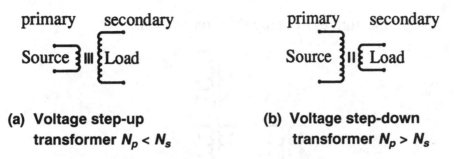

(a) **Voltage step-up transformer $N_p < N_s$**

(b) **Voltage step-down transformer $N_p > N_s$**

Figure 36. Voltage step-up and step-down transformers

Dot Notation

The sign of the voltage across mutually coupled coils may be determined using **dot notation**. The procedure of assigning the dots on a pair of mutually coupled coils is given below, using Figure 37. The numbers in the procedure correspond to the circled numbers in the figure.

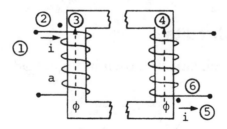

Figure 37. Assigning the dots on a pair of coupled coils

Procedure:

(1) Select a current direction in one of the coils.

(2) Assign a dot where the current enters the winding. (Note: This is the positive terminal with respect to point *a*.)

(3) Use the right-hand rule to assign flux direction.

(4) Assign opposite flux direction for the second coil.

(5) Use right-hand rule to find the current direction in the second coil which produces flux in the direction found in 4.

(6) Assign a dot where the current leaves the winding.

(7) Obtain simplified diagram as shown:

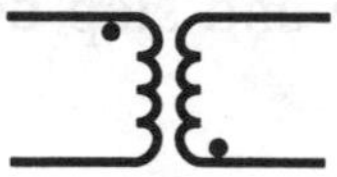

(8) Assign the sign to M using this convention:

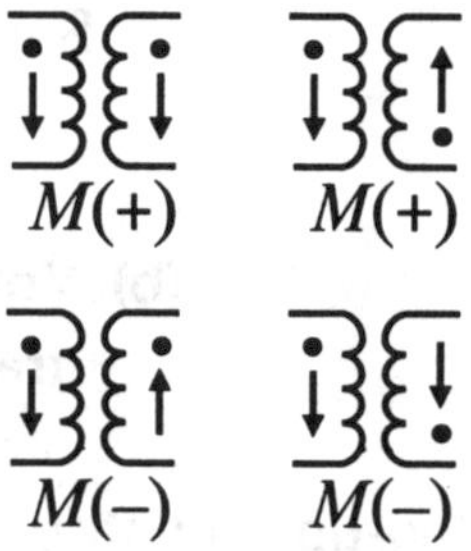

$$M(+) \qquad M(+)$$

$$M(-) \qquad M(-)$$

M = + (Both currents pass through coils and are either leaving or entering dots.)

M = − (If arrow indicating current direction through coil is entering the dot for one coil and leaving the dot for another.)

TRANSIENTS

Simple RL and RC Circuits

A **source-free RL circuit** is shown in Figure 38.

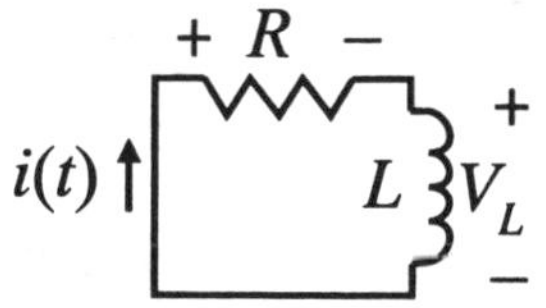

$$i(t) \uparrow \qquad + R - \qquad L \quad V_L$$

Figure 38. Source-free RL circuit

The following equation is produced by summing the voltages in the circuit:

$$v_R + v_L = Ri + L\frac{di}{dt} = 0.$$

The current $i(t)$ is:

$$i(t) = I_0 e^{\frac{-Rt}{L}} = I_0 e^{\frac{-t}{\tau}},$$

where I_0 is defined as the current $i(t)$ at time $t = 0$, and τ is the time constant:

$$\tau = \frac{L}{R},$$

as shown in Figure 39. The power dissipated in the resistor, p_R, is:

$$p_R = i^2 R = I_0^2 \, \text{Re}^{\frac{-2Rt}{L}},$$

and the total energy (in terms of heat) in the resistor is:

$$W_R = \frac{LI_0^2}{2}.$$

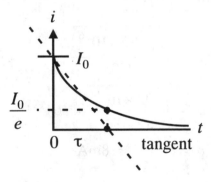

Figure 39. Time constant τ for a source-free RL circuit

EXAMPLE

A 30-mH inductor is in series with a $400\,\Omega$ resistor. If the energy stored in the coil at $t = 0$ is 0.96µJ, find the magnitude of the current at (a) $t = 0$; (b) $t = 100\mu s$; and (c) $t = 300\mu s$.

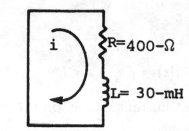

Figure 40. Inductor and resistor

SOLUTION

(a) Find the initial current ($i(0)$) by making use of the energy relationship for an inductor:

$$W = \frac{1}{2} Li(o)^2.$$

Since we are given W and asked to find i,

$$i(o) = \sqrt{\frac{2W}{L}}$$

$$i(o) = \sqrt{\frac{2(0.96 \times 10^{-6})}{0.03}}$$

$$i(o) = \sqrt{\frac{1.92 \times 10^{-6}}{3 \times 10^{-2}}} = \sqrt{64 \times 10^{-6}}$$

$$i(o) = 8 \times 10^{-3} = 8\text{mA}$$

(b) After $t = 0$ the current through the inductor is governed by the response of the series RL circuit.

$$i(t) = I_o e^{\frac{-Rt}{L}}.$$

To find i at 100μs,

$$i(100\mu s) = (0.008)\exp\left[\frac{-400(100 \times 10^{-6})}{0.03}\right]$$

$$i(100\mu s) = 0.008 / 2.64 = 3\text{mA}$$

(c) To find i at 300µs,

$$i(300\mu s) = (.008)\exp\left[\frac{-400\left(300 \times 10^{-6}\right)}{0.03}\right]$$

$$i(300\mu s) = (Cv(t))e^{-4} = (.008)(.018) = 0.15\text{mA}$$

A **source-free RC circuit** is shown in Figure 41.

Figure 41. Source-free RC circuit

The following equation is produced by summing the current through the resistor and capacitor:

$$C\frac{dv}{dt} + \frac{v}{R} = 0.$$

The voltage v(t) is:

$$v(t) = v(0)e^{\frac{-t}{RC}} = V_0 e^{\frac{-t}{RC}},$$

where V_0 is the voltage at time t = zero, and the time constant τ is:

$$\tau = RC,$$

as shown in Figure 42. The current $i(t)$ may be expressed as follows, where I_0 is the current at time t = zero:

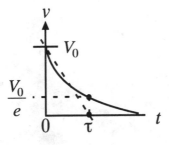

Figure 42. Source-free RC circuit

$$i(t) = i(0)e^{\frac{-t}{RC}} = I_o e^{\frac{-t}{RC}}.$$

Natural and Forced Response of RL and RC Circuits

The complete response of RL and RC circuits to the application of energy is composed of two responses, the **natural response** and the **forced response**. The natural response is the complementary solution of a linear differential equation, and has the form:

$$i_n = Ae^{-Pt}.$$

The forced response is the particular solution of an alinear differential equation, and has the form:

$$i_f = \frac{Q}{P}$$

for a sudden application of a DC source. P is a general function of time and Q is the forcing function (Q is constant for a suddenly applied DC source) in the question above. The complete current response is:

$$i(t) = \frac{Q}{P} + Ae^{-Pt},$$

The complete response is always:

Complete response = natural response + forced response

Total solution = complementary solution + particular solution

The procedure to find the complete response $f(t)$ of RL and RC circuits with DC sources is shown in table form on the next page.

	TABLE 1 **COMPLETE RESPONSE OF RL AND RC CIRCUITS** **WITH DC SOURCES**	
	RL	***RC***
1) Simplify the circuit by setting all independent sources to zero and determine:	R_{eq}, L_{eq} $\left(\tau = \dfrac{L_{eq}}{R_{eq}}\right)$	R_{eq}, C_{eq} $\left(\tau = R_{eq}C_{eq}\right)$
2) Consider: $\Rightarrow$ and use de-analysis to find:	$L_{eq} \approx$ short circuit $i_L(0^-)$	$C_{eq} \approx$ open circuit $v_c(0^-)$
3) Repeat procedure 2 to find the forced response:	i.e., $f(t)$ as $t \to \infty$ $f(\infty)$	
4) Obtain the total response as the sum of the natural and forced responses:	$f(t) = Ae^{\frac{-t}{\tau}} + f(\infty)$	
5) Determine $f(0^+)$ by considering the conditions:	$i_L(0^+) = i_L(0^-)$	$v_c(0^+) = v_c(0^-)$
6) Then:	$f(0^+) = A + f(\infty)$ and $f(t) = \left[f(0^+) - f(\infty)\right]e^{\frac{-t}{\tau}} + f(\infty)$	

The RLC Circuits

A parallel, **source-free RLC circuit** is shown in Figure 43.

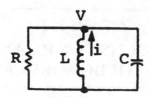

Figure 43. Parallel, source-free RLC circuit

Kirchhoff's Current Law produces the following equation for the parallel RLC circuit:

$$\frac{v}{R} + \frac{1}{L}\int_{t_0}^{t} v\,dt - i(t_0) + C\frac{dv}{dt} = 0$$

and the corresponding linear, second-order homogeneous differential equation is:

$$C\frac{d^2v}{dt^2} + \frac{1}{R}\frac{dv}{dt} + \frac{v}{L} = 0.$$

The natural response has the following form (as this is a source-free circuit, the forced response must be zero):

$$V = A_1 e^{s_1 t} + A_2 e^{s_2 t}$$

where

$$s_1 = \frac{-1}{2RC} + \sqrt{\left(\frac{1}{2RC}\right)^2 - \frac{1}{LC}}$$

$$s_2 = \frac{-1}{2RC} - \sqrt{\left(\frac{1}{2RC}\right)^2 - \frac{1}{LC}}$$

or

$$s_1 = -\alpha + \sqrt{\alpha^2 - \omega_0^2}$$

$$s_2 = -\alpha - \sqrt{\alpha^2 - \omega_0^2}$$

where the exponential damping coefficient, or neper frequency α, is:

$$\alpha = \frac{1}{2RC},$$

and the resonant frequency ω_0 is:

$$\omega_0 = \frac{1}{\sqrt{LC}}.$$

Three special responses of parallel RLC circuits are the cases of a) overdamped response, b) critically damped response, and c) underdamped response, as shown in Table 2. The response curves are shown in Figure 44.

TABLE 2 SPECIAL RESPONSE OF A PARALLEL RLC CIRCUIT		
a) Overdamped	b) Critical damping	c) Underdamped
1) $\alpha > \omega_0$ or if $LC > 4R^2C^2$	$\alpha = \omega_0$ or $LC = 4R^2C^2$ or $LC = 4R^2C$	$\alpha < \omega_0$
2) s_1 and $s_2 =$ negative real numbers, i.e., $\sqrt{\alpha^2 - \omega_0{}^2} < \alpha$ or $\left(-\alpha - \sqrt{\alpha^2 - \omega_0{}^2}\right)$ $< \left(-\alpha + \sqrt{\alpha^2 - \omega_0{}^2}\right)$ < 0	$s_1 = s_2 = \alpha$ $A_1 e^{\alpha t} + A_2 t e^{\alpha t}$	s and s_2 complex quantities.
3) $v(t) = A_1 e^{s_1 t} + A_2 e^{s_2 t}$		$v(t) = e^{-\alpha t}\left(A_1 e^{j\omega_d t} + A_2 e^{j\omega_d t}\right)$ where $\omega_d =$ $\sqrt{\omega_0{}^2 - \alpha^2} =$ Natural Resonant Frequency or

$$v(t) = e^{-\alpha t}$$

$$\left\{ (A_1 + A_2) \right.$$

$$\left[\frac{e^{j\omega_d t} + e^{-j\omega_d t}}{2} \right] +$$

$$j(A_1 - A_2)$$

$$\left. \left[\frac{e^{j\omega_d t} - e^{-j\omega_d t}}{2j} \right] \right\}$$

or

$$v(t) = e^{-\alpha t}$$

$$\left[(A_1 + A_2)\cos\omega_d t + (A_1 - A_2)\sin\omega_d t \right]$$

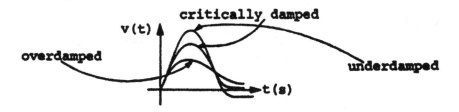

Figure 44. Three response curves for source-free parallel RLC circuits

A series, source-free RLC circuit is shown in Figure 45.

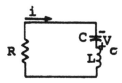

Figure 45. Series, source-free RLC circuit

Kirchhoff's Voltage Law produces the following equation:

$$Ri + \frac{1}{C}\int_{t_0}^{t} i\,dt + L\frac{di}{dt} - v_c(t_0) = 0,$$

and the corresponding second-order differential equation in terms of *i*:

$$L\frac{d^2i}{dt^2} + R\frac{di}{dt} + \frac{i}{C} = 0$$

or in terms of v_c:

$$LC\frac{d^2v_c}{dt^2} + RC\frac{dv_c}{dt} - v_c = 0.$$

Cases of a) overdamped response, b) critically damped responses, and c) underdamped response are summarized in Table 3.

<table>
<tr><td colspan="3" align="center">**TABLE 3**
SPECIAL RESPONSE OF SERIES RLC CIRCUIT</td></tr>
<tr><td>a) Overdamped</td><td>b) Critical damping</td><td>c) Underdamped</td></tr>
<tr>
<td>

1) $\alpha > \omega_0$

2) $s_1, s_2 = \dfrac{-R}{2L} \pm$

$\sqrt{\left(\dfrac{R}{2L}\right)^2 - \dfrac{1}{LC}}$

or

$= -\alpha \pm \sqrt{\alpha^2 - \omega_0^2}$

where $\alpha = \dfrac{R}{2L}$,

$\omega_0 = \dfrac{1}{\sqrt{LC}}$

3) $i(t) = A_1 e^{s_1 t} + A_2 e^{s_2 t}$
</td>
<td>

$\alpha = \omega_0$

$s_1 = s_2 = \alpha$

$i(t) = e^{-\alpha t}\left(A_1 t + A_2 t\right)$
</td>
<td>

$\alpha < \omega_0$

$s_{1,2} = -\alpha \pm j\omega_d$

$\omega_d = \sqrt{\omega_0^2 - \alpha^2}$

$i(t) = e^{-\alpha t}\left(B_1 \cos \omega_d t + B_2 \sin \omega_d t\right)$
</td>
</tr>
</table>

The general equation of a complete response of a second-order system in terms of voltage for an RLC circuit is given by:

$$v(t) = \underbrace{V_f}_{\text{forced response}} + \underbrace{Ae^{s_1 t} + Be^{s_2 t}}_{\text{natural response}}$$

where V_f is a constant (DC excitation).

AC CIRCUITS

Sinusoidal Current, Voltage, and Phase Angle

The sinusoidal forcing function in its general form is as follows:

$$v(t) = V_m \cos(\omega t + \theta)$$

where

V_m = Maximum value

ω = Angular frequency = $2\pi f = \dfrac{2\pi}{T}$ in $\dfrac{\text{radians}}{\text{sec}}$

f = Frequency = $\dfrac{1}{T}$ in $\dfrac{\text{cycles}}{\text{sec}}$ or hertz (Hz)

T = Period (time duration of 1 cycle = sec)

θ = Phase angle in degrees or radians

The voltage across resistance (R), inductance (L), or capacitance (C) is given below for the specified current.

<table>
<tr><td colspan="4" align="center">TABLE 4
RESISTANCE, INDUCTANCE, OR CAPACITANCE</td></tr>
<tr><td>Element</td><td>voltage</td><td>$i = I_m \sin \omega t$</td><td>$i = I_m \cos \omega t$</td></tr>
<tr><td>R</td><td>$V_R \quad =$</td><td>$RI_m \sin \omega t$</td><td>$V_R = RI_m \cos \omega t$</td></tr>
<tr><td>L</td><td>$V_L \quad =$</td><td>$\omega L I_m \cos \omega t$</td><td>$V_L = \omega L I_m(-\sin \omega t)$</td></tr>
<tr><td>C</td><td>$V_C \quad =$</td><td>$\dfrac{I_m}{\omega C}(-\cos \omega t)$</td><td>$V_C = \dfrac{I_m}{\omega C}\sin \omega t$</td></tr>
</table>

The current in R, L, or C for the specified voltage is given below in table form.

TABLE 5
CURRENT, R, L, OR C

Element	current		$v = V_m \sin \omega t$	$v = V_m \cos \omega t$
R	i_R	$=$	$\dfrac{V_m}{R}\sin \omega t$	$i_R = \dfrac{V_m}{R}\cos \omega t$
L	i_L	$=$	$\dfrac{V_m}{\omega L}(-\cos \omega t)$	$i_L = \dfrac{V_m}{\omega L}\sin \omega t$
C	i_C	$=$	$\omega C V_m \cos \omega t$	$i_C = \omega C V_m(-\sin \omega t)$

Voltage and current were expressed in earlier sections of this chapter in integral and differential form for the resistor, inductor, and capacitor, as follows:

$$i_R(t) = \frac{V_R(t)}{R}, \quad V_R(t) = i_R(t)R$$

$$i_L(t) = \frac{1}{L}\int_{-\infty}^{t} V_L(\tau)d\tau, \quad V_L(t) = L\frac{di_L(t)}{dt}$$

$$i_C(t) = C\frac{dV_c(t)}{dt}, \quad V_C(t) = \frac{1}{C}\int_{-\infty}^{t} i_C(\tau)d\tau$$

The characteristics of phase angle are summarized in Table 6.

TABLE 6
CHARACTERISTICS OF PHASE ANGLE IN A PURE ELEMENT

Element	Current and voltage phase angle relationship	Impedance magnitude	Diagram
R	Current and voltage in phase	R	
L	Current lags the voltage by 90° or $\frac{\pi}{2}$ rad.	ωL	

C	Current leads the voltage by $90°$ or $\dfrac{\pi}{2}$ rad.	$\dfrac{1}{\omega C}$	
Series RL	Current lags the voltage by $\tan^{-1}\left(\dfrac{\omega L}{R}\right)$.	$\sqrt{R^2 + (\omega L)^2}$	
Series RC	Current leads the voltage by $\tan^{-1}\left(\dfrac{1}{\omega CR}\right)$.	$\sqrt{R^2 + \left(\dfrac{1}{\omega C}\right)^2}$	

The Concept of Phasor

In general, the **phasor** form of a sinusoidal voltage or current is:

$$V = V_m\angle\theta° \text{ and } I = I_m\angle\theta°.$$

Thus, for the voltage source $v(t) = V_m \cos\omega t$, the corresponding phasor form is $V_m\angle\theta°$. For the current response $i(t) = I_m \cos(\omega t + \theta)$, the corresponding phasor form is $V_m\angle\theta°$. Most often, instead of using the maximum value of voltage or current, the rms value is used (see AC Circuit Analysis).

The following steps outline the procedure for transformation to and from the time domain and frequency domain. Current and voltage relationships in the time and frequency domain are shown in table form below, and illustrated in Figure 46.

Time domain → frequency domain:

$$i(t) = I_m \cos(\omega t + \theta) \rightarrow I = I_m\angle\theta$$

(1) Assume a sinusoidal function $i(t)$ in the time domain is given. Express $i(t)$ as a cosine wave with a phase angle.

(2) Using Euler's identity—$e^{j\theta} = \cos\theta + j\sin\theta$—express the cosine wave as the real part of a complex quantity.

(3) Drop the Re and the term $e^{j\omega t}$ to obtain the final phasor form (the frequency domain form).

Frequency domain → time domain:

(1) Given a phasor current or voltage in polar form in the frequency domain, express the complex expression in exponential form.

(2) Multiply the factor $e^{j\omega t}$ by the obtained exponential form.

(3) Apply Euler's identity and take the real part of the complex expression to obtain the time domain representation.

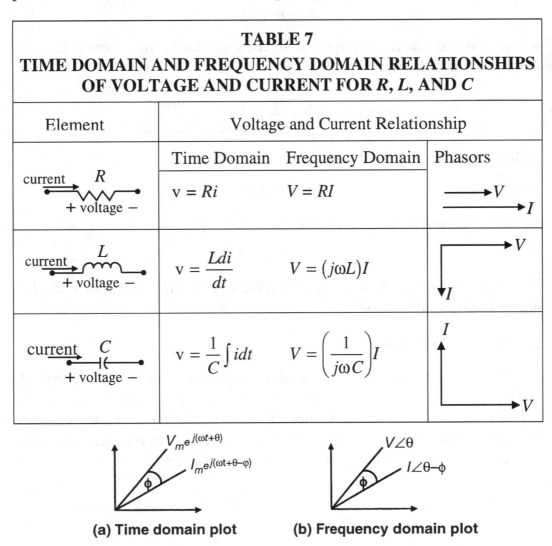

TABLE 7

TIME DOMAIN AND FREQUENCY DOMAIN RELATIONSHIPS OF VOLTAGE AND CURRENT FOR *R*, *L*, AND *C*

Element	Voltage and Current Relationship		
	Time Domain	Frequency Domain	Phasors
current R + voltage −	$v = Ri$	$V = RI$	
current L + voltage −	$v = \dfrac{Ldi}{dt}$	$V = (j\omega L)I$	
current C + voltage −	$v = \dfrac{1}{C}\int idt$	$V = \left(\dfrac{1}{j\omega C}\right)I$	

(a) Time domain plot   (b) Frequency domain plot

Figure 46. Time and frequency domain plot

$$V_m \text{ and } I_m \text{ are } \frac{1}{\sqrt{2}} \text{ times } V \text{ and } I$$

Impedance is a complex quantity with units of ohms, and is defined as:

$$\text{impedance } (Z) = \frac{\text{phasor voltage}}{\text{phasor current}} \text{[ohms]},$$

which in polar form is:

$$\mathbf{Z} = Z \angle \theta°,$$

and in rectangular form:

$$\mathbf{Z} = R + jX,$$

where X is the reactive component of the impedance. In a similar fashion, admittance is defined as:

$$\text{Admittance } (Y) = \frac{1}{Z} = \frac{\text{phasor current}}{\text{phasor voltage}},$$

with the following polar form:

$$\mathbf{Y} = Y \angle \theta°,$$

and the expected rectangular form:

$$\mathbf{Y} = G + jB.$$

The imaginary part of the admittance Y is the susceptance B. The units of admittance is mhos.

AC Circuit Analysis

Procedures similar to DC analysis and theorems are used for **AC analysis** except that they are in terms of phasor voltage and current (V and I) and impedance (Z) or admittance (Y). The following examples illustrate the application of familar theorems to AC circuits. In the case of source conversions, the general format is as shown in Figure 47.

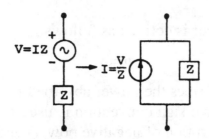

Figure 47. Source conversions

The rms, or effective, value of current and voltage are:

$$I_{eff} = I_{rms} = \sqrt{\frac{1}{T}\int_0^T [i(t)]^2 \, dt},$$

and

$$V_{eff} = V_{rms} = \sqrt{\frac{1}{T}\int_0^T [v(t)]^2 \, dt}.$$

(1) Effective value of $a \sin \omega t$ and $a \cos \omega t = \dfrac{a}{\sqrt{2}}$

(2) I_{eff} for sinusoidal current $i(t)$ equals $I_m \cos(\omega t - \theta)$

with $T = \dfrac{2\pi}{\omega}$; $\dfrac{I_m}{\sqrt{2}} = 0.707 I_m$

POWER

Instantaneous power is defined as follows:

$$p = vi.$$

This equation describes the power absorbed by the element as shown in Figure 48. The passive sign convention is used to differentiate between power generation (absorption of negative power) and power absorption by the element. This convention states that if the current enters the positive terminal then the sign of the product of the current and voltage may be used to describe the absorbed power. If the product is negative, negative power is absorbed by the element, or in other words, power is generated by the element.

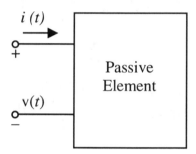

Figure 48. Power absorbed by an element

Instantaneous power in a resistive circuit is:

$$p = i^2 R = \frac{v^2}{R},$$

and for an inductive circuit:

$$p = Li\frac{di}{dt} = \frac{v}{L}\int_{-\infty}^{t} v\,dt,$$

and for a capacitive circuit:

$$p = Cv\frac{dv}{dt} = \frac{i}{C}\int_{-\infty}^{t} i\,dt.$$

Average power is defined mathematically as:

$$P = \frac{1}{t_2 - t_1}\int_{t_1}^{t_2} p(t)\,dt,$$

and for the sinusoidal steady state:

$$\text{Average power } (P) = \frac{1}{2} V_m I_m \cos\theta$$

$$= \underbrace{V_{rms} I_{rms}}_{\text{apparent power}} \cos\theta$$

where

$$V_{rms} = \frac{V_m}{\sqrt{2}}$$

$$I_{rms} = \frac{I_m}{\sqrt{2}}$$

Power factor (*pf*) is defined as a ratio of average power to apparent power:

$$\text{Power factor } (pf) = \frac{\text{average power}(P)}{\text{apparent power}(V_{rms} I_{rms})} = \cos\theta,$$

where apparent power is equal to the product of *rms* voltage and *rms* current as shown above. The angle (θ) is referred to as the *pf* angle. For a purely resistive load, voltage and current are in phase, i.e., $\theta = 0$ and *pf* = 1. Hence, apparent power = average power. For a purely reactive load, the phase difference between the voltage and current is either +90° or –90°. Hence, *pf* = 0. In general networks, $0 < pf < 1$.

Power factor correction is used to reduce electrical utility charges by changing the *pf* angle without changing the real power. The *pf* angle may be changed by altering the circuit reactance. The change in reactance required to change the *pf* angle from θ_1 to θ_2 is:

$$\Delta Q = P(\tan\theta_1 - \tan\theta_2)$$

where Q, the reactive power, is:

$$\underbrace{V_{rms} I_{rms}}_{\text{apparent power}} \sin\theta$$

in units of VAR, or volt-ampere reactance. The power factor can be corrected by adding inductance to a capacitive circuit, or adding capacitance to an inductive circuit. The capacitance in farads needed to correct the power factor is found by the application of the following equation:

$$C = \frac{\Delta Q}{2\pi f V^2},$$

where f is frequency.

Complex power, S, is the sum of the real average power and the reactive power

$$S = VIe^{j\left(\theta_v - \theta_i\right)}$$

$$= VI\cos\theta - j\,VI\sin\theta$$

$$= \underset{\text{real average power}}{P} - \underset{\text{reactive power}}{jQ,}$$

where

$$P = Re(VI^*)$$

$$Q = Im\,(VI^*)$$

The current and voltage are effective values, and I^* is the complex conjugated of I. The magnitude of the complex power S is the apparent power:

$$S = |VI^*|.$$

EXAMPLE

A circuit draws $4A$ at $25V_{rms}$, and dissipates $50W$. Find: (a) apparent power; (b) reactive power; (c) power factor and phase angle; and (d) impedance in both polar and rectangular forms.

SOLUTION

(a) The apparent power is

$$|S| = V_{eff}I_{eff} = (4)(25) = 100VA.$$

(b) Since

$$\vec{S} = P + jQ$$

and

$$|S| = \sqrt{P^2 + Q^2} = 100VA,$$

we can find Q because we are given P (dissipated power) $= 50W$.

Hence

$$Q = \sqrt{|S|^2 - P^2}$$

$$Q = \sqrt{100^2 - 50^2} = \sqrt{7,500} = 86.6 VA$$

(c) The power factor is defined as the ratio of dissipated power to apparent power. Hence,

$$pf = \frac{P}{|S|} = \frac{50}{100} = 0.5.$$

The phase angle is the $\cos^{-1} pf$, thus $\phi = \cos^{-1} 0.5 = 60°$.

(d) The magnitude of the impedance can be found from

$$|z| = \frac{V_{eff}}{I_{eff}} = \frac{25}{4} = 6.25\Omega.$$

We can therefore write z in polar form:

$$\vec{z} = |z| \angle \phi$$

$$\vec{z} = 6.25 \angle 60°$$

In rectangular form we must write

$$\vec{z} = 3.125 \pm j5.41\Omega$$

since we are not given any information to determine the polarity of the phase angle (that is, whether V lags or leads I). Thus the j term could be either plus or minus.

THREE-PHASE CIRCUITS

Three-Phase Systems

Figure 49 illustrates both positive, or ABC, sequence and negative, or CBA, sequence of voltages generated in a **three-phase system**. In the ABC sequence, $V_{A'A}$ reaches its peak before $V_{B'B}$, and $V_{B'B}$ reaches its peak before $V_{C'C}$. Reversing the rotation of the field magnet produces the CBA sequence in which $V_{C'C}$ reaches its peak before $V_{B'B}$, which in turn peaks before $V_{A'A}$.

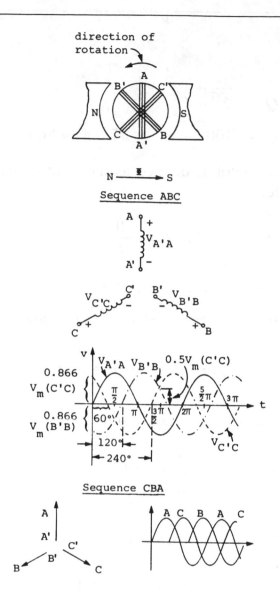

Figure 49. ABC and CBA sequences in three-phase system

At any instant of time, the summation of all three-phase voltages is zero:

$$\sum V_{A'A} + V_{B'B} + V_{C'C} = 0.$$

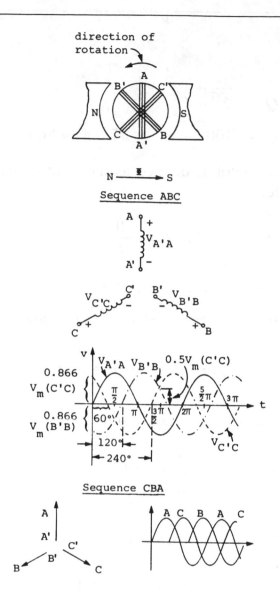

Figure 50. Summation of three-phase voltages

In a three-phase system, summarized in Figure 50, the three coils on the rotor are placed 120° apart as in Figure 51. (Assume each coil has an equal number of turns.)

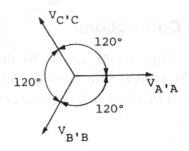

Figure 51. Spacing of coils on typical three-phase system

Three-phase voltages are listed in table form for positive and negative sequences.

TABLE 8	
THREE-PHASE SYSTEM VOLTAGES	
Sequence (positive phase sequence) 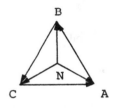	(Note: V_L = line voltage) $$V_{AN} = \left(\frac{V_L}{\sqrt{3}}\right)\angle 90°$$ $$V_{BN} = \left(\frac{V_L}{\sqrt{3}}\right)\angle -30°$$ $$V_{CN} = \left(\frac{V_L}{\sqrt{3}}\right)\angle -150°$$ $$V_{AB} = V_L\angle 120°$$ $$V_{BC} = V_L\angle 0°$$ $$V_{CA} = V_L\angle 240°$$
sequence (negative phase sequence) 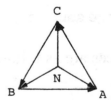	(Note: V_L = line voltage) $$V_{AN} = \left(\frac{V_L}{\sqrt{3}}\right)\angle -90°$$ $$V_{BN} = \left(\frac{V_L}{\sqrt{3}}\right)\angle 30°$$ $$V_{CN} = \left(\frac{V_L}{\sqrt{3}}\right)\angle 150°$$ $$V_{AB} = V_L\angle 240°$$ $$V_{BC} = V_L\angle 0°$$ $$V_{CA} = V_L\angle 120°$$

(**Note:** Phase reference line voltage V_{AB}.)

The Wye and Delta Connections

Two common configurations found in three-phase circuits are the **wye (*Y*)** and **delta (Δ) connections**, as shown in Figure 52. Figure 53 illustrates the connection of ideal voltage sources in wye configuration.

Y-Alternator   **Δ-Alternator**

Figure 52. Wye and delta connections

$$I_{coil} = I_{line} \qquad\qquad I_{coil} = \frac{1}{\sqrt{3}} I_{line}$$

$$V_{line} = \sqrt{3}\, V_{coil} \qquad\qquad V_{line} = V_{coil}$$

I_{coil} is more commonly referred to as I_{phase}.

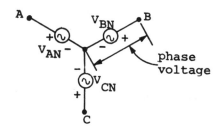

Figure 53. Wye-connected ideal voltage sources

Characteristics of balanced three-phase sources are as follows:

(1) $|V_{AN}| = |V_{BN}| = |V_{CN}|$ and $V_{AN} + V_{BN} + V_{CN} = 0$

(2) If $V_{AN} = V_P \angle 0°$ is the reference where $V_P = rms$ is the magnitude of any of the phase voltages, then $V_{BN} = V_P \angle{-120°}$ and $V_{CN} = V_P \angle -240°$ (positive phase or sequence *ABC*) or $V_{BN} = V_P \angle 120°$ and $V_{CN} = V_P \angle 240°$ (negative phase or sequence *CBA*).

Phasor diagrams of positive and negative sequences are shown in Figure 54 and line-phasor voltage relationships in Figure 55 for balanced three-phase circuits.

V_CN=V_P∠-240°
(V_P=phase voltage)
N
V_AN=V_P∠0°
V_BN=V_P∠-120°
V_BN=V_P∠120°
N
V_AN=V_P∠0°
V_CN=V_P∠240°

(a) Positive sequence **(b) Negative sequence**

Figure 54. Phasor diagrams of positive and negative sequences in balanced three-phase circuits

V_CN
V_AB
V_CA
V_AN
V_BN
V_BC

$$V_{\text{line}} = \sqrt{3}V$$

$$V_{AB} = \sqrt{3}V_P\angle 30°$$

$$V_{BC} = \sqrt{3}V_P\angle -90°$$

$$V_{CA} = \sqrt{3}V_P\angle -210°$$

Figure 55. Phasor diagrams of line and phase voltage for balanced three-phase circuits

A wye-connected load is shown in Figure 56. The phase power, P_p, is:

$$P_p - V_{\text{phase}} I_{\text{line}} \cos\theta,$$

where θ is the angle by which phase current lags phase voltage (for inductive loads, θ would be positive, and for capacitive loads, θ would be negative), and the total power P_t is:

$$\mathrm{V}_P I_P = V_P I_L = \frac{V_L I_L}{\sqrt{3}},$$

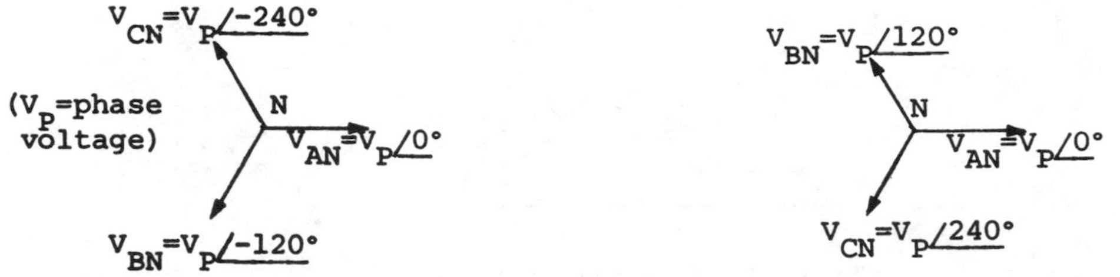

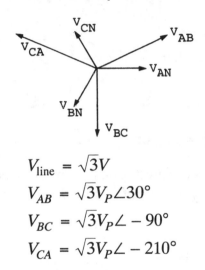

$$P_t = 3P_P, \text{ or } P_t = \sqrt{3} \cdot V_L I_L \cos\theta \text{ where } V_L = \sqrt{3}V_P.$$

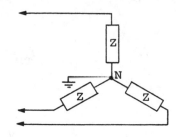

Figure 56. Wye-connected load

For a Δ-connected load, the phase power, P_p, is:

$$P_P = V_L I_P \cos\theta,$$

where

$$V_L I_P = V_P I_P = V_L \frac{I_L}{\sqrt{3}}.$$

The total power, P_t, is:

$$P_t = 3P_p \text{ or } P_t = \sqrt{3}V_L I_L \cos\theta.$$

The circuit and associated phasor diagram for a balanced delta-connected load with a wye-connected source is shown in Figure 57.

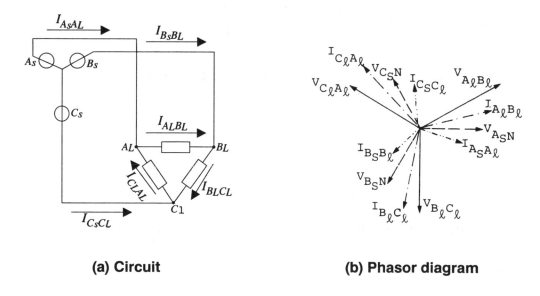

(a) Circuit (b) Phasor diagram

Figure 57. Balanced delta-connected load with wye-connected source

Referring to Figure 57, the voltages are:

$$V_{\text{phase}} = \left|V_{A_sN}\right| = \left|V_{B_sN}\right| = \left|V_{C_sN}\right|,$$

assuming that the line voltage:

$$V_{\text{line}} = \left|V_{A_sB_s}\right| = \left|V_{A_sC_s}\right| = \left|V_{C_sA_s}\right|$$

where

$$V_L = \sqrt{3}V_A \quad \text{and} \quad V_{A_sB_s} = \sqrt{3}V_{A_sN}\angle 30°.$$

Then the phase currents are:

$$I_{A_LB_L} = \frac{V_{A_sB_s}}{Z_p}, \; I_{B_LC_L} = \frac{V_{B_sC_s}}{Z_p} \quad \text{and} \quad I_{C_LA_L} = \frac{V_{C_sA_s}}{Z_p},$$

and the line currents are:

$$I_{A_LB_L} - I_{C_LA_L} = I_{A_sA_L}, \text{ etc.}$$

The three-phase currents are equal in magnitude:

$$I_P = \left|I_{A_sB_s}\right| = \left|I_{B_sC_s}\right| = \left|I_{C_sA_s}\right|,$$
$$I_L = \left|I_{A_sA_L}\right| = \left|I_{B_sB_L}\right| = \left|I_{C_sC_L}\right|,$$

and

$$I_L = \sqrt{3}I_P.$$

IDEAL TRANSFORMERS

An ideal transformer, like the one shown in Figure 58, has two magnetically coupled coils with N_1 and N_2 turns. The coefficient of coupling is unity, $k = 1$. The self-inductance of each coil is assumed to be infinite, $L_1 = L_2 = \infty$. Coil losses are negligible.

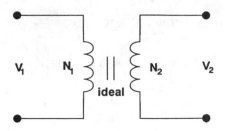

Figure 58. Ideal transformer

Due to the ideal nature of the transformer, its behavior can be described by a few simple relationships. The magnitude of the voltage per turn is the same for both coils, or:

$$\frac{V_1}{N_1} = \frac{V_2}{N_2}$$

Also the total current is the same for both coils,

$$I_1 N_1 = I_2 N_2.$$

The unity coupling yields the inductance relationship:

$$\frac{V_2}{V_1} = \frac{L_2}{L_1}$$

The symbol $\underset{\text{ideal}}{\|}$ used in the figure depicts the transformer as ideal. Ideal transformers are approximated by coils wound around ferromagnetic cores, which is in contrast to a linear transformer where the core is non-magnetic. Laminated sheets of magnetic material are often used as cores in ideal transformers. This ferromagnetic material is able to create a space with a high permeance, thus, most of the magnetic flux remains trapped inside the core. The magnetic core material results in a high degree of coupling between coils which share the same core. The high permeance of the magnetic material yields a high self-inductance. The magnetic cores are also very efficient, which allows the negligible loss approximation. The high efficiency, usually greater than 95%, also reflects the good power transfer from one coil to another.

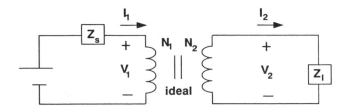

Figure 59. Ideal transformers can alter the impedance of the load

Ideal transformers can be used to raise or lower the impedance level of a load. An example is shown in Figure 59. The impedance seen by the source, $Z_{internal} - Z_{source}$, is:

$$Z_{IN} = \frac{V_1}{I_1}$$

but:

$$\frac{V_1}{I_1} = \frac{N_1}{N_2} \frac{V_2}{I_2}$$

The load impedance, Z_1, is $\dfrac{V_2}{I_2}$

Thus:

$$Z_{IN} = \frac{N_1}{N_2} Z_1$$

By altering the turns ratio, $\dfrac{N_1}{N_2}$, the impedance of the load can be matched to that of the source Z_s. Therefore, ideal transformers can be used to improve the power transferred from source to load.

In other analyses, ideal transformers are used in T-equivalent and π-equivalent circuits. The turns ratio can be changed to create an infinite number of equivalent circuits. Ideal transformers are also useful in avoiding negative inductors which may be present in some models.

FOURIER TRANSFORMS IN CIRCUITS

The Fourier transform can transfer a function that is aperiodic from the time domain into the frequency domain. While the Laplace transform also has this capability, the Fourier transform can be used with functions that are time-negative, that is $t < 0$, whereas with the Laplace transform, $t > 0$. The Laplace transform is used for the transient state of the circuit, while the Fourier transform can generate the steady-state response of a circuit that is excited by a sinusoidal source. Fourier transforms are commonly used in problems in communication theory and signal processing. The review of Fourier transforms in this section is very brief and elementary.

The Fourier transform is defined by the equation:

$$F(\omega) = f\{f(t)\} = \int_{-\infty}^{+\infty} f(t)e^{-j\omega t}dt$$

where f(t) is the function in the time domain and F(ω) is the corresponding function in the frequency domain. The inverse operation of the transform is defined by the equation:

$$f(t) = \frac{1}{2}\pi \int_{-\infty}^{+\infty} F(\omega)e^{j\omega t}d\omega.$$

Figure 60 shows the Fourier transform of a signal; some other common Fourier transforms are shown in the table. The convergence of the Fourier integral is dependent upon the function f(t). If the function is well behaved and is single-valued and encloses a finite area, then the integral will converge. An example is the Fourier transform of the step function shown in Figure 61. If the function is single-valued, but non-zero over an infinite interval, it will converge if the integral $\int |f(t)| \, dt$ exists and any discontinuities are finite. An example of such a function is a decaying exponential. Finally, the Fourier integral will not converge if f(t) is a constant. These cases are treated by defining a limit process, and the limiting value of the F(ω) is defined as the Fourier transform.

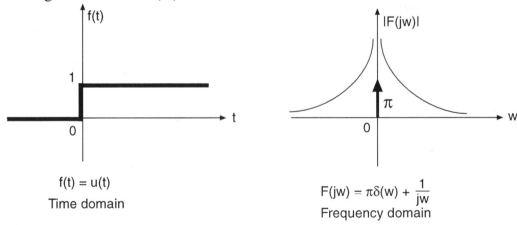

Figure 60. Time and frequency representations of a step function

TABLE OF FOURIER TRANSFORMS

f(t)	Function name	F(ω)
$\delta(t)$	impulse	1
A	constant	$2\pi A\delta(\omega)$
sgn(t)	signum	$\dfrac{2}{j\omega}$
u(t)	step	$\pi\delta(\omega) + \dfrac{1}{j\omega}$
$e^{-at}u(t)$	positive-time exponential	$\dfrac{1}{a + j\omega}$
$e^{at}u(-t)$	negative-time exponential	$\dfrac{1}{a - j\omega}$
$\cos \omega_0 t$	cosine	$\pi\left[\delta(\omega + \omega_0) + \delta(\omega - \omega_0)\right]$
$\sin \omega_0 t$	sine	$j\pi\left[\delta(\omega + \omega_0) - \delta(\omega - \omega_0)\right]$

While the Laplace transform is more widely used in circuit analysis, Fourier transforms are used in transient analysis, especially in convolution integrals, where a transfer function, H(ω), is used to relate the transform of the input X(ω) to the transform of the response Y(ω). Convolution in the frequency domain is represented as multiplication as shown.

$$Y(\omega) = X(\omega)H(\omega).$$

Consider the example below.

EXAMPLE

Find $i_o(t)$ if $i_g(t)$ is a signum function 20 sgn t A.

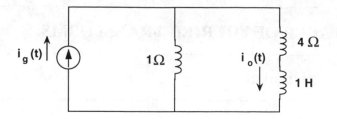

Figure 61. Circuit for example

SOLUTION

The Fourier transform of $I_g(t)$, $I_g(\omega) = 20 \left(\dfrac{2}{j\omega} \right) = \dfrac{40}{j\omega}$

The transfer function, $H(\omega)$ is the ratio of the I_o to I_g, or:

$$H(\omega) = \frac{1}{5 + j\omega}$$

Thus, $I_o(\omega) = I_g(\omega)H(\omega) = \dfrac{40}{j\omega(5 + j\omega)}$

Expanding into partial fractions and finding the constants gives:

$$I_o(\omega) = \frac{K_1}{j\omega} + \frac{K_2}{5 + j\omega}$$

$$K_1 = \frac{40}{5} = 8$$

$$K_2 = \frac{40}{-5} = -8$$

$$I_o(\omega) = \frac{8}{j\omega} - \frac{8}{5 + j\omega}$$

$$I_o(t) = 4 \operatorname{sgn} t - 8\,e^{-5t}\,u(t)$$

LAPLACE TRANSFORMS IN ELECTRIC CIRCUITS

In circuits, Laplace transforms are used to solve integro-differentiation problems which have several simultaneous equations. Equations in the time domain (t-domain) are transformed into simpler algebraic equations in the frequency domain (s-domain). Laplace transforms are best used on problems with constant coefficients and with simply defined initial and/or final conditions, such as circuits with initial currents and voltages which are varying with time. While the algebra in the s-domain is simple, often converting back to the t-domain, with the inverse transform it can be cumbersome, and partial fractions expedite the process.

Two functions that are commonly used are the step function and the impulse function. Figure 62 shows the step function in the time domain, along with its mathematical description. Similarly, Figure 63 depicts the impulse function.

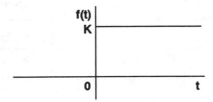

Figure 62. Step function

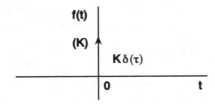

Figure 63. Impulse function

Some commonly used Laplace transform pairs are given in the table. All of these are valid if t > 0.

Laplace Transform Pairs

f(t)	Function name	F(s)
$\delta(t)$	impulse	1
$u(t)$	step	$\dfrac{1}{s}$
t	ramp	$\dfrac{1}{s^2}$
e^{-at}	exponential	$\dfrac{1}{(s+a)}$
$\sin \omega t$	sine	$\dfrac{\omega}{s^2 + a^2}$
$\cos \omega t$	cosine	$\dfrac{s}{s^2 + a^2}$
te^{-at}	damped ramp	$\dfrac{1}{(s+a)^2}$
$e^{-at} \sin \omega t$	damped sine	$\dfrac{\omega}{(s+a)^2 + \omega^2}$
$e^{-at} \cos \omega t$	damped cosine	$\dfrac{s+a}{(s+a)^2 + \omega^2}$

Circuits can also be simply transformed from the t-domain to the s-domain. Figure 64 shows three circuits, with a resistor (a), inductor (b), and capacitor (c), respectively, with their s-domain equivalents.

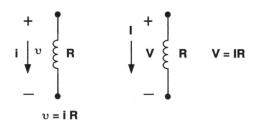

Figure 64(a). Circuit with resistor

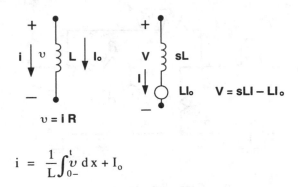

$$v = iR$$

$$V = sLI - LI_o$$

$$i = \frac{1}{L}\int_{0-}^{t} v\, dx + I_o$$

Figure 64(b). Circuit with inductor

$$V = \frac{T}{sC} + \frac{V_o}{s}$$

$$v = \frac{1}{C}\int_{0-}^{t} i\, dx + V_o$$

Figure 64(c). Circuit with capacitor

OPERATIONAL AMPLIFIERS

Basic Op-Amp with Feedback

Operational amplifiers make use of BJTs and other electronic devices to provide current or voltage gain. An ideal operational amplifier has infinite input impedance, infinite gain, infinite bandwidth, and zero output impedance. The basic operational amplifier with feedback is shown in Figure 65.

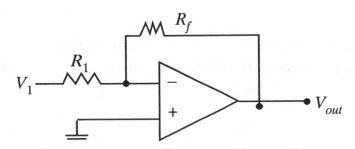

(a) Design schematic

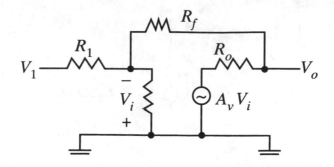

(b) Circuit diagram

Figure 65. Basic operational amplifier with feedback

Derived using the principle of superposition and the definition of voltage gain, the input voltage is

$$V_i = \frac{R_f}{R_f(1 + A_v)R_1} V_1.$$

The input voltage is approximately equal to

$$V_i \cong \frac{R_f}{A_v R_1} V_1$$

when

$$A_v >> 1$$
$$R_1 >> R_f.$$

The following example derives the output voltage equation for the basic operation amplifier with feedback. This circuit is also referred to as an inverting constant-gain circuit, as the sign of the input signal is changed at the output and the gain is a constant multiplier.

EXAMPLE

Determine the output voltage of the circuit in Figure 66. The following parameters are given: $R_i = 10^5 \, \Omega$, $R_o = 0$, $A = 10^5$. Let $R_1 = 10^5 \, \Omega$ and $R_2 = 10^7 \, \Omega$.

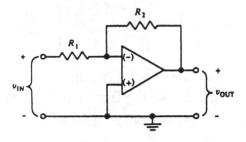

Figure 66. Circuit

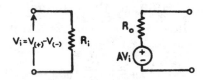

Figure 67. Model for op-amp

SOLUTION

By replacing the op-amp with the model of Figure 67, the result is the circuit in Figure 68. In order to keep track of the negative (−) and positive (+) input terminals, their locations in the new circuit have been shown.

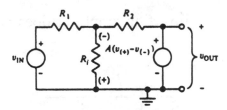

Figure 68. Resulting circuit

The voltage at the (−) input terminal $V_{(-)}$ is found by the node equation. Summing the currents leaving the (−) node:

$$\frac{V_{(-)} - V_{in}}{R_1} + \frac{V_{(-)}}{R_i} + \frac{V_{(-)} - A\left(V_{(+)} - V_{(-)}\right)}{R_2} = 0.$$

$V_{(+)} = 0$, so the equation is rewritten as

$$V_{(-)} \left[\frac{1}{R_1} + \frac{1}{R_i} + \frac{(1+A)}{R_2} \right] = \frac{V_{in}}{R_1}.$$

Referring to the values of R_1, R_i, R_2, and A, the last term in the square brackets is clearly the largest, so the first two terms in the brackets may be neglected. Moreover, $(1 + A)$ is nearly equal to A. Thus,

$$V_{(-)} \left[\frac{A}{R_2} \right] \cong \frac{V_{in}}{R_1}$$

$$V_{(-)} \cong \frac{R_2}{R_1} \frac{V_{in}}{A}$$

The output voltage is equal to the voltage of the dependent voltage source, which is $-AV_{(-)}$. Thus,

$$V_{out} \cong -\frac{R_2}{R_1} V_{in}.$$

Op-AMP Applications

Common operation amplifier applications include circuits which function as **adders**, **integrators**, **differentiators**, and **simple phase changers**. A noninverting constant-gain circuit is shown in Figure 69. The gain for this circuit is

$$A_v = \frac{R_f + R_1}{R_1}.$$

As expected, the noninverting amplifier does not change the sign of the input signal.

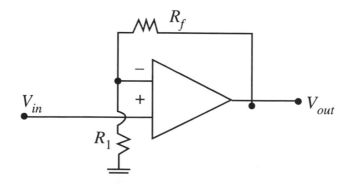

Figure 69. Noninverting constant-gain operation amplifier

A summing amplifier, or adder, is shown in Figure 70. This operational amplifier configuration provides a means to sum voltages, in this case, the three voltages V_1, V_2, and V_3. The output voltage is

$$V_o = -R'\left(\frac{V_1}{R_1} + \frac{V_2}{R_2} + \frac{V_3}{R_3}\right),$$

or

$$V_o = \frac{-R'}{R}\left(V_1 + V_2 + V_3\right), \text{ if } R_1 = R_2 = R_3 = R.$$

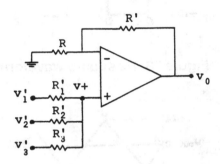

Figure 70. Summing amplifier

The output of the operational amplifier in Figure 71 is the integral of the input. This integrator circuit produces an output voltage as follows:

$$V_o = \frac{-1}{RC}\int V dt$$

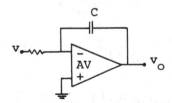

Figure 71. Integrator

The input to the integrator shown in Figure 96 is the +/– 10V, 250 Hz square waveform shown in Figure 73. Knowing that $C = 1\mu F$ and $R = 100k\,\Omega$, the output voltage waveform is determined.

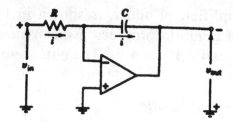

Figure 72. Integrator

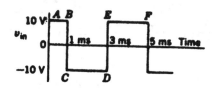

Figure 73. Hz square waveform

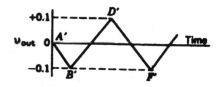

Figure 74. Output voltage waveform

The time constant of the circuit, *RC*, is

$$RC = 10^5 \Omega \times 1 \times 10^{-6} \text{F} = 0.1\text{s}.$$

Then

$$V_{out} = \frac{-1}{RC} \int V_{in} dt = -10 \int V_{in} dt.$$

The area under the curve is $\int V_{in} dt$. Starting from *A* toward *B* on the square wave, the area increases linearly. The final area at *B* is

$$\int V_{in} dt = (10\text{v}) \times (0.001\text{s}) = 0.01\text{sv}$$

then $$V_{out} = -10 \int V_{in} dt = (-10) \times (0.01) = -0.1\text{V}.$$

Thus, the voltage changes linearly from zero at *A'* to –0.1V at *B'*.

The area from C to D is negative and the magnitude of the area increases linearly from C to D. The total area from C to D is

$$(-10V) \times (0.002s) = -0.02sv$$

$$V_{out} = -10\int V_{in}dt = (-10) \times (-0.02) = +0.2V$$

At B', V_{out} is -0.1V. The linear change of V_{out} from B' to D' is $+0.2V$. Thus, the voltage at D' is $-0.1 + 0.2 = +0.1V$.

The area under the input voltage waveform increases linearly from E to F. This increasing area causes the voltage to fall linearly from D' to F'.

Thus, if a square wave is fed into the input of an integrator, the output voltage is the triangular wave form shown in Figure 74.

A differentiator circuit is shown in Figure 75, which as expected, is very similar to the integrator circuit of Figure 74. The output voltage is

$$V_o = -RC\frac{dV}{dt}.$$

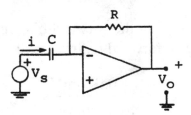

Figure 75. Differentiator

DIODES

Ideal Diode Equation

The current-voltage relationship and the diode circuit symbol are shown in Figure 76. The ideal diode equation relates diode current and voltage as follows:

$$i_D = I_0\left[\varepsilon^{\frac{V_D}{\eta T}} - 1\right]$$

where I_0 is the **saturation current** as shown in Figure 76 and η is an empirical constant. For the common semiconductor materials germanium and silicon, ε is equal to 1 and 2, respectively. The **volt-equivalent of the temperature**, V_T, is also required in the ideal diode equation above and is equal to

$$V_T = \frac{T}{11,600},$$

where T represents temperature in Kelvin.

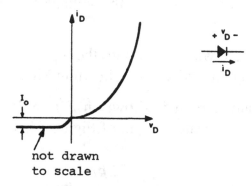

not drawn
to scale

Figure 76. Diode voltage-current relationship and circuit symbol

The inverse of the slope in the forward bias region of Figure 76 is the **forward resistance**, r_f. The forward resistance at room temperature is

$$r_f = \frac{0.026\text{mV}}{i_D}.$$

The **reverse resistance**, r_r, is the inverse of the slope in the reverse bias region and is usually assumed to be infinite in value.

The diode characteristic curve in Figure 76 provides a means of graphically analyzing diode circuits using the diode load line, as reviewed in the following example.

EXAMPLE

Each of the five load-lines in Figures 78 and 79 corresponds to the circuit in Figure 77. Find E_S (potential), R (resistance), I_R (current in the reverse direction), V_R (voltage in the reverse direction), and the mode in which the diode is operating.

SOLUTION

Start with the following method.

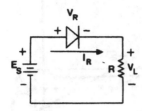

Figure 77. Circuit diagram

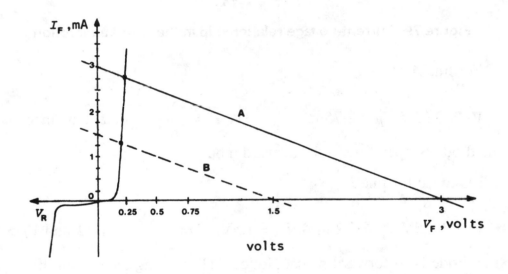

Figure 78. Current-voltage relationship in the forward direction

The endpoints of a load-line are given by

$$V = 0, I = \frac{E_S}{R}$$

and

$$I = 0, V = E_S$$

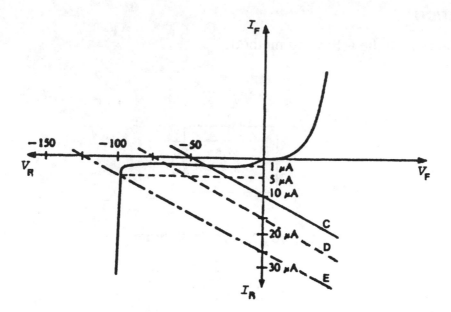

Figure 79. Current-voltage relationship in the reverse direction

For line A:

$$V_R = 0.25\text{V}, \ I_R = 2.75\text{mA}, \ E_S = 3V, \ R = \frac{3V}{3\text{mA}} = 1\text{k}\Omega \ \text{and since} \ V_R >$$

0, the diode is operating in the forward mode.

Likewise for line B:

$$V_R = 0.25\text{V}, \ I_R = 1.25\text{mA}, \ E_S = 1.5\text{V}, \ R = \frac{1.4\text{V}}{1.5\text{mA}} = 1\text{k}\Omega \ \text{and} \ V_R > 0,$$

so the diode is in forward mode. Notice that reducing the current by more than 50% had virtually no effect on the voltage across the diode in the forward mode.

Line C:

$$V_R = -45\text{V}, \ I_R = -1 \text{ A}, \ E_S = -50\text{V}, \ R = \frac{-50\text{V}}{-10\mu\text{A}} = 5\text{M}\Omega. \ \text{Since} \ V_R <$$

0, the diode is reverse-biased. Very little current flows.

Line D:

$$V_R = -70\text{V}, \ I_R = -1\mu\text{A}, \ E_S = -75\text{V}, \ R = \frac{-75\text{V}}{-15\mu\text{A}} = 5\text{M}\Omega, \ V_R < 0, \ \text{so}$$

the diode is reverse-biased. Note that increasing the voltage across the diode on reverse mode does not change the current.

Line E:

$$V_R = -100\text{V}, \ I_R = -5\mu\text{A}, \ E_S = -125\text{V}, \ R = \frac{-125\text{V}}{25\mu\text{A}} = 5\text{M}\Omega. \text{ Now the}$$

diode has broken down. At this point, V_R will remain at -100V as long as $E_S < -100$V. The diode will burn out if the current is not limited by a large resistance, since power $= I_R V_R$ and V_R is so large.

Diode Equivalent Circuits

The **DC** or **static resistance** is the resistance of the diode at a particular operating point.

$$R_{DC} = \frac{V_D}{I_D}$$

If the static resistance is known at the **particular operating point**, or **Q-point**, it can be modeled by a resistor of the appropriate value. After determining the conducting state of the diode ("on" or "off"), the equivalent circuitry is substituted for the diode. Resistors, batteries, and ideal diodes may be used to obtain simple diode equivalent circuits. (Often only the ideal diode is used to represent the real diode.) The value of the battery reflects the conduction physics of a silicon diode—a silicon diode does not reach conduction state until 0.7 volts.

The open-circuit equivalent, or "off" state, of a diode results when a voltage with the polarity shown in Figure 80(a) is applied. The "off" state also results when a voltage less than the value required to reach conduction state (the back-bias voltage) is applied, as in Figure 80(b). This value is 0.3 volts for germanium diodes and, as mentioned previously, 0.7 volts for silicon diodes. The "on" state is shown in Figure 80(c) for an ideal diode and in Figure 80(d) for a silicon diode.

(a) "Off" state of any diode

(b) "Off" state of a silicon diode

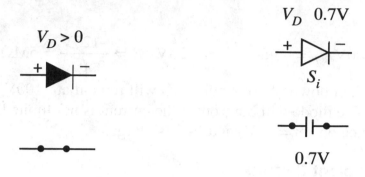

(c) "On" state of an ideal diode   (d) "On" state of a silicon diode

Figure 80. Conduction states and equivalent circuits

EXAMPLE

A common application of silicon diodes is shown in Figure 81. Predict the current I_2 as a function of V_1.

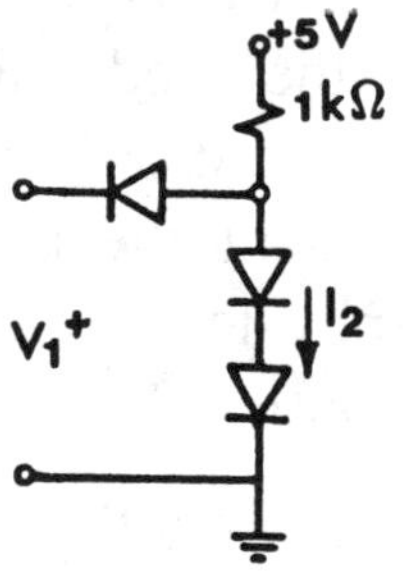

Figure 81. Silicon diodes

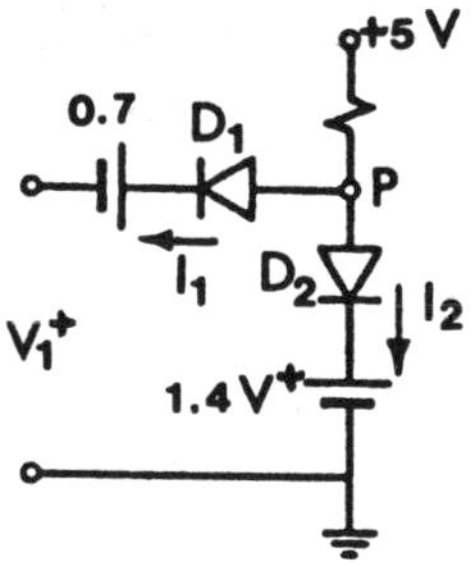

Figure 82. Ideal diode

SOLUTION

As a first step in the analysis, replace the diodes by appropriate circuit models. The two diodes in series are represented by an ideal diode and a source of $2 \times 0.7 = 1.4$V. (See Figure 82.)

V_P cannot exceed 1.4V because at that voltage D_2 is forward biased and current I_2 flows readily. Also, V_P cannot exceed $V_1 + 0.7$ because at that voltage D_1 is forward-biased and current I_1 flows readily.

The critical value is $V_P = 1.4 = V_1 + 0.7$ or $V_1 = 1.4 - 0.7 = 0.7$V. For $0 < V_1 < 0.7$V, D_1 is forward-biased and $I_2 = 0$. For $V_1 > 0.7$V, D_2 is forward-biased and $I_2 = \dfrac{V}{R} = \dfrac{(5 - 1.4)}{1,000} = 3.6$mA. The circuit thus provides a switchable constant current series.

Zener diodes operate differently in the reverse-bias region than the diodes discussed previously. While silicon diodes are modeled as open-circuits in the reverse-bias region, Zener diodes may be modeled by a short-circuit once an offset voltage is reached. The following example reviews Zener diode fundamentals.

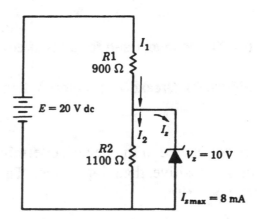

Figure 83. Zener diode

To determine if the Zener diode in Figure 83 is properly biased, the voltage-current relationship is examined. A Zencr diode is basically a semiconductor diode which is designed to operate in the breakdown region (see Figure 84).

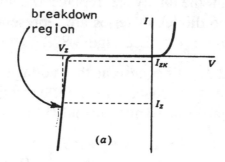

(a) The volt-ampere characteristic of an avalanche, or Zener, diode.

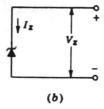

(b) The symbol used for a breakdown diode

Figure 84. Breakdown region of Zener diode

The anode is connected to the negative terminal of the source; hence, its cathode is more positive than its anode. The Zener, therefore, has proper bias voltage polarity.

Assume that the Zener diode is open. Then the voltage across it is in the same proportion to the total as R_2 is to the total resistance $(R_1 + R_2)$. Writing this statement in equation form and solving it for V_{Z0} (voltage across the open Zener) yields the familiar voltage diode equation.

$$V_{Z0} = E\left(\frac{R_2}{(R_1 + R_2)}\right)$$

$$V_{Z0} = 20\left(\frac{1,100}{2,000}\right) = 11V \text{ dc}$$

Note that $V_{Z0} > V_Z$ by 10 volts, and the Zener is properly voltage biased.

Because the Zener has proper voltage bias, the voltage across it is its V_Z of 10 volts. The same voltage is across R_2, making

$$I_2 = \frac{10V}{1,100} = 0.009A \text{ or } 9mA.$$

The voltage across R_1 is the difference between the voltage across R_2 and the Zener, and the source voltage (E), or

$$V_{R_1} = E - V_2 = 20 - 10 = 10V.$$

Then, the current through R_1 is

$$I_1 = \frac{10V}{900} = 0.011A \text{ or } 11mA$$

$$I_Z = I_1 - I_2 = 11mA - 9mA = 2mA$$

Therefore, the current through the Zener (I_Z) is less than I_{Zmax} of 8mA. The Zener has a negative open voltage greater than its V_Z and a current (I_Z) less than I_{Zmax}. Hence, it is properly biased.

Diode Applications

Diodes are commonly used as **full-wave** and **half-wave rectifiers**. A half-wave rectifier is shown in Figure 85 with its input and resulting output signals. The output voltage is explained for each half-cycle of the input voltage as follows.

1. **Positive half-cycle:** The polarity of the input voltage defines the "on" state for the ideal diode in the figure. The ideal diode may be represented by a short circuit. The output voltage is therefore equivalent to the input voltage for the first half of the period. (For a circuit with a silicon diode, the equivalent circuitry would be a 0.7 volts battery, and the output voltage would be equal to the input voltage—0.7 volts.)

2. **Negative half-cycle:** The polarity of the input voltage defines the "off" state of the ideal diode. This results in an open circuit equivalent for the negative half-cycle, and therefore zero voltage for the second half of the period.

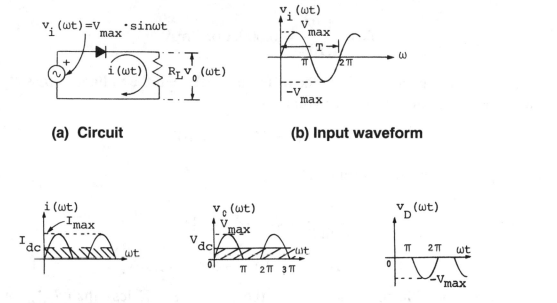

(a) **Circuit**   (b) **Input waveform**

(c) **Output Current**   (d) **Output voltage**   (e) **Voltage across the diode**

Figure 85. Half-wave rectifier

The load for the rectifier circuit in Figure 86, for the case of approximate U.S. line voltage ($C = 50 \times 10^{-6}$F, $R = 1,000\,\Omega$ and $V_1 = 165\,(\sin 377t)$), can easily be drawn. For simplicity, assume that the diode is a perfect rectangle.

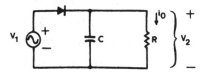

Figure 86. Rectifier circuit

First sketch the input voltage [Figure 87(a)]. Initially, the capacitor is fully charged to 165V at time t_1. In the time interval from t_1 to $5t_1$, the input and the diode are effectively removed from the circuit. During this time the capacitor discharges into the load, supplying the load current, and the circuit reduces to a resistance in parallel with a capacitance. [See Figure 87(b)]. In RC circuits, the voltage V_C decays exponentially with time constant RC. The voltage is thus of the form $V_C = 165 \exp\left(-\left(\dfrac{t - t_1}{RC}\right)\right)$.

This equation is plotted in Figure 87(c).

The equation only describes the output up to the time t_C shown in the figure because the charging of the capacitor starts again at this instant and the cycle is repeated. Thus, the actual waveform is as given in Figure 111(d). The load current has the same form as the output voltage because

$$i_0 = \frac{V_C}{R}.$$

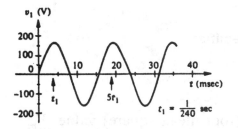

(a) Input voltage

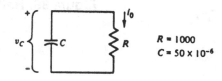

(b) Resistance in parallel with a capacitance

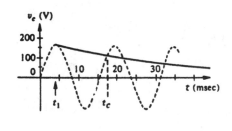

(c) Voltage

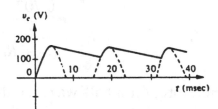

(d) Actual waveform

Figure 87. Addition of a capacitor to the basic half-wave rectifier circuit

The average dc values for current and voltage shown in Figure 85 are defined as follows:

$$I_{dc} = \frac{I_{max}}{\pi} = 0.318\, I_{max}$$
$$V_{dc} = 0.318 I_{dc} \times R_L = 0.318 V_{max}$$

Other factors of interest concerning half-wave rectifier circuits are the **ripple factor, efficiency,** and the **peak inverse voltage (PIV)**. The following example provides a review of these terms, and explains the procedure and equations needed to solve problems of this type.

EXAMPLE

For the half-wave rectifier shown in Figure 88, find (a) the I_{dc}, (b) the I_{rms}, (c) the ripple factor, r, (d) the rectifier efficiency η_r, and (e) the peak inverse.

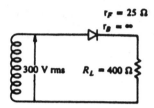

Figure 88. Half-wave rectifier

SOLUTION

(a) Since the input voltage is an rms (root mean square) value, V_m and I_m must be converted by

$$V_m = \frac{300}{0.707} = 425V$$

$$I_m = \frac{V_m}{\left(r_F + R_L\right)} = \frac{425}{425} = 1A$$

Therefore, for a half-wave rectifier,

$$I_{dc} = \frac{1}{2}\pi\int_0^\pi id\theta = \frac{I_m}{\pi} = \frac{1}{\pi} = 0.32A.$$

(b) For a half-wave rectifier

$$I_{rms} = \frac{I_m}{2} = \frac{1}{2} = 0.5A.$$

(c) By definition, the ripple factor is the ratio of the rms value of the ac component of the current to the dc component of the current, where

$$i(t)_{ac} = i(t) - I_{dc}$$

or

$$I^2_{ac,rms} = I^2_{rms} - I^2_{dc}$$

so $\quad r = \dfrac{\left(I_{ac,rms}\right)}{\left(I_{dc}\right)} = \dfrac{\sqrt{\left(I_{rms}^2 - I_{dc}^2\right)}}{I_{dc}} = \dfrac{\sqrt{(.5)^2 - (.32)^2}}{.32} = 1.21$

(d) The rectifier efficiency is the ratio of the dc power absorbed by R_L to the average power supplied

or $\qquad\qquad\qquad \eta_r = \dfrac{P_{dc}}{P_i}$

Since $\qquad\qquad\qquad P_i = I_{rms}^2\left(r_F + R_L\right)$

and $\qquad\qquad\qquad P_{dc} = I_{dc}^2 R_L$

it follows that

$$\eta_r = \frac{\left(I_{dc}^2 R_L\right)}{\left(I_{rms}^2\left(r_F + R_L\right)\right)} = \frac{\left(0.32^2(400)\right)}{\left(.5^2(25 + 400)\right)} = 38\%.$$

(e) The peak reverse voltage is the maximum voltage the diode sees when reverse-biased. In this circuit, no current flows when the diode is reverse biased, so

$$PIV = V_m = 425\text{V}.$$

Full-wave rectification is accomplished using a circuit such as in Figure 89. The average dc values are shown in the figure and defined as follows:

$$I_{dc} = \frac{2 \times I_{max}}{\pi} = 0.636 I_{max}$$
$$V_{dc} = 0.636 V_{max}$$

These dc values are twice that of the half-wave circuit, as expected. The output signal is found using the same method as itemized for the half-wave rectifier circuit.

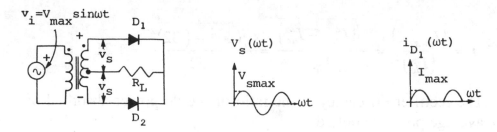

(a) Circuit (b) Waveform across secondary winding (c) Current in diode D_1

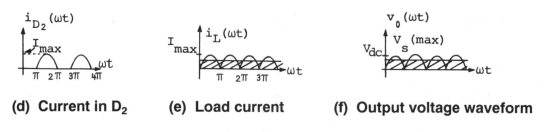

(d) Current in D_2 (e) Load current   (f) Output voltage waveform

Figure 89. Full-wave rectifier

Other common diode applications are **clipper** and **clamper networks**. Clipper circuits "clip" off part of the input signal without affecting the remaining part of the input signal. For example, the half-wave rectifier circuit discussed previously was a simple clipper circuit because it clipped off the negative half of the voltage without affecting the positive cycle.

An example of a symmetrical clipper is shown in Figure 90. It clips the positive and negative portions of the input sine wave, V_i, so the output, V_o, approximates a trapezoidal waveform. (See Figure 91.)

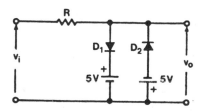

Figure 90. Symmetrical clipper

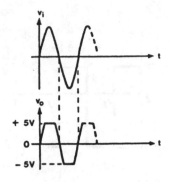

Figure 91. Reverse-biased diodes

In Figure 16, when V_i is less than 5V, both diodes are reverse-biased, and $V_o = V_i$. As soon as V_i is slightly more positive than 5V, diode D_1 is forward-biased (diode D_2 remains reverse biased). The output is clamped (maintained) at +5V and remains clamped at that value until V_i becomes less than 5V.

When V_i is between +5V and −5V, both diodes are reverse-biased again, and $V_o = -V_i$. As soon as V_i becomes more negative than −5V, D_2 conducts (D_1 is reverse-biased), and the output is now clamped to −5V. It remains clamped at this value until V_i is less negative than −5V.

Clamper circuits "clamp" the signal to some dc level. The simplest clamper circuit must include a resistive element, diode, and a capacitor. The basic methods outlined with the full- and half-wave rectifier circuit analysis apply for all diode circuits.

EXAMPLE

The circuit of Figure 92 is called a clamper. The input wave is shown on Figure 93.

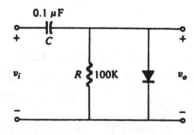

Figure 92. Clamper

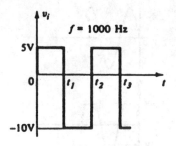

Figure 93. Input wave

SOLUTION

At the instant the input switches to the +5V state, the circuit will appear as shown in Figure 94. The input will remain in the +5V state for an interval of time equal to one-half the period of the waveform since the time interval $0 \rightarrow t_1$ is equal to the interval $t_1 \rightarrow t_2$.

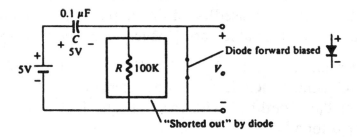

Figure 94. Input in +5V state

The period at V_1 is $T = \dfrac{1}{f} = \dfrac{1}{1,000} = 1\text{ms}$ and the time interval is the +5V state is $\dfrac{T}{2} = 0.5\text{ms}$.

Since the output is taken from directly across the diode, it is 0V for this interval of time. The capacitor, however, will rapidly charge to 5V, since the time constant of the network is not $\tau = RC \sim OC = 0$.

When the input switches to −10V, the circuit of Figure 95 will result.

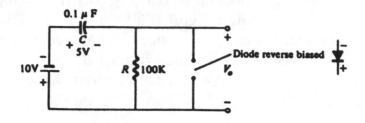

Figure 95. Input in –10V state

The time constant for the circuit of Figure 95 is

$$RC = 100 \times 10^8 \times 0.1 \times 10^{-6} = 10\text{ms}.$$

Since it takes approximately 5 time constants, or 50ms, for a capacitor to discharge, and the input is only in this state for 0.5ms, to assume that the voltage across the capacitor does not change appreciably during this interval of time is certainly a reasonable approximation. The output is therefore

$$V_0 = -10 - 5 = -15\text{V}.$$

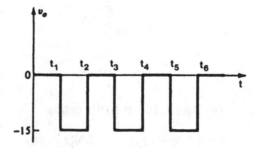

Figure 96. Output waveform

The resulting output waveform (V_0) is provided in Figure 96. The output is clamped to the negative region and will repeat itself at the same frequency as the input signal. Note that the swing of the input and output voltages is the same: 15V. For all clamper circuits the voltage swing of the input and output waveforms will be the same. This is in contrast to clipping circuits.

Diodes are also used in **logic gates**, such as the **AND** and **OR** gate. The basic diode AND gate is shown in Figure 97 with the corresponding truth table. Although Boolean algebra is not reviewed in this chapter, recall that an AND gate produces an output of 1 only if both inputs are 1. The inputs A and B are varied in Figure 97(d) for the four combinations shown in the truth table. For example, notice that the second configuration ($A = 0$, $B = 1$, $F = 0$) has a voltage source at input B, but does not show a voltage source for the A input. As with the previous diode applications, analysis is based upon the "off" or "on" state of the diodes.

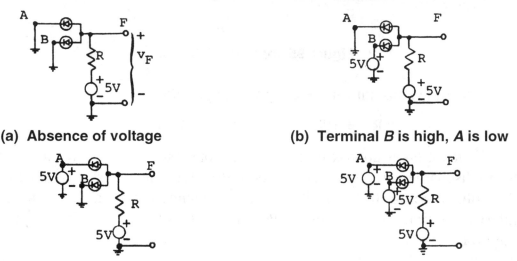

(a) **Absence of voltage** (b) **Terminal *B* is high, *A* is low**

(c) **Terminal *A* is high, *B* is low** (d) **Terminals *A* and *B* are high**

Inputs		Output
A	B	F
0	0	0
1	0	0
0	1	0
1	1	1

(e) Associated truth table

Figure 97. The diode AND gate

An absence of voltage sources tied to terminals A and B results in a low output (first entry in truth table). When terminal B is high, terminal A is low, a low output results. When terminal A is high and terminal B is low, low output results. When terminals A and B are high, high output results, as shown in the last entry of the truth table.

An OR gate, such as in Figure 98, produces an output of 1 if any or all of the inputs are 1. Although the different input variations of the circuit are not shown in Figure 98, the addition of a voltage source at the appropriate input(s) would result in the truth table configurations shown. For example, a voltage source at the A input only ($A = 1$, $B = 0$, $C = 0$) would produce an output $F = 1$, as shown in the fifth entry of the truth table. The following example illustrates an OR diode logic (DL) circuit.

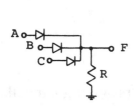

Inputs			Output
A	B	C	F
0	0	0	0
0	0	1	1
0	1	0	1
0	1	1	1
1	0	0	1
1	0	1	1
1	1	0	1
1	1	1	1

(a) The circuit   **(b) Associated truth table**

Figure 98. A diode OR gate

EXAMPLE

Verify that the **DL** gate shown can perform the exclusive OR logic.

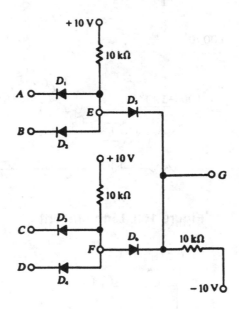

Figure 99. DL gate

SOLUTION

If either A or B is low, then D_1 or D_2 will conduct, and point E will be at V_D, low. If both are high, D_1 and D_2 are both off, and point E is high. Thus, D_1 and D_2 form the AND function $E = AB$ while similarly $F = CD$. The directions of D_5 and D_6 are reversed and they form an OR, $G = E + F$. (A high at E or F forward biases D_5 or D_6, the voltage at E or F is carried through to G, since the diode voltage drop is small.) Thus,

177

$$G = E + F = AB + CD.$$

With

$$B = D \text{ and } C = A$$
$$G = AD + AD = A \times D.$$

D_5 and D_6 form the final OR function besides providing cancellation of the 0.7V drop in the input diodes.

REVIEW PROBLEMS

PROBLEM 1

Calculate the magnitude of a line current in the circuit shown in Figure 100.

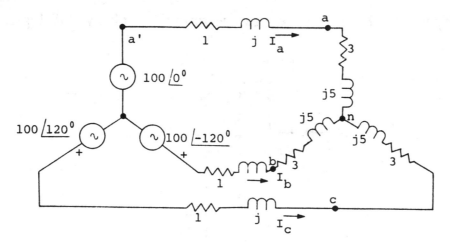

Figure 100. Line current

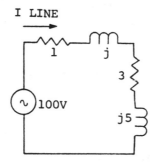

Figure 101. Simplified circuit

SOLUTION

The circuit is balanced because the load for each phase is the same, the magnitude of the source for each phase is the same, and the angle for each phase is displaced by 120°. Since the circuit is balanced, the magnitude of the line current in each phase is the same. To find the line current, Figure 100 is redrawn in Figure 101 to include only one phase.

The total impedance of one phase is $1 + j + 3 + j5 = 4 + j6\Omega$. The magnitude of the line current is:

$$\left|I_{\text{line}}\right| = \left|\frac{100}{4 + j6}\right| = \frac{100}{\sqrt{4^2 + 6^2}} = \frac{100}{7.21} = 13.85A.$$

PROBLEM 2

Use Kirchhoff's Current Law to write an integrodifferential equation for v(t) for the circuit shown.

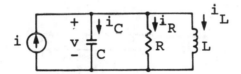

Figure 102. Parallel and series circuit

SOLUTION

Kirchhoff's Current Law applied to the upper node of the circuit yields the equation:

$$i = i_C + i_R + i_L.$$

The currents for each element i_C, i_R, and i_L can be expressed in terms of the same voltage v:

$$i_C = C\frac{dv}{dt}, \ i_R = \frac{1}{R}v, \ i_L = \frac{1}{L}\int_{-\infty}^{t}v \, d\tau.$$

Substituting these terms into the KVL equation yields the required integrodifferential equation:

$$i = C\frac{dv}{dt} + \frac{1}{R}v + \frac{1}{L}\int_{-\infty}^{t}v \, d\tau.$$

PROBLEM 3

Given an infinitely long straight filament carrying a current I, find the field H at point P:

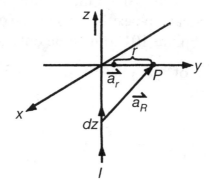

Figure 103. Field produced by filament with current I

SOLUTION

$$dH = \frac{Idz\boldsymbol{a}_z \times \left(r\boldsymbol{a}_r - z\boldsymbol{a}_z\right)}{4\pi\left(r^2 + z^2\right)^{3/2}}$$

$$= \frac{Idzr\boldsymbol{a}_\phi}{4\pi\left(r^2 + z^2\right)^{3/2}}$$

$$H = \frac{I}{4\pi} \int_{-\infty}^{\infty} \frac{rdz\boldsymbol{a}_\phi}{\left(r^2 + z^2\right)^{3/2}}$$

$$= \frac{I}{2\pi r}\boldsymbol{a}_\phi$$

PROBLEM 4

Find the voltage across an inductor, shown in Figure 104, whose inductance is given by:

$$L(t) = te^{-t} + 1$$

and the current through it is given by:

$$i(t) = \sin \omega t.$$

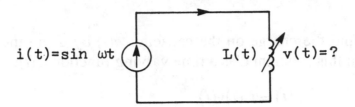

Figure 104. Simple inductor

SOLUTION

The voltage across an inductor is defined as $v(t) = \dfrac{d\phi}{dt}$ and $\phi = L\, i(t)$.

In this problem L is a time-varying inductance $L(t)$:

$$\phi(t) = L(t)\, i(t) = (te^{-t} + 1)\,(\sin \omega t)$$

the voltage becomes:

$$v(t) = \frac{d}{dt}\,[(te^{-t} + 1)\,(\sin \omega t)]$$

$$v(t) = (1 + te^{-t})\,(\omega \cos \omega t) + (\sin \omega t)(e^{-t} - te^{-t})$$

$$v(t) = (\omega \cos \omega t)\,(1 + te^{-t}) + (1 - t)e^{-t} \sin \omega t$$

PROBLEM 5

Consider the capacitor shown in Figure 105. The capacitance $C(t)$ is given by:

$$C(t) = C_0(1 + 0.5 \sin t).$$

The voltage across this capacitor is given by:

$$v(t) = 2 \sin \omega t.$$

Find the current through the capacitor.

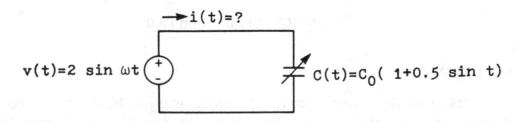

Figure 105. Simple capacitor

SOLUTION

We can find the charge on the capacitor $q(t)$ by using the definition $q(t) = C\,v(t)$. In this problem C is a time varying function $C(t)$:

$$q(t) = C(t)v(t)$$
$$q(t) = C_0(1 + 0.5\sin t)(2\sin \omega t).$$

Since $i(t) = \dfrac{dq}{dt}$, we have:

$$
\begin{aligned}
i(t) &= \frac{d}{dt}\big[C_0(1 + 0.5\sin t)(2\sin \omega t)\big] \\
&= (2\sin \omega t)(0.5C_0 \cos t) + C_0(1 + 0.5\sin t)(2\omega \cos \omega t) \\
i(t) &= C_0 \sin \omega t \cos t + 2\omega C_0 \cos \omega t(1 + 0.5\sin t)
\end{aligned}
$$

PROBLEM 6

For the circuit shown in Figure 106, find i and v as functions of time for $t > 0$.

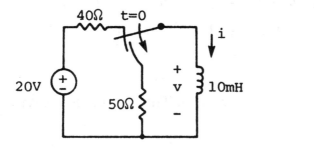

Figure 106. Circuit for Problem 6   **Figure 107. Circuit when $t < 0$**

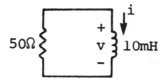

Figure 108. Circuit when $t \geq 0$

SOLUTION

First, find the current through the inductor i, just before the switch is thrown. Figure 107 shows the circuit at $t = 0^-$. In Figure 107,

$i = \dfrac{20v}{40\Omega} = 0.5A$. Figure 108 shows the circuit in Figure 106 at $t = 0^+$. In Figure 108, in order for the voltage drops to sum to zero around loop, the voltage v must be $-(50\Omega)(0.5A) = -25V$. The time constant is found to be:

$$\frac{L}{R} = \frac{10mH}{50\Omega} = \frac{1}{5,000}$$

Write the response:

$$i(t) = 0.5e^{-5,000t}A; \; t > 0$$
$$v(t) = -25e^{-5,000t}V; \; t > 0.$$

PROBLEM 7

Find R, L, and C for the networks shown in Figure 109.

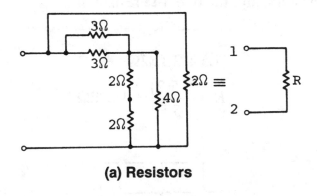

(a) Resistors

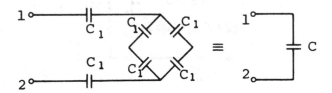

(b) Capacitors

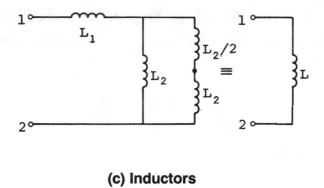

(c) Inductors

Figure 109. Component networks and equivalents

SOLUTION

(a) First, combine the parallel resistances (as shown in Figure 110), the two 3-Ω resistors, and the two 4-Ω resistors.

Finally:

$$(1.5 + 2)\Omega \| 2\Omega$$

$$R = \frac{3.5(2)}{5.5} = 1.272\Omega$$

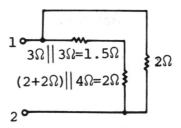

Figure 110. Combined parallel resistors

(b) Since capacitors combine the conductances (Figure 111), and finally,

$$C = \frac{1}{\dfrac{1}{C_1} + \dfrac{1}{C_1} + \dfrac{1}{C_1}} = \frac{1}{\dfrac{3}{C_1}}$$

$$C = \frac{C_1}{3} F.$$

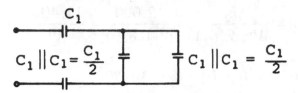

Figure 111. Combined capacitors

(c) Since inductors combine like resistances (Figure 112)

$$L = (L_1 + 0.6L_2)H.$$

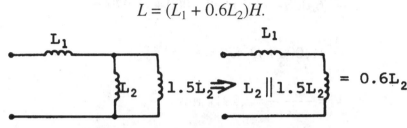

Figure 112. Combined inductors

PROBLEM 8

A balanced three-phase three-wire system supplies two balanced Y-connected loads. The first draws 6 kW at 0.8 PF lagging while the other requires 12 kW at 0.833 PF leading. If the current in each line is 8A rms, find the current in the: (a) first load; (b) second load; and (c) source phase.

SOLUTION

It does not matter how the load is connected. For any balanced 3-phase system,

$$P = |V| \, |I| \cos \theta$$

where P is the average power, $|V|$ is the rms voltage magnitude, $|I|$ is the rms current magnitude, and $\cos(\theta)$ is the power factor. θ is the angle by which the voltage leads the current in each line.

(a) For $P_1 = 6$ kW, $\cos(\theta_1) = 0.8$ lagging (that is, θ is negative),

$$\theta_1 = -\cos^{-1}(0.8) = -36.87°$$

$$|I_1| = \frac{P_1}{|V|\cos(\theta_1)} = \frac{(6,000)}{|V|(0.8)} = \frac{7,500}{|V|} A \text{ rms}$$

For the second load, $P_2 = 12$ kW, $\cos(\theta_2) = 0.833$ leading

$$\theta_2 = +\cos^{-1}(0.833) = 33.59°$$

$$|I_2| = \frac{P_2}{|V|\cos(\theta_2)} = \frac{12,000}{|V|(0.833)} = \frac{14,406}{|V|} A \text{ rms.}$$

We are also given that $|I_1 + I_2| = 8A$ rms, so

$$\frac{1}{|V|}|7,500\angle -36.87° + 14,406\angle +33.59°| = 8$$

$$\frac{1}{|V|}|6,000 - j4,500 + 12,000 + j7,979| = 8$$

$$\frac{1}{|V|}|18,000 + j3,479| = 8$$

$$|V| = \frac{18,331}{8} = 2,291V \text{ rms}$$

Finally,

$$|I_1| = \frac{7,500}{2,291} = 3.273A \text{ rms.}$$

(b) From (a)

$$|I_2| = \frac{14,406}{|V|} = \frac{14,406}{2,291} = 6.288A \text{ rms.}$$

(c) The source phase current is the same as the line current, so it is 8 A rms.

PROBLEM 9

Find i in the circuits of Figure 113 (a), (b), and (c).

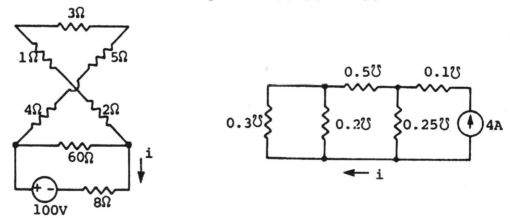

(a) Loop resistors in series

(b) Conductance

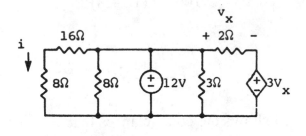

(c) Series combination

Figure 113. Circuits

SOLUTION

(a) To find the current i, combine resistors to form a single loop circuit. Note that, despite its complicated appearance, the five resistors in the upper part of the circuit are all in series.

$$R_{eq} = \frac{60(15)}{75} = 12\Omega$$

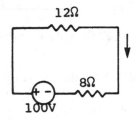

Figure 114. Equivalent resistance

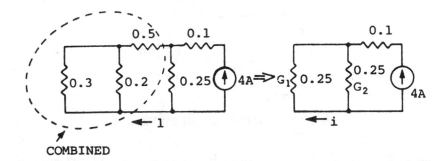

Figure 115. Combined resistors   **Figure 116. Equivalent circuit**

The sum of the resistors in the upper half of the network is in parallel with the 60Ω resistor. Figure 114 demonstrates the resulting circuit. KVL around the loop

$$100 = i\,(12 + 8)$$

gives

$$i = \frac{100}{20} = 5A.$$

(b) Figure 115 shows the conductances that are combined to form the circuit in Figure 116.

To find i, which is the current through the 0.25 conductance G_1 on the left, it is necessary to know the voltage across G_1. Since the voltage across G_1 and G_2 are the same, one can combine them. Remembering that $4A$ flows through the combined conductance of 0.5, calculate the voltage.

$$v = \frac{1}{G} = \frac{4}{0.5} = 8V.$$

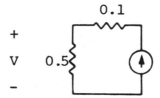

Figure 117. Simple conductance

The current sense of i is opposite the convention adopted, thus

$$i = -8(0.25)$$
$$i = -2A$$

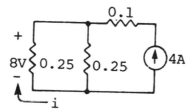

Figure 118. Flow through conductor

(c) Observe in Figure 113(c) that the 12-V source is connected across the 8 and 16Ω series combination on the left.

Hence,

$$i = \frac{V}{R} = \frac{12}{8+16} = \frac{12}{24} = 0.5A.$$

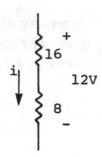

Figure 119. Series combination

PROBLEM 10

Find the E field due to a uniformly charged sphere by direct integration.

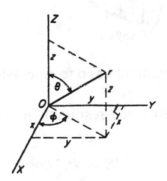

Figure 120. Relation of spherical and rectangular coordinates

SOLUTION

For a sphere of radius R, the charge per unit area is $q_s = \dfrac{q}{4\pi R^2}$. For convenience in integration, use spherical coordinates r, θ, and ϕ. These are defined in terms of the rectangular coordinates x, y, and z by

$$x = r \sin \theta \cos \phi$$
$$y = r \sin \theta \sin \phi$$
$$z = r \cos \theta$$

and are illustrated in Figure 120. Then construct a thin ring on the surface of the charged sphere of Figure 121 such that the ring is symmetrical about the z-axis (note that the coordinate system has been rotated) and subtends a half-angle θ at the center. An element of area dS is chosen with sides given by $Rd\theta$ and $R \sin \theta \, d\phi$. The charge on this area is $q_s R^2 \sin \theta d \theta d\phi$ and the field at P due to this charge has a magnitude

$$dE_P = \frac{q_s R^2 \sin \theta d\theta d\phi}{4\pi\varepsilon_0 a^2}$$

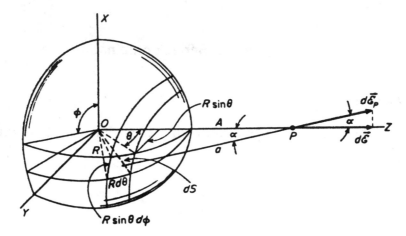

Figure 121. Surface element used to calculate field of charged sphere

Because of symmetry, the resultant field dE due to the ring is along OZ, so that

$$dE = dE_p \cos \alpha$$

Now integrate with respect to ϕ, using limits of 0 and 2π, to obtain

$$dE = \frac{q_s R^2 \sin \theta d\theta \cos \alpha}{2\varepsilon_0 a^2} \qquad (1)$$

Now

$$\cos \alpha = \frac{A - R\cos\theta}{a}$$

and

$$a^2 = A^2 + R^2 - 2AR\cos\theta$$

from which

$$a \, da = AR\sin\theta \, d\theta \qquad (2)$$

and

$$\cos \alpha = \frac{A^2 - R^2 + a^2}{2Aa} \qquad (3)$$

Substituting (2) and (3) into (1) gives

$$E = \frac{q_s R}{4\varepsilon_0 A^2} \int_{A-R}^{A+R} \frac{A^2 - R^2 + a^2}{a^2} \, da = \frac{q_s R^2}{\varepsilon_0 A^2} = \frac{q}{4\pi\varepsilon_0 A^2}$$

PROBLEM 11

Through the use of Ampere's circuital law, find the **H** field in all regions of an infinite length coaxial cable carrying a uniform and equal current I in opposite directions in the inner and outer conductors. Assume the inner conductor to have a radius of a(m) and the outer conductor to have an inner radius of b(m) and an outer radius of c(m). Assume that the cable's axis is along the z-axis.

SOLUTION

Through the use of symmetrical pairs of filamentary currents as shown in Figure 122(b), it can be argued that the **H** field in all regions will be in the ϕ direction and thus

$$H = \phi H_\phi.$$

(a) For a concentric amperian closed loop drawn in the region $(r_c < a)$ of the inner conductor, Ampere's circuital law becomes

$$\oint_\ell H \cdot dl = \oint_\ell \left(\phi H_\phi\right) \cdot \left(\phi r_c d\phi\right)$$

$$= H_\phi r_c \int_0^{2\pi} d\phi = H_\phi 2\pi r_c = I_{en}$$

(1)

Amperian closed path

(a) Graphical display for finding the H field inside and outside a conductor of finite cross section

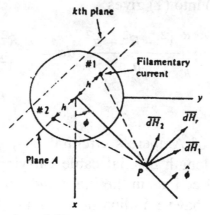

(b) Symmetrical pairs of filamentary currents produce a resultant field in the φ direction

Figure 122. Magnetic field in a coaxial cable

Now,

$$I_{en} = \frac{Ir_c^2}{a^2}$$

for the amperian closed loop inside the inner conductor. Thus, the last two terms in (1) become

$$H_\phi 2\pi r_c = I_{en} = \frac{Ir_c^2}{a^2}$$

yielding

$$H_\phi = \frac{Ir_c}{2\pi a^2}$$

and

$$H = \phi \frac{Ir_c}{2\pi a^2} \left(Am^{-1} \right) (r_c < A) \tag{2}$$

(b) For a concentric amperian closed loop drawn in the region ($a < r_c < b$), Ampere's circuital law becomes

$$\oint_\ell H \bullet dl = \oint_\ell \left(\phi\, H_\phi \right) \bullet \left(\phi r_c d\phi \right)$$

$$= H_\phi r_c \int_0^{2\pi} d\phi = H_\phi 2\pi r_c = I \tag{3}$$

where $I_{en} = I(A)$. Solving for H_ϕ from the last two terms in (3),

$$H = \frac{\phi I}{2\pi r_c}\left(Am^{-1}\right)\quad (a < r_c < b)\qquad(4)$$

(c) For a concentric amperian closed loop in the region $(b < r_c < c)$, Ampere's circuital law becomes

$$\oint_\ell H \bullet dl = \oint_\ell \left(\phi H_f\right) \bullet \left(\phi r_c d\phi\right)$$

$$= H_\phi r_c \int_0^{2\pi} d\phi = H_\phi 2\pi r_c = I_{en}\qquad(5)$$

Now,

$$I_{en} = I - I\left[\frac{\left(r_c^2 - b^2\right)}{\left(c^2 - b^2\right)}\right]$$

for the amperian closed loop inside the outer conductor. It should be noted that some of the enclosed current flows in the reverse direction. Substituting for I_{en} into (5) and solving for H_ϕ from the last two terms,

$$H = \phi\frac{I}{2\pi r_c}\left(\frac{c^2 - r_c^2}{c^2 - b^2}\right)\left(Am^{-1}\right)\quad (b < r_c < c)$$

(d) For a concentric amperian closed loop drawn in the region $(c < r_c)$, the enclosed current is found to be zero, and thus H is zero.

PROBLEM 12

The force field

$$F = ya_x - xa_y$$

is nonconservative, and the work done in opposing the field,

$$-\int_B^A F \bullet dl$$

depends on the path followed from B to A (shown in Figure 123). Let B be $(0, 1, 0)$ and let A be $(0, -1, 0)$. Determine the work done in following these paths consisting of straight line segments:

(a) $(0, 1, 0)$ to $(1, 1, 0)$ to $(1, -1, 0)$ to $(0, -1, 0)$;

(b) $(0, 1, 0)$ to $(0, -1, 0)$;

(c) $(0, 1, 0)$ to $(-1, 1, 0)$ to $(-1, -1, 0)$ to $(0, -1, 0)$.

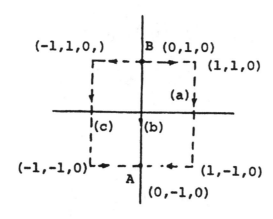

Figure 123. Work paths

SOLUTION

The paths are indicated as shown. Since

$$F = ya_x - xa_y,$$

and

$$dl = dx\,a_x + dy\,a_y,$$

and

$$W = -\int_{B}^{A} F \bullet dl,$$

(a) from $(0, 1, 0)$ to $(1, 1, 0)$

$$W_1 = -\int_{0,1,0}^{1,1,0} \left(y\,a_x - x\,a_y\right) \bullet \left(dx\,a_x + dy\,a_y\right)$$

$$= -\int_{0,1,0}^{1,1,0} ydx - xdy = -\int_{0}^{1} dx = -1$$

from $(1, 1, 0)$ to $(1, -1, 0)$

$$W_2 = -\int_{1,1,0}^{1,-1,0} ydx - xdy = -\int_{1}^{-1} -dy = -2$$

from $(1, -1, 0)$ to $(0, -1, 0)$

$$W_3 = -\int_{1,-1,0}^{0,-1,0} ydx - xdy = -\int_{1}^{0}(-1)dx = -1$$

The total work done in path a is

$$W_1 + W_2 + W_3 = W_a$$

$$= -4 \text{ Joules.}$$

(b) From $(0, 1, 0)$ to $(0, -1, 0)$, $dx = 0$, $x = 0$

$$\therefore W_b = \int_{1}^{-1} -0dy = 0$$

(c) From $(0, 1, 0)$ to $(-1, 1, 0)$ to $(-1, -1, 0)$ to $(0, -1, 0)$,

$$W_c = -\left[\int_{0}^{-1} dx - \int_{1}^{-1} -dy + \int_{-1}^{0} dx\right] = -[-1 - 2 - 1] = 4 \text{ Joules}$$

FE/EIT

Fundamentals of Engineering: AM Exam

CHAPTER 5

Statics

CHAPTER 5

STATICS

This chapter will review that portion of the study of mechanics that deals with bodies in equilibrium under the influence or action of forces, namely statics.

VECTOR FORCES

The action of one body on another produces force. A force has magnitude, direction, and sense and hence may be represented by a vector. There are three classifications of vectors:

(1) When the action of a vector is not confined to or associated with a unique line in space, then it is a **free vector**.

(2) When the quantity of a vector must maintain a certain unique line of action, then it is a **sliding vector**.

(3) When a unique point of application is defined for a vector, and therefore it occupies a specific position in space, then it is called a **fixed vector**.

In Figure 1, we have vector **V** and its negative −**V**. The sense of direction is measured by the angle θ.

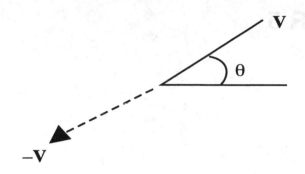

Figure 1. Vector V

Remember that vectors must obey the parallelogram law of equilibrium which states that two vectors V_1 and V_2 can be replaced by the resultant vector V: $V = V_1 + V_2$ (vector addition).

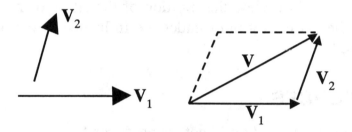

Figure 2. Vector addition

Figure 3 illustrates the use of the parallelogram method in vector subtraction.

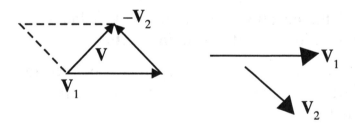

Figure 3. Vector subtraction

In three-dimensional problems, the rectangular components of a vector can be expressed in terms of **i, j,** and **k** unit vectors in the x, y, and z directions, respectively.

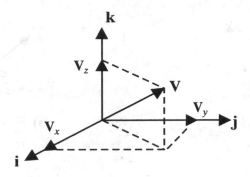

Figure 4. $V = i\,V_x + j\,V_y + k\,V_z$

The figure below shows $\mathbf{F}_x$ and $\mathbf{F}_y$, the rectangular components of a vector $\mathbf{F}$.

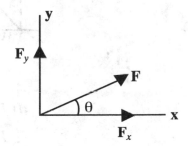

Figure 5. Rectangular components F_x and F_y of vector F

The magnitudes of the vectors, $\mathbf{F}$, $\mathbf{F}_x$ and $\mathbf{F}_y$ are related as shown below, where F is the magnitude of $\mathbf{F}$, F_x is the magnitude of $\mathbf{F}_x$, and F_y is the magnitude of $\mathbf{F}_y$:

$$F_x = F \cos \theta$$
$$F_y = F \sin \theta$$
$$F = \sqrt{F_x^2 + F_y^2}$$
$$\theta = \tan^{-1} \frac{F_y}{F_x}$$

In cases where the assignment of reference axes is not readily identifiable, use the following guide, as shown in Figure 6.

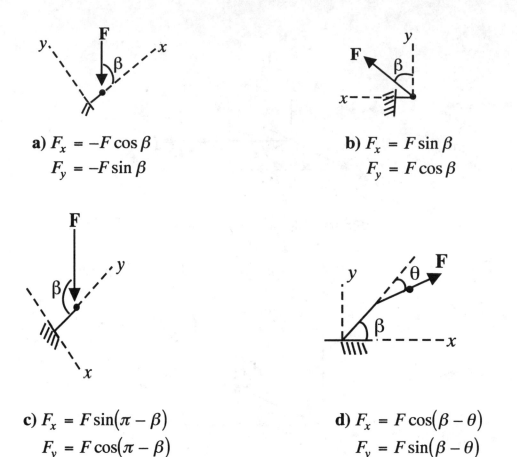

a) $F_x = -F\cos\beta$
$F_y = -F\sin\beta$

b) $F_x = F\sin\beta$
$F_y = F\cos\beta$

c) $F_x = F\sin(\pi - \beta)$
$F_y = F\cos(\pi - \beta)$

d) $F_x = F\cos(\beta - \theta)$
$F_y = F\sin(\beta - \theta)$

Figure 6. Assignment of reference axes

In the three-dimensional rectangular force system, we can resolve a force into its three components (as illustrated graphically in Figure 7):

$$F_x = F\cos\theta_x \qquad F = \sqrt{F_x^2 + F_y^2 + F_z^2}$$
$$F_y = F\cos\theta_y \qquad F = iF_x + jF_y + kF_z$$
$$F_z = F\cos\theta_z \qquad F = F(i\cos\theta_x + j\cos\theta_y + k\cos\theta_z)$$

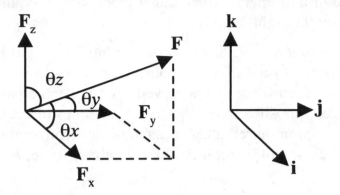

Figure 7. Rectangular components F_x, F_y, F_z of vector F

MOMENTS AND COUPLES

The tendency of a force to rotate a body about any axis that does not intersect its line of action and is not parallel to it is a **moment *M***. The moment of a force about a point *A* is equal to

$$M_A = r \times F$$

where **r** is a vector from point *A* to the point at which the force is applied, as shown in Figure 8. The magnitude of moment M_A is

$$M_A = rF \sin \theta$$

or

$$M_A = dF$$

where θ is the angle shown in the figure and *d* is known as the moment arm.

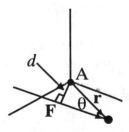

Figure 8. Geometry used to define the moment of a force about a point

The sense of a moment will be either clockwise or counterclockwise, as determined by the right-hand rule.

In a system where several forces are acting on a rigid body, we can move all the forces to an arbitrary point, *A*, provided a **couple** is introduced as well for each force that is moved. A couple is a pair of forces of equal magnitude, opposite direction, and parallel lines of action, which has a pure turning or moment effect. A system of non-concurrent forces such as that shown below can be replaced by a resultant force, *R*, and resultant couple, *M*.

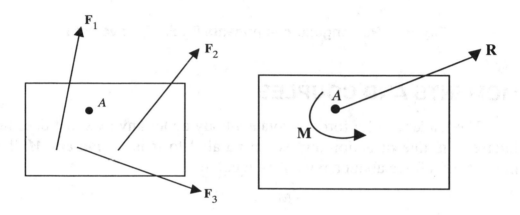

Figure 9. Resultant force and moment

The resultant force is

$$R = F_1 + F_2 + F_3 = \sum F$$

and the resultant couple is $M = M_1 + M_2 + M_3 = \sum d_x F$, where *d* is the moment arm of each force to point *A*.

TWO-DIMENSIONAL EQUILIBRIUM

The free-body diagram is the most useful tool in the solving of problems in mechanics. To review the construction of free-body diagrams:

(1) Decide which combination of bodies (or body) is to be isolated and make sure that one or more of the desired unknowns is involved in the choice.

(2) Isolate the bodies (or body) chosen by a diagram that show its complete external boundary.

(3) Show all forces that act on the isolated bodies (or body).

(4)   Choose coordinate axes.

In two-dimensional (and three-dimensional) equilibrium, the resultant moment and force vectors must be zero:

$$\sum F_x = 0$$
$$\sum F_y = 0$$
$$\sum M_A = 0$$

The location of the axis, A, about which moments are summed, is arbitrary. The magnitude of the resultant force and moment vectors must be zero.

The different types of equilibrium in two dimensions are shown in Figure 10.

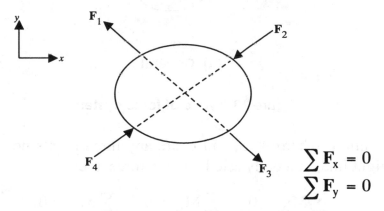

$$\sum F_x = 0$$
$$\sum F_y = 0$$

(a) Concurrent at a specific point

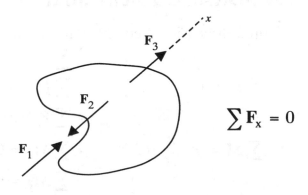

$$\sum F_x = 0$$

(b) Collinear

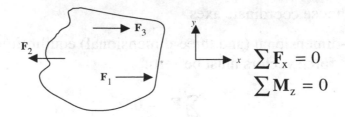

$$\sum F_x = 0$$
$$\sum M_z = 0$$

(c) Parallel

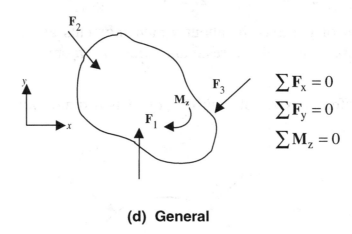

$$\sum F_x = 0$$
$$\sum F_y = 0$$
$$\sum M_z = 0$$

(d) General

Figure 10. Types of force systems

In addition, where *A, B,* and *C* are any three points not lying in the same straight line on a body acted on by a force, then

$$\sum M_A = 0 \qquad \sum M_B = 0 \qquad \sum M_C = 0.$$

THREE-DIMENSIONAL EQUILIBRIUM

In the case of three-dimensional equilibrium, we may write:

$$\sum F_x = 0$$
$$\sum \mathbf{F} = 0 \qquad \text{or} \qquad \sum F_y = 0$$
$$\sum F_z = 0$$

$$\sum \mathbf{M} = 0 \qquad \text{or} \qquad \sum M_x = 0$$
$$\sum M_y = 0$$
$$\sum M_z = 0$$

Complete equilibrium necessitates all six of these equations. Refer to the guide in Figure 11 to determine the actions of three-dimensional forces.

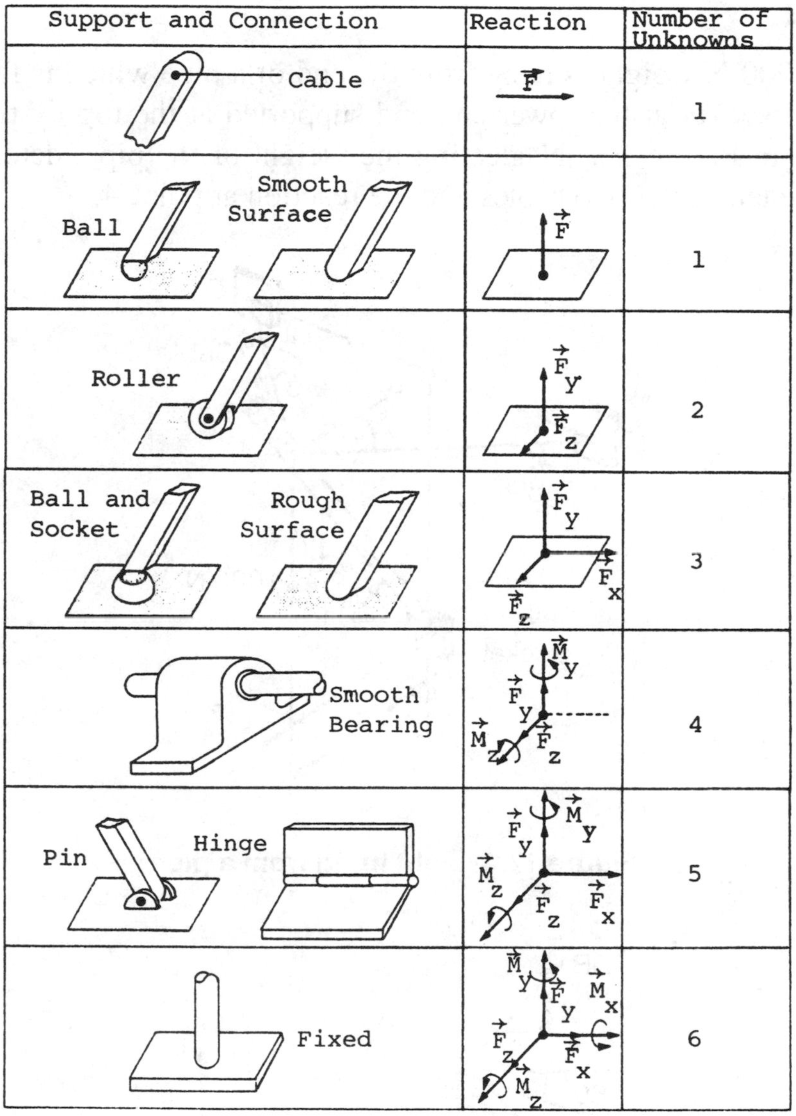

Support and Connection	Reaction	Number of Unknowns
Cable	$\vec{F}$	1
Ball — Smooth Surface	$\vec{F}$	1
Roller	$\vec{F}_y$, $\vec{F}_z$	2
Ball and Socket — Rough Surface	$\vec{F}_y$, $\vec{F}_x$, $\vec{F}_z$	3
Smooth Bearing	$\vec{M}_y$, $\vec{F}_y$, $\vec{M}_z$, $\vec{F}_z$	4
Pin — Hinge	$\vec{F}_y$, $\vec{M}_y$, $\vec{M}_z$, $\vec{F}_z$, $\vec{F}_x$	5
Fixed	$\vec{M}_y$, $\vec{F}_y$, $\vec{M}_x$, $\vec{F}_z$, $\vec{F}_x$, $\vec{M}_z$	6

Figure 11. Reactions at supports and connections in three-dimensional structures

Two- and three-dimensional equilibrium equations, free-body diagrams, and the information in Figures 10 and 11 provide a foundation for problems involving determinate reactions.

EXAMPLE

A 1,000 N weight is hung from the end of a pipe which is fastened to a ball and socket at the lower end and supported at the top by two cables as shown in Figure 12. Neglecting the weight of the pipe, determine the forces in each of the two cables and the reaction at point A.

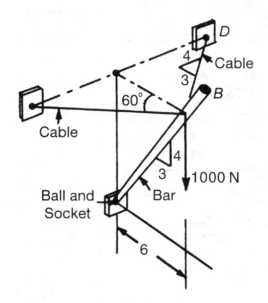

Figure 12. Weight hung from a pipe

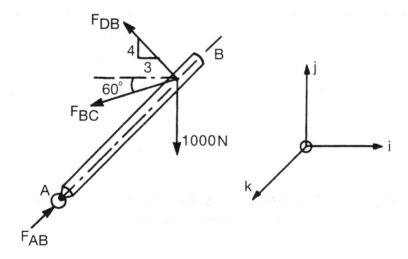

Figure 13. Reaction

SOLUTION

We isolate the pipe *AB* and obtain the free-body diagram shown in Figure 13. Recognizing that *AB* is a two-force member, we obtain the following equations:

$$F_{DB} = F_{DB}\left(-\frac{3}{5}\mathbf{i} - \frac{4}{5}\mathbf{k}\right)$$

$$F_{CB} = F_{CB}(-\cos 60°\mathbf{i} + \sin 60°\mathbf{k})$$

$$F_{AB} = F_{AB}\left(\frac{3}{5}\mathbf{i} + \frac{4}{5}\mathbf{k}\right)$$

or

$$F_{DB} = F_{DB}(-0.6\mathbf{i} - 0.8\mathbf{k})$$

$$F_{CB} = F_{CB}(-0.5\mathbf{i} + 0.866\mathbf{k})$$

$$F_{AB} = F_{AB}(0.6\mathbf{i} + 0.8\mathbf{j})$$

$$W = -1,000\mathbf{j}\ \text{N}$$

Applying the condition $\mathbf{F} = 0$, we have

$$(-0.6F_{BD} - 0.5F_{CB} + 0.6F_{AB})\hat{i} + (0.8F_{AB} - 1,000)\hat{j} + (-0.8F_{BD} + 0.866F_{BC})\hat{k} = 0$$

The components of this equation give us the three equations needed to find the three unknowns. Solving them yields

$$F_{AB} = 1,250\ \text{N}$$
$$F_{BD} = 705\ \text{N}$$
$$F_{BC} = 652\ \text{N}$$

ANALYSIS OF INTERNAL FORCES

To analyze the forces acting on a structure, it is necessary to analyze separate free-body diagrams of the members of the structure by dismembering the structure itself. The internal forces acting on each member (or combination) can be looked at.

A truss is made up of straight members connected at joints at the ends of each member. Hence, in trusses, the basic element is a triangle, and all members are two force members in either compression or tension. The external forces on a member in compression or tension are as shown in Figure 14.

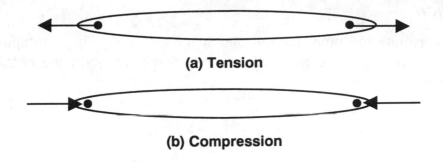

(a) Tension

(b) Compression

Figure 14. External forces on a member

Assume in simple trusses that all external forces are applied at the pin connections.

Examine the truss structure at each pin location to determine the direction and application of the forces acting at that location.

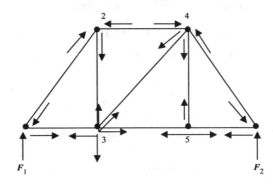

Figure 15. Truss

Apply equilibrium equations at each joint to determine the reactions. Examining the internal forces of a structure at each joint in this manner is called the method of joints.

We can also use the method of sections to look at the forces acting on an entire section. This method employs equilibrium equations on a section of a truss, as shown in Figure 16.

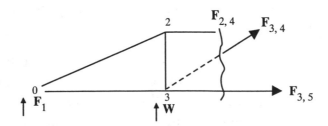

Figure 16. Section of truss

EXAMPLE

In the bridge truss of Figure 17, calculate the forces in members *UV* and *DE*.

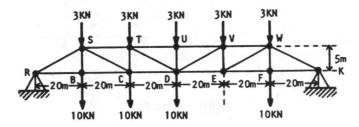

Figure 17. Bridge truss

SOLUTION

The free-body diagram is shown in Figure 18. The method of section will again be used. The section *aa* cuts through the truss intersecting members *UV* and *DE*. The reaction at *K* is determined using the equation

$$+\curvearrowleft \sum M_R = 0$$

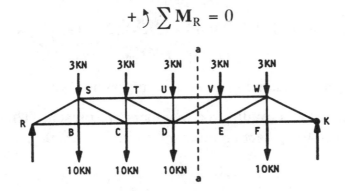

Figure 18. Free-body diagram

$-(13KN)(20m) - (13KN)(40m) - (13KN)(60m) - (3KN)(80m) - (13KN)(100m) + K(120m) = 0$

or

$$K = 25.8KN$$

The right portion of the truss *VWKE* cut off by the line *aa* in Figure 18 will be used as a free body to calculate the force in the three members. For force in member *DE*

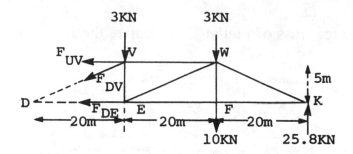

Figure 19. Right portion of truss

$$+ \, \text{)} \, \sum \mathbf{M}_V = 0$$

$$(25.8KN)\,(40m) - (13KN)\,(20m) - F_{DE}\,(5m) = 0$$
$$\therefore F_{DE} = +154KN = 154KN \text{ tension}$$

The force in member *UV* is determined by taking moments about joint *D*. From Figure 19,

$$+ \, \text{)} \, \sum \mathbf{M}_D = 0$$

$$(25.8KN)\,(60m) - (13KN)\,(40m) - (3KN)\,(20m) + (F_{UV)}\,(5m) = 0$$
$$\therefore F_{UV} = -194KN$$

The negative sign indicates F_{UV} to be in compression.

In many structures, multiforce members are present. These members have three or more forces acting on them, as in Figure 20.

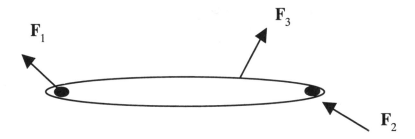

Figure 20. Multiforce members

DISTRIBUTED FORCES, CENTROIDS, AND CENTERS OF GRAVITY

Line distribution, in Newtons per meter $\left(\dfrac{N}{m}\right)$, occurs when a force is distributed along a line such as a suspended wire.

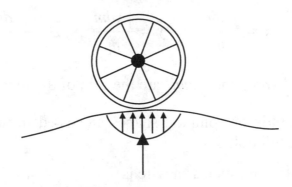

Figure 21. Line distribution

Area distribution, in $\dfrac{N}{m^2}$, occurs when force is distributed over an area.

Volume distribution occurs when force is distributed over the volume of a body, such as the earth's gravitational pull.

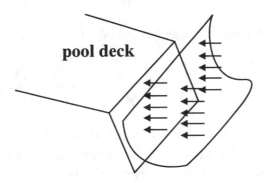

Figure 22. Area distribution—water against the wall of a pool

To find the center of gravity, apply the principle of moments—Varignon's Theorem. Varignon's Theorem states that the sum of individual moments about a point caused by multiple concurrent forces is equal to the moment of a resultant force about that point. The resultant gravitational force W about any axis equals the sum of the moments about the same axis of the incremental force *dw* acting on all infinitesimal elements of the body. As

$$W = mg$$

$$dw = gdm$$

the coordinates of the center of gravity are:

$$\bar{x} = \frac{\int xdm}{m} \qquad \bar{y} = \frac{\int ydm}{m} \qquad \bar{z} = \frac{\int zdm}{m},$$

where $\int xdm$, $\int ydm$, and $\int zdm$ are the sum of the moments.

The **centroids** of common shapes are listed in most engineering or mathematics handbooks.

The centroid of a line such as a wire is

$$\bar{x} = \frac{\int xdL}{L} \qquad \bar{y} = \frac{\int ydL}{L} \qquad \bar{z} = \frac{\int zdL}{L},$$

the centroid of areas is

$$\bar{x} = \frac{\int xdA}{A} \qquad \bar{y} = \frac{\int ydA}{A} \qquad \bar{z} = \frac{\int zdA}{A},$$

and the centroid of volume for a general body of volume is

$$\bar{x} = \frac{\int xdV}{V} \qquad \bar{y} = \frac{\int ydV}{V} \qquad \bar{z} = \frac{\int zdV}{V}.$$

For ease of calculation, use the elements that can be integrated in one continuous operation in the equation. Disregard higher order terms, choose a coordinate that best matches the region's boundaries, use first order system elements, and use a coordinate to the centroid of the element.

EXAMPLE

(a) Locate the centroid of the T-section shown in Figure 23.

(b) Also locate the centroid of the volume of the cone and hemisphere shown in Figure 24, the values of *r* and *h* being 6 m and 18 m, respectively.

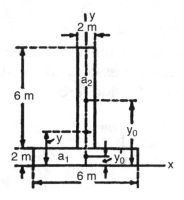

Figure 23. T section

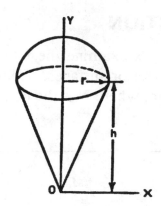

Figure 24. Cone and hemisphere

SOLUTION

(a) If axes are selected as indicated, it is evident from symmetry that $\bar{x} = 0$. By dividing the given area into areas a_1 and a_2 and by taking moments about the bottom edge of the area, $\bar{y}$ may be found as follows:

$$A\bar{y} = \sum(ay_0),$$

$$\bar{y} = \frac{12 \times 1 + 12 \times 5}{6 \times 2 + 6 \times 2} = 3 \text{ m}$$

(b) The axis of symmetry will be taken as the y-axis. From symmetry then $\bar{x} = 0$. By taking the x-axis through the apex of the cone as shown, the equation $V\bar{y} = \sum(vy_0)$ becomes

$$\left(\frac{1}{3}\pi r^2 h + \frac{2}{3}\pi r^3\right)\bar{y} = \frac{1}{3}\pi r^2 h \times \frac{3}{4}h + \frac{2}{3}\pi r^3\left(h + \frac{3}{8}r\right).$$

That is,

$$\frac{1}{3}\pi r^2(h + 2r)\bar{y} = \frac{1}{3}\pi r^2\left(\frac{3}{4}h^2 + 2rh + \frac{3}{4}r^2\right).$$

Therefore,

$$\bar{y} = \frac{\frac{3}{4}h^2 + 2rh + \frac{3}{4}r^2}{h + 2r}$$

$$= \frac{\frac{3}{4} \times (18)^2 + 2 \times 6 \times 18 + \frac{3}{4} \times (6)^2}{18 + 2 \times 6} = 16.2 \text{ m}$$

FRICTION

Let's examine the effects of dry friction acting on rigid bodies and their exterior surfaces. Consider Figure 25, and the associated free-body diagram, where **N** is the normal force and **F** is the friction force.

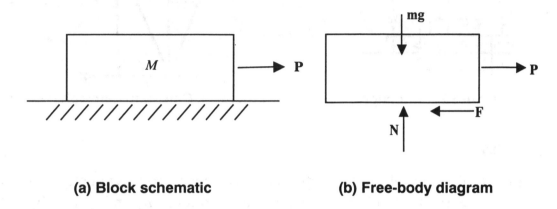

| (a) Block schematic | (b) Free-body diagram |

Figure 25. Sliding block

Obviously greater force is required to overcome friction and get the block moving than to keep it in motion once it is sliding across the plane surface. The frictional resistance up to the point of slippage is called static friction and is defined by

$$f_{s\,max} = \mu_s N,$$

where μ_s is the coefficient of static friction and N is the magnitude of the normal force on the block. Once the block is moving, kinetic friction takes over:

$$f_k = \mu_k N,$$

where μ_k is the coefficient of kinetic friction.

For a body on an incline, the body will not slide until the parallel component of the weight is greater than the friction force. The body will slide when the angle of incline equals a critical angle which can be related to the coefficient of friction:

$$\tan\theta = \frac{f}{N}$$

or

$$\tan\theta = \mu$$

Depending on whether we use μ_k or μ_s, θ is called the angle of static friction or kinetic friction.

EXAMPLE

A ladder of length L = 10m and mass M = 10kg leans against a frictionless vertical wall at an angle of 60° from the horizontal. The coefficient of static friction between the horizontal floor and the foot of the ladder is $\mu_s = 0.25$. A man of mass M = 70kg starts up a ladder. How far along the ladder does he get before the ladder begins to slide down the wall?

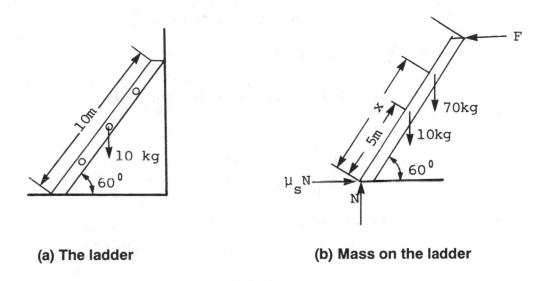

(a) The ladder   **(b) Mass on the ladder**

Figure 26. Force on a ladder

SOLUTION

The forces on the ladder are shown. The horizontal force on the foot of the ladder is equal to $\mu_s N$ only at the instant before the ladder begins to slide. We wish to find the position of the man at this instant. Because the vertical wall is frictionless, it can exert a force on the ladder only perpendicular to itself as shown.

Since the net force on the ladder is zero, we find, taking vertical components,

$$N - 10g - 70g = 0$$

and, from horizontal components,

$$\mu_s N - F = 0$$

Let x be the distance of the man along the ladder from the foot at the instant the ladder begins to slide. Equate the torque about the foot of the ladder to zero.

$$\frac{L}{2} mg \cos \theta + xMg \cos \theta - FL \sin \theta = 0$$

From the equation above,

$$N = 80g \text{ newtons.}$$

From this and the second equation,

$$F = 0.25 \times 80g = 20g \text{ newtons.}$$

From this and the third equation,

$$\frac{1}{2} mLg \cos \theta + xMg \cos \theta - 20gL \sin \theta = 0$$

$$x = \frac{20gL \sin \theta - \frac{1}{2} mLg \cos \theta}{Mg \cos \theta}$$

$$= \frac{200 \times 0.866 - \frac{1}{2} \times 10 \times 10 \times \frac{1}{2}}{70 \times \frac{1}{2}} = 4.2 \text{ meters}$$

A wedge machine and its free-body diagrams are shown in Figure 27.

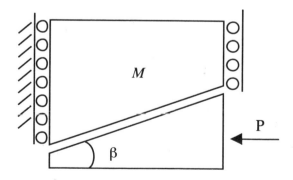

(a) Wedge machine schematic

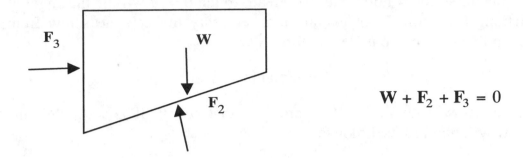

$$W + F_2 + F_3 = 0$$

(b) Free-body diagram on top component

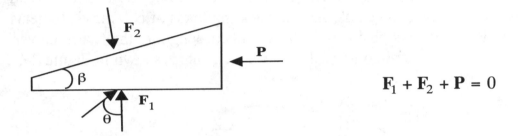

$$F_1 + F_2 + P = 0$$

(c) Free-body diagram on bottom component

Figure 27. Wedge machine

A screw is a common wedge machine, as shown in Figure 28.

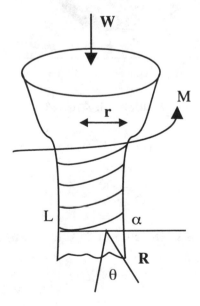

Figure 28. Common wedge machine

θ is the angle for **R** normal to the thread, so tan θ = *M* will be the angle of friction. The moment of equilibrium necessary to keep the screw from unwinding downward under the force **W** is

$$M = Wr \tan(\alpha + \theta).$$

The screw will remain in place provided that $\alpha < \theta$. If $\alpha > \theta$, then the screw will unwind itself downward.

MOMENT OF INERTIA

The area moment of inertia is used to determine the deflection and stresses of shafts and beams, and the buckling loads of columns. Moments of inertia are always positive and have units of length to the fourth power. An elementary area *A* composed of *i* area elements is shown in Figure 29.

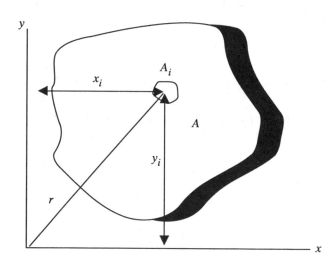

Figure 29. Area *A*

For area *A*, the moment of inertia with respect to the *x*-axis is

$$I_x = \sum_i y_i^2 A_i,$$

and the moment of inertia with respect to the *y*-axis is

$$I_y = \sum_i x_i^2 A_i.$$

The formal definitions of moment of inertia of a plane area are

$$I_x = \int_A y^2 dA,$$

which is the moment of inertia about the x-axis, and

$$I_y = \int_A x^2 dA,$$

which is the moment of inertia about the y-axis.

The polar moment of inertia may be informally defined as the resistance of an area to torsion. It is denoted by J, and like the area moment of inertia, has units of length to the fourth power. The Perpendicular Axis Theorem relates polar and area moments of inertia as follows:

$$J = I_x + I_y.$$

The polar moment of inertia in integral form is

$$J = \int_A \left(x^2 + y^2\right) dA.$$

The imaginary distance from a centroidal axis at which the area would not affect the moment of inertia is the radius of gyration, denoted by K, and defined as

$$K_x = \sqrt{\frac{I_x}{A}}$$

$$K_y = \sqrt{\frac{I_y}{A}}$$

REVIEW PROBLEMS

PROBLEM 1

A 200 N man is standing 3 m from the top of an 8 m ladder that leans against a smooth wall as shown in the figure. If the ladder is in equilibrium, determine the forces at A and D in Figure 30. Neglect the weight of the ladder.

SOLUTION

This problem can be solved by determining the line of action of $\mathbf{F}_D$ and then setting the x and y components of the force to zero. The lines of action of $\mathbf{F}_A$ and the 200 N gravity force are known and intersect at point C. (See Figure 30.)

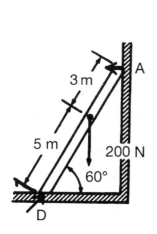

(a) Force equilibrium diagram

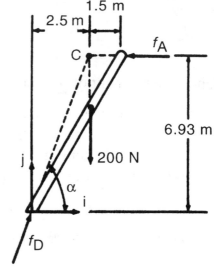

(b) Lines of action

Figure 30. Schematic of ladder in equilibrium

Since the ladder is a three-force member, the line of action of $\mathbf{F}_D$ must pass through point C. First we determine the angle α:

$$\tan\alpha = \frac{6.93}{2.5} = 2.772$$

$$\alpha = 70.16° \qquad \cos\alpha = 0.339 \qquad \sin\alpha = 0.94$$

$$(-F_A + 0.339F_D)i - (0.94F_D - 200)j = 0,$$

which yields:

$$-F_A = -0.339F_D$$

$$0.94\,F_D = 200 \qquad F_D = \frac{200}{0.94}$$

$$F_A = 0.339\left(\frac{200}{0.94}\right)$$

$$F_D = 213 \text{ N}$$

$$F_A = 72.2 \text{ N}$$

PROBLEM 2

In Figure 31, a 50-N tension is required to maintain the box B in equilibrium with force F. Calculate the magnitude of F given that $d = 10$ cm and $r = 5$ cm.

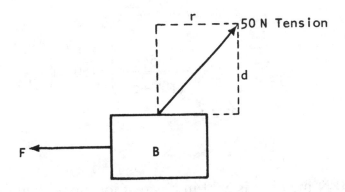

Figure 31. Forces on box

SOLUTION

The free-body diagram of the box is shown in Figure 32. It accounts for all forces acting on the box. Since only F is required, it is sufficient to consider only the x-direction. It is given that the box is in equilibrium, thus the summation of all the forces in the x-direction must be zero.

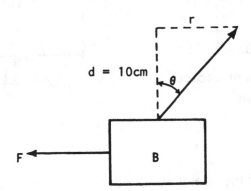

Figure 32. Free-body diagram of box

$$-F + (50 \text{ N}) (\sin\theta) = 0 \qquad (1)$$

From trigonometry,

$$\sin \theta = \frac{r}{\sqrt{10^2 + r^2}}.$$

Substituting for sinθ in equation (1) gives

$$F = (50 \text{ N}) \frac{r}{\sqrt{10^2 + r^2}}$$

But

$$r = 5 \text{ cm}$$

$$F = (50 \text{ N}) \left(\frac{5}{\sqrt{10^2 + 5^2}} \right) = (50 \text{ N}) \left(\frac{5}{\sqrt{100 + 25}} \right)$$

$$F = 22.4 \text{ N}$$

PROBLEM 3

A 2,000 N member is held in place at locations P and Q as shown in Figure 33. Determine the reactions at P and Q if the forklift is used to haul a 3,000 N load.

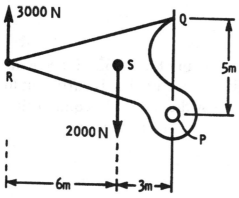

Figure 33. Position and forces
on member

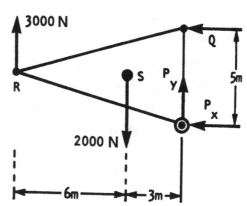

Figure 34. Free-body diagram

SOLUTION

The weight of the member acts along the center of gravity located at point S on the free-body diagram of Figure 34. The reaction at Q has been resolved into its x and y components. Assume the forces to act in the direction shown. The final sense of each force component will be known after the magnitudes of the forces are determined.

Taking moments about point P eliminates P_x and P_y and allows for the value of Q to be determined.

$$\sum M_P = 0$$
$$(3,000 \text{ N}) (9 \text{ m}) - (2,000 \text{ N}) (3 \text{ m}) - Q (5 \text{ m}) = 0$$
$$Q = 4,200 \text{ N}$$

P_x is determined by summing the horizontal components of all external forces and setting it equal to zero.

$$\therefore \sum F_x = 0: -P_x - Q \text{ or } -P_x - 4,200 \text{ N} = 0$$

$$P_x = -4,200 \text{ N}$$

Since P_x is negative, it means that its sense as shown in Figure 34 should be in the opposite direction. To determine P_y, all vertical forces are summed equal to zero.

$$\therefore \sum F_y = 0: 3,000 \text{ N} - 2,000 \text{ N} + P_y = 0$$
$$P_y = -1,000 \text{ N}$$

P_y is negative, thus it has an opposite sense to that shown in Figure 34. The forces acting on the member and their directions as determined above are shown in Figure 35.

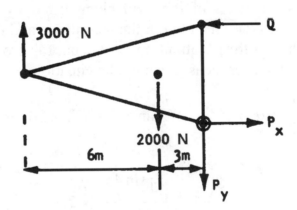

Figure 35. Resultant forces

PROBLEM 4

A crane lifts a load of 10,000 kg mass. The boom of the crane is uniform, has a mass of 1,000 kg, and a length of 10 m. Calculate the tension in the upper cable and the magnitude and direction of the force exerted on the boom by the lower pivot.

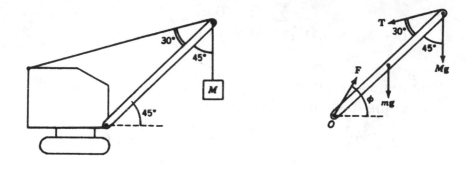

(a) Schematic of crane　　　　　　　**(b) Free-body diagram**

Figure 36. Crane lifting load

SOLUTION

Isolate the boom analytically and indicate all forces on it as in the right-hand portion of the figure, where **T** is the tension in the upper cable, **F** is the force exerted on the boom by the lower pivot, m is the mass of the boom, and M is the mass of the load being lifted by the crane. The magnitude of **T** is unknown and both the magnitude and direction of **F** are unknown. Set the net torque about point O equal to zero. If the length of the boom is S, this net torque is given by the equation:

$$\frac{S}{2} mg \sin 45° + SMg \sin 45° - ST \sin 30° = 0$$

$$\frac{g\left(\dfrac{m}{2} + M\right) \sin 45°}{\sin 30°} = T$$

Substitute the values given above.

$$T = \frac{9.8(500 + 10,000)\left(\dfrac{1}{\sqrt{2}}\right)}{\dfrac{1}{2}} = 1.46 \times 10^5 \, \text{N}$$

We can find F_x and F_y, the x and y components of **F** respectively, by requiring that both the x and y components of the net force on the boom be equal to zero.

$$\overset{+}{\rightarrow} \sum F_x = 0$$

$$F_x - T\cos15° = 0$$

$$F_x = 1.46 \times 10^5 \, (\cos15°)$$

$$F_x = 1.41 \times 10^5 \, \text{N}$$

$$+ \uparrow \sum F_y = 0$$

$$F_y - T\sin15° - mg - Mg = 0$$

$$F_y = 1.46 \times 10^5 \, (\sin15°) + 9.8(1{,}000 + 10{,}000)$$

$$F_y = 1.46 \times 10^5 \, \text{N}$$

So that the magnitude of **F** is:

$$F = \sqrt{F_x^2 + F_y^2} = 2.03 \times 10^5 \, \text{N}.$$

The angle ϕ that **F** makes with the horizontal is given by:

$$\tan\phi = \frac{F_x}{F_y} = \frac{1.46}{1.41} = 1.035$$

$$\phi = 46°$$

PROBLEM 5

Determine the forces acting on each member of the frame in Figure 37.

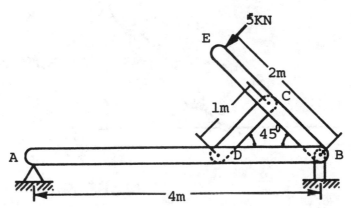

Figure 37. Frame and components

SOLUTION

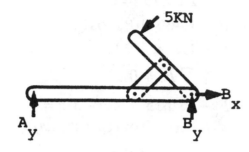

Figure 38. Forces on entire frame

Determine the reaction at *A* by calculating the moment at point B.

$$+ \circlearrowleft \sum M_B = 0; \; -(Ay)\,(4 \text{ m}) + (5 \text{ KN})\,(2\text{m}) = 0$$

$$A_y = 2.5 \text{ KN} \uparrow$$

Determine the remaining reactions by taking each member as a free body. Figure 39 shows a free-body diagram for each member.

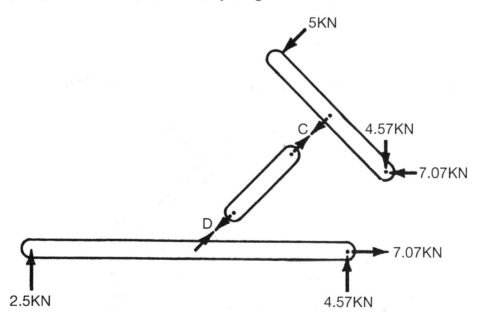

Figure 39. Forces on individual components

$$+ \circlearrowleft \sum M_B = 0; \; (-2.5 \text{ KN})\,(4\text{m}) - (D)\,(1\text{m}) = 0$$

$$D = 10 \text{ KN} \quad 45° \text{ (on member } AB)$$

$$C = 10 \text{ KN} \quad 45° \text{ (on member } BE)$$

$$\overset{+}{\rightarrow} \sum F_x = 0;\ B_x - 10\cos45° = 0$$

$$B_y = 7.07\ \text{KN}$$

$$+ \uparrow \sum F_y = 0;\ 2.5 + B_y - 10\cos45° = 0$$

$$B_y = 4.57\ \text{KN}$$

PROBLEM 6

First, find the centroid of the parabolic section shown in Figure 40. Then, determine the moments of inertia of the shaded area shown with respect to each of the coordinate axes. Finally, using the results from determining the moments of inertia of the shaded area, determine the radius of gyration of the shaded area with respect to each of the coordinate axes.

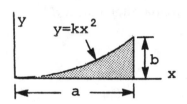

Figure 40. Parabolic section

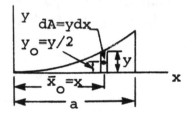

Figure 41. Vertical differential element

SOLUTION

Given $y = kx^2$, the value of k can be obtained from the point $x = a$, $y = b$. Hence, $k = \dfrac{b}{a^2}$.

$$y = \frac{b}{a^2} x^2 \tag{1}$$

or

$$x = \frac{a}{b^{\frac{1}{2}}} y^{\frac{1}{2}} \tag{2}$$

Choose a vertical differential element as shown in Figure 41. Then the total area A is

$$A = \int dA = \int y\,dx = \int_0^a \frac{b}{a^2}x^2\,dx = \left[\frac{b}{a^2}\frac{x^3}{3}\right]_0^a$$

$$= \frac{ab}{3} \tag{3}$$

The moment of the differential element with respect to the y-axis is $\overline{x}_o dA$. The moment of the total area with respect to this axis is, therefore,

$$\int \overline{x}_o dA = \int xy\,dx = \int_0^a x\left(\frac{b}{a^2}x^2\right)dx$$

$$= \left[\frac{b}{a^2}\frac{x^4}{4}\right]_0^a = \frac{a^2 b}{4} \tag{4}$$

The centroid $\overline{x}$ is that point which, when multiplied by the area, gives the same result for the moment as the integration of the differential moments $x_o dA$.

Thus,

$$\overline{x}A = \int \overline{x}_o dA$$

$$\overline{x}\frac{ab}{3} = \frac{a^2 b}{4}$$

$$\overline{x} = \frac{3}{4}a \tag{5}$$

Similarly, the moment of the differential element with respect to the x-axis is $\overline{y}_o dA$, and the moment of the total area is

$$\int \overline{y}_o dA = \int \frac{y}{2}y\,dx = \int_0^a \frac{1}{2}\left(\frac{b}{a^2}x^2\right)^2 dx$$

$$= \frac{ab^2}{10}$$

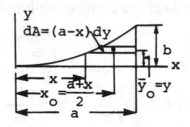

Figure 42. Horizontal element

Thus,

$$\bar{y}_o = \int \bar{y}_{el} dA$$

$$\bar{y}\frac{ab}{3} = \frac{ab^2}{10}$$

$$\bar{y} = \frac{3}{10}b \qquad (6)$$

The same result will be obtained by using a horizontal element as shown in Figure 42. For example, the moments with respect to the coordinate axes are:

$$\int \bar{x}_o dA = \int \frac{a+x}{2}(a-x)dy = \int_0^b \frac{a^2 - x^2}{2}dy$$

$$= \frac{1}{2}\int_0^b \left(a^2 - \frac{a^2}{b}y\right)dy = \frac{a^2b}{4},$$

$$\int \bar{y}_o dA = \int y(a-x)dy = \int y\left(a - \frac{a}{b^{\frac{1}{2}}}y^{\frac{1}{2}}\right)dy$$

$$= \int_0^b \left(ay - \frac{a}{b^{\frac{1}{2}}}y^{\frac{3}{2}}\right)dy = \frac{ab^2}{10}$$

Hence, equations (5) and (6) follow.

Using the vertical differential element, compute the moment of inertia. Since all portions of this element are not at the same distance from the x-axis, treat the elements as a thin rectangle.

The moment of inertia of the element with respect to the x-axis is

$$dI_x = \frac{1}{3}y^3 dx = \frac{1}{3}\left(\frac{b}{a^2}x^2\right)^3 = \frac{1}{3}\frac{b^3}{a^6}x^6 dx$$

$$I_x = \int dI_x = \int_0^a \frac{1}{3}\frac{b^3}{a^6}x^6 dx = \frac{ab^3}{21} \qquad (7)$$

Similarly,

$$dI_y = x^2 dA = x^2(y\,dx) = x^2\left(\frac{b}{a^2}x^2\right)dx$$

$$= \frac{b}{a^2}x^4 dx$$

$$I_y = \int dI_y = \int_0^a \frac{b}{a^2}x^4 dx = \frac{a^3 b}{5} \qquad (8)$$

The radii of gyration are

$$k_x^2 = \frac{I_x}{A} = \frac{\dfrac{ab^3}{21}}{\dfrac{ab}{3}} = \frac{b^2}{7}$$

$$k_x = \sqrt{\frac{1}{7}}b,$$

$$k_y^2 = \frac{I_y}{A} = \frac{\dfrac{a^3 b}{5}}{\dfrac{ab}{3}} = \frac{3}{5}a^2 \qquad (9)$$

$$k_y = \sqrt{\frac{3}{5}}a$$

PROBLEM 7

The wheels of a small wagon are separated by a distance d, and the center of mass is a distance h above the ground. The wagon is at rest on a hill of slope angle θ, and between the wheels and the surface of the hill the coefficient of static friction is μ. How steep a hill can the wagon rest on without tipping over or sliding?

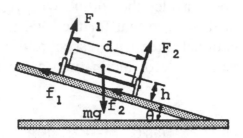

Figure 43. Forces on wagon

SOLUTION

The wagon is acted on by three forces: gravity and two contact forces at the wheels. Both the direction and the magnitudes of the contact forces are unknown. Consequently, we have four unknown force components, which are denoted by F_1, F_2, f_1, and f_2 in Figure 43. Since we have only three equilibrium equations, this problem normally is statically indeterminate in the sense that f_1 and f_2 cannot be determined separately. However, we are now interested only in the condition when the wagon is on the verge of sliding or on the verge of tipping. In these cases, we have additional relations imposed between the variables. When the wagon is on the verge of sliding, the friction forces are fully developed at both wheels, and, as we recall, are then simply related to the force components normal to the plane. If we let the symbols F_1, F_2, f_1, and f_2 denote the forces that are obtained when the wagon is on the verge of sliding, we have

$$f_1 = \mu F_1 \quad \text{and} \quad f_2 = \mu F_2.$$

If we combine these relations with the general conditions for equilibrium,

$$\sum F_x = f_1 + f_2 - mg \sin \theta_1 = 0$$
$$\sum F_y = F_1 + F_2 - mg \cos \theta_1 = 0$$

we obtain $\mu \, mg \cos \theta_1 = mg \sin \theta_1$ or $\tan \theta_1 = \mu$.

In other words, in order to prevent sliding, we must have $\theta < \theta_1$.

When the wagon is on the verge of tipping, the forces F_1 and f_1 will be zero since then the contact between the upper wheel and the plane will be broken. Then, if we consider the torque with respect to the contact point of the lower wheel, we see that for the total torque to be zero, the lever arm of the gravitational force with respect to this point must be zero. This will occur when the angle of inclination of the plane has the value given by

$$\tan \theta_2 = \frac{d}{2h}$$

and tipping will be prevented if $\theta < \theta_2$. If $\theta_1 = \theta_2$, it follows that tipping and sliding will occur simultaneously when $\mu = \dfrac{d}{2h}$. If μ is less than $\dfrac{2}{dh}$, sliding will occur before tipping as the angle θ is increased. The opposite, of course, occurs if μ is larger than $\dfrac{d}{2h}$.

PROBLEM 8

A small pump is mounted on a concrete slab which, in turn, rests on four concrete posts. Two of the posts have settled slightly so that the slab must be leveled. The foreman decides to raise the low side with two large wedges located as drawn on Figure 44. Fortunately, there is a concrete floor on which the bottom wedge can be fastened. If μ_s between the two wedges is 0.4 and between the wedge and the concrete 0.6, and if the motor slab transmits a 1,000 N vertical force to the wedge, determine the force **P** required for lifting the slab.

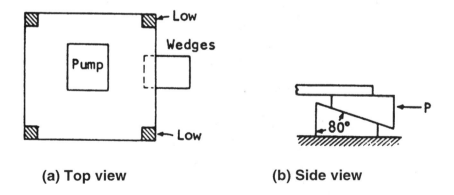

| (a) Top view | (b) Side view |

Figure 44. Pump mounted on concrete slab

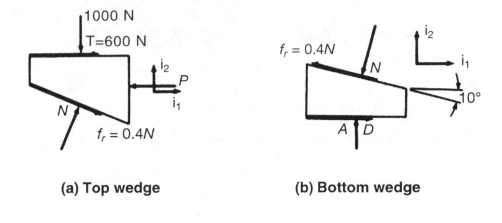

(a) Top wedge **(b) Bottom wedge**

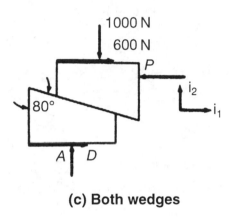

(c) Both wedges

Figure 45. Free-body diagrams

SOLUTION

The free-body diagrams are shown in Figure 45. Notice that Figure 45c, showing the two wedge system, has only the external forces shown. The forces between the wedges are equal and opposite and canceled out by Newton's Third Law. If the sum of all external forces are set equal to zero, the system is in equilibrium, that is, nothing moves. Any greater force will start lifting the slab.

$$\xrightarrow{+} \sum F_{i_1} = 0; \ 600 + D - P = 0 \tag{1}$$

$$+ \uparrow \sum F_{i_2} = 0; \ -1{,}000 + A = 0$$

so $\qquad A = 1000 \ \text{N}$

The bottom wedge, as described, is fastened to the floor. The sum of the forces must be equal to zero throughout. This means that the force **D** is entirely reactive and does not depend on any coefficient of friction or the normal force **A**. The equilibrium equations are, from Figure 45b,

$$\overset{+}{\rightarrow}\sum F_{i_1} = 0;\ D - 0.4N\cos 10° - N\sin 10° = 0 \tag{2}$$

$$+\uparrow \sum F_{i_2} = 0;\ A - N\cos 10° + 0.4N\sin 10° = 0$$

or
$$1{,}000 - N\cos 10° + 0.4N\sin 10° = 0. \tag{3}$$

Solving equations (2) and (3) simultaneously for D yields

$$D = 1{,}000\,\frac{0.4\cos 10° + \sin 10°}{\cos 10° - 0.4\sin 10°}$$

$$= 621\ \text{N}$$

Putting this value into equation (1) yields

$$P = 1{,}221\ \text{N}$$

The force **P** needed by this method is greater than the 1,000 N needed for a direct lift.

PROBLEM 9

A capstan is used to lower a crate from an elevated loading platform to the ground. When held stationary on the incline, the crate applies a force $\mathbf{F}_2$ of 5,000 N to the rope wound with two turns about the capstan, while it takes a force $\mathbf{F}_1$ of 100 N to hold the crate in place.

(a) Calculate the coefficient of friction between the rope and the capstan.

(b) Using this coefficient of friction, compute the force $\mathbf{F}_2$ that will be held when the rope is wound with three turns.

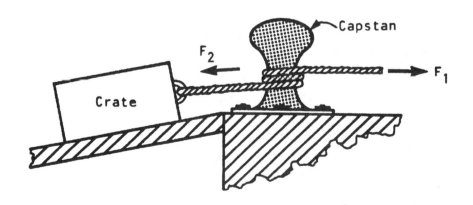

Figure 46. Capstan lowering a crate

SOLUTION

The equation relating the tensions at the beginning and end of a rope wrapped around a fixed circular cylinder is

$$\ell n \frac{T_2}{T_1} = \mu\left(\theta_2 - \theta_1\right). \tag{1}$$

Since the rope is wrapped two full turns around the capstan, we have:

$$\left(\theta_2 - \theta_1\right) = 2(2\pi) = 4\pi \text{ rad.}$$

Given are:

$$F_1 = 100 \text{ N}, F_2 = 5{,}000 \text{ N}$$

so

$$4\pi\mu = \ell n \frac{5{,}000}{100} = \ell n 50 = 3.91.$$

Solving for μ, we get

$$\mu = \frac{3.91}{4\pi} = 0.31.$$

To analyze the problem when the rope is wrapped three times about the capstan, we first modify equation (1) by taking antilogs, yielding

$$\frac{T_2}{T_1} = e^{\mu\left(\theta_2 - \theta_1\right)}.$$

So, using $\theta_2 - \theta_1 = 3(2\pi) = 6\pi$ rad., we get

$$T_2 = \left(100 \text{ N}\right)e^{(0.31)(6\pi)}$$
$$= 34{,}493 \text{ N}$$

FE/EIT

Fundamentals of Engineering: AM Exam

CHAPTER 6

Dynamics

CHAPTER 6

DYNAMICS

Dynamics is divided into areas: **kinematics** (geometry of motion) and **kinetics** (force-acceleration relationships). Kinematics will be limited to particle and planar (two dimensional) motion of vehicles, projections, and rotating bodies. Kinetics will include force, acceleration, work, energy, impulse, momentum, and vibration.

KINEMATICS

Linear Particle Motion

Velocity (v) is the rate of change of the position (s) of a particle with time (t).

$$v = \frac{ds}{dt}.$$

Acceleration is the rate of change of velocity

$$a = \frac{dv}{dt} = \frac{d^2s}{dt^2}, \text{ and also } a = \frac{vdv}{ds}.$$

As an example, let

$$s = 18 + 8t - 2t^2$$

where s = position in meters and t = time in seconds.

Position at $t = 10$ sec is

$$s = 18 + 8 \times 10 - 2 \times 10^2 = -10.2 \text{ m.}$$

Velocity at $t = 10$ sec is

$$v = \frac{ds}{dt} = 8 - 4t = -32 \text{ m/sec.}$$

Acceleration at $t = 10$ sec is

$$a = \frac{dv}{dt} = -4 \text{ m/sec}^2.$$

Distance traveled from $t = 0$ to $t = 10$ seconds is a little more involved since the particle reverses directions when the velocity ($v = 8 - 4t$) becomes 0 at $t = \frac{8}{4} = 2$ sec. The velocity is zero at $t = \frac{8}{4} = 2$ sec, thus the particle changes direction. The distance traveled from $t = 0$ to $t = 10$ sec is the sum of the distances in each direction. See Figure 1 for an illustration of this problem.

$$\text{Total distance} = 8 + 26 + 102 = 136 \text{ m}$$

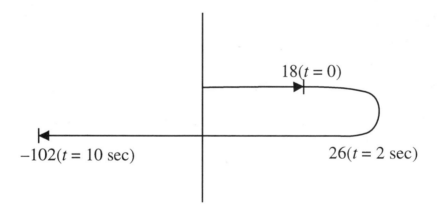

Figure 1. Movement of a particle

Constant Velocity and Constant Acceleration

Constant velocity and constant acceleration are frequent problems in dynamics.

At constant velocity (v), integrating

$$ds = vdt$$

$$s = s_o + vt$$

where s_o = position at $t = 0$.

The position of particle (s) at time (t) is equal to its initial position (s_o) plus its velocity (v) multiplied by time.

Constant acceleration (a), integrating

$$dv = adt$$
$$v = v_o + at$$

where v_o = initial velocity at $t = 0$. Substituting s for v and rearrange terms,

$$s = s_o + v_o t + \left(\frac{1}{2}\right)at^2$$
$$v^2 = v_o^2 + 2a(s - s_o)$$
$$(v + v_o)t = 2\,(s - s_o)$$

where v_o = velocity at $t = 0$.

Projectile Motion

Projectiles have motion in two dimensions simultaneously, the horizontal x- direction and the vertical y-direction. These components are independent of one another. The projectile travels in the x-direction at constant velocity, and thus its position at time, t, is

$$x = x_o + v_x t$$

where (x_o) is the initial position and v_x is the x-component of the velocity v. Movement in the y-direction occurs with constant acceleration, or gravity (g) and

$$v_y = v_{yo} - gt$$
$$y = y_o + v_{yo}t - \left(\frac{1}{2}\right)gt^2$$
$$v_y^2 = v_{yo}^2 - 2g(y - y_o)$$

Projectile problems may be presented with various surface geometries. Some examples are horizontal surface requiring horizontal and vertical positions, maximum horizontal distance, or maximum vertical height [shown in Figure 2(a)]; surface at an angle requiring the horizontal and vertical distances [shown in Figure 2(b)]; point of impact fixed, more than one solution may be possible[shown in Figure 2(c)]; and object in projectile path, many solutions are possible [shown in Figure 2(d)].

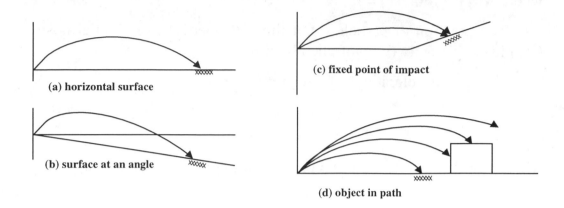

Figure 2. Projectile motion

As an example of projectile motion, consider the problem given in Figure 3. Initial velocity is 30.5 m/sec at an upward slope of 30°. The ground slopes downward at an angle of 12° to a horizontal distance of 152.4 meters. Determine the horizontal distance to projectile impact.

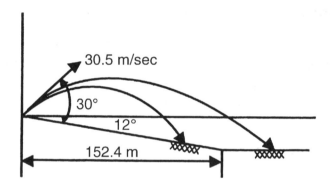

Figure 3. Projectile impact

There are two possible flight patterns: the projectile could hit the horizontal surface (Figure 4), or the projectile could hit the sloping surface (Figure 5). First, assume the projectile hits the horizontal surface.

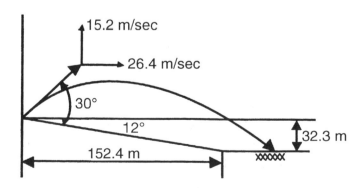

Figure 4. Landing on the horizontal surface

Initial computations show

$$v_x = 30.5 \cos 30° = 26.4 \text{ m/sec}$$
$$x = 26.4t$$
$$v_{yo} = 30.5 \sin 30° = 15.2 \text{ m/sec}$$

$$y = y_o + v_{yo}t - \left(\frac{1}{2}\right)gt^2$$

At x 152.4 m, $y = -152.4 \tan 12° = -32.3$ m. Substituting for y and solving for t,

$$-32.3 = 0 + 15.2t - \left(\frac{9.8}{2}\right)t^2$$

$$t = -1.45 \text{ sec}, 4.555 \text{ sec}$$

Reject $t < 0$, thus at $t = 4.555$ sec results in $x = 120.3$ m. Since 120.3 m < 152.4 m, the assumption used is incorrect, and the projectile hits on the slope.

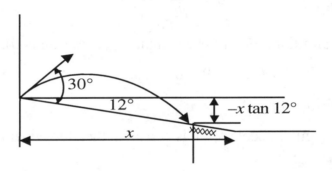

Figure 5. Hitting a slope

Next, assume that the projectile hits the slope. The equations of motion are

$$x = 26.4t$$
$$y = -x \tan 12° \text{ at impact found from geometry, and}$$

$$y = y_o + v_{yo}t - \left(\frac{1}{2}\right)gt^2$$

Substituting, we get

$$y = -x \tan 12° = (-26.4t) \tan 12° = 0 + 15.2t - \left(\frac{9.8}{2}\right)t^2.$$

Solving $\quad$ $t = 0$ sec, 4.25 sec.

Substituting $\quad$ $x = 26.4(4.25) = 112.2$ m.

The correct solution, therefore, is $x = 112.2$ m, and the projectile hits the sloping surface.

Rotational Motion

Rotation has similarities to linear motion in that essentially the same equations may be used with the variables having rotational meanings.

Rotational motion is movement around a circle; the change in position (α) is measured in angles and defined as angular velocity (ω).

$$\omega = \frac{d\theta}{dt}$$

Angular acceleration (α) is the rate of change of angular velocity.

$$\alpha = \frac{d\omega}{dt} = \frac{d^2\theta}{dt^2}$$

When the angular velocity is constant (acceleration is 0), then

$$\theta = \theta_o + \omega t$$

where θ_o = position at $t = 0$.

When the angular acceleration is constant, then the equations of motion are

$$\omega = \omega_o + \alpha_o t$$

$$\theta = \theta_o + \omega_o t + \left(\frac{1}{2}\right)\alpha t^2$$

$$\omega^2 = \omega_o^2 + 2\alpha\,(\theta - \theta_o)$$

where θ_o = position at $t = 0$, ω_o = angular velocity at $t = 0$, α = angular acceleration, and t = time.

Tangential Velocity and Acceleration

The velocity of a particle rotating a distance (r = constant) about a fixed point is the tangential velocity

$$v_t = r\omega$$

where r = radius and ω = rotational velocity.

Acceleration has two components: tangential and radial. The tangential component of acceleration (a_t) is

$$a_t = r\alpha.$$

The radial component, (a_r), is directed back toward the center of rotation and has a magnitude of

$$a_r = r\omega^2 = \frac{v_t^2}{r}$$

where α = angular acceleration, ω = angular velocity, and v_t = tangential velocity.

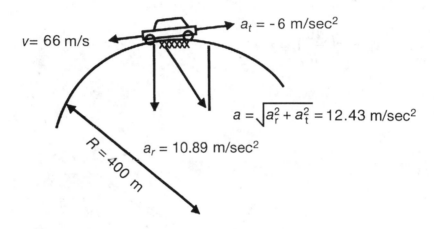

v= 66 m/s

$a_t = -6$ m/sec^2

$a = \sqrt{a_r^2 + a_t^2} = 12.43$ m/sec^2

$a_r = 10.89$ m/sec^2

$R = 400$ m

Figure 6. Motion on a curvature

Use Figure 6 as an example. Suppose a car is traveling around a curve. The radius of curvature is 400 m, and the car is traveling at 45 m/sec while decelerating at 6 m/sec^2. Determine the tangential velocity.

Radial acceleration is

$$a_r = \frac{v_t^2}{r} = \frac{66^2}{400} = 10.89 \text{ m/sec}^2.$$

Tangential acceleration is

$$a_t = -6 \text{ m/sec}^2$$

Total acceleration is the resultant of both radial and tangential acceleration.

$$a = \sqrt{a_r^2 + a_t^2} = \sqrt{10.89^2 + (-6.0)^2} = 12.43 \text{ m/sec}^2$$

Motion in Polar Coordinates (*r* = variable)

Equations of motion in polar coordinates with the radius of curvature variable (shown in Figure 7) are

$$a_r = \frac{d^2r}{dt^2} - r\left(\frac{d\theta}{dt}\right)^2 = \frac{d^2r}{dt^2} - r\omega^2$$

$$a_\theta = r\left(\frac{d^2\theta}{dt^2}\right) + 2\left(\frac{dr}{dt}\right)\left(\frac{d\theta}{dt}\right) = r\alpha + 2\left(\frac{dr}{dt}\right)\omega$$

$$v_r = \frac{dr}{dt}$$

$$v_\theta = r\left(\frac{d\theta}{dt}\right) = r\omega$$

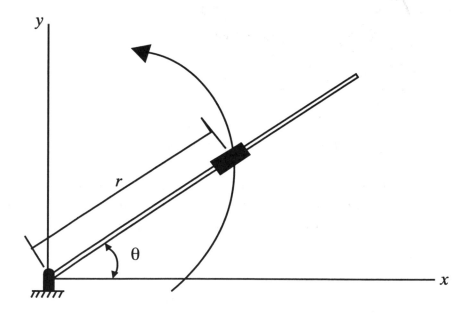

Figure 7. Motion in polar coordinates

Relative and Related Motion

Relative motion is the movement of one object *A* with respect to a second object *B*. The motion of observer *A* = motion of observer *B* + the difference between *A* and *B*.

acceleration	$a_B = a_A + a_{B/A}$
velocity	$v_B = v_A + v_{B/A}$
position	$x_B = x_A + x_{B/A}$

These equations apply to linear, two-dimensional, and rotational motion.

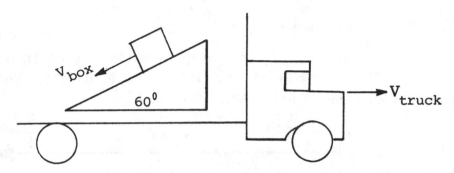

Figure 8. Relative motion inside and outside a truck

Look at Figure 8. Suppose a box starts sliding at a constant velocity down the ramp of a truck inclined at 60° while the truck is still moving. If an observer outside the truck sees the box moving down vertically, and the speed of the box with respect to the moving ramp is 4 m/sec, then what is the speed of the truck?

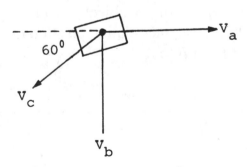

Figure 9. Velocity of the block

The absolute velocity of the block (Figure 9) is equal to the velocity of the block with respect to the moving ramp, V_c, summed with the velocity of the truck, V_a.

$$V_b = V_a + V_c$$
$$\rightarrow \sum V_x = 0$$
$$V_a - V_c \cos 60° = 0$$
$$\therefore V_a = 4\left(\frac{1}{2}\right) = 2\text{m/scc}$$

The speed of the truck is 2 m/sec.

Linear motion of two objects may be shown as follows. The position of object B with respect to object A is a vector to the right while the position of A with respect to B is a vector to the left.

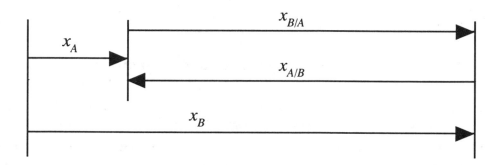

Figure 10. Vector diagram of linear motion

With **two-dimensional motion**, two objects are traveling in different directions. The relative position of object B with respect to object A is a vector from A to B. Likewise, the relative position of object A with respect to object B is a vector from B to A.

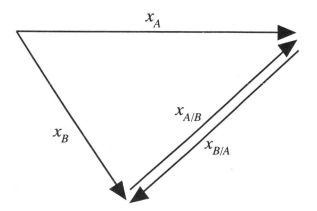

Figure 11. Two-dimensional motion

With **dependent motion**, two objects are connected by a rope of fixed length. When object A moves, then object B must move by a proportional amount. The amount of movement is determined by either observation or computation. The related motion of the first set of objects can usually be determined by observation. When object A moves downward then object B moves upward by the same amount. The related motion of the second and third set of objects is determined by finding the rope length from some fixed point. The derivative of the rope length with respect to time gives the velocity and acceleration. The constant is the sum of all irrelevant lengths of rope.

Figure 12. Rope length $= x_A + x_B +$ constant

$$\frac{dL}{dt} = v_A + v_B = 0, \; v_A = -v_B$$

$$\frac{d^2L}{dt^2} = a_A + a_B = 0, \; a_A = -a_B$$

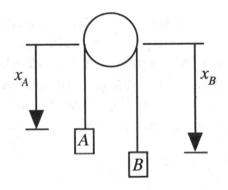

Figure 12. Rope length (a)

Figure 13. $L = x_A + 2x_B + c$

$$\frac{dL}{dt} = v_A + 2v_B = 0, \; v_A = -2v_B$$

$$\frac{d^2L}{dt^2} = a_A + 2a_B = 0, \; a_A = -2a_B$$

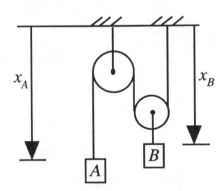

Figure 13. Rope length (b)

Figure 14. $L_1 = x_A + 2(x_A - x_C) + c_1$

$$\frac{dL_1}{dt} = 3v_A - 2v_C = 0, \; 3v_A = 2v_C$$

$L_2 = x_B + x_C + c_2$

$$\frac{dL_2}{dt} = v_B + v_C = 0, \; v_C = -v_B$$

Substituting, we get $3v_A = -2v_B$.

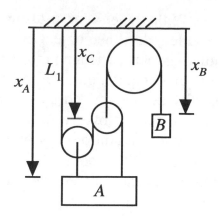

Figure 14. Rope length (c)

Rotational motion of gears and belts is also dependent. Again, the relation of position, velocity, or acceleration depends on the geometry. Two different examples are shown in Figures 15 and 16. In the first example, the distance of movement along the rim surface (or number of gear teeth) is the same for all gears. In the second example, the radius changes, and thus geometry changes, must be considered.

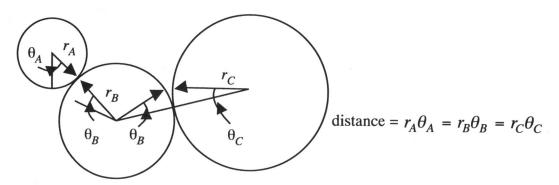

distance $= r_A\theta_A = r_B\theta_B = r_C\theta_C$

Figure 15. Rotational motion

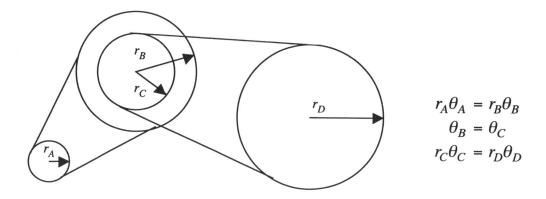

$$r_A\theta_A = r_B\theta_B$$
$$\theta_B = \theta_C$$
$$r_C\theta_C = r_D\theta_D$$

Figure 16. Radius change

Plane motion of rigid bodies is the topic of discussion in the next set of paragraphs. There, we will make a more thorough study. The first problem, Figure 17, shows two objects, *A* and *B*, connected by a link moving along definite paths. The second problem, Figure 18, shows a wheel rolling without sliding along a horizonal surface.

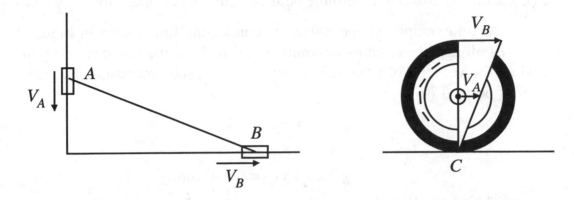

Figure 17. Two linked objects in motion

Figure 18. Wheel rolling w. horizontal sliding

Plane Motion of Rigid Bodies

Plane motion is rigid body motion in two dimensions; rolling wheels are an example. Rigid body motion is the sum of a translational component and the rotation around a fixed axis.

Plane motion	=	Translation	+	Rotation
x_B	=	x_A	+	$x_{B/A}$
v_B	=	v_A	+	$v_{B/A}$
a_B	=	a_A	+	$a_{B/A}$

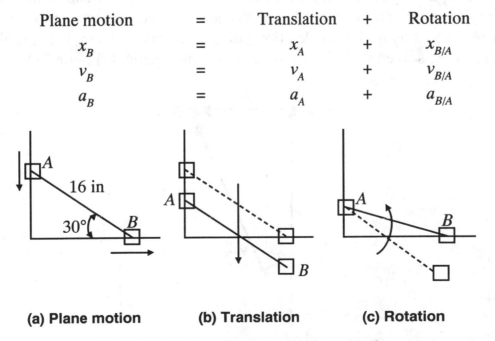

(a) Plane motion   **(b) Translation**   **(c) Rotation**

Figure 19. Vector diagrams of plane motion

Velocity for plane motion may be found by several methods. One method is by working with the horizontal and vertical portion (*x* and *y* components) of the velocity equation. A second approach is to use the vector polygon. A third approach is to use the instantaneous center of rotation. A fourth approach, not covered here, is to use vector mathematics (*i, j, k* unit vectors) to determine both velocity and acceleration.

As an example, suppose that the connecting link shown in Figure 19 moves along the set paths at points *A* and *B*. Find the velocity of point *B* when the velocity of point *A* is a constant 24 m/sec downward. The velocity of point *B* is

$$v_B = v_A + v_{B/A}$$
$$v_B = v_A + r_{AB}\,\omega_{AB}$$
$$v_B = 24 + v_{B/A} = 24 + 16\omega_{AB}$$

The vertical and horizontal components of the equation give

$$\text{vertical} \qquad 0 \qquad = 24 + v_{B/A}\cos 30°$$
$$\text{horizontal} \quad v_B = v_{B/A}\sin 30°$$

The results are $v_{B/A} = 27.7$ m/sec, $\omega_{AB} = 1.73$ radians/sec counterclockwise, and $v_B = 13.86$ m/sec.

The vector polygon for the velocity equation is shown in Figure 20 and can be solved by trigonometry. The velocity vectors from either side of the equal sign begin from the same starting point and end at the same stopping point. This concept can be visualized more clearly when there are more vectors as in the acceleration polygon discussed later. This problem can also be solved with the instantaneous center method (Figure 21).

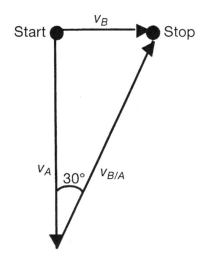

Figure 20. Vector polygon method

The instantaneous center, point C, is found by drawing radial lines from both points A and B. The body is temporarily hinged and rotated about point C. The rotational velocity vector is

$$\omega_{AB} = \frac{v_A}{r_{CA}} = \frac{24}{(16 \cos 30°)} = 1.73 \text{ rad/sec.}$$

The linear velocity of point B is

$$v_B = \omega_{AB}\, r_{CB} = 1.73(16 \sin 30°) = 13.86 \text{ m/sec.}$$

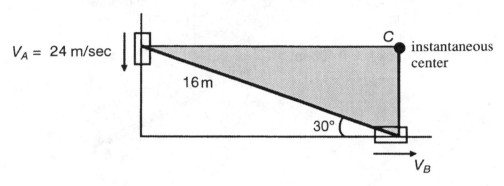

Figure 21. Instantaneous center method

As a second example, consider the large spool rolling to the right without slipping shown in Figure 22. The point of contact with the ground is the instantaneous center. If the rope is moving to the right with a velocity of 4 m/sec, then the rotational velocity is

$$\omega = \frac{4 \text{ m/sec}}{(2 \text{ m})} = 2 \text{ rad/sec.}$$

The velocity of any point is equal to the rotational velocity times the distance from that point to the instantaneous center (point C).

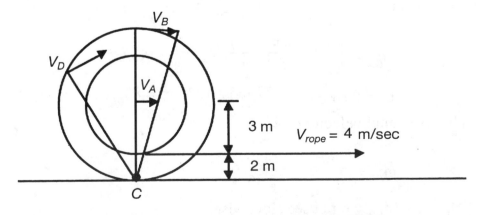

Figure 22. Large spool rolling without slipping

As a third example, consider the mechanism *ABDE* shown in Figure 23. Some of the necessary calculations are superimposed on the same sketch. The instantaneous center of member *BD* at point *C* is also shown. Assume that the member *AB* is rotating at 6 rad/sec clockwise. Find the rotational velocity of *BD* and *DE*, and find the linear velocity of point *D*.

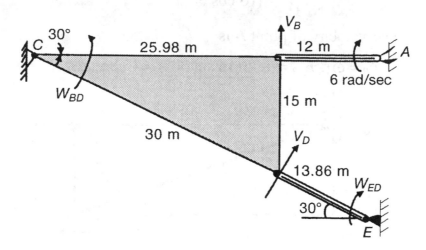

Figure 23. Diagram of mechanism *AB DE*

The instantaneous center for member *AB* is at point *A*, and the instantaneous center for member *ED* is at point *E*.

The linear velocity of each point is

$$v_B = r_{AB}\, \omega_{AB} = 12 \text{ m}(6 \text{ rad/sec}) = 72 \text{ m/sec}$$
$$v_D = r_{ED}\, \omega_{ED} = (13.86 \text{ m})\omega_{ED}$$

For a mechanism such as this, we focus our efforts on the middle member *BD,* which has the instantaneous center at point *C*. Since the velocity of point *B* is 72 m/sec, the rotational velocity of *BD* and the linear velocity of *D* are

$$\omega_{BD} = \frac{v_B}{r_{CB}} = \frac{(72 \text{ m}/\text{sec})}{25.98 \text{ m}} = 2.77 \text{ rad/sec}$$

$$v_D = \omega_{BD} r_{CD} = (2.77 \text{ rad/sec})30 \text{ m} = 83.14 \text{ m/sec}$$

The rotational velocity of *ED* is

$$\omega_{ED} = \frac{v_D}{r_{ED}} = \frac{(83.14 \text{ m}/\text{sec})}{13.86 \text{ m}}$$

$$\omega_{ED} = 6 \text{ rad/sec clockwise}$$

The mechanism of the third example can also be solved by either the plane motion equation (Figure 24) or by the vector polygon (Figure 25). Both of the methods are abbreviated below. To solve the mechanism, we focus our attention on the middle member *BD*.

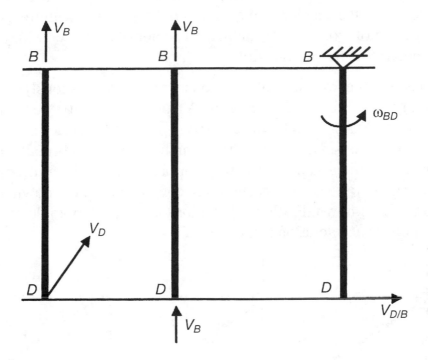

Figure 24. Plane motion

Solving this problem by the plane motion equation for *BD*,

$$(13.86 \text{ m}) \, \omega_{ED} \, \sin \, 30° = 72 \text{ m/sec} + (15 \text{ m}) \, \omega_{BD}$$

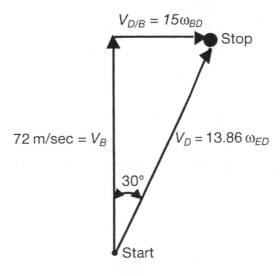

Figure 25. Vector polygon

Acceleration for plane motion can have six components whereas velocity has three components. Each term of the acceleration equation can have both radial and tangential components. To find acceleration, the velocity as discussed previously must first be determined. Acceleration may be found by working with the horizonal and vertical portion (*x* and *y* components) of the acceleration equation or by working with the geometry of the vector polygon. Vector mathematics, not covered here, may also be used to determine the acceleration.

Consider the example of the connecting link previously discussed for velocity and redrawn in Figure 26. Values for velocity were $v_A = 0.61$ m/sec (constant), $v_B = 13.86$ m/sec, and $\omega_{AB} = 1.73$ rad/sec. Even though point *A* has a constant velocity, the member *AB* will normally have an angular acceleration, and point *B* will normally have a linear acceleration. The line of action of the acceleration components are known, but the direction is not known. Further calculations are necessary to determine the direction of the acceleration components.

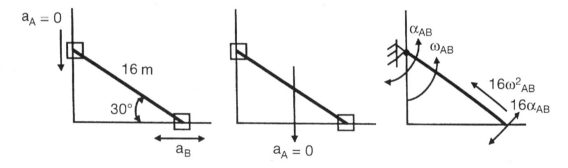

Figure 26. Plane acceleration

$$a_B = a_A + a_{B/A}$$
$$a_B = 0 + r_{AB}\,\omega_{AB}^{\,2} + r_{AB}\,\alpha_{AB}$$
$$a_B = 0 + 16 \text{ m}(1.73 \text{ rad/sec})^2 + 16 \text{ m}(\alpha_{AB})$$

Using either the *x* and *y* components or the vector polygon gives the solution as: $a_B = 55.43$ m/sec² to the left and $\alpha_{AB} = 1.73$ rad/sec² counterclockwise. The directions of the acceleration components may be found most easily by referring to the vector polygon (Figure 27).

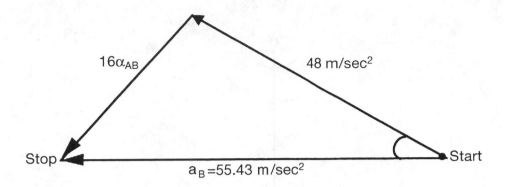

Figure 27. Vector polygon

Assume the angular acceleration of *AB* is 8 rad/sec^2 clockwise. Using Figure 28, find the radial and tangential acceleration of points *B* and *D*.

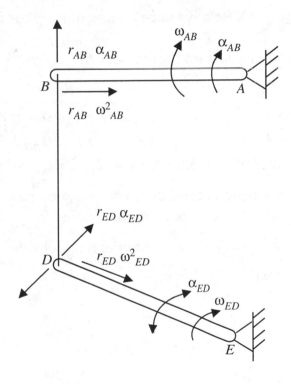

Figure 28. Acceleration of points *B* and *D*

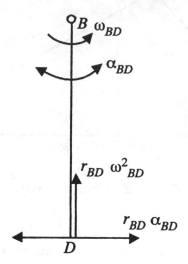

Figure 29. Relative acceleration of member *BD*

The plane motion equation for member *BD* is

$$a_D = a_B + a_{D/B}$$
$$r_{ED}\,\alpha_{ED} + r_{ED}\,\omega_{ED}^2 = r_{AB}\,\alpha_{AB} + r_{AB}\,\omega_{AB}^2 + r_{BD}\,\alpha_{BD} + r_{BD}\,\omega_{BD}^2$$
$$13.86\alpha_{ED} + 13.86(6^2) = 12(8) + 12(6^2) + 15\alpha_{BD} + 15(2.77^2)$$
$$13.86\,\alpha_{ED}\sin 30° + 498.8 = 96 + 432 + 15\alpha_{BD} + 115.2$$

The directions of the acceleration components are found by comparing the directions on the vector polygon in Figure 30.

$$\alpha_{BD} = 17.73 \text{ rad/sec}^2 \text{ counterclockwise}$$
$$\alpha_{ED} = 38.40 \text{ rad/sec}^2 \text{ clockwise}$$

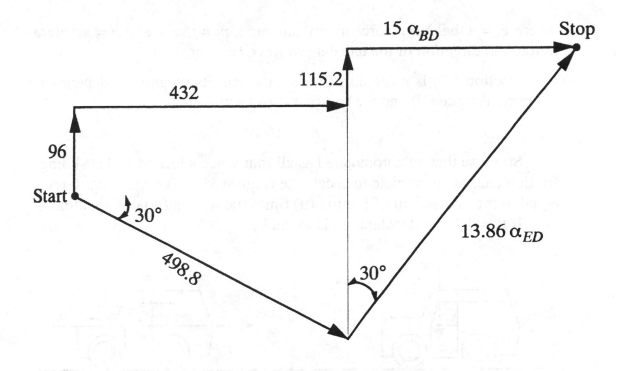

Figure 30. Resultant vector polygon

KINETICS

The study of kinetics covers force = acceleration relationships. Topics studied in kinetics include: force acceleration, work energy, power, impulse momentum, and impact.

Mass and Weight

Weight (*w*) relates the mass (*m*) of an object by the acceleration of gravity (*g*).

$$w = mg$$

On the Earth's surface the average acceleration of gravity is

$$g = 9.81 \text{ m/sec}^2.$$

Force and Acceleration of Particles

Force-acceleration of particles are related by Newton's second law. When there is an unbalanced force on an object, the object will accelerate in the direction of the unbalanced vector force. The relationship is

$$F = ma$$

where F = unbalanced force in any direction, m = mass, and a = acceleration in the direction of the unbalanced force (x, y, or z).

Friction (F_f) is a force that resists motion. Its magnitude depends on the normal force (N) and the coefficient of friction (μ).

$$F_f = \mu N$$

Suppose that an automobile has all four wheels locked and is sliding; friction causes the vehicle to decelerate (Figure 31). The frictional force is equal to the coefficient of friction (μ) times the weight (w) of the automobile. If $\mu = 0.4$, the deceleration is found by

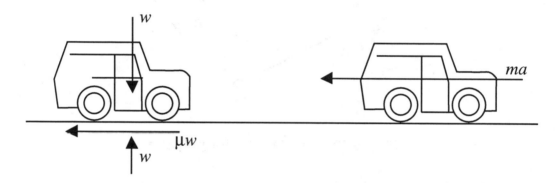

Figure 31. Sliding automobile

$$F = ma$$

$$\mu w = \left(\frac{w}{g}\right) a$$

$$a = \mu g$$

If the coefficient of friction is $\mu = 0.4$, then the deceleration is

$$a = 0.4(9.81 \text{ m/sec}^2) = 3.92 \text{ m/sec}^2$$

The problem of the sliding automobile becomes much more complicated when ideal conditions are not present. The first difficulty is that the assumed coefficient of friction varies considerably depending on the surface condition. Also, the solution becomes more difficult when all wheels are not sliding or when part of the wheels are sliding part of the time. To solve the problem some questionable assumptions must be made.

Two equations are needed when two weights are connected by a rope as shown in Figure 32. The $F = ma$ equation is applied to the free-body diagram of each weight.

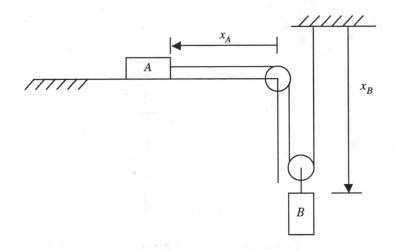

Figure 32. Weights connected by rope

Assume μ = coefficient between the surface and the weight w_A. For block A to move from rest or accelerate, the tensile force (T) in the rope must be larger than the frictional resistance, μw_A.

After it has been established that the weights are moving, the relative acceleration must be determined. The relation of the acceleration of block A to block B is determined by considering dependent motion studied previously. Since the length of the rope remains constant

$$L = x_A + 2x_B + \text{constant}$$

$$\frac{dL}{dt} = v_A + 2v_B = 0$$

$$\frac{d^2L}{dt^2} = a_A + 2a_B = 0, \; a_A = -2a_B$$

Assume the direction of the force on each block is positive and write the force equation for each (Figures 33 and 34).

Block A

$$T - \mu w_A = \left(\frac{w_A}{g}\right) a_A$$

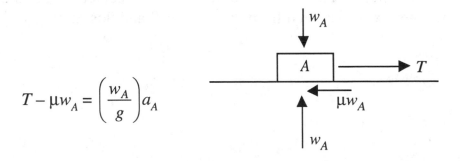

Figure 33. Force diagram for block A

Block *B*

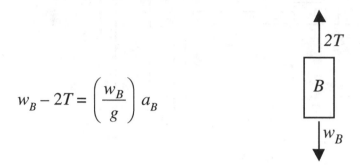

$$w_B - 2T = \left(\frac{w_B}{g}\right) a_B$$

Figure 34. Force diagram for block B

Solving provides

$$a_A = \frac{2(w_B - 2\mu w_A)g}{(4w_A + w_B)}; a_B = 2a_A; T = \mu w_A + \frac{2w_A(w_B - 2\mu w_A)}{(4w_A + w_B)}$$

Centripetal Force

Rotational motion can be expressed as the sum of two forces: tangential and centripetal (directed inward). **Centripetal force**, F_c, is the force associated with the normal path of the object.

$$F_c = ma_n = \frac{mv_t^2}{r}$$

where m = mass of the object, a_n = normal (radial) acceleration, v_t = tangential velocity, and r = radius of the rotation.

Figure 35 shows a simple pendulum consisting of a small mass, m, attached to the end of a wire length l; the other end of the wire is attached to a fine point A. When the mass is displaced slightly, it oscillates with simple harmonic motion along the arc of a circle with center A. (Assume: arc $OB = x$, where x is measured from 0; $\angle OAB = \theta$ and θ is small.)

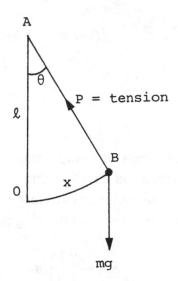

Figure 35. Simple pendulum

To find the acceleration along arc *OB*, note line the force *mg* sin θ, directed along the tangent at *B* is responsible for the acceleration along the arc *OB* (Figure 36). The tension *P* has no component in this direction.

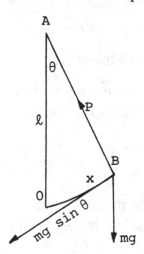

Figure 36. Acceleration component of simple pendulum

Therefore, $-mg \sin \theta = ma$, where *a* is the acceleration along the arc *OB*.

Note, the reason for the minus sign is that the force *mg* sin θ is directed toward *O* while the displacement *x* is measured along the arc from *O*.

Since θ is small, sin θ ≈ θ so that $-mg\,\theta = ma$

$$a = -g\theta$$

Since

$$\ell\theta = x$$

$$a = -g\left(\frac{x}{\ell}\right)$$

Work and Energy

The law of conservation of energy states that energy cannot be created nor destroyed. **Energy** is divided into kinetic and potential components. **Kinetic energy** is associated with movement of a body. The kinetic energy (*KE*) of an object of mass (*m*) moving at velocity (*v*) is defined as

$$KE = \left(\frac{1}{2}\right)mv^2$$

Potential energy (*PE*) of an object is relative to its position in a gravitational field. An object mass (*m*) raised to a height (*y*) above a particular point has potential energy of

$$PE = mgy$$

$$PE = wy$$

where *w* = *mg* is the weight of the object.

The potential energy of a linear spring, with a constant (*k*) is the work needed to compress the spring a distance (*x*).

$$PE = \left(\frac{1}{2}\right)kx^2$$

Work is defined as the process of changing the energy of an object. The work (*W*) done by an object is the integral of the force component (*F*) over all the increments of distance (*ds*).

Work of a force is

$$\text{Work} = \int F ds$$

where Work = total work added to all objects, *F* = force component in the direction of movement, and *ds* = the increment of movement. When the force is constant over a distance (*d*), then

$$\text{Work} = Fd$$

The work done in moving an object from point 1 to point 2 is denoted by W_{1-2}. During any process, the change in total energy is zero.

$$KE_1 + \text{Work}_{1-2} = KE_2$$

where KE_1 = kinetic energy of the object at position 1, KE_2 = kinetic energy at position 2, and Work_{1-2} = total work involved from position 1 to position 2. To note the ease of the energy solution approach to certain problems, consider the two blocks shown in Figure 37. Weight A is 445 N weight B is 890 N, the coefficient of friction is 0.4, and the initial velocity of B is 1.21 m/sec downward. Find the velocity of both blocks after block B has moved downward 3.03 m.

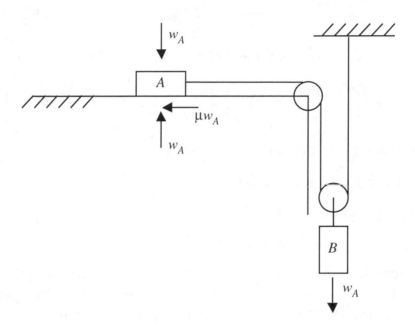

Figure 37. Schematic of a two block system

Using dependent motion studied previously, we determine the related movement and velocity of both blocks. When block B moves downward 3.03 m, then block A moves horizontal to the right 6.1 m. Also, when block B is moving downward 1.21 m/sec, then block A is moving to the right at 2.42 m/sec. The work of block B moving down is positive, but the work of block A is the negative frictional resistance. Internal work is not considered. Tensile force in the rope is found later by working separately with the free-body diagram of either weight. Substituting into the work-energy equation gives

$$KE_1 + \text{Work}_{1-2} = KE_2$$

$$KE_1 = \left\{\left(\frac{1}{2}\right)\left(\frac{w_A}{g}\right)v_{A1}^2 + \left(\frac{1}{2}\right)\left(\frac{w_B}{g}\right)v_{B1}^2\right\}$$

$$\text{Work}_{1-2} = \left\{-\mu w_A d_A + w_B d_B\right\}$$

$$KE_2 = \left\{\left(\frac{1}{2}\right)\left(\frac{w_A}{g}\right)v_{A2}^2 + \left(\frac{1}{2}\right)\left(\frac{w_B}{g}\right)v_{B2}^2\right\}$$

Substituting

$$KE_1 = \left\{\left(\frac{1}{2}\right)\left(\frac{445}{9.8}\right)\times 2.42^2 + \left(\frac{1}{2}\right)\left(\frac{890}{9.8}\right)\times 1.21^2\right\} = \{133 + 67\} \text{ joules}$$

$$\text{Work}_{1-2} = \{-0.4 \times 445 \times 6.1 + 890 \times 3.03\} = \{-1{,}085 + 2{,}696\} \text{ joules}$$

$$KE_2 = \left\{\left(\frac{1}{2}\right)\left(\frac{445}{9.8}\right)v_{A2}^2 + \left(\frac{1}{2}\right)\left(\frac{890}{9.8}\right)v_{B2}^2\right\} = \left\{22.7v_{A2}^2 + 50.5v_{B2}^2\right\}$$

Substituting into the energy equation gives

$$\{133 + 67\} + \{-1{,}085 + 2{,}696\} = \{22.7v_A^2 + 50.5v_B^2\}.$$

Using $v_A = 2v_B$ and solving,

$$v_A = 7.29 \text{ m/sec and } v_B = 3.65 \text{ m/sec}.$$

The tensile force in the rope connecting the two weights may be found by dealing with either weight. The force diagram for block A is shown in Figure 38. When block *A* is used, the tensile force is found as follows:

$$KE_1 + \text{Work}_{1-2} = KE_2$$

$$\frac{1}{2}\left(\frac{w_A}{g}\right)v_{A1}^2 + \left(-\mu w_A + T\right)d = \frac{1}{2}\left(\frac{w_A}{g}\right)v_{A2}^2$$

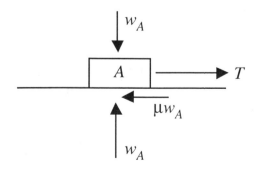

Figure 38. Force diagram for block A

Using the values found previously and substituting gives

$$\frac{1}{2}\left(\frac{445}{9.8}\right)2.42^2 + (-0.4 \times 445 + T)6.1 = \frac{1}{2}\left(\frac{445}{9.8}\right)7.29^2$$

$$133 + (-178 + T)6.1 = 1210 \text{ Nm}$$

Solving gives $T = 356$ N.

The tensile force in the rope of 356 N is reasonable when compared to the boundary possibilities. A force of 178 N (μw_A) is needed to move weight A. If weight B is stationary, the tensile force is 445 N $\left(\frac{w_B}{2}\right)$. When the weights are moving, the actual tensile force must be between these two bounds, and in this case the tensile force must be 356 N.

$$178 \text{ N} \leq T \leq 445 \text{ N}$$

The previous problem involving the two weights could have been solved by using $F = ma$. The accelerations could have been found as discussed previously. After the accelerations were found, the velocity could have been found by using the equations discussed at the beginning of the chapter. Impulse-momentum, discussed later, could also have been used. When velocity, distance, and work are involved, the energy method is usually preferred.

As a generalization, when either force or acceleration is needed, then the force-acceleration method is usually the most convenient solution approach. When velocity and work are related, then work-energy is usually the preferred solution approach. Lastly, when velocity and time are related directly, then impulse-momentum is usually the preferred solution approach.

Related	**Preferred Solution Approach**
Force, Acceleration	Force-Acceleration
Work, Velocity, Displacement	Work-Energy
Time, Velocity	Impulse-Momentum

Potential Energy

The potential energy concept can be used to solve certain problems more conveniently than the work-energy method. Problems involving elastic springs can often be solved more easily by using potential energy. For other engineering applications, potential energy can be extended beyond the mechanical energy definition used here. Potential energy can be in the form of voltage, water pressure, water head, or chemical as in explosives.

Potential energy of a compressed linear spring is the work needed to compress the spring and is

$$PE = \left(\frac{1}{2}\right)kx^2$$

where PE = potential energy, k = linear spring constant, and x = amount of spring compression. Potential of a weight at a certain distance above a particular point is

$$PE = wy$$

where w = weight and y = vertical distance.

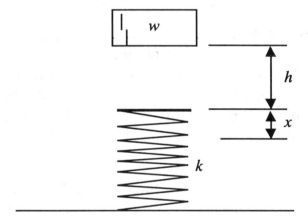

Figure 39. Spring compression

Suppose a weight of w is dropped a height of h on a spring having a spring constant of k (Figure 39). Determine the amount of spring compression (x). The potential energy equation can be written as

$$KE_1 + PE_1 = KE_2 + PE_2$$

where KE = kinetic energy and PE = potential energy. Continuing with the solution gives

$$0 + w(h + x) = 0 + \frac{1}{2}\left(kx^2\right)$$

where the KE = initial and final kinetic energies are 0, and x = compression of the spring. Solving gives

$$x = \left(\frac{w}{k}\right) \pm \sqrt{\left(\frac{w}{k}\right)^2 + \left(\frac{2wh}{k}\right)}$$

where $\dfrac{w}{k}$ = the static deflection.

If the weight is attached permanently to the spring so it will not "hop off," then the weight will vibrate in harmonic motion, as discussed later.

Vibration will be around static equilibrium $\left(x = \dfrac{w}{k} \right)$ with an amplitude of

$$\sqrt{\left(\frac{w}{k}\right)^2 + \left(\frac{2wh}{k}\right)}.$$

Determine the additional spring compression of the problem shown in Figure 40. A weight is dropped on a linear spring as shown. Assume the necessary data as follows: 22.2 N weight is dropped 0.91 m, initial velocity of the weight is 3.05 m/sec downward, the spring has an initial compression of 0.076 m, and the spring constant is 1730 N/m.

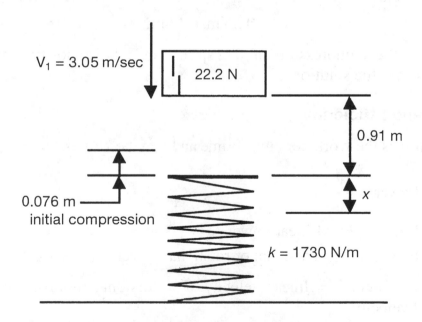

Figure 40. Additional spring compression

$$x_1 = 0.0758 \text{ m}$$
$$x_2 = x + 0.0758 \text{ m}$$
$$v_1 = 3.05 \text{ m/sec}$$
$$v_2 = 0 \text{ m/sec}$$

The energy equation is written as

$$KE_1 + PE_1 = KE_2 + PE_2$$

$$\left(\frac{1}{2}\right)\left(\frac{w}{g}\right)v_1^2 + w(h+x) + \left(\frac{1}{2}\right)kx_1^2 = \left(\frac{1}{2}\right)\left(\frac{w}{g}\right)v_2^2 + \left(\frac{1}{2}\right)kx_2^2$$

$$\left(\frac{1}{2}\right)\left(\frac{22.2}{9.81}\right)3.05^2 + 22.2(0.91+x) + \left(\frac{1}{2}\right)(1730)(0.0758)^2 =$$

$$0 + \left(\frac{1}{2}\right)(1730)(x+0.0758)^2$$

$$10.5 + 20.2 + 22.2x + 4.97 = 865x^2 + 131.1x + 4.97$$

Solving gives the additional compression of the spring.

$$x = -0.26 \text{ m}, 0.134 \text{ m}$$

Since the compression of the spring must be a positive number, $x = 0.134$ m is the solution.

Power and Efficiency

Power is the work per unit of time and may be written as

$$\text{Power} = \frac{W}{\Delta t}$$

$\text{Power} = Fv$ Linear power

$\text{Power} = T\omega$ Torsional or rotational power

where F = force, v = linear velocity, T = torsional moment, and ω = rotational velocity.

For torsional power, suppose a drill using 1,500 watts (1,500 Nm/sec) is turning the drill bit at 300 revolutions/minute. The torsional moment is

$$T = \frac{\text{Power}}{(2\pi f)} = \frac{1,500}{\left(\dfrac{2\pi 300}{60}\right)} = 47.7 \text{ Nm}$$

where f = frequency = 300 rev/min/60 sec/min = 5 rev/sec.

Also, suppose a 2 horsepower (one horsepower = 746 Nm/sec) drill is turning the drill bit at 300 rev/min. The torsional moment is

$$T = \frac{\text{Power}}{(2\pi f)} = 2 \times \frac{746 \text{ Nm / sec}}{2\pi(5)}$$

$$T = 47.5 \text{ Nm}$$

The **efficiency** of a process is the amount of output power or work obtained from the system compared to the amount of input or energy. The efficiency of an ideal system is unity.

$$\text{Efficiency} = \frac{\text{output}}{\text{input}}$$

Often problems involving power require the conversion of work or power from one system of units to another such as mechanical, thermal, or electrical.

Suppose that water is dropped into a mine 5,000 feet deep (h) at 20 gallons per minute (Q) for the purpose of cooling the air. With water weighing 8.33 lb/gal (g) the mechanical energy is

Power = $Q\,\gamma h$

Power = 20 gal/min × 8.33 lb/gal × 5,000 feet

Power = 833,000 ft-lb/min

This amount of mechanical power would produce 833,000/33,000 = 25.24 horsepower, 25.24 × 0.746 = 18.83 kilowatts, or 25.24 × 42.44 = 1,071 Btu/min. When a generator at an assumed efficiency of 90 percent is used to retrieve the electrical power, we would get 0.90 × 18.83 = 17 kilowatts. The energy that is not retrieved first as electrical energy is lost as heat. The energy required to pump the water back out of the mine would again increase the air temperature.

An automobile having a mass of 1,200 kilograms and traveling at 15 m/sec has

$$\text{Energy} = \left(\frac{1}{2}\right)mv^2 = \left(\frac{1}{2}\right)1,200 \times 15^2 = 135,000 \text{ Nm}$$

If this conversion was really 100 percent efficient, then a 100 watt (100 Nm/sec) light bulb would burn for $135,000/100/60 = 22.5$ min.

Impulse and Momentum

The **momentum** of an object is the product of its mass (m) and its velocity (v). Momentum is conserved, thus the sum of momentum of a system is always equal to the same constant total. The total momentum of the objects before a collision is equal to the sum of the momentums of the objects after a collision.

$$m_1 v_1 + m_2 v_2 = m_1^1 v_1^1 + m_2^1 v_2^1$$

Impulse is the change in momentum or the integral of the force (F) acting on the object with respect to time (dt).

$$\text{Impulse} = \int F dt \text{ (linear impulse)}$$

$$\text{Impulse} = \int T dt \text{ (angular impulse)}$$

Integrating $F = ma = \dfrac{mdv}{dt}$ as follows

$$\int F dt = \int m dv$$

results in the impulse-momentum equation

$$mv_1 + \int F dt = mv_2$$

where mv_1 = momentum at position one, mv_2 = momentum at position two, and $\int F dt$ = impulse between position one and position two.

Determine the time required to stop the sliding automobile in Figure 41.

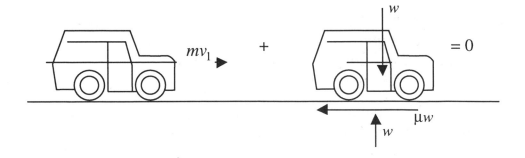

Figure 41. Force diagram on sliding automobile

$$mv_1 + \int F dt = mv_2$$

$$\left(\frac{w}{g}\right)v + \mu w t = 0$$

Solving gives $t = \dfrac{v}{(\mu g)}$.

The beauty of the impulse-momentum approach is more evident when the force is not constant. The impulse is the area under the F/t curve, such as shown in Figure 42. Solving such problems by either the force-acceleration method or the energy method would require more effort.

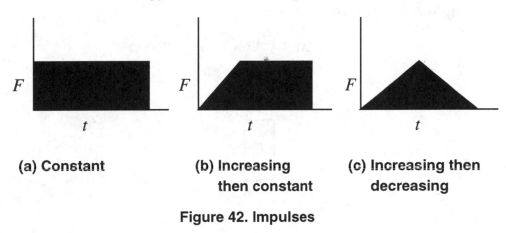

| (a) Constant | (b) Increasing then constant | (c) Increasing then decreasing |

Figure 42. Impulses

Both impulse and momentum are vector quantities. For this reason, two equations are required for problems involving two weights as considered previously. Briefly consider the problem in Figure 43.

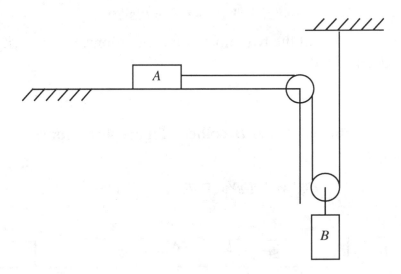

Figure 43. Schematic of block example

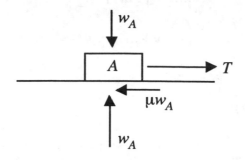

Figure 44. Forces on block A

Weight A (Figure 44):

$$m_A v_{A1} + (-\mu w_A + T)t = m_A v_{A2}$$

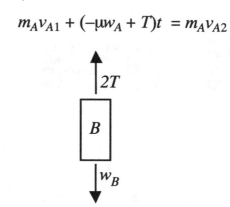

Figure 45. Forces on block B

Weight B (Figure 45)

$$m_B v_{B1} + (w_B - 2T)t = m_B v_{B2}$$

Using $v_A = 2v_B$ and the two momentum equations, the velocity at time two can be determined.

Impact

When two objects A and B collide (Figure 46), momentum is conserved. That is

$$m_A v_{A1} + m_B v_{B1} = m_A v_{A2} + m_B v_{B2}$$

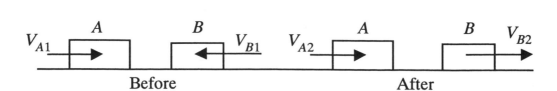

Figure 46. Force diagram for block A

The velocities are related by the **coefficient of restitution**:

$$e = \frac{v_{B2} - v_{A2}}{v_{A1} - v_{B1}}$$

The coefficient of restitution varies from $0 \leq e \leq 1.0$. Two unknown velocities may be solved by using the two equations.

Special cases of impact are perfectly elastic impact ($e = 1.0$), perfectly plastic impact ($e = 0$), impact with one mass infinite, and oblique impact.

With **perfectly elastic impact ($e = 1$)**, the kinetic energy

$$KE = \left(\frac{1}{2}\right)mv^2$$

is conserved.

With **perfectly plastic impact ($e = 0$)**, the two objects stick together after impact and have the same final velocity. The impact equation is

$$m_A v_{A1} + m_B v_{B1} = (m_A + m_B)v'.$$

Two clay objects would normally involve plastic impact.

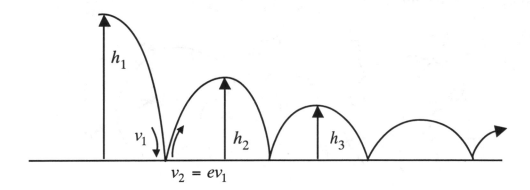

Figure 47. Ball striking the floor

When **one mass is infinite,** such as a ball striking a floor or wall (Figure 47), the momentum equation is unnecessary and the velocity is related by

$$v_2 = ev_1.$$

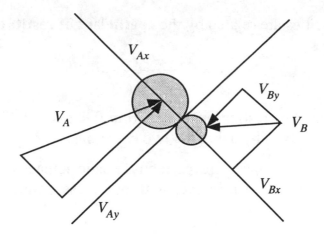

Figure 48. Oblique impact

With **oblique impact** (Figure 48), the momentum along the line of impact is determined in the same way as linear impact. The momentum and velocity transverse to the line of impact is not affected when the friction between the surfaces is neglected.

Two-Dimensional Rigid Body Motion

Kinetics of two-dimensional rigid body motion (Figure 49) involves two force-acceleration equations (x and y components) and one moment equation about some point.

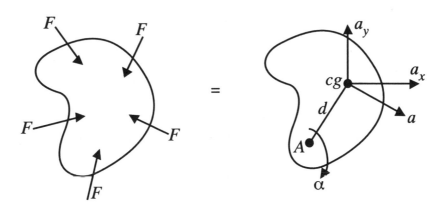

Figure 49. Force diagram during rigid body motion

$$F_x = ma_x$$
$$F_y = ma_y$$
$$M_A = I_A \alpha = I_{cg} \alpha + m(a)d$$

where F_x and F_y = force components, m = mass, a_x and a_y = linear acceleration components of the center of gravity (cg), M_A = moment of forces about point A, I_A = mass inertia about point A, I_{cg} = mass inertia about the center of gravity, a = component of linear acceleration normal to a line connecting points A and cg, α = angular acceleration, and d = distance from point A to the center of gravity.

Rigid body motion can be divided into three cases: translation only, rotation only, and general plane motion.

Determine the forces at the front and rear tires of the automobile as it slides to a stop. Assume a 13320 N car and a coefficient of friction of 0.5. Wheel base and center of gravity are shown in Figure 50.

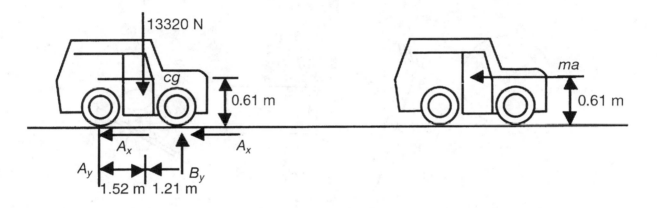

Figure 50. Forces on sliding automobile

Linear acceleration

$$F = ma,$$

$$\mu w = \left(\frac{w}{g}\right)a,$$

$$a = \mu g$$

$$a = 0.5 \times 9.8 = 4.9 \text{ m/sec}^2$$

Moment about rear

$$M_A = mad$$

$$13320 \times 1.52 - 2.73B_y = -\left(\frac{13,320}{9.8}\right)4.9 \times 0.61$$

$$B_y = 8,880 \text{ N}$$

For this problem the front tires carry two-thirds of the car weight as it slides to a stop. The force on the rear tires can be found by summing moments about the front tires in a similar manner or by summing forces in the vertical direction.

Rotation

Problems having rotation constrained about a fixed point require the mass moment of inertia. One equation is necessary to find the angular acceleration.

$$M_A = I_A \alpha = I_{cg} \alpha + m(a)d$$

where point A is often the center of gravity. The linear acceleration components are required to find the forces at the point of rotation.

Rotation about a fixed point could involve such objects as a spinning disk [Figure 51(a)], a beam hinged at one end [Figure 51(b)], a plate hinged about one corner [Figure 51(c)], or a wheel rolling on a large axle [Figure 51(d)].

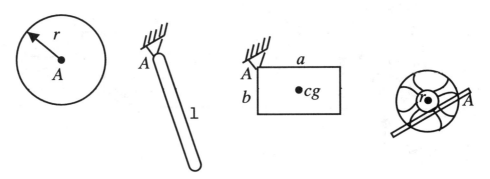

(a) Spinning disk   (b) Hinged beam   (c) Hinged plate   (d) Rolling wheel

Figure 51. Rotation of objects

Inertia

Newton's First Law of Motion states that if an object is at rest, its inertia will act upon it to keep it at rest. Likewise, an object in motion will remain in motion. The mass inertia of an object about its center of gravity (*cg*) is dependent upon its shape and size.

Mass inertia of the objects sketched previously are:

Spinning disk $I_{cg} = \left(\dfrac{1}{2}\right) mr^2$

Beam about *cg* $I_{cg} = \left(\dfrac{1}{12}\right) ml^2$

Plate about *cg* $I_{cg} = \left(\dfrac{1}{12}\right) m(a^2 + b^2)$

Wheel about cg $I_{cg} = mk^2$

where m = mass and r, l, a, and b = object dimensions, and k = radius of gyration of the wheel. The radius of gyration of any object is $k = \sqrt{\dfrac{I}{m}}$.

The transfer axis theorem must be used to find the mass inertia about a point some distance d from the center of gravity. The transfer axis theorem states

$$I_A = I_{cg} + md^2$$

where d = distance from the center of gravity to point A.

Thus, the mass inertia for the beam, plate, and wheel results in

Beam $I_A = \left(\dfrac{1}{12}\right)ml^2 + m\left(\dfrac{1}{2}\right)^2 = \left(\dfrac{1}{3}\right)ml^2$

Plate $I_A = \left(\dfrac{1}{12}\right)m\left(a^2 + b^2\right) + m\left[\left(\dfrac{a}{2}\right)^2 + \left(\dfrac{b}{2}\right)^2\right] = \left(\dfrac{1}{3}\right)m\left(a^2 + b^2\right)$

Wheel $I_A = mk^2 + mr^2$

The beams of the frame in Figure 52 weigh 2198 N/m. Find the mass moment of inertia about the center of gravity and point A.

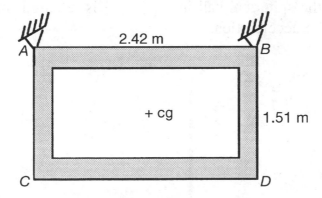

Figure 52. Hanging frame

The mass inertia of each beam about their respective centers of gravity is

$$I_{AB} = I_{CD} = \left(\frac{1}{12}\right) m l^2 = \left(\frac{1}{12}\right)\left(2.42 \times \frac{2198}{9.8}\right)2.42^2 = 268 \text{ mN sec}^2$$

$$I_{AC} = I_{BD} = \left(\frac{1}{12}\right)\left(1.51 \times \frac{2198}{9.8}\right)1.51^2 = 65.2 \text{ mN sec}^2$$

Combining the results and using the transfer axis theorem gives

$$I_{cg} = 2 \times 268 + 2 \times 65.2 + 2\left(2.42 \times \frac{2198}{9.8}\right)0.756^2 + 2\left(1.51 \times \frac{2198}{9.8}\right)1.21^2$$

$$I_{cg} = 2278 \text{ mN sec}^2$$

Transferring the mass inertia to point A results in

$$I_A = 2278 + \left(7.88 \times \frac{2198}{9.8}\right)(0.756^2 + 1.21^2) = 5875 \text{ m N sec}^2$$

General Plane Motion

Plane motion could have both linear and angular acceleration components. The equations stated previously are

$$F_x = ma_x$$
$$F_y = ma_y$$
$$M_A = I_A \alpha = I_{cg} \alpha + m(a)d$$

Suppose the spherical ball in Figure 53 is released from rest. Determine the angular acceleration.

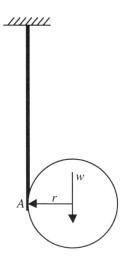

Figure 53. Rotation of spherical ball

The angular acceleration is

$$M_A = I_{cg}\,\alpha + m(a)d$$

$$wr = \left(\frac{1}{5}\right)\left(\frac{w}{g}\right)r^2\alpha + \left(\frac{w}{g}\right)(r\alpha)r = \left(\frac{6}{5}\right)\left(\frac{w}{g}\right)r^2\alpha$$

$$\alpha = \left(\frac{5}{6}\right)\left(\frac{g}{r}\right)$$

The tensile force is

$$F_y = ma_y = mr\alpha$$

$$w - T = \left(\frac{w}{g}\right)\left(\frac{5}{6}\right)\left(\frac{g}{r}\right)r = \left(\frac{5}{6}\right)w$$

$$T = \frac{w}{6}$$

Use Figure 54 as a second example. Suppose that both a pipe and cylinder are rolling without sliding on a sloping surface. Assume that the mass and outside radius of both objects are the same. Determine which will roll the fastest.

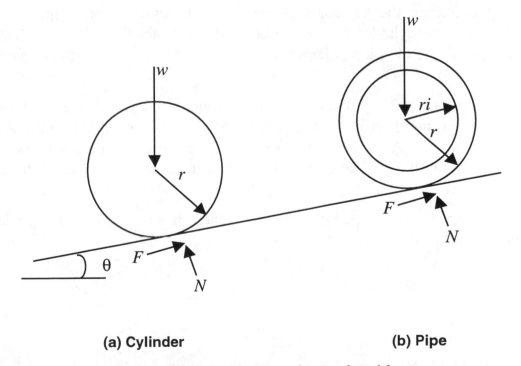

(a) Cylinder   (b) Pipe

Figure 54. Rolling objects and associated forces

Since the cylinder and pipe are rolling without sliding, moments are summed at the contact point for each object. The cylinder has an angular acceleration of

$$M_A = I_{cg}\,\alpha + m(a)d$$

$$wr\sin\theta = \left[\left(\frac{1}{2}\right)\left(\frac{w}{g}\right)r^2\right]\alpha + \left(\frac{w}{g}\right)(r\alpha)r = \left(\frac{3}{2}\right)\left(\frac{w}{g}\right)r^2\alpha$$

$$\alpha = \left(\frac{2g\sin\theta}{3r}\right)$$

The pipe has an angular acceleration of

$$wr\sin\theta = \left[\left(\frac{1}{2}\right)\left(\frac{w}{g}\right)\left(r^2 - r_i^2\right)\right]\alpha + \left(\frac{w}{g}\right)(r\alpha)r$$

$$wr\sin\theta = \left[\left(\frac{1}{2}\right)\left(\frac{w}{g}\right)\left(3r^2 - r_i^2\right)\right]\alpha$$

$$\alpha = \frac{(2gr\sin\theta)}{\left(3r^2 - r_i^2\right)}$$

Comparing the angular acceleration of the cylinder and pipe, it is noted that the cylinder will accelerate and roll faster than the pipe. The mass inertia of the pipe is larger than a cylinder having the same outside radius and mass.

In the previous problem, both the cylinder and pipe rolled without sliding. The question is, at what angle will a round object roll and slide simultaneously? A rectangular block will begin to slide on a sloping surface when $\tan\theta = \mu$. Therefore, when the coefficient of friction is 0.60, a rectangular object will begin to slide at an angle at or exceeding 31°.

Determine the slope angle that the sphere in Figure 55 will roll and slide simultaneously.

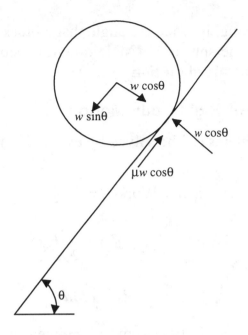

Figure 55. Rolling sphere

When the sphere is sliding, the angular acceleration is

$$M_{cg} = I_{cg}\alpha$$

$$\mu w r \cos\theta = \left(\frac{2}{5}\right)\left(\frac{w}{g}\right)r^2\alpha$$

$$\alpha = \left(\frac{5}{2}\right)\frac{\mu g}{r}\cos\theta$$

When the sphere is just beginning to slide $a_{cg} = r\alpha$, and the linear acceleration is

$$F = ma$$

$$w\sin\theta - w\cos\theta = \left(\frac{w}{g}\right)r\left[\left(\frac{5}{2}\right)\frac{\mu g}{r}\cos\theta\right]$$

Solving $$\tan\theta = \frac{7\mu}{2}.$$

When the coefficient of friction is 0.6, a block will begin to slide at a slope of 31° and a sphere will begin to roll and slide at an angle of 65°. In general, the cylinder, pipe, or sphere will begin to roll and slide simultaneously at an angle roughly twice the angle that a block will begin to slide. If no friction exists, the sphere will slide down the slope without rolling; this is known as **constrained motion**.

Energy Methods for Rigid Body Motion

Rigid body problems can be solved by examining the energy relationships of the system.

$$KE_1 + \text{Work}_{1-2} = KE_2$$

where

$$KE = \left(\frac{1}{2}\right)m(v_{cg})^2 + \left(\frac{1}{2}\right)I_{cg}\omega^2$$

and

$$W_{1-2} = \int F\,ds + \int M\,d\theta$$

Variables are KE = kinetic energy, v_{cg} = linear velocity of the center of gravity, ω = rotational velocity, I_{cg} = mass inertia at the center of gravity, F = component of force along the line of movement, ds = increment of movement, M = moment, and $d\theta$ = increment of rotation.

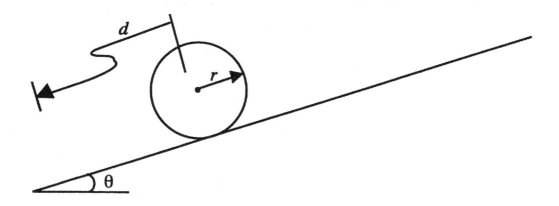

Figure 56. Rolling cylinder

Determine the rotational velocity of a cylinder after it has rolled a distance of d down a slope (Figure 56). Assume that the initial velocity = 0 and the cylinder rolls without sliding.

$$KE_1 + W_{1-2} = KE_2$$

$$0 + wd\sin\theta = \left(\frac{1}{2}\right)m\left(v_{cg}\right)^2 + \left(\frac{1}{2}\right)I_{cg}\omega^2$$

$$wd \sin \theta = \left(\frac{1}{2}\right)\left(\frac{w}{g}\right)(r\omega)^2 + \left(\frac{1}{2}\right)\left[\left(\frac{1}{2}\right)\left(\frac{w}{g}\right)r^2\right]\omega^2$$

$$wd \sin \theta = \left(\frac{3}{4}\right)\left(\frac{w}{g}\right)r^2\omega^2$$

Solving $\qquad \omega = \sqrt{\dfrac{(4gd \sin \theta)}{\left(3r^2\right)}}.$

Use Figure 57 as a second example. Determine the rotational velocity of cylinder A when it has traveled a distance d. Assume no sliding, weight and radius of both cylinders are the same, and the initial velocity = 0. The relationship of the rotational velocities is $\omega_B = 2\omega_A$.

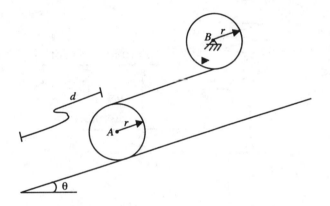

Figure 57. Two rolling cylinders

$$KE_1 + W_{1-2} = KE_2$$

$$0 + wd \sin \theta = \left(\frac{1}{2}\right)\left(\frac{w}{g}\right)(r\omega_A)^2 + \left(\frac{1}{2}\right)\left[\left(\frac{1}{2}\right)\left(\frac{w}{g}\right)r^2\right]\omega_A^2$$

$$+ \left(\frac{1}{2}\right)\left[\left(\frac{1}{2}\right)\left(\frac{w}{g}\right)r^2\right]\omega_B^2$$

$$wd \sin \theta = \left(\frac{7}{4}\right)\left(\frac{w}{g}\right)r^2\omega_A^2$$

Solving
$$\omega_A = \sqrt{\frac{(4gd\sin\theta)}{(7r^2)}} \ .$$

Mechanical Vibration

Simple harmonic motion results from a single mass vibrating about a position of equilibrium. The focus of this discussion is on problems that have a single degree of freedom, no damping, no forcing function, and a linear spring.

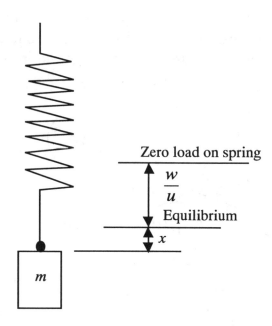

Figure 58. Simple harmonic motion

Suppose a mass is displaced a distance x from the position of equilibrium in the vertical plane (Figure 58). The unbalanced force and the force-acceleration relation give

$$F = ma$$

$$-kx = \frac{md^2x}{dt^2}$$

where k = spring constant, m = mass, x = displacement, and $\frac{d^2x}{dt^2}$ = acceleration of the mass. The differential equation is

$$\frac{md^2x}{dt^2} + kx = 0.$$

The solution of the differential equation gives

Position $\qquad x = x_m \sin\left[\sqrt{\frac{k}{m}}\, t + \theta\right]$

Velocity $\qquad v = \frac{dx}{dt} = x_m \sqrt{\frac{k}{m}}\cos\left[\sqrt{\frac{k}{m}}\, t + \theta\right]$

Acceleration $\qquad a = \frac{d^2x}{dt^2} = -x_m\left(\frac{k}{m}\right)\sin\left[\sqrt{\frac{k}{m}}\, t + \theta\right]$

Variables are x_m = maximum amplitude, θ = phase angle, t = time,

and $\sqrt{\dfrac{k}{m}}$ = angular velocity. Other quantities are:

Maximum values $\qquad x = x_m, v = x_m\sqrt{\frac{k}{m}}, a = x_m\left(\frac{k}{m}\right)$

Period $\qquad T = \dfrac{2\pi}{\sqrt{\dfrac{k}{m}}}$

Frequency $\qquad f = \dfrac{1}{T} = \dfrac{\sqrt{\dfrac{k}{m}}}{2\pi}$

Consider two examples. Maximum displacement = 0.050 m, k_1 = 5,000 N/m, k_2 = 4,000 N/m, and m = 60 kg.

For springs in parallel, the spring force is shown in Figure 59.

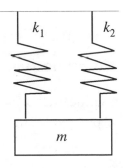

Figure 59. Springs in parallel

Assume the mass is moved a distance of one. For springs in parallel, the spring force is

$$k = k_1 + k_2 = 5,000 + 4,000 = 9,000 \text{ N/m}$$

Maximum values are $x = 0.05$ m, $v = 0.61$ m/sec, $a = 7.50$ m/sec^2. Maximum velocity occurs at zero displacement, and maximum acceleration occurs at maximum displacement. Period is 0.51 sec per cycle, and frequency is 1.95 cycles per sec.

Springs in series is illustrated in Figure 60.

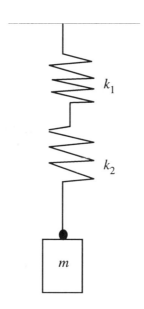

Figure 60. Springs in series

Assume a load = 1 is applied to the springs. Total displacement resulting from both springs is

$$\text{Displacement} = \frac{1}{k} = \frac{1}{k_1} + \frac{1}{k_2}.$$

The spring constant of two springs in series is $\dfrac{1}{k} = \dfrac{1}{4,000} + \dfrac{1}{5,000}$ and $k = 2,222$ N/m. Maximum values are $x_m = 0.05$ m, $v = 0.30$ m/sec, $a = 1.85$ m/sec^2. Period is 1.03 sec per cycle and frequency is 0.97 cycles per second.

VIBRATIONS

Free Vibration

A vibration describes an oscillatory motion of a body. A simple system is shown in the figure. A free vibration with no external forces is described by the equation:

$$y'' + \left(\frac{k}{m}\right)y = 0$$

where k is the spring constant.

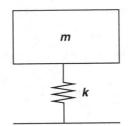

only vertical movement

If $\omega_n = \sqrt{\left(\dfrac{k}{n}\right)}$ is substituted into the equation, then the equation has the general solution:

$$y = A \sin \omega_n t + B \cos \omega_n t$$

or:

$$y = C \sin(\omega_n t + \varphi)$$

where:

$$C = \sqrt{\left(A^2 + B^2\right)} \text{ and } \tan\varphi = \frac{B}{A}.$$

In this representation, y is called the simple harmonic function of time, ω_n is the natural circular frequency, C is the amplitude of the displacement y, and φ is the phase angle. The simple harmonic motion function is periodic with a period of $\tau_n = \dfrac{2\pi}{\omega_n}$. The frequency, f_n is defined as

$$\frac{1}{\tau_n} = \frac{\omega_n}{2\pi}.$$

Damped Vibration

Consider the figure below, where the rate of extension is proportional to the force applied through the damping constant c. Thus the force is c times the rate of extension. Therefore, the system is described by the equation:

$$my'' + cy' + ky = 0$$

which has the arbitrary solution:

$$y = Ae^{rt}$$

Where A is an arbitrary constant and r is a characteristic parameter. Thus,

$$(mr^2 + cr + k)Ae^{rt} = 0$$

which is satisfied nontrivially with:

$$mr^2 + cr + k = 0.$$

The characteristic equation has two roots by:

$$r = \frac{-c}{2m} \pm \sqrt{\left(\frac{c}{2m}\right)^2 - \frac{k}{m}}$$

Except for the case in which $\left(\dfrac{c}{2m}\right)^2 = \dfrac{k}{m}$, the roots are distinct. If the roots are called r_1 and r_2, the general solution is:

$$y = A_1 e^{r_1 t} + A_2 e^{r_2 t}$$

If $\left(\dfrac{c}{2m}\right)^2 = \dfrac{k}{m}$, there is only one repeated root, $r = \dfrac{-c}{2m}$, then the general solution is:

$$y = A_1 e^{-(c/2m)t} + A_2 t e^{-(c/2m)t}$$

then:

$$A_1 = y_o \text{ and } A_2 = v_o + \left(\frac{c}{2m}\right)y_o$$

with the initial conditions, $y(0) = y_o$ and $y'(0) = v_o$.

In this case the damping is critical, that is, $c = c_{crit}$:

$$c_{crit} = 2\sqrt{km} = 2m\omega_d.$$

If $c > c_{crit}$, the system is overdamped or the damping is supercritical. The general solution is:

$$y = e^{-(c/2m)t}\left(A_1 \sin \omega_d t + A_2 \cos \omega_d t\right)$$

Forced Vibration

The differential equation for a system with a spring damper is:

$$my'' + cy' + ky = P\sin \omega t$$

The general solution is composed of two parts: a particular solution and a complementary solution. A particular solution may be of the form $y = Y \sin(\omega t - \varphi)$.

The general solution is of the form:

$$y = y_c(t) + Y \sin(\omega t - \varphi).$$

REVIEW PROBLEMS

PROBLEM 1

An electric motor is used to lift a 7120 N block at a rate of 3.05 m/ min. How much electric power (watts) must be supplied to the motor, if the motor lifting the block is 60 percent efficient?

SOLUTION

The power requirement of the motor is the power exerted in lifting the block. The power exerted by the motor is the same as the power exerted by the force F in lifting the block. This is

$$P = Fv.$$

Since the block is moving at a constant velocity the power exerted by the motor is

$$P = Fv = (7{,}120)\left(\frac{3.05}{60}\right) = 359 \text{ Nm/sec}$$

or, in terms of horsepower,

$$P = \frac{267}{550} = 0.485 \text{ hp.}$$

This is the power required to lift the block at the velocity required, and this is the power that the motor has to produce. However, since the motor is only 60 percent efficient, the power input to the motor must be greater. Thus,

$$P_{in} = \frac{P_{out}}{\varepsilon}$$

or $$P_{in} = \frac{0.485}{0.60} = 0.81 \text{ hp}$$

and the power input in terms of the electric power supplied to the motor is

$$P_{in} = 0.81 \times 746 = 605 \text{ watts.}$$

PROBLEM 2

Two similar cars, A and B, are connected rigidly together and have a combined mass of 4 kg. Car C has a mass of 1 kg initially; A and B have a speed of 5 m/sec; and C is at rest as shown in Figure 61.

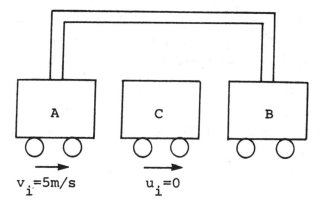

Figure 61. Cars rigidly connected

Assuming a perfectly inelastic collision between A and C, what is the final speed of the system?

SOLUTION

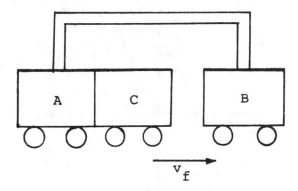

Figure 62. Inelastic collision

A perfectly inelastic collision means that the two colliding bodies stick together and move with the same velocity after the collision, as shown in Figure 62. From the Principle of Conservation of Linear Momentum, we may write

Total Momentum Before Collision = Total Momentum After Collision

Thus,

$$4(v_i) + 0 = (4 + 1)\,(v_f).$$

Solving for the final velocity, v_f:

$$v_f = \frac{4}{5}v_i = \frac{4}{5}(5 \text{ m/sec}) = 4 \text{ m/sec.}$$

PROBLEM 3

Two masses, $m_1 = a$ kg and $m_2 = b$ kg, have velocities $u_1 = b$ m/sec in the $+ x$ direction and $u_2 = a$ m/sec in the $+ y$ direction. They collide and stick together. What is the measure of the angle to the horizontal?

SOLUTION

The total x and y components of linear momentum must be conserved after the collision. The mass of the body resulting after the collision is

$$m = m_1 + m_2$$

and the velocity v is inclined at angle to the x-axis. We know that the total momentum vector is unchanged, and we can write down the x and y components of momentum (shown in Figure 63).

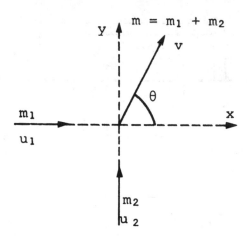

Figure 63. Components of momentum

	INITIAL MOMENTUM	**FINAL MOMENTUM**
x component	$m_1 u_1$	$(m_1 + m_2)v \cos \theta$
y component	$m_2 u_2$	$(m_1 + m_2)v \sin \theta$

Thus,

$$m_1 u_1 = (m_1 + m_2)v \cos \theta$$

$$m_2 u_2 = (m_1 + m_2)v \sin \theta$$

$$\therefore \tan \theta = \frac{m_2 u_2}{m_1 u_1}$$

$$= \frac{b \times a}{a \times b} = 1$$

Hence, $\theta = 45°$.

PROBLEM 4

A boat travels directly upstream in a river, moving with constant but unknown speed v with respect to the water. At the start of this trip upstream, a bottle is dropped over the side. After 15 minutes the boat turns around and heads downstream. It catches up with the bottle when the bottle has drifted one mile downstream from the point at which it was dropped into the water. What is the current in the stream?

SOLUTION

Consider a coordinate system at rest with respect to the water. Then the water is at rest and it is the banks which appear to move upstream. The bottle is at rest with respect to the water. From the point of view of this coordinate system, it is just as though the boat were moving at speed v in a perfectly still pond. We can see that the return trip downstream must also take 15 minutes. Once it is known that the round trip takes a half hour, we can see that the current in the river must be 2 miles per hour since the bottle moves one mile in a half hour.

PROBLEM 5

If the coefficient of sliding friction for steel on ice is 0.05, what force is required to keep a man weighing 150 pounds moving at constant speed along the ice?

SOLUTION

To keep the man moving at constant velocity, we must oppose the force of friction tending to retard his motion with an equal but opposite force (see Figure 64).

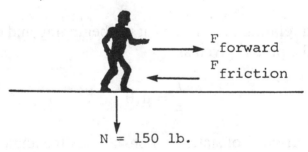

Figure 64. Constant velocity on ice

The force of friction is given by:

$$F = \mu_{kinetic}\, N.$$

By Newton's Third Law

$$F_{forward} = F_{friction}.$$

Therefore,

$$F_{\text{forward}} = \mu_{\text{kinetic}} N$$

$$F_{\text{forward}} = (0.05)(667 \text{ N}) = 33.4 \text{ N}$$

PROBLEM 6

In Figure 65, a man applies a force F of 880 N to a belt, wrapped four times around a pipe PQ, to draw water from a well. Given that the belt is just about to slip, calculate a) the coefficient of static friction between the belt and the pipe, and b) F, if the belt is wrapped twice around the pipe.

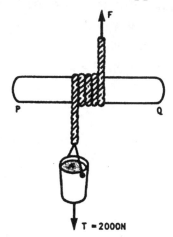

Figure 65. Belt around a pipe

SOLUTION

The equation relating the tensions at the beginning and end of the belt wrapped around the pipe is given as

$$ln\frac{T}{F} = \mu_s \theta \qquad (1)$$

where μ_s is the coefficient of static friction and θ is the angle subtended by the belt when in contact with the pipe. θ is given in radians and is multiplied by the number of turns that the belt is wrapped on the pipe.

Thus,

$$\theta = 4(2\pi \text{ rad}) = 25.1 \text{ rad.}$$

From equation (1),

$$\mu_s = \ell n\left(\frac{T}{F}\right)\left(\frac{1}{25.1 \text{ rad}}\right)$$

$$= \left[\ell n\left(\frac{2,000 \text{ N}}{880 \text{ N}}\right)\right]\left(\frac{1}{25.1 \text{ rad}}\right)$$

$$\mu_s = 0.033$$

b) From equation (1),

$$\frac{T}{F} = e^{\mu_s\theta}$$

or
$$F = \frac{T}{e^{\mu_s\theta}} \qquad (2)$$

Now $\theta = 2$ turns $(2\pi \text{ rad}) = 12.6$ rad.

Calculating F from equation (2) gives

$$F = \frac{2,000 \text{ N}}{e^{(0.033)(12.6)}}$$

$$= \frac{2,000}{1.52} = 1,315.8 \text{ N}$$

PROBLEM 7

A skid weighing 500 N and carrying 9,500 N of paper is being pulled up onto a loading dock (Figure 66). The static and kinetic coefficients of friction are $m_s = 0.30$ and $m_k = 0.20$, respectively. What is the magnitude of the force F (1) when the skid begins to move upward; (2) while the skid is moving; and (3) to prevent the skid from sliding downward?

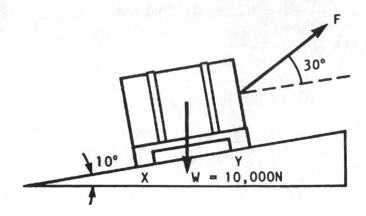

Figure 66. Loading a skid

SOLUTION

This problem may be solved by resolving forces into normal and tangential compounds with respect to the incline, to find values of the frictional force. However, this procedure actually does more than necessary. A more direct, geometrical procedure is possible. It is based on the fact that the combined normal and frictional forces, that is, the reaction of the incline on the skid, is directed at an angle ϕ defined by the friction coefficient μ and the equation $\tan \phi = \mu$.

This magnitude of the combined weight W of the skid and paper is

$$W = 500 \text{ N} + 9{,}500 \text{ N} = 10 \text{ kN}$$

The free-body diagram for part (1) is shown in Figure 67.

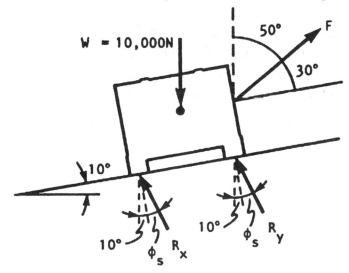

Figure 67. Free-body diagram

Noting that R_x and R_y have the same direction (same angle of friction ϕ_s), draw a force triangle including the weight W, the force F, and the sum $R = R_x + R_y$. The triangle is closed since there is no acceleration. The direction of R will be different for each part of this problem. For part (1)

$$\tan\phi_s = \mu_s = 0.30$$
$$\phi_s = 16.7°$$

This angle is measured from the normal, as shown in Figure 68, so the actual direction of R is given by $10° + 16.7° = 26.7°$. The force triangle, then, is

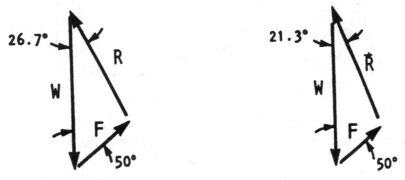

Figure 68. Force diagrams

Using the law of sines,

$$\frac{F}{\sin 26.7°} = \frac{W}{\sin[180° - (50° + 26.7°)]}$$
$$F = 4.78 \text{ kN, direction shown}$$

The situation is similar for part (2) except now the kinetic coefficient must be used. Therefore,

$$\tan\phi_k = \mu_k = 0.20$$
$$\phi_k = 11.3°$$

The direction of $\vec{R}$ is given by $10° + 11.3° = 21.3°$. Consequently,

$$\frac{F}{\sin 21.3°} = \frac{W}{\sin[180° - (50° + 21.3°)]}$$
$$F = 3.29 \text{ kN, direction shown}$$

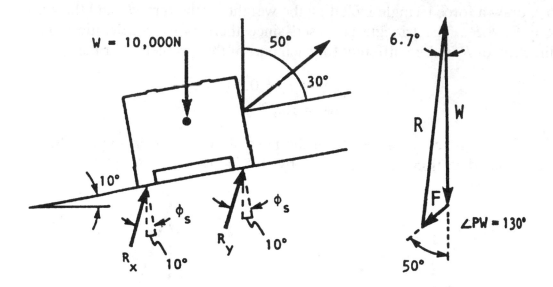

Figure 69. Motion of the skid   **Figure 70. Force triangle**

For part (3), consider the frictional force to be opposite the downward motion of the skid, so that the sense of R_x and R_y has changed considerably (see Figure 69). Again, $\phi_s = 16.7°$, but now the resulting direction of R is given by $16.7° - 10° = 6.7°$. The force triangle for this situation is shown in Figure 70.

Using the law of sines,

$$\frac{F}{\sin 6.7°} = \frac{W}{\sin\left[180° - (130° + 6.7°)\right]}$$
$$F = 1.7501 \text{ kN}$$

However, notice in Figure 70 that F is directed from the head of the vector W to the tail of the vector R, as was done in Figure 68, and is now pointing downward. In other words, it would take a push of more than 1.7501 kN along the direction of F to start the skid moving. Thus, the answer to (3) is that no force F is needed to keep the skid from sliding down; it will not slide down under its own weight.

PROBLEM 8

A small pump is mounted on a concrete slab which, in turn, rests on four concrete posts (Figure 71). Two of the posts have settled slightly, so that the slab must be leveled. The foreman decides to raise the low side with two large wedges located as drawn on the figure. Fortunately, there is a concrete floor on which the bottom wedge can be fastened. If μ_s between the two wedges is 0.4 and between the wedge and the concrete 0.6, and if the motor slab transmits a 4450 N vertical force to the wedge, determine the force P required for lifting the slab.

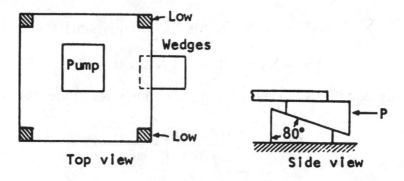

Top view   Side view

Figure 71. Pump mounted on a concrete slab

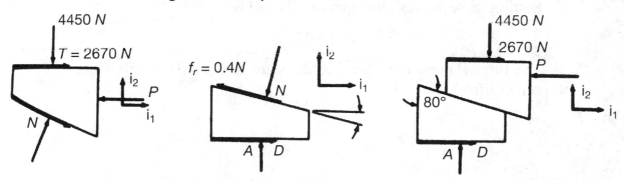

Figure 72. Free-body diagrams

SOLUTION

The free-body diagrams are shown in Figure 72. Notice that part (c), showing the two wedge system, has only the external forces shown. The forces between the wedges are equal and opposite and cancel out by Newton's Third Law. If the sum of all the external forces are set equal to zero, the system is in equilibrium. That is, nothing moves. Any greater force will start lifting the slab.

$$^{+\downarrow}\sum F_{i_1} = 0; \qquad 2670 + D - P = 0 \qquad (1)$$

$$^{+\uparrow}\sum F_{i_2} = 0; \qquad -4{,}450 + A = 0$$

so $\qquad\qquad\qquad A = 4{,}450 \text{ N}.$

The bottom wedge, as described, is fastened to the floor. The sum of the forces must be equal to zero throughout. This means that the force D is entirely reactive and does not depend on any coefficient of friction or the normal force A. The equilibrium equations are, from diagram (2b),

$$^{+\downarrow}\sum F_{i_1} = 0; \qquad D - 0.4 \cos 10° - N \sin 10° = 0, \tag{2}$$

$$^{+\uparrow}\sum F_{i_2} = 0; \qquad A - N \cos 10° + 0.4\, N \sin 10° = 0$$

or
$$4{,}450 - N \cos 10° + 0.4\, N \sin 10° = 0. \tag{3}$$

Solving equations (2) and (3) simultaneously for D yields

$$D = 4{,}450 \frac{0.4 \cos 10° + \sin 10°}{\cos 10° - \ 0.4 \sin 10°}$$
$$= 2{,}757 \ \text{N}$$

Putting these values into equation (1) yields

$$P = 5{,}421 \ \text{N}$$

The force P needed by this method is greater than the 4,450 N needed for a direct lift.

FE/EIT

Fundamentals of Engineering: AM Exam

CHAPTER 7

Mechanics of Materials

CHAPTER 7

MECHANICS OF MATERIALS

The study of Mechanics of Materials covers two important areas: 1) dynamics, which covers bodies in motion, and 2) statics, which deals with bodies of matter at rest.

For a basic review of statics, see Chapter 5. We will continue the discussion of statics here. When a body is held at rest and exposed to external forces (such as gravity), the tendency of the body is to change shape or to be deformed. Stress can be defined as a body's internal resistance to these external forces. This chapter will cover various aspects of stress and the resultant deformation—strain. This will include its application to bodies such as beams and columns.

STRESS AND STRAIN

Remember that **stress** is thought of in terms of unit stress and total stress. The total resistance to an external force (expressed in pounds, kips, or newtons) or other force dimension is called total stress. The resistance over a unit area of a body is called unit stress.

Unit stress is expressed in units of pounds per square inch or kips per square inch or other force per unit area. In this review, stress refers to unit stress. The various types of stress are 1) direct or simple stress, which can be in the form of tension, compression, or shear; 2) indirect stress, which applies to bending or torsion; and 3) combined stress, which is any combination of stresses 1) and 2).

To review, direct stress (simple) is developed under direct loading, such as simple tension and compression. When the load is applied (applied force) axially (axial loading), we have simple tension and compression. When equal, opposite, and parallel forces cause two surfaces to slide relative to each other, simple shear occurs.

We can calculate the magnitude of simple stress from the formula:

$$\text{Stress, } \sigma = \frac{F(\text{Force})}{A(\text{Area})},$$

where: F = External force causing stress (i.e., N)
           A = Area on which stress is acting (m²)
           σ = Average unit stress (i.e., N/m²)

While there are several types of stress/strain responses of materials when subjected to one or more loads, for our purposes, we will refer to the most useful behavioral response, which is a **linear elastic response**. Linear elastic response is characterized by stress proportional to strain, independent of time, and strain recoverable upon load removal. This response is called **Hooke's Law**.

If a beam is undergoing simple tension or compression and has the same cross-sectional area throughout, then the stress will be the same throughout the length of the body, as shown in Figure 1.

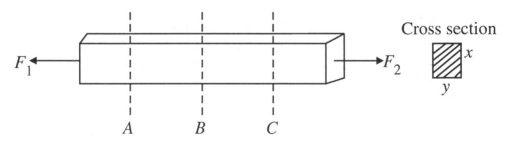

$$\text{Stress at } A, B, \text{ or } C = \frac{F(\text{N})}{A(\text{m}^2)}$$

Figure 1. Stress on a beam of uniform cross-sectional area

However, if the cross section varies in total area as in Figure 2, then the largest stress will be carried on the smallest area. This is because the load must be carried by all areas of the body—otherwise failure will occur.

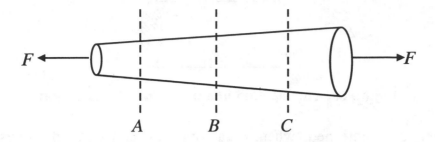

$$\sigma_C < \sigma_B < \sigma_A;\ \text{Area } A < \text{Area } B < \text{Area } C$$

Figure 2. Stress on a body of varying cross-sectional area

Note that in Figures 1 and 2, the areas resisting the external forces are **perpendicular** to the direction of the application of those forces. It is also important to note that we assume no bending occurs in the beam under compression. Therefore, the force is applied through the centroidal axis of the straight member.

As stated earlier, the resultant deformation of a rigid body is called **strain** and can be measured from the formula:

$$\text{Unit Strain } (\varepsilon) = \frac{\text{New length} - \text{Original length}}{\text{Original length}}.$$

Strain is always related to these simple stresses—tension, compression, and shear. Remember that the deformation is always measured in the direction of the applied force.

The elongation of an axially loaded body experiencing normal stress is:

$$\delta = \frac{FL_o}{EA}$$

where L_o is the original length of the body and E is the modulus of elasticity.

SHEAR

In the **Stress and Strain** section, we examined the resultant stress when force is applied to the area of a rigid body in a perpendicular direction, as in Figure 3.

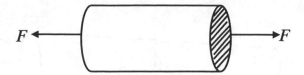

Figure 3. Force applied in a perpendicular direction

However, as mentioned, when equal opposite and parallel forces cause two surfaces to slide relative to each other, simple **shear** occurs. In other words, when the resisting area is **parallel** to the applied force (external), simple shear develops.

In Figure 4, the two pieces of wood are held together by a simple wooden dowel.

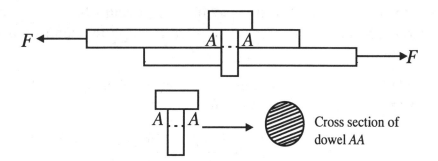

Figure 4. Resisting area is parallel to the applied force

The circular area, *AA*, of the dowel is subject to shear strain by the force, *F*. In this case, the magnitude of the stress is determined by:

$$\text{Stress, } \sigma = \frac{F(\text{Force})}{A(\text{Area})}.$$

Of course, if the dowel were to fail, it would shear across the surface, *A*, as shown in Figure 5.

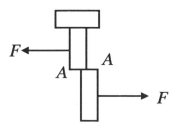

Figure 5. Failure across surface *A*

Another form of shear would occur in an operation such as hole punching, as in Figure 6.

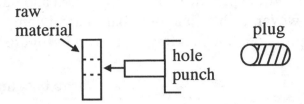

Figure 6. Hole punching

In this case, the shear area is taken to be the cylindrical surface of the plug, and the shear stress is still calculated by:

$$\sigma = \frac{F}{A},$$

except A is now the outer cylindrical surface.

TENSION AND COMPRESSION

Tension occurs when a body such as the block in Figure 7 is acted on by two equal and opposite forces, F. Tension will cause the block to tend to stretch or be pulled apart.

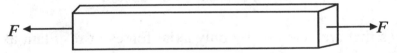

Figure 7. Block in tension

If the forces act in the opposite direction from those in Figure 7, then **compression** occurs (shown in Figure 8). These compressive forces tend to crush or shorten the body.

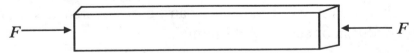

Figure 8. A block in compression

Remember that, although the forces acting on a body are equal and occurring in equilibrium, tension or compression is always present. These forces are acting in an axial direction.

It is important to distinguish between axial tension and axial compression. In axial tension, the length of a long body subjected to axial tension will not normally be a factor. However, in axial compression, length plays an important role. Obviously a long length of bar subjected to axial compression will experience both compression and buckling, as shown in Figure 9a. However, a short length of bar in axial compression will only experience compression, not buckling, as shown in Figure 9b.

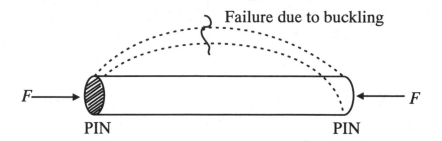

(a) Compression and buckling on a long bar

(b) Compression only on a short bar

Figure 9. Axial compression

Bodies that are acted on by only axial forces or resultant axial forces are called two-force members.

BEAMS

A member that bends elastically in order to resist transverse forces and loads is called a **beam**. To examine our beams, we'll agree that the value of unknown forces or moments can be discovered if we apply the following condition of static equilibrium:

(1) The sum of all forces acting on the beam in the x and y direction is zero:

$$\sum F_x = 0, \ \sum F_y = 0$$

(2) The sum of all moments acting on the beam is zero:

$$\sum M = 0.$$

These conditions apply to a statically determinate beam only. Examples of statically determinate beams are:

(1) A simple supported beam with supports at each end and forces applied in between, Figure 10a,

(2) A cantilever beam supported at one end (i.e., by a wall or clamp) with force(s) applied along its length, Figure 10b, and

(3) An overhanging beam with the force(s) applied between the end of the beam and the support point, Figure 10c.

In all cases, we assume that the forces are known values, and the resistance (or reaction at the supports) and the wall moments are unknown.

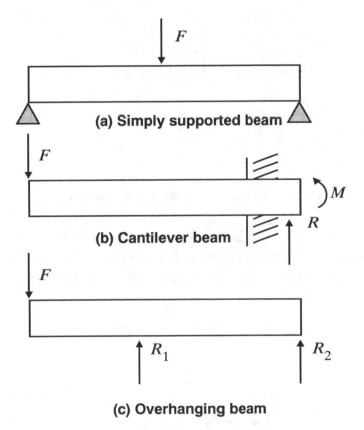

(a) Simply supported beam

(b) Cantilever beam

(c) Overhanging beam

Figure 10. Beam supports

Let's look at a simply supported beam when a load is applied, as in Figure 11. First, remember that the sum of all forces equals zero, and the sum of all moments equals zero.

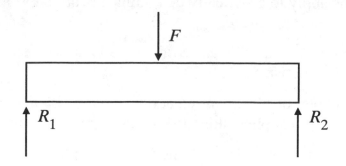

Figure 11. Load applied to a simply supported beam

Under loading, assuming that the elastic limit of the material is not exceeded, the bar will bend as shown in Figure 12.

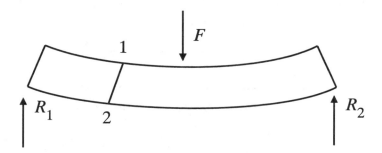

Figure 12. Beam bends upon loading

As we can see, some of the bar is in compression and some of it is in tension. In addition to bending, certain sections of the bar are trying to slip past one another in shear. This shearing tendency must be resisted by the material fiber.

If we cut the beam, along section 1 – 2, we see the acting forces more clearly.

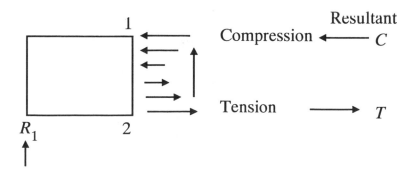

Figure 13. Section 1 – 2 of loaded beam

Because the greatest forces of compression and tension lie along the top and bottom edges of the beam, a resultant arrow for total compression and total tension will be placed at the outer edges. All forces in the *xy* plane equal zero:

$$C - T = 0; C = T$$

The resultant compression and tension are equal, but act in opposite directions. This effect is a couple (equal, opposite, and parallel forces) which produces a resisting moment. This resisting moment is equal and opposite to the moment produced by R_1, around the opposite end of beam $1 - 2$. Otherwise, the sum of all moments would not be zero. (Neglect the weight of the beam.)

For ease of discussion, use the beam portion to the left of a section in determining the solutions to beam problems. Referring to Figure 11, we apply the condition to calculate the unknown reactions:

$$\sum F_y = 0$$

therefore

$$R_1 + R_2 - F = 0, \ R_1 + R_2 = F.$$

Because F is centrally located on the beam:

$$R_1 = \frac{F}{2}$$

and

$$R_2 = \frac{F}{2}.$$

In cases where the load is uniformly distributed over the entire length, the result is the same. A uniform load is usually indicated by weight per linear measurement. The total uniform load may be calculated by multiplying the uniform load by the total length of the beam.

For cantilever beams, such as the one shown in Figure 14, the wall must carry the load on the beam, and the resistance at the wall is equal to the load itself, whether the load is uniform or concentrated:

$$F - R = 0$$

therefore

$$R = F.$$

Because we know that the beam is in static equilibrium and that the total moment is zero, we can calculate the moment at the wall, M. Recall that a moment is force multiplied by distance:

$$F\ell - M = 0$$

For a uniform load, assume that the force is acting at the midpoint of the load on the beam. In this case:

$$F\left(\frac{\ell}{2}\right) - M = 0$$

$$F\left(\frac{\ell}{2}\right) = M$$

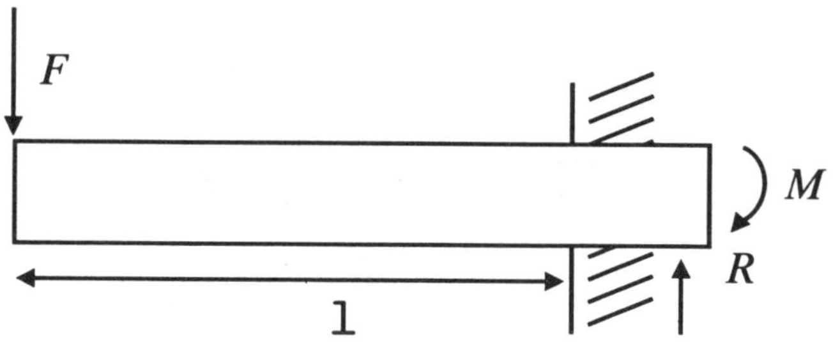

Figure 14. Cantilever beam

Knowing the shear force at a section of a beam can also be helpful in its design. The shear force is simply the sum of all forces acting vertically, to the left of that particular section that we are examining. To find shear force, it is helpful to plot a shear force diagram. All external forces are plotted along the beam. Upward forces are considered positive and downward forces are given a negative sign. In other words, if the force acts upward on the left side of a cross section of interest or downward on the right side, that is considered **positive shear**. If the force acts in the opposite direction, that is **negative shear**. Cases of positive and negative shear are illustrated in Figure 15.

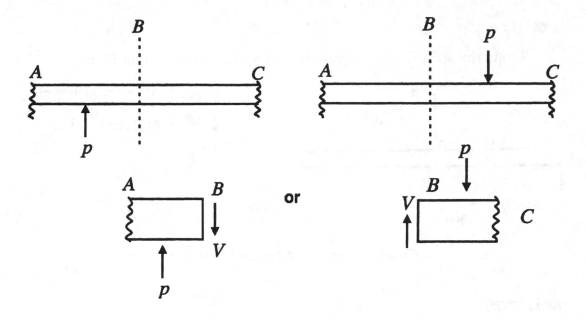

(a) Positive shear

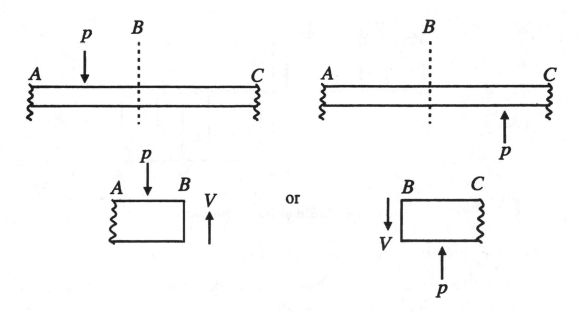

(b) Negative shear

Figure 15. Shear stresses

EXAMPLE

Draw the shear force diagram for the system as shown in Figure 16.

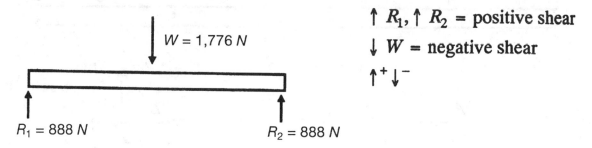

$\uparrow R_1, \uparrow R_2$ = positive shear

$\downarrow W$ = negative shear

$\uparrow^+ \downarrow^-$

Figure 16. Stresses applied to beam

SOLUTION

Figure 17 shows the correct shear force diagram for this problem.

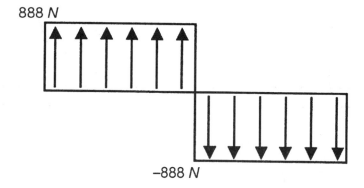

Figure 17. Shear force diagram

Of course, directly at each support, the shear forces are zero.

In the case of a uniformly distributed load, the shear force diagram is developed by calculating the resistance at each end and drawing a line between the endpoints. We know the shear forces acting on each section will change incrementally as we move along the beam resulting in a line passing through the midpoint of the beam.

EXAMPLE

Draw the shear force diagram for the beam under uniform loading as shown in Figure 18.

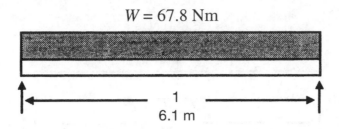

$$W = 67.8 \text{ Nm}$$

1
6.1 m

Figure 18. Beam under uniform loading

SOLUTION

Figure 19 shows the correct shear force diagram for this problem.

$$\text{Total WT} = 4,440 \text{ N}$$
$$R_1 + R_2 = 4,440 \text{ N}$$
$$R_1 = R_2 = 2,220 \text{ N}$$

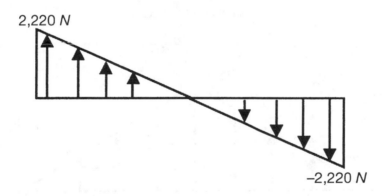

2,220 *N*

–2,220 *N*

Figure 19. Shear force diagram for beam under uniform loading

BENDING MOMENT DIAGRAM

A **bending moment diagram** is used to illustrate bending moment changes along a beam. The sum of the moments due to forces acting to the left of a section will give the bending moment for that section of the beam. In order to maintain equilibrium, these external bending moments must be resisted by the beam material. Bending occurs as the beam material undergoes stress and resists these bending moments.

EXAMPLE

Draw the bending moment diagram for the beam as shown in Figure 20. The 8,880 N force is applied at the midpoint of the beam.

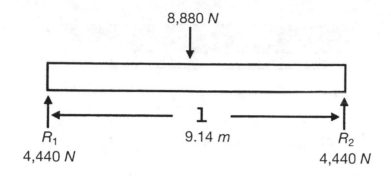

8,880 N

R_1
4,440 N

1
9.14 m

R_2
4,440 N

Figure 20. Forces applied to beam to induce bending

SOLUTION

Obviously the bending moment is greatest at the center of the beam:

$$\sum M = 0$$
$$M = (4.57)(4,440)$$
$$= 20,290 \text{ Nm}$$

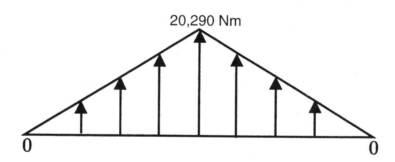

20,290 Nm

0   0

Figure 21. Bending moment diagram

If the effect of the bending moment causes a concave upward shape, this is called **positive bending moment**, as illustrated in Figure 22.

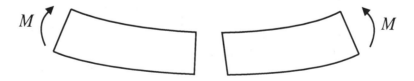

M M

Figure 22. Positive bending moment

If the effect is a downward convex bending movement, this is called a **negative bending movement**, as shown in Figure 23.

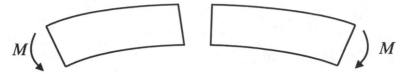

Figure 23. Negative bending moment

Figure 24 summarizes the shear and bending moment diagrams for two common types of loading.

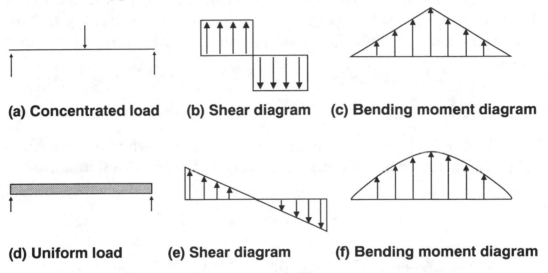

(a) Concentrated load **(b) Shear diagram** **(c) Bending moment diagram**

(d) Uniform load **(e) Shear diagram** **(f) Bending moment diagram**

Figure 24. Shear and bending diagram summary

Beams which are loaded with both concentrated and distributed loads, as in the following example, necessarily have more complicated bending moment and shear diagrams.

The maximum stress along a cross section of a beam is along the outer edges, and the stress is zero along the neutral axis, as shown in Figure 25.

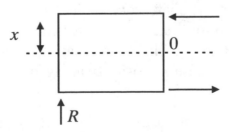

Figure 25. Stresses on the cross section of a beam

The maximum fiber stress, σ_F, is:

$$\sigma_F = \frac{M}{Z}$$

where Z, the section modulus, is:

$$Z = \frac{I_c}{C}.$$

The centroidal moment of inertia of the beam's cross section is denoted I_c in the equation above. The distance from the neutral axis to the top or bottom surface (most distant from the neutral axis) is the quantity C. Note that the moment of inertia is generally listed in the table form for common objects.

TORSION

When two equal and opposite twisting moments, which exist in parallel planes, act upon a shaft, then the shaft is said to be in **torsion**.

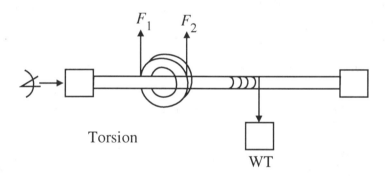

Figure 26. Torsion

A shaft in torsion may be rotating or it may be stationary. If it is rotating, it will do so in a uniform manner, such as a hoist. In the above figure, looking down the shaft from the left-hand end, if F_2 is greater than F_1, the shaft will tend to rotate in a counterclockwise direction. Because of the weight attached to the shaft, the shaft will also tend to rotate in a clockwise direction. These opposite twisting movements put the shaft in **torsion**.

The twisting moment, or torque, has units of in-lb or N-m. Referring to Figure 26 above, if F_2 is 2225 N and F_1 is 890 N and the pulley radius is 0.203 m, then the torque (T) is:

$$T = (2,225 \text{ N} - 890 \text{ N}) \times 0.203 \text{ m}$$

$$= 271 \text{ Nm}$$

If we assume that the system is in equilibrium and that the radius of the shaft is 0.051 m., then the weight (WT) equals 5,340 N. In a shaft with several pulleys on it, the torque available along the length of the shaft will vary according to each pulley size.

Torsion shearing stress occurs when any cross-sectional area of the shaft tends to shear across the adjacent face due to the torsion applied to the body. The resistance of the material fibers per unit area is torsional shearing stress. Examine the torque wrench on the lug nut of the wheel shown in Figure 27.

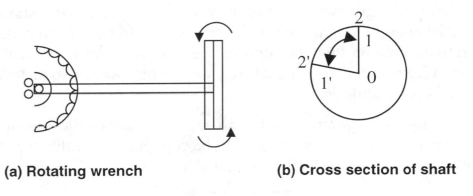

(a) Rotating wrench   (b) Cross section of shaft

Figure 27. Torque wrench

The elongation 1-1' is proportional to the distance from the center of the shaft. Therefore, 2-2' is greater than 1-1' in deformation. If the shear stress at 2 is $6.89 \times 10^7 \text{ N/m}^2$ and the radius from $0 \rightarrow 2$ is 0.051 m., then the shearing stress at a point halfway between 0 and 2 would equal half that amount or $3.45 \times 10^7 \text{N/m}^2$.

If we define σ_s as the maximum shearing stress, due to torsion, at the outer fiber of a uniform, solid circular member (in N/m^2), then to find the maximum safe shearing stress use:

$$\sigma_s = \frac{16T}{\pi d^3},$$

for a hollow circular shaft, where d_o is the outer diameter and d_i is the inner diameter:

$$\sigma_s = \frac{16Td_o}{\pi\left(d_o{}^4 - d_i{}^4\right)}.$$

COLUMNS

A body or member, which is in compression (axial loading), is referred to as a **column**. Compression of a short beam may be determined using the familiar equation F/A. For a relatively long column, of course, material defects, misalignment, and unknown initial stresses will affect the behavior of the material and the maximum load. Localized buckling or sudden bending are typical sources of failure in columns.

Because of the previously mentioned factors, maximum safe axial loads are found using several column design factors that determine the shape and size of the column. For our purposes in this discussion, both ends of the column are pinned or fixed.

Column length is a very important factor in determining maximum load. Also, cross-sectional area and moment of inertia can be important in determining column strength. However, because the moment of inertia can be found from the cross-sectional area, we combine these two factors into the radius of gyration (r).

The radius of gyration is the distance from the axis to a point in a plane where all the area is imagined to be concentrated so that the movement of inertia is unchanged, as illustrated in Figure 28.

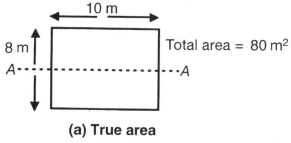

(a) True area

or

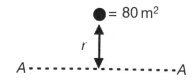

(b) Idealized schematic of area

Figure 28. Radius of gyration

Then the radius of gyration, r, equals:

$$r = \sqrt{\frac{I}{A}},$$

where I is the moment of inertia, and A is the total area as shown in the figure. Therefore, along with end conditions, factors governing column strength include 1) length and 2) radius of gyration. The ratio of length to radius of gyration is the slenderness ratio:

$$\text{Slenderness Ratio} = \frac{\ell}{r}.$$

There are generally three types of compression bodies — short, intermediate, and long—depending on their slenderness ratio. Typical slenderness ratios range from 80 to 120. In short compression bodies, the slenderness ratio $\frac{\ell}{r}$ has no effect on load performance, and the ultimate stress of the material is found from the equation:

$$\sigma = \frac{F}{A}.$$

In long columns, the length is of primary importance because slender columns can fail in buckling. Their strength can be defined by the Euler formula:

$$\sigma = \frac{\pi^2 E}{\left(\frac{\ell}{r}\right)^2},$$

where E is the modulus of elasticity, in units of N/m^2 (or appropriate equivalent units), and the column ends are pinned. The effective (or critical) slenderness ratio takes other end mount configurations into account using the end restraint coefficient C as follows:

$$\text{effective slenderness ratio} = \frac{C\ell}{r}.$$

End restraint coefficients are listed in Figure 29 for various end mount configurations. Note that for equivalent cases, the end mount configuration in Figure 29a is the strongest followed by the configuration in Figure 29d, Figure 29c, and Figure 29b.

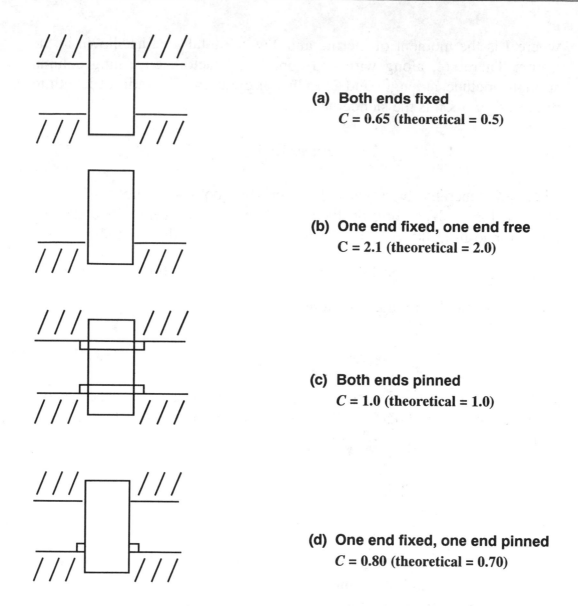

(a) Both ends fixed
$C = 0.65$ (theoretical = 0.5)

(b) One end fixed, one end free
$C = 2.1$ (theoretical = 2.0)

(c) Both ends pinned
$C = 1.0$ (theoretical = 1.0)

(d) One end fixed, one end pinned
$C = 0.80$ (theoretical = 0.70)

Figure 29. End restraint coefficients, *C*

COMBINED STRESSES

In the earlier sections of this chapter, it was shown that direct axial loading or bending can induce tensile (or compressive) stresses. In addition, it was shown that torsion or direct shearing forces can cause shear stress. When the same kind of stresses act simultaneously on a specific area, these stresses may be added to produce a **combined** effect. If these stresses act along the same line (**collinear**), then their resultant may be found **algebraically**. These stresses must be added **vectorially** if they do not act along the same line. For further information on resolving concurrent force systems into resultants, consult the chapter on statics.

In situations of combined tension or compression, we will demonstrate the principle of **superposition**. For this purpose, combined axial and bending stresses in beams will be examined. This method can also be used for combined direct and torsional shear situations. Examine the beam in Figure 30, with a uniformly distributed load and subjected to the axial tensile force F.

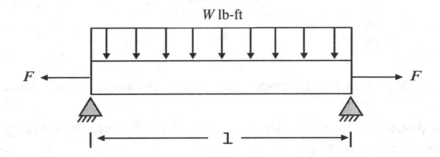

Figure 30. Uniform load distributed on a beam subjected to axial tensile forces

To determine the combined stresses at any given point, first determine the stresses due individually to axial loading and to the uniform load and superimpose their effects to get the combined result.

The tensile stress due to the axial force F is:

$$\sigma_1 = \frac{F}{A},$$

where A is the cross section of the beam and it is assumed that σ_1 acts equally at all points on the cross sections, as shown in the next figure.

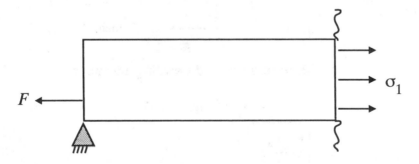

Figure 31. Tensile stress on beam

The uniform load W causes the beam to bend, which induces a stress at each cross section. The stresses vary from maximum compression at the top of the beam to maximum tension at the bottom of the beam, as shown in Figure 32.

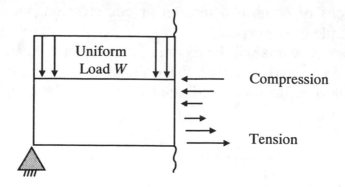

Figure 32. Tensile and compressive stresses due to uniform load *W*

As discussed in an earlier section of this chapter, the bending stress (maximum fiber stress) is:

$$\sigma_2 = \frac{M}{\left(\dfrac{I_c}{C}\right)}.$$

For design purposes, use the maximum values of σ_2 located at the extreme outer fibers of the beam. Also, note that for a uniformly loaded beam, on a simple span, the bending moment is greatest at the midpoint of the beam, which is also where the greatest stress values are located.

Axial and bending stresses are combined in Figure 33.

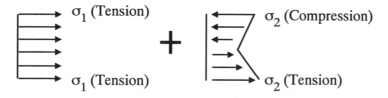

(a) Addition of axial and bending stresses

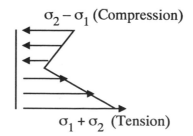

(b) Resultant stress

Figure 33. Combining stresses

Algebraically:

$$\sigma_{Total} = \sigma_1 \pm \sigma_2$$

or

$$\sigma_{Total} = \frac{F}{A} \pm \frac{M}{\left(\dfrac{I_c}{C}\right)}.$$

To determine sign convention, in this case, examine the top and bottom fibers of the beam to determine whether they are in tension or compression. In the case of the bottom fibers, they are in tension due to axial load F and also in tension due to the bending moment so it is proper to add both resultant stresses, as shown in Figure 34.

$$\sigma_{Bottom} = \frac{F}{A} + \frac{M}{\left(\dfrac{I_c}{C}\right)}$$

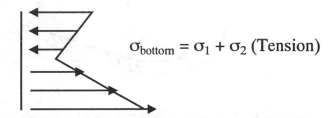

$$\sigma_{bottom} = \sigma_1 + \sigma_2 \text{ (Tension)}$$

Figure 34. Resultant stresses on bottom fibers of beam

In the case of the top fibers, they are in tension due to axial load F, but in compression due to the bending moment, so it is necessary to subtract one stress value from the other, as in Figure 35.

$$\sigma_{Top} = \frac{F}{A} - \frac{M}{\left(\dfrac{I_c}{C}\right)}$$

$$\sigma_{Top} = \sigma_2 - \sigma_1 \text{(Compression)}$$

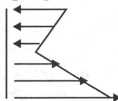

Figure 35. Resultant stresses on top fibers of beam

Remember to always identify tension or compression at the beam fibers to help maintain proper sign convention.

THIN-WALLED PRESSURE VESSELS

When a pressure vessel has a diameter at least ten times the thickness of its wall, it is considered a **thin-walled pressure vessel**, such as a boiler drum. The forces tending to rupture the vessel act perpendicular to the surface of the vessel. These forces tend to rupture the vessel along the seam parallel to the element of the shell longitudinally and along a seam corresponding to the vessel's circumference transversely.

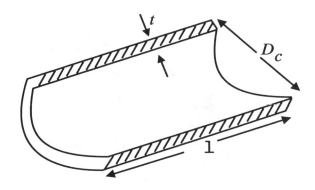

Figure 36. Longitudinal section of a thin-walled pressure vessel

Although D_c is shown as an outer diameter, as this section deals with thin-walled vessels, outer or inner diameter may be used in equations.

As shown in Figure 37, the pressure is distributed uniformly along the curved surface. Only components acting perpendicular to the longitudinal surface tend to cause failure.

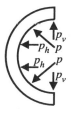

(a) Uniform pressure

(b) Vertical and horizontal components of the uniform pressure

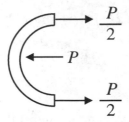

(c) Effect of all horizontal pressure components

Figure 37. Pressure distributed in a thin-walled pressure vessel

Notice how the vertical components of the force p will cancel themselves out because they act in equal and opposite directions (Figure 37b). If force P is the total effect of all horizontal components of p acting against the curved surface (Figure 37c), then we calculate P as follows:

P = the pressure $p \times$ the area of the curved surface on the longitudinal plane, or

$$P = p\, D_c \ell.$$

Because the equations in this section refer to *thin*-walled vessels, it is usually not necessary to specify inner or outer diameter when using D_c. It is the resistance of the material that holds the pressure force in equilibrium in the longitudinal section. If the resistance is shared equally by both sections, then:

$$P = \frac{P}{2} + \frac{P}{2}$$

as shown in Figure 37c.

Then, based on force equal to stress times the area, the total resistive force is:

$$2\left(\frac{P}{2}\right) = (2\ell t)\sigma_t$$
$$P = 2\ell t\sigma_t$$

where

$$\sigma_t \; = \text{Tangential stress in material, N/m}^2$$
$$2\ell t = \text{Total area of resistance, m}^2$$

Equating resistive and pressure forces:

$$(2\ell t)\sigma_1 = pD_c\ell$$

$$\sigma_t = \frac{pD_c}{2t},$$

where

σ_t = Average tangential stress, N/m^2

p = Internal pressure in cylinder, N/m^2

D_c = Cylinder diameter, m

t = Thickness of plate, m

To determine the force along each longitudinal seam of the vessel, refer back to:

$$P = pD_c\ell.$$

If each seam carries half of the total force P, then:

$$F = \frac{pD_c\ell}{2}.$$

where

F = Force on the longitudinal seam ℓ, N

p = Internal pressure in cylinder, N/m^2

D_c = Cylinder diameter, m

ℓ = Length of seam, m

The total pressure acting in the longitudinal plane is:

$$P = pa$$

$$P = p\frac{\pi D_c^2}{4}$$

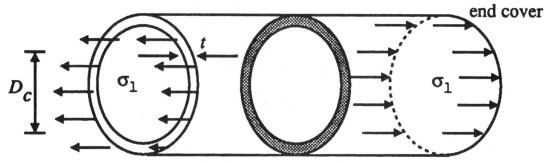

Figure 38. Longitudinal stresses σ_ℓ in a thin-walled pressure vessel

The pressure force must be balanced by resistive forces in the thin ring of metal on the transverse section which is approximately equal to its circumference $\pi D_c \times$ thickness t:

$$P = (\pi D_c t)\sigma_\ell.$$

Equating pressure force and resistive force to determine the longitudinal stress σ_ℓ (shown in Figure 38):

$$(\pi D_c t)\sigma_\ell = p\left(\frac{\pi D_c^2}{4}\right)$$

$$\sigma_\ell = \frac{pD_c}{4t}$$

COMBINED STRESSES – LOAD COMBINATIONS

There are numerous engineering applications where members are subjected to two or more types of loads at the same time. These situations are referred to as combined stresses. There are four different load combinations: (1) axial and torsional loads, (2) axial and flexural loads, (3) torsional and flexural loads, and (4) torsional, flexural, and axial loads. The material is always assumed not to be sressed beyond its elastic limit, thus justifying the principle of superposition. The superposition principle allows the development of several analytical methods which examine the stress conditions imposed by the combined loads.

Axial and Torsional Stresses

Several engineering situations require a member to resist both axial and torsional loads. Examples include a screw and a drill shaft. When a screw is driven by a screwdriver, it is both turned and pushed simultaneously. Consider the tube shown below.

The tube is subjected to the axial force P and the torque T. With superposition, the forces can be separated into the axial force and the torque acting alone. The axial force on the tube is analyzed and the stress induced at any cross-section along the length is the simple uniform normal stress distribution with intensity σ_x. The member subjected to the torque has a shear stress induced at any cross-section of τ_{xv}. The stress varies linearly from zero at the center to a maximum value at the outside surface. To evaluate the most severe stress condition which may exist in the tube, the principal stresses and maximum shear stress can be computed with the use of Mohr's circle.

Axial and Flexural Stresses

The combined action of axial and flexural stresses frequently occur in structural members, such as traffic light frames. Consider the structure shown below.

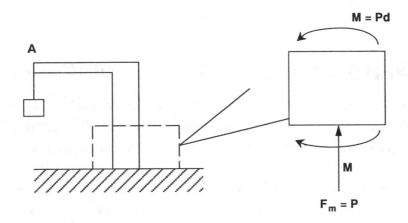

A weight is hanging from point A; this weight combined with the weight of the beam induces a normal force $F_n = P$ and a bending moment $M = Pd$ at any cross-section of the vertical member. The combined effects of F_n and M are determined by the principle of superposition. The resultant stress can be written as:

$$\sigma_y = \frac{F_n}{A} + \frac{M_u v}{I_u}$$

where u is the principle centroidal axis.

In this case, the fiber of zero stress may not coincide with the neutral axis, but may be shifted. The extend of the shift is dependent upon the relative magnitudes of the normal stresses produced by F_n and M_u.

Torsional and Flexural Stresses

An example of a member subjected to both torsional and flexural stresses is a crank shaft of an automobile. Consider the idealized rod on the next page. Force F is flexural, while T is the torque. Then again using superposition, the forces σ_x and τ_{xv} fare computed separately. Once the composite stress element is determined, Mohr's circle is used to determine the principal stresses and the maximum shear stress at the point.

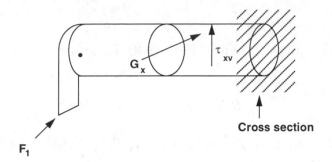

Cross section

F_1

Torsional, Flexural and Axial Stresses

Like the problems with two combined stresses, problems with members subjected to three stresses are solved using the principle of superposition. All three stresses are commonly exerted on structural and machine members; one example is a shaft keyed to bevel gears.

In the simplest forms of these problems the stresses are exerted uniformly on the member. If the member is not of uniform composition, the problem becomes far more complex and is not easily solved. For each problem, the number and types of stress should first be defined. The free body diagrams should be drawn for each individual stress component. When the magnitudes of the individual stresses are computed, they are then combined to yield the total stress exerted by the loads.

REVIEW PROBLEMS

PROBLEM 1

Construct the shear force and bending moment diagrams for the beam shown in Figure 39.

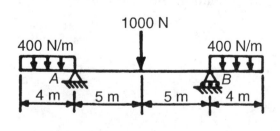

Figure 39. Shear force and bending moment diagram

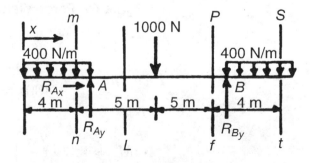

Figure 40. Loading diagram

SOLUTION

The loading diagram is shown in Figure 40. Reactions at the supports are calculated to be:

$$\sum F_x = 0 \qquad\qquad R_{Ax} = 0$$

$$\sum M_A = 0 + 400(4)(10+2) - R_{By}(10) + 1,000\ (5) - 400(4)(2) = 0$$

$$R_{By} = \frac{19,200 + 5,000 - 3,200}{10} = 2,100\ \text{N}$$

Because the loading is symmetric $R_{Ay} = R_{By} = 2,100$ N. Check whether the beam is in equilibrium:

$$\sum F_y = 0$$

$$R_{Ay} + R_{By} - (400)(4) - (400)(4) - 1,000 = 0$$

$$2,100 + 2,100 - 1,600 - 1,600 - 1,000 = 0$$

$$0 = 0$$

Beam is in vertical equilibrium and calculated values of R_{Ay} and R_{By} are correct.

The free-body diagram for a portion of the beam to the left of section *mn* (refer to Figure 40) is shown in Figure 41.

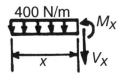

Figure 41. Force diagram left of section *mn*

$$0 < x \le 4$$

$$V_x + 400x = 0$$

$$V_x = -400x$$

$$M_x + 400(x)\left(\frac{x}{2}\right) = 0$$

$$M_x = -400\frac{x^2}{2} = -200x^2$$

The free-body diagram for a portion of the beam to the left of section *KL* (refer to Figure 40) is shown in Figure 42.

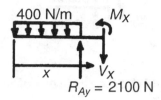

Figure 42. Force diagram left of section *KL*

$$4 < x \leq 9$$
$$V_x - 2,100 + 400(4) = 0$$
$$V_x = 500 \text{ N}$$
$$M_x + 400(4)(x - 4 + 2) - 2,100(x - 4) = 0$$
$$M_x = 2,100x - 8,400 - 1,600x + 3,200$$
$$M_x = 500x - 5,200$$

Figure 43 illustrates a portion of the beam to the left of section *Pf* (refer to Figure 40).

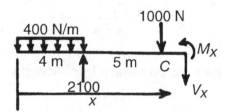

Figure 43. Force diagram left of section *Pf*

$$9 < x \leq 14$$
$$V_x + 1,000 - 2,100 + 400(4) = 0$$
$$V_x = 2,100 - 1,000 - 1,600 = -500 \text{ N}$$
$$M_x + 1,000(x - 9) - 2,100(x - 4) + 400(4)(x - 4 + 2) = 0$$
$$M_x = -1,000x + 9,000 + 2,100x - 8,400 - 1,600x + 3,200$$
$$M_x = -500x + 3,800$$

The portion of the beam to the right of section *St* (refer to Figure 40) is shown in Figure 44.

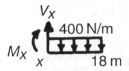

Figure 44. Force diagram of section *St*

$$V_x - 400(18 - x) = 0 \qquad \frac{M_x + 400(18 - x)(18 - x)}{2} = 0$$

$$V_x = -400x + 7{,}200 \qquad M_x = -200(18 - x)^2$$

Multiplied out:

$$M_x = -200x^2 + 7{,}200x - 64{,}800$$

This section of the beam, $14 < x \leq 18$, can also be analyzed by looking at the loads to the left of the cut.

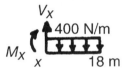

Figure 45. Summary force diagram

$$V_x + 400(x - 14) - 2{,}100 + 1{,}000 - 2{,}100 + 400(4) = 0$$
$$V_x = -400x + 7{,}200$$

Summing the moments:

$$\frac{M_x + 400(x - 14)(x - 14)}{2 - 2{,}100(x - 14) + 1{,}000(x - 9) - 2{,}100(x - 4) + \left(x - \dfrac{4}{2}\right)} = 0$$

$$M_x = -200x^2 + 7{,}200x - 64{,}800$$

The summary force diagram for this problem is shown in Figure 45.

The shear force and bending moment diagrams are then plotted by substituting for x in the various expressions for V_x and M_x (Figures 46 and 47).

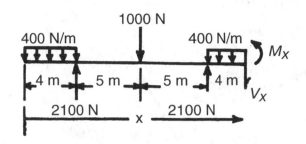

Figure 46. Shear force diagram

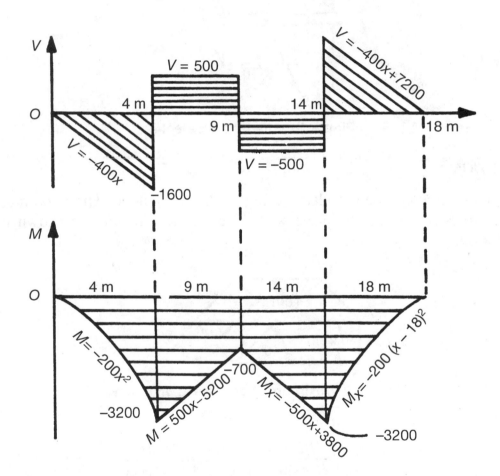

Figure 47. Bending moment diagram

PROBLEM 2

A 60 cm structural steel bar $\frac{1}{2}$ by 4 cm in cross section is to support an axial tensile load with allowable normal and shearing stresses of 18,000N/cm^2 and 8,000N/cm^2, respectively, and with an allowable elongation of 0.05 cm. Determine the maximum permissible load.

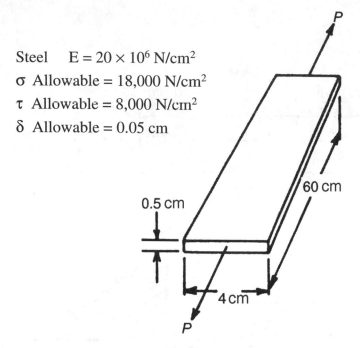

Steel $E = 20 \times 10^6 \text{ N/cm}^2$

σ Allowable = 18,000 N/cm^2

τ Allowable = 8,000 N/cm^2

δ Allowable = 0.05 cm

Figure 48. Stresses on steel bar

SOLUTION

This force can be calculated using shear stress alone. The maximum shear stress occurs on the plane with an orientation of 45°, as shown in Figure 49.

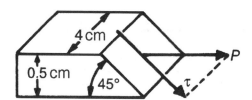

Figure 49. Maximum shear stress on beam

$$\tau = \frac{F}{A} = \frac{P \sin 45°}{(0.5 \text{ cm} / \sin 45°)4 \text{ cm}} = \frac{0.707P}{(0.707)4 \text{ cm}^2}$$

$$\tau = \frac{P}{4 \text{ cm}^2}$$

$$P = 4\tau = 4(8,000)$$

$$P = 32,000 \text{ N}$$

It still remains for us to determine whether the extension for this load exceeds the allowable elongation:

$$\delta = \frac{PL}{AE} = \frac{(32{,}000 \text{ N})(60 \text{ cm})}{(2 \text{ cm}^2)(20 \times 10^6 \text{ N}/\text{cm}^2)} = 0.048 \text{ cm}$$

This is within the allowable range of elongation, therefore:

$$P_{max} = 32{,}000 \text{ N}$$

PROBLEM 3

The beam of Figure 50 has a rectangular cross section $^1/_3$ m wide 1 m deep and a span of 12 meters. It is subjected to a uniformly distributed load of 100 N per meter and concentrated loads of 600 N and 1,200 N at 2 m and 7 m, respectively, from the left support. Determine the maximum fiber stress at the center of the beam.

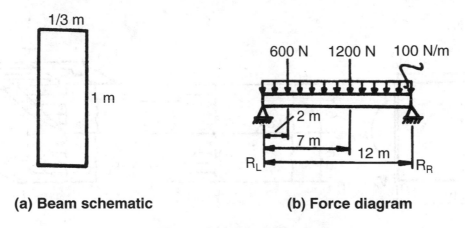

(a) Beam schematic **(b) Force diagram**

Figure 50. Beam diagram

SOLUTION

The reactions are evaluated from a free-body diagram of the entire beam and moment equations with respect to each of the two reactions. By this method, the reactions are evaluated independently, and summation of forces may be used to check the results. $\sum M = 0$ about the right support. Therefore,

$$0 = -12R_L + (100)(12)\left(\frac{12}{2}\right) + (1{,}200)(5) + 600(10)$$

$$12R_L = 19{,}200$$
$$R_L = 1{,}600 \text{ N}$$

$\sum M = 0$ about the left support. Therefore:

$$0 = 12\,R_R + 600(2) + 100\left(\frac{12}{2}\right)(12) + 1{,}200(7)$$

$$12\,R_R = 16{,}800$$
$$R_R = 1{,}400 \text{ N}$$

Check: $\sum F_y = 0$

$$600 + 1{,}200 + 100 \times 12 - 1{,}600 - 1{,}400 = 0$$
$$0 = 0$$

The left reaction, R_L, is 1,600 N and the right reaction, R_R, is 1,400 N, both upward. Figure 51 is a free-body diagram of the left half of the beam.

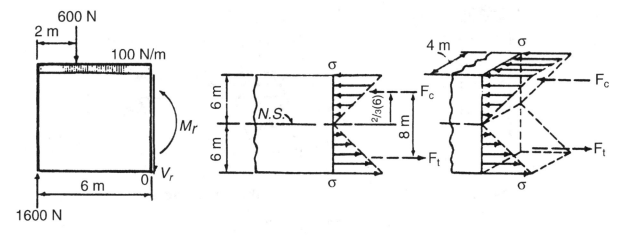

| (a) Free-body diagram | (b) Force diagram | (c) Force diagram in 3-D perspective |

Figure 51. Forces on left half of beam

The equation $\sum M_r = 0$ gives:

$$+ M_r + 600(4) + 100(6)(3) - 1{,}600(6) = 0,$$

from which

$$M_r = 5{,}400 \text{ N/m}.$$

The moment, M_r, is the resultant of the flexural stresses indicated in Figure 51b and c in which F_C and F_T are the resultants of the compressive and tensile stresses, respectively. The resultants F_C and F_T (which act through the centroids of the wedge-shaped stress distribution diagram of

Figure 51c) are located through the centroids of the triangular stress distribution diagrams of Figure 52b. The magnitude of the couple M_r is:

$$M_r = F_C(8)$$

or

$$M_r = F_T(8).$$

The stress, σ, is:

$$\sigma = \frac{F_c}{(6)(4)\left(\dfrac{1}{2}\right)},$$

therefore:

$$
\begin{aligned}
F_c &= 12\sigma \\
M_r &= F_c(8) \\
5{,}400 &= (12\sigma)(8) \\
\sigma_{max} &= 56.25 \text{ N/m}^2 \text{ } C \text{ at top and } T \text{ at bottom}
\end{aligned}
$$

PROBLEM 4

Shown in Figure 52 is a simply supported beam with a triangular loading. What is the deflection curve of this beam?

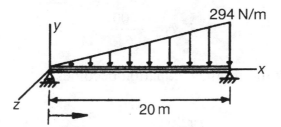

Figure 52. Beam with triangular loading

SOLUTION

This problem will be solved by integrating the fourth order differential equation of the curvature due to loading

$$EI\frac{d^4y}{dx^4} = w$$

The equation for the loading is

$$w = \frac{20 \text{ N} / \text{m} \, (x)}{20 \text{ m}} = x \, \text{N} / \text{m}^2.$$

Integrating the loading gives the shear

$$EI \frac{d^3 y}{dx^3} = \frac{x^2}{2} + c_1.$$

Integrating the shear gives the moment

$$EI \frac{d^2 y}{dx^2} = \frac{x^3}{6} + c_1 x + c.$$

The moments at the ends of the beam are both zero. At $x = 0$,

$$EI(0) = \frac{0}{6} + c_1 \times 0 + c_2 = 0$$

$$c_2 = 0$$

At $x = 20$,

$$EI(0) = \frac{20^3}{6} + c_1 \times 20$$

$$c_1 = \frac{-400}{6}$$

Substituting the moment equation becomes

$$EI \frac{d^2 y}{dx^2} = \frac{x^3}{6} - \frac{400x}{6}$$

Integrating the moment gives the slope

$$EI \frac{dy}{dx} = \frac{x^4}{24} - \frac{400x^2}{12} + c_3.$$

Integrating the slope gives the deflection

$$EI y = \frac{x^5}{120} - \frac{400x^3}{36} + c_3 x + c_4.$$

The deflections at the ends of the beam are both zero. At $x = 0$,

$$EI(0) = \frac{(0)^5}{120} - \frac{400(0)^3}{36} + c_3 \times 0 + c_4$$

$$c_4 = 0$$

At $x = 20$,

$$EI(0) = \frac{(20)^5}{120} - \frac{400(20)^3}{36} + c_3(20)$$

$$c_3 = \frac{88,888.9 - 26,666.7}{20} = 3,110$$

Substituting yields

$$EIy = \frac{x^5}{120} - \frac{400x^3}{36} + 3,110x.$$

Thus, the equation of the deflection curve of the beam is

$$y = \frac{1}{EI}\left(\frac{x^5}{120} - \frac{400x^3}{36} + 3,110x\right).$$

PROBLEM 5

Two small lathes are driven by the same motor through a 0.5 m diameter steel shaft, as shown in Figure 53 (a) on the next page. Determine the maximum shear stress in the shaft due to twisting.

SOLUTION

We begin the analysis by idealizing the situation as shown in Figure 53(b) on the next page. Here we represent each pulley loading by its static equivalent of a force of 25 N through the axis of the shaft and a couple about the z axis of $6(20 - 5) = 90$ Nm. Because each pulley is supported by a pair of immediately adjacent bearings, we make the idealization that the 25 N transverse forces are balanced by the bearing reactions in such a way that there is negligible shear force and bending moment transmitted beyond the bearings. In this case, it is only necessary for the motor to supply a torque M_A, as shown.

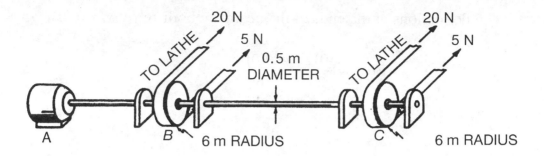

(a) Lathes diagram

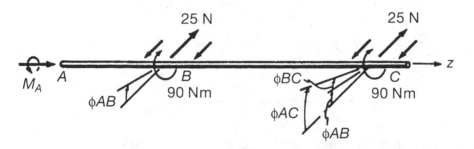

(b) Force diagram

Figure 53. Shear stress on shaft

Establishing moment equilibrium, we have, since all moment vectors are parallel to z, $\sum M_A = 0$ if:

$$M_A - 90 - 90 = 0$$
$$M_A = 180 \text{ Nm}$$

The twisting moments in sections AB and BC of the shaft are then clearly

$$M_{AB} = 180 \text{ Nm} \qquad M_{BC} = 90 \text{ Nm}$$

The maximum shear stress occurs at the outside of the shaft in section AB. Using equation:

$$\sigma_s = \frac{16T}{\pi d^3},$$

where the torque (T) here is the twisting moment in section AB:

$$\sigma_s = \frac{(16)(180 \text{ Nm})}{\pi (0.5 \text{ m})^3}$$

$$= 7,333.9 \text{ N / m}^2$$

PROBLEM 6

Determine the required section modulus Z for a beam AB to support the distributed load shown in Figure 54 if $q = 4{,}000$ N/m and the allowable bending stress $\sigma_w = 16{,}000$ N/m². Neglect the weight of the beam.

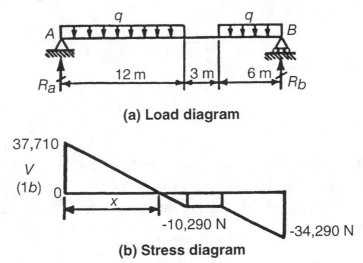

(a) Load diagram

(b) Stress diagram

Figure 54. Forces on beam

SOLUTION

1) To locate the section of maximum bending moment, it is helpful to construct a shear force diagram, shown in Figure 54. The reactions at the supports are:

$$R_a = 37{,}710 \text{ N} \qquad R_b = 34{,}290 \text{ N}$$

and the distance x defining the point of zero shear is given by the equation:

$$R_a - qx = 0$$

from which $x = \dfrac{R_a}{q} = 9.43$ m. At this distance from support A, the bending moment is a maximum:

$$M_{max} = R_a x - \frac{qx^2}{2}$$

$$= (37{,}710 \text{ N})(9.43 \text{ m}) - \frac{(4{,}000 \text{ N}/\text{m})(9.43 \text{ m})^2}{2}$$

$$= 177{,}755.5 \text{ Nm}$$

The required section modules, from $\sigma = \dfrac{M}{Z}$ is:

$$Z = \frac{M}{\sigma}$$
$$= \frac{177,755.5 \, \text{Nm}}{16,000 \, \text{N} / \text{m}^2}$$
$$= 11.1 \, \text{m}^3$$

PROBLEM 7

A 0.305 m-by-0.406 m wooden cantilever beam weighing 730 N/m carries an upward concentrated force of 17,800 N at the end, as shown in Figure 55. Determine the maximum bending stresses at a section 1.83 m from the free end.

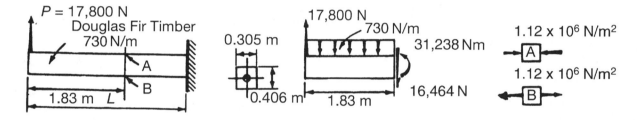

(a) Beam schematic (b) Cross section (c) Free-body diagram (d) Summary of forces

Figure 55. Cantilever beam

SOLUTION

A free-body diagram for a 1.83 m. segment of the beam is shown in Figure 55c. The weight, 730 N/m, is considered as a uniformly distributed external load and the beam is then considered massless. To keep this segment in equilibrium requires a shear of 17,800 − 730(1.83) = 16,464 N and a bending moment of 17,800(1.83) − 730(1.83) = 31,238 Nm at the cut section. Both these quantities are shown with their proper sense in Figure 55. By inspecting the cross-sectional area, the distance from the neutral axis to the extreme fibers is seen to be 0.2 m, hence, $c = 0.2$ m. This is applicable to both the tension and the compression fiber.

Therefore,

$$I_{zz} = \frac{bh^3}{12} = \frac{0.305(0.406)^3}{12} = 1.7 \times 10^{-3} \, m^4$$

$$\sigma_{max} = \frac{Mc}{I} = \frac{31,238(0.305)0.2}{0.0017} = 1.12 \times 10^6 \, N/m^2$$

From the sense of the bending moment shown in Figure 55c, the top fibers of the beam are seen to be in compression and the bottom ones in tension. In the answer given, the positive sign applies to the tensile stress, and the negative sign applies to the compressive stress. Both of these stresses decrease at a linear rate toward the neutral axis where the bending stress is zero. The normal stresses acting on infinitesimal elements at A and B are shown in Figure 55d.

PROBLEM 8

A beam with overhanging ends (Figure 56) carries a uniform load of intensity q = 146 kN/m on each overhang. Assuming that the beam is a $W30 \times 172$ section with $E = 2.07 \times 10^{11} \, N/m^2$, determine the maximum normal stress in the beam.

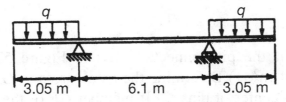

Figure 56. Overhanging beam

SOLUTION

A $W30 \times 172$ section has the following properties:

nominal size	$0.762 \times 0.381 \, m^2$
depth of section	0.759 m
area	$0.0327 \, m^2$
I	$3.28 \times 10^{-3} \, m^4$

Maximum normal stress occurs at a point where moment is maximum. This is at the midpoint of the beam.

In order to find the moment, the reaction forces need to be determined. The beam is symmetrically loaded; therefore, the reactions are equal.

By vertical equilibrium:

$$\sum F_y = 0,$$
$$(2)(3.05)(146 \text{ kN/m}) - 2R = 0$$
$$R = 445 \text{ kN}$$

The moment at the midpoint of the beam by moment equilibrium is:

$$\sum M = 0$$
$$M_{max} + (445 \text{ kN})(3.05 \text{ m}) - (146 \text{ kN/m})(4.57 \text{ m})(3.05 \text{ m}) = 0$$
$$M_{max} = 678 \text{ kNm}$$

and σ_{max} is:

$$\sigma_{max} = \frac{M_{max} \times C}{I}$$
$$= \frac{(678 \text{ kNm})(0.759 \text{ m})}{3.28 \times 10^{-3} \text{ m}^4}$$
$$= 1.57 \times 10^8 \text{ N/m}^2$$

PROBLEM 9

Member *GF* of the pin-connected truss in Figure 57 has a cross-sectional area of 2.4 m². 1) Determine the axial stress in *GF*. The lengths shown are center to center of pins. 2) If member *CF* of the pin-connected truss is a ⁷/₈ m diameter rod, determine the axial stress in *CF*. The lengths shown are center to center of pins.

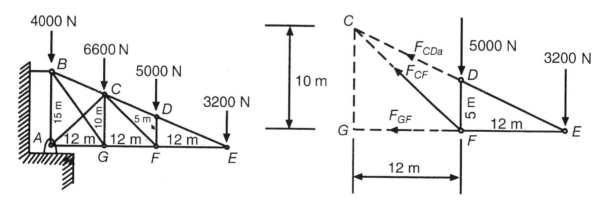

Figure 57. Truss   **Figure 58. Force diagram of truss**

SOLUTION

In general, to determine the forces in the truss members, the reactions for the whole structure should be calculated. Since the truss in this problem is a cantilever truss, the member forces can be found without finding the reaction.

1) To find the axial force in GF, make a section cut a-a as shown in Figure 58. By taking the moment about point C, F_{CD} and F_{CF} will not contribute since their lines of action go through C. Therefore, the only unknown is F_{GF}:

$$F_{GF}(10) + 5{,}000(12) + 3{,}200(24) = 0$$

$$F_{GF} = -13{,}680 = 13{,}680 \text{ N compression}$$

The axial stress in GF is:

$$\sigma_{GF} = \frac{F_{GF}}{A_{GF}} = \frac{13{,}680}{2.4} = 5{,}700 \text{ N/m}^2 \ C.$$

2) To find the axial force in CF, again determine the moment. (The vertical component of F_{CF} passes through the point D and contributes no moment.)

The horizontal component of F_{CF} is:

$$F_{CF_x} = F_{CF}\left(\frac{12}{\sqrt{12^2 + 10^2}}\right)$$

$$\sum M_D = F_{CF}\left(\frac{12}{\sqrt{12^2 + 10^2}}\right)(5) - 13{,}680(5) + (3{,}200)(12) = 0$$

$$F_{CF} = 7{,}810 \text{ N tension}$$

Axial stress in CF:

$$\sigma_{CF} = \frac{F_{CF}}{A_{CF}}$$

where

$$A_{CF} = \frac{\pi d^2}{4} = \frac{\pi\left(\frac{7}{8}\right)^2}{4} = 0.0601 \text{ m}^2$$

$$\sigma_{CF} = \frac{7{,}810}{0.6} = 12{,}988 \text{ N/m}^2 \ T$$

PROBLEM 10

A thin-walled pressure vessel is subjected to an internal gauge pressure. Using Figures 59 and 60, determine the normal stresses on an infinitesimal element.

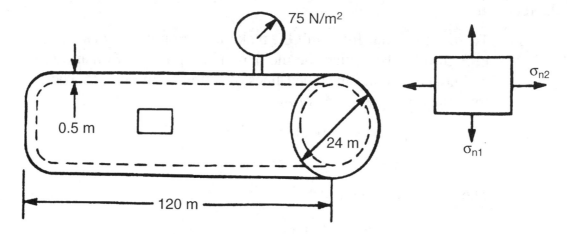

Figure 59. Pressure vessel　　　　　　**Figure 60. Free-body diagram**

SOLUTION

The equations for the normal stresses $(\sigma_n)_1$ and $(\sigma_n)_2$ for a thin cylinder acted on by internal pressure p, at a point far from the ends of the cylinder, are:

$$(\sigma_n)_2 = \frac{pr}{t} \tag{1}$$

and

$$(\sigma_n)_1 = \frac{pr}{2t}. \tag{2}$$

The internal pressure is 75 N/m² above atmospheric pressure. This is the same as the net internal pressure, or the equivalent internal pressure if the external pressure were zero. Since this is the pressure used to derive (1) and (2), we can use it without modification for this problem.

From (1)

$$(\sigma_n)_2 = \frac{\left(75\,\text{N}/\text{m}^2\right)(12\text{m})}{\left(\dfrac{1}{2}\text{m}\right)} = 1,800\,\text{N}/\text{m}^2 \tag{3}$$

From (2)

$$(\sigma_n)_1 = \frac{(75\text{N}/\text{m}^2)(12\text{m})}{2\left(\frac{1}{2}\text{m}\right)} = 900 \text{ N}/\text{m}^2 \tag{4}$$

It is seen from (3) and (4) that both components of normal stress are much larger in value than the pressure that caused them. This can be accounted for by the fact that the internal pressure acts over a large area to create certain forces that must be balanced by forces in the cylinder acting over small areas. This produces rather large stresses in the cylinder.

Also note that the axial stress $(\sigma_n)_1$ is half as large as the tangential stress $(\sigma_n)_2$.

Equations (1) and (2) should be used only where $t \ll r$ and away from the ends of the cylinder.

PROBLEM 11

The steel shaft of Figure 61a is in equilibrium under the torques shown. Determine the maximum shearing stress in the shaft in English units.

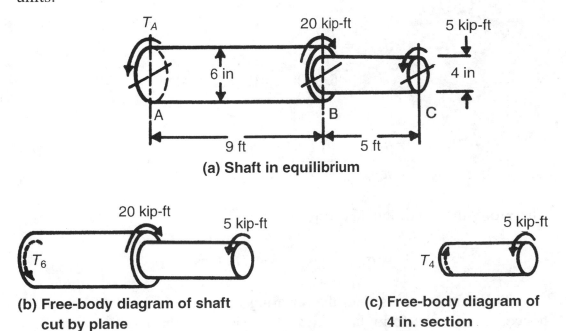

(a) Shaft in equilibrium

(b) Free-body diagram of shaft cut by plane

(c) Free-body diagram of 4 in. section

Figure 61. Steel shaft

SOLUTION

In general, free-body diagrams should be drawn in order to evaluate the resisting torque correctly. Such diagrams are shown in Figures 61b and 61c, where in 61b, the shaft is cut by any transverse plane through the 6-inch segment, and T_6 is the resisting torque on this section. Similarly, in Figure 61c, the plane is passed through the 4-inch section, and T_4 is the resisting torque on this section. The location of the maximum shearing stress is not apparent; hence, the stress must be checked at both sections. Thus, from Figure 61b:

$$\sum M = 0, \; T_6 = 20 - 5 = 15 \text{ ft-kips} = 15,000\,(12) \text{ in-lb,}$$

and

$$\sigma_{\max} = \frac{T_6 c}{I} = \frac{15,000(12)(3)}{\left(\frac{\pi}{2}\right)(3^4)} = \frac{40,000}{3\pi} \text{ psi.}$$

From Figure 61c,

$$\sum M = 0,$$
$$T_4 = 5 \text{ ft-kips} = 5,000(12) \text{ in-lb,}$$

and

$$\sigma_{\max} = \frac{T_4 c}{I}$$
$$= \frac{5,000(12)(2)}{\left(\frac{\pi}{2}\right)(2^4)} = \frac{15,000}{\pi} \text{ psi;}$$
$$\frac{15,000}{\pi} > \frac{40,000}{3\pi}$$

Therefore, the maximum shearing stress is

$$\sigma_{\max} = \frac{15,000}{\pi} = 4,774.6 \text{ psi.}$$

This stress is less than the shearing proportional limit of any steel; hence, the torsion formula applies. Note that had the larger torque been carried by the smaller section, the maximum stress would obviously occur in the small section and only one stress determination would have been required.

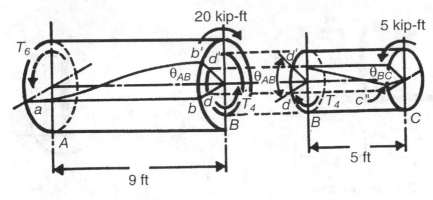

(d) Segments *AB* and *BC*

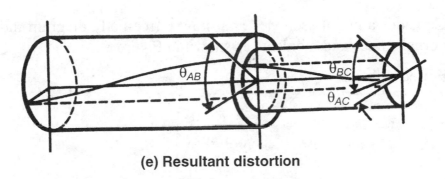

(e) Resultant distortion

Figure 62. Torque diagrams

As an aid to visualizing the distortion of the shaft, the segments *AB* and *BC* and the torques acting on them are drawn in Figures 62d and 62e with the distortions greatly exaggerated. As the resultant torque of 15 ft-kips twists segment *AB* through the angle θ_{AB}, points *b* and *d* move to *b'* and *d'* respectively, and segment *BC* may be considered as a rigid body rotating through the same angle, point *c* moving to *c'*, after which the torque of 5 ft-kips acting on *BC* twists this part of the shaft back through the angle θ_{BC}, point *c'* moving back to *c''*. The resultant distortion for the entire shaft is shown in Figure 62e.

PROBLEM 12

Calculate the internal forces and moments acting at sections 1 and 2 in the structure shown.

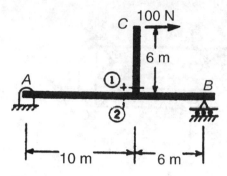

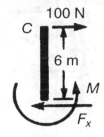

Figure 63. Forces on structure

Figure 64. Forces on structure part 1

SOLUTION

Consider a cut at section 1 and draw a free-body diagram indicating the internal forces and moments as shown in Figure 64.

For equilibrium

$$\sum F = 0$$
$$\therefore F_x - 100 = 0$$
$$\therefore F_x = 100 \text{ N}$$

$\sum M = 0$ about the cut

$$\therefore M - 6 \times 100 = 0$$
$$\therefore M = 600 \text{ Nm}$$

To get the internal forces and moment at section 2, first determine the reactions at the supports. See Figure 65.

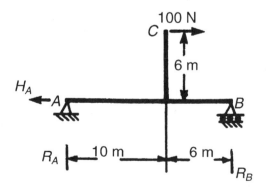

Figure 65. Reactions at structure supports

$F = 0$ (horizontal forces)

$$\therefore -H_A + 100 = 0$$
$$\therefore H_A = 100 \text{ N}$$

$\sum M = 0$ at support A +

$$\therefore 100 \times 6 - 16R_B = 0$$
$$\therefore R_B = 37.5 \text{ N}$$

$\sum M = 0$ at support B +

$$100 \times 6 + 16R_A = 0$$
$$\therefore R_A = -37.5 \text{ N}$$

Now consider a cut through section 2 and draw a free-body diagram as shown in Figure 66.

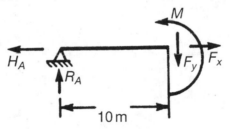

Figure 66. Free-body diagram

$\sum F_y = 0$

$$\therefore R_A - F_y = 0$$
$$\therefore F_y = R_A = -37.5 \text{ N}$$

$\sum F_x = 0$

$$\therefore F_x - H_A = 0$$
$$\therefore F_x = H_A = 100 \text{ N}$$

$\sum M = 0$ about the cut +

$$-M + 10R_A = 0$$
$$\therefore M = -10 \times 37.5$$
$$= 375 \text{ Nm clockwise}$$

FE/EIT

Fundamentals of Engineering: AM Exam

CHAPTER 8

Chemistry

CHAPTER 8

CHEMISTRY

This chapter is a brief review of general chemistry, reviewing such fundamental concepts as nomenclature and equations to redox reactions and acid-base equilibria. Since being able to recognize and identify chemicals is of primary importance, we will start there.

NOMENCLATURE

A chemical formula is a representation of a compound in terms of its constituent atoms and their relative numbers. Chemical formulas may be empirical or molecular. The **empirical formula** of any compound gives the *relative number* of atoms in each element in the compound. It is the simplest formula of a material compound that can be derived solely from its components. The molecular formula of a substance indicates the *actual number* of atoms in a molecule of a substance. To determine the molecular formula of a compound, one must calculate the empirical formula and then extrapolate to the molecular formula via molecular weight. It is easiest to remember that a molecular formula is simply a multiple of an empirical formula.

Now, let's look at naming inorganic compounds (nomenclature for organic compounds is discussed in the Organic Chemistry section). Binary compounds consist of two elements. The formula of a binary compound identifies the two elements present and ends in "-ide" (e.g., NaCl = sodium chloride). If a metal is bonded to a nonmetal, the metal is named first. If a metal element has only two possible oxidation states, use the suffix "-ous" for the lower state and "-ic" for the higher state. For example,

$FeCl_2$ = ferrous chloride [iron (II) chloride]

$FeCl_3$ = ferric chloride [iron (III) chloride]

When naming binary covalent compounds formed between two non-metals, a third system is preferred. The numbers of each atom in the molecule are specified by a Greek prefix: di-, tri-, tetra-, penta-, and so on. For example, N_2O_5 = dinitrogen pentoxide.

Ternary (three element) compounds are usually made up of an element and a radical. To name these compounds, each component making up the compound is identified. The positive component is written first and the negative one second. For example, in $CaCO_3$, Ca is the element, and CO_3 is the radical anion: $CaCO_3$ ($Ca^{+2} + CO_3^{-2}$) = calcium carbonate.

Binary acids use the prefix "hydro-" in front of the stem (or full name) of the nonmetallic element and place the suffix "-ic" at the end (e.g., HCl = hydrochloric acid).

Ternary acids are slightly more complicated. They may be examined along with salts containing polyatomic anions. Both oxy-acids and oxy-ions are named according to their oxygen content. Anions with more oxygen atoms end in "-ate," while their counterparts end in "-ite." Acids are defined almost the same way. Acids with more oxygen atoms end in "-ic,"and acids with fewer end in "-ous." If there are more than two types of anions or acids, prefixes are also added. These naming conventions are summarized in the table below.

TABLE 1 SUFFIX NOMENCLATURE				
Oxidation State	**Anion**	**Acid**	**Example**	**Name**
+1	hypo- -ite	hypo- -ous	HClO	hypochlorous acid
+3	-ite	-ous	$HClO_2$	chlorous acid
+5	-ate	-ic	$HClO_3$	chloric acid
+7	per- -ate	per- -ic	$HClO_4$	perchlorous acid

A simple rule of thumb is "-ate/-ic...-ite/-ous."

Partial neutralization of an acid that is capable of furnishing more than one H+ per acid molecule produces salts that are called acid salts. When only one acid salt is formed, the salt can be named by adding the prefix "bi-" to the name of the anion of the acid (e.g., $NaHSO_4$ = sodium bisulfate). The salt can also be named by specifying the presence of H. For example, Na_2HPO_4 = sodium hydrogen phosphate or disodium hydrogen phosphate. In writing formulas, there are a couple of general observations to keep in mind:

(1) Metals have positive oxidation numbers while nonmetals (and most common radical ions except the ammonium ion) have negative oxidation numbers.

(2) A radical ion is a group of elements that remain bonded as a group even when involved in the formation of compounds.

Some basic rules for writing formulas are:

(1) Represent the symbols of the components using the positive part first and the negative part second.

$$(NH_4)(SO_4) = \text{ammonium sulfate}$$

(2) Indicate the respective oxidation number above and to the right of each symbol.

$$(NH_4)^{+1}(SO_4)^{-2}$$

(3) Write the subscript number equal to the oxidation number of the other element or radical, and omit the subscript "1" as well as any + or – signs.

$$(NH_4)^{+1} (SO_4)^{-2} = (NH_4)_2(SO_4)$$

(4) As a general rule, the subscript numbers are reduced to their lowest terms. Hence, Ca_2O_2 becomes CaO. There are some exceptions. Hydrogen peroxide H_2O_2 and acetylene C_2H_2 are two.

EQUATIONS

Now that simple inorganic nomenclature has been established, let's look at equations. An **equation** is a chemical sentence. It gives information about the states of the reactants and products, their relative molar proportions, and the possible directions of the reaction. The formula of each substance is followed by an indication of state (e.g., s, l, g, aq). Remember that state *does* depend on temperature and pressure, so when writing an equation, be sure to check for these values. If none are given, assume standard temperature and pressure (STP) values (1 atm, 273 K).

Aqueous solutions may contain strong electrolytes (which dissociate into ions readily), weak electrolytes (which dissociate to a small extent), or nonelectrolytes (which do not dissociate at all). If a substance is a strong electrolyte, it is written in its dissociated form. For example, sodium chloride would be written in aqueous solution as $Na^+(aq) + Cl^-(aq)$. Strong electrolytes include salts (a metal ion with a nonmetal or polyatomic ion) and strong acids and bases (HCl, NaOH). Weak electrolytes and non-electrolytes are generally written in undissociated form. These include weak acids and bases, most nonpolar substances, and many organic materials.

Any substances in the system whose quantities do not change during the reaction are not included in the equation. Since their quantities and states remain constant, they do not affect the net reaction. For example,

$$Ag^+(aq) + NO_3^-(aq) + Na^+(aq) + Cl^-(aq) \rightleftharpoons$$
$$AgCl(s) + Na^+(aq) + NO_3^-(aq)$$

should be written

$$Ag^+(aq) + Cl^-(aq) \rightleftharpoons AgCl(s).$$

The bottom equation is called a net equation because it only involves the net reacting components of the system. This is usually the part of the reaction in which we are interested. Finally, equations are not complete until they are properly balanced. The law of conservation of mass must be observed when writing an equation. No quantities of elements can suddenly appear or disappear; the same number of atoms must be on either side of the equation. For

$$2H_2(g) + O_2(g) \rightleftharpoons 2H_2O(1),$$

there are four H atoms on the left and four H atoms on the right. Oxygen is balanced the same way. In general, a properly balanced equation is the starting point in solving many chemical problems.

EXAMPLE

Balance the following by filling in the missing species and proper coefficient:

(a) $NaOH +$ _____ $\rightarrow NaHSO_4 + HOH$

(b) $PCl_3 + 3HOH \rightarrow$ _____ $+ 3HCl$

(c) $CH_4 +$ _____ $\rightarrow CCl_4 + 4HCl$

SOLUTION

To balance chemical equations you must remember that ALL atoms (and charges) must be accounted for. The use of coefficients in front of compounds is a means to this end. Thus,

(a)   NaOH + _____ → NaHSO$_4$ + HOH

On the right side of the equation, you have 1 Na, 3 H's, 5 O's, and 1 S. This same number of elements must appear on the left side. However, on the left side, there exists only 1 Na, 1 O, and 1 H. You are missing 2 H's, 1 S, and 4 O's. The missing species is H$_2$SO$_4$, sulfuric acid. You could have anticipated this since a strong base (NaOH) reacting with a strong acid yields a salt (NaHSO$_4$) and water. The point is, however, that H$_2$SO$_4$ balances the equation by supplying all the missing atoms.

(b)   PCl$_3$ + 3HOH → _____ + 3HCl

Here, the left side has 1 P, 3 Cl's, 6 H's, and 3 O's. The right has 3 H's and 3 Cl's. You are missing 1 P, 3 O's, and 3 hydrogens. Therefore, P(OH)$_3$ is formed.

(c)   CH$_4$ + _____ → CCl$_4$ + 4HCl

Here, there are 1 C, 8 Cl's, and 4 H's on the right and 1 C and 4 H's on the left. The missing compound, therefore, contains 8 Cl's and thus is 4 Cl$_2$. One knows that it is 4 Cl$_2$ rather than Cl$_8$ or 8 Cl because elemental chlorine gas is a diatomic or 2 atom molecule.

STOICHIOMETRY

The next fundamental review is that of stoichiometry. **Stoichiometry** is really chemical arithmetic. Basically, it involves measuring relative amounts and proportions of reactants and products in chemical reactions. To perform such measurements, a few concepts must first be outlined.

One **mole** of a substance is the standard chemical unit for "amount." It contains Avogadro's number of particles (atoms, molecules, ions, electrons, etc.), approximately 6.02×10^{23}. The definition of the mole is

$$\text{number of moles} = \frac{\text{mass}}{\text{molecular weight}} = \frac{\text{g}}{\text{g/mol}}.$$

The gram-atomic weight of any element is defined as the mass, in grams, which contains one mole of atoms of that element. For example, approximately 12.0 g of carbon, 16.0 g of oxygen, and 32.1 g of sulfur each contain one mole of atoms.

The molecular weight (formula weight) of a molecule or compound is determined by the addition of its component atomic weights. For example, look at the formula weight (F.W.) of $CaCO_3$:

$$F.W.\ CaCO_3 = 1(40) + 1(12) + 3(16) = 100\ g/mol.$$

The formula for molecular weight is given below:

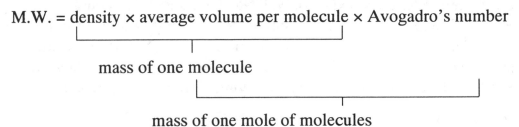

M.W. = density × average volume per molecule × Avogadro's number

mass of one molecule

mass of one mole of molecules

Finally, equivalent weights are the amounts of substances that react completely with one another in chemical reactions. In *electrolytic* reactions, the equivalent weight is defined as that weight which either receives or donates one mole of electrons at an electrode. For *oxidation-reduction* reactions, an equivalent is defined as the quantity of a substance that either gains or loses one mole of electrons. In *acid-base* reactions, an equivalent of an acid is defined as the quantity of acid that supplies one mole of H^+. An equivalent of base supplies one mole of OH^-.

It is important to note that a given substance may have any of several equivalent weights, depending on the particular reaction in which it is involved. For example, for Fe^{3+}:

$Fe^{3+} + e^- = Fe^{2+}$ one equivalent weight per mole; eq wt = 56 g/eq

$Fe^{3+} + 3e^- = Fe^0$ three equivalent weights per mole; eq wt = $(\frac{1}{3})(56) =$
18.7 g/eq

Stoichiometric calculations utilize reaction equations. Since stoichiometry involves examining relative amounts and/or proportions of reactants and products, it is very important that the equations be properly balanced. The coefficients in chemical equations provide the ratios in which moles of one substance react with moles of another. Although the coefficients may represent numbers of molecules, they also represent the number of moles of reactants and products required. For the equation, $C_2H_4 + 3O_2 \rightleftharpoons 2CO_2 + 2H_2O$, the number of moles of O_2 consumed is always equal to three times the number of moles of C_2H_4 that react.

Usually, reactants and products are not set up in a neat economical package containing correct stoichiometric ratios. Some reagents may be in excess of their needed ratios and will not be completely consumed in the reaction. Chemical reactions can only proceed as far as their least abundant reactant will allow (similar to the strong chain/weakest link idea). The reactant is called **limiting reagent**. It is always consumed first in the chemical reaction, and it determines the amount of product that will be formed unless equilibrium is reached first (see the section on Equilibrium). To perform limiting reagent calculations, you must modify your calculations according to the amounts of reagents present. Calculate the number of moles of each reagent and compare them to the number of actual moles needed (according to the stoichiometric ratios and actual amounts of reagents you have present). Whatever amount of reactant present that is less than the amount required is the limiting reagent (and will determine the quantities of product formed).

This brings us to "yields" of reactions. The **theoretical yield** of a given product is the maximum yield that can be obtained from a given reaction if the reaction goes to completion (rather than to equilibrium). For example:

$$50 \text{ g O}_2 \times \frac{18 \text{ g H}_2\text{O}}{16 \text{ g O}} = 56.25 \text{ g H}_2\text{O} \text{ [water is } \left(\frac{16}{18}\right) \text{ oxygen } \left(\frac{2}{18}\right) \text{ hydrogen]}$$

The **percentage yield** is a measure of the efficiency of a reaction. It is defined as

$$\text{percentage yield} = \frac{\text{actual yield}}{\text{theoretical yield}} \times 100\%.$$

We may also look at **percentage compositions**, the percentage of the total mass contributed by each element:

$$\text{percentage composition} = \frac{\text{mass of element in compound}}{\text{mass of compound}} \times 100\%$$

Remember that at "STP," standard temperature and pressure, 273 K and 1 atm, 1 mole of any ideal gas occupies 22.4 liters. In other words, the molar volume of an ideal gas is 22.4 liters/mol. Density can be converted to molecular weight using this relationship:

M.W. = (density)(molar volume)

(g/mol) = (g/l)(l/mol)

STATES OF MATTER

Matter occupies space and possesses mass. It is found in three states or phases: solid, liquid, and gas. A solid has both definite volume and shape. A liquid has definite volume, but takes the shape of its container. A gas has neither definite shape nor definite volume. Usually, temperature and pressure are the primary factors that determine the state of a substance. We will first review solids.

The properties of solids are as follows:

(1) They retain their shape and volume when transferred from one container to another.

(2) They are virtually incompressible.

(3) They exhibit extremely slow rates of diffusion.

In a solid, the attractive forces between the atoms, molecules, or ions are relatively strong. The particles are held in a rigid structural array, wherein they exhibit only vibrational motion. When solids are heated at certain pressures, some vaporize without passing through the liquid phase. This is called sublimation. The heat required to change one mole of a solid completely to vapor is called the molar heat of sublimation, ΔH_{sub}. Note that $\Delta H_{sub} = \Delta H_{fus} + \Delta H_{vap}$.

Next, we move to liquids. A liquid is composed of molecules constantly moving in a random fashion; however, attractive forces between molecules prevent it from being a gas. These attractive forces hold the molecules close together, so that increasing the pressure has little effect on the volume. As a result, liquids are virtually incompressible. Also, changes in temperature cause only small volume changes. Liquids diffuse more slowly than gases, but their rates increase with increasing temperature. The heat of vaporization of a substance is the number of calories required to convert 1g of liquid to 1g of vapor without a change in temperature. The reverse process is called the heat of condensation, and involves the removal of the same amount of heat energy. The heat needed to vaporize 1 mole of a substance is called the molar heat of vaporization or the molar enthalpy of vaporization, ΔH_{vap}. Again, note that $\Delta H_{vap} = \Delta H_{vapor} - \Delta H_{liquid}$. We can also look at the change from a solid to a liquid, fusion. The number of calories needed to change 1g of a solid substance (at the melting point) to 1g of liquid (at the melting point) is called the heat of fusion. Note that $\Delta H_{fus} = \Delta H_{liquid} - \Delta H_{solid}$.

When the rate of evaporation equals the rate of condensation, the system is in equilibrium. Vapor pressure is the pressure exerted by gas molecules in equilibrium with their liquid. This pressure increases with increasing temperature. To determine the vapor pressure of an ideal solution at a particular temperature, we can use **Raoult's law**. This states that the vapor pressure is equal to the mole fraction of a solvent in the liquid phase multiplied by the vapor pressure of the pure solvent at the same temperature:

$$P_{solution} = X_{solvent} \, P^0_{solvent}$$

or

$$P_A = X_A \, P^0_A$$

where P_A is the vapor pressure with solute added, P^0_A is the vapor pressure of pure A, and X_A is the mole fraction of A in the solution (A is assumed to be nonvolatile).

EXAMPLE

The vapor pressures of pure benzene and toluene at 60°C are 385 and 139 Torr, respectively. Calculate (a) the partial pressures of benzene and toluene, (b) the total vapor pressure of the solution, and (c) the mole fraction of toluene in the vapor above a solution with 0.60 mole fraction toluene.

SOLUTION

The vapor pressure of benzene over solutions of benzene and toluene is directly proportional to the mole fraction of benzene in the solution. The vapor pressure of pure benzene is the proportionality constant. This is analogous to the vapor pressure of toluene. This is known as Raoult's law. It may be written as

$$P_1 = X_1 \, P^0_1$$
$$P_2 = X_2 \, P^0_2$$

where 1 and 2 refer to components 1 and 2, P_1 and P_2 represent the partial vapor pressure above the solution, P^0_1 and P^0_2 are the vapor pressures of pure components, and X_1 and X_2 are their mole fractions. Solutions are called ideal if they obey Raoult's law.

The mole fraction of a component in the vapor is equal to its pressure fraction in the vapor. The total vapor pressure is the sum of the vapor's component partial pressures.

To solve this problem one must

(1) calculate the partial pressures of benzene and toluene using Raoult's law;

(2) find the total vapor pressure of the solution by adding the partial pressures; and

(3) find the mole fraction of toluene in the vapor.

One knows the mole fraction of toluene in the solution is 0.60 and, thus, one also knows the mole fraction of benzene is (1 − 0.60) or 0.40. Using Raoult's law:

$$P^\circ_{benzene} = 385 \text{ Torr} \quad P^\circ_{toluene} = 139$$

(a) $P_{benzene} = (0.40)(385 \text{ Torr}) = 154.0 \text{ Torr}$

$P_{toluene} = (0.60)(139 \text{ Torr}) = 83.4 \text{ Torr}$

(b) $P_{total} = 154.0 + 83.4 = 237.4 \text{ Torr}$

(c) The mole fraction of toluene in the vapor =

$$X_{toluene, vap} = \frac{P_{toluene}}{P_{toluene} + P_{benzene}} = \frac{83.4}{237.4} = 0.351.$$

This brings us to gases. Gases, remember, have no fixed volume, so they assume the volumes of their containers. Gases are measured in terms of pressure, which is defined as "force per unit area." Standard atmospheric pressure is used in many problems and can be expressed in several ways:

$$14.7 \text{ psi} = 760 \text{ mm Hg} = 760 \text{ torr} = 1 \text{ atm}.$$

A familiar equation used in gas calculations is the ideal gas equation (or ideal equation of state):

$$PV = nRT,$$

where P is pressure, V is volume, T is temperature, n is number of moles, and R is the gas constant.

Molecules of the hypothetical ideal gas have no attraction for one another and have no intrinsic volume; they are "point masses." Several equations are derived from the ideal gas law. They are shown in Table 2.

TABLE 2
GAS LAW CORRELATIONS

Law	Definition (k = constant)	Form
Boyle's	$T = k, PV = k, V \propto \dfrac{1}{P}$	$P_1 V_1 = P_2 V_2$
Charles'	$P = k, \dfrac{V}{T} = k, V \propto T$	$\dfrac{V_1}{T_1} = \dfrac{V_2}{T_2}$
Gay-Lussac	$V = k, \dfrac{P}{T} = k, P \propto T$	$\dfrac{P_1}{T_1} = \dfrac{P_2}{T_2}$
Combined Gas	$n = k, V \propto \dfrac{1}{P} \propto T$	$\dfrac{P_1 V_1}{T_1} = \dfrac{P_2 V_2}{T_2}$
Avogadro's	if $P_1 = P_2$ and $T_1 = T_2, V \propto n$	$\dfrac{V_2}{V_1} = \dfrac{n_2}{n_1}$

EXAMPLE

What pressure is required to compress 5 liters of gas at 1 atm pressure to 1 liter at a constant temperature?

SOLUTION

In solving this problem, one uses Boyle's Law: The volume of a given mass of gas at a constant temperature varies inversely with the pressure. This means that, for a given gas, the pressure and the volume are proportional, at a constant temperature, and their product equals a constant.

$$P \times V = k$$

where P is the pressure, V is the volume, and k is a constant. From this one can propose the following equation:

$$P_1 V_1 = P_2 V_2,$$

where P_1 is the original pressure, V_1 is the original volume, P_2 is the new pressure, and V_2 is the new volume.

In this problem, one is asked to find the new pressure and is given the original pressure and volume and the new volume.

$$P_1V_1 = P_2V_2 \qquad\qquad P_1 = 1 \text{ atm}$$
$$V_1 = 5 \text{ liters}$$

$$1 \text{ atm} \times 5 \text{ liters} = P_2 \times 1 \text{ liter} \qquad P_2 = ?$$

$$\frac{1 \text{ atm} \times 5 \text{ liters}}{1 \text{ liter}} = P_2 \qquad\qquad V_2 = \text{liter}$$

$$5 \text{ atm} = P_2$$

Sometimes we have mixtures of gases. The pressure exerted by each gas in a mixture is called its partial pressure. The total pressure exerted by a mixture is equal to the sum of the partial pressures of the gases in the mixture. This is **Dalton's law of partial pressures**:

$$P_T = P_a + P_b + P_c \ldots$$

The ideal gas obeys exactly the mathematical statement of the ideal gas law; however, most gases are not ideal. Real gases act in a less ideal way, especially under conditions of increased pressure and/or decreased temperature. Real gas behavior approaches that of ideal gases as the gas pressure becomes very low.

Last, we'll look at effusion and diffusion. **Effusion** is the process in which a gas escapes from one chamber of a vessel by passing through a very small opening or orifice. **Graham's law of effusion** states that the mean molecule velocity and, hence, the rate of effusion (ρ) is inversely proportional to the square root of the density of the gas:

$$\text{rate of effusion} \propto \sqrt{\frac{1}{\rho}},$$

and

$$\frac{\text{rate of effusion (A)}}{\text{rate of effusion (B)}} = \sqrt{\frac{\rho_B}{\rho_A}} = \sqrt{\frac{MW_B}{MW_A}}$$

where M.W. is the molecular weight of each gas, and where temperature is the same for both gases.

EXAMPLE

Two gases, HBr and CH_4, have molecular weights 81 and 16, respectively. The HBr effuses through a certain small opening at the rate of 4 ml/sec. At what rate will the CH_4 effuse through the same opening?

SOLUTION

The comparative rates or speeds of effusion of gases are inversely proportional to the square roots of their molecular weights. This is written

$$\frac{\text{rate}_1}{\text{rate}_2} = \frac{\sqrt{MW_2}}{\sqrt{MW_1}}$$

For this case $\dfrac{\text{rate}_{HBr}}{\text{rate}_{CH_4}} = \dfrac{\sqrt{MW_{CH_4}}}{\sqrt{MW_{HBr}}}$

One is given the rate_{HBr}, MW_{CH_4}, and MW_{HBr} and asked to find rate CH_4.

Solving for rate CH_4:

$$\frac{\text{rate}_{HBr}}{\text{rate}_{CH_4}} = \frac{\sqrt{MW_{CH_4}}}{\sqrt{MW_{HBr}}} \qquad \text{rate}_{HBr} = 4 \text{ ml/sec}$$

$$\text{rate}_{CH_4} = ?$$

$$\frac{4 \text{ ml/sec}}{\text{rate}_{CH_4}} = \frac{\sqrt{16}}{\sqrt{81}} \qquad MW_{CH_4} = 16$$

$$MW_{HBr} = 81$$

$$\text{rate}_{CH_4} = \frac{4 \text{ ml/sec} \times \sqrt{81}}{\sqrt{16}}$$

$$= \frac{4 \text{ ml/sec} \times 9}{4} = 9 \text{ ml/sec}$$

Mixing of molecules of different gases by random motion and collision until the mixture becomes homogeneous is called **diffusion**. Graham's law of diffusion states that the relative rates at which gases will diffuse will be inversely proportional to the square roots of their respective densities or molecular weights:

$$\text{rate} \propto \frac{1}{\text{mass}} \quad \text{(where, again, } T_1 = T_2\text{)}$$

and

$$\frac{\text{rate 1}}{\text{rate 2}} = \frac{\sqrt{MW_2}}{\sqrt{MW_1}} \left(\text{or } \frac{r_1}{r_2} = \frac{\sqrt{d_2}}{\sqrt{d_1}} \right)$$

SOLUTIONS

Often in chemistry, we work with solutions; therefore, it is important that we understand some concepts of solution chemistry. A **solution** is a homogeneous mixture of substances. They may be gaseous, liquid, or solid. **Concentration** quantifies the amount of solute in a solution. Some concentration units are defined in Table 3:

TABLE 3 CONCENTRATION UNITS		
Unit	**Definition**	**Formula**
Mole fraction	$\dfrac{\text{\# moles of one component of solution}}{\text{total \# moles of all components in solution}}$	$X_A = \dfrac{n_A}{n_A + n_B + n_C + \ldots}$
Mole percent	Mole fraction expressed as %	$(X_A)(100\%)$
Weight fraction	$\dfrac{g \text{ one component of solution}}{\text{total } g \text{ of all components in solution}}$	$W_A = \dfrac{g_A}{g_A + g_B + g_C + \ldots}$
Weight percent	Weight fraction expressed as %	$(W_A)(100\%)$
Molarity	Moles of solute per liter of solution	$M = \dfrac{n \text{ solute}}{\ell \text{ solution}}$
Molality	Moles of solute per kg of solvent	$m = \dfrac{n \text{ solute}}{\text{kg solvent}}$
Normality	# equivalents of solute per liter of solution	$N = \dfrac{\text{equiv solute}}{\ell \text{ of solution}}$

EXAMPLE

Calculate the molarity of a solution containing 10.0 grams of sulfuric acid in 500 ml of solution (MW of $H_2SO_4 = 98.1$).

SOLUTION

The molarity of a compound in a solution is defined as the number of moles of the compound in one liter of the solution. In this problem, one is told that there are 10.0 grams of H_2SO_4 present. One should first calculate the number of moles that 10.0 g represents. This can be done by dividing 10.0 g by the molecular weight of H_2SO_4.

$$\text{number of moles} = \frac{\text{amount present in grams}}{\text{molecular weight}}$$

$$\text{number of moles of } H_2SO_4 = \frac{10.0 \text{ g}}{98.1 \text{ g/mole}} = 0.102 \text{ moles}$$

Since molarity is defined as the number of moles in one liter of solution, and since, one is told that there is 0.102 moles in 500 ml ($\frac{1}{2}$ of a liter), one should multiply the number of moles present by 2. This determines the number of moles in H_2SO_4 present in 1,000 ml.

Number of moles in 1,000 ml = $2 \times 0.102 = 0.204$

Because molarity is defined as the number of moles in 1 liter, the molarity (M) here is 0.204 M.

Now that concentration units have been defined, we can look at **solubility**, the concentration of dissolved solute in a saturated solution. A **saturated** solution is one in which solid solute is in equilibrium with dissolved solute, and no more solute will go "into solution." **Unsaturated** solutions contain less solute than required for saturation. **Supersaturated** solutions contain more solute than required for saturation (this is meta-stable state). Solubility may be affected by changes in temperature or pressure, but the exact change depends on the solution. The solubility of most *solids* in liquids increases with increasing temperature. For *gases* in liquids, the solubility usually decreases with increasing temperature. To analyze the change in solubility due to change in temperature, we may use the following equation:

$$\log \frac{K_2}{K_1} = \frac{-\Delta H^O}{2.303R}\left(\frac{1}{T_2} - \frac{1}{T_1}\right)$$

where K_2 = solubility constant at T_2, K_1 = solubility constant at T_1 (see the section on Equilibrium for a detailed definition of the solubility constant) and ΔH^O = enthalpy change when the solute dissolves in the solvent at standard conditions. A positive ΔH^O indicates that solubility increases with increasing temperature. Pressure has very little effect on the solubility of liquids or solids in liquid solvents; however, the solubility of gases in liquid (or solid) solvents always increases with increasing pressure.

Some solids are only sparingly soluble in solutions. The equilibrium constant for sparingly soluble compounds is termed the solubility product, K_{sp}. When performing calculations on sparingly soluble compounds, it is important to have a balanced equation for the dissolution of the compound. For example, let's look at the reaction

$$Ag_2CrO_4(s) \rightleftharpoons 2Ag^+(aq) + CrO_4^{-2}(aq), K_{sp} = 8.5 \times 10^{-8}.$$

The solubility of Ag_2CrO_4 at room temperature in moles/liter is determined as follows:

$$Ag_2CrO_4(s) \rightleftharpoons 2Ag^+(aq) + CrO_4^{-2}(aq)$$

start	a	0	0
equil	$a-x$	$2x$	x

$K_{sp} = [Ag^+]^2[CrO_4^{-2}] = 8.5 \times 10^{-8}$ (Ag_2CrO_4 is not included, because it is a solid)

Now, synthesize this information to determine x:

$$(2x)^2(x) = 8.5 \times 10^{-8}$$
$$2x^3 = 8.5 \times 10^{-8}$$
$$x = 3.5 \times 10^{-3}$$

recalling that the solubility product is equal to the product of the concentrations of the ions, each raised to the power of its coefficient.

Aqueous solutions are a very important part of chemistry. Ionic compounds generally dissolve readily in water, but there are some exceptions.

TABLE 4
SOLUBLE IONS

Ion	Solubility	Exceptions
Nitrates, NO_3^-	All soluble	none
Chlorates, ClO_3^-	"	"
Acetates, CH^3COO^-	"	"
Sulfates, SO_4^{-2}	Soluble	$BaSO_4$, $SrSO_4$, $PbSO_4$ are insoluble $CaSO_4$, Ag_2SO_4, $HgSO_4$ are slightly insoluble
Chlorides, Cl^-	"	AgCl (insoluble), Hg_2Cl_2 (insoluble), $PbCl_2$ (slightly soluble)
Bromides, Br^-	"	AgBr (insoluble), Hg_2Br_2 (insoluble), $PbBr_2$ (soluble)
Iodides, I^-	"	AgI (insoluble), Ag_2I_2 (insoluble), PbI_2 (soluble)
Hydroxides, OH^-	Insoluble	Group IA metals (Li, Na, …) are soluble $Sr(OH)_2$, $Ca(OH)_2$ are slightly soluble
Carbonates, CO_3^{-2}	Insoluble	Group IA metals, $(NH_4)_2(CO_3)$ are soluble
Phosphates, PO_4^{-3}	"	Group IA metals, $(NH_4)_3(PO_3)$ are soluble
Sulfides, S^{-2}	"	Group IA, IIA metals, $(NH_4)_2S$ are soluble
Common salts of NH_4^+, Na^+, K^+	Almost all soluble	

We looked at vapor pressure when we reviewed states of matter. Vapor pressure is an example of a **colligative property**, one that depends on the number of solute particles in the solution. The colligative property law states that the freezing point, boiling point, and vapor pressure of a solution differ from those of the pure solvent by amounts directly proportional to the molal concentration of the solute. The vapor pressure of an aqueous solution is always lowered by the addition of more solute (which also causes the boiling point to be raised—boiling point elevation). The freezing point is always lowered by the addition of solute. The formulas are:

freezing point depression $\quad \Delta T_f = -K_f m$

boiling point elevation $\quad \Delta T_b = -K_b m$

where $\Delta T = T_{\text{solution}} - T_{\text{pure solvent}}$, and m = molality of solute. K_f and K_b represent constants.

EXAMPLE

The freezing point constant of toluene is 3.33°C per mole per 1,000 g. Calculate the freezing point of a solution prepared by dissolving 0.4 mole of solute in 500 g of toluene. The freezing point of toluene is –95.0°C.

SOLUTION

The freezing point constant is defined as the number of degrees the freezing point will be lowered per 1,000 g of solvent per mole of solute present. The freezing point depression is related to this constant by the following equation:

freezing point depression = molality of solute × freezing point constant

The molality is defined as the number of moles per 1,000 g of solvent. Here one is given that 0.4 moles of solute are added to 500 g of solvent; therefore, there will be 0.8 moles in 1,000 g.

$$\frac{0.4 \text{ moles}}{500 \text{ g}} = \frac{0.8 \text{ moles}}{1,000 \text{ g}}$$

The molality of the solute is thus 0.8 m. One can now find the freezing point depression. The freezing point constant for toluene is 3.33°.

$$\text{freezing point depression} = \text{molality} \times 3.33°$$
$$= 0.8 \times 3.33° = 2.66°$$

The freezing point of toluene is thus lowered by 2.66°.

$$\text{freezing point of solution} = (-95°C) - 2.66° = -97.66°C.$$

Another colligative property is osmotic pressure. Osmosis is the diffusion of a solvent through a semipermeable membrane into a more concentrated solution. The osmotic pressure of a solution is the minimum pressure that must be applied to the solution to prevent the flow of solvent from pure solvent into the solution. The formula for osmotic pressure in very dilute solutions is

$$\Pi = cRT,$$

where Π is osmotic pressure, c is concentration in molality or molarity, R is the gas constant, and T is temperature in Kelvins.

PERIODICITY

Now that we're familiar with compounds, let's familiarize ourselves with the periodic table and its elements. **Periodic law** states that chemical and physical properties of elements are periodic functions of their atomic numbers. The periodic table provides a systematic representation of these chemical and physical properties. Vertical columns are called groups, and each contain a family of elements possessing similar chemical properties. The horizontal rows in the table are called periods. The elements lying in the two rows just below the main part of the table are called the inner transition elements. In the first of these rows are elements 58 through 71, called the lanthanides or rare earth elements. The second row consists of elements 90 through 103, the actinides. Group IA elements are the alkali metals; they have a single S electron in the outer orbital. Group IIA elements are the alkaline earth metals; they have two S electrons in the outer orbital. Group VIIA elements are the halogens, and the Group VIIIA elements are the noble gases. The Group B elements are the semimetals and transition elements. For the Group A elements, the column numbers indicate the number of filled valence shell electron orbitals (since the Group VIIIA noble gases have eight electrons in their valence shells, they are the most stable of all elements). Group B elements are harder to classify since they commonly possess several valence states.

The periodic table provides a lot of information, and various trends can be outlined in its design. Figure 1 defines some of these trends or periodicity.

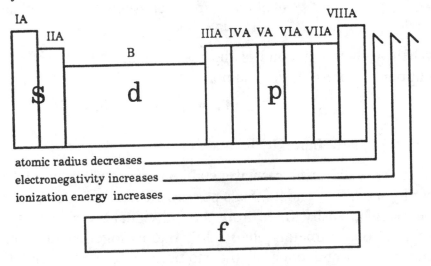

Figure 1. General characteristics of periodic table

Figure 1 illustrates periodic trends (for the full periodic table, see page 658) in atomic size, electronegativity, and ionization energy. The electronegativity of an element is a number that measures the relative strength with which the atoms of the element attract valence electrons in a chemical bond. (Recall that ionic bonding occurs when electrons are transferred during the formation of a bond, whereas electrons are shared in covalent bonding.) Ionization energy is defined as the energy required to remove an electron from an isolated atom in its ground state.

EXAMPLE

Distinguish a metallic bond from an ionic bond and from a covalent bond.

SOLUTION

The best way to distinguish between these bonds is to define each and provide an illustrative example of each.

When an actual transfer of electrons results in the formation of a bond, it can be said that an ionic bond is present. For example,

$$2K° \quad + \quad \ddot{S}: \quad \rightarrow \quad 2K^+ \quad + \quad :\ddot{S}:^{2-} \quad \rightarrow \quad K_2S$$

| potassium atoms | sulfur atom | potassium ions (unlike ions due to transfer of electrons from potassium to sulfur) | sulfur ion | ionic bond due to the attraction of unlike ions |

When a chemical bond is the result of the sharing of electrons, a covalent bond is present. For example:

$$:\ddot{Br}• \quad + \quad •\ddot{F}: \rightarrow :\ddot{Br}:\ddot{F}:$$

These electrons are shared by both atoms.

A pure crystal of elemental metal consists of millions of atoms held together by metallic bonds. Metals possess electrons that can easily ionize, i.e., they can be easily freed from the individual metal atoms. This free state of electrons in metals binds all the atoms together in a crystal. The free electrons extend over all the atoms in the crystal, and the bonds formed between the electrons and positive nucleus are electrostatic in nature. The electrons can be pictured as a "cloud" that surrounds and engulfs the metal atoms.

The periodic table also reveals the number of electrons in the valence shell of an atom. The "A" group numbers describe the number of electrons that are filling the valence shell of an atom in that column. This is not a foolproof rule, but it helps to generalize valence shell occupancies and vacancies when determining bonding or ion charges.

The table also follows the sequence for filling electron orbital subshells (s, p, d, f, etc.). Recall the mnemonic device for electron distribution shown in Figure 2.

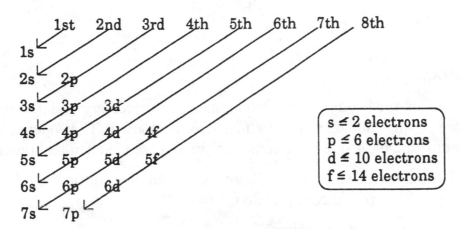

Figure 2. Electron distributions

Also, remember that the filling of orbitals follows several rules. Only two atoms may occupy an orbital at a time, and their spins must be paired, or opposite. If we look across the periodic table, we may see the trends of electron addition. Look at Figure 3 for example:

	1s	2s	$2p_x$	$2p_y$	$2p_z$	
3_{Li}	↿⇂	↿⇂				$1s^2 2s^1$
4_{Be}	↿⇂	↿⇂				$1s^2 2s^2$
6_C	↿⇂	↿⇂	↿⇂	↿⇂		$1s^2 2s^2 2p^2$
8_O	↿⇂	↿⇂	↿⇂	↿⇂	↿	$1s^2 2s^2 2p^4$

Figure 3. Electron addition

Note: The number of electrons generally follows the atomic number of the element. Since the atomic number represents the number of protons in the element, a neutral atom would have the same number of electrons as protons. Also, note that Hund's rule is in effect—electrons fill all empty subshells within a level before they pair up in a subshell.

EXAMPLE

The faint light sometimes seen over marshland at night, the "will-o'-the-wisp," is believed to come about as a result of the burning of a compound of phosphorus (P) and hydrogen (H). What is the formula of this compound?

$$
\begin{array}{c}
\text{H} \\
\overset{\times\bullet}{} \\
\text{H}\overset{\times}{\underset{\bullet}{}}\ \text{P}\overset{\times}{\underset{\bullet}{}}\ \text{H} \\
\overset{}{\bullet\bullet}
\end{array}
$$

SOLUTION

To find the formula of this compound, it is necessary to determine the valence of the elements from which it is composed. The valence of an element is the number of electrons that are involved in chemical bonding.

To find the valence of phosphorus and hydrogen, consider their atomic number and electronic configuration.

Hydrogen: Atomic number = 1

Electronic configuration = $1s^1$

Phosphorus: Atomic number = 15

Electronic configuration = $1s^2\ 2s^2\ 2p^6\ 3s^2\ 3p^3$

The outer electrons are $1s^1$ for hydrogen and $3p^3$ for phosphorus. It takes one additional electron to fill hydrogen's s orbital; its valence is one. It takes three more electrons to fill phosphorus's p orbital; its valence is three. Elements react with the purpose of filling all their orbitals with the maximum number of electrons by either a transfer of electrons or by sharing electrons.

It would take three hydrogen atoms to complete phosphorus's outer orbital. In turn, each electron of phosphorus would serve to complete the outer orbital of each hydrogen atom. This can be pictured in an electron-dot formula as shown above.

In this figure, the x's represent the outer electrons of hydrogen and dots represent the electrons in the outer shell of phosphorus. The formula of this compound is, thus, PH_3.

EQUILIBRIUM

Now let's look at a specific type of chemical state: equilibrium. When a system is in a state of equilibrium, both the forward and reverse reactions take place at the same rate. There is no spontaneous forward or reverse reaction favored, and the concentrations of reactants and products no longer change with time. If the system is disturbed by an outside stress (change in temperature, pressure, or concentration, for example), it adjusts to a new equilibrium. Chemical equilibrium provides useful information in areas such as kinetics, thermodynamics, and the compositions of chemical systems.

We work with chemical equilibrium by using K_{eq}, the equilibrium constant. It is usually written in the form of a fraction, with product values in the numerator and reactant values in the denominator. For the reaction $aA + bB \rightleftharpoons eE + fF$:

$$K_{eq} = \frac{[E]^e [F]^f}{[A]^a [B]^b}$$

where [A-F] indicates the thermodynamic activity. This relationship is known as the mass action equation, and

$$\frac{[E]^e [F]^f}{[A]^a [B]^b}$$

is the mass action expression. It is very important to note that pure solids and pure liquids are not included in the expression, since their concentrations are fairly constant at any given temperature. If the reaction involves solutions, we express concentration in terms of molarity, molality, etc. If the reaction involves gases, we express concentration as pressures. Thus, for the reaction

$$NH_3(g) + HCl(l) \rightleftharpoons NH_4^+(aq) + Cl^-(aq)$$

$$K_{eq} = \frac{[NH_4^+][Cl^-]}{P_{NH_3}}.$$

It is also useful to note that the size of the K_{eq} value provides an indication of the direction of the reaction. If the K_{eq} value is large (e.g., 10^5), we know that there must be a large concentration of products. The reaction must favor the formation of products. If the K value is small, reactants are favored.

Kinetic information can be gathered by analyzing the mass action expression of a reversible reaction. The rate of an elementary chemical reaction is proportional to the concentrations of the reactants raised to powers equal to their stoichiometric coefficients in the balanced equation. For the equation, $aA + bB \rightleftharpoons eE + fF$:

$$\text{rate}_{\text{forward}} = k_f[A]^a[B]^b$$
$$\text{rate}_{\text{reverse}} = k_r[E]^e[F]^f$$

where k_f and k_r are the rate constants for the forward and reverse reactions, respectively. If we arrange this information into the form of the mass action expression, the relationship between K_{eq} and rate can be observed, as shown below:

$$K_{eq} = \frac{[E]^e[F]^f}{[A]^a[B]^b} = \frac{k_f}{k_r} \quad (\text{at equilibrium rate}_f = \text{rate}_r).$$

Chemical equilibrium also provides thermodynamic information. If we use the symbol Q to represent the mass action expression for a reaction at any given time, we can determine that reaction's favored direction. Q is written using the same concentrations and form as K_{eq}, so we may say that

when $Q < K$ then products favored

when $Q = K$ then reaction at equilibrium

when $Q > K$ then reactants favored

Q may also be used in Gibb's free energy determinations:

$$\Delta G = \Delta G^0 + 2.303 \, RT \, \log Q,$$

where ΔG is the free energy change under conditions other than standard conditions, and ΔG^0 is the free energy under standard conditions. At equilibrium, $Q = K$, and the products and reactants have the same total Gibb's free energy such that $\Delta G = 0$. Therefore,

$$\Delta G^0 = -2.303 RT \, \log K_{eq} = -RT \ln K_{eq}.$$

In some situations, gases are also expressed in terms of concentration rather than pressure. We can differentiate between using concentration values and pressure values by using K_c and K_p, respectively. K_c and K_p are related by the ideal gas equation, $PV = nRT$. Since $P = \left(\dfrac{n}{V}\right)RT$, we can

substitute $\dfrac{n}{V}$ (concentration) into the mass action expression:

$$K_p = \frac{P_E^e P_F^f}{P_A^a P_B^b} = \frac{[E]^e (RT)^e [F]^f (RT)^f}{[A]^a (RT)^a [B]^b (RT)^b} = \frac{[E]^e [F]^f}{[A]^a [B]^b} (RT)^{(e+f)-(a+b)}$$

Therefore, $K_p = K_c (RT)^{\Delta n}$, where Δn represents the change in the number of moles of gas upon going from reactants to products.

K_{eq} can also be used to determine the status of other equilibrium states of the reaction at the same temperature. For example, if a chemist performs the reaction

$$2NO\ (g) + Br_2\ (g) \rightleftharpoons 2NOBr\ (g)$$

where $K_{eq} = 100$ and the initial pressure of the reactants is 1 atm, we have enough information to determine the quantity of NOBr formed. First, write the equilibrium expression from the balanced equation:

$$K_{eq} = \frac{[NOBr]^2}{[NO]^2 [Br_2]} = 100.$$

To find out how much NOBr is produced, we have to know how many moles of NO and Br_2 reacted. Then, we can find the number of grams produced. The equilibrium expression is based on the concentrations of reactants and products. We can express concentrations as moles per liter. This means that if the volume and concentration of NOBr is known, we can find moles (since mol/liter × liter = moles). If we express the concentration as $\dfrac{n}{V}$, the expression becomes

$NO\ (g) + \frac{1}{2}Br_2 \rightleftharpoons NOBr\ (g)$

$$K = \frac{\left(\dfrac{n_{NOBr}}{V}\right)^2}{\left(\dfrac{n_{NO}}{V}\right)^2 \left(\dfrac{n_{Br_2}}{V}\right)}.$$

Let x = moles of NOBr formed. Then, x moles of NO and $\dfrac{x}{2}$ moles of Br_2 are consumed (since the coefficients of the reaction show a 2:2:1 ratio for NOBr:NO:Br$_2$). Now,

$$K = 100 = \frac{n_{NOBr}^2 V}{n_{NO}^2 n_{Br_2}} = \frac{x^2 V}{(2-x)^2 (1-0.5x)}$$

$$2NO + Br_2 \rightleftharpoons 2NOBr$$

start	2	1	0
equil	$2-x$	$1-0.5x$	x

If x moles of NOBr form and we started with 2 moles of NO, then, at equilibrium, we have $(2 - x)$ moles of NO left. We started with only 1 mole of Br_2, of which $0.5x$ moles form NOBr; thus, we only have $1 - 0.5x$ moles of Br_2 left. To determine the quantity of NOBr formed, we now have to calculate the volume.

$$V = \frac{nRT}{P} = \frac{(3\,mol)\left(0.821\dfrac{liters-atm}{mol-K}\right)(273\,K)}{1\,atm} = 673 \text{ liters}$$

Now that V is known:

$$K = \frac{x^2(673)}{(2-x)^2(1-0.5x)} = 100$$

We solve for x either by factoring or by the quadratic equation,

$$x = \frac{b \pm \sqrt{b^2 - 4ac}}{2a},$$

and obtain $x = 0.923$ moles = moles of NOBr formed. Now, use the molecular weight of NOBr to determine the grams produced (101.53 g).

One last bit of useful information involves LeChatelier's principle. It states that when a system at equilibrium is disturbed by the application of a stress, it reacts to minimize the stress and attain a new equilibrium position.

TABLE 5
LE CHATELIER'S PRINCIPLE

Stress	Result
Increase in concentration of reactants	Increase in amount of product formed
Decrease in concentration of reactants	Decrease in amount of product formed
Increase in temperature	Exothermic reaction: shift to left
	Endothermic reaction: shift to right
Increase in pressure	Shift in position of equilibrium in direction of fewest number of moles of gaseous reactant or product
Catalyst	Speeds approach to equilibrium, but K_{eq} does not change
Addition of inert gas	Increases pressure, but K_{eq} is not affected

ACIDS AND BASES

Next, we come to a familiar topic in chemistry. There are several definitions of acids and bases. The Arrhenius theory states that acids are substances that ionize in water to give H^+ ions, and bases are substances that produce OH^- ions in water. The Bronsted-Lowry theory defines acids simply as proton donors and bases as proton acceptors. Finally, the Lewis theory defines an acid as an electron pair acceptor and a base as an electron pair donor.

Several factors influence the strength of acids. The greater the number of oxygens bound to the element "E" in the hydroxy compound, H_xEO_y, the stronger the acid. This is also a positive correlation with oxidation state of E. In addition, as we move down a group in the periodic table, the strength of the oxoacids decreases.

Acids and bases are often examined in terms of acid-base equilibria in aqueous solution. First, we can study the ionization of water and the concept of pH. For the equation:

$$H_2O + H_2O \rightleftharpoons H_3O^+ + OH^-, K_w = [H_3O^+][OH^-] = 1.0 \times 10^{-14} \text{ at } 25°C.$$
$$(\text{or } K_w = [H^+][OH^-])$$

$[H_3O^+][OH^-]$ is the product of ionic concentrations, and K_w is the dissociation, or ionization, constant for water. When we think of acids, we often think of pH. pH is related to K_w as follows:

$$pH = -\log [H^+]$$
$$pOH = -\log [OH^-]$$
$$pK_w = pH + pOH = 14.0$$

In a neutral solution, pH = 7.0, the concentration of acids and bases are equal. In an acidic solution, pH is less than 7.0; in basic solutions, pH is greater than 7.0. Note that since K_w varies with temperature (as do all equilibrium constants), neutral pH may differ from 7.0 when the temperature differs from 25°C.

The dissociation of weak electrolytes (weak acids and bases) can be defined in the same way. For the equation:

$$A^- + H_2O \rightleftharpoons HA + OH^-, \quad K_b = \frac{[HA][OH^-]}{[A^-]},$$

where K_b is the base ionization constant. Here, A^- is acting as the base (conjugate base).

For the reaction:

$$HA + H_2O \rightleftharpoons A^- + H^- (H_3O^+), \quad K_a = \frac{[H^+][A^-]}{[HA]},$$

where K_a is the acid ionization constant, and HA is the acid. For any conjugate acid-base pair, the two constants are related to K_w as follows:

$$K_w = K_a K_b.$$

Thus,

$$K_w = [H^+][OH^-].$$

For polyprotic acids, there is more than one dissociation constant. For example:

$$H_2S \rightleftharpoons H^+ + HS^- \qquad K_{a1} = \frac{[H^+][HS^-]}{[H_2S]}$$

$$HS^- \rightleftharpoons H^+ + S^{-2} \qquad K_{a2} = \frac{[H^+][S^{-2}]}{[HS^-]}$$

Also, $K_{a1} \gg K_{a2}$, since it is easier to "pull off" the first H^+ than the second. The total K_a is

$$K_a = K_{a1} \times K_{a2} = \frac{\left[H^+\right]^2\left[S^{-2}\right]}{\left[H_2S\right]}.$$

Acids and bases are used extensively in buffer systems. **Buffer solutions** are equilibrium systems that resist changes in acidity, maintaining constant pH when acids or bases are added to them. The most effective pH range for any buffer is at or near the pH where the acid and salt concentrations are equal (that is pK_a). The pH for a buffer is given by

$$pH = pK_a + \log\frac{\left[A^-\right]}{\left[HA\right]} = pK_a + \log\frac{[\text{base}]}{[\text{acid}]},$$

which is obtained very simply from the equation for weak acid equilibrium.

Hydrolysis refers to the action of salts of weak acids or bases with water to form acidic or basic solutions. Some examples are shown below.

Salts of Weak Acids and Strong Bases: Anion Hydrolysis

For $C_2H_3O_2^- + H_2O \rightleftharpoons HC_2H_3O_2 + OH^-$ $K_h = \frac{\left[HC_2H_3O_2\right]\left[OH^-\right]}{\left[C_2H_3O_2^-\right]}$

$K_h = \dfrac{K_w}{K_a}$

$K_a = \dfrac{\left[H^+\right]\left[C_2H_3O_2^-\right]}{\left[HC_2H_3O_2\right]}$

Salts of Strong Acids and Weak Bases: Cation Hydrolysis

For $NH_4^+ + H_2O \rightleftharpoons H_3O^+ + NH_3$ $K = \dfrac{\left[H_3O^+\right]\left[NH_3\right]}{\left[NH_4^+\right]}$

$K_h = \dfrac{K_w}{K_b}$

$K_1 = \dfrac{\left[NH_4^+\right]\left[OH^-\right]}{\left[NH_3\right]}$

Hydrolysis of Salts of Polyprotic Acids

For $S^{-2} + H_2O \rightleftharpoons HS^- + OH^-$
$$K_{h1} = \frac{K_w}{K_{a2}} = \frac{[HS^-][OH^-]}{[S^{-2}]}$$

$HS^- + H_2O \rightleftharpoons H_2S + OH^-$
$$K_{h2} = \frac{K_w}{K_{a1}} = \frac{[H_2S][OH^-]}{[HS^-]}$$

In chemistry, titration is often used as an analytical tool. Titration is the process of determining the amount of a solution of known concentration that is required to react completely with a certain amount of a sample that is being analyzed. The solution of known concentration is called a standard solution, and the sample being analyzed is the unknown. The concentration unit, normality, is used rather than molarity. Recall that equivalents are used in normal concentration units, and here an equivalent is defined as a substance that releases one mole of either protons or hydroxyl ions. One may define equivalents as

$$\text{equiv}_A = V_A N_A \text{ and equiv}_B = V_B N_B,$$

where V is the volume of solution in liters, and N is the normality in equivalents per liter. At the equivalence point, $eq_A = eq_B$ and $V_A N_A = V_B N_B$. The equivalence point occurs when equal numbers of equivalents of acid and base have reacted. It is often useful to look at titration curves. For example, look at the strong acid-strong base curve in Figure 4.

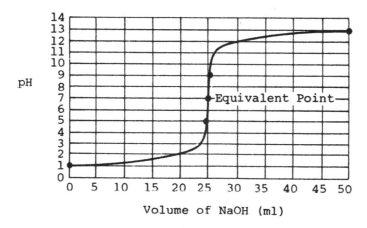

Figure 4. Titration of 0.1 M HCL with 0.1 M NaOH

At the equivalence point, the solution is neutral because neither of the ions of the salt solution undergoes hydrolysis.

One last term related to acid-base chemistry is the term amphoteric. An **amphoteric** substance is one that may act as an acid or a base. For example, aluminum hydroxide, $AL(OH)_3$, can donate H^+ or OH^- ions depending on the concentration of H^+ or OH^- ions from other compounds in the solution.

OXIDATION-REDUCTION

We will now review oxidation-reduction or "redox" reactions. **Oxidation** is defined as a reaction in which atoms or ions undergo an increase in oxidation state (they lose electrons to become more positive). **Reduction** is defined as a reaction in which atoms or ions undergo a decrease in oxidation state (they gain electrons and become more negative). The term "oxidation state" can be used interchangeably with the term "oxidation number." **Oxidation number** can be defined as the charge that an atom would have if both of the electrons in each bond were assigned to the more electronegative element. The following are basic rules for assigning oxidation numbers:

(1) The oxidation number of any element in its elemental form is zero.

(2) The oxidation number of any monatomic ion is equal to the charge on that ion.

(3) The sum of all the oxidation numbers of all of the atoms in a neutral compound is zero (or, more generally, the sum of the oxidation numbers of all the atoms in a given species is equal to the net charge on that species).

Recall that a redox reaction involves an oxidizing and a reducing agent. The oxidizing agent is reduced and the reducing agent is oxidized.

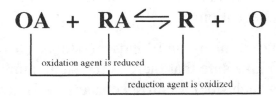

Figure 5. Oxidation and reduction equilibrium

Like any other chemical equation, a "redox" reaction equation must also be properly balanced (as illustrated in Figure 5). The transfer of electrons makes it a little tricky, but here are a couple of step-by-step methods:

The Oxidation-Number-Change Method

(1) Assign oxidation numbers to each atom in the equation.

(2) Note which atoms change oxidation number and calculate the number of electrons transferred per atom during the reaction.

(3) Sometimes, more than one atom of an element that changes oxidation number is present. If so, calculate the number of electrons transferred per formula unit.

(4) Make the number of electrons gained equal to the number of electrons lost.

(5) Once the coefficients from step 4 have been attained, the remainder of the equation can be balanced by inspection. Add H^+ and H_2O (in acidic solution), or OH^- and H_2O (in basic solution), as required.

Sometimes, you don't know (or don't want to calculate) the oxidation numbers of each atom. You may use the ion-electron (or half-reaction) method to balance your equation. Here the reaction is split in half: the oxidizing part and the reducing part.

The Ion-Electron Method

(1) First, determine which of the substances present are involved in the redox reaction.

(2) Break the overall reaction into two half-reactions; one for the oxidation step and one for the reduction step. Note: The half-reactions are written in the same directions that they appear in the original equation.

(3) Balance the numbers and kinds of atoms on each side of the equation (make sure that there is the same number of each kind of atom on each side) for all species *except* H and O.

(4) Balance the number of O atoms first by adding H_2O as required; then, balance the H atoms (for acidic solutions, balance with H^+; for basic solutions, use OH^-).

(5) Balance the reactions electrically by adding electrons to either side. The total electric charge should be the same on the left and right sides.

(6) Multiply the two balanced half-reactions by the appropriate factors so that the same number of electrons is transferred in each.

(7) Add these half-reactions to obtain the balanced overall reaction (the electrons should cancel from both sides of the final equation).

Redox reactions are a very important part of electrochemistry, and we can gain a better understanding of them by looking at their electrochemical applications.

EXAMPLE

Balance the equation for the following reaction taking place in aqueous acid solution:

$$Cr_2O_7^{2-} + I_2 \rightarrow Cr^{3+} + IO_3^-$$

SOLUTION

The equation in this problem involves both an oxidation and a reduction reaction. It can be balanced by using the following rules: (1) Separate the net reaction into its two major components: the oxidation process (the loss of electrons) and the reduction process (the gain of electrons). For each of these reactions, balance the charges by adding H^+, if the reaction is occurring in an acidic medium, or OH^- in a basic medium. (2) Balance the oxygens by adding H_2O. (3) Balance hydrogen atoms by addition of H. (4) Combine the two half-reactions, so that all charges from electron transfer cancel out. These rules are applied in the following example.

The net reaction is

$$Cr_2O_7^{2-} + I_2 \rightarrow Cr^{3+} + IO_3^-$$

The oxidation reaction is

$$I_2^0 \rightarrow 2IO_3^- + 10e^-.$$

The I atom went from oxidation number of O in I_2 to +5 in IO_3^-, because O always has a –2 charge. You begin with I_2, therefore, 2 moles of IO_3^- must be produced and 10 electrons are lost, 5 from each I atom.

Recall, the next step is to balance the charges. The right side has a total of 12 negative charges. Add 12 H$^+$'s to obtain

$$I_2 \rightarrow 2IO_3^- + 10e^- + 12H^+.$$

To balance the oxygen atoms, add 6H$_2$O to the left side, since there are 6 O's on the right, thus,

$$I_2 + 6H_2O \rightarrow 2IO_3^- + 10e^- + 12H^+.$$

Hydrogens are already balanced. There are 12 on each side. Proceed to the reduction reaction:

$$Cr_2O_7^{2-} + 6e^- \rightarrow 2Cr^{3+}.$$

Cr began with an oxidation state of +6 and went to +3. Since $2Cr^{3+}$ are produced, and you began with $Cr_2O_7^{2-}$, a total of 6 electrons are added to the left. Balancing charges: the left side has 8 negative charges and the right side has 6 positive charges. If you add 14H$^+$ to the left, they balance. Both sides now have a net +3 charge. The equation can now be written.

$$Cr_2O_7^{2-} + 6e^- + 14H^+ \rightarrow 2Cr^{3+}$$

To balance oxygen atoms, add 7H$_2$O's to the right. You obtain

$$Cr_2O_7^{2-} + 6e^- + 14H^+ \rightarrow 2Cr^{3+} + 7H_2O.$$

The hydrogens are also balanced, 14 on each side. The oxidation reaction becomes

$$I_2 + 6H_2O \rightarrow 2IO_3^- + 10e^- + 12H^+.$$

The reduction reaction is

$$Cr_2O_7^{2-} + 6e^- + 14H^+ \rightarrow 2Cr^{3+} + 7H_2O.$$

Combine these two in such a manner that the number of electrons used in the oxidation reaction is equal to the number used in the reduction. To do this, note that the oxidation reaction has 10e$^-$ and the reduction 6e$^-$. Both are a multiple of 30. Multiply the oxidation reaction by 3, and the reduction reaction by 5, obtaining

oxidation: $3I_2 + 18H_2O \rightarrow 6IO_3^- + 30e^- + 36H^+$

reduction: $5Cr_2O_7^{2-} + 30e^- + 70H^+ \rightarrow 10Cr^{3+} + 35H_2O$

Add these two half-reactions together.

$$3I_2 + 18H_2O \rightarrow 6IO_3^- + 30e^- + 36H^+$$
$$+ \qquad 5Cr_2O_7^{2-} + 30e^- + 70H^+ \rightarrow 10Cr^{3+} + 35H_2O$$
$$\overline{3I_2 + 18H_2O + 5Cr_2O_7^{2-} + 30e^- + 70H^+ \rightarrow 10Cr^{3+} + 35H_2O + 30e^- + 36H^+}$$

Simplifying, you obtain

$$3I_2 + 5Cr_2O_7^{2-} + 34H^+ \rightarrow 6IO_3^- + 10Cr^{3+} + 17H_2O.$$

This is the balanced equation.

ELECTROCHEMISTRY

First, we will look at electrochemical cells. These include things like common flashlight batteries to larger salt solution cells. Cells are important chemical "translators." They can convert electrical energy into chemical energy, or they may convert chemical energy into electrical energy.

Reactions that do not occur spontaneously can be forced to take place by supplying energy through an external current. These are called electrolytic reactions. In **electrolytic cells**, electrical energy is converted to chemical energy.

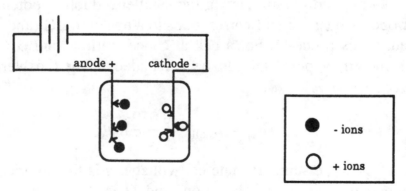

Figure 6. Simple battery

The other type of electrochemical cell is the galvanic (or voltaic cell). Flashlight batteries are of this type (see Figure 6). In galvanic cells, chemical energy is converted to electrical energy (the opposite of electrolytic cells). The salt bridge illustrated in Figure 7 is an example of a galvanic cell. Since the energy conversion process proceeds in the opposite direction in galvanic cells as compared to electrolytic cells, their anodes and cathodes are switched. In galvanic cells, the anode is negative, and the cathode is positive. Electrons flow from the negative electrode to the positive electrode.

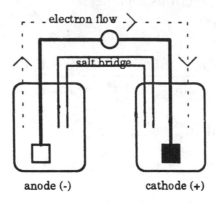

Figure 7. Salt bridge

The force driving the electrons is called the electromotive force (emf) and is measured in volts (V), where 1 V = 1 J/coulomb. The greater the tendency, or potential, of the two half-reactions to occur spontaneously, the greater will be the emf of the cell. The emf of the cell is called the cell potential, or E_{cell}. The cell potential for a Zn/Cu cell may be written as

$$E^0_{cell} = E^0_{Cu} - E^0_{Zn},$$

where the E^0's are the standard reduction potentials (these are generally provided in a table of reduction potentials). The overall standard cell potential is obtained by subtracting the smaller reduction potential from the larger one. A positive emf corresponds to a negative ΔG (and, therefore, to a spontaneous process). For a cell at concentrations and conditions other than standard, a potential can be calculated using the Nernst equation below:

$$E_{cell} = E^0_{cell} - \frac{0.059}{n} \log(Q),$$

where E^0_{cell} is the standard state cell voltage, n is the number of electrons exchanged in the reaction equation, and Q is the mass action quotient. Other interpretations of the Nernst equation are arranged below.

In terms of cell potential: $E = E^0 - \dfrac{RT}{nF} \ln Q$ $E = E^0 - \dfrac{0.059}{n} \log(Q)$

In terms of Gibb's free energy: $\Delta G = -nFE$ $\Delta G = G^0 + 2.30RT \log(Q)$

In the above equations, F represents a faraday, the electrical charge on one mole of electrons. One faraday is approximately 96,500 coulombs per mole of electrons.

EXAMPLE

Calculate the voltage of the cell Fe; Fe^{+2} || H^+; H_2 if the iron half cell is at standard conditions but the H^+ ion concentrations is .001M.

SOLUTION

The voltage (E) of a cell is found using the Nernst equation because it involves the use of concentration factors. It is stated

$$E = E^0 - \frac{RT}{nF}\ln Q,$$

where R is 8.314 joules per degree, F is 96,500 coulombs, n is the number of moles of electrons transferred, and Q is the concentration term. $T = 25°C$, by definition of standard conditions, in this equation (or 298K).

But to solve the problem we must first obtain E^0. This is done by writing down the appropriate half-reactions. Oxidation is the loss of electrons, and reduction is the gain of electrons.

Reaction	Type	$E°_{red}$
$Fe \rightarrow Fe^{+2} + 2e^-$	Oxidation	+.44
$2H^+ + 2e^- \rightarrow H_2$	Reduction	0

Next, take the algebraic sum of the E^0_{red} and E^0_{oxid}, which gives E^0.

$$E^0 = +.44 + 0 = +.44.$$

Now set up the concentration term.

$$\ln Q = \ln \frac{\left[H^+\right]^2}{\left[Fe^{+2}\right]} = \ln \frac{(.001)^2}{(1)}$$

Standard conditions always mean a concentration of 1M. Substituting all these terms into the Nernst equation, one calculates E to be

$$E = +.44 - \frac{.059}{2}\ln\frac{10^{-6}}{1} = .85\text{volt}.$$

Now, we'll take quite a different turn. In electrochemistry, we can also include the behavior of electrons and photons. First, let's review some atomic structure theory. The ground state is the lowest energy state available to the atom. The excited state is any state of energy higher than that of the ground state. The formula for changes in energy, ΔE, is

$$\Delta E = E_{final} - E_{initial}.$$

When an electron moves from the ground state to an excited state, it absorbs energy. Conversely, when an electron moves from an excited state back down to the ground state, it emits energy. This exchange of energy is the basis for atomic spectra.

We can now look at the Bohr theory of the hydrogen atom. To the hydrogen atom, Bohr applied the concept that the electron can exist in only certain stable energy levels and that when the electronic state of the atom changes, it must absorb or emit exactly that amount of energy equal to the difference between the final and initial states:

$$\Delta E = E_a - E_b.$$

The equation below measures the energy difference between states a and b, where n = the (quantum) energy level, E = energy, e = charge on the electron, a_0 = Bohr radius, and z = atomic number:

$$E_a - E_b = \frac{z^2 e^2}{2a_0}\left[\frac{1}{n_a^2} - \frac{1}{n_b^2}\right].$$

The Rydberg-Ritz equation permits calculation of the spectral lines of hydrogen:

$$\frac{1}{\lambda} = R\left[\frac{1}{n_a^2} - \frac{1}{n_b^2}\right],$$

where R = 109,678 cm^{-1} (Rydberg constant), n_a and n_b are quantum numbers for states a and b, and λ is the wavelength of light emitted or absorbed.

EXAMPLE

The Rydberg-Ritz equation governing the spectral lines of hydrogen

is $\frac{1}{\lambda} = R\left(\frac{1}{n_1^2} - \frac{1}{n_2^2}\right)$, where R is the Rydberg constant, n_1 indexes the

series under consideration (n_1 = 1 for the Lyman series, n_1 = 2 for the Balmer series, n_1 = 3 for the Paschen series), $n_2 = n_1 + 1, n_1 + 2, n_1 + 3,$ …indexes the successive lines in a series, and λ is the wavelength of the line corresponding to index n_2. Thus, for the Lyman series, n_1 = 1 and the first two lines are 1,215.56 $\overset{\circ}{A}$ ($n_2 = n_1 + 1 = 2$) and 1,025.83 $\overset{\circ}{A}$ ($n_2 = n_1 + 2 = 3$). Using these two lines, calculate two separate values of the Rydberg constant. The actual value of this constant is $R = 109,678$ cm^{-1}.

SOLUTION

The first thing to do is to convert the wavelengths from $\overset{\circ}{A}$ to more manageable units, i.e., centimeters. Using the relationship $1\overset{\circ}{A} = 10^{-8}$ cm, the first two Lyman lines are 1,215.56 $\overset{\circ}{A} = 1,215.56 \times 10^{-8}$ cm for $n_2 = 2$, and 1,025.83 $\overset{\circ}{A} = 1,025.83 \times 10^{-8}$ cm for $n_2 = 3$. Solving the Rydberg-Ritz equation for R, one obtains

$$R = \left(\lambda \left(\frac{1}{n_1^2} - \frac{1}{n_2^2} \right) \right)^{-1} .$$

For the first line,

$$R = \left(\lambda \left(\frac{1}{n_1^2} - \frac{1}{n_2^2} \right) \right)^{-1} = \left(1,215.56 \times 10^{-8} \text{cm} \left(\frac{1}{1^2} - \frac{1}{2^2} \right) \right)^{-1}$$

$$= 109,689 \text{ cm}^{-1}$$

and for the second line,

$$R = \left(\lambda \left(\frac{1}{n_1^2} - \frac{1}{n_2^2} \right) \right)^{-1} = \left(1,025.83 \times 10^{-8} \text{cm} \left(\frac{1}{1^2} - \frac{1}{3^2} \right) \right)^{-1}$$

$$= 109,667 \text{ cm}^{-1}$$

The first of these is 0.0100% greater than the true value, and the second is 0.0100% less than the true value.

Recall that light behaves as if it were composed of tiny packets, or quanta, of energy (now called photons). The energy of a photon is defined as

$$E_{\text{photon}} = h\upsilon,$$

where *h* is Planck's constant, and v is the frequency of the light. The frequency can be further broken down to make the equation even more elementary:

$$E = \frac{hc}{\lambda},$$

where *c* is the speed of light, and λ is the wavelength of light.

The electron is restricted to specific energy levels in the atom; it is quantized. Specifically,

$$E = \frac{-A}{n^2},$$

where $A = 2.18 \times 10^{-11}$ erg, and *n* is the quantum number.

Finally, we'll look at components of atomic structure (illustrated in Figure 8). The number of protons and neutrons in the nucleus is called the **mass number**, which corresponds to the isotopic atomic weight. The **atomic number** is the number of protons found in the nucleus.

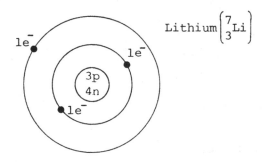

Figure 8. Lithium, $_3^7$Li   Electron(–), Proton(+), Neutron(0)

The electrons in the outermost shell are valence electrons. When these electrons are lost or partially lost (through sharing), the oxidation state is assigned a positive value for the element. If valence electrons are gained by an atom, its oxidation number is taken to be negative.

KINETICS

Now, we'll move on to another important area of chemistry, kinetics. **Kinetics** is the study of the rates of reactions. The measurement of reaction rate is based on the rate of appearance of a product or disappearance of a reactant. It is usually expressed in terms of a change in the concentration of one of the participants per unit time:

$$\text{rate of reaction} = \frac{\text{change in concentration}}{\text{time}} = \frac{\text{moles/liter}}{\text{sec}}.$$

For the general reaction $2AB \rightarrow A_2 + B_2$:

$$\text{average rate} = \frac{\left[AB\right]_{t2} - \left[AB\right]_{t1}}{t_2 - t_1} = -\frac{\Delta\left[AB\right]}{\Delta t},$$

where $\left[AB\right]_{t2}$ represents the concentration of AB at time t_2. There are a few important factors that control the rate of a reaction:

(1) The nature of the reactants and products (i.e., the nature of the transition state formed). Some elements and compounds, because of the bonds broken or formed, react more rapidly with each other than others do.

(2) The surface area exposed. Since most reactions depend on the reactants coming into contact with each other, increasing the surface area exposed proportionally increases the rate of the reaction.

(3) Concentrations. The reaction rate usually increases with increasing concentrations of reactants and products.

(4) Temperature. For most reactions, the reaction rate increases as temperature increases.

The Arrhenius equation relates rate to temperature and energy:

$$k = Ae^{\frac{-E_a}{RT}}$$

where k = Rate constant

   A = Arrhenius constant

   E_a = Activation energy

   R = Universal gas constant

   T = Temperature in Kelvins

EXAMPLE

What activation energy should a reaction have so that raising the temperature by 10°C at 0°C would triple the reaction rate?

SOLUTION

The activation energy is related to the temperature by the Arrhenius equation which is stated

$$k = Ae^{\frac{-E_a}{RT}}$$

where A is a constant characteristic of the reaction, e is the base of natural logarithms, E is the activation energy, R is the gas constant (8.314 J mol^{-1} deg^{-1}), and T is the absolute temperature. Taking the natural log of each side:

$$\ell nk = \ell nA - \frac{E}{RT}.$$

For a reaction that is three times as fast, the Arrhenius equation becomes

$$3k = Ae^{\frac{-E}{R\left(T+10°\right)}}$$

Taking the natural log:

$$\ell n3 + \ell nk = \ell nA - \frac{E}{R\left(T+10°\right)}$$

Subtracting the equation for the final state from the equation for the initial state:

$$\ell nk = \ell nA - \frac{E}{RT}$$

$$-\left(\ell n\,3 + \ell nk = \ell nA - \frac{E}{R(T+10°)}\right)$$

$$-\ell n3 = -\frac{E}{RT} + \frac{E}{R(T+10°)}$$

Solving for E:

$$\ell n3 = \frac{E}{RT} - \frac{E}{R(T+10°)} \qquad R = 8.314 \text{ J/mole K}$$

$$T = 0 + 273 = 273$$

$$-\ell n3 = \overline{\left(\dfrac{-E}{8.314 \text{ J/mole K}}\right)} (273\text{K}) + \overline{\left(\dfrac{E}{8.314 \text{ J/mole K}}\right)} (283)\text{K}$$

$$-1.10 = \overline{\left(\dfrac{-E}{2,269.72 \text{ J/mole K}}\right)} + \overline{\left(\dfrac{E}{2,269.72 \text{ J/mole K}}\right)}$$

$$(2,269.72 \text{ J/mole K})(2,352.86 \text{ J/mole K}) \times (-1.10) =$$

$$\left(\dfrac{-E}{2,269.72 \text{ J/mole K}} + \dfrac{E}{2,352.86 \text{ J/mole K}}\right)$$

$(2,269.72 \text{ J/mole K}) \ (2,352.86 \text{ J/mole K})$

$$-5.874 \times 10^6 \text{ J}^2/\text{mole}^2 = (-E)(2,352.86 \text{ J/mole}) + E \ (2,269.72 \text{ J/mole})$$

$$-5.874 \times 10^6 \text{ J}^2/\text{mole}^2 = 8.314 \times 10^1 \text{ J/mole} \times E$$

$$7.06 \times 10^4 \text{ J/mole} = E$$

When the temperature of the reaction mixture is very low or the activation energy is very large, k is small. If we take the natural log of both sides,

$$\ln k = \ln A - \dfrac{E_a}{RT}$$

$$(y = b + mx)$$

we can plot ln (k) versus $\dfrac{1}{T}$. The straight line plot will give a slope $= \dfrac{-E_a}{R}$ and an intercept with the ordinate $= \ln(A)$. For two different temperatures of the same reaction:

$$\ln\dfrac{k_2}{k_1} = -\dfrac{E_a}{R}\left(\dfrac{1}{T_2} - \dfrac{1}{T_1}\right) \quad \text{or} \quad \log\dfrac{k_2}{k_1} = -\dfrac{E_a}{2.303R}\left(\dfrac{1}{T_2} - \dfrac{1}{T_1}\right).$$

Activation energy E_a is the energy necessary to cause a reaction to occur. It is the difference in energy between the transition state (or activated complex) and the reactants. Figure 9 illustrates the concept of activation energy.

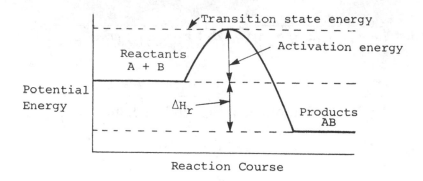

Figure 9. Activation energy

In an exothermic process, energy is released and ΔH_2 is negative. In an endothermic process, energy is absorbed and ΔH_2 is positive. For a reversible reaction, the energy liberated in the exothermic reaction is equal to the energy absorbed in the endothermic reaction (the energy of the reaction, ΔH_2, is also equal to the diffcrence between the activation energies of the opposing reactions:

$$\Delta H_2 = E_{a \text{ reverse}} - E_{a \text{ forward}}$$

As mentioned earlier, the rate of an irreversible reaction is directly proportional to the concentration of the reactants raised to some power. If the reaction

$$A + B \rightarrow P$$

is an elementary reaction, the rate is proportional to

$$[A]^x[B]^y.$$

The order of the reaction with respect to A is x, and the order with respect to B is y. For this reaction, the rate law is

$$\text{rate} = \text{k}[A]^x[B]^y, \text{k} = \text{rate constant.}$$

EXAMPLE

Assume that one A molecule reacts with two B molecules in a one-step process to give AB_2. (a) Write a rate law for this reaction. (b) If the initial rate of formation of AB_2 is 2.0×10^{-5} M/sec and the initial concentrations of A and B are 0.30 M, what is the value of the specific rate constant?

SOLUTION

(a) The overall equation for this reaction is

$$A + 2B \rightarrow AB_2.$$

Since no other information is provided about the reaction, the rate law for the reaction is assumed to be written

$$\text{rate} = k\,[A][B]^2,$$

where k is the rate constant and [ ] indicates concentration.

(b) One can solve for k using the rate law when the rate, [A] and [B], are given as they are in this problem.

$$\text{Rate} = k\,[A][B]^2$$

$$2.0 \times 10^{-5} \text{ M/sec} = k(0.30 \text{ M})(0.30 \text{ M})^2$$

$$\frac{2.0 \times 10^{-5} \text{ M/sec}}{(0.30 \text{ M})(0.30 \text{ M})^2} = k$$

$$k = 7.41 \times 10^{-4} \text{M}^{-2}\text{sec}^{-1}$$

There are several orders of reactions. Below are guidelines to determine zero, first, second, and third order reactions.

ORDERS OF REACTIONS

Zero order: rate = k

> If the reaction rate remains constant regardless of changes in reactant concentration, it is a zero order reaction.

First order: rate = k[A]

> If the reaction rate is doubled by doubling the concentration of the reactant, the order with respect to the reactant is 1.

Second order: rate = $k[A]^2$; rate = $k[2a]^2 = 4ka^2$

> If the rate is increased by a factor of four when the concentration of a reactant is doubled, it is second order with respect to that component.

Third order: rate = $k[A]^3$; rate = $k[2a]^3 = 8ka^3$

> The rate of a third order reaction would undergo an eightfold increase when the concentration is doubled.

Another way to think about rate is to look at rates of appearance or disappearance of products or reactants. For the reaction:

$$aA + bB \rightarrow eE + fF$$

$$\frac{1}{a}\left(\frac{-\Delta A}{\Delta t}\right) = \frac{1}{b}\left(\frac{-\Delta B}{\Delta t}\right) = \frac{1}{e}\left(\frac{-\Delta E}{\Delta t}\right) = \frac{1}{f}\left(\frac{-\Delta F}{\Delta t}\right)$$

$$\qquad \text{disappearance} \qquad\qquad \text{appearance}$$

METALS AND NONMETALS

Elements can be divided into three general categories: metals, semi-metals, and nonmetals. We can further simplify the categories into metals and nonmetals. Metals comprise most of the elements on the periodic table, and most periodic tables have a line dividing the metals and nonmetals. Metals are excellent conductors of electricity; they possess a shiny, lustrous surface, are malleable, are usually solids (mercury is a liquid), and emit electrons when exposed to heat or short wavelength radiation. Metals rarely form diatomic molecules. Instead, they usually bond to nonmetals in an ionic bond (NaCl, LiOH, KBr). Gold is an interesting example of a metal. Gold is actually a noble metal because even concentrated acids do not attack it. Only a mixture of concentrated HCl and concentrated HNO^3 in a 3:1 ratio (aqua-regia) can dissolve gold (watch out for this in problem solving!).

The middle of the periodic table is primarily composed of semimetals and transition metals. In general, they are classified in terms of their conductivity. Semimetals are poor conductors of electricity but increase their conductivity with increasing temperature. These metals are electronically characterized as having an incomplete "d" subshell or may form ions with an incomplete "d" subshell (the elements Zn, Cd, and Hg do, however, have a complete "d" subshell and so are not included in the transition metal group). The metals in groups IB through VIIIB of the periodic table exhibit multiple valence states. These metals have two (sometimes one) "s" electrons in the outer orbit, and "d" electrons are added one orbit down with each successive element formed. These "d" electrons have significantly different reactivity than the "s" electrons in the outer orbit and lead to multiple valence states depending on whether or not they react.

Nonmetals are among the most abundant substances in the universe. Nonmetals include the noble gases, the halogens, and the elements C, N, P, O, S, and H. Nonmetals may bond to metals to form ionic salts, or they may bond with each other covalently to form various compounds. Also, bonding in nonmetals may be nonpolar or polar. Remember, electronegativity still follows periodic trends within the nonmetal groups! Now, let's look at some of these nonmetal groups.

The noble, or inert, gases (Group VIIIA) are so named because of their "reluctance" to bond with other atoms. Since their "s" and "p" orbitals are completed, they have a filled valence shell (an octet) and so are stable as atomic particles. Under ordinary conditions, they do not react with other molecules, and they exist naturally as monatomic gases.

The halogens (Group VIIA) are a very important group of nonmetals. They exist as diatomic molecules, but they also react readily with metals to form ionic salts. They may also react with oxygen to form various compounds. Halogens are very electronegative and form strong acids. In addition, they are good oxidizing agents; and each halogen can oxidize any of the halogens below it on the periodic table. (However, they cannot oxidize anything above them.) Their valence state is -1, and they have an electron configuration of ns^2np^5.

Hydrogen is, in a sense, a misfit element. It cannot truly be classified with any type of element group beyond its "nonmetallic" classification. Its electron configuration is 1s, and it naturally exists as a diatomic molecule; however, it is one of the most common elements in the universe and exists in many other forms as well (water, organics, acids, bases, etc.). Hydrogen reacts with almost all of the elements to form hydrides, binary compounds consisting only of hydrogen and one other element (e.g., H_2O, HCl).

Carbon is one of the most abundant elements on the earth. It is the backbone element of all organic compounds, and forms most of the biological and polymeric compounds that we see everyday. The electron configuration of carbon is $2s^22p^2$, and it has only four valence electrons. This allows it to form many strong covalent bonds at its four sites.

The other nonmetals form vital compounds, and are also abundant throughout the earth. Nitrogen makes up most of the atmosphere and forms such compounds as ammonia, various oxides, and amino acids—the building blocks of proteins. Phosphorous is found in many biological molecules and makes up part of the helical structure of the DNA molecule. Finally, sulfur is present in various oxides and acids, but it is also prevalent within the earth's crust, rising in a gaseous form from the cracks in the surface.

ORGANIC CHEMISTRY

This brings us to organic chemistry. In general, organic chemistry focuses primarily on nonmetallic compounds, involving the chemistry of carbon and its compounds. Many carbon compounds are **hydrocarbons**, compounds that contain carbon and hydrogen. Carbon is a unique element in that it has four bonding sites. As a result, it may form single, double, or triple bonds. It may also form ringlike structures or long hydrocarbon chains. Another phenomenon of organic molecules is that even though two compounds may have the same chemical formulas, they may not have the same chemical properties. Since the carbon atoms may bond to each other in any of several ways, several different structures may form. These are called isomers. Isomers may be structural or conformational; the molecules may differ in their actual physical makeup, or they may simply be rotated or inverted enough to prevent them from being the same molecule. For example, the formula C_5H_{12} can be drawn several ways:

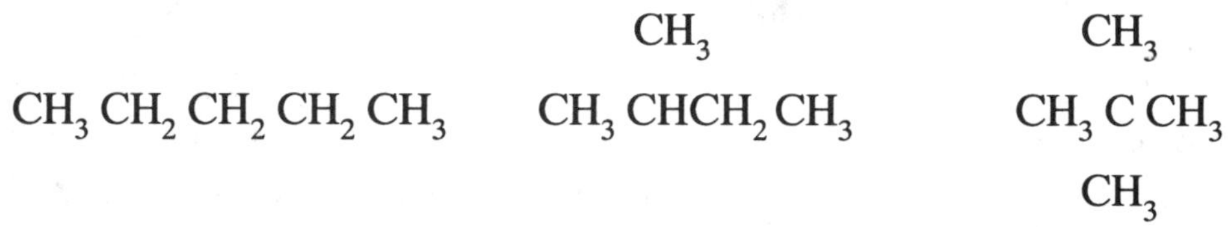

$$CH_3\ CH_2\ CH_2\ CH_2\ CH_3$$

$$CH_3\ \overset{\displaystyle CH_3}{\overset{\displaystyle |}{CH}}CH_2\ CH_3$$

$$CH_3\ \overset{\displaystyle CH_3}{\underset{\displaystyle CH_3}{\overset{\displaystyle |}{\underset{\displaystyle |}{C}}}}\ CH_3$$

(a) Pentane **(b) 2-methyl-butane** **(c) 2,2-dimethyl-propane**

Figure 10. Structures of C_5H_{12}

For compounds with double or triple bonds, isomers may be the result of a change in the position of the multiple bond:

$$CH_2 = CHCH_2CH_3 \qquad\qquad CH_3CH = CHCH_3$$

butene 2-butene

Or, they may simply have groups arranged in different ways:

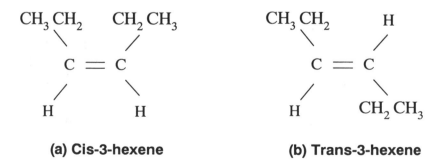

(a) Cis-3-hexene **(b) Trans-3-hexene**

Figure 11. Conformations of 3-hexene

We will first look at alkanes, the simplest organic molecule. **Alkanes** are hydrocarbons with single bonds only. Their structural formula is $C_nH_{2n + 2}$. They are saturated compounds (meaning that they have no multiple bonds), and may take the form of a straight chain or a ring. Nomenclature defines an organic molecule's nature and structure. Prefixes and suffixes indicate substituents, functional groups, and bonding type. Alkanes always end with the suffix "-ane." The prefix depends on the number of carbons in the longest continuous chain of the molecule.

Some prefixes are outlined below:

TABLE 6 CHAIN LENGTH PREFIXES	
# of Carbons	**Prefix**
1	meth-
2	eth-
3	prop-
4	but-
5	pent-
6	hex-

Here are some suffixes as well:

TABLE 7 STRUCTURAL SUFFIXES	
Structure	**Suffix**
Single bond	-ane
Double bond	-ene
Triple bond	-yne

Alkanes are generally nonpolar, unreactive molecules. The boiling point, melting point, density, and viscosity of alkanes increase as the length of the carbon chain increases.

EXAMPLE

Name the following alkanes: (a) CH_4, (b) CH_3CH_3, (c) $CH_3 \!-\! CH_2$,

and (d) $CH_3CH_2CH_2CH_3$.

$$CH_3$$

SOLUTION

Four steps can be followed in naming alkanes.

(1) In naming open-chain alkanes, first find the longest chain of carbon atoms.

(2) Write down the parent name.

(3) Identify any side chains.

(4) Number these side chains and add their names and location as a prefix to the name of the parent compound.

These steps are illustrated in the naming of the four compounds above.

$$\text{(a)} \quad H-\underset{\displaystyle H}{\overset{\displaystyle H}{\underset{|}{\overset{|}{C}}}}-H$$

This compound contains only one carbon atom and is the simplest of all the alkanes. It is called methane.

$$\text{(b)} \quad H-\underset{\displaystyle H}{\overset{\displaystyle H}{\underset{|}{\overset{|}{C}}}}-\underset{\displaystyle H}{\overset{\displaystyle H}{\underset{|}{\overset{|}{C}}}}-H$$

This is a two-carbon alkane. A chain of two carbon atoms is given the root "eth." The parent names of alkanes are formed by adding the suffix "ane" to the root name of the longest carbon chain. This compound is called ethane.

```
                    H
                    |
         H    H—C—H
         |      |
(c)   H— C———— C—H
         |      |
         H      H
```

The longest chain in this compound is three carbons long. It is not significant that the chain is bent. The root used in naming three carbon chains is "prop." The name of this compound is propane.

```
            H   H   H   H
            |   |   |   |
(d)   H— C — C — C — C—H
            |   |   |   |
            H   H   H   H
```

The longest chain here is four carbons long. The root used in naming four carbon chains is "but." The name of this compound is butane.

Alkenes are unsaturated hydrocarbons with one or more carbon-carbon double bonds. They have the general formula C_nH_{2n}. Since alkenes have another bond, they have two fewer hydrogens than their alkanal counterparts. Alkenes are named in much the same way as alkanes (the location of the double bond must be specified; however, naming compounds can be complicated and tedious. This way, you will be able to recognize the compounds quickly). Alkenes with one to four C's are gases, with five to fifteen C's are liquids, and with sixteen or more C's are solids. Alkenes show relatively higher reactivity than alkanes, and many reactions focus on "attacking" the double bond. Addition reactions saturate the double bond and create alkanes. Cleavage reactions break the double bond and create two new products. Dehydration, dehalogenation, dehydrohalogenation, and application of heat create alkenes from alkanes.

EXAMPLE

Write the chemical structures for each compound listed.

(a) 1-Hexene

(b) 3-Methyl-1-butene

(c) 2, 4-Hexadiene

(d) 1-Iodo-2-methyl-2-pentene

(e) 2-Chloro-3-methyl-2-hexene

(f) 6, 6-Dibromo-5-methyl-5-ethyl-2, 3-heptadiene

SOLUTION

(1) Look at the complete name of the compound and pick out the parent name. It is usually the last word of the complete name, and it denotes the longest continuous chain that contains the carbon-carbon double bond. (All of the structures are alkenes.)

(2) Write out the carbon skeleton that makes up the parent chain. Determine the number of double bonds present by examining the suffix of the parent name. For example, "ene" means one double bond, where as "diene" means two.

(3) Position the double bond (or bonds) in the carbon skeleton as specified by the number directly (usually) in front of the parent name. For example, if the compound is 2-pentene, one would write

$$C - C - C = C - C$$
$$5 \quad 4 \quad 3 \quad 2 \quad 1$$

(Recall, the position of the double bond is given by the number of the first doubly bonded carbon encountered when numbering from the end of the chain nearest the double bond.)

(4) Position the functional group substituents on the chain as specified by the number directly in front. For example, 3-methyl-2-pentene would be:

$$\overset{\displaystyle C}{\underset{\displaystyle \underset{5 \quad 4 \quad 3 \quad 2 \quad 1}{C - C - C = C - C}}{|}}$$

The structures of the compound in (a) – (f) become:

(a) $CH_3CH_2CH_2CH_2CH = CH_2$

(b) $CH_2 = CH-\underset{\underset{\displaystyle CH_3}{|}}{CH}-CH_3$

(c) $CH_3-CH = CH-CH = CH - CH_3$

(d) $CH_3CH_2CH = \underset{\underset{\displaystyle CH_3}{|}}{C}-CH_2I$

(e) $CH_3CH_2CH_2C = C-CH_3$
                      | |
                     CH_3 Cl

(f)
$$CH_3-CH=C=CH-\underset{\underset{CH_3}{|}}{\overset{\overset{CH_3}{|}}{C}}-\underset{\underset{Br}{|}}{\overset{\overset{Br}{|}}{C}}-CH_3$$
                                  |
                                 CH_2
                                  |
                                 CH_3

To see how this process works, examine how structure (f) was written. The parent name is heptadiene. The prefix "hepta" indicates that seven carbons are present in the skeleton: C—C—C—C—C—C—C. The 2, 3 indicates the positions of the two double bonds—it is a diene. So, one can write

$$
\begin{array}{ccccccc}
C - C = C = C - C - C - C \\
1 \quad 2 \quad 3 \quad 4 \quad 5 \quad 6 \quad 7
\end{array}
$$

With this numbering system, the substituents are now added as specified by the 6 for the bromines and 5 for the methyl (CH_3) and ethyl groups.

$$
\begin{array}{cccc}
 & & CH_3 & Br \\
 & & | & | \\
C-C=C=C-C & -C-C \\
1 \ 2 \ 3 \ 4 & | & | \ 7 \\
 & CH_2 & Br \\
 & | \\
 & CH_3
\end{array}
$$

And now only the hydrogens need to be added to obtain:

$$
\begin{array}{cc}
 & CH_3 \quad Br \\
 & | \qquad | \\
CH_3CH=C=CHC & -C-CH_3 \\
 & | \qquad | \\
 & CH_2 \quad Br \\
 & | \\
 & CH_3
\end{array}
$$

Alkynes are unsaturated hydrocarbons containing triple bonds. They have the general formula C_nH_{2n-2}. Alkynes are named in the same way as alkenes, except the suffix "-ene" is replaced with "-yne." The hydrogens in terminal alkynes are relatively acidic, and the dipole moment is small, but larger than that of an alkene. Other physical properties are essentially the same as alkanes and alkenes. Alkynes undergo many of the same types of addition, cleavage, and dehydration reactions as alkenes.

Organic molecules may also form cyclic structures. Triangular, square planar, and various other regular and irregular polygonal structures may be formed. One of the most important types of structures are aromatic compounds. These are six membered rings with alternating double and single bonds. An example of this is benzene, C_6H_6:

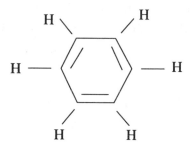

Figure 12. Benzene ring

Other organic compounds include those created by functional groups, additional groups of elements that "add on" to the hydrocarbon skeleton. Functional groups often determine the chemical properties of organic compounds. Some elemental functional groups include oxygen, nitrogen, and sulfuric compounds. Some of the most common are those of oxygen. Alcohols, ethers, aldehydes, ketones, and carboxylic acids are among the most common oxygen containing organic compounds.

TABLE 8
NOMENCLATURE OF FUNCTIONAL GROUPS

Structure/Functional Group	Name
$-\overset{\mid}{\underset{\mid}{C}}-\overset{\mid}{\underset{\mid}{C}}-$	ALKANE
$\overset{}{\underset{}{>}}C=C\overset{}{\underset{}{<}}$	ALKENE
$-C\equiv C-$	ALKYNE
(pentagon)	CYCLOALKANE (cyclopentane)
(hexagon with inscribed)	AROMATIC RING (benzene)
$-CH_3$	METHYL GROUP
$-CH_2CH_3$	ETHYL GROUP
$-CH_2CH_2CH_3$	PROPYL GROUP
$-OH$	ALCOHOL
(hexagon)$-OH$	PHENOL
$-NH_2$, $-NA-$, $-N-$	AMINE
$-C-O-C-$	ETHER
$-\overset{}{C}-\overset{}{C}-$ with O below (epoxide ring)	EPOXIDE
$-C\overset{\nearrow O}{\underset{\searrow OH}{}}$	CARBOXYLIC ACID
$-C\overset{\nearrow O}{\underset{\searrow H}{}}$	ALDEHYDE
$-C\overset{\nearrow O}{\underset{\searrow C-}{}}$	KETONE

INORGANIC CHEMISTRY

Inorganic chemistry covers a vast number of topics and compounds with every known type of physical and structural characteristics. While organic chemistry is usually defined as the study of molecules which contain carbon, inorganic chemistry refers to everything else. Often carbon structures are studied in inorganic chemistry also, although not in the combinations with oxygen and hydrogen, like the proteins and carbohydrates found in organic chemistry. Since this review is brief, it will only touch on the main topics, and even then in only a cursory manner. For a more complete review of the subject, the reader is advised to consult one of the many textbooks on inorganic chemistry.

Nonmolecular Solids - Most of the important substances, including the elements themselves, are in the form of nonmolecular solids. The elements that are metals are held together by delocalized electrons in closely packed arrays. Carbon and silicon have infinite networks of more localized bonds. Other molecules are in ionic arrays. Glasses and polymers are held together either by well-defined arrays or infinite arrays. Semiconductors, ceramics, superconductors, and alloys all have nonmolecular structures.

Metals have physical characteristics which are quite different from other compounds. These include high reflectivity, high electrical conductance, high thermal conductance, and the mechanical properties of strength and ductility. All metals have one of three basic structures: the atoms may be packed as cubic or hexagonal close-packed arrays, or in body-centered cubic array.

Interstitial compounds are defined as the combination of relatively large transition metal atoms with small metalloid or nonmetal atoms, such as hydrogen or boron. The interstitial compounds have structures of the metal host lattice with the smaller atoms occupying the interstices. Only occasionally do the arrays correspond to known packing arrangements. Interstitial compounds have great hardness, great brittleness, and high melting points. Some have luster, malleability, and good conductivity, as is found in metals.

Ionic crystals are usually thought of as salts; some examples include NaF, KCl, and CsI. In these salts, the cations and anions are isoelectronic and the radius ratios are all similar. The cation and anion are assumed to be in contact and the internuclear distance is the sum of the radii. In an ionic structure, each ion is surrounded by ions of the opposite charge; the number of surrounding ions is known as the coordination number of the ion. In NaCl, the cation has a coordination number of 6. While the ionic model is often accurate, x-ray crystallographic analysis of several crystals, including NaCl, show that the electron distribution does not always correspond to the exact requirements. Thus, the ionic model is only a model, and its requirement of fixed ratios sometimes is violated.

Elements in Group IV (except lead), boron, phosphorous, arsenic, selenium, and tellurium, all form covalent solids. In the case of diamond, the structure can be simply described as all atoms are equivalent and each atom is surrounded by a tetrahedon of four other atoms. Each atom forms a localized two-electron bond with each of its neighbors.

Structure defects are common in all crystalline solids. A Schottky defect, in ionic crystals, occurs when vacant cation and anion sites are present in numbers proportional to the stoichiometry. A Frenckel defect, on the other hand, describes the case when an ion occupies a normally vacant interstitial site. Both Schottky and Frenckel defects are stoichiometric defects. Nonstoichiometric defects include Farbe defects, which occur when a metal ion has a different oxidation state from the others in the solid. Defects arising from impurities in the solid include p-type (for positive) and n-type (negative), which are common in semiconductors. In each case, an atom is substituted by another foreign one, leaving a charge imbalance and resulting in electrons wandering throughout the solid, hence giving the compound its semiconductor property.

Group I Elements include Li, Na, K, Rb, and Cs. These are also known as the alkali metals. Each has a single s electron surrounding a noble gas core. The chemistry of these elements is predominantly cationic, although some degree of covalent bonding may occur in certain cases.

Group II Elements include Be, Mg, Ca, Sr, Ba, and Ra. Their chemistry is predominately covalent. Due to increased nuclear charge, the atomic nuclei of Group II elements is smaller than the Group I metals. Considering the series from Ca to Ra: the hydration tendencies of the crystalline salts increases, while the solubilities of sulfates, nitrates, and chlorides decreases. The rates of reaction of the metals with hydrogen increases.

Group III Elements include Al, Ga, In, and Ti. While boron is in Group III, its characteristics are slightly different from the other elements. While the other Group III elements form cationic complexes, boron does not. Al is the most common metal in the earth's crust and is easily mined. The other elements in this group are found only in trace amounts. Gallium, indium, and thallium are all soft, white, relatively reactive metals.

Group IV Elements include C, Si, Ge, Sn, and Pb. Unlike Groups I and II which have fairly similar properties, the elements in Group IV are very different from each other. Carbon is nonmetallic; silicon is essentially nonmetallic; Ge is metalloid; and Sn and Pb are metals. Bonding among the elements decreases in strength, as C-C bonds are the strongest and Pb-Pb bonds are the weakest.

Group V Elements are N, P, As, Sb, and Bi. N and P have chemistry which is essentially always covalent, while As, Sb, and Bi show tendencies toward cationic behavior. Oxides of N are acidic, while those of Bi are basic. Similarly, halides made with these elements have increasing ionic characteristics.

Group VI Elements O, S, Se, Te, and Po have electron configurations that are two electrons short of a noble gas. Their chemistry is essentially nonmetallic covalent, with the exception of Po. While there are great differences in the chemistry of O and S, more gradual variations exist throughout the rest of the sequence. Thermal stability of the H_2X compounds decreases. The elements have an increasing metallic character and an increasing tendency to form anionic complexers.

Halogens include F, Cl, Br, I, and At. The atoms are only one electron short of the noble gas configuration and are thus highly reactive. All halogens exist in nature as diatomic molecules. The chemistry is essentially nonmetallic. When a halogen atom forms a bond with another atom more electronegative than itself, the bond will be polar with a partial positive charge on the halogen.

REVIEW PROBLEMS

PROBLEM 1

Balance the following by filling in missing species and proper coefficient:

(1) $NaOH +$ _____ $\rightarrow NaHSO_4 + HOH$

(2) $PCl_3 + 3HOH \rightarrow$ _____ $+ 3HCl$

(3) $CH_4 +$ _____ $\rightarrow CCl_4 + 4HCl$

SOLUTION

To balance chemical equations you must remember that ALL atoms (and charges) must be accounted for. The use of coefficients in front of compounds is a means to this end. Thus,

(1) $\qquad$ $NaOH + \underline{\hspace{2cm}} \rightarrow NaHSO_4 + HOH$

On the right side of the equation, you have 1 Na, 3 H's, 5 O's, and 1 S. This same number of elements must appear on the left side. However, on the left side, there exists only 1 Na, 1 O, and 1 H. You are missing 2 H's, 1 S, and 4 O's. The missing species is H_2SO_4, sulfuric acid. You could have anticipated this since a strong base (NaOH) reacting with a strong acid yields a salt ($NaHSO_4$) and water. The point is, however, that H_2SO_4 balances the equation by supplying all the missing atoms.

(2) $\qquad$ $PCl_3 + 3HOH \rightarrow \underline{\hspace{2cm}} + 3HCl$

Here, the left side has 1 P, 3 Cl's, 6 H's, and 3 O's. The right side has 3 H's and 3 Cl's. You are missing 1 P, 3 O's, and 3 hydrogens. Therefore, $P(OH)_3$ is formed.

(3) $\qquad$ $CH_4 + \underline{\hspace{2cm}} \rightarrow CCl_4 + 4HCl$

Here, there are 1 C, 8 Cl's, and 4 H's on the right and 1 C and 4 H's on the left. The missing compound, therefore, contains 8 Cl's and thus it is $4Cl_2$. One knows that it is $4Cl_2$ rather than Cl_8 or $8Cl$ because elemental chlorine gas is a diatomic or 2 atom molecule.

PROBLEM 2

Calculate the mole fractions of ethyl alcohol, C_2H_5OH, and water in a solution made by dissolving 9.2 g of alcohol in 18 g of H_2O. The M.W. of $H_2O = 18$, M.W. of $C_2H_5OH = 46$.

SOLUTION

Mole fraction problems are similar to percent composition problems. A mole fraction of a compound tells us what fraction of 1 mole of solution is due to that particular compound. Hence,

$$\text{mole fraction of solute} = \frac{\text{moles of solute}}{\text{moles of solute } + \text{ moles of solvent}} .$$

The solute is the substance being dissolved into or added to the solution. The solvent is the solution to which the solute is added.

The equation for calculating mole fractions is

$$\frac{\text{moles } A}{\text{moles } A \; + \; \text{moles } B} = \text{mole fraction } A .$$

Moles are defined as grams/molecular weight (M.W.). Therefore, first find the number of moles of each compound present and then use the above equation.

$$\text{moles of } C_2H_5OH = \frac{9.2 \text{ g}}{46.0 \text{ g/mole}} = .2 \text{ mole}$$

$$\text{moles of } H_2O = \frac{18 \text{ g}}{18 \text{ g/mole}} = 1 \text{ mole}$$

$$\text{mole fraction of } C_2H_5OH = \frac{.2}{1 + .2} = .167$$

$$\text{mole fraction of } H_2O = \frac{1}{1 + .2} = .833$$

Note: The sum of the mole fractions is equal to 1.

PROBLEM 3

What is the maximum weight of SO_3 that could be made from 25.0 g of SO_2 and 6.0 g of O_2 by the following reaction?

$$2SO_2 + O_2 \rightarrow 2SO_3$$

SOLUTION

From the reaction, one knows that for every 2 moles of SO_3 formed, 2 moles of SO_2 and 1 mole of O_2 must react. Thus, to find the amount of SO_3 that can be formed, one must first know the number of moles of SO_2 and O_2 present. The number of moles is found by dividing the number of grams present by molecular weight:

$$\text{number of moles} = \frac{\text{number of grams}}{\text{M.W.}}.$$

For O_2: M.W. = 32

$$\text{no. of moles} = \frac{6.0 \text{ g}}{32.0 \text{ g/mole}} = 1.875 \times 10^{-1} \text{ moles}$$

For SO_2: M.W. = 64

$$\text{no. of moles} = \frac{25.0 \text{ g}}{64.0 \text{ g/mole}} = 3.91 \times 10^{-1} \text{ moles}$$

Because 2 moles of SO_2 are needed to react with 1 mole of O_2, 3.75×10^{-1} moles of SO_2 will react with 1.88×10^{-1} moles of O_2. This means that $3.91 \times 10^{-1} - 3.75 \times 10^{-1}$ moles or $.16 \times 10^{-1}$ moles of SO_2 will remain unreacted. In this case, O_2 is called the limiting reagent because it determines the number of moles of SO_3 formed. There will be twice as many moles of SO_3 formed as there are O_2 reacting.

no. of moles of SO_3 formed = $2 \times 1.875 \times 10^{-1}$ moles

$$= 3.75 \times 10^{-1} \text{ moles}$$

The weight is found by multiplying the number of moles formed by the molecular weight (M.W. of $SO_3 = 80$).

weight of $SO_3 = 3.75 \times 10^{-1}$ moles $\times 80$ g/mole = 30.0 g

PROBLEM 4

The following reaction

$$2H_2S(g) \rightleftharpoons 2H_2(g) + S_2(g)$$

was allowed to proceed to equilibrium. The contents of the two-liter reaction vessel were then subjected to analysis and found to contain 1.0 mole H_2S, 0.20 mole H_2, and 0.80 mole S_2. What is the equilibrium constant K_{eq} for this reaction?

SOLUTION

This problem involves substitution into the equilibrium constant expression for this reaction:

$$K_{eq} = \frac{[H_2]^2[S_2]}{[H_2S]^2}.$$

The equilibrium concentration of the reactant and products are $[H_2S]$ = 1.0 mole/2 liters = 0.50 M, $[H_2]$ = 0.20 mole/2 liters = 0.10 M, and $[S_2]$ = 0.80 mole/2 liters = 0.40 M, Hence, the value of the equilibrium constant is

$$K_{eq} = \frac{[H_2]^2[S_2]}{[H_2S]^2} = \frac{(0.10)^2(0.40)}{(0.50)^2} = 0.016$$

for this reaction.

PROBLEM 5

The ionization constant for acetic acid is 1.8×10^{-5}.

(1) Calculate the concentration of H^+ ions in a 0.10 molar solution of acetic acid.

(2) Calculate the concentration of H^+ ions in a 0.10 molar solution of acetic acid in which the concentration of acetate ions has been increased to 1.0 molar by addition of sodium acetate.

SOLUTION

(1) The ionization constant (K_a) is defined as the concentration of H^+ ions times the concentration of the conjugate base ions of a given acid divided by the concentration of unionized acid. For an acid, HA:

$$K_a = \frac{\left[H^+\right]\left[A^-\right]}{[HA]}$$

where K_a is the ionization constant, $[H^+]$ is the concentration of H^+ ions, $[A^-]$ is the concentration of the conjugate base ions, and $[HA]$ is the concentration of unionized acid. The K_a for acetic acid is stated as

$$K_a = \frac{\left[H^+\right]\left[\text{acetate ion}\right]}{\left[\text{acetic acid}\right]} = 1.8 \times 10^{-5}.$$

The chemical formula for acetic acid is $HC_2H_3O_2$. When it is ionized, one H^+ is formed and one $C_2H_3O^-$ (acetate) is formed, thus the concentration of H^+ equals the concentration of $C_2H_3O^-$:

$$[H^+] = [C_2H_3O^-].$$

The concentration of unionized acid is decreased when ionization occurs. The new concentration is equal to the concentration of H^+ subtracted from the concentration of unionized acid:

$$[HC_2H_3O] = 0.10 - [H^+].$$

Since $[H^+]$ is small relative to 0.10, one may assume that $0.10 - [H^+]$ is approximately equal to 0.10:

$$0.10 - [H^+] \cong 0.10.$$

Using this assumption and the fact that $[H^+] = [C_2H_3O^-]$, K_a can be rewritten as

$$K_a = \frac{\left[H^+\right]\left[H^+\right]}{0.10} = 1.8 \times 10^{-5}.$$

Solving for the concentration of H^+:

$$\left[H^+\right]^2 = \left(1.0 \times 10^{-1}\right)\left(1.8 \times 10^{-5}\right) = 1.8 \times 10^{-6}$$
$$\left[H^+\right] = \sqrt{1.8 \times 10^{-6}} = 1.3 \times 10^{-3} M$$

The concentration of H^+ is thus 1.3×10^{-3} M.

(2) When the acetate concentration is increased, the concentration of H^+ is lowered to maintain the K_a. The K_a for acetic acid is stated as

$$K_a = \frac{\left[H^+\right]\left[C_2H_3O^-\right]}{\left[HC_2H_3O\right]} = 1.8 \times 10^{-5}.$$

As previously shown for acetic acid equilibria in a solution of 0.10 molar acid, the concentration of acid after ionization is

$$[HC_2H_3O] = 0.10 - [H^+].$$

Because $[H^+]$ is very small compared to 0.10, $0.10 - [H^+] \cong 0.10$ and:

$$[HC_2H_2O] = 0.10 \text{ M}.$$

In this problem, we are told that the concentration of acetate is held constant at 1.0 molar by addition of sodium acetate. Because we now know the concentrations of the acetate and the acid, the concentration of H^+ can be found:

$$\frac{\left[H^+\right]\left[C_2H_3O^-\right]}{\left[HC_2H_3O\right]} = 1.8 \times 10^{-5}$$
$$\frac{\left[H^+\right]\left[1.0\right]}{\left[0.10\right]} = 1.8 \times 10^{-5}$$
$$\left[H^+\right] = 1.8 \times 10^{-6} M$$

PROBLEM 6

A chemist dissolves $BaSO_4$ in pure water at 25°C. If $K_{sp} = 1 \times 10^{-10}$, what is the solubility of the barium sulfate in the water?

SOLUTION

The solubility of a compound is defined as the limiting concentration of the compound in a solution before precipitation occurs. To find the solubility of the barium sulfate, you need to know the concentration of its ions in solution. $BaSO_4$ will dissociate into ions because it is salt. There will be an equilibrium between these ions and the $BaSO_4$. The equilibrium can be measured in terms of a constant, K, called the solubility constant. The K_{sp} is expressed in terms of the concentrations of the ions. As such, to answer the question, you want to represent this K_{sp}. For this reaction, the equation is

$$BaSO_4 \rightleftharpoons Ba^{++} + SO_4^{=}$$
$$K_{sp} = [Ba^{+2}]\{SO_4^{-2}\} = 1 \times 10^{-10}$$

Let $x = [Ba^{+2}]$. Thus, $x = [SO_4^{-2}]$, also, since both ions will be formed in equimolar amounts. Therefore, $x \times x = 1 \times 10^{-10}$. Solving:

$$x = 1 \times 10^{-5}\,M = [Ba^{+2}] = [SO_4^{-2}].$$

PROBLEM 7

"Hard" water contains small amounts of the salts calcium bicarbonate $(Ca(HCO_3)_2)$ and calcium sulfate $(CaSO_4$, molecular weight = 136 g/mole). These react with soap before it has a chance to lather, which is responsible for its cleansing ability. $Ca(HCO_3)_2$ is removed by boiling to form insoluble $CaCO_3$. $CaSO_4$ is removed by reaction with washing soda $(Na_2CO_3$, molecular weight = 106 g/mole) according to the following equation:

$$CaSO_4 + Na_2CO_3 \rightarrow CaCO_3 + Na_2SO_4.$$

If the rivers surrounding New York City have a $CaSO_4$ concentration of 1.8×10^{-3} g/liter, how much Na_2CO_3 is required to "soften" (remove $CaSO_4$) the water consumed by the city in one day (about 6.8×10^9 liters)?

SOLUTION

We must determine the amount of $CaSO_4$ present in 6.8×10^9 liters and, from this, the amount of Na_2CO_3 required to remove it.

The number of moles per liter, or molarity, of $CaSO_4$ corresponding to 1.8×10^{-3} g/liter is obtained by dividing this concentration by the molecular weight of $CaSO_4$. Multiplying by 6.8×10^9 liters gives the number of moles of $CaSO_4$ that must be removed. Hence:

$$\text{moles } CaSO_4 = \frac{\text{concentration(g/liter)}}{\text{molecular weight of } CaSO_4} \times 6.8 \times 10^9 \text{ liters}$$

$$= \frac{1.8 \times 10^{-3} \text{ g/liter}}{136 \text{ g/mole}} \times 6.8 \times 10^9 \text{ liters}$$

$$= 9.0 \times 10^4 \text{ moles}$$

From the equation for the reaction between $CaSO_4$ and Na_2CO_3, we see that one mole of $CaSO_4$ reacts with one mole of Na_2CO_3. Hence, 9.0×10^4 moles of Na_2CO_3 are required to remove all the $CaSO_4$. To convert this to mass, we multiply by the molecular weight of Na_2CO_3 and obtain

$$\text{mass } Na_2CO_3 = \text{moles } Na_2CO_3 \times \text{molecular weight } Na_2CO_3$$

$$= 9.0 \times 10^4 \text{ moles} \times 106 \text{ g/mole}$$

$$= 9.5 \times 10^6 \text{ g} = 9.5 \times 10^6 \text{ g} \times 1 \text{ kg}/1{,}000 \text{ g}$$

$$= 9.5 \times 10^3 \text{ kg}$$

which is about 10 tons.

PROBLEM 8

For the following voltaic cell, write the half-reactions, designating which is oxidation and which is reduction. Write the cell reaction and calculate the voltage (E^0) of the cell from the given electrodes. The cell is

$$Cu; Cu^{+2} \| Ag^{+1}; Ag.$$

SOLUTION

In a voltaic cell, the flow of electrons creates a current. Their flow is regulated by two types of reactions that occur concurrently—oxidation and reduction. Oxidation is a process where electrons are lost and reduction where electrons are gained. The equation for these are the half-reactions. From the cell diagram, the direction of the reaction is always left to right.

$$Cu \leftarrow Cu^{2+} + 2e^- \qquad \text{oxidation}$$

$$\leftarrow 2Ag^+ + 2e^- \rightarrow 2Ag \qquad \text{reduction}$$

Therefore, the combined cell reaction is

$$\leftarrow Cu + 2Ag^+ \rightarrow Cu^{2+} + 2Ag.$$

To calculate the total E^0, look up the value for the E^0 of both half-reactions as reductions. To obtain E^0 for oxidation, reverse the sign of the reduction E_0. Then, substitute into $E^0_{cell} = E^0_{red} + E^0_{ox}$. If you do this, you find

$$E^0_{cell} = -(E^0_{red} \; Cu) + E^0_{red} \; Ag^{+1}$$

$$= -.34 + .80$$

$$= .46 \text{ volt}$$

PROBLEM 9

For the following oxidation-reduction reaction, (1) write out the two half-reactions and balance the equation, (2) calculate ΔE^0, and (3) determine whether the reaction will proceed spontaneously as written:

$$Fe^{2+} + MnO_4^- + H^+ \rightarrow Mn^{2+} + Fe^{3+} + H_2O$$

(1) $Fe^{3+} + e^- \rightleftharpoons Fe^{2+}, \; E^0 = 0.77eV$

(2) $MnO_4^- + 8H^+ + 5e^- \rightleftharpoons Mn^{2+} + 4H_2O, \; E^0 = 1.51eV$

SOLUTION

(1) The two half-reactions of an oxidation = reduction reaction are the equation for the oxidation process (loss of electrons) and the reduction process (gain of electrons). In the overall reaction, you begin with Fe^{2+} and end up with Fe^{3+}. It had to lose an electron to accomplish this. Thus, you have oxidation:

$$Fe^{2+} \rightarrow Fe^{3+} + e^-.$$

Note: This is the reverse of the reaction given with $E^0 = .77eV$. As such, the oxidation reaction in this problem has $E^0 = -.77eV$. The reduction must be

$$MnO_4^- + 8H^+ + 5e^- \rightarrow Mn^{2+} + 4H_2O,$$

since in the overall reaction, you see $MnO_4^- + H^+$ go to Mn^{2+}, which suggests a gain of electrons. This is the same reaction as the one given in the problem, $E^0 = 1.51eV$. To balance the overall reaction, add the oxidation reaction to the reduction reaction, such that all electron charges disappear. If you multiply the oxidation reaction by 5, you obtain:

$$5Fe^{2+} \rightarrow 5Fe^{3+} + 5e^-$$

$$MnO_4^- + 8H^+ + 5e^- \rightarrow Mn^{2+} + 4H_2O$$

$$5Fe^{2+} + MnO_4^- + 8H^+ \rightarrow 5Fe^{3+} + Mn^{2+} + 4H_2O$$

Note: Since both equations contained $5e^-$ on different sides, they canceled out. This explains why the oxidation reaction is multiplied by five. Thus, you have written the balanced equation.

(2) The ΔE^0 for the overall reaction is the sum of the E^0 for the half-reactions, i.e.,

$$\Delta E^0 = E_{red} + E_{oxid}.$$

You know E_{red} and E_{oxid}; $\Delta E^0 = 1.51 - .77 = 0.74 eV$.

(3) A reaction will only proceed spontaneously when $\Delta E^0 = $ a positive value. You calculated a positive ΔE^0, which means the reaction proceeds spontaneously.

PROBLEM 10

The ketone acid $(CH_2CO_2H)_2CO$ undergoes a first-order decomposition in aqueous solution to yield acetone and carbon dioxide:

$$(CH_2CO_2H)_2CO \rightarrow (CH_3)_2CO + 2CO_2$$

(1) Write the expression for the reaction rate.
(2) The rate constant k has been determined experimentally as 5.48×10^{-2}/sec at 60°C. Calculate $t_{\frac{1}{2}}$ at 60°C.

(3) The rate constant at 0°C has been determined as 2.46×10^{-5}/sec. Calculate $t_{\frac{1}{2}}$ at 0°C.

(4) Are the calculated half-lives in accord with the stated influence of temperature on reaction rate?

SOLUTION

(1) For a chemical decomposition, the rate of the reaction is equal to the product of the rate constant (k) and the concentration of the compound decomposing. Thus:

$$Rate = k [(CH_2CO_2H)_2CO].$$

(2) Because the rate is only proportional to $[(CH_2CO_2H)_2CO]$, the reaction is first-order. For a first-order reaction, the half-life $t_{\frac{1}{2}}$ is related to k by the following equation:

$$t_{\frac{1}{2}} = \frac{0.693}{k}$$

Solving for $t_{\frac{1}{2}}$:

$$t_{\frac{1}{2}} = \frac{0.693}{5.48 \times 10^{-2}/sec} = 12.65\,sec.$$

(3) One can solve for $t_{\frac{1}{2}}$ at 0°C using the same equation:

$$t_{\frac{1}{2}} = \frac{0.693}{2.46 \times 10^{-5}/sec} = 2.82 \times 10^4\,sec.$$

(4) In general, the speed of a chemical change is approximately doubled for each ten degrees rise in temperature. The temperature rises 60°, from 0°C to 60°C. Therefore, the rate should double six times or the ratio of the $t_{\frac{1}{2}}$ at 0°C to the $t_{\frac{1}{2}}$ at 60°C is $2^6 = 64$.

$$\frac{t_{\frac{1}{2}}\,0°}{t_{\frac{1}{2}}\,60°} = \frac{2.82 \times 10^4\,sec}{12.65\,sec} = 2.23 \times 10^3$$

This is much greater than the expected ratio of 64.

PROBLEM 11

(1) A reaction proceeds five times as fast at 60°C as it does at 30°C. Estimate its energy of activation. (2) For a gas phase reaction with $E_A = 40,000$ cal/mole, estimate the change in rate constant due to a temperature change from 1,000°C to 2,000°C.

SOLUTION

The actuation energy E_A can be related to the rate constants k_1 (at temperature T_1) and k_2 (at temperature T_2) by the Arrhenius equation:

$$\log\frac{k_2}{k_1} = -\frac{E_a}{2.303R}\left(\frac{1}{T_2} - \frac{1}{T_1}\right)$$

where R = universal gas constant.

(1) You are told a reaction proceeds five times as fast at 60° as it does at 30°C. Therefore, if k_1 = rate constant at 30°C = 303K with T_1 = 303K, then $k_2 = 5k_1$ at 60°C = 333K with T_2 = 333K. You are given R. Substitute these values into the Arrhenius equation and solve for E_A. Rewriting and substituting:

$$E_a = \frac{-2.303R}{\dfrac{1}{T_2} - \dfrac{1}{T_1}}\log\frac{k_2}{k_1} = \frac{(-2.303)(1.987)\left(\dfrac{1\text{ kcal}}{1,000\text{ cal}}\right)}{\left(\dfrac{1}{333} - \dfrac{1}{303}\right)}\log 5$$

$$= (15.4\text{ kcal/mole})(.699) = 10.8\text{ kcal/mole}.$$

Note: 1 kcal/1,000 cal is a conversion factor to obtain the correct units.

To answer (2) find $\dfrac{k_2}{k_1}$ from the Arrhenius equation. Rewriting and substituting:

$$\frac{k_2}{k_1} = \text{antilog}\left(\frac{E_a}{2.303R}\left(\frac{1}{T_2} - \frac{1}{T_1}\right)\right)$$

$$= \text{antilog}\left(\frac{-40,000}{(2.303)(1.987)}\left(\frac{1}{2,273} - \frac{1}{1,273}\right)\right)$$

$$= \text{antilog}\,3.02 = 1.05 \times 10^3$$

That is, the rate should be about 1,050 times as great at 2,000°C as at 1,000°C.

PROBLEM 12

Four liters of octane gasoline weigh 3.19 kg. Calculate the volume of air required for its complete combustion at STP.

SOLUTION

To answer this problem, you need to write the balanced equation for the combustion of octane gasoline. This means knowing the molecular formula of octane gasoline and what is meant by combustion. Octane is a saturated hydrocarbon, i.e., it is an alkane. A saturated hydrocarbon means a compound that contains only single bonds between the carbon-to-carbon and carbon-to-hydrogen bonds. Alkanes have the general formula C_nH_{2n+2}, where n = number of carbon atoms. Since the prefix "oct" means eight, you know there are 8 carbon atoms, which indicates that 18 hydrogen atoms are present. Thus, gasoline octane has the formula C_8H_{18}. Now, combustion is the reaction of an organic compound with oxygen to produce CO_2 and H_2O. With this in mind, you can write the balanced equation for the reaction:

$$2C_8H_{18} + 25O_2 \rightarrow 16CO_2 + 18H_2O.$$

To determine the volume of air required for combustion, you need the volume of O_2 required, since 21 percent of air is oxygen (O_2). To find the amount of O_2 involved, use the fact that at STP (standard temperature and pressure) 1 mole of any gas occupies 22.4 liters. Thus, if you know how many moles of O_2 were required, you would know its volume. You can find the number of moles by using stoichiometry. You have 3.19 kg or 3,190 g (1,000 g = 1 kg) of octane gasoline. The molecular weight (M.W.) of octane is 114 grams/mole. Thus, since

$$\text{mole} = \frac{\text{grams (weight)}}{\text{M.W.}}, \text{ you have } \frac{3,190}{114} = 27.98 \text{ moles of gasoline.}$$

From the equation's coefficients, you see that for every 2 moles of gasoline, 25 moles of O_2 are required. Thus, for this number of moles of gasoline, you need

$$(27.98)\,\frac{25}{2} = 349.78 \text{ moles of } O_2.$$

Recalling that 1 mole of gas occupies 22.4 liters at STP, 349.78 moles of O_2 occupies (349.78)(22.4) = 7,835.08 liters. Oxygen is 21% of the air. Thus, the amount of air required is

$$\frac{7,835.08 \text{ liters}}{.21 \text{ liters } O_2}\,O_2 = 37,309.9 \text{ liters air}.$$

FE/EIT

Fundamentals of Engineering: AM Exam

CHAPTER 9

Computers

CHAPTER 9

COMPUTERS

FLOWCHARTS

People tend to relate easily to pictures, which is why programmers use diagrams to communicate among themselves. A diagram provides a clear picture that allows a designer to visualize a problem. A flowchart is a type of diagram that is a good way to describe a basic algorithm.

Flowchart Symbols

There are three basic flowchart symbols that are used to represent algorithms (see Figure 1): 1) the oval symbol is either a beginning or termination box, 2) the rectangular block is either a command or processing block, and 3) the diamond box is a decision box. In addition, we will use the parallelogram to represent input/output as shown in Figure 1(d).

Flowchart templates will also include symbols for subroutines or procedure calls, symbols for peripheral devices such as disk drives, and additional symbols for such things as communications links. However, since we are only concerned with representing algorithms using flowcharts, we will only need the basic symbols shown in Figure 1.

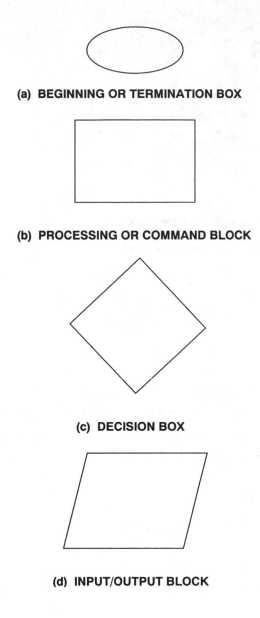

(a) BEGINNING OR TERMINATION BOX

(b) PROCESSING OR COMMAND BLOCK

(c) DECISION BOX

(d) INPUT/OUTPUT BLOCK

Figure 1. Common Flowchart Symbols

Basic Logic Symbols

There are three fundamental logic structures used to describe algorithms using flowcharts:

1.　Simple Sequencing

2.　Decision Making

3.　Repetition or Looping

Figure 2 shows how each is represented using a flowchart.

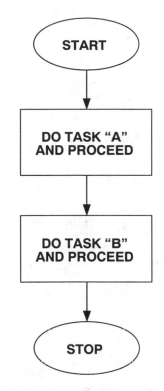

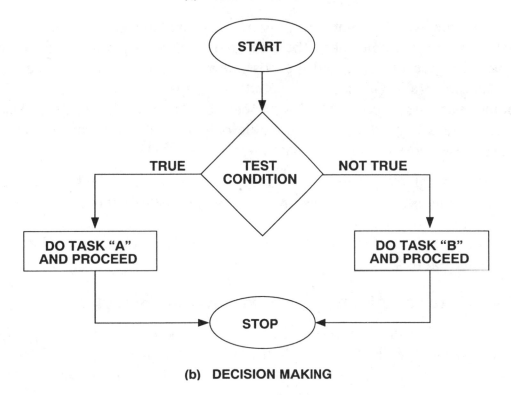

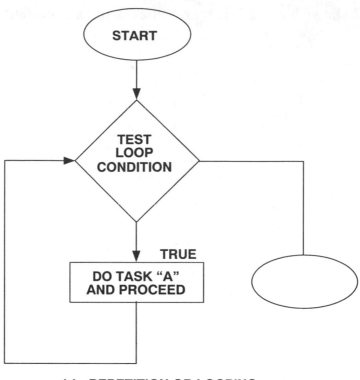

(c) REPETITION OR LOOPING

Figure 2. Fundamental Logic Structures

The decision box, shown in Figure 2(b), can have several forms. The first is with a variable that is being tested followed by a question mark, depicted inside the box, and the possible results shown outside the box (see Figure 3(a)). Other forms include a comparison of a variable with another variable or constant (>, <, =, etc.) as shown in Figure 3(b). Also, when there are more than two possible outcomes, a colon can be placed between two possible variables, as shown in Figure 3(c).

Process blocks generally contain one or more assignment statements, however, the use of the equal sign for assignment statements is considered poor form, with the equal sign being reserved for test conditions in a decision box. Therefore, arrows are used to assign values to variables as shown in Figure 4.

Flowcharts and Algorithms as Design Methodologies

In an early stage of design, flowcharts can be used as a technique for system design, when a basic algorithm is not already known. Process blocks can contain a general description of what needs to be done. Then, at the next level of refinement, a new flowchart can be created that replaces the general description with one or more boxes that show specifically, step by step, how that general objective will be accomplished.

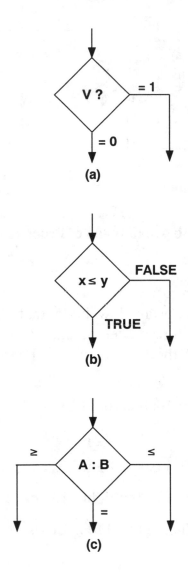

Figure 3. Decision Box Forms

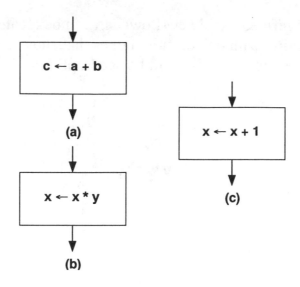

Figure 4. Examples of Process Box

EXAMPLE

Create an algorithm, using flowcharts, that can be used to design an embedded system that will read a temperature from a heat sensor in Kelvin and output the range of the temperature in Fahrenheit (temp), with the following specifications:

1. If 0 <= temp <= 10, then light LED #1

2. If 10 < temp <= 20, then light LED #2

3. If 20 < temp <= 30, then light LED #3

4. If 30 < temp <= 40, then light LED #4

5. If 40 < temp, then light all four LEDs

SOLUTION

First, we create a flowchart that describes the algorithm in general terms as shown in Figure 5.

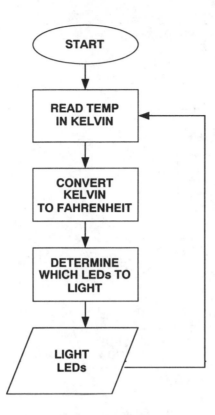

Figure 5. High-Level Flowchart for Embedded Heat Sensor System

Then we create a more detailed flowchart that replaces the process box containing the words "Convert Kelvin to Fahrenheit" with a process box containing specific assignment statements for the conversion. Also, we replace the process box containing the words "Determine Which LEDs to Light" with several decision boxes that perform that task. Finally, for the sake of clarity, we replace the single input/output box with several input/output boxes, which show which LEDs to light, as shown in Figure 6.

It is important to note that flowcharts that represent algorithms may be created before the software and hardware have been designed. The algorithm in the above example could be implemented with a microprocessor system with a small program in ROM (Read Only Memory), or, if the program was small enough, using a microcontroller with ROM and RAM (Random Access Memory) on board, or even only using hardware—such as a system of logic gates and comparators. After the hardware was designed, and if needed, a computer language would be selected to implement the software.

Sometimes, in the design process, at as necessary to back up more than one level, if it becomes apparent that the design is on the wrong track. If, in the above example, it became necessary to back up all the way to the

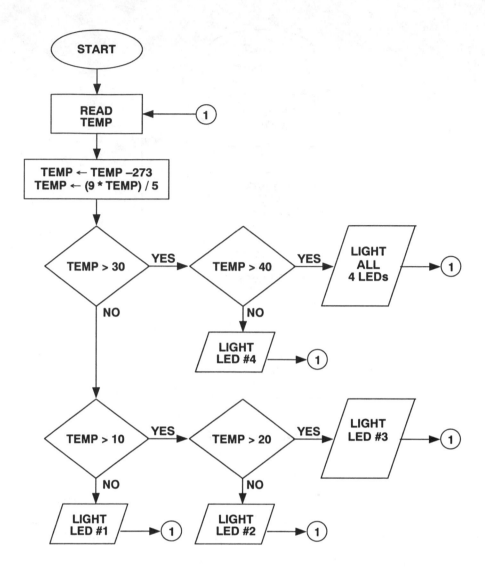

**Figure 6. Flowchart of Algorithm for Embedded System
with Heat Sensor and LEDs**

algorithmic level, then the flowchart in Figure 6 might, for instance, be changed. It would have one output box, but process boxes should be added to assign the value of which LEDs to light to a variable that was determined at a lower level of the design process—perhaps hardware or software.

PSEUDOCODE

Pseudocode is a combination of a computer programming language and English. Pseudocode is used extensively in computer science literature to represent algorithms and is also used as a design methodology by programmers and software engineers.

Pseudocode as a Structured Language

In order to understand why pseudocode has become so widely used to represent algorithms and as a design philosophy, it is important to be familiar with the basic constructs and syntax of Pascal, because Pascal and Pascal-like languages, such as ADA and C, are used the most in pseudocode.

Pascal-Based Pseudocode

Pascal was originally designed in 1971 as a language for teaching and for constructing system software. An earlier language, ALGOL (which stands for algorithmic language), played an important role in providing some particulars, such as Pascal's block-structured layout, but more importantly in emphasizing simplicity and elegance in design.

Pascal is a block-structured language. In order to show what we mean by "block-structured," we will present an example of a simple Pascal program, not from the standpoint of teaching the reader to program in Pascal, but only so the reader will be able to recognize and understand Pascal-based pseudocode. We will then show an example of pseudocode that describes the same algorithm as the Pascal program.

Before we go over this program line by line, we will describe its general structure, especially its block structure. Then we will fill in the gaps with a line-by-line examination.

The line numbers in Figure 7 are not part of Pascal, but are shown in this figure for the purpose of identification. Line number 1 shows the program statement with "PROGRAM" being a reserved word of Pascal and "DoubleForMonth" being an identifier which was created by the programmer as the program's name. Pascal is not case sensitive, an element that allows the programmer the flexibility to create his own style and add to the readability of a program. In this particular program, all of the reserved words consist of capital letters and all of the identifiers consist of one or more English words combined with the first letter of each English word capitalized. The one exception is the identifier "Cntr," which first appears on line 11.

The brackets to the left of Figure 7 mark the blocks of the program "DoubleForMonth." The blocks of Pascal programs are made up of three parts:

1. The header, which consists of the program or subprogram statement followed by the constant, type, and variable declarations.

The header for the main program block in Figure 3.1 consists of lines 1–11.

2. Declarations of subprograms. The subprogram declaration part of the main program block in Figure 7 consists of lines 13–32.

3. The body of statements to be executed. The body of the main program block in Figure 7 consists of lines 34–45.

There are two types of subprograms in Pascal: procedures and functions. The second block in Figure 7, which includes lines 13–32, consists of a procedure declaration for the procedure "ComputeMonth" and has these three main parts:

1. The header, which consists of the procedure statement and a variable declaration, includes lines 18–22.

2. Declarations of subprograms within this block. The subprogram declaration part of this block is found on lines 18–24.

3. The body of statements to be executed. The body of the procedure "ComputeForMonth" is found on lines 26–32.

The second type of subprogram in Pascal is the function. The third block in Figure 7, which includes lines 18–24, consists of a function declaration for the function "Double" and has these three main parts:

1. The header, which consists of the function statement and is found on line 18.

2. Declarations of subprograms within this block. There are no subprogram declarations in the function "Double," but either procedures or functions could have been declared within this function, if needed.

3. The body of statements to be executed, which is found on lines 20–24.

```
 1 ┌─  PROGRAM DoubleForMonth:
 2 │
 3 │         CONST
 4 │                   Size = 30;
 5 │         TYPE
 6 │                   Dollars = REAL;
 7 │                   Thirty = ARRAY (1..Size) OF Dollars:
 8 │          VAR
 9 │                   Month : Thirty;
10 │                   FirstDay : Dollars;
11 │                   Cntr : INTEGER;
12 │
13 │┌─ PROCEDURE ComputeMonth (InitialAmount : Dollars;
14 ││                                  VAR ThirtyDays : Thirty);
15 ││  VAR
16 ││                   Day : INTEGER;
17 ││
18 ││┌─ FUNCTION Double (DollarAmount : Dollars) : Dollars;
19 │││
20 │││        BEGIN (* Begin Double *)
21 │││
22 │││                Double := DollarAmount * 2;
23 │││
24 ││└─   END; (* End Double *)
25 ││
26 ││        BEGIN (* Begin ComputeMonth *)
27 ││
28 ││            ThirtyDays [1] ; = InitialAmount;
29 ││            FOR Day := 1 TO Size − 1 DO
30 ││               ThirtyDays [Day+1] := Double (ThirtyDays [Day]
31 ││
32 │└─   END; (* End ComputeMonth *)
33 │
34 │        BEGIN (* DoubleForMonth *)
35 │
36 │            READLN ('Enter Initial Amount $', Firstday; 12:2)
37 │            ComputeMonth (FirstDay, Month);
38 │            Cntr := 1;
39 │            WHILE Cntr < Size DO
40 │               BEGIN (* Begin While *)
41 │                   WRITELN ('Day', Cntr, "$', Month [Cntr];1
42 │                   Cntr := Cntr + 1
43 │               END (* End While *)
44 │
45 └─────── END. (* End DoubleForMonth *)
```

Figure 7. Example of a Pascal Program

Each block of a Pascal program is made up of a program or subprogram. An unlimited number of subprograms may be declared in a program or subprogram and they may be nested to any level. Each block has a header which includes the program or subprogram statement and constant, type, and variable declarations, if needed, followed by subprogram declarations, if any, followed by the body of statements to be executed. Each subprogram is a block, which is contained within the main program, which is also a block, and each may contain one or more smaller subprograms within it, which are also blocks. This is what we mean when we say Pascal is a block-structured language—blocks contained within blocks within blocks, and so on.

Figure 8 shows approximately what a monitor screen might look like if this program had been run. The user enters .01, or the equivalent of one penny, and the initial amount is doubled for each day of the month with the final result being in excess of $5 million.

```
Enter initial amount    $.01
Day   1 $                 .01
Day   2 $                 .02
Day  30 $           5368709.12
```

Figure 8. Execution of Program "DoubleForMonth"

Figure 9 shows what the basic algorithm of the program might look like if it were represented by pseudocode.

```
type
      dollars = dollars and cents
      thirty = array [days of month] of dollars


var
      initial_amount : dollars
      month : thirty
begin
      read initial_amount
      COMPUTE_MONTH - double initial_amount repeatedly
                      for each day of month


      write the entire array month


end
```

Figure 9. Pseudocode of Algorithm for Figure 7

One of the biggest advantages of pseudocode is that painstaking details of a computer language can be omitted. As seen in Figure 9, there are no program or subprogram statements; the types are defined with either English or a combination of English and Pascal reserved words; and details of the read and write statements are left out. Also, semicolons, which normally mark the end of Pascal statements, unless an END follows, are not used. That doesn't mean that program or subprogram statements, or detailed type descriptions, or any of the other things we left out aren't used in pseudocode; they often are. What matters is what combination of reserved words of the computer language and English can best give the most succinct representation of the algorithm, at the level of refinement that is necessary in a particular situation.

When using pseudocode, tasks to be performed are capitalized, followed by a short description of what the task does, in English. Procedure calls are also capitalized, with an informal description of their parameters in parentheses. Reserved words of the language are often highlighted in bold and identifiers are often italicized. Also, it is considered preferable to show assignment statements using arrows, similar to assignment statements in flowcharts.

There is considerable variance from one pseudocode representation to another. The reader should bear in mind that there are some forms of pseudocode with strict rules, but the most important thing is to give an exact, step-by-step description of the algorithm that is being represented.

We will show examples of FORTRAN-based pseudocode in the next two sections. While it is worth pointing out that ADA, which is based on Pascal, is gradually replacing Pascal as the language of choice for teaching and for use in pseudocode, a student or professional who is familiar with Pascal can nearly always understand ADA-based pseudocode. That is also true with C-based pseudocode, another Pascal-like language. Also, there are a couple of more simple, but important, Pascal structures, that still need to be demonstrated, which we will show in the following sections.

The Concept of a Well-Structured Program

Pseudocode is a structured language. It is useful for representing algorithms in a way that is easily understandable. In the preceding section we demonstrated the concept of block-structure, however, there is more to a well-structured program than a block structure. There is also the important concept of one point of entry and one point of exit for each program module (a module is a group of statements that perform a specific task).

While an algorithm shown with pseudocode is not the same thing as a program, it should also be well structured so that it is easily understandable. Also, a program implemented from the algorithm is much more likely to be well structured, if the algorithm is well structured—whether it is shown with pseudocode or a flowchart.

We will begin our explanation of the one entry-one exit rule by contra example. The flowchart in Figure 10 shows an algorithm that violates the one entry-one exit rule.

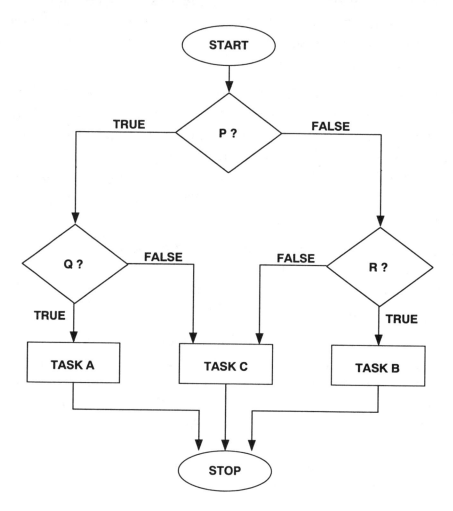

Figure 10. Violation of One Entry-One Exit Rule

Figure 11 shows how easily this problem can be solved using Pascal-based pseudocode.

```
if P and Q then
        TASK-A
else if not P and R then
        TASK-B
else    TASK-C
```

Figure 11. Solution to One Entry-One Exit Problem

Stepwise Refinement as a Design Tool

When a program is designed, the process usually begins with a diagram called a structure chart, which shows the high-level general structure of the program. The next step is to represent the main program modules with a high-level pseudocode representation that leaves a lot of details out by giving a general description in English of what certain tasks do. Then the detailed design phase begins with the program details being filled in with pseudocode or perhaps with detailed flowcharts. Then the detailed design is converted to actual code. This process is called stepwise refinement.

We will attempt to show the process of stepwise refinement by presenting an algorithm for computing a Fourier transform.

The computer implementation of the FFT on an array which contains the sample of the function to be transformed involves performing what is called a bit reversal on the array. For example, if the index of the array is 6, which is represented in binary by 110, its bit reversal, which makes the first bit last and the second bit second to last and so on, is 011, or decimal 3. If an FFT were to be performed on a sample of eight, the reorder would be 0, 4, 2, 6, 1, 5, 2, 7. This makes it possible to perform a two-point transform on each adjacent two points in the array, taking the principal of decomposition to its limit.

Figure 12 shows a FORTRAN-based pseudocode representation for an FFT algorithm. Although Pascal is considered a more structured language than FORTRAN, once the concepts of a well-structured program are understood, they can be carried over to another language. A well-structured algorithm represented by pseudocode should not have GO TO statements; everything should be sequential. If the algorithm was converted to a flowchart, it should not look "like spaghetti." In fact, none of the lines connecting boxes should cross. Figure 12 shows loops nested to three levels, but that is consistent with well-structuredness.

447

```
SUBROUTINE FFT (F, log₂ of N)
COMPLEX F(1024), W, W2, TEMP
PI ← 3.141593
N ← 2 raised to log₂ of N
Reorder F – perform bit reorder
DO 5 loop from LEVEL = 1 to log₂ of N
MX2 ← 2**LEVEL
M ← MX2/2
W2 ← (1.0,0.0)
W ← (COS(PI/M, −SIN(PI/M))
DO 5 loop from IU = 1 to M
        DO 4 loop from I = IU to N increment by MX2


4                    compute two point transforms


5        W ← W2*W
DO 6 loop from I = 1 to N
6        F(I) ← F(I) divided by N
RETURN
END
```

Figure 12. FFT Algorithm

In Figure 12, the variable MX2 represents $2M$ from the above FFT discussion. Also *IU*, which means "integer *U*," represents *U* from the FFT discussion and the variable LEVEL represents the level of decomposition of equations (4) and (5). The variables *N*, *M*, and *W* are taken directly from the discussion of the FFT.

The last loop divides each of the elements of the array *F* by *N*, resulting in some loss of efficiency, about 14%. However, the FFT is so much more efficient than the straightforward implementation of the discrete transform that it hardly matters.

The algorithm shown in Figure 12 is at a fairly high level of stepwise refinement. We won't show the precise steps needed to perform the bit reversal, but we will take the DO 4 loop, which computes the two-point transforms to their next level of refinement.

```
DO 4 loop from I = IU  to N increment by MX2
   IP ← I + MX2
   TEMP ← F(IP)*W2
   F(IP) ← F(I)─TEMP
   F(I) ← F(I)+TEMP
```

Figure 13. Pseudocode for Two-Point Transform

Figure 13 shows the pseudocode which would replace the English words "compute two-point transforms" in Figure 12. The second line represents the complex multiplication and the last two lines represent the additions of equations (6) and (7). As can be seen, once the detailed design phase is complete, the conversion to actual code is rather straightforward.

DATA STORAGE AND TRANSMISSION

We will first cover how data is stored for use by computers. Then we will cover a transition topic Data Transfer, which isn't really data transmission, but allows us to develop some concepts that we use in the description of data transmission.

Units of Data Storage

The most basic unit of storage is the bit, or binary digit, which has a value of 0 or 1.

A byte is a group of 8 bits.

A word is 1, 2, 4, or 8 bytes, depending on the size of a computer's CPU registers.

A kilobyte is 2^{10} or 1,024 bytes.

A megabyte is 2^{20} or 1,046,516 bytes.

A gigabyte is 2^{30} or 1,073,741,824 bytes.

Data Storage

Data is stored for use in computers in several different ways: registers, RAM (Random Access Memory), ROM (Read Only Memory), and peripheral storage devices, such as electromagnetic disks and tape drives. For peripheral storage devices we will concentrate on electromagnetic disks because, as their capacity has increased by orders of magnitude, their relative importance has increased accordingly.

Registers

Registers are the fastest memory devices used in computers. Registers can be accessed about three or four times as fast as the main memory, or the memory unit of a computer, which is made up of RAM.

Registers generally hold one word of data. A word varies from computer to computer from two bytes (or 16 bits) to eight bytes (or 64 bits). A word is the amount of data that can be read from, or written to, the memory unit in one memory cycle. A typical memory cycle takes about 80 nano-seconds.

Memory cycles can be further divided up into clock cycles, with a memory cycle taking three or four clock cycles. A clock cycle may take 20 nano-seconds, although there is considerable variation from computer to computer. A register, being faster than RAM, can be read from or written to in one clock cycle.

Registers are usually part of the central processing unit (CPU), sometimes called the brains of the computer. However, registers can have other uses. The interface between the computer and a peripheral device—such as a printer, disk drive, or monitor—has what is called a command register. CPUs communicate with peripheral devices by storing a command in the command register and also may receive a response by reading what is called a response register.

In order to show how registers work, we first need to introduce the concept of the logic gate, because logic gates are used, together with other devices, to form a register. A logic gate is a digital electronic device that has one or more inputs and one output. For any gate, the inputs and the outputs can only have two possible logic values, logic 0 or logic 1.

Ranges of voltage levels are used to represent logic 0 and logic 1 in digital electronics. A typical range for logic 0 might be 0.0 V to 0.5 V and a typical range for logic 1 might be 3.5 V to 5.0 V, with voltages in-between these two ranges not allowed, if the circuit is to work properly.

Figure 14(a) shows the graphical symbol for a very common logic gate, the AND gate. The input variables A and B are assumed to have logic values of either 0 or 1. The output $A * B$ is read A AND B, and the truth table in Figure 14(b) shows the possible input and output values for an AND gate. Actually AND gates may have more than two inputs, but the important thing to remember is that the only time the output is logic 1 is if all of the inputs are logic 1.

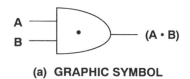

(a) GRAPHIC SYMBOL

A	B	A · B
0	0	0
0	1	0
1	0	0
1	1	1

(b) TRUTH TABLE

Figure 14. AND Gate

The only other kind of gate that we need to describe, in order to show how registers work, is the inverter. Figure 15 shows the graphical symbol for an inverter. An inverter is such a simple device that we won't need to show its truth table. An inverter simply inverts its input: if the input is a 0, the output is a 1, and if the input is a 1, the output is a 0.

A ————▷○———— A′

Figure 15. Inverter

Registers are formed with the combination of gates and a device called a flip-flop, which is a device that can be used to store a single binary digit. The R-S flip-flop, which is shown in Figure 16(a), is a basic type of flip-flop. The inputs include the R and S inputs, the clock-pulse input (CP), and the preset and clear inputs, represented by Pr and Cl. The only outputs are the Q and Q' outputs. The Q' output is always the complement of Q, Q' is 0 when Q is 1 and vice versa. The logic values of Q and Q' represent the current state of the flip-flop.

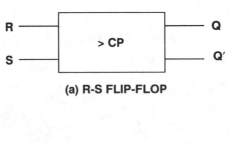

(a) R-S FLIP-FLOP

(b) CLOCK PULSE

S	R	Q(t + 1)	Comments
0	0	Q(t)	No Change
0	1	0	Clear
1	0	1	Set
1	1	?	Not Allowed

(c) State Table

Figure 16. Clocked R-S Flip-Flop

The clock pulse, shown in Figure 16(b), represents an electronic signal whose voltage varies from the range of logic 0 to the range of logic 1 and back again, with the transitions being so fast that the signal can be classified as a "square wave." Figure 16(c) shows the state table for an *R-S* flip-flop with the transition to the next state being triggered by a transition of the clock pulse.

Figure 16 shows a rising edge- or positive edge-triggered flip-flop. If there had been a little circle at the input of the clock pulse in Figure 16(a), similar to the little circle at the output of the inverter in Figure 15, we would know that it was a negative edge-triggered flip-flop. However, since there is no little circle, we know that it is positive edge-triggered.

We know this is an *R-S* flip-flop by the transition table. The transition table defines the type of flip-flop. There are other types of flip-flops, with different state tables, but we only need to cover *R-S* flip-flops to show how registers work.

The way a positive edge-triggered *R-S* flip-flop is used to store a binary digit is:

1. The inputs are set according to the state table, prior to the rising edge of the clock pulse:

   - $R = 0, S = 1$, to store a 1 or

   - R = 1, S = 0, to store a 0.

2. The *R-S* inputs are held during the rising edge of the clock pulse, causing the Q output to assume the appropriate next state value:

   - $Q = 1$, if $R = 0$ and $S = 1$ or

   - $Q = 0$, if $R = 1$ and $S = 0$.

3. Following the transition, the *R-S* inputs are both set to logic 0 so the next rising edge (the next clock cycle) will result in the *Q* output being left unchanged.

The preceding three steps show how an *R-S* flip-flop can be used to store a binary digit in conjunction with a clock pulse. In addition, the Pr and Cl inputs are preset (set to 1) or clear to 0, overriding the clock pulse.

A four-bit register that uses *R-S* flip-flops is shown in Figure 17. The data inputs are I_1, I_2, I_3, and I_4. The clock pulse is connected to all four flip-flops and consists of continuous pulses. The circle under the triangle of each flip-flop indicates that this is a negative edge-triggered flip-flop.

The load input is connected to all four flip-flops via the AND gates. When the load is 0 the inputs to each *R* and *S* is 0, and Q remains in its previous state. When the load is 1 the inputs to each *R* and *S* is I_n and $I_n{}'$, thus each output A_n will show the value of $I_n{}'$.

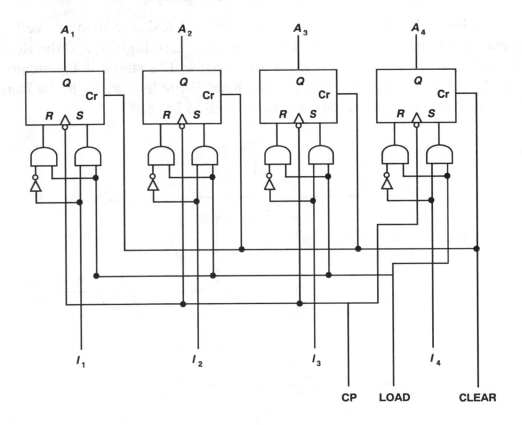

Figure 17. 4-Bit Register

Random Access Memory

The main memory or memory unit of a computer is made up of Random Access Memory. Random Access Memory also has many other uses. For example, a laser printer will have RAM so that fonts can be downloaded and also to act as a data buffer. Peripheral devices and interfaces between computers and peripheral devices often have use for RAM. In addition, imbedded systems based on microprocessors also need RAMs of various sizes, although, if the memory requirements are small enough, the RAM may be on board the microprocessor chip and we may refer to it as a microcontroller.

In a computer, RAM is organized into words with each word being the size of the registers that are part of the CPU—varying from two bytes to eight bytes. The storage capacity of a computer's main memory varies anywhere from about one mega-byte, for a simple computer, to multiples of giga-bytes, for the more powerful supercomputers.

A logic diagram of the smallest unit of RAM, the memory cell, is shown in Figure 18. When the Select line is high, or logic 1, and the Read/Write line is low, or logic 0, the Data-in input will be stored in the memory cell. When both the Select line and the Read/Write line are high, the Data-out line is enabled, allowing the memory cell to be read.

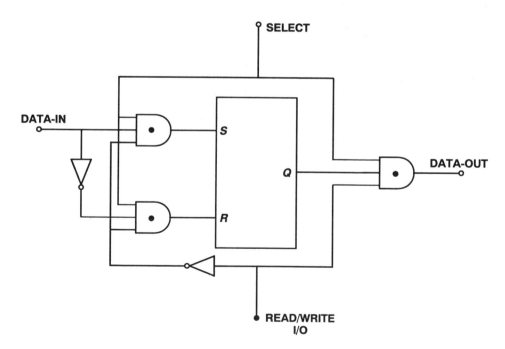

(a) Logic Diagram of Memory Cell

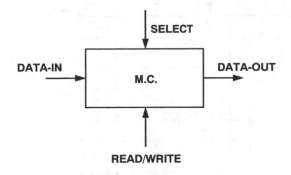

(b) Block Diagram

Figure 18. Memory Cell

In order to show how RAM works, we need to introduce the concept of the decoder, which is a device that is used to address the word in RAM that is accessed. To put it another way, looking at the memory cell in Figure 18, the Select line of each memory cell in the word that is being addressed would be high, and the decoder is the device that causes this to happen.

The logic diagram of a 2×4 decoder is shown in Figure 19(a) and its truth table is shown in Figure 19(b). Briefly, the way a decoder works is, if there are N input lines, there are 2^N output lines, with only one of the output lines high. Often a decoder is simply shown with a block diagram, with the input lines on one side and the output lines on the other. Decoders can also be cascaded, used in a parallel configuration, or both at the same time to greatly increase the addressing capability. Part of the reason RAM is slower to access than registers is the "depth" of the decoder used to address multi-mega-words of information.

X	Y	Z_0	Z_1	Z_2	Z_3
0	0	1	0	0	0
0	1	0	1	0	0
1	0	0	0	1	0
1	1	0	0	0	1

(a) Truth Table

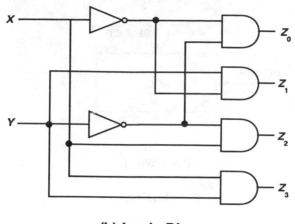

(b) Logic Diagram

Figure 19. 2 × 4 Decoder

We also need to introduce one more type of logic gate to show how RAM works. The OR gate is shown in Figure 20. The important thing to remember about the OR gate is that regardless of whether it has two inputs, or three or more, all it takes is for one input to be high and the output will be high.

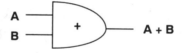

Figure 20. OR Gate

There are other types of logic gates, such as the EXCLUSIVE-OR gate, whose output is high if one, and only one, of the inputs is high. Also, there is the NAND gate, which behaves like an AND gate with an inverter at its output and the NOR gate, which is like an OR gate with its output inverted. However, to show how RAM works we only need the AND and OR gates, and the inverter.

A 4 × 3 RAM is shown in Figure 21. The two address lines can address four words each whose contents will be output on the data lines when a word is addressed.

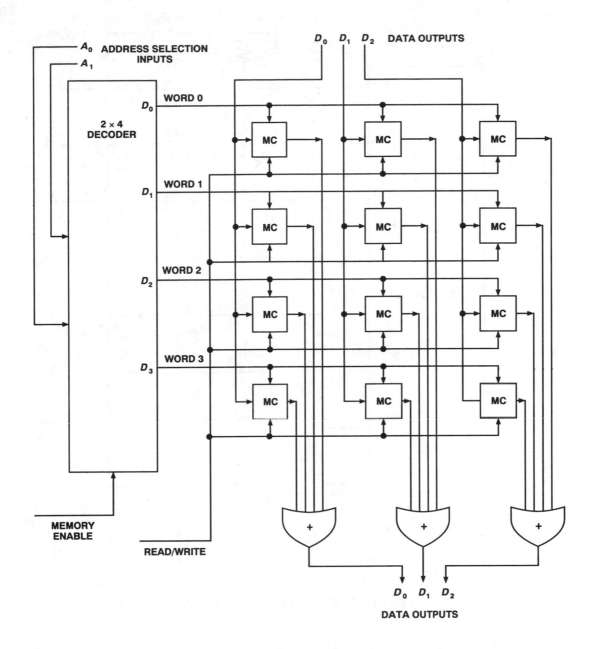

Figure 21. 4 × 3 RAM

Read Only Memory

A Read Only Memory (ROM) cell is much simpler than a RAM cell. Figure 22 shows eight word lines W_0–W_7 with diodes connected to four bit lines B_0–B_3. If a word is addressed and there is a diode connection between that word line and a bit line, then that bit will be logic 1, otherwise it will be logic 0. The diode connections on the word lines not addressed have no effect because current cannot flow backward through a diode.

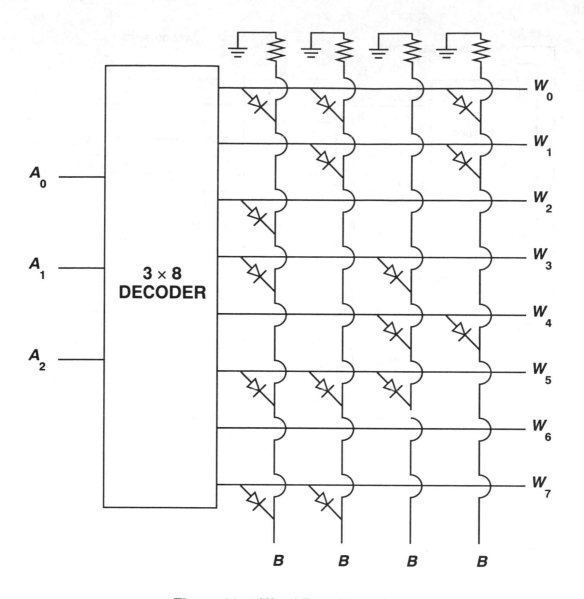

Figure 22. 8 Word By 4 Bits ROM

The biggest advantage of ROM is that the data stored in it is not lost when the power is turned off.

Electromagnetic Disk

Disk drives are formatted in electromagnetic tracks, with the outermost track being the largest physically and each succeeding track taking the shape of a slightly smaller circle contained in the previous track. A floppy disk might have 80 tracks, while hard disks usually have thousands. A drive will usually store the same amount of data on each track regardless of its physical size.

A cylinder is a group of two or more concentric tracks. If a disk has one two-sided platter, then each corresponding track on the top and bottom sides of the disk is a cylinder. If a drive has four two-sided platters, then each cylinder will consist of eight concentric tracks.

A disk's tracks are subdivided into sectors. Personal computer disk drives usually have sectors of 512 bytes.

A cluster is made up of the corresponding sectors of the tracks that are included in the same cylinder. If a cylinder has eight tracks, then the first sector of each of the eight tracks represents the first cluster and the second sector of each of the eight tracks represents the second sector and so on. A cluster is usually the smallest unit of file storage on a computer disk drive.

Data Transfer

In a computer system, it is desirable to be able to transfer data between any two registers. This means there must be a data path between each flip-flop in one register and the corresponding flip-flop in every other register. If the number of data paths is equal to r, then $(2^r - 1)n$ data paths, where n is the number of flip-flops in each register, are required. This would lead to a horrendous increase in the complexity and cost of the system. However, a data transfer system called a "bus system" can greatly simplify transmission between registers.

Multiplexers

In order to show how a bus system works, we need to introduce the concept of the multiplexer. A multiplexer, as shown in Figure 23, can be thought of as a device that performs the inverse operation of a decoder. A multiplexer is a digital function that receives information in 2^n input lines, n select lines, and transmits information in a single output line.

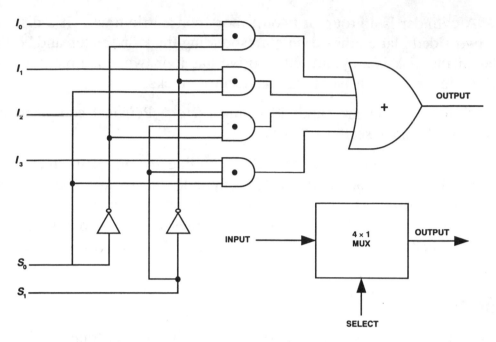

Figure 23. 4 × 1 Multiplexer

A group of wires that transmits binary information between registers is called a bus. This concept is analogous to commuter transportation that relies on buses rather than private cars.

A bus system is formed with a bus line (a group of wires), multiplexers, and decoders. Figure 24 shows how multiplexers are used to select the outputs of one of the registers for transmission onto the bus line, and Figure 25 shows how decoders are used to select one of the registers to receive the contents of the register selected by the multiplexers.

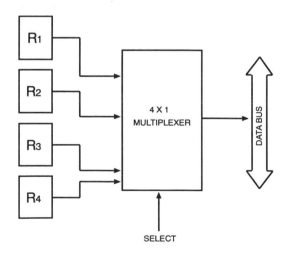

(a) Detailed Block Diagram

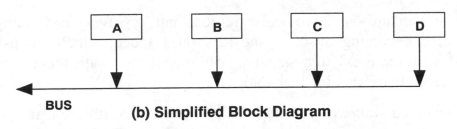

(b) Simplified Block Diagram

Figure 24. Bus System for Four Registers

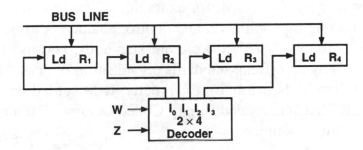

Figure 25. Transfer from Bus to Decoder

If the contents of Register B are to be transferred to Register A, then the inputs to the bus system should have these values: $X = 0$, $Y = 1$, $W = 0$, and $Z = 0$. Thus, the contents of Register B would be selected by the decoder, transmitted to the bus line, and received by Register A, which would be selected by the decoder.

Data Transmission

The world of data transmission is designed for, built around, and interfaced by, standards and protocols. These standards and protocols, by describing in fine detail precisely the form transmitted data must take, makes possible "plug-compatible" connections between completely different types of computers, or between the same type of computer running completely different software, or from computers to data communication equipment (DCE) and then to phone lines, that may or may not run across national boundaries, and then to different types of DCEs and computers on the other end.

The standards and protocols are constantly evolving and changing, with some becoming obsolete and new ones added, which are usually upgrades of some existing standard of protocol, and with these changes being driven by advancing technology.

The word *standard* and the word *protocol* have different meanings, although they are sometimes used almost interchangeably. World and national standards organizations have defined standards for technologies as diverse as programming languages, flexible magnetic media, and microprocessor systems. But these are not protocols because they are not standards for data transmission.

On the other hand, companies will sometimes develop their own protocols for internal use. IBM, for example, at one time had eight different ways of coding alphanumeric and control characters to be transmitted. These were protocols, but they were not standards, because they had not been sanctioned by an official standards organization such as ANSI (American National Standards Institute). Eventually, IBM settled on one protocol for coding, EBCDIC (Extended Binary Coded Decimal Interchange Code), which did become a standard.

We will give a more formal definition for *protocol* here, but a good way to look at a protocol is as an interface. For example, if a computer under development is to be connected to a modem, by means of an RS-232 interface—an Electronic Industries Association (EIA) recommended standard—then all the computer designers need to be concerned with is that inputs to the interface conform with the RS-232 standard and the protocol supported by the modem. Thus, a protocol allows an engineer to think of what is on the other side of an interface as a black box that will provide the correct output if it receives the correct inputs.

It is the nature of data transmission that the standard protocols provide interfaces that allow the transmission of data anywhere—from two computers sitting on the same desk to various worldwide networks. It is for this reason that standard protocols are the foundation for the study of data transmission.

Coding

Digital computers process numbers and other characters, such as letters of the alphabet and certain special characters. Errors can crop up when data is transmitted to peripheral devices or to other computers, or even during internal transfer of data as described earlier in this chapter. In this section we will discuss data handling and error detection.

Most handling of alphanumeric characters is done using the American National Code for Information Interchange (ASCII). There have been competing codes, such as EBCDIC, which we discussed in the previous section. Although EBCDIC has increasingly fallen into disuse, it is still used by IBM mainframe computers.

ASCII uses the rightmost seven bits of each byte to represent 128 characters including the letters of the alphabet, the ten decimal digits, punctuation marks, and certain special non-printable characters. The leftmost, or most significant bit of each byte, is called the "parity bit" and is used for error detection.

Figure 26 shows the ASCII character set. The CR and LF characters, when transmitted to a printer or to a monitor, will cause a carriage return and a line feed. The FF character, when transmitted to a printer, will cause a form feed. The ACK (for ACKnowledge message), NAK (for Not AcKnowledge message), and SYN (for SYNchronize transmission) characters are special non-printable characters used for data transmission.

Bits 0 to 3 Second Hex Digit (LSB)	Bits 4 to 6 First Hex Digit (MSB)							
	0	1	2	3	4	5	6	7
0	NUL	DLE	SP	0	@	P		p
1	SCH	DC1	!	1	A	Q	a	q
2	STX	DC2	"	2	B	R	b	r
3	ETX	DC3	#	3	C	S	c	s
4	EOT	DC4	S	4	D	T	d	t
5	ENQ	NAK	%	5	E	U	e	u
6	ACK	SYN	&	6	F	V	f	v
7	BEL	ETB	'	7	G	W	g	w
8	BS	CAN	(	8	H	X	h	x
9	HT	EM	)	9	I	Y	i	y
A	LF	SUB	*	:	J	Z	j	z
B	VT	ESC	+	;	K	[	k	{
C	FF	FS	,	<	L	/	l	/
D	CR	GS	~	=	M	]	m	}
E	SO	RS	.	>	N	^	n	≈
F	SI	US	/	?	O	_	o	DEL

Figure 26. ASCII Character Set

The following is a more formal definition for protocol: computer protocols define in fine detail precisely the form data must take before it is transmitted, the rate at which the data is transmitted, and how the data is to be checked for errors.

Although ASCII does not define a transmission rate and it is generally referred to as a standard or a character code, it is also considered to be a protocol, a coding protocol. This is because it includes special control characters, like ACK, that were expressly designed for data transmission, and also because it provides a means for different types of computers to communicate or interface with each other. The keyword is interface; protocols provide interfaces between differing types of equipment and differing types of software modules.

ASCII is often used for transmission over cables or phone lines with the leftmost bit, or most significant bit, used for error detection. The most significant bit is called the parity bit or check bit. If "odd" parity checking is used, the parity bit is set to a 1 if the first seven bits contain an even number of 1's. If "even" parity checking is used, the parity bit is set to a 1 if the first seven bits contain an odd number of 1's.

Because telephones and cables usually only allow transmission over a single line, the ASCII characters must be transmitted in serial form as shown in Figure 27.

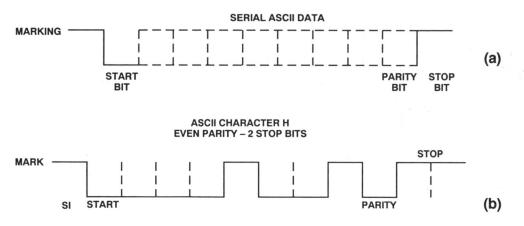

Figure 27. Serial Data Transmission

Serial data transmission usually starts the transmission by lowering the voltage on the transmission line for a specified time period. The start bit in Figure 27, then transmits the character bits including the parity bit, and then raises the signal voltage for one or two bits, the stop bit in Figure 27(a) and Figure 27(b). After that, the transmitter can transmit the next character by lowering the signal, the start bit again, or idle by keeping the signal high.

This is known as "asynchronous" transmission because there is no clock pulse synchronizing the sending and receiving devices as described in the section on data transfer.

The way an error is detected by a receiving device is by realizing that if odd parity is used and the number of 1's is even, at least one bit must be invalid. Even parity works the same way, in reverse. Parity checking is an effective error-checking method when the error rate is low enough that there is almost never more than one incorrect bit in each byte.

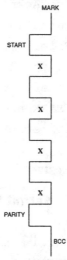

Figure 28. Parity Checks

What was described in the above paragraph is called vertical parity checking. Longitudinal parity can be added, as shown in Figure 28, by transmitting a block check character (BCC) at the end of each message. This is capable of detecting all 1-, 2-, and 3-bit errors, and all odd-numbered and some even-numbered errors. The even-numbered errors in the same rows and columns will not be detected, as shown by the boxes marked with Xs in Figure 28. The percentage of redundant information for characters is (n + 8)/7n * 100%, which works out, for 128 character blocks, to 1.5% redundant information.

Kermit Protocol

Kermit is a protocol developed in the early 1980s at Columbia University for the purpose of transmitting data between computers of different types, such as from microcomputers to mainframes. We won't describe the entire Kermit protocol, but only the Kermit packet, which is shown in Figure 29.

MARK Start of header; usually ASCII SOH.

LEN Length of packet excluding MARK and CHECK

                fields; expressed as ASCII decimal digits.

SEQ Modulo packet sequence number.

TYPE Type of packet; some of which are:

                D Data Packet

                ACK Acknowledgement Packet (data field

                    empty)

                NAK Negative Acknowledgement Packet

                  (data field empty)

                Z End of File.

DATA Data Field; contains 0 to 91 characters.

CHECK Block check on characters in the packet

                excluding MARK and CHECK itself. If SUM

                is the arithmetic sum of the ASCII

                characters,

                SUM = char(SUM + ((SUM AND 192/64)AND 63)

Figure 29. Kermit Packet

Kermit packets whose type field is either the ACK or NAK ASCII control characters are usually transmitted from the receiver to the sender. The way Kermit works is:

1. The sender sends a data packet.

2. If the receiver acknowledges by transmitting back on ACK packet, the sender transmits the next data packet.

3. If the receiver transmits a negative acknowledgement because the CHECK field didn't match, or the SEQ field was off, the sender retransmits the current packet.

The AND operator in the CHECK field in Figure 29 is similar in function to the AND gate, except every corresponding bit in two bytes is ANDed and it is implemented by software.

Kermit is an example of a byte-oriented protocol. We will give an example of a bit-oriented protocol in the next section. Also, we didn't say anything about the transmission medium or the electrical characteristics of the connectors, but those also will be described in later sections.

Cables

RS-232 Interface and EIA Standard Cables

One of the best known communications standards is the RS-232 interface, first adopted in 1960. *RS* stands for recommended standard. Before serial interfaces were standardized, every company that manufactured communications equipment used a different interface configuration. Thus, interconnecting computers and communication equipment from different vendors required building level converters and special cables and connectors. To facilitate such communication, the Electronic Industries Alliance (EIA) adopted the RS-232 standard. This global standard has seen successive revisions, the last time in 1987, with the RS-232-D (also known as EIA-232-D).

The RS-232 is used for all types of communication between computers and peripherals. The maximum data rate is 19.2 kilobits per second and the maximum length is 50 feet. A 25-pin connector called a DB-25 is usually used, but sometimes a 9-pin connector called a DB-9 is used.

Since the RS-232 is a digital interface, the voltage levels of the pins represent either a logic 0 or a logic 1. Figure 30 shows the voltage levels of a DB-25 connector.

```
-15 to -5V Mark, logic 1
-5 to -3V Noise margin
-3 to +3V Transition region
+3 to +5V Noise margin
+5 to +15 Space, logic 0
```

Figure 30. Voltage Levels of a DB-25 Connector

Figure 31 shows the circuit functions of the pins used for control purposes and the pins used for actual data transmission. The signals transmitted and received by pins 2 and 3, if represented in graphical form, would look like the serial data transmission shown in Figure 27, with very rapid transition from high to low voltage.

Pin 4 RTS, Request to Send. The transmitter
     signals that it is ready to send data.

Pin 5 CTS, Clear to Send. The receiver signals
     that it is ready to accept data.

Pin 6 DSR, Data Set Ready. For use with modems.
     Means the modem is connected to the
     telephone line.

Pin 8 DCD, Data Carrier Detect. For use with
modems. Means the modem has found
a modem on the other end of the telephone line.

Pin 20 DTR, Data Terminal Ready. The transmitter
signals that it is powered up.

Pin 2 TD, Transmitted Data. The transmitter
transmits data on this pin.

Pin 3 RD, Received Data. The receiver receives
data on this pin.

Figure 31. Pin Circuit Functions

Although the RS-232 interface can be used to connect two computers, it was primarily meant to connect data terminal equipment (DTE) such as computers or terminals with data communication equipment (DCE) such as modems. However, the RS-232 interface is handy for connecting two computers directly, as shown in Figure 32, in what is called a null modem configuration, in which the serial ports of two computers are fooled into thinking they are connected to a modem.

Computer 1			Computer 2
Function	Pin No.	Pin No.	Function
Frame Ground	1	1	Frame Ground
Transmitted Data	2	3	Received Data
Received Data	3	2	Transmitted Data
Request to Send	4	5	Clear to Send
Clear to Send	5	4	Request to Send
Data Set Ready	6	20	Data Terminal Ready
Signal Ground	7	7	Signal Ground
Data Carrier Detect	8	20	Data Terminal Ready
Data Terminal Ready	20	6	Data Set Ready
Data Terminal Ready	20	8	Data Carrier Detect

Figure 32. Possible RS-232 Connection of Two Computers

Pin 6 of each computer is connected to Pin 20 of the other computer so that it appears to each computer that it is connected to a modem. Also, Pins 9 and 20 are jumpered together to simulate a carrier signal.

If the above configuration was used to transmit a file from one computer to another using Kermit, the transmitter and receiver would signal back and forth to each other using Pin 4, Request to Send, and Pin 5, Clear to Send, that they were ready to transmit and receive data. This is known as handshaking. According to the Kermit protocol, the transmitter would send a data packet, the receiver would reply either with an acknowledgement packet (ACK), or a negative-acknowledgement packet (NAK). Then the transmitter would either send the next packet, or in the case of a NAK, retransmit the previous packet. This process would then continue until the file was transmitted.

The concept of protocol layers is very important in data transmission. Kermit, which is a software-oriented protocol, would be a higher layer then the RS-232 interface, which is the physical layer. If an application program ran Kermit in the background and allowed, for example, users on two computers to view a common spreadsheet, it would be a higher layer still. We will say more about layers in the next section.

Upgrades of RS-232

The RS-449 was developed as an eventual replacement for this RS-232. The RS-449 is a mechanical standard supported by the RS-422-A, which is an electrical standard. When the RS-449, which comes in a 9-pin and 37-pin configuration, is operating with the RS-422-A electrical standard, it is capable of data rates of 2 megabits per second with a maximum cable length of 200 feet. The RS-232 achieves this data rate by modulating the transmitted signal with an inverse copy of the same signal on another wire, thus allowing greater immunity to noise.

The EIA 530, which uses a 25-pin connector, has been growing in popularity. The advantage of the EIA 530 is that it allows digital connections of up to 500 feet.

Coaxial Cable, Twisted Pairs, and Fiber-Optic Cable

Coaxial Cable

Coaxial cable consists of an outer layer of insulation, an outer conductor (usually woven wire), an inner layer of insulation, and a core conductor. The outer conductor acts as both a ground and a shield from noise. Coaxial cable is the medium of choice for cable television and also for most computer network installations, although most of the newer networks are installed using twisted pair cabling.

The thickness of "coax" varies from about ¼" to 1" and it is not very flexible. It is, however, great for data. It offers a large bandwidth, high immunity from electrical interference, and a low error rate. When used in a local area network (LAN), a type of computer network in which computers are fairly close to each other—usually within a thousand feet—it uses a type of signaling called baseband signaling, which is shown in Figure 33.

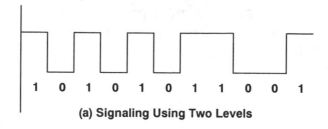

(a) Signaling Using Two Levels

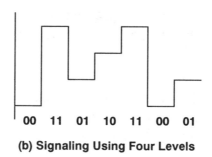

(b) Signaling Using Four Levels

Figure 33. Baseband Signaling

Baseband signaling is for strictly digital transmission, and it may be only 0's and 1's or it may be multilevel to increase the throughput. If it is multilevel, it is quickly converted to binary by the receiver.

Ethernet is a type of LAN that was originally developed by the Xerox Corporation and has since become a standard sanctioned by the Institute of Electrical and Electronic Engineers (IEEE). An Ethernet LAN can connect up to 1,024 computers with a maximum distance of 2.5 kilometers. The maximum distance of any cable segment is 500 meters, with segments connected by repeaters which strengthen the signals.

Like Kermit, which we described earlier, Ethernet uses a byte-oriented protocol, although it is somewhat different especially since it requires a source and destination address. An Ethernet packet is shown in Figure 34. Ethernet is not the only LAN that has become standard of course; the Token Ring developed by IBM has also become an IEEE standard.

PREAMBLE	DEST. ADDR.	SOURCE ADDR.	TYPE	USER DATA	FCS
BYTES: 8	6	6	2	46-1500	4

Figure 34. Ethernet Packet

Twisted Pairs

Twisted pairs are also used for Ethernet and other types of LANs. Twisting a pair of cables improves immunity to degradation of the signal and outside interference. Twisted pairs generally operate at a data rate of 4 megabits per second, although shielded twisted pairs have been used for much higher data rates.

Twisted pairs are usually connected with RJ-45 connectors similar to the connectors used on a standard telephone, except they are larger and are capable of connecting eight wires (four twisted pairs). Also, DB-9 connectors are sometimes used.

The advantages of twisted pairs are that they are more flexible and less expensive to install.

Fiber-Optic Cable

A fiber-optic cable consists of a thin glass filament enclosed in a protective cladding. One or more cables are enclosed in a loose sheathing. Fiber-optic cables are much more difficult to connect than coaxial cable or twisted pairs and require special technical expertise and equipment to handle.

Fiber-optic cables easily support data rates of 100 megabits per second and are capable of data rates in the multi-gigabit per second range.

The American National Standards Institute (ANSI) has developed a standard for a fiber-optic network called Fiber Distributed Data Interface (FDDI), which is a wide area network (WAN) that can cover distances of up to 125 and is meant primarily to be a backbone connecting LANs. The network runs at 100 megabits per second.

Telephone Lines

Telephone lines have actually been used for digital data transmission between computers since the early 1960s when AT&T made available what they called DSO links, which allowed data rates of 64 kilobits per second. However, it has been in the last ten years that revolutionary progress has been made with the installation of digital switches and fiber-optic trunks connecting central offices, those huge switches that serve an entire mid-sized city.

Now the ITU-T, an international standards organization for telecommunications, is promoting a standard called Integrated Services Digital Network (ISDN) which will make possible one network for voice, data, and video. Working in conjunction with Asynchronous Transfer Mode (ATM), which is yet another standard protocol, ISDN should make possible Metropolitan Area Networks (MANs), which work as efficiently as LANs, using the public telephone network.

There is also the Internet, an extension of the Defense Department's ARPANET, which has become a worldwide network. The Internet is just beginning to use ISDN to achieve higher data rates.

However, analog technology, which we will cover in the next section, is still important for transmitting data between computers. In the following section, we will cover some of the concepts of digital transmission over telephone lines.

Analog

Nearly all telephones are connected to local central offices with twisted pairs, which use an analog signal with a bandwidth of 3,000 Hz. from 300 Hz. to 3,300 Hz., which was meant for the transmission of voice. A phone line can be plugged into a modem, which stands for modulator-demodulator. Modems, which are also called data circuit terminating equipment (DCE), can be connected to computers, which are sometimes called data terminating equipment (DTE), and can thus transmit digital data to a modem and a computer somewhere on the telephone network.

Figure 35 shows different modulation methods used by modems, which include amplitude modulation, frequency modulation, and phase shift keying. Also, more than one amplitude level, frequency, or phase angle can be used so that a signal change can represent more than just one bit. In fact, there is a modulation method called quadrature amplitude modulation (QAM) which combines two amplitude levels with four phases for eight possible values, or three bits, for each signal change.

Although sometimes confused, there is a difference between the baud rate and the bit rate. The baud rate is the number of signal changes per second, and the bit rate is the number of bits per second. If a modem uses QAM and has a baud rate of 3,200, it will have a bit rate of 9,600 bits per second.

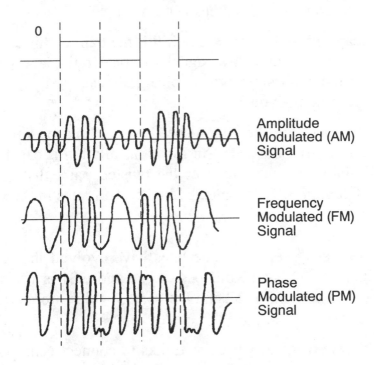

Figure 35. Modulation Methods

Modems have come a long way. The first modems transmitted data at a rate of 300 bits per second. Today's modems commonly exceed 20 kilobits per second. They are achieving higher data rates in several different ways:

1. Using sophisticated modulation techniques such as QAM,

2. Using bit-oriented protocols that don't have stop and start bits for every byte,

3. Transmitting over double twisted pair phone lines that use the extra pair for synchronization,

4. Electronic techniques such as equalization, and

5. Error detection and correction

However, today's modems are pushing the envelope. In 1933, Harry Nyquist developed a theory that the bit rate cannot exceed twice the bandwidth of an allocated channel. For a voice grade line of 3,000 Hz, this would allow a maximum bit rate of 6,000. However, this theory applies to simple signals with only binary values. Also, C.E. developed a formula that relates transmission speed to signal power and error rates. Shannon stated that as the power increased so did the error rate, creating a limitation on the speed a link could operate. Shannon's law is shown on the following page.

$$C = B \log_2 (1 + S/N)$$

C is the capacity in bits per second; B is the bandwidth; and S/N is the signal to noise ratio. For a low signal to noise ratio, a capacity of 30 kilobits per second is possible over a voice-grade channel, but modems are not likely to get much beyond that.

Eventually there will be a high-speed digital link to every telephone, making modems all but obsolete. An ISDN installation is capable of transmitting 144 kilobits per second over the twisted pairs that are in place. Other types of cabling offer promise of higher data rates in the future.

Digital

Digital services over telephone lines have evolved in increments of the digital signal. DSO is 64 Kbits per second and DS1 is 1.544 Mbits per second. There is also DS2 or T2 and DS3 or T3 which are multi-Mbits per second.

T1 lines were originally used as trunks to connect central offices; 24 voice conversations were sampled at a rate of 8,000 samples per second by pulse code modulators (PCMs), plus 8,000 bits were added for network control, for a total of 1.544 Mbits per second.

The samples taken by PCMs of calls coming in to the central office over twisted pairs are eight bits each, so that 24 voice channels will be combined in frames of 192 bits plus one bit for synchronization, for a total of 193 bits for each frame.

When T1 lines were made available as a way to connect computer networks, usually LANs that were at a distance, companies used time division multiplexing (TDM) to give each computer in the LAN a time slice, which is then demultiplexed at the LAN at the other end of the T1 line. TDMs are similar to the multiplexers we described in Section 4.2 except they automatically select a new input line for each time interval. T1 lines used to connect computer networks are called trunks or backbones.

IBM developed a bit-oriented protocol called Synchronous Data Link Control (SDLC) for data transmission over high-speed links between networks. An SDLC frame is shown in Figure 36. A standard very similar to SDLC, called HDLC, has been sanctioned by the ITU-T.

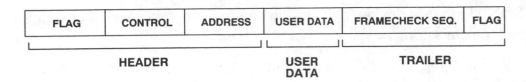

Figure 36. SDLC Frame

The SDLC uses a cyclic redundancy check (CRC) to check for errors. A CRC treats the message as a binary number (a polynomial) and divides it using modulo 2 arithmetic by what is called a generator polynomial and appends the remainder to the end of the message. The message is then checked at the other end by the same generator polynomial.

Messages of bit-oriented protocols are usually called frames, while messages of byte-oriented protocols are usually called packets. Frames are more likely to be checked by hardware, while packets are more likely checked by software. Frames usually are by low-level protocols, usually what is called the data link layer.

The International Standards Organization (ISO) is promoting what it calls the Open System Interface (OSI) reference model, which has seven layers of protocols as shown below:

7. Applications

6. Presentation

5. Session

4. Transport

3. Network

2   Data Link

1. Physical

The top five layers are considered more software-oriented. Kermit, which we described in an earlier section, would be considered the Transport layer. A program that ran Kermit in the background, which allowed two users to communicate directly, would be considered the Application or Presentation layer. ATM, which we already described, would be considered the Network layer because it involves packet switching. SDLC would be considered the Data Link layer. Coaxial cable is an example of the physical layer.

How well the OSI reference model will be adhered to still remains to be seen. Also, there is a standard called Synchronous Optical Network

(SONET) that is designed to tap the enormous potential of fiber-optics for data transmission.

One thing everybody agrees on is that there is a telecommunications revolution taking place, and that the information superhighway will continue to evolve as technology advances.

SPREADSHEETS

In its simplest form, a spreadsheet is a two-dimensional display of data. The horizontal entities are called rows and the vertical entities are called columns. The intersections of the rows and columns are called cells.

What first appears when a spreadsheet program is run is called a worksheet. The main part of the worksheet is made up of a grid that marks the invidivual cells. Most spreadsheet programs allow the user to turn the grid lines on and off, and the printout of the display may or may not show the cell borders.

At the top of the main part of the worksheet are letters such as A, B, C, etc., which identify the columns, and to the left of the main part of the worksheet are numbers which identify the rows. A typical spreadsheet will allow about 256 columns with the letters following the sequence A–Z, then AA–AZ, and so on, to IV. The number of rows is typically about 8,192, which is 2^{13}.

Other parts of the worksheet include: 1) the menu bar, which has pull-down menus such as edit, formula, help, etc., 2) the tool bar, which allows the user to use tools such as scroll capability, and 3) the formula bar, which displays formulas that are being entered into a cell or have already been entered into a cell. Various spreadsheets may also include as part of the worksheet a status bar or perhaps a title bar.

Entries are made in the active cell by typing. The active cell is selected either by use of the arrow keys or by using a mouse to move a pointer to a particular cell, and then clicking a mouse button—either way the selected cell becomes highlighted. The user types data into the active (or highlighted cell), then presses either enter or an arrow key. The arrow keys cause what the user has typed to be entered into the cell, and then cause an adjacent cell to be selected (or highlighted). Pressing the enter key causes the data to be entered, but the same cell is still highlighted.

If a user wants to edit a cell, the user invokes the cell edit command by pressing a function key. When a cell is being edited, the arrow keys

476

move the insertion point one space at a time, rather than to an adjacent cell. Also, during a cell edit the delete key will only delete one character. Normally, the delete key will delete the entire contents of the selected cell. The user presses the enter key when the cell edit is completed.

There are three kinds of entries that can be made in spreadsheet cells: labels, values, and formulas. Labels are text used for the purpose of describing data, usually a row of numbers to the right of a label or a column of numbers below a label. Values are numerical data. Values can be formatted in various ways:

1.	Integers or reals with or without commas between every third digit (the number of decimal places can vary usually up to seven places).

2.	Alignment—left-justified, right-justified, or centered.

3.	Money amounts with dollar signs and two decimal places.

4.	As a percent followed by a a percent sign.

If, for example, .095 is a value that had been entered in a cell, and the cell is formatted by a menu or keystroke command to be a percent, then the value in the cell would be changed to 9.5%.

A formula is an equation that may include mathematical operators, references to other cells, functions such as trigometric or logarithmic functions, special spreadsheet functions such as average or sum, and integer or real numbers. The value that is shown in a cell containing a formula is not the formula, but the value that is the result of the formula.

A formula is entered by selecting a cell and invoking the formula command. Then the user types the formula which appears on the formula bar near the top of the worksheet. When the user presses the enter key, the value that is the result of the formula appears in the selected cell. If a formula had already been entered in the selected cell, the formula would have appeared on the formula bar when the cell was selected.

```
menu BAR

tool BAR

formula BAR  |   B8   |   = A6 + A7
           A     B      C      D      E      F      G      H
1

2

3

4

5      Addition of Cells B6 and B7

6            300

7            400

8            700

9
```

Figure 37. Entering Formula

Figure 37 shows how a spreadsheet would appear just after a formula had been entered in cell B8, which added the contents of cells B6 and B7. The formula is shown on the menu bar and the result is shown in cell B8.

Spreadsheets are menu-driven. A command may be accessed by using a mouse to move a pointer to a pull-down menu, then clicking it, and then moving the pointer to a menu command and clicking the mouse again. A command also may be accessed by holding down the ALT key and typing a letter that is underlined on one of the pull-down menus and then by typing a letter that is underlined on one of the commands that is part of the menu. Also, a command may be accessed directly by typing a backslash and then the command. For our purposes, it doesn't really matter how a command is accessed, we will concentrate on capabilities that all spreadsheets have. The use of many of the features of a spreadsheet is intuitively obvious by examining the menus, or failing that, the help menu or a manual.

Spreadsheets give the user the ability to design their own display. Individual columns can be widened if the values or labels, entered in a column, require more space. The default setting for columns is usually about ten digits. Also, a user can enter a title in a cell above a display of data, and if the title is wider than the width of the cell, the user can continue to type, overriding the grid lines (see Figure 37).

An important feature of spreadsheets is that they give the user the flexibility to make changes. Rows or columns can be inserted. The results of a formula can be reformatted. If, for example, a column contained the sum of several rows to the left of the column and it was decided that it would be better if the sums were expressed as whole numbers, then the cells containing the sums could be reformatted as integers.

Ranges and Addresses

A range is a rectangular region on the spreadsheet. It may consist of a single cell, a row, a column, or a region made up of two or more columns or rows.

An address of a cell is the letter and the number that identify the column and the row that intersect at that cell. A range is identified by the address of the cell at the upper left corner of the rectangle and the address of the cell at the lower right corner of the range. For example. B2..D3 would identify a six-cell range that includes the cells with the addresses B2, C2, D2, B3, C3, and D3.

A common way to designate a range is by pressing one of the buttons on the mouse with the cell pointer over the upper left corner cell of the range and by dragging it to the lower right corner cell of the range and then clicking it. A range can, of course, also be designated by keystroke commands. Once a range is designated it can be moved, copied, erased, or filled. A range can be filled with a value, say the integer 1,000, or if the step option of the fill command is chosen, by incremental values starting with 1,000.

One of the more useful applications of ranges, from the standpoint of engineering, is its use in calculating a list. For example, the formula for the thermal conductivity of silicon is given by:

$$K(T) = \frac{K_0}{\left(T - T_0\right)}$$

If we wanted to calculate the list of values of the thermal conductivity of silicon for temperatures from 200 Kelvin to 700 Kelvin, we could first designate the range A8..A18. Once the range A8..A18 (which is strictly a vertical range in this case, so it is designated by its uppermost and lower-most cells) is designated, we could invoke the fill command. We could use the fill command to fill the range with 200 by step 50.

After the range has been filled in, we could enter the values 350 and 68 in cells B3 and B4 to represent K_0 and T_0, respectively. We could then enter the following formula in cell B8:

$$= \$B\$4/(A8 - \$B\$3)$$

The use of the dollar sign in a cell address means the absolute value of the address, so $\$B\$4$ and $\$B\$3$ refer to the absolute cell addresses B4 and B3, while A8, in the above formula, refers to the relative cell address A8. The next step is to copy the formula in cell B8 to the range B9..B18. When we copy the formula to that range, the absolute addresses $\$B\$3$ and $\$B\$4$ will stay the same and the relative address A8 will change to A9 through A18, because spreadsheets assume, when a formula is copied or moved, that its location is being changed, not its logic. We should also point out that it is sometimes convenient to use a partial absolute address in a formula such as $\$E9$ or $G\$6$.

Once the formula has been entered and copied to cells B8 through B18, the values that represent the result of the formula should appear. The next step is to enter the labels K_0 and T_0 in cells A3 and A4 and the labels $T(K)$ and $K(W/cm - K)$ in cells A6 and B6, respectively. The resulting spreadsheet is shown in Figure 38.

menu BAR

tool BAR

formula BAR

	A	B	C	D	E	F	G	H
1								
2								
3	$K0$	350						
4	$T0$	68						
5								
6	$T(K)$	K $(W/cm{-}K)$						
7		-----------------						
8	200	2.65						
9	250	1.92						
10	300	1.51						

11	350	1.24
12	400	1.05
13	450	0.92
14	500	0.81
15	550	0.73
16	600	0.66
17	650	0.60
18	700	0.55

Figure 38. Thermal Conductivity of Silicon

Another use of spreadsheets is to display a cost-benefit analysis. The ideal failure rate versus time curve for system components is shown in Figure 39.

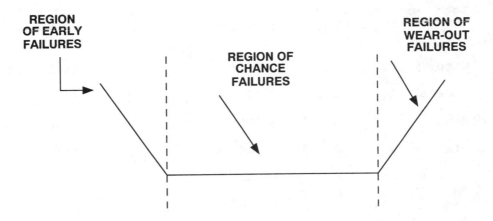

Figure 39. Ideal Failure Rate vs. Time Curve

The first part of the curve, the region of early failures, can be avoided with techniques such as subjecting devices to a burn-in period prior to installation. The last part of the curve is often avoided because obsolescence due to technological advancement requires replacement prior to wear-out.

Let us assume that Company XYZ sells and, under contract agreement, maintains a simple device that is made up of a microprocessor, three RAM chips, and two peripheral interface adapters. Company XYZ is trying to decide to purchase the components for this device from one of two suppliers. The first supplier's components are less expensive but have a higher failure rate. The second supplier's components are more expensive but have a lower failure rate.

The failure rate, or chance of failure over a specific time period, is given by:

$$F(t) = 1 - \exp\left(-((n * t) / theta)\right)$$

where *n* is the number of components, *t* is the time period, and *theta* is the mean time between failure of each component.

menu BAR

tool BAR

formula BAR

	A	B	C	D	E	F	G	H
1		Supplier 1			Supplier 2			
2	*THETA*		.03			.07		
3	Tech. expense		$2000			$2000		
4								
5	Comp	Nbr	Each	Cst#1		Nbr	Each	Cst#2
6	Microp	1	$ 100	$ 100		1	$150	$ 100
7	RAM	3	$ 100	$ 300		3	$150	$ 450
8	PIA	2	$ 100	$ 200		2	$150	$ 300
9				-----				-----
10	Total for unit			$ 600				$ 750
11	Nbr units			50				50
12				-----				-----
13	Tot for all units			$3000				$4500
14	Expected repair cost			$1050				$ 215
16				-----				-----
17	Total cost			$4150				$4715

Figure 40. Cost-Benefit Analysis

Figure 40 shows the cost-benefit analysis of purchasing components from the two potential suppliers. The label "Tech. expense" in cell A3 refers to the expense of having a technician make a repair in the event of failure. It is assumed to be the cost of flying the technician to the site, hotel accommodations, and salary. The total cost of repair of a unit is the tech. expense plus the cost of one component.

The total cost for one unit is computed by entering the formula "= SUM (D6 : D8)" in cell D9 and a similar formula in cell H9–SUM being a spreadsheet function.

It is possible to name a range using spreadsheets, which is a very useful feature. The total for all units is computed by first naming the range in D10 (a range can be only one cell) as Cst#1, and entering the formula "= 50 * Cst#1" in cell D15 and a similar formula in cell H13. The expected repair cost is computed by entering the formula "= (1 – exp – ((7 * 24) / cost" and entering appropriate formulas in D17 and H17 to add the total for all unit to the expected repair cost.

The spreadsheet in Figure 40 can easily be modified as the cost or number of components change, or the mean time between failure varies, or as other factors change. Of course, spreadsheets in the real world are more complicated, but once the basic concepts are understood it is a smooth transition from the simple to the complex.

We said earlier that there are three kinds of entries that can be made in cells. Actually, there is a fourth one: macros. Macros used in spreadsheets are similar to macros used in word processors and editors in that they save a series of keystrokes or commands, with the difference being that they are saved in a cell. Sometimes it is useful to allow room at the top of the main worksheet area for macros. It is also useful to save templates of spreadsheets that are used over and over with just the labels typed in, and useful macros saved in cells at the top or near the bottom of the main worksheet.

REVIEW PROBLEMS

PROBLEM 1

The octal representation of a number is 63, what is the binary representation of this number?

SOLUTION

The number 63_{oct} can also be rewritten in decimal form.

$$63_{oct} = 8^1 * 6 + 8^0 * 3$$
$$= 8 * 6 + 1 * 3$$
$$= 48 + 3$$
$$= 51$$

In binary, the base is 2. Therefore numbers are written as $2^n, 2^{n-1}, \ldots, 2^2, 2^1, 2^0$, with each written as either a 0 or 1. Thus to write 51 in binary, divide by a power of 2. Since 51 falls between $2^5 = 32$ and $2^6 = 64$, 51 will have 6 binary digits, from 2^5 to 2^0.

$$\frac{51}{2^5} = \frac{51}{32} = 1 + 19 \text{ remainder}$$

and

$$\frac{19}{2^4} = 1 + 3 \text{ remainder}$$

$$\frac{3}{2^3} = 0 + 3 \text{ remainder}$$

$$\frac{3}{2^2} = 0 + 3 \text{ remainder}$$

$$\frac{3}{2^1} = 1 + 1 \text{ remainder}$$

$$\frac{1}{2^0} = 1 \text{ with no remainder.}$$

Therefore, the binary representation of 63_{oct} is 110011. Many calculators also do these conversions, eliminating the long division process.

PROBLEM 2

In the following program, if $N = 2$, what is the value of R?

```
INPUT N
S = 0;  P = 1;  R = 2
FOR I = 1 to N
P = P + 1
S = S + P
NEXT I
```

SOLUTION

In this problem, the question asks for the value of R if $N = 2$. According to the code, R is set equal to 2 ($R = 2$), and then the value of R is not changed after this initial assignment.

To further show this point, see how the other values change.

Initially, $N = 2$, $S = 0$, $P = 1$, $R = 2$

$I = 1$ TO 2

$I = 1$

$P = P + 1 = 1 + 1 = 2$

$S = S + P = 0 + 2 = 2$

R must be 2 since no changes have been made to R.

and when $I = 2$

$P = P + 1 = 2 + 1 = 3$

$S = S + P = 2 + 3 = 5$,

but $R = 2$.

PROBLEM 3

After a set of computations, a calculator (which stores 8 significant digits) returns a value of 9.99999999 instead of the exact value of 10. Will this error present problems in engineering computation?

SOLUTION

This question asks what problems, if any, could result when a calculator returns a value which is slightly different from the exact value. While the small error may be insignificant at this stage, after many iterations, a small round off error can be increased, leading to more substantial errors. Therefore, this type of round off error may present problems if the calculator is used to perform iterations.

PROBLEM 4

Given the section section below, what is the value of cell B4?

	A	B
1	0	= A1^2 − A1
2	3	= A2^2 − A2
3	6	= A3^2 + A2
4	9	= A4 + B3
5	12	

SOLUTION

The formula given for B4 is A4 + B3, but the value for B3 is defined by the formula A3^2 + A2. Solve for B3 first:

B3 = A3^2 + A2

$\quad$ = 6^2 + 3

$\quad$ = 36 + 3

$\quad$ = 39

Now B3 = 39, thus

B4 = A4 + B3

$\quad$ = 9 + 39

B4 = 48.

PROBLEM 5

What is the decimal equivalent of the binary number 1011010?

SOLUTION

The binary number is easily converted to the decimal number:

$1011010 = 1*2^6 + 0*2^5 + 1*2^4 + 1*2^3 + 0*2^2 + 1*2^1 + 0*2^0$

$\quad = 64 + 0 + 16 + 8 + 0 + 2 + 0$

$\quad = 90.$

Alternatively, if your calculator converts from binary to decimal, a few keystrokes will arrive at the same answer.

PROBLEM 6

What is the value of Y returned by the program segment?

```
X = 1
Y = -2
Z = -X
IF Z > 0 Z= 1
RETURN
```

SOLUTION

In this problem, you are asked for the value of Y. Y is initially assigned a value of -2, then Z is set equal $-X = -1$. The conditional statement involving Z follows. Thus since no further operations are performed on Y, its value remains at -2.

PROBLEM 7

The cells C2 through C12 of a spreadsheet contain the series of values 5, 10, 15,... Cell D3 contains the formula 2*C2 + 7. If the formula is copied to cells D4 through D12, what is the value in cell D8?

SOLUTION

For this question, list the values in the cells C2 through C8.

	C
2	5
3	10
4	15
5	20
6	25
7	30
8	35

Now the formula for cell D8 will be 2*C7 + 7. Since the value for C7 is 30, then D8 is

$$D8 = 2*C7 + 7$$
$$= 2*30 + 7$$
$$= 67.$$

PROBLEM 8

The significant part of Register A of a computer CPU contains 1101, while the significant part of Register B contains 0110. An NAND operation is performed on the two registers. What is the result?

SOLUTION

The NAND function is a combination of AND and NOT functions. The AND function performed of 1101 and 0110 is a comparison. If the same digits are present in both places, then a 1 is returned for the digit; if not, a 0 is returned.

So 1101 AND 0110 yields 0100.

The NOT function reverses the values of the digits. That is, 0 becomes 1, and 1 becomes 0. Therefore 0100 becomes 1011.

PROBLEM 9

An ASCII computer system is composed of 8 bit bytes and two byte words. How many words are required to store the expression COMPUTER?

SOLUTION

The ASCII system represents 256 different characters with 8 bits. With 2 byte words, the number of words required to store the expression COMPUTER is equal to the number of characters divided by 2. COMPUTER has 8 characters, $^8/_2 = 4$. Therefore, 4 of the two byte words are needed. If the question asked how many 8 bit bytes were needed to store the characters, the answer would be 8 of the 8 bit bytes, or one 8 bit byte for each individual character.

PROBLEM 10

The OR circuit shown below will result in what binary output?

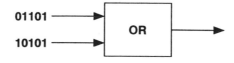

SOLUTION

The OR function will return a value of 1 if either of the input values is 1 and a value of 0 if both input values are 0. Knowing this definition, align the input values.

input 1   01101
input 2   10101

Look at each individual digit. In the first digit place, both inputs are 1, so the result will be 1. In the second digit place, both inputs are 0, so the result will be 0. For the third digit, both inputs are 1, so again, the result will be 1. In the fourth and fifth places, an input is 1 and the other input is 0, so the result will be 1. With all the digits together, the result is 11101.

PROBLEM 11

What are the possible contents of a cell in a spreadsheet, and what is the function of a macro in a spreadsheet?

SOLUTION

The contents of a cell in a spreadsheet may be either a numerical value, a label, or a formula. However, these contents cannot be mixed within the same cell. That is, a single cell cannot contain both a label and a formula.

In a spreadsheet, a macro is a grouping and recording of instructions that the users originally executes manually. The recorded macro can thus be used repetitively as one command, instead of the chain of commands. A macro eliminates the tedious repetitive instructions and reduces them to a single keystroke, saving time and reducing errors.

PROBLEM 12

Looking at the given flowchart, what is the output is $X = -2$?

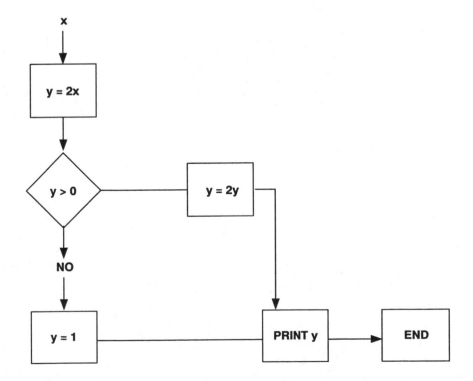

SOLUTION

In this simple flowchart, the input X determines the value of Y. Y is then compared to 0.

If $Y > 0$, the value of Y is set to $2*Y$. If Y is not > 0, or in other words, if $Y <= 0$, then Y is set to 1.

If $X = -2$, then $Y = 2*(-2) = -4$. In this case, $Y < 0$, or Y follows the NO pathway for the comparison. Y is then set to 1. So the output is $Y = 1$, or 1.

FE/EIT

Fundamentals of Engineering: AM Exam

CHAPTER 10

Thermodynamics

CHAPTER 10

THERMODYNAMICS

PROPERTIES

The state of a medium is defined by the properties of that medium. Properties are divided into two major categories:

(1) **Intensive properties** which are independent of the mass. Pressure (P), density (ρ), and temperature (T) are examples of intensive properties.

(2) **Extensive properties** which vary directly with the mass of the medium. Volume (V), total enthalpy (H), total internal energy (U), and mass (m) are examples of extensive properties.

An extensive property divided by the mass is called a specific property and can be used in the same manner as the intensive property. Specific volume (v), enthalpy (h), entropy (s), and internal energy (u) are examples of specific properties.

The specific volume is the total volume divided by the mass

$$v = \frac{V}{m}$$

and the density is the inverse of the specific volume

$$\rho = \frac{1}{v}.$$

The enthalpy, a derived property, is equal to the internal energy plus the product of pressure and specific volume. This relationship can be developed by considering the effect of fluid flow on the internal energy. Thus, enthalpy is

$$h = u + Pv.$$

For a pure substance, one that is homogeneous, of constant chemical composition, and with only one work mode (compressibility), two independent intensive or specific properties are required to fix the state of the medium. Thus, the necessity for strict understanding of the difference between extensive and intensive properties.

The utility of properties is their ability to define the state of a medium and to relate to each other to define new, useful relationships. Some properties are defined as a result of physical occurrences, pressure being a prime example. Defined as a force per unit area normal to the force,

$$P = \frac{F}{A}$$

pressure is considered absolute in this case. Most pressure is measured as gauge pressure, the difference between the absolute and the atmospheric. Gauge pressure is either positive or negative (vacuum). Pressure relationships in equation form are

$$P_{abs} = P_{atm} + P_{gauge}$$

where P_{abs} = Absolute pressure

P_{atm} = Atmospheric pressure

P_{gauge} = Gauge pressure (positive or vacuum)

Figure 1 shows the relationship between the gauge, absolute, and atmospheric pressures.

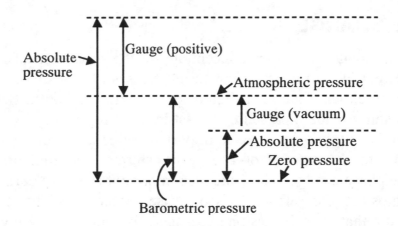

Figure 1. Pressure measurement for both positive gauge and vacuum situations

In every case, the value of the property is defined at a finite state point. Properties are designated as point functions, in contrast to energy transfers (heat and work) which are path functions. Heat and work will be defined later.

Thermodynamic Systems

Throughout the study of thermodynamics, the medium, and the actions associated with the medium, i.e., the flow of matter and energy transfer, must be described in terms of the boundary used to isolate the medium from other media or the surroundings. Generally, the boundary is the means of identifying the type of analysis to be performed. As will be seen later, the type of analysis may determine which properties are logically used. Two types of thermodynamic systems are frequently used:

(1) An **open system** is one that allows for the flow of matter and the transfer of energy across the system boundary. Problems analyzed using this analysis are referred to as flow problems. Additionally, the term **control volume** is used to specify open systems. The control volume is any fixed volume in space through which fluid flow takes place. Its surface is called a control surface. Turbines, compressors, and nozzles are analyzed using the control volume.

(2) A **closed system** allows energy to cross the system boundary without the flow of matter. A fixed mass characterizes this type of problem.

The importance of choosing the correct system will be clear after the discussion of the First and Second Laws, processes, and cycles.

PHASE CHANGE

Thermodynamic studies concentrate on the properties of substances and the effect of energy transfers. In most cases, the medium under consideration is either a gas or a liquid, or a mixture of both. Seldom is a complete study made of a solid, at least in the introductory levels. Transformation from liquid to vapor is important, as is any phase change, primarily due to the amount of energy transferred (required or liberated) during the phase change. There are also important property definitions and relationships that come from study of phase interactions. The most important medium that experiences phase changes is water. The study of water, especially in the form of steam, led to the development of the science of thermodynamics.

Since we generally deal with pure substances as defined above, we will consider only those in this discussion. Water is a pure substance because it retains its chemical composition through all three phases (solid, liquid, vapor). On the other hand, air will decompose into individual elements as the temperature is reduced, altering the chemical composition. For this reason, mixtures of gases, such as air, can be considered pure at temperatures and pressures that keep them in the gaseous phase.

Figures 2 and 3 are three-dimensional schematics of the *P-V-T* surface for a pure substance. They show that pure substances can exist only in the vapor, liquid, or solid phase in certain regions.

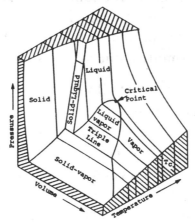

Figure 2. *P-V-T* surface for a substance that contracts on freezing

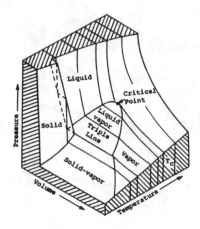

Figure 3. *P-V-T* surface for a substance that expands on freezing

The following information applies to these diagrams:

(1) The **critical point** is the point beyond which the substance exists as a gas. At the critical point, the saturated liquid and saturated vapor are identical, and the heat of vaporization, h_{fg}, is zero.

(2) The pressure, temperature, and specific volume at the critical point are called **critical properties:** P_c, T_c, and v_c.

(3) In the **liquid-vapor region**, liquid and vapor exist as a saturated mixture. Any change in the heat transfer (energy) at constant pressure will change the ratio of the liquid to the vapor. One hundred percent liquid describes the saturated liquid line, **SLL**, while 100 percent vapor describes the saturated vapor line, **SVL**. Any increase in energy from the SLL causes vapor to form. Any decrease in energy from the SVL causes liquid to form. The temperature is constant during the vaporization process and is referred to as the **saturation temperature**. Temperature and pressure are not independent intensive properties in the liquid-vapor region.

The change in enthalpy associated with a phase change from solid to liquid is the latent heat of fusion. The change in enthalpy associated with a phase change from liquid to vapor is the latent heat of vaporization.

A useful representation of the three-dimensional phase diagram is the two-dimensional equivalent. The *P-T* diagram describes the interaction of the phases experienced by the medium. Figures 4 and 5 are for substances which expand on freezing and for substances which contract on freezing, respectively. For these diagrams, the following terms apply:

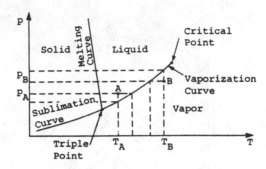

Figure 4. *P-T* **diagram for a substance that expands on freezing**

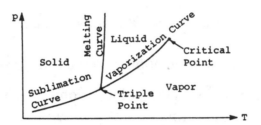

Figure 5. *P-T* **diagram for a substance that contracts on freezing**

(1) The **triple point** is the point at which all three phases can coexist in equilibrium.

(2) The **sublimation curve** is the curve along which the solid phase may exist in equilibrium with the vapor phase.

(3) The **vaporization curve** is the curve along which the liquid phase may exist in equilibrium with the vapor phase.

(4) The **melting curve** is the curve along which the solid phase may exist in equilibrium with the liquid phase.

(5) In Figure 4, State A is known as a subcooled liquid or a compressed liquid. State B is known as a super heated vapor.

Several other useful diagrams can be obtained as a result of plotting different property comparisons.

These diagrams are used to describe property relationships and to solve problems in which the medium is either water or Freon. In each case, a vapor dome is described by the SLL and SVL. Understanding the vapor dome and the property interactions associated with the dome is important in the solution of cycles, especially vapor power cycles. Figures 6 to 9 represent the common combinations used in thermodynamics.

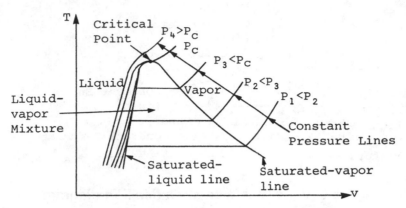

Figure 6. Vapor dome on a *T-v* diagram

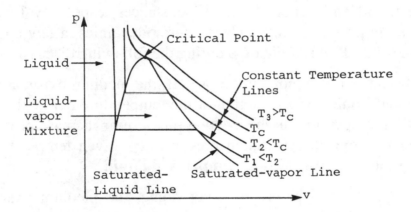

Figure 7. Vapor dome on a *P-v* diagram

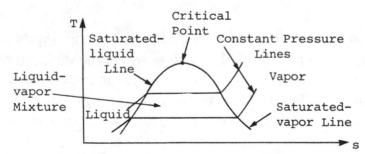

Figure 8. Vapor dome on a *T-s* diagram

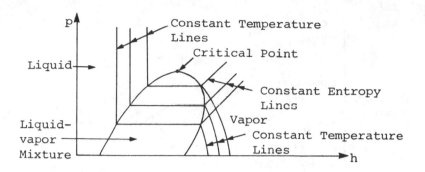

Figure 9. Vapor dome on a *P-h* (Mollier) diagram

Vapor Dome

Since liquid and vapor phases of substances, especially Freon and water, are so important in the study of thermodynamics, a few additional notes are in order. Refer to Figure 6 during the following discussion.

(a) In the liquid region on the far left, the medium exists as a saturated liquid. Any reduction of the temperature below the saturation temperature at the existing pressure or increase of the pressure above the saturation pressure at a given temperature will produce a **subcooled** or **compressed liquid**.

(b) On the far right of the vapor dome, the medium exists as a saturated vapor. Any increase in temperature above the saturation temperature at a given pressure results in a **superheated vapor**.

(c) The line used to construct the left side of the vapor dome is called the saturated liquid line and is where the medium exists as a **saturated liquid**. Any increase in the temperature when the medium is at its saturation temperature at a given pressure will result in vaporization. Similarly, the saturation pressure at a given temperature is the pressure, below which, the medium will vaporize.

(d) The line used to construct the right side of the vapor dome is called the saturated vapor line and is where the medium exists as a **saturated vapor**. Any decrease in the temperature when the medium is at its saturation temperature at a given pressure will result in condensation. Similarly, the saturation pressure at a given temperature is the pressure, above which, the medium will condense.

(e) Finally, between the saturated liquid and the saturated vapor line lies the **saturated mixture** region or the **liquid-vapor mixture**. Here the temperature and pressure are not independent intensive properties. The quality, as defined below, becomes important when fixing the state of the medium. Saturated mixtures increase in vapor content as more energy is added, or become more liquid as energy is removed.

Common notation used around the vapor dome includes:

f = Saturated liquid

g = Saturated vapor

fg = Difference between values of properties for a liquid and a gas, i.e., $h_{fg} = h_g - h_f$, heat of vaporization.

In the liquid-vapor mixture region, temperature and pressure are not independent properties. To assist in the fixing of states in this region, the ratio of the mass of the vapor to the total mass defines the quality, which is used as an intensive property. The quality is defined only under the dome and ranges from 0 on the SLL to 1 on the SVL. The quality in equation form is

$$x = \frac{m_g}{m_g + m_f} = \frac{m_{vapor}}{m_{total}}$$

where m_g = Mass of vapor

m_f = Mass of liquid

Knowledge of the quality is useful in the calculation of other properties, such as enthalpy and entropy, using the following relationship:

$$P = P_f + x P_{fg} = x P_g + (1 - x) P_f$$

where P = Any property (v, u, h, s)

x = Quality

The moisture content is extremely important in the design and operation of steam turbines. It is defined as

$$y = 1 - x.$$

To illustrate how properties are determined in the various regions, water will be used as an example, since steam tables are readily available:

(1) With T and P known, determine where on the vapor dome the state point is located. This is accomplished by looking up T_{sat} for the given pressure and comparing it to the state point temperature, T. If,

$$T > T_{sat}, \text{ then } \textbf{superheated vapor}, \text{ or}$$

$$T = T_{sat}, \text{ then } \textbf{saturated mixture}, \text{ or}$$

$$T < T_{sat}, \text{ then } \textbf{compressed liquid}, \text{ or}$$

$$T > T_{critical}, \text{ then } \textbf{superheated vapor}.$$

(2) If a **compressed liquid** state exists at pressure less than 7.5 MPa, a good approximation is to look up the properties for the saturated liquid (f) at the state point temperature.

(3) If a **superheated state** enters the superheated vapor tables with the known properties and determine the needed values.

(4) If the quality is given, then the state point must be in the **saturated mixture** region. Here, use the procedures outlined above.

(5) With T and v known, look up v_f and v_g at the prescribed T. If

$$v < v_f, \text{ then } \textbf{compressed liquid}, \text{ or}$$

$$v > v_g, \text{ then } \textbf{superheated vapor}, \text{ or}$$

$$v_f < v < v_g, \text{ then } \textbf{saturated mixture} \text{ region},$$

follow steps 2, 3, or 4 above as appropriate.

(6) Given any two properties which are independent intensive properties, the procedures above can be used if one property is either temperature, T, or pressure, P.

THERMODYNAMIC PROCESSES

When a thermodynamic system changes from one state to another, it is said to execute a process. The process is described in terms of the end states and is influenced by the energy transfers that occur as the medium changes states. When a medium at an initial state experiences changes that cause it to undergo several processes and then returns to its original state, it has experienced a cycle.

Throughout thermodynamics, special processes are used to model actual devices in an attempt to predict the outcome of the actions of these devices. Cycles are combinations of these processes and are the root of the study of heat engines and refrigerators. Processes most commonly experienced are:

(1) **Isothermal process**: one that occurs at constant temperature

(2) **Isobaric process**: one that occurs at constant pressure

(3) **Isometric/isochoric process**: one that occurs at constant volume

(4) **Adiabatic process**: one that occurs with no heat transfer across the system boundary

(5) **Quasiequilibrium process**: one that occurs as a succession of equilibrium states such that at every instant the system involved departs only infinitesimally from the equilibrium state

(6) **Reversible process**: one that occurs such that the initial state of the system can be restored with no observable effect on the system or the surroundings. Also known as an ideal process

(7) **Irreversible process**: one that occurs such that the initial state of the system cannot be restored without observable effects on the system or the surroundings

(8) **Isentropic process**: one that occurs at constant entropy. Also known as an adiabatic-reversible process

(9) **Polytropic process**: one that obeys the relationship $PV^n =$ constant. Normally a reversible process with an associated heat transfer

IDEAL GASES

It is generally accepted that gases at low density obey what is known as the ideal gas equation of state:

$$Pv = RT$$

where R = specific gas constant.

Rearranging this equation and introducing the compressibility factor, Z, we have

$$Z = \frac{RT}{Pv}$$

When the compressibility factor equals one, then an ideal gas exists. The assumption of an ideal gas can be made even if the compressibility factor differs slightly from one. If the pressure is low, below 10 MPa or so, depending on the gas, and if the temperature is about twice the critical temperature, the ideal gas assumption is considered valid. Other forms of the ideal gas equation of state are

$$PV = mRT$$

$$PV = n\overline{R}T$$

where m = Mass of the gas

n = Number of moles of the gas

$\overline{R}$ = Universal gas constant

In addition to the equation of state, ideal gases have other important relationships used throughout thermodynamic analysis. For an ideal gas, internal energy and enthalpy are functions of temperature only,

$$u = u(T), \qquad h = h(T)$$

From the previous definition of enthalpy, replacing Pv with RT in accordance with the equation of state produces

$$h = u + RT.$$

Two important relationships used to connect internal energy and enthalpy to temperature variations are the constant volume and constant pressure specific heats. The constant volume specific heat is defined as

$$C_v = \left(\frac{\partial u}{\partial T} \right)_v$$

and the constant pressure specific heat is defined as

$$C_p = \left(\frac{\partial h}{\partial T} \right)_p.$$

Several other specific heat relations are frequently used,

$$C_p - C_v = R$$

and

$$k = \frac{C_p}{C_v}.$$

As will be seen later in cycle analysis, changes in internal energy, enthalpy, and entropy are important to the analysis. For ideal gases, the evaluation of these changes are directly related to the properties at the beginning and ending states. Often, all that is needed is the temperature variation, i.e., $T \rightarrow T_o$. Using this notation, the following relationships are presented:

(1) Internal energy change

$$u - u_o = \int_{T_o}^{T} C_v dT = C_v(T - T_o)$$

(2) Enthalpy change

$$h - h_o = \int_{T_o}^{T} C_p dT = C_p(T - T_o)$$

(3) Entropy change

$$s - s_o = \int_{T_o}^{T} \frac{C_v dT}{T} + R\ln\frac{v}{v_o} = C_v\ln\frac{T}{T_o} + R\ln\frac{v}{v_o}$$

$$s - s_o = \int_{T_o}^{T} \frac{C_p dT}{T} - R\ln\frac{P}{P_o} = C_p\ln\frac{T}{T_o} - R\ln\frac{P}{P_o}$$

The values obtained using constant specific heats are reasonable approximations. For better results, variable specific heats can be used in concert with tabulated data for the various gases. When using the tables, knowledge of the temperature is sufficient for direct evaluation of u, h, and s at a given state point.

For an ideal gas, variations in properties can be represented on T-s and P-v diagrams as shown in Figures 10 and 11:

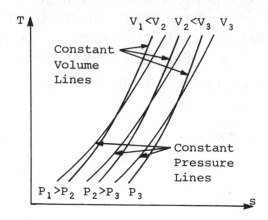

Figure 10. *T-s* diagram for an ideal gas

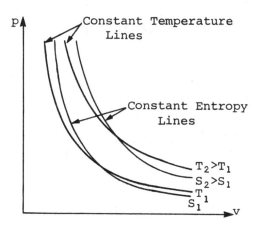

Figure 11. *P-v* diagram for an ideal gas

The reversible polytropic process for an ideal gas is one for which the pressure-volume relation is given by

$$Pv^n = \text{Constant}.$$

The polytropic processes for various values of n are shown on the P-v and T-s diagrams, in Figures 12 and 13:

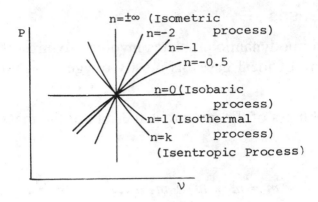

Figure 12. Polytropic processes on a *P-v* diagram

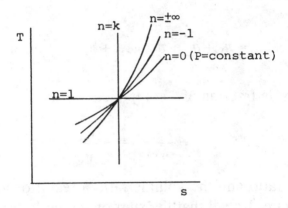

Figure 13. Polytropic processes on a *T-s* diagram

For a polytropic process, the properties are related according to the relationship below:

$$\frac{T_2}{T_1} = \left(\frac{P_2}{P_1}\right)^{\frac{(n-1)}{n}} = \left(\frac{v_1}{v_2}\right)^{(n-1)}$$

Many thermodynamic processes are modeled as isentropic. These require additional property relationships based on the Gibbs equations. Thus, for an isentropic process,

$$\frac{T_2}{T_1} = \left(\frac{P_2}{P_1}\right)^{\frac{k-1}{k}} = \left(\frac{v_1}{v_2}\right)^{k-1}$$

Mixture of Gases

Many thermodynamic problems involve mixtures of ideal gases. Air, itself a mixture of ideal gases, is mostly oxygen and nitrogen, at normal temperatures.

The total mass of the mixture is the sum of the masses of the components:

$$m = m_1 + m_2 + m_3 + \ldots + m_n = \sum_i^n m_i$$

The total number of moles of the mixture is the sum of the moles of the components:

$$n = n_1 + n_2 + n_3 + \ldots + n_n = \sum_i^n n_i$$

Define the mole fraction of a component, x_i, as

$$x_i = \frac{n_i}{n} = \frac{P_i}{P} = \frac{v_i}{v}$$

with the pressure ratio and the volume ratio a result of applying the ideal gas equation of state. Recall that the sum of the mole fractions is equal to one. Using the mole fraction and molar values of h, u, s, C_p, and C_v, along with pressure, provides the following series of relationships used to determine properties of mixtures of ideal gases:

Enthalpy

$$\bar{h} = \sum_i x_i \bar{h}_i$$

Internal energy

$$\bar{u} = \sum_i x_i \bar{u}_i$$

Entropy

$$\bar{s} = \sum_i x_i \bar{s}_i$$

Specific heat

$$\bar{C}_p = \sum_i x_i \bar{C}_{pi}$$

Specific heat

$$\overline{C}_v = \sum_i x_i \overline{C}_{vi}$$

Pressure

$$P_i = x_i P$$
$$P = \sum_i x_i P$$

Finally, the equivalent molecular weight of the mixture, M, is found using

$$M = \sum_i x_i M_i .$$

A similar series of equations can be generated by defining the mass fraction as the mass of a component divided by the total mass. Then using property values based on mass fractions instead of mole fractions, the mixture values are calculated. Both provide necessary information concerning the mixture, and the use of one over the other is merely a convenience of the problem solution.

ENERGY, HEAT, AND WORK

Since for a given closed system the work done is the same in all adiabatic processes between equilibrium states, a fundamental property of the medium in the system can be defined such that the change between equilibrium states is equal to the adiabatic work, as below:

$$E_2 - E_1 = W_{adiabatic}$$

Work will be discussed later. The energy is a fundamental property and is defined in the following word equation:

$E =$ Internal Energy + Kinetic Energy + Potential Energy

where

(1) **Internal energy, U,** is an extensive property since it depends on the mass of the system. It represents the energy modes on the microscopic level, such as the energy associated with nuclear spin, molecular binding, magnetic dipole moment, etc.

(2) **Kinetic energy, *KE*,** is energy a body possesses due to bulk motion. For example, the kinetic energy of a system of mass, *m*, with velocity *v* is given by

$$KE = \frac{1}{2}mv^2.$$

(3) **Potential energy, *PE*,** is the energy a body possesses due to its position in a potential field. For example, the potential energy of a system having a mass, *m*, and an elevation, *z*, above a defined plane in a gravitational field with a constant gravitational constant, *g*, is given by

$$PE = mgz.$$

Whereas energy is a property and has a finite value at a fixed point, heat and work are transient phenomena and are not defined at a point. Systems never possess heat or work. Heat and work cross the boundary of a system undergoing a change of state and are only observable at the boundary. Both are path functions and are represented by inexact differentials. Heat is represented by δQ and work by δW. When integrated across a process, in a closed system from state 1 to 2, the amount of heat that crosses the boundary is represented by $_1Q_2$, and similarly for work, $_1W_2$.

Heat, *Q*, is the form of energy that is transferred across a system boundary as a result of temperature differences. Heat travels from the highest temperature to the lowest temperature. Positive heat transfer is heat addition to a system, and negative heat transfer is heat removed from a system. The details of heat transfer are saved for a complete series of courses that investigate the three modes of heat transfer, conduction, convection, and radiation. These topics are reviewed later.

Work, *W*, is classically defined as a force, *F*, applied through a distance, *dx*. In integral form,

$$W = \int_1^2 Fdx.$$

In a thermodynamic sense, work is an interaction between a system and its surroundings where the sole effect of the system on the surroundings is the raising of a weight. Work done by a system is considered positive, and work done on a system is considered negative.

There are many work modes used in the analysis of thermodynamic processes. These include compressibility, stretched wire work, surface film work, magnetic work, and electrical work. Since we are concentrating on the pure substance, compressibility is the only work mode being considered. In Figure 14, a gas contained in a closed system is expanded from state 1 to state 2 as a result of a higher pressure inside than outside.

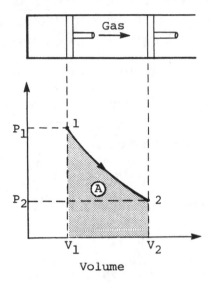

Figure 14. Work done on a simple compressible system

For any small expansion in which the volume of the gas increases by dV, the work done by the gas is

$$W = \int_{1}^{2} P dV.$$

The integral value is the area under the curve on the $P\text{--}v$ diagram. Since we can go from state 1 to state 2 along many different paths, it is evident that the amount of work represented under the curve is a function of both the end states and the path the process follows while going from state 1 to state 2. As previously mentioned, work is a path function, represented mathematically as an inexact differential.

During the analysis of energy transfers associated with the first law, work will be described as:

(1) **System boundary work**: work associated with the movement of a boundary such as that which occurs during a $P\text{--}v$ expansion or compression.

(2) **Shaft work**: work associated with the rotation of a shaft.

(3) **Flow work**: work associated with the flow of a fluid. This is most often tied to the definition of enthalpy.

First Law

Before any discussion of the first law, it is customary to discuss the conservation of mass. Mass can neither be created nor destroyed; it must be strictly accounted for. For any system, conservation of mass states that:

mass added − mass removed = change in the mass stored

For the closed system, the mass is fixed since there is no exchange of mass with the surroundings. Thus, the mass at any state point is constant. Symbolically, this is represented by

$$m_1 = m_2 = m_3 = \ldots$$

For the open system, one that allows for mass transfer across the boundary, conservation of mass is stated as:

$$\dot{m}_{in} - \dot{m}_{out} = \frac{dm}{dt}$$

where $\dot{m}_{out}$ = Mass flow rate out of the control volume

$\dot{m}_{in}$ = Mass flow rate into the control volume

$\frac{dm}{dt}$ = Rate of change in the mass in the control volume

Specific applications will be addressed for each version of the first law discussed. **Note:** The conservation of mass is often referred to as the continuity equation and will be referred to as such from now on.

As with the continuity equation, the first law of thermodynamics can be simply stated via a word equation:

energy input − energy output = change in stored energy

This rather simple equation is the basis for the development of every application of the first law and many of the applications used in heat transfer. Mastery of the first law is essential in the analysis of work producing machines and in any device that exchanges heat with the surroundings.

Observations have led to the formulation of the first law for cycles, which in equation form is

$$\oint dQ = \oint dW$$

where $\oint dQ$ = Cyclic integral of the heat transfer

$\oint dW$ = Cyclic integral of work

and the units are System International.

The first law applied to the closed system undergoing a process and changing from state 1 to state 2 is

$$\delta Q - \delta W = dE$$

where δQ = Heat transferred to the system during the process

δW = Work transferred from the system during the process

E = The total energy of the system and a property of the medium

The net change of the energy of the system is always equal to the net transfer of energy across the system boundary in the form of heat and work.

For analysis purposes it is important to look at continuity for the closed system. Via the continuity equation, the mass is constant. Thus, the mass at any state point can be represented as m. The integrated form of the first law becomes

$$_1Q_2 - {}_1W_2 = U_2 - U_1 + \frac{m\left(v_2^2 - v_1^2\right)}{2} + mg\left(z_2 - z_1\right)$$

where $_1Q_2$ = The heat transferred during the process from 1 to 2

$_1W_2$ = The work done by or in the system during the process from 1 to 2

$U_2 - U_1$ = The change in internal energy

$\dfrac{m\left(v_2^2 - v_1^2\right)}{2}$ = The change in kinetic energy

$mg\left(z_2 - z_1\right)$ = The change in potential energy

Two additional notes concerning this equation:

(1) Only changes in internal energy and kinetic and potential energy can be determined with this equation. Absolute values are not easily obtained.

(2) The first step in applying the first law is to determine the appropriate boundary description—open or closed.

A sign convention used in thermodynamics, although not universal, and applied equally to open and closed systems is

work in is –   work out is +

heat in is +   heat out is –

The general forms of the equations of continuity and the first law for an open system with multiple inlets and exits are, respectively,

$$\sum \dot{m}_{in} - \sum \dot{m}_{out} = \frac{dm}{dt}$$

$$\dot{Q}_{cv} - \dot{W}_{cv} = \frac{dE_{cv}}{dt} + \sum \dot{m}_e \left(h_e + \frac{V_e^2}{2} + gz_e \right) - \sum \dot{m}_i \left(h_i + \frac{V_i^2}{2} + gz_i \right)$$

where $\dot{Q}_{cv}$ = Rate of heat transfer into the control volume

$\dot{W}_{cv}$ = Work rate that crosses or displaces the control volume

$\frac{dE_{cv}}{dt}$ = Rate of change of the energy inside the control volume

$\sum \dot{m}_e \left(h_e + \frac{V_e^2}{2} + gz_e \right)$ = Rate of energy flowing out as a result of mass transfer

$\sum \dot{m}_i \left(h_i + \frac{V_i^2}{2} + gz_i \right)$ = Rate of energy flowing in as a result of mass transfer

Taking the basic equation and applying it to the steady-state, steady-flow process, a primary form used in thermodynamic analysis requires the following assumptions:

(1) The control volume does not move relative to the coordinate frame.

(2) The state of the mass at each point in the control volume does not change with time.

(3) The mass flux does not vary with time.

(4) The rates at which heat and work cross the control surface remain constant.

(5) With the requirement of one inlet, one exit produces:

Continuity equation, $\dot{m}_i = \dot{m}_e = \dot{m}$

First law

$$\dot{Q}_{cv} - \dot{W}_{cv} = \sum \dot{m}_e \left(h_e + \frac{v_e^2}{2} + gz_e \right) - \sum \dot{m}_i \left(h_i + \frac{v_i^2}{2} + gz_i \right)$$

Start up operations and time dependent, unsteady situations are analyzed using the uniform-state, uniform-flow equations. Assumptions for this model are:

(1) The control volume remains constant relative to the coordinate frame.

(2) The state of the mass may change with time in the control volume, but at any instant of time the state is uniform throughout the entire control volume.

(3) The state of the mass crossing all the areas of flow is constant with respect to the control surface, but the mass flow rates may vary with time. Thus:

Continuity equation, $\left(m_2 - m_1 \right)_{cv} + \sum m_e - \sum m_i = 0$

First law

$$Q_{cv} - W_{cv} = \sum m_e \left(h_e + \frac{v_e^2}{2} + gz_e \right) - \sum m_i \left(h_i + \frac{v_i^2}{2} + gz_i \right)$$
$$+ \left(m_2 \left(u_2 + \frac{v_2^2}{2} + gz_2 \right) - m_1 \left(u_1 + \frac{v_1^2}{2} + gz_1 \right) \right)_{cv}$$

In this equation, the rate expressions for the heat, work, and mass flow terms have not been forgotten: integration over time in the development provides total quantities in lieu of rates.

Second Law

The study of the second law and entropy is predicated on the understanding of heat engines, the Carnot cycle, and reversible and irreversible processes. The latter have been previously discussed. Here, the study will begin with the heat engine and refrigerator, followed by the Carnot cycle. The purpose is to place limitations on real devices not obvious by the first law. For example, it is possible to satisfy the first law and violate the second law. Without this check, heat could flow from cold to hot, a concept that is naturally alien to intuition.

A heat engine is a system that operates in a cycle while only heat and work cross its boundaries. The work is the desired result of a heat engine, having a positive (out) sign. Referring to Figure 15, heat is transferred from the high-temperature reservoir, T_H, to the low-temperature reservoir, T_L.

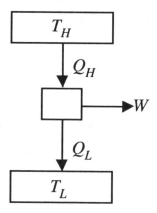

Figure 15. Heat engine

A steam power plant is a heat engine that receives heat from a high-temperature reservoir at the boiler, rejects heat to a low-temperature reservoir at the condenser, and delivers useful work. There are many other heat engines that will be discussed later.

The efficiency of a heat engine is defined as the ratio: the net work delivered to the surroundings divided by the heat received from the high-temperature source. Additionally, the work produced in our simple model is equal to the difference between the heat added and the heat rejected. In equation form,

$$\eta = \frac{W}{Q_H} = \frac{Q_H - Q_L}{Q_H} = 1 - \frac{Q_L}{Q_H}$$

where Q_H = Amount of heat added to the heat engine

   Q_L = Amount of heat rejected by the heat engine

   W = Net work produced by the engine, $Q_H - Q_L$

Refrigerators and heat pumps are heat engines working in reverse. Work is required (input) in order to move heat from a low-temperature reservoir to a high-temperature reservoir. While this appears to fail intuition, remember that heat cannot travel from low to high on its own, only when aided by another energy transfer, work. Figure 16 illustrates the concept of a refrigerator or heat pump,

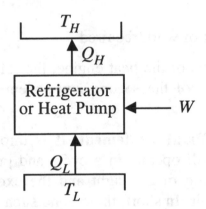

Figure 16. Refrigerator/heat pump

where the values of Q_H, Q_L, and W have particular functions depending on the device. For example,

   Q_H = Heating capacity of a heat pump

   Q_L = Cooling/refrigeration capacity of the refrigerator or air conditioner

   W = Work required to make the cycle operate

The effectiveness of refrigerators and heat pumps is not measured by efficiency, rather by using the coefficient of performance, COP. Values for the coefficient of performance greater than one are not uncommon, and are actually expected. The COP for a refrigerator is

$$\beta_R = \frac{Q_L}{W} = \frac{Q_L}{Q_H - Q_L} = \frac{1}{\dfrac{Q_H}{Q_L} - 1}$$

and the COP for a heat pump is

$$\beta_{HP} = \frac{Q_H}{W} = \frac{Q_H}{Q_H - Q_L} = \frac{1}{1 - \dfrac{Q_L}{Q_H}}$$

where in general terms

Q_L = Amount of heat transferred from the low-temperature reservoir

Q_H = Amount of heat transferred from the high-temperature reservoir

W = Net amount of work required

With the definitions of the heat engine, the refrigerator, and the heat pump in hand, the first of the second law statements can be presented. These are:

(1) **The Kelvin-Plank Statement**: It is impossible to construct a device that will operate in a cycle and produce no effect other than the raising of a weight and the exchange of heat with a single reservoir. In short, there is no such thing as a perfect heat engine—there must be heat rejected.

(2) **The Clausius Statement**: It is impossible to construct a device that operates in a cycle and produces no effect other than the transfer of heat from a cooler body to a hotter body. In short, heat does not flow uphill, cooler to hotter.

There are other limits on the effectiveness of the devices previously discussed. The Carnot cycle is the reversible approximation of the ideal heat engine or refrigerator. It consists of reversible processes that form a reversible cycle. Since the cycle is reversible, a Carnot heat engine can be reversed to operate as a Carnot refrigerator/heat pump. When the cycle operates between two temperature reservoirs, high and low, the cycle consists of the four processes depicted in Figure 17. These four processes are the same for any Carnot cycle.

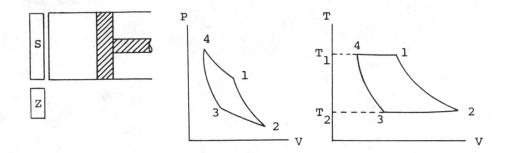

Figure 17. Carnot cycle on *P-v* and *T-v* diagrams

Process 1-2

A reversible adiabatic process in which the temperature of the working fluid decreases from the high temperature to the low temperature.

Process 2-3

A reversible isothermal process in which heat is transferred to or from the low-temperature reservoir.

Process 3-4

A reversible adiabatic process in which the temperature of the working fluid increases from the low temperature to the high temperature.

Process 4-1

A reversible isothermal process in which heat is transferred to or from the high-temperature reservoir.

As a result of the development of the Carnot cycle, two propositions have been formulated regarding the efficiency of the Carnot cycle.

(1) It is impossible to build an engine that operates between two thermal reservoirs and is more efficient than a reversible engine operating between the same thermal reservoirs.

(2) All Carnot engines operating between the same thermal reservoirs have the same efficiency.

From the development of a Thermodynamic Temperature Scale, the efficiency of the reversible heat engines and the COP of refrigerators and heat pumps can be expressed as a function of the thermal reservoir temperatures. Thus,

$$\eta_{th} = 1 - \frac{T_L}{T_H}$$

$$\beta_R = \frac{1}{\dfrac{T_H}{T_L} - 1}$$

$$\beta_{HP} = \frac{1}{1 - \dfrac{T_L}{T_H}}$$

where T_L = Low-temperature reservoir

T_H = High-temperature reservoir, both temperatures are absolute

Finally, the efficiency of a heat engine is always less than one, $\eta_{th} <$ 1, and the efficiency of an irreversible engine is less than that of a reversible engine, $\eta_I < \eta_R$.

So far we have discussed cycles made up of processes, most of which have been reversible. Before turning to the evaluation of processes to determine if they are progressing in accordance with the second law, it is important to mention the Inequality of Clausius. Simply stated, for any irreversible cycle, the following cyclic integral must apply:

$$\oint \frac{\delta Q}{T} \le 0$$

Satisfaction of this requirement indicates that a cycle is obeying the second law; therefore, it is capable of occurring if it also satisfies the first law.

It can be shown that for two reversible processes operating in a cycle, the end points alone define the quantity:

$$dS = \left(\frac{\delta Q}{T} \right)_{rev}$$

where δQ = Heat supplied to the system

T = Absolute temperature of the system

dS = Change in the property called entropy

A few notes are required at this point.

(1) The equation is valid for any reversible process.

(2) Entropy, S, is an extensive property, and it is a function of the end points of the process only, a point function. Thus, since it is independent of the path, the value of the change in entropy is the same for reversible and irreversible processes. The change in the entropy of a closed system can be found by integrating

$$S_2 - S_1 = \int_1^2 \left(\frac{\delta Q}{T} \right)_{rev}$$

In the case of an irreversible process, the entropy change will be exactly the same as for the reversible process. So what is the difference between the two? In the irreversible process, a certain amount of the energy transferred is lost, not available for use later on. The entropy change for an irreversible process in a closed system becomes

$$S_2 - S_1 \overset{>}{=} \int_1^2 \frac{\delta Q}{T}$$

The second law, just like the first law, is applied to many different situations: open and closed systems, and steady-state and unsteady problems. Since continuity has been previously reviewed with the first law, only the second law equations for each situation will be presented.

The general form of the second law for the control volume is

$$\frac{dS_{cv}}{dt} + \sum \dot{m}_e s_e - \sum \dot{m}_i s_i = \int_A \left(\frac{\dot{Q}_{cv}/A}{T} \right) dA + \int_V \left(\frac{L \dot{W}_{cv}/V}{T} \right) dVA$$

This expression states that the rate of change of entropy inside the control volume, plus the net rate of entropy flow out, is equal to the sum of two terms: the integrated heat transfer term and the positive, internal irreversibility term.

For the steady-state, steady-flow case, the general equation reduces to

$$\sum \dot{m}_e s_e - \sum \dot{m}_i s_i \overset{>}{=} \int_A \left(\frac{\dot{Q}_{cv}/A}{T} \right) dA$$

where the removal of the irreversibility term requires the inequality. For an adiabatic process, with a single inlet and a single exit, the equation reduces to $s_e \geq s_i$.

For the uniform-state, uniform-flow case, the general equation becomes

$$\left(m_2 s_2 - m_1 s_1\right)_{cv} + \sum m_e s_e - \sum m_i s_i = \int_o^t \left(\frac{\dot{Q}_{cv} + L\, \dot{W}_{cv}}{T}\right) dt .$$

Additional notes concerning the second law are necessary to understand the total importance it has in thermodynamics. Looking first at the reversible steady-state, steady-flow process with one inlet and one exit, there are three important results:

(1) When the process is both reversible and adiabatic,

$$w = -\int_i^e v\, dP + \frac{\left(v_i^2 - v_e^2\right)}{2} + g\left(z_i - z_e\right).$$

(2) Taking this equation one step further by specifying that the work is zero and the fluid is incompressible, after integration we obtain Bernoulli's equation:

$$v\left(P_e - P_i\right) + \frac{\left(v_e^2 - v_i^2\right)}{2} + g\left(z_e - z_i\right) = 0$$

(3) If the process is reversible and isothermal,

$$T\left(s_e - s_i\right) = \frac{\dot{Q}_{cv}}{\dot{m}} = q .$$

Entropy is a way to determine the direction of time. As with time, entropy will always be positive in the total universe. This is referred to as the principle of the increase in entropy. For any isolated system,

$$ds_{isol} \geq 0$$

and for a control volume interacting with the surroundings

$$\frac{dS_{cv}}{dt} + \frac{dS_{surr}}{dt} \geq 0 .$$

Finally, there are two important property relationships that are applicable for reversible or irreversible processes since they provide a means for evaluation of the change in entropy needed above.

$$TdS = dU + PdV$$

$$TdS = dH - VdP$$

AVAILABILITY-IRREVERSIBILITY

The maximum work that can be done by a system is called the **availability**. This maximum work is achieved when the work is reversible, with the system undergoing a reversible process until it achieves equilibrium with the surroundings. Calculation of the availability depends, in part, on the type of analysis being performed, that is, closed or open system. For the closed system, boundary variations and the work associated with them must be considered since this reduces the total available work. Availability, per unit mass, neglecting kinetic and potential energy effects, is given by

$$\phi = \left(w_{rev}\right)_{max} - w_{surr}$$

where $\left(w_{rev}\right)_{max} = \left(u - T_o s\right) - \left(u_o - T_o s_o\right)$

$$w_{surr} = -P_o\left(v - v_o\right)$$

thus $\qquad \phi = \left(u - u_o\right) + P_o\left(v - v_o\right) - T_o\left(s - s_o\right)$

where u, v, and s are the internal energy, specific volume, and entropy of the system and u_o, v_o, and s_o are the internal energy, specific volume, and entropy of the surroundings.

For the open system there is no boundary work, and thus no work to the surroundings. The availability is the reversible work and is in the general form:

$$\dot{W}_{rev} = \sum \dot{m}_i \Psi_i - \sum \dot{m}_e \Psi_e$$

where $\quad \Psi = \left(h - T_o s + \dfrac{V^2}{2} + gz\right) - \left(h_o - T_o s_o + gz_o\right),$

and those symbols without subscript are either inlet or exit values as per the previous equation.

Irreversibility is the difference between the reversible work and the actual work accomplished. It is defined as

$$I = W_{rev} - W_{cv}$$

where W_{rev} = The reversible work

W_{cv} = The work crossing the control volume

The irreversibility is expressed for a control volume experiencing a uniform-state, uniform-flow process as

$$I = \sum m_e T_o s_e - \sum m_i T_o s_i + m_2 T_o s_2 - m_1 T_o s_1 - Q_{cv}$$

where the subscripts e = Exit

i = Inlet

o = Surroundings

1 = State 1

2 = State 2

This is the most general form of the irreversibility relationship from which the others are developed. For a steady-state, steady-flow process the equation becomes

$$I = \sum m_e T_o s_e - \sum m_i T_o s_i - Q_{cv}$$

and for the system of fixed mass the equation reduces to

$$_1 I_2 = m T_o (s_2 - s_1) - {_1 Q_2}.$$

Finally, if the process taking place was a reversible one, the irreversibility would be equal to zero. Such is the case in the ideal processes that describe ideal cycles.

Components

Cycles used to produce power are designed based on specific needs and are improved by the addition of components which increase efficiency or otherwise influence operating conditions. This section will introduce these components and briefly discuss their operation and application.

Pumps and **compressors** are used to increase the pressure of the medium flowing through them. Pumps are used when the medium is a liquid and compressors are used when gases are flowing. Both devices require work and while increasing the pressure they also add energy to the medium.

Boilers, **superheaters**, and **evaporators** all take energy from some source and increase the energy of the flowing medium. In the case of boilers and superheaters, the energy required comes from a large source such as a nuclear reactor or the flame from an oil or gas burner. In the boiler, the phase of the medium usually changes from liquid to vapor whereas in the superheater additional energy is added to a vapor to move farther into the superheated region. The evaporator also uses phase changes but the energy source is often much smaller and at lower temperatures such as air at ambient conditions. As the medium in the evaporator "boils," the energy source cools.

Condensers, as the name implies, change the phase of the medium from a vapor to a liquid. Condensers are heat exchangers which normally operate by having two distinct flow channels, one with the vapor that is condensed and one with a cooling fluid, usually water. The cooling fluid absorbs enough energy to cause condensation.

Turbines and **throttling valves** are both used to reduce the pressure and the associated energy level of the vapor. Turbines make this energy change as the fluid flows over a series of blades which change the thermal energy to a mechanical form, usually shaft work. The shaft is connected to a generator or the blades of a helicopter or to a compressor in jet engines. The throttling valve reduces the pressure and causes some of the liquid to flash to vapor prior to evaporation.

Economizers and **regenerators** use waste heat in the exhaust to precondition incoming air or liquids from the condenser prior to pumping. In both cases, the preconditioning reduces the need for energy in the form of fuel. A method for warming the incoming water is the use of **feedwater heaters**. These come in two types, open, where the water is mixed directly with bleed steam, and closed which is more like a conventional heat exchanger in that the hot and cold streams are kept separated.

Nozzles and **diffusers** change the velocity of the medium, increasing or decreasing the velocity depending on the conditions of the flow. Diffusers are often used to slow the flow while increasing the pressure, an important aspect in the design of supersonic aircraft engines. Nozzles are used to accelerate the flow to produce thrust for the operation of jet aircraft.

For any of these components, there is an efficiency known as the **component efficiency** or the **isentropic efficiency** which compares the actual operation to the operation if it took place reversibly. In all cases, this efficiency must be less than one. For components receiving work, the actual work required will be more than the reversible work provided. For components producing work, the actual work will be less than the reversible work which could be generated. Component efficiencies will be seen in example problems.

CYCLES

Cycles are divided into two categories: power and refrigeration. This section will concentrate on power cycles; the next section will concentrate on air conditioning and refrigeration.

Power cycles are divided into two major categories: vapor power cycles and air-standard cycles. Vapor power cycles use external heat to produce steam, the working fluid used to power the cycle. Air-standard cycles use combustion of a fuel within the engine as the source of the energy to drive the cycle. Since vapor power cycles have been around the longest, we will start with them.

The Rankine cycle is the idealization of the steam (vapor) power cycle. Figure 18 illustrates the simple steam power plant.

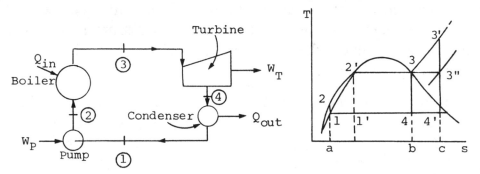

Figure 18. Simple steam power plant that operates on the Rankine cycle

The Rankine cycle consists of the following idealized processes:

Process 1-2

Reversible adiabatic (isentropic) pumping

Process 2-3

Constant-pressure heat addition in the boiler

Process 3-4

Reversible adiabatic (isentropic) expansion

Process 4-1

Constant pressure heat rejection from the condenser.

Assuming steady-state, steady-flow processes throughout, the continuity equation becomes

$$\dot{m}_1 = \dot{m}_2 = \dot{m}_3 = \dot{m}_4.$$

Neglecting kinetic and potential energy in each component, the first law for each component reduces to

Boiler $\qquad \dot{Q}_{in} = \dot{m}(h_3 - h_2)$

Turbine $\qquad \dot{W}_T = \dot{m}(h_3 - h_4)$

Condenser $\quad \dot{Q}_{out} = \dot{m}(h_4 - h_1)$

Pump $\qquad \dot{W}_p = \dot{m}(h_2 - h_1) = \dot{m}v_1(P_2 - P_1)$

The last equation is possible since the fluid is incompressible and the process reversible. The thermal efficiency is the net work output divided by the energy added. In the efficiency equation, the mass flow rate has been divided out of the equation.

$$\eta_{th} = \frac{w_{net}}{q_{in}} = \frac{w_T - w_P}{q_{in}} = \frac{(h_3 - h_4) - (h_2 - h_1)}{h_3 - h_2}$$

and

$$w_{net} = q_{in} - q_{out} = (h_3 - h_2) - (h_4 - h_1)$$

The Rankine cycle efficiency can be increased by lowering the exhaust pressure from the turbine, increasing the pressure during heat addition, or superheating the steam.

The Rankine cycle with superheater seen in Figure 19 is used to increase the efficiency by increasing the mean temperature of heat addition with no increase in the maximum cycle pressure.

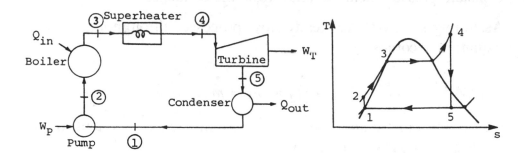

Figure 19. Rankine cycle with superheater

The continuity equation has not changed; however, the first law has a few subtle differences.

Boiler/Superheater $\quad \dot{Q}_{in} = \dot{m}\left(h_4 - h_2\right)$

Turbine $\qquad\qquad \dot{W}_T = \dot{m}\left(h_4 - h_5\right)$

Condenser $\qquad\quad \dot{Q}_{out} = \dot{m}\left(h_5 - h_1\right)$

Pump $\qquad\qquad\; \dot{W}_p = \dot{m}\left(h_2 - h_1\right) = \dot{m}\,v_1\left(P_2 - P_1\right)$

and the thermal efficiency becomes

$$\eta_{th} = \frac{w_{net}}{q_{in}} = \frac{w_T - w_p}{q_{in}} = \frac{\left(h_4 - h_5\right) - \left(h_2 - h_1\right)}{h_4 - h_2}$$

and

$$w_{net} = q_{in} - q_{out} = \left(h_4 - h_2\right) - \left(h_5 - h_1\right)$$

A second improvement over the original Rankine cycle is the Reheat cycle which was developed to take advantage of the increased efficiency associated with higher pressures. Figure 20 depicts an ideal Reheat cycle.

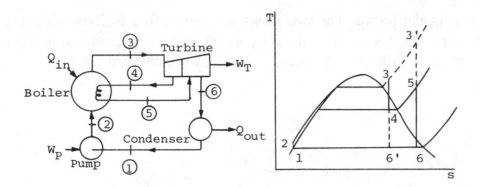

Figure 20. The ideal Reheat cycle

Notice that with the higher pressure comes the penalty of increased moisture content at state point 6'. The reheating of the flow after it leaves the high-pressure portion of the turbine allows expansion to a more reasonable moisture content. The turbine is divided into high- and low-pressure portions; however, these may be nothing more than taps. As in the other cases, continuity remains essentially the same, except for two extra state points. The first law analysis becomes

Boiler $\qquad \dot{Q}_{in} = \dot{m}\left[\left(h_3 - h_2\right) + \left(h_5 - h_4\right)\right]$

Turbine $\qquad \dot{W}_T = \dot{m}\left[\left(h_3 - h_4\right) + \left(h_5 - h_6\right)\right]$

Condenser $\quad \dot{Q}_{out} = \dot{m}\left(h_6 - h_1\right)$

Pump $\qquad \dot{W}_P = \dot{m}\left(h_2 - h_1\right) = \dot{m}\,v_1\left(P_2 - P_1\right)$

and thermal efficiency becomes

$$\eta_{th} = \frac{w_{net}}{q_{in}} = \frac{w_T - w_p}{q_{in}} = \frac{\left(h_3 - h_4\right) + \left(h_5 - h_6\right) - \left(h_2 - h_1\right)}{h_4 - h_2}$$

and

$$w_{net} = q_{in} - q_{out} = \left(h_3 - h_2\right) + \left(h_5 - h_4\right) - \left(h_6 - h_1\right)$$

The last of the vapor power cycles is the regenerative cycle. This cycle increases the average temperature at which heat is added in the boiler by taking some of the flow out of the turbine early and mixing it with the remaining flow, thus increasing the average temperature of the water entering the pump. The two flows are mixed in a feedwater heater, the number of heaters is determined by economic considerations, and are fed back into the boiler via the pump. Figure 21 illustrates the regenerative cycle.

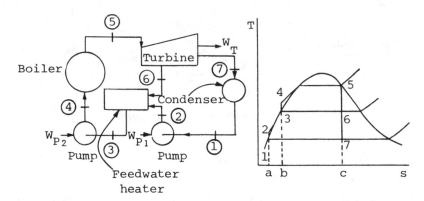

Figure 21. Regenerative cycle with open feedwater heater

Continuity for this cycle is somewhat more complex. Based on a one kilogram flow at points 3, 4, and 5, the remaining flows are some fraction of the initial kilogram. The flow at points 7, 1, and 2 is $(1 - m_1)$ and the flow at 6 is m_1. Based on the one kilogram flow, the following energy transfers apply:

$$q_{in} = h_5 - h_4$$
$$w_T = (h_5 - h_6) + (1 - m_1)(h_6 - h_7)$$
$$q_{out} = h_1 - h_7$$
$$w_{p2} = h_4 - h_3 = v_3(P_4 - P_3)$$
$$w_{p1} = h_2 - h_1 = v_1(P_2 - P_1)$$

where the energy balance around the feedwater heater is

$$m_1 h_6 + (1 - m_1)h_2 = h_3$$

producing the thermal efficiency

$$\eta_{th} = \frac{w_T - (1 - m_1)w_{p1} - w_{p2}}{h_5 - h_4}$$

<table>
<tr><th colspan="5">TABLE 1
RANKINE CYCLE COMPARISON CHART</th></tr>
<tr>
<th>Device</th>
<th>Ideal Rankine</th>
<th>With Superheater</th>
<th>Reheat</th>
<th>Regenerative*</th>
</tr>
<tr>
<td>Boiler $\dot{Q}_{in}$ =</td>
<td>$\dot{m}(h_3 - h_2)$</td>
<td>$\dot{m}(h_4 - h_2)$</td>
<td>$\dot{m}\left[(h_3 - h_2) + (h_5 - h_4)\right]$</td>
<td>$q_{in} = h_5 - h_4$</td>
</tr>
<tr>
<td>Turbine $\dot{W}_T$ =</td>
<td>$\dot{m}(h_3 - h_4)$</td>
<td>$\dot{m}(h_4 - h_5)$</td>
<td>$\dot{m}\left[(h_3 - h_4) + (h_5 - h_6)\right]$</td>
<td>$w_T = (h_5 - h_6) +$
 $(1 - m_1)(h_6 - h_7)$</td>
</tr>
<tr>
<td>Condenser $\dot{Q}_{out}$ =</td>
<td>$\dot{m}(h_4 - h_1)$</td>
<td>$\dot{m}(h_5 - h_1)$</td>
<td>$\dot{m}(h_6 - h_1)$</td>
<td>$q_{out} = h_1 - h_7$</td>
</tr>
<tr>
<td>Pump(s) $\dot{W}_p$ =</td>
<td>$\dot{m}(h_2 - h_1) =$
 $\dot{m}v_1(P_2 - P_1)$</td>
<td>$\dot{m}(h_2 - h_1) =$
 $\dot{m}v_1(P_2 - P_1)$</td>
<td>$\dot{m}(h_2 - h_1) =$
 $\dot{m}v_1(P_2 - P_1)$</td>
<td>$w_{P_2} = h_4 - h_3 =$
 $v_3(P_4 - P_3)$
 $w_{P_1} = h_2 - h_1 =$
 $v_1(P_2 - P_1)$</td>
</tr>
<tr>
<td>Efficiency η_{th} =</td>
<td>$\dfrac{(h_3 - h_4) - (h_2 - h_1)}{h_3 - h_2}$</td>
<td>$\dfrac{(h_4 - h_5) - (h_2 - h_1)}{h_4 - h_2}$</td>
<td>$\dfrac{(h_3 - h_4) + (h_5 - h_6) - (h_2 - h_1)}{h_4 - h_2}$</td>
<td>$\dfrac{w_T - (1 - m_1)w_{P_1} - w_{P_2}}{h_5 - h_4}$</td>
</tr>
</table>

* The regenerative Rankine cycle is best analyzed using a per mass basis equation.

The next series of power cycles are the air-standard power cycles. While the working fluid is not all air and the cycles are actually open, power cycles can be effectively modeled using air as the primary working fluid, and a closed cycle can approximate the actual engine operation. The following assumptions apply to air-standard engines:

(1) A fixed mass of air is the working fluid and the air is always an ideal gas.

(2) The combustion process is replaced by a heat transfer from an external source.

(3) The cycle is completed by heat transfer to the surroundings.

(4) All processes are internally reversible.

(5) Air has a constant specific.

The Air-Standard Carnot cycle is the standard against which all other air-standard heat engines are compared. The Carnot cycle has been previously discussed, as have the isentropic relations that assist in specifying state point data. The isentropic relations can also be used to fix the thermal efficiency in terms of the isentropic pressure ratio and isentropic compression ratio as follows:

$$\text{Isentropic pressure ratio: } r_{ps} = \frac{P_1}{P_4} = \frac{P_2}{P_3} = \left(\frac{T_3}{T_2}\right)^{\frac{k}{(1-k)}}$$

$$\text{Isentropic compression ratio: } r_{vs} = \frac{V_4}{V_1} = \frac{V_3}{V_2} = \left(\frac{T_3}{T_2}\right)^{\frac{1}{(1-k)}}$$

Thus, the efficiency of the Carnot cycle is

$$\eta_{th} = 1 - r_{ps}^{\frac{(1-k)}{k}} = 1 - r_{vs}^{1-k}.$$

Engines such as the spark ignition engine, the compression ignition engine, and the gas turbine engine have been modeled using ideal cycles. These cycles are then compared to Carnot to see how they measure up. Remember, no cycle can be *more* efficient than the Carnot cycle.

The spark ignition engine has been modeled by the Air-Standard Otto cycle using a closed system. Figure 22 illustrates the processes used to model the spark ignition engine.

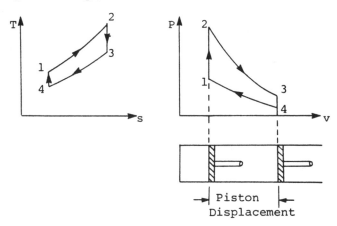

Figure 22. Air-Standard Otto cycle

The processes associated with the Otto cycle are:

Process 1-2

Constant volume heat addition

Process 2–3

Isentropic expansion

Process 3–4

Constant volume heat rejection

Process 4–1

Isentropic compression

For the closed system, the mass is fixed and is given by m. Application of the first law for the closed system results in

$$Q_{in} = {}_1Q_2 = U_2 - U_1 = mC_v(T_2 - T_1)$$
$$Q_{out} = {}_3Q_4 = U_3 - U_4 = mC_v(T_3 - T_4)$$

and a thermal efficiency of

$$\eta_{th} = \frac{W_{net}}{Q_{in}} = \frac{Q_{in} - Q_{out}}{Q_{in}} = 1 - \frac{(T_3 - T_4)}{(T_2 - T_1)} = 1 - \frac{1}{r_v^{(k-1)}}$$

where $r_v = \dfrac{V_3}{V_2} = \dfrac{V_4}{V_1}$ is known as the compression ratio. It is interesting to note that the Otto cycle efficiency increases with increased compression ratio. Also, the network is simple heat in, minus heat out.

The compression ignition engine has been modeled by the Air-Standard Diesel cycle using a closed system. Figure 23 illustrates the process used to model the compression ignition engine.

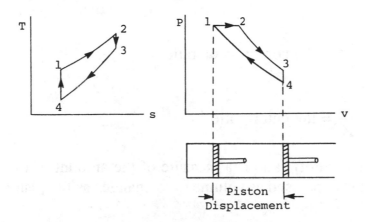

Figure 23. The Diesel cycle

The processes associated with the Diesel cycle are:

Process 1-2

Constant pressure heat addition

Process 2-3

Isentropic expansion

Process 3-4

Constant volume heat rejection

Process 4-1

Isentropic compression

For the closed system, the mass is fixed and is given by m. Application of the first law for the closed system results in

$$Q_{in} = {}_1Q_2 = H_2 - H_1 = mC_p(T_2 - T_1)$$
$$Q_{out} = {}_3Q_4 = U_3 - U_4 = mC_v(T_3 - T_4)$$

with the C_p in process 1–2 a result of the combination of properties. The thermal efficiency is

$$\eta_{th} = \frac{W_{net}}{Q_{in}} = \frac{Q_{in} - Q_{out}}{Q_{in}} = 1 - \frac{(T_3 - T_4)}{k(T_2 - T_1)}$$

$$\eta_{th} = 1 - \frac{1}{r_v^{k-1}}\left[\frac{r_c^k - 1}{k(r_c - 1)}\right]$$

where $\quad r_v = \dfrac{V_4}{V_1}$ = the compression ratio

$\quad r_c = \dfrac{V_2}{V_1}$ = the cutoff ratio

Recall that the cutoff ratio is a measure of the amount of time that fuel is injected and is expressed as volume ratio changes as the piston moves.

<table>
<tr><th colspan="3" align="center">TABLE 2
OTTO, DIESEL COMPARISONS</th></tr>
</table>

Process	Otto	Diesel
Heat Addition $Q_{in} =$	$U_2 - U_1 = mC_v(T_2 - T_1)$	$H_2 - H_1 = mC_p(T_2 - T_1)$
Heat Rejection $Q_{out} =$	$U_3 - U_4 = mC_v(T_3 - T_4)$	$U_3 - U_4 = mC_v(T_3 - T_4)$
Compression Ratio $r_v =$	$\dfrac{V_3}{V_2} = \dfrac{V_4}{V_1}$	$\dfrac{V_4}{V_1}$
Efficiency ηth	$1 - \dfrac{(T_3 - T_4)}{(T_2 - T_1)} = 1 - \dfrac{1}{r_v^{(k-1)}}$	$1 - \dfrac{(T_3 - T_4)}{k(T_2 - T_1)} = 1 - \dfrac{1}{r_v^{(k-1)}}\left[\dfrac{r_c^k - 1}{k(r_{c-1})}\right]$

For both Otto and Diesel cycles there is one power stroke for every four strokes represented on the *T-s* diagram. The strokes are intake, compression, power, and exhaust. Thus, if an engine operates at 4,000 Revolutions Per Minute (RPM), there are 2,000 power strokes in that period. Recall that a revolution will include two strokes. Each piston will have a power stroke every three one-hundreths of a second at 4,000 RPM.

The gas turbine engine has been modeled by the Air-Standard Brayton cycle using both a closed and an open system. In both cases there is flow through each component, thus necessitating a control volume analysis of the components. Figure 24 illustrates the processes used to model the gas turbine engine.

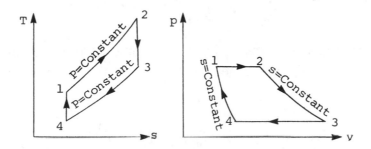

Figure 24. Brayton cycle

The processes associated with the Brayton cycle are:

Process 1-2

Constant pressure heat addition

Process 2-3

Isentropic expansion

Process 3-4

Constant pressure heat rejection

Process 4-1

Isentropic compression

As stated above, a control volume analysis is required on each component of the Brayton cycle. Since each device has a single inlet/exit, the mass flow rate will be constant. Application of the first law produces

$$\dot{Q}_{in} = \dot{m} C_p (T_2 - T_1)$$

$$\dot{Q}_{out} = \dot{m} C_p (T_4 - T_3)$$

and a thermal efficiency of

$$\eta_{th} = \frac{\dot{W}_{net}}{\dot{Q}_{in}} = \frac{\dot{Q}_{in} - \dot{Q}_{out}}{\dot{Q}_{in}} = 1 - \frac{(T_3 - T_4)}{(T_2 - T_1)}$$

The turbine produces the power; however, some of that power is used to turn the compressor. Thus, the net work can be calculated using either the heat difference or

$$\dot{W}_{net} = \dot{W}_T - \dot{W}_c = \dot{m} C_p (T_2 - T_3) - \dot{m} C_p (T_1 - T_4)$$

$$\eta_{th} = 1 - \frac{1}{r_p^{\frac{k-1}{k}}}$$

where $r_p = \dfrac{P_1}{P_4} = \dfrac{P_2}{P_3}$ = the pressure ratio.

Figure 25 depicts the open and closed Brayton cycles. In the open cycle, the heat is rejected to the air, much the same as is done in most turbine applications. In the closed cycle, there is a heat exchanger present to remove heat.

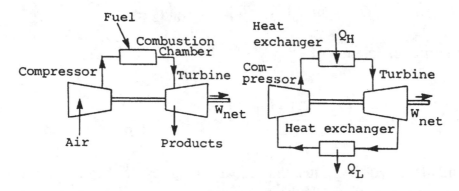

Figure 25. A gas turbine operating on the Brayton cycle

In an effort to recover some of the heat that escapes as exhaust, a regenerator is added to the Brayton cycle. This addition increases the cycle efficiency of the turbine. Assuming a perfect regenerator, one where the amount of heat carried to the regenerator as exhaust is exactly equal to the amount of heat picked up by the incoming air, we have the cycle seen in Figure 26.

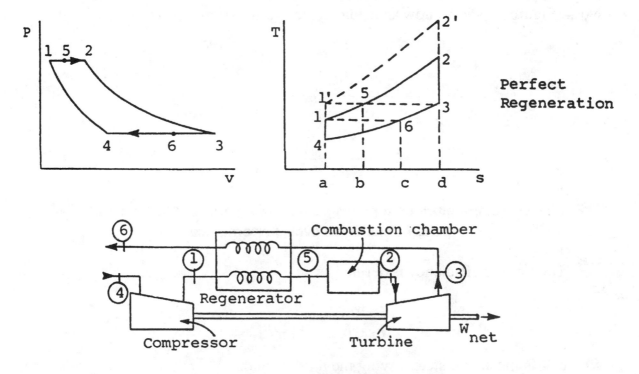

Figure 26. Brayton cycle with regenerator

Continuity remains the same, and the first law produces

$$\dot{W}_{net} = \dot{m}\,C_p\!\left(T_2 - T_3\right) - \dot{m}\,C_p\!\left(T_2 - T_4\right)$$

$$\dot{Q}_{in} = \dot{m}\,C_p\!\left(T_2 - T_5\right) = \dot{m}\,C_p\!\left(T_2 - T_3\right)$$

and a thermal efficiency of

$$\eta_{th} = \frac{\left(T_2 - T_3\right) - \left(T_1 - T_4\right)}{\left(T_2 - T_3\right)} = 1 - \frac{T_4}{T_2}\left(\frac{P_1}{P_4}\right)^{\frac{(k-1)}{k}}$$

The ideal cycles are just that, ideal. In real cycles there are deviations caused by many reasons. If there is piping, as there is in the steam power plant, then there will be piping losses. These are due to frictional effects and heat transfer that cause a loss in pressure. These losses cause a decrease in the entropy and the availability. Condensers have losses associated with cooling the liquid below the saturation temperature, thus causing it to be heated more than necessary.

Pumps and turbines have losses associated with nonisentropic (irreversible) behavior. For this case, the turbine/pump efficiencies are defined as a comparison of the actual work to the adiabatic-reversible (isentropic) work. Figure 27 shows how an actual device varies from isentropic.

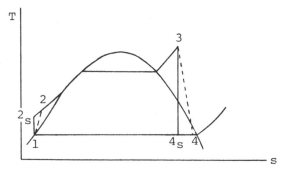

Figure 27. Temperature-entropy diagram showing effect of turbine and pump inefficiencies on cycle performance

The turbine efficiency is defined as

$$\eta_t = \frac{w_t}{h_3 - h_{4s}} = \frac{h_3 - h_4}{h_3 - h_{4s}}$$

where   4 is the actual state leaving the turbine, and
        4s is the state after the isentropic expansion.

A similar equation can be developed for the pump. Here, the actual work required will be more than the isentropic, thus keeping the efficiency less than 100 percent; the actual work must be in the denominator.

$$\eta_p = \frac{h_{2s} - h_1}{w_p} = \frac{h_{2s} - h_1}{h_2 - h_1}$$

Every mechanical device has a similar efficiency.

AIR CONDITIONING AND REFRIGERATION

Vapor compression refrigeration is the most common form of refrigeration and "air conditioning." Conditioning is accomplished by changing the makeup of the air by removing dust or water vapor, or adding water vapor if necessary. The description of the vapor compression refrigeration cycle will be given first; followed by a problem that addresses "conditioning" the air.

The vapor compression refrigeration cycle is essentially the same as the Rankine cycle but in reverse. The only difference is that the pump is replaced by an expansion valve. The following processes make up the cycle:

Process 1-2

Isentropic compression

Process 2-3

Constant pressure heat rejection

Process 3-4

Adiabatic throttling process

Process 4-1

Constant pressure heat addition

Figure 28 shows the Vapor Compression Refrigeration cycle.

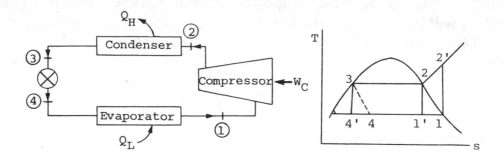

Figure 28. The ideal Vapor Compression Refrigeration cycle

For a refrigerator or air conditioner, $\dot{Q}_L$ is the quantity of interest. Used as a heat pump, $\dot{Q}_H$ is the quantity of interest. In both cases, the capacity of the device may be specified in BTUs or in tons. Cooling capacity is a term frequently used when referring to $\dot{Q}_L$.

The continuity equation is based on steady-state, steady-flow, with one inlet/exit. Thus, the mass flow rate is constant. Applying the first law produces the following:

Compressor $\quad \dot{W}_c = \dot{m}(h_2 - h_1) = \dot{m}\,C_p(T_2 - T_1)$

Condenser $\quad \dot{Q}_H = \dot{m}(h_3 - h_2) = \dot{m}\,C_p(T_3 - T_2)$

Valve $\quad\quad\ \ h_3 = h_4$

Evaporator $\quad \dot{Q}_L = \dot{m}(h_1 - h_4) = \dot{m}\,C_p(T_1 - T_4)$

The coefficient of performance for the refrigerator or air conditioner is

$$\beta_R = \frac{\dot{Q}_L}{\dot{W}_c} = \frac{h_1 - h_4}{h_2 - h_1}$$

and for the heat pump

$$\beta_{HP} = \frac{\dot{Q}_H}{\dot{W}_c} = \frac{h_2 - h_3}{h_2 - h_1}.$$

The easiest way to solve vapor compression refrigeration problems is to plot them on a Freon chart (see Figure 29). The availability of constant entropy lines makes this chart extremely easy to use.

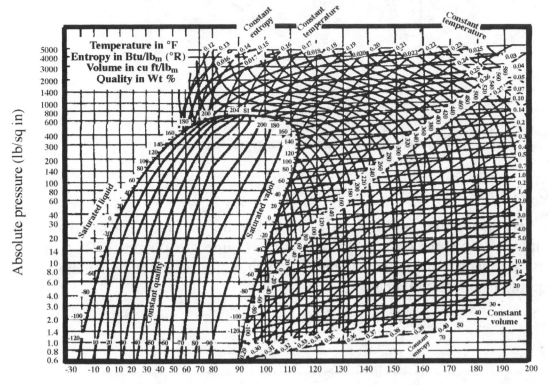

Enthalpy (Btu per lb$_{in}$ above saturated liquid at -40 °F)

Figure 29. Pressure-enthalpy diagram for Freon-22 refrigerant

The problem below is an excellent review of the use of the psychrometric chart when dealing with conditioning of the air.

EXAMPLE

Psychrometric charts are indispensable when calculating the mass of water removed and the refrigeration required in certain systems. Using a psychrometric chart, determine these two quantities for the following system:

> Initial state:
>
> $t_i = 80°$ F
>
> humidity = 40%
>
> Final state:
>
> $t_f = 50°$ F
>
> humidity = 100%
>
> Amount of airflow
>
> 2,000 cfm incoming air processed

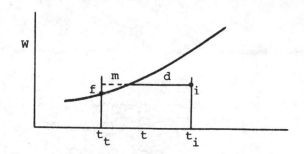

Figure 30. Schematic of refrigeration system

SOLUTION

By using the psychrometric chart, the initial (and final) enthalpy, weight of moisture (per lb dry air), and volume are obtained. By using mass and energy balances, the mass of H_2O removed and the refrigeration required can be calculated.

Initial state properties

$t_i = 80°$ F

humidity $= 40\%$

enthalpy $= h_i = 29$ BTU/lb dry air

mass of moisture $= m_i = 62$ grains/lb dry air

volume $= V_i = 13.78$ ft³/lb dry air

Final state properties

$t_f = 50°$ F

humidity $= 100\%$

$h_f = 20.4$ BTU/lb dry air

$m_f = 53$ grains/lb dry air

$V_f = 13.0$ ft³/lb dry air

Therefore, the amount of water to be separated out per pound of dry air is

$$m_{sep.} = m_i - m_f = 62 - 53$$
$$= 9 \text{ grains}$$

In conjunction with the mass balance on air and water, the energy balance yields, the refrigeration requirements (per lb of dry air) as the decrease in enthalpy:

$$-Q = h_i - h_f - \left(m_i - m_f\right)h_w$$

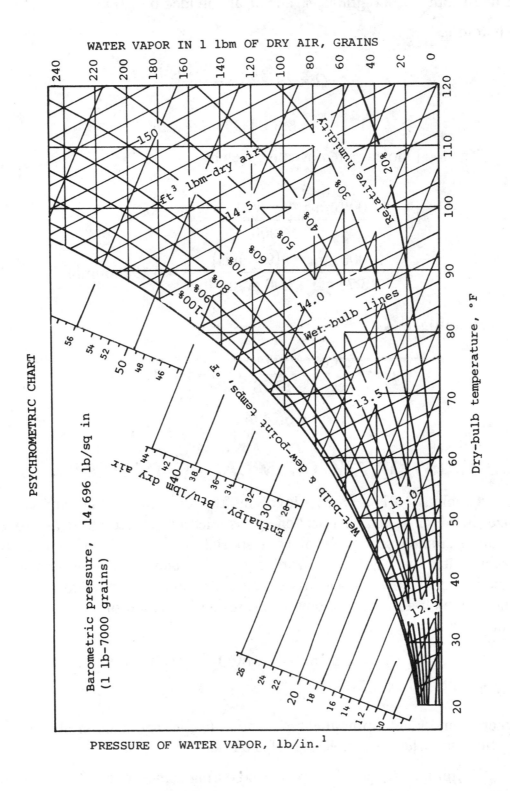

Figure 31. Psychrometric chart for air

where h_w is the enthalpy of saturated H_2O liquid at 50° F, h_w = 18.1 BTU. Since 1 lbm = 7,000 grains, m_i and m_f are divided by 7,000.

Therefore,

$$-Q = 29 - 20.4 - \frac{9(18.1)}{7,000}$$

$$= 8.6 \text{ BTU/lbm dry air}$$

The total moisture removed is given by

$$M_T = \frac{2,000\,\text{cfm}}{V_i}\frac{\left(m_i - m_f\right)}{7,000}$$

$$= \frac{2,000\,\text{cfm}}{13.78\,\text{cf}}\frac{\left(9\,\text{grains}\right)}{7,000\,\text{grains/lbm}} = 0.19 \text{ lbm/min}$$

and the refrigeration

$$(-Q)\cdot\left(\frac{\text{cfm}}{\text{cf}}\right) = \frac{2,000}{13.78} \times 8.6 = 1,248 \text{ BTU/min}$$

$$= 6.24 \text{ tons}$$

COMBUSTION AND CHEMICAL REACTIONS

Combustion is a process involving the reaction of a fuel and an oxidizer in which stored chemical energy is released. The combustion process is often studied separately or as a special subset of chemical reactions because it moves quickly toward completion and is so important to the production of power from fossil fuels. A complete combustion reaction, one in which all carbon atoms result in the formation of carbon dioxide, can be represented as

$$C_xH_y + \underbrace{aO_2 + 3.76aN_2}_{\text{air}} \rightarrow bCO_2 + cH_2O + dO_2 + eN_2$$

where x and y determine fuel type, and a, b, c, d, and e are moles of other participants when one mole of fuel is burned.

Definitions frequently experienced during combustion calculations and discussions include:

(1) **Theoretical Air (*TA*)** is the minimum amount of air that supplies enough oxygen to ensure complete combustion of all elements in the fuel. Realize that the nitrogen is a nonparticipant in the oxidation of the fuel, although it can form pollutants if excess oxygen is present.

(2) **Excess Air (*EA*)** is the amount of air supplied over and above the theoretical air. This will normally ensure complete combustion, but it can lead to the formation of pollutants, especially compounds involving nitrogen.

(3) **Air-Fuel Ratio (*AF*)** is the ratio of the mass of theoretical air to the mass of the fuel. The inverse is the Fuel-Air Ratio (*FA*).

(4) The combustion efficiency η_{comb} is

$$\eta_{comb} = \frac{FA \text{ ideal}}{FA \text{ actual}}$$

The useful result of the combustion process is the liberation of heat used to power the heat engines previously discussed. The combustion process occurring in a steady-state, steady-flow device at constant pressure and with no work is depicted in Figure 32.

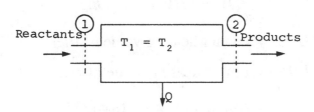

Figure 32. Combustion process

Applying the first law and neglecting potential and kinetic energy leads to

$$Q = H_2^P - H_1^R = \Delta H$$

where Q = Heat flow in

H_1^R = Enthalpy of the reactants at state 1

H_2^P = Enthalpy of the products at state 2

If the reactants and products are at the same temperature, the quantity ΔH is the enthalpy of reaction.

Before discussing the first and second laws as they apply to the combustion process, several explanations concerning enthalpy of reacting components are necessary:

(1) **The standard enthalpy of formation** (h_f^o) of a compound is the enthalpy of reaction for the formation of the compound from its elements at 25°C and 1 atm. The enthalpy of formation of an element is zero.

(2) **Exothermic reactions** $(\Delta H < 0)$ are those that liberate heat.

(3) **Endothermic reactions** $(\Delta H > 0)$ are those that absorb heat.

(4) **The heating value of a fuel** is numerically equal to its **enthalpy of reaction** but with opposite sign:

$$H_1^R - H_2^P = -\Delta H$$

(5) **Heating values** are normally presented as "higher" and "lower." The higher heating value occurs when the water in the products is still a liquid, while the lower heating value occurs when the water is a vapor. The difference in the heating values is the enthalpy of evaporation of the water. In equation form:

$$HHV = LHV + m_{H_2O} h_{fg}$$

where HHV = Higher heating value of fuel

LHV = Lower heating value of fuel

m_{H_2O} = Amount of water formed

h_{fg} = Enthalpy of evaporation of water

(6) The **total molal enthalpy** at any temperature and pressure is

$$\bar{h}_{T,P} = \bar{h}_f^o + \left(\bar{h}_{T,P} - \bar{h}_{298(atm)} \right)$$

where $\bar{h}_{T,P} - \bar{h}_{298(atm)}$ = Difference in enthalpy between any given state and the enthalpy at the reference state of 298K and 1 atm.

$\bar{h}_f^o$ = enthalpy of formation of a substance.

(7) **Standard enthalpy** of reaction is $\Delta H° = H_2^° - H_1^°$.

(8) **Adiabatic flame temperature** is the temperature of the products when the combustion occurs adiabatically and with no work or changes in kinetic or potential energy.

With the definitions in hand and an understanding of the basic combustion process, application of the first law to a steady-state, steady-flow chemically reacting process while neglecting kinetic and potential energy produces

$$Q_{cv} - W_{cv} = \sum_P n_e \left(\overline{h}_f + \overline{h}\right)_e - \sum_R n_i \left(\overline{h}_f + \overline{h}\right)_i$$

where R, P = The reactants and products, respectively

n_i = Moles of reactants

n_e = Moles of products

$\overline{h}_f$ = Molal enthalpy of formation

$\overline{h}$ = $\overline{h}_f^o - \overline{h}_{298}^o$ of a substance, which can be found directly from the tables

Similarly, for the second law, for any reactive process we have

$$\Delta S = S_P - S_R - \sum \frac{Q_{cv}}{T} \geq 0$$

where S_P = Entropy of products

S_R = Entropy of reactants

$\sum \dfrac{Q_{cv}}{T}$ = Entropy change due to heat transfer

For the steady-state, steady-flow process under consideration, the following apply:

(1) Reversible work

$$W_{rev} = \sum_R n_i \left(h_f^o + \Delta\overline{h} - T_o\overline{s}\right)_i - \sum_P n_e \left(h_f^o + \Delta\overline{h} - T_o\overline{s}\right)_e$$

(2) Irreversibility

$$I = \sum_P n_e T_o \bar{s}_e - \sum_R n_i T_o \bar{s}_i - Q_{cv}$$

(3) Availability

$$\Psi = (h - T_o s) - (h_o - T_o s_o)$$

Determination of the absolute base entropy value is accomplished via the third law of thermodynamics. The third law states that the entropy of a pure crystalline substance is zero at the absolute zero of temperature. The value can be determined using

$$\bar{S}_{T,P} = \bar{S}_T^o - \bar{R} \ln\left(\frac{P}{0.1}\right)$$

where $\bar{S}_{T,P}$ = Absolute entropy at 0.1 MPa and temperature T

P = Pressure in MPa

$\bar{R}$ = Universal gas constant

For any chemical reaction to proceed as discussed, it must satisfy the Gibbs function criteria, that is, the chemical reaction is only possible if the Gibbs function for the products is less than the Gibbs function of the reactants. The Gibbs function itself is defined as

$$G = H - TS.$$

For a chemical reaction carried out at constant temperature and pressure,

$$\Delta G = \Delta H - T\Delta S \leq 0.$$

The last topic dealing with reactions is chemical equilibrium. Applying the Gibbs function to a reactive system, we find that a chemical reaction carried out at constant pressure and temperature can proceed only if the Gibbs function of the system will continually decrease. The reaction will stop when the Gibbs function of the system has reached a minimum. Thus, we can say that the equilibrium composition of any reactive system of known temperature and pressure is governed by $dG_{T,P} = 0$. To find the equilibrium composition, an expression for dG in terms of the moles of reactants and products is needed:

$$dG = VdP - SdT + \sum_i u_i dN_i$$

where $u_i = \left(\dfrac{\partial G}{\partial N_i}\right)_{P,T,N_i}$

N_i = Number of moles of each chemical species within the system at some time

When $dG_{T,P} = 0$, a minor amount of mathematical manipulation produces

$$\ln K = \frac{\Delta G^o}{RT}$$

where K = the equilibrium constant

$$\Delta G^o = c_c \overline{g}_C^o + d_d \overline{g}_D^o - a_a \overline{g}_A^o - b_b \overline{g}_B^o$$

$\overline{g}_C^o, \overline{g}_D^o, \overline{g}_B^o, \overline{g}_A^o$ = Standard Gibbs functions

a, b, c, d = The stoichiometric coefficients

The value of K takes on many forms depending on available information. If partial pressures are known, then

$$K = \frac{(P_C)^c (P_D)^d}{(P_A)^a (P_B)^b}$$

where P_A, P_B, P_C, P_D = Partial pressures of the chemical constituents

A similar expression for K can be obtained by replacing the partial pressures with the activity coefficients. If mole fractions are used in place of the partial pressures, then the fraction must be multiplied by

$$(P)^{c+d-a-b}.$$

HEAT TRANSFER

While thermodynamics concerns itself with the macroscopic exchange of energy, heat transfer deals with the specifics. Three modes of heat transfer—conduction, convection, and radiation—are commonly studied separately and then combined to model real problems. The following is a brief discussion of these modes.

(1) **Conduction** is the transfer of heat in a material due to molecular motion in the material. A temperature gradient must exist to act

as the potential for the flow of heat. The heat will flow from the high temperature to the cooler temperature. Fourier's law of conduction expresses the rate of heat transfer within the medium,

$$q = -kA \frac{dT}{dx}$$

where q = Heat transfer rate [W]

k = Thermal conductivity [W/m³K]

A = Area normal to the direction of the flow [m²]

T = Temperature [K]

x = Direction [m]

and, the negative sign is necessary since the flow of heat is in the direction opposite to the thermal gradient.

There are similar equations for each coordinate direction. Often the heat transfer is equated to a simple electrical circuit with a flow, a potential, and a resistance. The heat transfer is the flow, the temperature gradient is the potential, and the resistance is determined by the physical dimensions and properties of the material concerned. The following equations apply in this case:

$$q = \frac{kA\Delta T}{L} = \frac{\Delta T}{R_{th}}$$

where L = The thickness of the material in the direction of the heat flow

R_{th} = The conductive resistance

$$R_{th} = \frac{L}{kA}$$

Conduction through several materials of the same area normal to the flow can be treated as a series circuit with the resistance summed. Parallel circuits are needed when heat flows through different materials with varying normal areas. It is important to note that the rate of heat transfer is constant through a composite material. This fact allows for calculation of intermediate surface temperatures.

(2) **Convection** is the transfer of heat due to motion of a fluid near the surface of an object. Forced convection occurs when the fluid is placed into motion by a fan, pump, moving object, or due to the wind. Free convection occurs when the flow of the fluid is induced by buoyancy—a situation noticeable on roads during the summer.

Newton's law of cooling applies to convection problems, regardless of the type: free or forced.

$$q = hA(T_s - T_\infty)$$

where h = Convective heat transfer coefficient

T_s = Surface temperature

T_∞ = Fluid temperature

A = Area normal to the heat transfer

The convective heat transfer coefficient can be found through an energy balance at the surface or through evaluation of the Nusselt number:

$$Nu = \frac{hx}{k}$$

where x can be the length of a flat plate, diameter of a cylinder or sphere, or other characteristic dimension specified. Solution for h is simple once the Nusselt number is known. For forced convection, the Nusselt number is a function of the Reynolds and Prandtl numbers,

$$Nu = f(Re, Pr)$$

where

$$Re = \frac{\rho U_\infty x}{\mu}$$

$$Pr = \frac{\upsilon}{\alpha}$$

and U_∞ = Fluid velocity

ρ = Density

μ = Dynamic viscosity

$$v \quad = \text{Kinematic viscosity}$$

$$x \quad = \text{Characteristic dimension}$$

$$\alpha \quad = \text{Thermal diffusivity}$$

For free convection, the Nusselt number is a function of the Grashof number and the Prandtl number:

$$Nu = f_2(Gr,Pr)$$

where

$$Gr = \frac{g\beta(T_S - T_\infty)L^3}{v^2}$$

and g = Gravitational acceleration

β = Volumetric thermal expansion coefficient

L = Surface length

with other variables being previously defined. As with conduction, convection can be expressed as a circuit with the convection resistance defined as

$$R_{th} = \frac{1}{hA}$$

and the convection and conduction resistances are summed when a combined mode problem is solved. Again, the heat transfer rate is constant through the circuit.

(3) **Radiation heat transfer** is due to thermal radiation. Radiation heat transfer is temperature dependent, to the fourth power, and can occur without a medium. Black bodies are perfect emitters and absorbers. A perfect emitter obeys the Stefan-Boltzmann Law,

$$q = \sigma A T^4$$

where A = Surface area

σ = Stefan-Boltzmann constant

T = Absolute temperature

There are few perfect emitters, such as black bodies; thus, it is normal to deal with gray bodies that emit some fraction of the energy of the black body. The emissivity of such bodies is defined as the ratio of the energy emitted compared to the energy emitted by a black body at the same temperature.

$$\varepsilon = \frac{q_{\text{gray}}}{q_{\text{black}}}$$

Thus, $$q_{\text{gray}} = \sigma \varepsilon A T^4$$

The net exchange of energy due to radiation heat transfer involves shape, view, or configuration factors. These factors geometrically predict the amount of energy departing one body and arriving at another. We all realize that if all the sun's energy arrived on earth it would be very hot. It is the shape factor that predicts the actual fraction that arrives. Thus, the net radiation exchange between two bodies is

$$q_{1\rightarrow 2} = \sigma A_1 F_{1-2}\left(T_1^4 - T_2^4\right)$$

where F_{1-2} represents the net effect of shape view and configuration factors between the two bodies.

GAS DYNAMICS: FLOW THROUGH NOZZLES AND BLADE PASSAGES

The differential from of the conservation equations is most often abandoned at this point in favor of the integral equivalents. Thus, the conservation of mass for a control volume (open system) becomes:

$$\frac{\partial}{\partial t}\int_V \rho dV + \int_A \rho \vec{v} \bullet d\vec{A} = 0$$

where $\quad \dfrac{\partial}{\partial t}\displaystyle\int_V \rho dV$ = Rate of change of mass within the control volume

$\displaystyle\int_A \rho v dA$ = Net rate of mass efflux through the control surface

For an incompressible flow (ρ = Constant),

$$\int_A \rho \vec{v} \bullet d\vec{A} = 0$$

Similarly, the conservation of momentum expressed as an integral becomes:

$$\sum F_j = \frac{1}{g_c}\left[\frac{d}{dt}\int_V V_j \rho dV + \int_A v_j \rho v_{rn} dA\right]$$

For the steady-state, steady-flow process we have:

$$\sum F_j = \frac{1}{g_c}\left[\sum \dot{m}_e (v_e)_j - \sum \dot{m}_i (v_i)_j\right]$$

where $\dot{m}_i, \dot{m}_e$ = Rate of mass entering and leaving the C.V.

   v_i, v_e = Velocity of the mass entering and leaving the C.V.

   i = x, y, z (directions)

At this juncture, it is important to introduce the concepts of the speed of sound and the Mach number. The Mach number is defined by:

$$M = \frac{v}{c}$$

where v = Local gas speed

   c = Local speed of sound

For an ideal gas $c = \sqrt{kRT}$, where $k = \frac{C_p}{C_v}$ as previously defined.

The Mach number is used to define the relative speed of the flow as follows:

   if $M > 1$,   the flow is supersonic

   if $M = 1$,   the flow is sonic

   if $M < 1$,   the flow is subsonic

Within the flowfield it is necessary to calculate properties. Of particular importance are the local isentropic properties that would be obtained at any point in a flowfield if the fluid at that point were decelerated from local conditions to zero velocity following a frictionless adiabatic (isentropic) process.

For an ideal gas the isentropic stagnations (denoted by the subscript 0) are:

$$\frac{P_0}{P} = \left[1 + \frac{k-1}{2}M^2\right]^{\frac{k}{(k-1)}}$$

$$\frac{T_0}{T} = 1 + \frac{k-1}{2}M^2$$

$$\frac{\rho_0}{\rho} = \left[1 + \frac{k-1}{2}M^2\right]^{\frac{1}{(k-1)}}$$

Another important property set represents the conditions at the throat of a nozzle. These conditions can be found by noting that $M = 1$ at the throat. These properties (denoted by an asterisk *) are referred to as critical pressure, critical temperature, and critical density and are given below as ratios to the stagnation properties.

$$\frac{P^*}{P_0} = \left(\frac{2}{k+1}\right)^{\frac{k}{(k-1)}}$$

$$\frac{T^*}{T_0} = \left(\frac{2}{k+1}\right)$$

$$\frac{\rho^*}{\rho_0} = \left(\frac{2}{k+1}\right)^{\frac{1}{(k-1)}}$$

Area variations directly effect the flow properties in an isentropic flow. The following equation is applicable:

$$\frac{dA}{A} = \frac{dP}{\rho V^2}\left(1 - M^2\right)$$

where M = Mach number

dA = Change in the area

dP = Change in the pressure

Since we have considered normal shocks, it is now possible to complete the discussion of flow in a converging-diverging nozzle. The pressure distribution through the nozzle for different back pressures is shown in Figure 33.

In Regime 1 the flow is subsonic throughout (i and ii). At condition (iii), the flow at the throat is sonic, that is $M_t = 1$.

In Regime 2 the exit flow is subsonic, a consequence of $P_e = P_b$.

In Regime 3 the back pressure is higher than the exit pressure but not sufficiently high to sustain a normal shock in the exit plane.

In Regime 4 the flow adjusts to the lower back pressure through a series of oblique expansion waves.

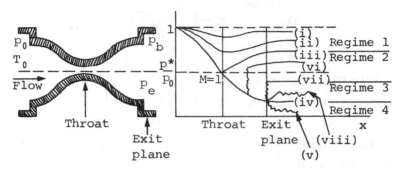

Figure 33. Pressure distribution vs. nozzle position

Operating conditions for nozzles and diffusers are optimized to ensure peak performance. Efficiencies and the coefficients of discharge and velocity make comparison between like devices a simple task. Comparison is followed by optimization in the design process.

(1)   Nozzle efficiency is defined:

$$n_N = \frac{\text{Actual kinetic energy at nozzle exit}}{\text{Kinetic energy at nozzle exit with isentropic flow to same exit pressure}}$$

(2)   The coefficient of discharge C_p is defined by the relation:

$$C_p = \frac{\text{Actual mass rate of flow}}{\text{Mass rate of flow with isentropic flow}}.$$

(3)   The efficiency of a diffuser is defined:

$$n_p = \frac{\left(1 + \dfrac{k-1}{2}M_1^2\right)\left(\dfrac{P_{02}}{P_{01}}\right)^{\frac{(k-1)}{K}} - 1}{\dfrac{k-1}{2}M_1^2}$$

where

   (a)   states 1 and 01 are the actual and stagnation states of the fluid entering the diffuser.

(b) states 2 and 02 are the actual and stagnation states of the fluid leaving the diffuser.

(4) The velocity coefficient C_v is defined:

$$C_v = \frac{\text{Actual velocity at nozzle exit}}{\text{Velocity at nozzle exit with isentropic flow and same exit pressure}}$$

REVIEW PROBLEMS

PROBLEM 1

Determine the final equilibrium state in English units when 2 lbm of saturated liquid mercury at 1 psia is mixed with 4 lbm of mercury vapor at 1 psia and 1,400°F. During the process the pressure in the cylinder is kept constant and no energy is lost between the cylinder and mercury.

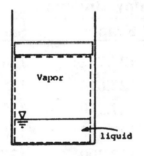

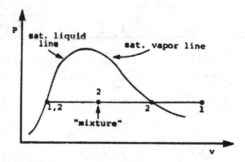

Figure 34. (a) The control mass   **(b) The process representation**

SOLUTION

Since the amount of liquid might change during the process, the liquid or only the vapor cannot be taken as the control mass. Instead, take the entire 6 lbm of mercury. By assumption, no energy transfer as heat occurs, but the volume is expected to change, resulting in an energy transfer as work. The only energy stored within the control mass is the internal energy of the mercury; the energy balance, made over the time for the process to take place, is therefore (Figures 34 and 35)

$$W \quad = \quad \Delta U$$

energy   increase in
input   energy storage

where $\Delta U = U_2 - U_1$

The work calculation is made easy by the fact that the pressure is constant. When the piston moves an amount dx, the energy transfer as work from the environment to the control mass is

$$dW = PAdx = -PdV.$$

Integrating,

$$W = \int_1^2 -PdV = P(V_1 - V_2).$$

Combining with the energy balance obtain

$$U_2 + PV_2 = U_1 + PV_1 \qquad (1)$$

TABLE 3
PROPERTIES OF SATURATED MERCURY

P, psia	T,°F	Enthalpy, Btu/lbm		
		Sat. liq.	Evap.	Sat. vap.
0.010	233.57	6.668	127.732	134.400
0.020	259.88	7.532	127.614	135.146
0.030	276.22	8.068	127.540	135.608
0.050	297.97	8.778	127.442	136.220
0.100	329.73	9.814	127.300	137.114
0.200	364.25	10.936	127.144	138.080
0.300	385.92	11.639	127.047	138.086
0.400	401.98	12.159	126.975	139.134
0.500	415.00	12.568	126.916	139.484
0.600	425.82	12.929	126.868	139.797
0.800	443.50	13.500	126.788	140.288
1.00	457.72	13.959	126.724	140.683
2.00	504.93	15.476	126.512	141.988
3.00	535.25	16.439	126.377	142.816
5.00	575.70	17.741	126.193	143.934

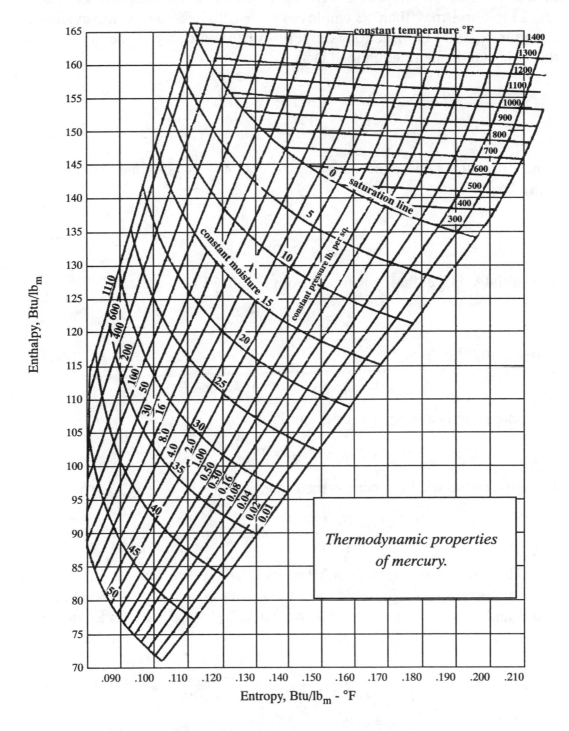

Figure 35. Thermodynamic properties of mercury

To evaluate the initial terms assume that the liquid is in an equilibrium state and the vapor is in an equilibrium state, even though they are not in equilibrium with one another. The graphical and tabular equations of state, Figure 35 and Table 3 for the thermodynamic properties of saturated mercury, may then be employed for each phase. Since the available equation-of-state information is in terms of the enthalpy property, express the right-hand side of equation (1) as

$$U_1 + PV_1 = M_{l_1} u_{l_1} + M_{v_1} u_{v_1} + P\left(M_{l_1} v_{l_1} + M_{v_1} v_{v_1}\right)$$
$$= M_{l_1} h_{l_1} + M_{v_1} h_{v_1}$$

Now, from the tables, the initial liquid enthalpy is (saturated liquid at 1 psia)

$$h_{l_1} = 13.96 \text{ Btu/lbm}$$

$$T_1 = 457.7°\text{F}$$

The initial vapor enthalpy is found from Figure 35 as

$$h_{v_1} = 164 \text{ Btu/lbm.}$$

Substituting the numbers,

$$U_1 + PV_1 = 2 \times 13.96 + 4 \times 164 = 684 \text{ Btu.}$$

The final state is a state of equilibrium, for which

$$U_2 + PV_2 = M(u + Pv)_2 = Mh_2.$$

The enthalpy in the final state is therefore

$$h_2 = \frac{684 \text{ Btu}}{6 \text{ lbm}} = 114 \text{ Btu / lbm.}$$

The final pressure and enthalpy may be used to fix the final state. Upon inspection of Figure 35, the final state is a mixture of saturated liquid and vapor at 1 psia and the "moisture" $(1 - x)$ is about 21 percent (0.79 quality). Alternatively, the information in Table 1, could have been used.

$$114 = \left(1 - x_2\right) \times 13.96 + x_2 \times 140.7$$
$$x_2 = 0.79$$

PROBLEM 2

The gauge pressure in an automobile tire when measured during winter at 32°F was 30 N/m². The same tire was used during the summer, and its temperature rose to 122°F. If we assume that the volume of the tire did not change, and no air leaked out between winter and summer, what is the new pressure as measured on the gauge?

SOLUTION

From one season to another, the only properties of the gas that will change are pressure and temperature. The mass (hence the number of moles) and the volume will remain the same. If it is assumed that this gas is ideal, then

$$PV = n\overline{R}T \tag{1}$$

where P = Pressure of the gas

V = Volume of the gas

n = Number of moles

$\overline{R}$ = Gas constant

T = Temperature of the gas

Rearranging equation (1) to solve for P gives

$$P = \left(\frac{n}{V}\right)\overline{R}T. \tag{2}$$

Since n and V are constant, equation (2) shows that pressure is directly proportional to temperature. That is, $\dfrac{P}{T} = \dfrac{n\overline{R}}{V} = $ constant. Therefore,

$$\frac{P_1}{T_1} = \frac{P_2}{T_2} = \frac{n_1\overline{R}}{V_1} = \frac{n_2\overline{R}}{V_2} \tag{3}$$

where P_1 = Initial pressure

T_1 = Initial temperature

P_2 = Final pressure

T_2 = Final temperature

n_1 and n_2 are initial and final moles, respectively. V_1 and V_2 are initial and final volume, respectively.

The moles and volume are not changing; therefore, $n_1 = n_2$ and $V_1 = V_2$. Consequently, equation (3) can be written as

$$\frac{P_1}{T_1} = \frac{P_2}{T_2}.$$ (4)

Before equation (4) can be used, the pressure and temperature must be in absolute scales.

$$\frac{T_C}{5} = \frac{T_F - 32}{9}$$ (5)

and

$$P = 14.7 \text{ AN/m}^2 + \text{GN/m}^2$$ (6)

where T_C = Temperature in degrees centigrade

T_F = Temperature in degrees Fahrenheit

AN/m² = Absolute Newtons per meter squared

GN/m² = Gauge Newtons per meter squared

Using equations (5) and (6),

$$122°F = 50°C = (50 + 273)K = 323K$$

and

$$P = 14.7 + 30 = 44.7 \text{ AN/m}^2.$$

These can now be inserted into equation (4) to give

$$\frac{44.7}{273} = \frac{P_2}{323}.$$

Therefore,

$$P_2 = \left[\frac{(44.7)(323)}{273} \right] \text{AN/m}^2$$

$$= 3.65 \times 10^5 \text{ AN/m}^2$$

or from equation (6),

$$52.9 \text{ AN/m}^2 = 14.7 \text{ AN/m}^2 + x \text{ GN/m}^2$$

$$P_2 = (52.9 - 14.7) \text{ GN/m}^2$$

$$= 38.2 \text{ GN/m}^2$$

PROBLEM 3

A container which has a volume of $0.1 m^3$ is fitted with a plunger enclosing 0.5 kg of steam at 0.4 MPa. Calculate the amount of heat transferred and the work done when the steam is heated to 300°C at constant pressure.

SOLUTION

For this system changes in kinetic and potential energy are not significant. Therefore,

$$Q = m(u_2 - u_1) + W$$

$$W = \int_1^2 PdV = P\int_1^2 dV = P(V_2 - V_1) = m(P_2 v_2 - P_1 v_1)$$

Therefore,

$$Q = m(u_2 - u_1) + m(P_2 v_2 - P_1 v_1) = m(h_2 - h_1)$$

$$v_1 = \frac{V_1}{m} = \frac{0.1}{0.5} = 0.2 = 0.001084 + x_1(0.4614)$$

$$x_1 = \frac{0.1989}{0.4614} = 0.4311$$

Then

$$h_1 = h_f + x_1 h_{fg}$$
$$= 604.74 + 0.4311 \times 2133.8 = 1,524.6$$
$$h_2 = 3,066.8$$
$$Q = 0.5(3,066.8 - 1,524.6) = 771.1 \text{ kJ}$$
$$W = mP(v_2 - v_1) = 0.5 \times 400(0.6548 - 0.2)$$
$$= 91.0 \text{ kJ}$$

Therefore,

$$U_2 - U_1 = Q - W = 771.1 - 91.0 = 680.1 \text{ kJ}.$$

The heat transfer can be calculated from u_1 and u_2 by using

$$Q = m(u_2 - u_1) + W$$
$$u_1 = u_f + x_1 u_{fg}$$
$$= 604.31 + 0.4311 \times 1,949.3 = 1,444.6$$
$$u_2 = 2,804.8$$

and

$$Q = 0.5(2,804.8 - 1,444.6) + 91.0 = 771.1 \text{ kJ}$$

PROBLEM 4

Steam at 3 MPa, 300°C leaves the boiler and enters the high-pressure turbine (in a reheat cycle) and is expanded to 300 kPa. The steam is then reheated to 300°C and expanded in the second stage turbine to 10 kPA. What is the efficiency of the cycle if it is assumed to be internally reversible?

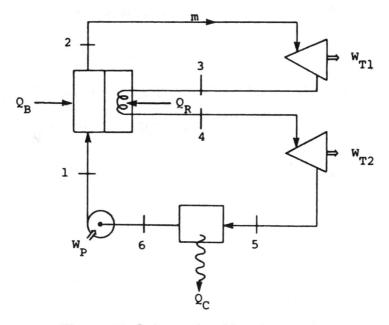

Figure 36. Schematic of heating cycle

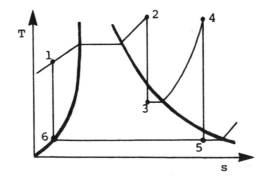

Figure 37. *T-s* diagram for heating cycle

SOLUTION

The efficiency η can be obtained from the following equation:

$$\eta = \frac{\dot{W}_{t_1} + \dot{W}_{t_2} - \dot{W}_p}{\dot{Q}_b - \dot{Q}_r} \qquad (1)$$

To calculate $\dot{W}_{t_1}$ assume that the turbine is adiabatic and neglect kinetic and potential energy changes. Applying the first law to the turbine,

$$\dot{W}_{t_1} = \dot{m}(h_2 - h_3).$$

From the steam tables,

$$h_2 = 2{,}993.5 \text{ kJ/kg}$$
$$s_2 = 6.5390 \text{ kJ/kg} - \text{K}$$

To find h_3 for the internally reversible adiabatic process $2 \rightarrow 3$:

$$s_2 = s_3 = 6.5390 \text{ kJ/kg} - \text{K}$$

At state 3,

$$s_{f_3} = 1.6718 \text{ kJ/kg} - \text{K} \qquad h_{f_3} = 561.47 \text{ kJ/kg}$$

$$s_{fg_3} = 5.3201 \text{ kJ/kg} - \text{K} \qquad h_{fg_3} = 2{,}163.8 \text{ kJ/kg}$$

$$s_{g_3} = 6.9919 \text{ kJ/kg} - \text{K} \qquad h_{g_3} = 2{,}725.3 \text{ kJ/kg}$$

$$s_2 = s_3 = s_{f_3} + x_3 s_{fg_3}$$

$$6.5390 = 1.6718 + x_3(5.3201)$$

$$x_3 = 0.915$$

$$h_3 = h_{f_3} + x_3 h_{fg_3}$$
$$= 561.47 + 0.915(2{,}163.8)$$
$$= 2{,}542 \text{ kJ/kg}$$

$$\frac{\dot{W}_{t_1}}{\dot{m}} = h_2 - h_3$$

$$= 2{,}993.5 - 2542$$
$$= 452 \text{ kJ/kg}$$

Similarly, to find $\dot{W}_{t_2}$

$$\dot{W}_{t_2} = \dot{m}(h_4 - h_5)$$

From the steam tables,

$$h_4 = 3{,}069.3 \text{ kJ/kg}$$
$$s_4 = 7.7022 \text{ kJ/kg} - \text{K}$$

To find h_5, note that

$$s_4 = s_5$$

At state 5,

$$s_{f_5} = 0.6493 \text{ kJ/kg} - \text{K}$$
$$h_{f_5} = 191.83 \text{ kJ/kg}$$
$$s_{fg_5} = 7.5009 \text{ kJ/kg} - \text{K}$$
$$h_{fg_5} = 2{,}392.8 \text{ kJ/kg}$$
$$s_{g_5} = 8.1502 \text{ kJ/kg} - \text{K}$$
$$h_{g_5} = 2{,}584.7 \text{ kJ/kg}$$
$$s_4 = s_5 = s_{f_5} + x_5 s_{fg_5}$$
$$x_5 = 0.949$$
$$h_5 = h_{f_5} + x_5 h_{fg_5}$$
$$h_5 = 191.83 + 0.949(2{,}392.8)$$
$$h_5 = 2{,}463 \text{ kJ/kg}$$

$$\therefore \frac{\dot{W}_{t_2}}{\dot{m}} = h_4 - h_5$$

$$= 3{,}069.3 - 2{,}463$$
$$= 606 \text{ kJ/kg}$$

To obtain $\dot{W}_p$, assume that $\dot{W}_p = \dot{m}\,v_6(p_1 - p_6)$.

From the steam tables,

$$v_6 = v_{f_6}$$
$$= 1.0102 \times 10^{-3} \text{ m}^3\text{/kg}$$

Thus,

$$\frac{\dot{W}_p}{\dot{m}} = 1.0102(30 - 0.1)10^5 \times 10^{-6}$$

$$= 3.0 \text{ kj/kg}$$

To obtain $\dot{Q}_b$, use

$$\dot{Q}_b = \dot{m}(h_2 - h_1)$$

$$h_1 = h_6 + \frac{\dot{W}_p}{\dot{m}}$$

$$= 191.8 + 3.0$$

$$= 194.8 \text{ kJ/kg}$$

$$\frac{\dot{Q}_b}{\dot{m}} = 2,993.5 - 194.8$$

$$= 2,799 \text{ kJ/kg}$$

To find $\dot{Q}_r$,

$$\dot{Q}_r = \dot{m}(h_4 - h_3)$$

$$\frac{\dot{Q}_r}{\dot{m}} = 3,069.3 - 2,542$$

$$= 527 \text{ kJ/kg}$$

From equation (1) then

$$\eta = \frac{452 + 606 - 3}{2,799 + 527}$$

$$= 0.317$$

PROBLEM 5

Steam leaves the boiler in a steam turbine plant at 2 MPa, 300°C and is expanded to 3.5 kPa before entering the condenser. Compare the following four cycles:

(1) A superheated Rankine cycle.

(2) A reheat cycle, with steam reheated to 300°C at the pressure when it becomes saturated vapor.

(3) A regenerative cycle, with an open feedwater heater operating at the pressure where steam becomes saturated vapor.

(4) A regenerative cycle, with a closed feedwater heater operating at the pressure where steam becomes saturated vapor.

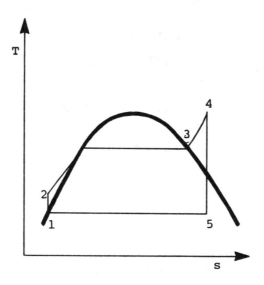

Figure 38. Rankine cycle

SOLUTION

(1) Referring to Figure 38, the steam tables show that

$$h_4 = 3,025 \text{ kJ/kg}$$
$$s_4 = 6.768 \text{ kJ/kg} - \text{K}$$

At $P = 3.5$ kPa,

$$s_g = 8.521 \text{ kJ/kg} - \text{K}$$
$$s_f = 0.391 \text{ kJ/kg} - \text{K}$$

Since $s_5 = s_4$, steam at 5 is a mixture of liquid and vapor. The quality is found as

$$x_5 = \frac{s_5 - s_f}{s_{fg}}$$
$$= \frac{6.768 - 0.391}{8.130}$$
$$= 0.785$$

Therefore,

$$h_5 = h_f + x_5 h_{fg}$$
$$= 112 + 0.785(2,438)$$
$$= 2,023 \text{ kJ/kg}$$

hence

$$w_{45} = h_4 - h_5$$
$$= 3,025 - 2,023$$
$$= 1,002 \text{ kJ/kg}$$

Now

$$w_{12} = h_1 - h_2$$
$$= v_f(p_1 - p_2)$$
$$= 0.0010(0.0035 - 2) \times 10^3 \text{ kJ/kg}$$
$$= -2 \text{ kJ/kg}$$

Therefore, the net work output is

$$w = w_{45} + w_{12} = 1,000 \text{ kJ/kg}$$

Heat input is

$$q_{42} = h_4 - h_2$$

But

$$h_2 = h_1 - w_{12} = 112 + 2 = 114 \text{ kJ/kg}$$

therefore,

$$q_{42} = 3,025 - 114 = 2,911 \text{ kJ/kg}$$

Thus,

$$\eta = \frac{w}{q_{42}} = \frac{1,000}{2,911} = 0.344$$

Also

$$\text{Specific Steam Consumption} = \frac{3,600}{w} = \frac{3,600}{1,000} = 3.6 \text{ kg/kWh}$$

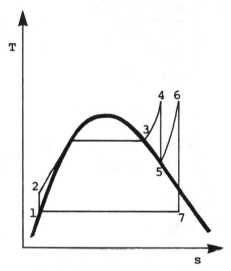

Figure 39. Reheat cycle

(2) Refer to Figure 39, and note that since

$$s_5 = s_{sat} = s_4 = 6.768 \text{ kJ/kg} - \text{K}$$

the pressure at reheat point 5 can be found using the steam tables. Interpolating between 0.55 MPa and 0.6 MPa gives

$$P_5 = 0.588 \text{ MPa.}$$

Then

$$
\begin{aligned}
h_5 &= 2,753 + \frac{0.588 - 0.55}{0.60 - 0.55}(2,757 - 2,753) \\
&= 2,753 + \frac{0.038}{0.05} \times 4 \\
&= 2,756 \text{ kJ/kg}
\end{aligned}
$$

As 6 and 5 are on the same isobar, by interpolation

$$h_6 = 3,065 + \frac{0.588 - 0.5}{0.60 - 0.5}(3,062 - 3,065)$$

$$= 3,065 + \frac{0.088}{0.1}(-3)$$

$$= 3,062.4 \text{ kJ/kg}$$

$$s_6 = 7.460 + 0.88(7.373 - 7.460)$$

$$= 7.460 + 0.88(-0.087)$$

$$= 7.384 \text{ kJ/kg} - \text{K}$$

At $P = 3.5$ kPa,

$$s_g = 8.521 \text{ kJ/kg} - \text{K}$$

$$s_f = 0.391 \text{ kJ/kg} - \text{K}$$

Since $s_7 = s_6$, the quality at 7 is found as

$$x_7 = \frac{7.384 - 0.391}{8.130} = 0.86.$$

Then

$$h_7 = 112 + 0.86(2,438)$$

$$= 112 + 2,095 = 2,207 \text{ kJ/kg}$$

The net work output is given by

$$w = w_{45} + w_{67} + w_{12}$$

$$= (3,025 - 2,765) + (3,062.4 - 2,207) - 2$$

$$= 1,122.4$$

The heat input is

$$q = q_{42} + q_{65}$$

$$= 2,911 + (h_6 - h_5)$$

$$= 2,911 + (3,062.4 - 2,756)$$

$$= 3,217.4$$

Therefore,

$$\eta = \frac{1,122.4}{3,217.4} = 0.349$$

and

$$\text{s.s.c.} = \frac{3,600}{w} = \frac{3,600}{1,122.4} = 3.2 \text{ kg/kWh.}$$

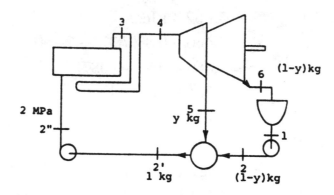

Figure 40. (a) Equipment schematic for regenerative cycle

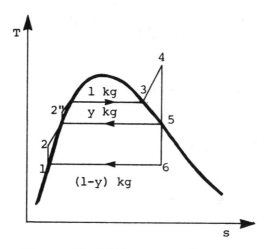

Figure 40. (b) Regenerative cycle

(3) Refer to Figures 40 (a) and 40 (b). The work is as in (b)

$$w_{45} = 269 \text{ kJ/kg}$$

Next determine the amount of steam bled off at 5. Consider an energy balance for the open feedwater heater with

$$h_{2'} = yh_s - (1-y)h_2$$

which gives

$$y = \frac{h_{2'} - h_2}{h_5 - h_2}$$

To find the value for $h_{2'}$, enter the steam tables. At 5 the pressure is known ($P = 0.588$ MPa) and the state of the steam is given as saturated vapor. Therefore, by interpolating between the values of 0.5 MPa and 0.6 MPa, obtain

$$h_{2'} = 656 + \frac{0.588 - 0.55}{0.60 - 0.55}(670 - 656)$$
$$= 656 + \frac{0.038}{0.05} \times 14$$
$$= 666.6 \text{ kJ/kg}$$

Then

$$y = \frac{666.6 - 114}{2,756 - 114}$$
$$= \frac{552.6}{2,642}$$
$$= 0.209$$

Hence,

$$w_{56} = (1 - y)(h_5 - h_6)$$
$$= 0.791(2,756 - 2,023)$$
$$= 580 \text{ kJ/kg}$$

also

$$w_{2'2''} = v_f(P_{2'} - P_{2''})$$
$$= 0.0011(0.588 - 2) \times 10^3$$
$$= -1.1 \times 1.412$$
$$= -1.55 \text{ kJ/kg}$$

Therefore,

$$w = w_{45} + w_{56} + w_{12} + w_{2'2''}$$
$$= 269 + 580 - 0.791 \times 2 - 1.55$$
$$= 845.87 \text{ kJ/kg}$$

The heat input is

$$q_{42"} = 3,025 - (666.6 + 1.55)$$
$$= 2,356.8 \text{ kJ/kg}$$

The efficiency of this cycle is

$$\eta = \frac{w}{q_{42"}} = \frac{845.87}{2,356.8} = 0.3595$$

and

$$\text{s.s.c.} = \frac{3,600}{w} = \frac{3,600}{845.9} = 4.25 \text{ kg/k Wh..}$$

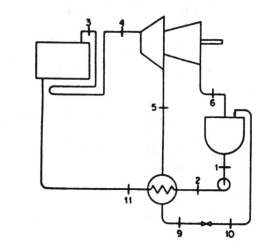

Figure 41. (a) Equipment diagram including closed heater

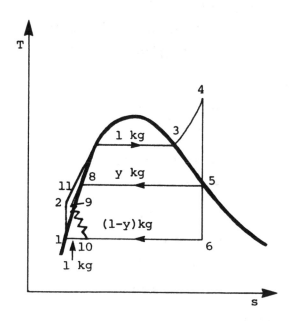

Figure 41. (b) A regenerative cycle with closed heater

(4) Refer to Figures 41 (a) and 41 (b). The work is as in part (b).

$$w_{45} = 269 \text{ kJ/kg}$$

Heat balance for the heater as a closed system gives

$$h_{21} = yh_5 - (1-y)h_2$$

giving

$$y = \frac{h_{11} - h_2}{h_5 - h_9}$$

Now in finding the enthalpies in the feed line, it is usual to make the following assumptions:

i. Neglect the feed pump term.

ii. Assume the enthalpy of the compressed liquid to be the same as that of the saturated liquid at the same temperature.

iii. Assume the states of the condensate extracted from the turbine, before and after throttling, to be the same as that of the saturated liquid at the lower pressure of the throttled liquid.

Using these assumptions

$$h_2 = h_1$$
$$h_{11} = h_8$$
$$h_9 = h_{10} = h_1$$

whence

$$y = \frac{h_8 - h_1}{h_5 - h_1}$$
$$= \frac{666.6 - 112}{2,756 - 112} = 0.209 \text{ kJ/kg}$$

Also,

$$w_{56} = 580 \text{ kJ/kg.}$$

Therefore,

$$w = w_{45} + w_{56} + w_{12}$$
$$= 269 + 580 - 2 = 847 \text{ kJ/kg}$$

Heat input $q_{411} = 2,358.4$ kJ/kg.

Then

$$\eta = \frac{w}{q_{411}} = \frac{847}{2,358.4} = 0.360$$

and

$$\text{s.s.c.} = \frac{3,600}{w} = \frac{3,600}{847} = 4.25 \text{ kg/k Wh.}$$

PROBLEM 6

(1) One kilogram of air at 101.35 kPa, 21°C is compressed in an Otto cycle with a compression ratio of 7 to 1. During the combustion process, 953.66 kJ of heat is added to the air. Compute (a) the specific volume, pressure, and temperature at the four points in the cycle, (b) the air standard efficiency, and (c) the mep (mean effective pressure) and hp of the engine, if it uses 1 kg/min of air.

(2) Calculate the efficiency for a Carnot cycle operating between the maximum and minimum temperatures of the Otto cycle (Figure 42).

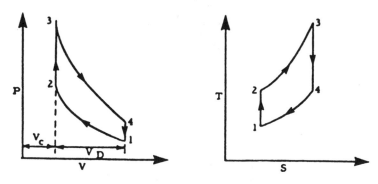

Figure 42. Otto cycle

SOLUTION

(1) (a) At state 1,

$$P_1 = 101.35 \text{ kPa}$$
$$T_1 = 294\text{K}$$

The specific volume, v_1, is determined by using the perfect gas equation of state.

$$v_1 = \frac{RT_1}{P_1}$$
$$= \frac{0.287(294)}{101.35}$$
$$= 0.8325 \text{ m}^3/\text{kg}$$

At 2, the specific volume can be obtained by using the compression ratio.

$$\frac{v_2}{v_1} = \frac{1}{7}$$

or

$$v_2 = \frac{v_1}{7}$$
$$= \frac{0.8325}{7}$$
$$= 0.1189 \text{ m}^3/\text{kg}$$

The pressure (P_2) is obtained from the isentropic relation.

$$P_2 = P_1\left(\frac{v_1}{v_2}\right)^k$$
$$= 101.35\left(\frac{0.8325}{0.1189}\right)^{1.4}$$
$$= 1,545.6 \text{ kPa}$$

The temperature (T_2) is

$$T_2 = T_1\left(\frac{v_1}{v_2}\right)^{k-1}$$
$$= 294\left(\frac{0.8325}{0.1189}\right)^{1.4-1}$$
$$= 640.4\text{K}$$

At state 3, $v_3 = v_2 = 0.1189$ m³/kg. The temperature here can be calculated from the quantity of heat supplied since

$$Q_{in} = mc_v(T_3 - T_2)$$

or solving for T_3,

$$T_3 = \frac{Q_{in}}{mc_v} + T_2$$

$$= \frac{953.66}{1(0.7243)} + 640.4$$

$$= 1,957.1 \text{K}$$

The pressure (P_3) is

$$P_3 = \frac{RT_3}{v_3}$$

$$= \frac{0.287(1,957.1)}{0.1189}$$

$$= 4,724 \text{ kPa}$$

At 4,

$$v_4 = v_1 = 0.8325 \text{ m}^3/\text{kg},$$

and the pressure is

$$P_4 = P_3\left(\frac{v_3}{v_4}\right)^k$$

$$= 4,724\left(\frac{0.1189}{0.8325}\right)^{1.4}$$

$$= 309.7 \text{ kPa}$$

The temperature T_4 is

$$T_4 = T_3\left(\frac{v_3}{v_4}\right)^{k-1}$$

$$= 1,957.1\left(\frac{0.1189}{0.8325}\right)^{1.4-1}$$

$$= 898.5 \text{K}$$

(b) The efficiency of the Otto cycle is defined as

$$\eta = \frac{Q_{in} - Q_{out}}{Q_{in}} \times 100 \tag{1}$$

where

$$Q_{in} = 953.66 \text{ kJ}$$

and

$$\begin{aligned}
Q_{out} &= mc_v(T_4 - T_1) \\
&= 1(0.7243)(898.5 - 274) \\
&= 452.3 \text{ kJ}
\end{aligned}$$

Therefore,

$$\begin{aligned}
\eta &= \frac{953.66 - 452.3}{953.66} \times 100 \\
&= 53\%
\end{aligned}$$

(c) The mep is

$$\text{mep} = \frac{W_{net}}{v_1 - v_2}$$

where

$$\begin{aligned}
W_{net} &= q_{in} - q_{out} \\
&= 953.66 - 452.3 \\
&= 501.36 \text{ kJ}
\end{aligned}$$

Thus,

$$\text{mep} = \frac{501.36}{0.8325 - 0.1189} = 702.6 \text{ kPa}$$

The horsepower is

$$\text{hp} = \dot{m} W_{net} = 501.36 \text{ kW}$$
$$501 \text{ kW} \cong 672 \text{ hp}$$

(2) The maximum and minimum temperatures of the Otto cycle are

$$T_{max} = 1{,}957.1 \text{K}$$
$$T_{min} = 294 \text{K}$$

The Carnot cycle efficiency is

$$\eta = \frac{T_{max} - T_{min}}{T_{max}} \times 100$$
$$= \frac{1,957.1 - 294}{1,957.1} \times 100$$
$$= 85\%$$

which is comparatively higher than the Otto cycle efficiency.

PROBLEM 7

Consider an air standard Diesel cycle. At the beginning of compression, the temperature is 300K and the pressure is 101.35 kPa. If the compression ratio is 15 and during the process 1,860 kJ/kg of air are added as heat, calculate: (a) the maximum cycle pressure and temperature, (b) the thermal efficiency of the cycle, and (c) the mep.

SOLUTION

(a) Referring to the figure for the states, and using the ideal gas equation of state

$$Pv = RT \tag{1}$$

the specific volume at state d is

$$v_d = \frac{RT_d}{P_d}$$
$$= \frac{0.287(300)}{101.35}$$
$$= 0.8495 \text{ m}^3/\text{kg}$$

Process $c \rightarrow d$ is an isochoric (constant volume) process. Hence,

$$v_c = v_d = 0.8495 \text{ m}^3/\text{kg}$$

The compression ratio is

$$r_v = \frac{v_d}{v_a} = 15$$

or

$$= \frac{v_d}{15}$$

$$= \frac{0.8495}{15}$$

$$= 0.0566 \text{ m}^3/\text{kg}$$

Process $d \rightarrow a$ is an isentropic process. Therefore,

$$\frac{T_a}{T_d} = \left(\frac{v_d}{v_a}\right)^{k-1}$$

or

$$T_a = 300\left(\frac{0.8495}{0.0566}\right)^{1.4-1}$$

$$= 886.5\text{K}$$

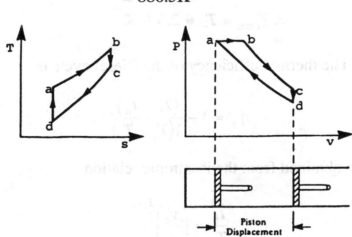

Figure 43. Diesel cycle

Also,

$$\frac{P_a}{P_d} = \left(\frac{v_d}{v_a}\right)^{k}$$

or

$$P_a = 101.35\left(\frac{0.8495}{0.0566}\right)^{1.4}$$

$$= 4,495 \text{ kPa}$$

$$\therefore P_{max} = P_a = 4,495 \text{ kPa}$$

The maximum temperature can be obtained as follows. From the first law, assuming constant specific heats, the heat supplied is

$$Q_{in} = Q_{ab} = C_p(T_b - T_a)$$

or

$$T_b = \frac{Q_{ab}}{C_p} + T_a$$

$$= \frac{1860}{1.0035} + 886.5$$

$$= 2,740 \text{K}$$

$$\therefore T_{max} = T_b = 2,740 \text{K}$$

(b) The thermal efficiency of the Diesel cycle is

$$\eta_{th} = 1 - \frac{(T_c - T_d)}{k(T_b - T_a)} \qquad (2)$$

T_c can be obtained from the isentropic relation

$$\frac{T_b}{T_c} = \left(\frac{v_c}{v_b}\right)^{k-1} \qquad (3)$$

where

$$v_b = \frac{RT_b}{P_b} \text{ from equation (1)}$$

$$= \frac{0.287(2,740)}{4,495}$$

$$= 0.1749 \text{ m}^3/\text{kg}$$

Substituting into (3),

$$\frac{T_b}{T_c} = \left(\frac{0.8495}{0.1749}\right)^{1.4-1}$$

or

$$\frac{T_b}{T_c} = 1.88$$

Solving for T_c,

$$T_c = \frac{2,740}{1.88}$$
$$= 1,457.5 K$$

From equation (2), then,

$$\eta_{th} = 1 - \frac{(1,457.5 - 300)}{1.4(2,740 - 886.5)}$$
$$= 1 - \frac{1,157.5}{2,594.9}$$
$$= 0.554$$

(c) The mean effective pressure (mep) is defined as

$$mep = \frac{W_{net}}{v_d - v_a} \qquad (4)$$

where

$$W_{net} = \eta_{th} Q_{in}$$
$$= 0.554(1,860)$$
$$= 1,030.44 \text{ kJ/kg}$$

Substituting into (4),

$$mep = \frac{1,030.44}{(0.8495 - 0.0566)}$$
$$= 1,299.6 \text{ kPa}$$

PROBLEM 8

The adiabatic efficiencies of the compressor and turbine used in an air-standard Brayton cycle are 85% and 90%, respectively. If the cycle operates between 14.7 and 55 psia and if the maximum and minimum temperatures are 1,500°F and 80°F, respectively, compute the thermal efficiency of the cycle. Assume constant specific heats.

SOLUTION

Use the accompanying figure to refer to the different states. The thermal efficiency of the cycle is calculated using the formula

$$\eta_{th} = \frac{W_{act}}{Q_H} \tag{1}$$

where

$$W_{act} = W_{turb.} + W_{comp.} \tag{2}$$

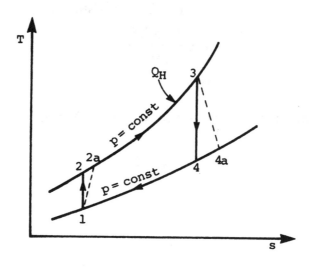

Figure 44. Brayton cycle

For this problem, the processes in the turbine and compressor are not reversible, and so the work done will be less than the work if the processes were reversible. Using the given efficiencies, it can be written

$$W_{act}\bigg|_{turb.} = \eta_{turb.} \times W_{theo.}\bigg|_{turb.} \tag{3}$$

and

$$W_{act}\bigg|_{comp.} = \frac{W_{theo}\bigg|_{comp.}}{\eta_{comp.}} \qquad (4)$$

where

$$W_{theo.}\bigg|_{turb.} = h_3 - h_4 = c_p(T_3 - T_4) \qquad (5)$$

and

$$-W_{theo.}\bigg|_{comp.} = h_2 - h_1 = c_p(T_2 - T_1) \qquad (6)$$

To find the temperatures at states 2 and 4, use the isentropic relation

$$\frac{T_a}{T_b} = \left(\frac{P_a}{P_b}\right)^{\frac{k-1}{k}}.$$

At state 2,

$$T_2 = T_1\left(\frac{P_2}{P_1}\right)^{\frac{k-1}{k}}$$

$$= 540\left(\frac{55}{14.7}\right)^{0.286}$$

$$= 787.6°R$$

At state 4,

$$T_4 = T_3\left(\frac{P_4}{P_3}\right)^{\frac{k-1}{k}}$$

$$= 1,960\left(\frac{14.7}{55}\right)^{0.286}$$

$$= 1,343.9°R$$

With these values, and $c_p = 0.24$ Btu/lbm–°R, from equations (5) and (6),

$$w_{theo.}\Big|_{turb.} = 0.24(1,960 - 1,343.9)$$

$$= 147.9 \text{ Btu/lbm}$$

and

$$-w_{theo.}\Big|_{comp.} = 0.24(787.6 - 540)$$

$$= 59.42 \text{ Btu/lbm}$$

Substituting into equations (3) and (4),

$$w_{act}\Big|_{turb.} = 0.90(147.9) = 133.1 \text{ Btu/lbm}$$

$$-w_{act}\Big|_{comp.} = \frac{59.42}{0.85} = 69.9 \text{ Btu/lbm}$$

From equation (2), then,

$$w_{act} = 133.1 - 69.9 = 63.2 \text{ Btu/lbm}$$

The only term unknown in equation (1) is the heat added to the system during process 2-3 (Q_H). However,

$$Q_H = h_3 - h_{2a} = c_p(T_3 - T_{2a}) \tag{7}$$

where T_{2a} is the actual temperature at state 2, and can be found using the efficiency of the compressor. Hence,

$$\eta_{comp} = \frac{T_2 - T_1}{T_{2a} - T_1} = 0.85$$

or

$$T_{2a} = \left(\frac{T_2 - T}{0.85}\right) + T_1$$

$$= \left(\frac{787.6 - 540}{0.85}\right) + 540$$

$$= 831.3°R$$

Equation (7) then gives

$$Q_H = 0.24(1,960 - 831.3)$$
$$= 270.89$$

Finally, using equation (1), the efficiency of the cycle is calculated as

$$\eta_{th} = \frac{63.2}{270.89} = 0.233$$

or

$$\eta_{th} = 23.3\%$$

PROBLEM 9

A standard vapor compression refrigeration cycle uses Freon-22 as the working fluid to provide three tons of cooling capacity. If the condenser operates at 140°F and the evaporator operates at 50°F, compute in English units (a) the mass flow rate of the Freon-22, (b) the horsepower required for the compressor, and (c) the heat transferred in the condenser. Assume the compression process to be reversible and adiabatic.

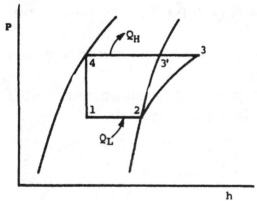

Figure 45. Refrigeration cycle

SOLUTION

Since the process has been assumed to be reversible and adiabatic, it will also be isentropic. Assuming the throttling process to be adiabatic, then it is also isenthalpic (constant enthalpy). Furthermore, assume that the condenser and evaporator operate at constant pressure. Then this cycle can be plotted on a P-h diagram as shown in Figure 45.

The values of the various properties at the different states shown in Figure 45 are taken from the P-h diagram for Freon-22, as shown in Figure 46. The procedure is as follows:

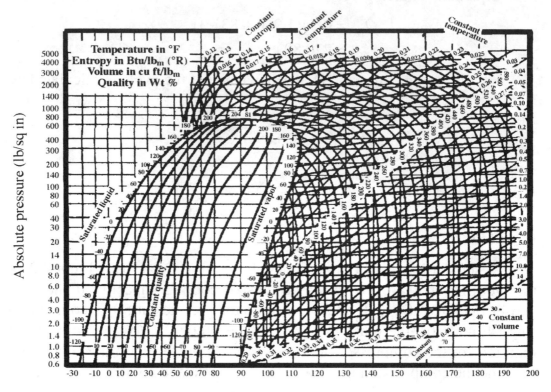

Enthalpy (Btu per lb$_{in}$ above saturated liquid at -40 °F)

Figure 46. Pressure-enthalpy diagram for Freon-22 refrigerant

At state 3' the temperature is known to be 140°F, and the state is saturated vapor. Therefore, from Figure 46

$$P_{3'} = P_3 = 350 \text{ psia}.$$

At state 4

$$P_4 = P_{3'} = 350 \text{ psia}$$
$$T_4 = T_{3'} = 140°F$$

Hence,

$$h_4 = 52 \text{ Btu/lbm}.$$

At state 1, since process 1-4 is isenthalpic

$$h_1 = h_4 = 52 \text{ Btu/lbm}.$$

At state 2 the temperature is known to be 50°C, and the state is saturated vapor. Hence, from Figure 46,

$$P_2 = 100 \text{ psia}$$
$$h_2 = 109 \text{ Btu/lbm}$$
$$s_2 = 0.218 \text{ Btu/lbm–°R}$$

State 3: Process 2-3 is an isentropic process and state 3, due to the compression, lies in the superheated region. Futhermore, $P_3 = P_{3'} = 350$ psia. Hence,

$$s_3 = s_2 = 0.218 \text{ Btu/lbm–°R}$$
$$h_2 = 109 \text{ Btu/lbm}$$

From Figure 46,

$$h_3 = 123 \text{ Btu/lbm}$$
$$T_2 = 180°F$$

Now that the values of the various properties have been obtained, we can solve the problem.

(a) Consider the evaporator and write an energy balance around it to find the heat absorbed by the Freon-22. Neglecting potential and kinetic energies, we can write

$$q_L = h_2 - h_1$$
$$= 109 - 52$$
$$= 57 \text{ Btu/lbm}$$

It is known, however, that the evaporator is to absorb three tons or 36,000 Btu/hr. Hence, the required mass flow rate is

$$\dot{m} = \frac{\dot{Q}_L}{q_L}$$
$$= \frac{36,000}{57}$$
$$= 631.58 \text{ lbm/hr}$$

(b) Consider the compressor and write an energy balance around it, neglecting potential and kinetic energies.

$$-w = h_3 - h_2$$
$$= 123 - 109$$
$$= 14 \text{ Btu/lbm}$$

or

$$w = -14 \text{ Btu/lbm}$$

The total work production is

$$\dot{W} = \dot{m}w$$
$$= 631.58(-14)$$
$$= -8,842.12 \text{ Btu/hr}$$

However, 1 hp = 2,545 Btu/hr, and hence the compressor will need

$$p = \frac{8,842.12}{2,545} = 3.48 \text{ hp}$$

(c) The heat load of the condenser can be computed in two ways: either by writing an energy balance around it, or by writing the overall energy balance around the refrigerator. Here the second way is used. Hence,

$$\dot{W} = \dot{Q}_H + \dot{Q}_L$$

Solving for $\dot{Q}_H$ gives

$$\dot{Q}_H = \dot{W} - \dot{Q}_L$$
$$= -8,842.12 - 36,000$$
$$= -44,842.12 \text{ Btu/hr}$$

The heat transferred per unit mass is

$$q_H = \frac{\dot{Q}_H}{\dot{m}}$$
$$= \frac{-44,842.12}{631.58}$$
$$= 71 \text{ Btu/lbm}$$

PROBLEM 10

A converging nozzle has air flowing through it. In English units, calculate the stagnation temperature T_o and pressure P_o if at point A within the nozzle, $P_A = 40$ psia, $T_A = 2,000°R$, $V_A = 500$ ft/sec, and A_A (cross-sectional area) = 0.2 ft². Also calculate the sonic velocity, Mach number at this section and the exit area A_B, exit pressure P_B, temperature T_B, and velocity V_B if the exit Mach number is one. Assume air to be an ideal gas with $k = 1.40$.

SOLUTION

The stagnation temperature is

$$T_o = T_A + \frac{k-1}{2kR} V_A^2.$$

Therefore,

$$T_o = 2,000°R + \frac{(1.4-1)(500)^2 \, \text{ft}^2/\sec^2}{2 \times 1.4 \times 53.35 \dfrac{\text{ft} \cdot \text{lb}}{\text{lbm R}} \times \dfrac{32 \, \text{lbm ft}}{\text{lb sec}^2}}$$

$$= 2,021 \, R$$

The stagnation pressure is

$$P_o = P_A \left(\frac{T_o}{T_A} \right)^{\frac{k}{(k-1)}}.$$

Therefore,

$$P_o = 40 \frac{\text{lb}}{\text{in}^2} \times \left(\frac{2,021}{2,000} \right)^{\frac{1.4}{(1.4-1)}}$$

$$= 41 \, \text{lb/in}^2$$

The sonic velocity is

$$C_A = \sqrt{kRT_A}$$

$$C_A = \left(1.4 \times 53.35 \frac{\text{ft} \cdot \text{lb}}{\text{lbm R}} \times 2,000 \, R \times 32.2 \frac{\text{lbm} \cdot \text{ft}}{\text{lb sec}^2} \right)^{\frac{1}{2}}$$

$$C_A = 2,193 \, \text{ft/sec}$$

The Mach number is

$$M_A = \frac{V_A}{C_A} = \frac{500}{2,193} = 0.228.$$

The exit pressure is

$$\gamma_c = \frac{P_B}{P_o} = 0.528.$$

Therefore,

$$P_B = 0.528 P_o = 0.528(41 \text{ psia}) = 21.65 \text{ lb/in}^2$$

The exit velocity is

$$V_B = C_B = \left(\frac{2k}{k+1} RT_o\right)^{\frac{1}{2}}$$

$$= \left(\frac{2 \times 1.4}{1.4+1} \times 53.35 \frac{\text{ft} \bullet \text{lb}}{\text{lbm R}} \times 32.2 \frac{\text{lbm ft}}{\text{lb sec}^2}\right)^{\frac{1}{2}}$$

$$= 2,013 \text{ ft/sec}$$

The exit temperature is

$$T_B = \frac{2}{k+1} T_o = \left(\frac{2}{1.4+1}\right)(2,021 \text{ R})$$

$$T_B = 1,684 \text{ R}$$

To calculate the exit area, the mass rate of flow is required. Therefore,

$$\rho_A = \frac{P_A}{RT_A} = \frac{40 \dfrac{\text{lb}}{\text{in}^2} \times 144 \text{ in}^2 / \text{ft}^2}{53.35 \dfrac{\text{ft} \bullet \text{lb}}{\text{lbm R}} 2,000 \text{ R}}$$

$$\rho_A = 0.054 \text{ lbm/ft}^3$$

$$\rho_B = \frac{P_B}{RT_B} = \frac{21.65 \times 144}{53.35 \times 1,684}$$

$$\rho_B = 0.035 \text{ lbm/ft}^3$$

Using the equation of continuity,

$$A_B = \frac{\rho_A A_A V_A}{\rho_B V_B} = \frac{0.054 \times 0.2 \times 500}{0.035 \times 2,013} = 0.077 \text{ft}^2.$$

FE/EIT

Fundamentals of Engineering: AM Exam

CHAPTER 11

Fluids

CHAPTER 11

FLUIDS

FLUID PROPERTIES

A fluid is defined as a substance that cannot resist a shear stress by static deformation. Both liquids and gases are fluids and are distinguished from solids by the above definition. There are many properties of fluids to which numerical values can be given. **Density**, ρ, is defined as the mass of a small fluid element divided by its volume. Often, **specific weight**,

$$\gamma = \rho g,$$

is more useful since density and gravitational acceleration usually occur together. Both density and specific weight are dimensional quantities; common units for density are kg/m^3 and $slug/ft^3$, and lbf/ft^3 is the typical unit for specific weight. **Specific gravity**, on the other hand, is dimensionless and is defined as the ratio of a fluid's density to the density of some reference fluid. For liquids, water is the reference fluid; for gases, air is used (at a standard temperature and pressure).

Viscosity, another important property of fluids, is the ratio of the local shearing stress to the rate of shearing strain of a fluid element in a moving fluid. For simple shear flows where velocity component μ in the x-direction is a function of only the normal coordinate y, the shear stress, τ, :

$$\tau = \mu \frac{du}{dy},$$

where μ is called the coefficient of viscosity. This linear relation applies only to **Newtonian** fluids. Fortunately, most common fluids, such as air, water, oil, etc., are Newtonian. The shear stress on a solid surface is equal but opposite to that applied to a fluid wetting the surface. Thus, frictional forces on surfaces can be found if the velocity gradient $\dfrac{du}{dy}$ (also called the rate of shearing strain) and coefficient of viscosity μ are known. Units for μ are the pascal-second in the SI system, and lbf-sec/ft^2 in the English system. **Kinematic viscosity,** υ, is defined as:

$$\upsilon = \frac{\mu}{\rho},$$

commonly given in units of ft^2/sec or cm^2/sec.

EXAMPLE

A block weighing 445 N and having an area of 0.186 m^2 slides down an inclined plane as shown in Figure 1, with a constant velocity. An oil gap between the block and the plane is 0.0254 cm thick, the inclination of the plane is 30° to the horizontal, and the velocity of the block is 1.83 m/s. Find the viscosity of the lubricating film.

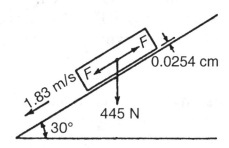

Figure 1. Forces on block

SOLUTION

The coefficient of viscosity μ (mu) is defined as the ratio:

$$\frac{\text{Shearing stress } \tau}{\text{Rate of shearing strain}\left(\dfrac{du}{dy}\right)}$$

and may be compared with the modulus of rigidity of a solid.

Rate of shearing strain is given by $\dfrac{du}{dy}$, and hence:

$$\mu = \frac{\tau}{\dfrac{du}{dy}}$$

or

$$\tau = \mu \frac{du}{dy}.$$

μ is also called the absolute or dynamic viscosity and has units of N-sec/m^2.

In this problem, the component of the weight acting down the plane is opposed by a viscous force exactly equal and opposite to it. Therefore,

$$F = 445 \sin 30° = 222.5 \text{ N}.$$

Hence:

$$\tau = \frac{F}{A} = \frac{222.5}{0.186} = 1196 \text{ N/m}^2$$

but

$$\tau = \mu \frac{du}{dy}.$$

Assuming a linear inverse in fluid speed from zero at the surface of the inclined plane to 1.83 m/s at the lower block surface:

$$\frac{du}{dy} = \frac{1.83 \text{ m/s}}{0.000254} = 7,205 \text{ s}^{-1}$$

Therefore:

$$\mu = \frac{\tau}{\dfrac{du}{dy}} = \frac{1,196 \text{ N/m}^2}{7,205 \text{ s}^{-1}} = 0.166 \text{ N-sec}/\text{m}^2$$

Vapor pressure, p_v, is defined as the pressure at which a liquid will boil at a given temperature; p_v depends greatly on temperature, and its value can be obtained from charts. In flows of liquids, local fluid pressures typically decrease as velocity increases. If the local pressure falls below p_v, local boiling or *cavitation* may occur.

With an increase in pressure, all fluids compress, and an increase in density results. The **coefficient of compressibility**, α, is given by:

$$\alpha = \frac{1}{V_o}\left(\frac{\partial V}{\partial p}\right)_T$$

where p denotes pressure and V, volume, for a constant temperature.

The **bulk modulus**, E, is the reciprocal of compressibility:

$$E = \frac{1}{\alpha} = V_o\left(\frac{\partial p}{\partial V}\right)_T,$$

with typical units of psi, atm, or kPa.

When a liquid forms an interface with a second liquid or gas, a tensional force exists at the interface. The **coefficient of surface tension**, σ, is a measure of this tensional force per unit length of the surface:

$$\sigma = \frac{F}{2L}.$$

The height of capillary action in a tube (Figure 2) can be found using the surface tension and the specific weight of the fluid.

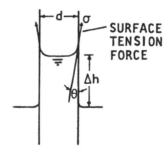

Figure 2. Capillary action in a tube

Taking the summation of forces in the vertical direction of the water in the tube that has risen above the reservoir level yields:

$$\sigma\pi d - \gamma(\Delta h)\left(\frac{\pi d^2}{4}\right) = 0$$

yielding
$$\Delta h = \frac{4\sigma}{\gamma d}$$

assuming the angle, θ, is equal to zero.

FLUID STATICS

The fundamental equation that describes the pressure field in a fluid at rest is

$$\nabla p = \rho g$$

where g is the acceleration vector due to gravity. If we adopt a coordinate system where z is "up" vertically, g acts downward (opposite to the direction of increasing z), the equation above reduces to:

$$\frac{dp}{dz} = -\rho g$$

when applied to gases with large height differences, such as the atmosphere density in a variable. For liquid applications ρ can be assumed to be constant with negligible error. For constant ρ and g:

$$p_2 - p_1 = -\rho g(z_2 - z_1),$$

where 1 and 2 represent any two positions in the same fluid. At a liquid surface, the pressure must equal the pressure of the air (or other fluid) immediately above the surface. For liquids exposed to atmospheric pressure, p_{atm}, the local pressure at some depth h (measured from the surface) is:

$$p = \rho g h + p_{atm},$$

where ρ is the density of the liquid. Often, it is more convenient to use gage (sometimes spelled "gauge") pressure, defined as the absolute pressure minus p_{atm}:

$$p_{gage} = p_{abs} - p_{atm}$$

where absolute pressure is measured with respect to a true zero pressure reference. In the liquid discussed above, the gage pressure would equal $\rho g h$.

The equation: $p_2 - p_1 = -pg(z_2 - z_1)$ can be applied in piecewise fashion to determine the pressure difference across a **simple manometer**.

A manometer consisting of n different substances with different specific gravities is shown in the figure. The following equation is used to determine the pressure difference $(P_A - P_n)$:

$$\left(P_A - P_n\right) = \left(P_A - P_{A_1}\right) + \left(P_{A_1} - P_{A_2}\right) + \left(P_{A_2} - P_{A_3}\right) + \left(P_{A_3} - P_{A_4}\right) + \ldots + \left(P_{An_{-1}} - P_n\right)$$

$$= -\gamma_1 z_1 - \gamma_2 z_2 + \gamma_3 z_3 + \gamma_4 z_4 \ldots - \gamma_n z_n$$

where

$\gamma_1, \gamma_2, \gamma_3, \gamma_4, \ldots, \gamma_n$ = the specific weights of the substances,

$z_1, z_2, z_3, z_4, \ldots, z_n$ = the distances between two successive points in the columns of the manometer.

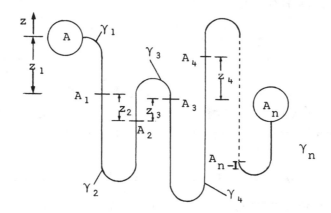

Figure 3. Simple manometer

Note: The distances $z_1, z_2, z_3, z_4, \ldots, z_n$ are considered as positive if the end point, A_3, is at a higher position than the start point, A_2 (Distance z_3), or as negative if the end point, A_1, is at a lower position than the start point, A (Distance z_1).

In order to determine the force acting on a submerged surface, we must specify the magnitude, the direction, and the line of action of the resultant force F_R.

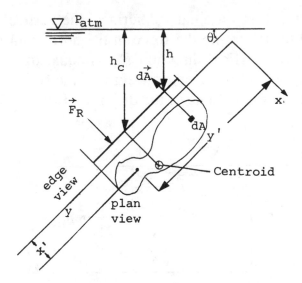

Figure 4. Plane submerged surface

The magnitude of the resultant force acting on the submerged surface is:

$$F_R = \gamma h_c A$$

where

      A is the surface area

      h_c is the depth from the free surface to the centroid of the area on which the force acts, and

      γ is the specific weight of the fluid.

The direction of F_R is normal to the surface, and the line of action passes through the points x', y', which can be located by:

$$y' = y_c + \frac{I_c}{A_{yc}} \qquad \frac{I_c}{A_{yc}} > 0$$

$$x' = x_c + \frac{\left(I_{xy}\right)_c}{A_{yc}}$$

where

      I_c, $(I_{xy})_c$ are the moments of inertia about its center gravity axes, and

      x_c, y_c are the center of gravity coordinates.

For a force acting on a curved surface, the vertical projection of the surface is used to determine the force in the horizontal direction F_{Ry} and z'. The force in the vertical direction F_{Rz} is equal to the volume of fluid displaced multiplied by the specific weight of the fluid. It acts through the center of gravity of the volume of the displaced fluid.

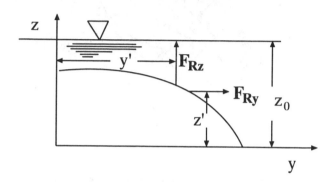

Figure 5. Two-dimensional curved submerged surface

Table 1 is a review of the geometry needed to solve fluid statics problems.

TABLE 1 LOCATION OF CENTROID, AREA, AND MOMENT OF INERTIA OF COMMON SHAPES		
Rectangle:		$A = b \cdot h$
Triangle:		$A = b \cdot h/2$
Circle:		$A = \pi D^2/4$

The resultant vertical force exerted on a body by a static fluid in which it is submerged or floating is called the **buoyant force**. The magnitude of this force is

$$F_z = \int \rho g (z_2 - z_1) dA = \rho g V$$

where

ρ = Density of the fluid

g = Gravitational constant

V = Volume of the body

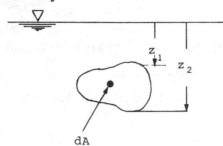

Figure 6. Buoyant force

The buoyant force for an incompressible fluid goes through the centroid of the volume displaced by the body.

For a completely submerged body (Figure 7), the center of gravity, G, must be directly below the center of buoyancy, B, to satisfy the condition for stability (stable equilibrium) as in Figure 6. The vertical alignment of B and G is important for stability. If G and B coincide, neutral equilibrium is obtained. In a floating body stable equilibrium can be achieved even when G is above B. The magnitude of the length GA serves as a measure of the stability of a floating body.

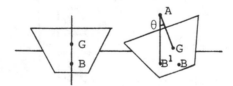

Figure 7. Completely submerged body and floating body

When a container of fluid undergoes constant uniform linear acceleration **a** (in any direction), the equation $\nabla p = \rho g$ may still be applied, by substituting $g - a$ for the vector **g**, i.e.:

$$\nabla p = \rho\,(g - a).$$

In other words, all the hydrostatic equations above remain valid, but with a different constant of gravity ($g - a$ instead of g). The surface of an accelerating container will align itself perpendicularly to the vector $g - a$. The pressure increases linearly with a coordinate along the direction of $g - a$, rather than simply along the direction of g in hydrostatics.

When a container of liquid rotates at a constant angular velocity about the vertical axis, the equation above is still valid, with the centripetal acceleration equal to:

$$a = -r\omega^2 i_r,$$

where

r = The radial distance from the axis of rotation

ω = The magnitude of the angular velocity

i_r = The unit coordinate in the radial direction,

and pressure is:

$$p = \text{Constant} - \rho g z + \frac{1}{2}\rho r^2 \omega^2.$$

EXAMPLE

A gate 5 ft wide is hinged at point B and rests against a smooth wall at point A. Compute (a) the force on the gate due to seawater pressure; (b) the horizontal force P exerted by the wall at point A; and (c) the reactions at the hinge B (Figure 8).

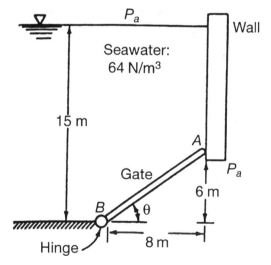

Figure 8. Submerged gate

SOLUTION

(a) By geometry the gate is 10 m long from A to B, and its centroid is halfway between, or at elevation 3 m above point B. The depth h_{CG} is thus $15 - 3 = 12$ m. The gate area is $5 \times 10 = 50$ m². Neglect p_A as acting on both sides of the gate. The hydrostatic force on the gate is:

$$F = p_{CG}A = \rho g h_{CG}A = (64 \text{ N/m}^3)(12 \text{ m})(50 \text{ m}^2) = 38{,}400 \text{ N}$$

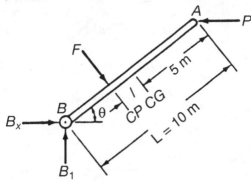

Figure 9. Free-body diagram

(b) First we must find the center of pressure of F. A free-body diagram of the gate is shown in Figure 9. The gate is a rectangle and hence

$$I_{xy} = 0 \text{ and } I_{xx} = \frac{bL^3}{12} = \frac{\left[(5\text{m}) \times (10\text{m})^3\right]}{12} = 417 \text{ m}^4. \text{ The ambient pressure}$$

p_a is neglected if it acts on both sides of the plane; e.g., the other side of the plane is inside a ship or on the dry side of a gate or dam. In this case $p_{CG} = \rho g h_{CG}$, and the center of pressure becomes independent of specific weight:

$$y_{CP} = -\frac{I_{xx} \sin\theta}{h_{CG}A}$$

$$x_{CP} = -\frac{I_{xy} \sin\theta}{h_{CG}A}$$

The distance I from the CG to the CP is given by the equation above, since p_a is neglected:

$$I = -y_{CP} = +\frac{I_{xx} \sin\theta}{h_{CG}A} = \frac{\left(417\text{m}^4\right)\left(\dfrac{6}{10}\right)}{(12\text{m})\left(50\text{m}^2\right)} = 0.417\text{m}.$$

The distance from point B to force F is thus $10 - I - 5 = 4.583$ m. Summing moments counterclockwise about B gives:

$$PL \sin\theta - F(5 - I) = P(6 \text{ m}) - (38{,}400 \text{ N})(4.583 \text{ m}) = 0$$

or

$$P = 29{,}300 \text{ N}$$

(c) With F and P known, the reactions B_x and B_z in Figure 9 are found by summing forces on the gate:

$$\sum F_x = 0 = B_x + F \sin \theta - P = B_x + 38{,}400(0.6) - 29{,}300$$

and
$$B_x = 6{,}300 \text{ N}$$

$$\sum F_z = 0 = B_z - F \cos \theta = B_z - 38{,}400(0.8)$$

and
$$B_z = 30{,}700 \text{ N}.$$

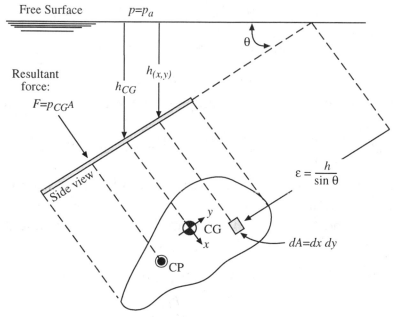

Figure 10. Hydrostatic force and center of pressure on an arbitrary plane surface of area *A* inclined at an angle θ below the free surface.

HYDRAULICS AND FLUID MACHINES

The first step in the solution of control volume problems is to choose a control volume. This basic step is most critical since the degree of difficulty of the problem can often be greatly reduced by a wise choice of control volume. Next, evaluate the net outflux of mass (the control surface integral). Finally, equate this to the negative of the unsteady control volume integral. In many cases, if the flow is steady, this volume integral will vanish.

Often, a control volume will cut through a duct or pipe where the flow is predominantly in one direction. In such cases, an **average velocity**:

$$v = \frac{Q}{A}$$

is defined where Q is the **volume flow rate** across the pipe's cross section and A is the cross-sectional area. In the control volume equation, then, the **mass flux** across this surface is simply:

$$\dot{m} = \rho v A.$$

The conservation of mass law is:

$$\rho_1 A_1 v_1 = \rho_2 A_2 v_2,$$

or for an incompressible fluid where $\rho_1 = \rho_2$:

$$A_1 v_1 = A_2 v_2.$$

In Cartesian coordinates, incompressible continuity is expressed as:

$$\frac{\partial u}{\partial x} + \frac{\partial v}{\partial y} + \frac{\partial w}{\partial z} = 0,$$

where u, v, and w are the x, y, and z components of velocity. For steady incompressible frictionless flow along a streamline between points 1 and 2, the following Bernoulli energy equation applies:

$$\frac{p_1}{\rho} + \frac{v_1^2}{2} + g z_1 = \frac{p_2}{\rho} + \frac{v_2^2}{2} + g z_2.$$

This equation is useful for duct or pipe flows, particularly when there are changes in cross-sectional areas and/or elevations. If the elevation increases ($z_2 > z_1$) or if the area decreases ($A_2 < A_1$ and thus $v_2 > v_1$ by the conservation of mass), it can be seen that the pressure p_2 must decrease accordingly to satisfy the equation. Often it is more convenient to rewrite the equation above in terms of the equivalent column height of fluid, or **head**. Dividing by g, the equation above can be written:

$$H = \frac{p_1}{\gamma} + \frac{v_1^2}{2g} + z_1 = \frac{p_2}{\gamma} + \frac{v_2^2}{2g} + z_2$$

where $\gamma = \rho g$, and H is called the total head or total Bernoulli head. H is also equivalent to the height of the Energy Grade Line (EGL).

In most practical problems, friction cannot be neglected, and there may be work added to the flow (by a pump), work extracted from the flow (by a turbine), or heat transferred to or from the fluid. In this case, a much more general Bernoulli equation must be developed. Specifically, the total head H in the equation above does not remain constant, but rather changes whenever friction, work, or heat transfers are present. From the Bernoulli energy equation:

$$\frac{p_1}{\rho g} + \frac{v_1^2}{2g} + z_1 = \frac{p_2}{\rho g} + \frac{v_2^2}{2g} + z_2 + h_s + h_{total}$$

where h_s = shaft work head, h_{total} = the total amount of head loss due to friction, heat transfer, etc. Here 1 and 2 are locations at an inlet and outlet of a control volume. The shaft work head, h_s:

$$h_s = \frac{\dot{W}_s}{\left(\dot{m} g\right)},$$

is the head associated with work done by the fluid,

where $\dot{W}_s$ = the shaft power (work per unit time) done by the fluid.

For a pump, let:

$$h_s = -E_p,$$

where E_p = the energy added per unit weight of the fluid (dimensions of head, i.e., height of fluid).

For a turbine, let E_T be the energy extracted from the fluid per unit weight. In this case:

$$h_s = E_T.$$

The power required by a pump is given by:

$$\dot{W}_p = \frac{Q \gamma E_p}{\eta_p},$$

where

$\quad Q \quad$ = The volumetric flow rate

$\quad \gamma \quad$ = The specific weight of the fluid

$\quad \eta_p$ = The pump efficiency.

The power produced by a turbine is given by:

$$\overset{\bullet}{W}_t = Q \gamma E_T \eta_t$$

where η_t = The turbine efficiency.

EXAMPLE

(a) Three kilonewtons of water per second flow through this pipeline reducer. Calculate the flow rate in cubic meters per second and the mean velocities in the 300 mm and 200 mm pipes (Figure 11).

(b) Thirty newtons of air per second flow through the reducer of the preceding problem, the air in the 300 mm pipe having a weight density of 9.8 N/m³. In flowing through the reducer, the pressure and temperature will fall, causing the air to expand and producing a reduction of density. Assuming that the weight density of the air in the 200 mm pipe is 7.85 N/m³, calculate the mass and volume flow rates and the velocities in the two pipes.

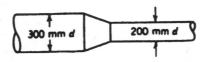

Figure 11. Dimensions of pipeline

SOLUTION

(a) Q: volumetric flow rate is:

$$Q = A_{cs}v$$

if density is essentially constant.

$\overset{\bullet}{G}$ is the weight flow rate:

$$Q = \frac{\overset{\bullet}{G}}{\gamma} = \frac{3 \times 10^3 \, \text{N/s}}{9.8 \times 10^3 \, \text{N/m}^3} = 0.306 \ \text{m}^3\text{/s}$$

$$v_{300} = \frac{Q}{A} = \frac{0.306}{\frac{\pi}{4}(0.3)^2} = 4.33 \ \text{m/s}$$

$$v_{200} = \frac{0.306}{\frac{\pi}{4}(0.2)^2} = 9.74 \text{ m/s}$$

or

$$Q_{300} \text{ mm pipe} = Q_{200} \text{ mm pipe:}$$

$$v_{200} = v_{300}\left(\frac{r_{300}}{r_{200}}\right)^2 = 4.33\left(\frac{.3}{.2}\right)^2 = 9.74 \text{ m/s}$$

(b)

$$Q_{300} = \frac{\dot{G}}{\gamma_1} = \frac{30 \text{ N/s}}{9.8 \text{ N/m}^3} = 3.06 \text{ m}^3/\text{s}$$

$$Q_{200} = \frac{\dot{G}}{\gamma_2} = \frac{30 \text{ N/s}}{7.85 \text{ N/m}^3} = 3.82 \text{ m}^3/\text{s}$$

$$v_{300} = \frac{Q_{300}}{A} = \frac{3.06}{\frac{\pi}{4}(0.3)^2} = 43.3 \text{ m/s}, \quad v_{200} = \frac{3.82}{\frac{\pi}{4}(0.2)^2} = 121.6 \text{ m/s}$$

$$\dot{m} = A\rho v = \text{Constant} = \frac{\dot{G}}{g_n} = \frac{30 \text{ N/s}}{9.81 \text{ m/s}^2} = 3.06 \text{ kg/s}$$

$$\dot{m} = \text{Mass flow rate}$$

$$\dot{G} = \text{Weight flow rate}$$

To check:

$$\dot{m} = \frac{\gamma_{300}Q_{300}}{g_n} = 9.8 \times \frac{3.06}{9.81} = 3.06 \text{ kg/s}$$

$$\dot{m} = \frac{\gamma_{200}Q_{200}}{g_n} = 7.85 \times \frac{3.82}{9.81} = 3.06 \text{ kg/s}$$

The theoretical velocity of a jet issuing from an orifice can be derived from the Bernoulli energy equation, as shown in the following example.

EXAMPLE

Using Figure 12, (a) Determine the velocity of efflux from the nozzle in the wall of the reservoir of the figure. (b) Find the discharge through the nozzle.

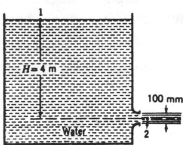

Figure 12. Flow through nozzle from reservoir

SOLUTION

(a) The jet issues as a cylinder with atmospheric pressure around its periphery. The pressure along its centerline is at atmospheric pressure for all practical purposes. Bernoulli's equation is applied between a point on the water surface and a point downstream from the nozzle,

$$\frac{v_1^2}{2g} + \frac{p_1}{\gamma} + z_1 = \frac{v_2^2}{2g} + \frac{p_2}{\gamma} + z_2.$$

With the pressure datum as local atmospheric pressure, $p_1 = p_2 = 0$; with the elevation datum through point 2, $z_2 = 0$, $z_1 = H$. The velocity on the surface of the reservoir is zero (practically); hence:

$$0 + 0 + H = \frac{v_2^2}{2g} + 0 + 0$$

and

$$v_2 = \sqrt{2gH} = \sqrt{2 \times 9.806 \times 4} = 8.86 \text{ m/s}$$

which states that the velocity of efflux is equal to the velocity of free fall from the surface of the reservoir. This is known as Torricelli's theorem.

(b) The discharge Q is the product of velocity of efflux and area of stream:

$$Q = A_2 v_2 = \pi \, (0.05 \text{ m})^2 \, (8.86 \text{ m/s}) = 0.07 \text{ m}^3/\text{s} = 70 \text{ l/s}.$$

MOMENTUM

In many fluid flow problems, the total force on a solid object or wall is desired, for example, in determining the required bolt strength on flanges in a piping system, or the total thrust produced by a jet engine. The control volume or integral technique may be applied here by utilizing the law of conservation of linear momentum.

The result is the integral conservation of momentum law for a control volume,

$$\frac{d}{dt}\iiint_{cv} \rho v \, dv + \iint_{cs} \rho v (v_r \cdot \mathbf{n}) dA = \sum \mathbf{F}$$

where v_r is the velocity of the fluid relative to the control surface, $\mathbf{n}$ is the unit outward normal vector, and $\sum \mathbf{F}$ is the total force acting on the control volume when the control volume is considered as a free body. Note that this equation is a *vector* equation, and thus represents in general three components that may have to be evaluated separately.

In most cases, the control volume is fixed, $v_r = v$, and the equation above reduces to

$$\frac{\partial}{\partial t}\iiint_{cv} \rho v \, dv + \iint_{cs} \rho v (v_r \cdot \mathbf{n}) dA = \sum \mathbf{F}$$

The technique for solving problems with the integral conservation of momentum equation involves first choosing an appropriate control volume, then determining the flux terms and (if nonzero) the unsteady control volume term. Typically, the unknown—some force on the right-hand side of the equation above—can then be obtained.

In general, the force term consists of surface forces due to pressure and friction, body forces such as gravity (and possibly electromagnetic forces), and other forces acting on the control surface such as the tension force in a bolt through which the control surface is sliced. It is important to keep two facts in mind:

1) $\sum \mathbf{F}$ is the *vector* sum of all forces acting on the control volume, and

2) $\sum \mathbf{F}$ include(s) *all* forces acting on both solid and fluid material in the control volume.

It is usually best to draw a free-body diagram of the control volume, showing all forces acting on it. If the desired result is the force acting on a solid wall *by* the fluid flow, remember to change the sign since any force in the equation above must be applied on the control volume or control surface.

For flowfields involving sections of pipe flow as inlets or exits, the surface integral in the equation above reduces to:

$$\iint_{cs} \rho v(v \cdot \mathbf{n})dA = \sum_{\text{outlets}} \dot{m}v - \sum_{\text{inlets}} \dot{m}v$$

where $\dot{m} = \rho Q$.

Also, for such sections, the pressure is typically constant over the cross-sectional area A; thus, the pressure force on the area is simply pA acting in the direction opposite to the unit outward normal vector $\mathbf{n}$. Although absolute pressure is implied in the above, gage pressure is often more convenient since atmospheric pressure may be subtracted uniformly over the entire control surface without changing the problem.

EXAMPLE

Consider a jet that is deflected by a stationary vane, such as is given in Figure 13. If the jet speed and diameter are 100 ft/s and 1 in., respectively, and the jet is deflected 60°, what force is exerted on the vane by the jet?

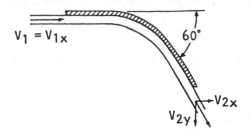

Figure 13. Flow of jet in stationary vane

SOLUTION

$$F_x = \sum_{cs} \mu \rho v \cdot A + \frac{d}{dt} \int_{cv} \mu \rho dv \tag{1}$$

If the flow is steady, the second term on the right of equation (1) will be zero, which leaves the following:

$$F_x = \sum_{cs} \mu \rho v \cdot A \tag{2}$$

At section 1, the velocity is constant over the section and the area vector A_1 is in the reverse direction of the velocity vector v. Therefore, for this part of the control surface, we have:

$$\sum_{cs} \mu \rho v \cdot A = v_{1x} \rho \left(-v_1 A_1 \right).$$

By a similar analysis for section 2 (in this case, the velocity v_2 and area A_2 have the same sense), we get:

$$\sum_{cs} \mu \rho v \cdot A = v_{2x} \rho v_2 A_2.$$

However, $v_1 A_1 = v_2 A_2 = Q$, so when these substitutions are made, equation (2) becomes:

$$F_x = \rho Q (v_{2x} - v_{1x}). \tag{3}$$

In a similar manner the force in the y direction, F_y, will be:

$$F_y = \rho Q (v_{2y} - v_{1y}). \tag{4}$$

Since the forces given by equations (3) and (4) are the forces exerted by the vane on the jet, we obtain the forces of the jet on the vane by simply reversing the sign on F_x and F_y. First solve for F_x, the x component of force of the vane on the jet, by using equation (3):

$$F_x = \rho Q (v_{2x} - v_{1x}). \tag{3}$$

Here, the final velocity component in the x direction is:

$$v_{2x} = 100 \cos 60° \text{ ft/s}.$$

Hence,

$$v_{2x} = 100 \times 0.500 = 50 \text{ ft/s}$$

also,

$$v_{1x} = 100 \text{ ft/s}$$

and

$$Q = v_1 A_1 = 100 \, \frac{0.785}{144} = 0.545 \text{ ft}^3/\text{s}.$$

Therefore,

$$F_x = 1.94 \text{ lbf-s}^2/\text{ft}^4 \times 0.545 \text{ ft}^3/\text{s} \times (50 - 100) \text{ ft/s} = -52.9 \text{ lbf}.$$

Similarly determined, the y component of force on the jet is:

$$F_y = 1.94 \text{ lbf-s}^2/\text{ft}^4 \times 0.545 \text{ ft}^3/\text{s} \times (-86.6 \text{ ft/s} - 0) = -91.6 \text{ lbf}$$

Then the force on the vane will be the reactions to the forces of the vane on the jet, or:

$$F_x = +52.9 \text{ lbf}$$
$$F_y = +91.6 \text{ lbf}$$

DIMENSIONAL ANALYSIS AND SIMILITUDE

It is generally desirable to express a given set of dimensional variables in a flowfield in terms of dimensionless parameters (or "Pi's"). These parameters provide universal measures of flow regimes and effectively reduce the number of independent variables. They are also necessary in order to obtain scaling laws to predict prototype performance based on measurements on a (typically smaller) model. Examples of dimensionless parameters are given in Table 2.

TABLE 2 FORCE RATIOS		
Name of Ratio	**Definition**	**Physical Meaning**
Reynolds number, Re	$\dfrac{v\ell\rho}{\mu}$	$\dfrac{\text{Inertia force}}{\text{Viscous force}}$
Froude number, Fr	$\dfrac{v^2}{(\ell g)}$	$\dfrac{\text{Inertia force}}{\text{Gravity force}}$
Weber number, We	$\dfrac{v^2\ell\rho}{\sigma}$	$\dfrac{\text{Inertia force}}{\text{Surface tension force}}$
Mach number, M	$\dfrac{v}{a}$	$\dfrac{\text{Inertia force}}{\text{Elastic force}}$
Euler number, Eu	$\dfrac{\Delta\rho}{\rho v^2}$	$\dfrac{\text{Pressure force}}{\text{Inertia force}}$

The Buckingham Pi technique provides a systematic way to determine dimensionless parameters from a given set of dimensional variables. The following procedure is invoked in the Buckingham Pi technique:

1) Count the total number of variables, n.

2) List the dimensions of each variable (as shown in Table 3). This is typically done in terms of the four primary dimensions—mass, length, time, and temperature. Alternately, force can replace mass as a primary dimension.

3) Count the total number of primary dimensions (typically three or four), and let j equal this number. Note: If the dimensional analysis fails in the steps below, return here, decrease j by one, and then repeat the analysis.

4) You now expect to find $k = n - j$ dimensionless parameters $\Pi_1, \Pi_2, ..., \Pi_k$. To find these, you first need to select j variables as "repeating variables." Choose variables that do not by themselves form a dimensionless group, but that represent all of the primary dimensions involved in the problem. There are "preferred" choices, such as velocity and density, which will generate recognizable Πs, such as the Reynolds number, etc.

5) Form a power product consisting of the j repeating variables and each of the remaining k variables. By forcing the exponent of each dimension to be zero, $\Pi_1, \Pi_2, ..., \Pi_k$ are found.

Note that although your Πs may be dimensionless, they may not be of a form suitable for your particular application. It is perfectly valid to multiply or divide two or more Πs together to form a new Π set. In fact, since each Π by itself is dimensionless, any Π multiplied by another Π raised to any exponent must also be dimensionless. The new set of Πs formed in this manner is no more or less valid than the first set; the "correct" set is that which is most suitable to the problem at hand. Note also that such a rearrangement of parameters may be used sometimes to obtain "standard" Πs such as the Reynolds number, the Froude number, etc., even if these do not result directly from your dimensional analysis.

The best way to learn this technique is to practice on many problems. True dynamic similarity between a model and a prototype can only exist if each Π for the model exactly matches the corresponding Π of the prototype. When such is the case, it is possible to scale up from the model to the prototype to predict its performance. These concepts of dimensional analysis and similitude are thus of paramount significance to designers who test small models before building a full-scale prototype.

TABLE 3 DIMENSIONS OF FLUID-MECHANICS QUANTITIES			
		Dimensions	
Quantity	*Symbol*	*(MLT Θ)*	*(FLT Θ)*
Angle	θ	None	None
Angular velocity	ω	T^{-1}	T^{-1}
Area	A	L^2	L^2
Density	ρ	ML^{-3}	FT^2L^{-4}
Force	F	MLT^{-2}	F
Kinematic viscosity	v	L^2T^{-1}	L^2T^{-1}
Length	L	L	L
Mass flux	$\dot{m}$	MT^{-1}	FTL^{-1}
Moment, torque	M, T	ML^2T^{-2}	FL
Power	P	ML^2T^{-3}	FLT^{-1}
Pressure, stress	p, τ	$ML^{-1}T^{-2}$	FL^{-2}
Specific heat	c_p, c_v	$L^2T^{-2}\,\Theta^{-1}$	$L^2T^{-2}\,\Theta^{-1}$
Speed of sound	a	LT^{-1}	LT^{-1}
Strain rate	i	T^{-1}	T^{-1}
Surface tension	σ	MT^{-2}	FL^{-1}
Temperature	T	Θ	Θ
Thermal conductivity	k	$MLT^{-3}\,\Theta^{-1}$	$FT^{-1}\,\Theta^{-1}$
Velocity	v	LT^{-1}	LT^{-1}
Viscosity	μ	$ML^{-1}T^{-1}$	FTL^{-2}
Volume	v	L^3	L^3
Volume flux	Q	L^3T^{-1}	L^3T^{-1}

EXAMPLE

The thrust F of a screw propeller is known to depend upon the diameter d, speed of advance v, fluid density ρ, revolutions per second N, and the coefficient of viscosity μ of the fluid. Find an expression for F in terms of these quantities.

SOLUTION

The general relationship must be $F = \phi(d, v, \rho, N, \mu)$, (where ϕ represents "a function of"), which can be expanded as the sum of an infinite series of terms giving:

$$F = A\left(d^m v^P \rho^q N^r \mu^s\right) + B\left(d^{m'} v^{P'} \rho^{q'} N^{r'} \mu^{s'}\right) + \dots,$$

where A, B, etc. are numerical constants and m, p, q, r, and s are unknown powers. Since, for dimensional homogeneity, all terms must be dimensionally the same, this can be reduced to:

$$F = Kd^m v^P \rho^q N^r \mu^s \qquad (1)$$

where K is a numerical constant.

The dimensions of the dependent variable F and the independent variables d, v, ρ, N, and μ are

$$[F] = [\text{Force}] = [MLT^{-2}]$$
$$[d] = [\text{Diameter}] = [L]$$
$$[v] = [\text{Velocity}] = [LT^{-1}]$$
$$[\rho] = [\text{Mass density}] = [ML^{-3}]$$
$$[N] = [\text{Rotational speed}] = [T^{-1}]$$
$$[\mu] = [\text{Dynamic viscosity}] = [ML^{-1}T^{-1}]$$

Substituting the dimensions for the variables in (1),

$$[MLT^{-2}] = [L]^m [LT^{-1}]^P [ML^{-3}]^q [T^{-1}]^r [ML^{-1}T^{-1}]^s.$$

Equating powers of $[M]$, $[L]$, and $[T]$:

$$[M], \quad 1 = q + s; \qquad (2)$$
$$[L], \quad 1 = m + p - 3q - s; \qquad (3)$$
$$[T], \quad -2 = -p - r - s. \qquad (4)$$

Since there are five unknown powers and only three equations, it is impossible to obtain a complete solution, but three unknowns can be determined in terms of the remaining two. If we solve for p and q, we get

$q = 1 - s$ from (2)

$p = 2 - r - s$ from (4)

$m = 1 - p + 3q + s = 2 + r - s$ substituting (2) and (4) into (3).

Substituting these values in (1),

$$F = Kd^{2+r-s}v^{2-r-s}\rho^{1-s}N^r\mu^s,$$

and regrouping the powers,

$$F = K\rho v^2 d^2 \left(\frac{\rho v d}{\mu}\right)^{-s} \left(\frac{dN}{v}\right)^r$$

Since s and r are unknown, this can be written

$$F = K\rho v^2 d^2 \phi\left\{\frac{\rho v d}{\mu}, \frac{dN}{v}\right\}. \tag{5}$$

At first sight, this appears to be a rather unsatisfactory solution, and (5) indicates that:

$$F = KC\rho v^2 d^2$$

where C is a constant to be determined experimentally and is dependent on the values of $\dfrac{\rho v d}{\mu}$ and $\dfrac{dN}{V}$.

EXAMPLE

A marine research facility uses a towing basin to test models of proposed ship hull configurations. A new hull shape utilizing a bulbous underwater bow is proposed for a nuclear-powered aircraft carrier that is to be 300 m long. A 3-m model has been tested in the towing tank and was found to have a maximum practical hull speed of 1.4 m/s. What is the anticipated hull speed for the prototype?

SOLUTION

In the study of ship hulls, surface tension and compressibility effects are not significant. Therefore, for geometrically similar bodies, dynamic similarity occurs when:

$$\left(\frac{v^2}{\ell g}\right)_m = \left(\frac{v^2}{\ell g}\right)_p \quad \text{and} \quad \left(\frac{\rho v \ell}{\mu}\right)_m = \left(\frac{\rho v \ell}{\mu}\right)_p$$

Experience has shown that the Froude number is of greater significance than the Reynolds number in this particular application. Thus, the fluid used in the towing tank is generally water. The Froude number alone is maintained between model and prototype, and empirical corrections are made to compensate for the differences that exist between the Reynolds numbers.

Hence, we ignore the viscous effects, as measured by the Reynolds number, and concentrate on the hull's wave-making characteristics, as measured by the Froude number:

$$\left(\frac{v^2}{\ell g}\right)_m = \left(\frac{v^2}{\ell g}\right)_p$$

Since the gravitational acceleration is the same for model and prototype, the anticipated prototype velocity becomes:

$$v_p = v_m \left(\frac{\ell_p}{\ell_m}\right)^{\frac{1}{2}}$$

or

$$v_p = 1.4 \text{ m/s} \left(\frac{300 \text{ m}}{3 \text{ m}}\right)^{\frac{1}{2}} = 14 \text{ m/s}$$

PIPE FLOW AND CHANNEL FLOW

Fluid flow can be categorized into two fundamental types: internal (or bounded) flow and external (or unbounded) flow. This chapter considers the former, where the flow is surrounded by walls, as in the flow of water through a pipe. An important dimensionless parameter in pipe flows is the **Reynolds number**, defined as

$$\text{Re} = \frac{\rho v d}{\mu} = \frac{v d}{\nu},$$

where

      v = The average velocity through a cross section of the pipe

      d = The pipe diameter

μ = The viscosity

ρ = the density

ν = The kinematic viscosity $\left(\nu = \dfrac{\mu}{\rho} \right)$

Average velocity is simply the volume flow rate Q divided by cross-sectional area $\dfrac{\pi d^2}{4}$. For pipe flows where Re is less than about 2,300, the flow is **laminar**, i.e., smooth and steady. For Re $\geq$ 2,300, the pipe flow becomes **turbulent**, i.e., unsteady, three-dimensional, and irregular fluctuating eddies or vortices. Laminar pipe flows can be predicted analytically, while experiments must be used to guide any attempts at analyzing turbulent flow. Most practical pipe flow problems are turbulent.

For flow along a pipe, the steady one-dimensional energy equation may be applied:

$$\frac{p_1}{\rho g} + \alpha_1 \frac{v_1^2}{2g} + z_1 = \frac{p_2}{\rho g} + \alpha_2 \frac{v_2^2}{2g} + z_2 + \frac{\dot{W_s}}{\dot{m} g} + h_{total}$$

where,

$\dot{W_s}$ = The shaft power (work per unit time) done by the fluid,

z = The vertical height,

$\dot{m}$ = The mass flow rate through the pipe,

α = The kinetic energy correction factor, and

h_{total} = The total head loss (dimensions of length) from inlet 1 to outlet 2.

$\dot{W_s}$ is positive for a turbine, which draws power *from* the fluid, but negative for a pump, which supplies power *to* the fluid. The total head loss is typically split into two parts:

$$h_{total} = \sum h_f + \sum h_m$$

The first term on the right is the sum of all the Moody-type frictional losses. These losses are associated with frictional losses along the inner wall of long, straight sections of pipe. The Moody Chart is a collection of semi-empirically obtained values of the frictional loss as a function of

Reynolds number Re and pipe roughness factor $\dfrac{\varepsilon}{d}$. These losses are plotted in terms of the nondimensional Darcy friction factor f:

$$f = \frac{h_f}{\left(\dfrac{L}{d}\right)\left(\dfrac{v^2}{2g}\right)},$$

where L is the total length of the pipe.

The following steps should be taken to determine the head loss with known conditions:

(1) Evaluate the Reynolds number.

(2) Obtain the relative roughness, $\dfrac{\varepsilon}{d}$, from the Moody Chart.

(3) Obtain the friction factor, f, using the appropriate curve from the Moody Chart.

(4) Find the head loss using the friction factor.

The friction factor for laminar flow (Re < 2,300) can be approximated by:

$$f = \frac{64}{Re}.$$

The most common method of determining friction factor in turbulent flow is by use of the Moody Chart. It can also be approximated by the Swamee & Jain equation:

$$f = \frac{0.25}{\left[\log_{10}\left(\dfrac{\varepsilon/d}{3.7} + \dfrac{5.74}{Re^{0.9}}\right)\right]^2}.$$

The second component of h_{total} comes from the so-called "minor" losses. These are losses associated with parts of the piping system other than long, straight pipe sections, such as valves, bends, or elbows, sudden changes in pipe diameter, inlets, exits, etc. Again, empirical values of these losses can be obtained from tables or charts. The nondimensional minor loss coefficient K is typically the listed value, defined as:

$$K = \frac{h_m}{\dfrac{v^2}{(2g)}}$$

For a constant diameter section of the pipe system, $\sum h_m$ is simply $v^2/(2g)$ multiplied by $\sum K$, the sum of all the minor loss coefficients along the pipe section.

For pipes of different diameters in *series*, volume flow rate Q must be the same along each section (for steady flow in the mean), and h_f and h_m must be summed independently in each section, then added to obtain the total head loss h_{total}. For pipes in *parallel*, however, the volume flow rate may be different in each parallel section. If the parallel pipes branch off at one point A and later rejoin at a point B as shown in Figure 14:

$$Q_A = Q_B = Q_1 + Q_2 + Q_3,$$

whereas the total head, along any of the three pipes from A to B must be identical since p_A and p_B are the same regardless of which pipe (1, 2, or 3) is under consideration. Another general rule is that the net volume flow rate into any junction must be zero, analogous to the statement that the net current into any junction in an electrical circuit must be zero. Also, the net head loss around any closed loop must be zero, just as in electrical circuits the net voltage drop around any closed loop must be zero.

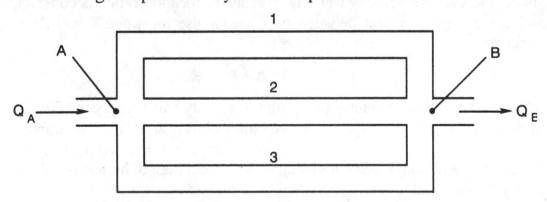

Figure 14. Parallel pipe system

For pipes with a cross section other than circular, the **hydraulic diameter** is defined as:

$$D_h = \frac{4A}{P},$$

where

A = The cross-sectional area

P = The wetted perimeter

Wetted perimeter refers to the portion of the perimeter in contact with the fluid. Once D_h has been calculated, the Moody Chart can be used to obtain friction factors based on D_h, which is basically the diameter of an equivalent round pipe that would give the same losses as the actual nonround pipe.

Open channel flow is somewhat similar to pipe flow except that, with a free surface exposed to atmospheric pressure, there can be no streamwise pressure gradient. The fluid flows due to gravity alone, with the flow rate determined by a balance between gravitational and frictional forces. A reasonable analysis can be obtained by using the Moody Chart for pipe flow with the hydraulic diameter of the channel. Instead, engineers prefer the **hydraulic radius**, defined as one-fourth of the hydraulic diameter:

$$\text{hydraulic radius} = R_h = \frac{A}{P} = \frac{D_h}{4},$$

where

A = The cross-sectional area of the fluid in the channel

P = The wetted perimeter (which does *not* include the free surface)

For uniform flow in long, straight, inclined channels of a constant shape, the average velocity v at any streamwise location remains constant, and the energy equation between two streamwise locations 1 and 2 reduces to:

$$h_f = y_1 - y_2 = L \sin \alpha,$$

where h_f is the frictional head loss which is exactly balanced by the change in surface height $y_1 - y_2$. In the equation above, L is the streamwise distance from 1 to 2 and α is the inclination angle with respect to the horizontal. Frictional head loss can also be expressed in terms of the Darcy friction factor f as:

$$h_f = f \frac{Lv^2}{8gR_h}.$$

Combining the last two equations, and introducing the Chézy constant $C = \left(\dfrac{8g}{f}\right)^{\frac{1}{2}}$, the velocity in the channel is found:

$$v = C(R_h S)^{\frac{1}{2}} = C(R_h \sin \alpha)^{\frac{1}{2}},$$

where S is the slope or hydraulic gradient. Typically, volume flow rate Q is the unknown in a channel flow problem. The procedure is to find the Chézy constant C for the given channel, and then to use the above equation to find v. Finally, Q = volume flow rate = vA.

In some cases, direct empirical relationships for C are available, but in most cases, C is found by the Manning correlation:

$$C = \frac{1.49}{n} R_h^{\frac{1}{6}} \ (R \text{ in units of feet}),$$

when n is the Manning coefficient, a nondimensional roughness coefficient that can be obtained from empirical tables.

In practice, the calculation of Chézy's coefficient can be bypassed by combining the equation for velocity and the Manning correlation:

$$v = \frac{1.49}{n} R_h^{\frac{2}{3}} (\sin \alpha)^{\frac{1}{2}} \ (R_h \text{ in ft, } v \text{ in ft/s})$$

or

$$v = \frac{1.0}{n} R_h^{\frac{2}{3}} (\sin \alpha)^{\frac{1}{2}} \ (R_h \text{ in m, } v \text{ in m/s}).$$

To find the volume flow rate, look up n for the channel (n depends greatly on the amount of roughness on the walls of the channel), calculate v using the appropriate equation above for inclination angle α and hydraulic radius R_h, and finally calculate $Q = vA$.

Another feature unique to open channel flows is the hydraulic jump. Here, a high-velocity supercritical flow (the Froude number is greater than one) is suddenly slowed to subcritical ($F_r < 1$) as the fluid depth increases and the velocity decreases across the hydraulic jump. The ratio of fluid heights downstream (y_2) and upstream (y_1) of a stationary hydraulic jump is:

$$\frac{y_2}{y_1} = \frac{1}{2}\left[\left(1 + 8F_{r_1}^2\right)^{\frac{1}{2}} - 1\right]$$

where F_{r_1} is the Froude number upstream:

$$F_{r_1} = \left[\frac{v_1^2}{(y_1 g)} \right]^{\frac{1}{2}}.$$

In problems where the hydraulic jump is not stationary as, for example, with a surge caused by a sudden gate closure, it is most convenient to transform the frame of reference to that of a stationary hydraulic jump, apply the fluid height ratio above, and then transform back to the original frame of reference.

EXAMPLE

A water transmission pipe having the diameter shown conducts water with flow rate of 0.5 m³/s. The relative roughness of the pipe, $\frac{\varepsilon}{D}$, is 3×10^{-3}. Find the pressure loss over unit length of the pipe.

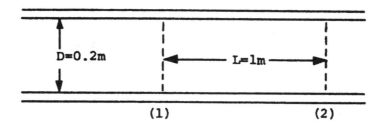

Figure 15. Dimensions of pipe

SOLUTION

Applying the general flow equation to compute the total head loss,

$$h_{\text{total}} = \frac{p_1}{\rho g} + \alpha_1 \frac{v_1^2}{2g} + h_1 - \frac{p_2}{\rho g} - \alpha_2 \frac{v_2^2}{2g} - h_2. \tag{1}$$

Assuming that the pipe is horizontal, then $h_1 = h_2$. With uniform internal pipe cross section, $v_1 = v_2$ since $A_1 = A_2$, and flow rate Q is constant throughout the pipe length. Substituting these conditions into (1), we obtain:

$$h_{\text{total}} = \frac{1}{\rho g}(p_1 - p_2) \tag{2}$$

Now,

$$h_{\text{total}} = f \frac{L}{D} \frac{v^2}{2g} \tag{3}$$

and, therefore,

$$p_1 - p_2 = \rho h g = f \rho \frac{L}{d} \frac{v^2}{2}. \tag{4}$$

The friction factor, f, is a function of the Reynolds number and the relative roughness, $\frac{\varepsilon}{d}$. The Reynolds number, Re, is obtained from:

$$\text{Re} = \frac{\rho v d}{\mu}. \tag{5}$$

The velocity of flow may be calculated from the flow rate equation:

$$v = \frac{Q}{A} = \frac{0.5}{\pi(0.1)^2} = 15.95 \, \text{m/s}$$

The parameters $\rho = 9.99 \times 10^2$ Kg/m^3 and $\mu = 10 \times 10^{-4}$ Kg/m-sec can be assumed for water at 20°C. The Reynolds number, therefore, becomes

$$\text{Re} = \frac{\left(9.99 \times 10^2\right)(0.2)(15.95)}{10 \times 10^{-4}}$$
$$= 3.18 \times 10^6$$

Referring to the Moody Chart to obtain the friction factor when knowing the Reynolds number and the relative roughness, we find $f = 0.014$. Substituting values into equation (4),

$$p_1 - p_2 = \frac{(0.014)\left(9.99 \times 10^2\right)\left(15.95^2\right)}{(0.2)(2)}$$
$$= 8.89 \times 10^3 \, Pa$$

EXAMPLE

What slope is required to produce a flow of 400 m^3/s at a uniform depth of 4 m in a trapezoidal earth channel with a base width of 6 m and side slopes of 1 vertical on 2 horizontal? Use a Manning coefficient of $n = 0.025$.

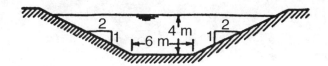

Figure 16. Dimensions of channel

SOLUTION

The Chézy formula is:

$$Q = AC\sqrt{R_h S}. \qquad (1)$$

The Manning correlation is:

$$C = 1.5\frac{R_h^{\frac{1}{6}}}{n}. \qquad (2)$$

The hydraulic radius is:

$$R_h = \frac{A}{P} = \frac{\dfrac{4(22+6)}{2}}{6+2\sqrt{4^2+8^2}} = \frac{56}{23.9} = 2.34\,\text{m}.$$

From equation (2),

$$C = 1.5\frac{R_h^{\frac{1}{6}}}{n} = 1.5\frac{2.34^{\frac{1}{6}}}{0.025} = 69.$$

Hence, upon solving equation (1) for S,

$$S = \frac{Q^2}{C^2 A^2 R_h} = \frac{400^2}{69^2 \times 56^2 \times 2.34} = 0.0046.$$

FLOW MEASUREMENT

There are two categories of devices that measure fluid flows: local velocity meters and volume flow meters. In addition, manometers are used to measure pressure in fluid flows as discussed previously in the fluid statics section.

Consider now the **pitot tube**, which is simply a slender tube with a hole in the front, aligned with the flow. The pressure at the nose of any body in an incompressible flow is the stagnation pressure p_o. Thus, p_o can be measured by connecting the opposite end of the pitot tube to a pressure meter (such as a manometer). The static pressure p can also be measured in a flow, either by a separate pressure tap or with additional holes in the pitot probe itself.

Bernoulli's equation is used to calculate the velocity from the pressure difference between p_o and p as follows (neglecting gravity):

$$p_o = p + \frac{1}{2}\rho v^2,$$

hence,

$$v = \left(\frac{2(p_o - p)}{\rho}\right)^{\frac{1}{2}}.$$

The pitot tube and pitot-static tube (which contains holes for both stagnation and static pressure) are local-velocity meters since they can easily be traversed through the fluid flow. Often it is only necessary to measure the volume flow rate in a pipe flow. The three most common volume flow meters are the orifice meter, the venturi meter, and the flow nozzle. All three work on the principle that pressure in an incompressible flow decreases as the velocity increases through a throat of a smaller area than the pipe's cross-sectional area. This is nothing more than Bernoulli's equation, and so the three devices are called Bernoulli obstruction devices.

In all three devices, a static pressure tap is located near the throat, and a second tap is located just upstream of the device. If there were no losses, the pressure difference between these two would give the average velocity (and, hence, the volume flow rate) by Bernoulli's equation and the integral conservation of mass. Of course, fluid that flows through any real device will not be inviscid, and frictional losses are taken into account through a **discharge coefficient** C_d which is always less than 1.0. (Empirical formulae for C_d can be obtained for any of the three devices.) The final expression for the volume flow rate is:

$$Q = C_d A_t \left[\frac{2(p_1 - p_2)}{\rho(1 - \beta^4)}\right]^{\frac{1}{2}},$$

Fluids

where

p_1 and p_2 = The pressure upstream of the throat and near the throat respectively,

A_t = The throat (minimum) area, and

β = The ratio of the throat diameter to the upstream pipe diameter.

Three coefficients commonly used with volume flow meters are defined as follows. The coefficient of contraction is defined as:

$$C_c = \frac{A_v}{A_t},$$

where

A_v = Area contracted and

A_t = Meter throat area.

The coefficient of velocity is defined as:

$$C_v = \frac{v_{2\text{actual}}}{v_{2\text{ideal}}},$$

where

$v_{2\text{actual}}$ = Actual mean velocity of the flow

$v_{2\text{ideal}}$ = Ideal velocity (no friction).

The coefficient of discharge is defined as:

$$C_d = \frac{Q_{\text{actual}}}{Q_{\text{ideal}}},$$

where

Q_{actual} = Actual flow rate

Q_{ideal} = Ideal flow rate,

also

$$C_d = C_v C_c.$$

Note: The value of the coefficients are determined experimentally.

A **weir** is an obstruction in the bottom of a channel over which the flow must deflect. The volume flow rate per unit width, q, is proportional to $H^{\frac{3}{2}}$ for a sharp-crested weir, i.e.:

$$q = \frac{2}{3} C_W (2g)^{\frac{1}{2}} H^{\frac{3}{2}},$$

where H is the height of the upstream flow above the crest of the weir, and C_W is the weir coefficient. The weir coefficient is an empirically determined coefficient that accounts for the losses associated with end effects, friction, etc. Typically,

$$C_W \approx 0.611 + \frac{0.075H}{Y},$$

where Y is the height of the crest of the weir. Once q is determined, the total discharge (or volume flow rate) Q is then simply q multiplied by the width of the weir.

For a broad-crested weir, i.e., one with a flat top, the surface of the fluid on top of the weir usually sinks to a height h above the crest, where $h \approx \frac{2H}{3}$. The discharge q per unit width then becomes:

$$q = c(2g)^{\frac{1}{2}} h^{\frac{3}{2}},$$

where c is the discharge coefficient of the weir, which must be empirically determined and is usually tabulated as a function of weir geometry (c also varies with h).

For flow through small orifices, the flow rate, Q, is given by

$$Q = C_D a (2gh)^{\frac{1}{2}}$$

where

a = The cross-sectional area of the orifice,

h = The difference in the head from one side of the orifice to the other, and

C_D = A discharge coefficient which again must be determined empirically.

EXTERNAL FLOW

The *no-slip* boundary condition requires that the velocity of a fluid immediately adjacent to a solid wall be equal to the velocity of the wall itself. In the usual frame of reference where the wall is stationary with fluid flowing over it, the fluid velocity right next to the wall must be zero. This no-slip condition leads to what is referred to as a **boundary layer**. A boundary layer is a thin fluid layer near the wall which experiences velocity variations. Inside a boundary layer, the fluid velocity goes from some finite value at the boundary layer edge to zero at the wall in a very short distance. Since viscous shear stress is proportional to viscosity μ and velocity gradient, the shear stress is quite large in a boundary layer, especially very close to the wall where the velocity gradient is steepest. This shear stress, by Newton's third law, imposes a frictional drag force on the wall in the same direction as the flow above the boundary layer.

Boundary layers can be either laminar (smooth and steady) or turbulent (quite unsteady and irregular). For uniform flow along a semi-infinite flat plate, the laminar boundary layer solution can be obtained exactly (albeit with the help of a digital computer), but turbulent boundary layers are too complex to solve exactly, even with the fastest computers. Turbulent boundary layer results are found empirically or semi-empirically.

For engineering analyses, the three quantities of most significance are the boundary layer thickness δ, the skin friction coefficient C_f, and the displacement thickness δ^*. δ^* is usually defined as the distance from the wall where the velocity μ has increased to 99 percent of the freestream velocity v. Letting τ_w denote the shear stress acting on the wall by the fluid, C_f is the skin friction coefficient:

$$C_f = \frac{2\tau_w}{\rho v^2}.$$

Displacement thickness is defined as the distance to which streamlines outside the boundary layer are displaced away from the wall, and results from the fact that the fluid inside the boundary layer carries less mass flow than it would have in the absence of the wall. See Figures 17 and 18. The displacement thickness is:

$$\delta^* = \int_0^\infty \left(1 - \frac{u}{v}\right) dy.$$

For laminar flow on a flat plate, expressions for δ, C_f, and δ^* to be used for engineering calculations according to the Blasius solution are:

$$\frac{\delta}{x} \qquad C_f \qquad \frac{\delta *}{x}$$

$$\frac{4.91}{\text{Re}_x^{\frac{1}{2}}} \quad \frac{1.328}{\text{Re}_x^{\frac{1}{2}}} \quad \frac{1.73}{\text{Re}_x^{\frac{1}{2}}}$$

where $\text{Re}_x = v\dfrac{x}{n}$ is the Reynolds number based on the length from the plate leading edge.

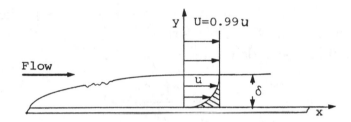

Figure 17. Boundary layer thickness

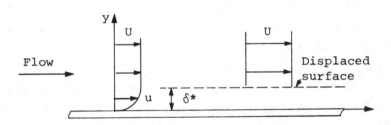

Figure 18. Displacement thickness

At a Reynolds number greater than about 300,000 based on v and x (the distance along the plate in the flow direction), the laminar boundary layer begins to oscillate and becomes turbulent. Empirical expressions for δ, C_f, and $\delta *$ can be found in the literature for turbulent flow.

Skin friction is not the only source of drag on bodies—such as automobiles, baseballs, submarines, and airplanes—moving through a fluid. The uneven distribution of pressure forces along the body surface can produce significant (often dominating) drag forces as well. For nonstreamlined or blunt bodies in particular, the boundary layer along the body surface cannot remain attached and separates off the surface. This leads to a gross imbalance of pressure (pressure being very high on the front end and very low on the back end of the body) and a large pressure drag.

The total aerodynamic drag on a body usually must be found by experimentation. Drag is expressed nondimensionally by a **drag coefficient**, C_D, defined as:

$$C_D = \frac{\text{Drag Force}}{\frac{1}{2}\rho v^2 A}$$

where

v = The freestream velocity

A = An area,

typically the projected frontal area, but sometimes (as in the case of airplane wings or flat plates) the platform area as listed in the last table. The drag coefficient has been determined to be:

$$C_D = \frac{1.328}{\sqrt{\text{Re}_x}}$$

for laminar boundary layer flow over a flat plate.

In general, a flow with a laminar boundary layer produces much less skin friction drag than a flow with a turbulent boundary layer. However, turbulent boundary layers are much more resilient to flow separation, and hence can lead to less pressure drag. In engineering analysis, one can sometimes force the flow to be turbulent in order to decrease the overall drag. The dimples on a golf ball are one such example. The dimples force the boundary layer to be turbulent, which delays separation and decreases the pressure drag. Since pressure drag dominates on bluff bodies such as spheres, the net effect is a decrease in total drag.

Lift, an upward force that is exerted on an object as it passes through a fluid, can be analyzed in much the same way as drag. Namely, a lift coefficient, C_L, is defined as:

$$C_L = \frac{\text{Lift Force}}{\frac{1}{2}\rho v^2 A}.$$

EXAMPLE

Air at 100°F is flowing over a flat plate 1 m wide. Estimate the boundary layer thickness 1 m from the leading edge. Also, determine the drag force. The air speed is 7.2 m/s.

SOLUTION

The boundary layer thickness δ can be estimated from the equation:

$$\frac{\delta}{x} = \frac{5}{\sqrt{Re_x}}$$

The kinematic viscosity of air at 100°F is $v = 1.8 \times 10^{-4}$ m²/sec. The density is $\rho = 2.20 \times 10^{-3}$ kg/m³. Therefore,

$$Re_x = \frac{v_0 x}{v} = \frac{7.2 \times 1}{1.8 \times 10^{-4}} = 4 \times 10^4$$

and

$$\delta = \frac{5 \times 1}{2 \times 10^2}\, m = 0.025 \text{ m.}$$

In general, the drag coefficient is:

$$C_D = \frac{\text{drag}}{\dfrac{1}{2}\rho v^2 A}$$

where

v = The upstream velocity and

A = The cross-sectional area.

For laminar boundary layer flow over a flat plate, the drag coefficient has been found to be:

$$C_D = \frac{1.328}{\sqrt{Re_x}}.$$

Therefore:

$$C_D = \frac{1.328}{\sqrt{4 \times 10^4}}$$
$$= 6.6 \times 10^{-3},$$

and the drag force is:

$$\text{Drag} = 0.5\rho\, C_D v^2 A$$
$$= (0.5)(2.2 \times 10^{-3})(6.6 \times 10^{-3})(7.2^2)(1^2)$$
$$= 3.8 \times 10^{-4} \text{ N}$$

EXAMPLE

A parachutist weighs 175 N and has a projected frontal area of 2 m² in free fall. His drag coefficient based on frontal area is found to be 0.80. If the air temperature is 70°F, determine his terminal velocity.

SOLUTION

It is convenient to express the drag of a bluff body in terms of a nondimensional parameter, C_D, called drag coefficient:

$$C_D = \frac{\text{Drag}}{\frac{1}{2}\rho v^2 A}$$

or

$$\text{Drag} = C_D \frac{1}{2}\rho v^2 A,$$

with A the projected frontal area of the bluff body normal to the flow direction.

At terminal velocity, the parachutist's weight is balanced by his drag:

$$W = C_D \frac{1}{2}\rho v^2 A$$

The density of air at normal atmospheric pressure and 70°F is $\rho = 0.00233$ kg/m³. Therefore,

$$v^2 = \frac{W}{C_D \left(\frac{1}{2}\right)\rho A}$$

$$= \frac{175}{0.80\left(\frac{1}{2}\right)(0.00233)(2)}$$

and

$$v_{\text{terminal}} = 30 \text{ m/s}$$

COMPRESSIBLE FLOW

There are several flow phenomena, such as choking, shock waves, etc., which occur only when a fluid flow is highly compressible. Compressibility becomes important when the **Mach number** becomes greater than about 0.3. The Mach number, defined earlier in the Force Ratio table, is the ratio of an object's speed to the speed of sound in the medium through which the object is traveling:

$$M = \frac{v}{a}.$$

For a perfect gas, the speed of sound a is:

$$a = (kRT)^{\frac{1}{2}}$$

where

k = The ratio of specific heats $\dfrac{C_p}{C_v}$,

R = The gas constant, and

T = The *absolute* temperature.

When M is less than one, the flow is subsonic, while supersonic flows are those with Mach numbers greater than one.

Most compressible flow problems encountered by engineers involve the flow of a gas in a duct. Of these, three different simplifications enable the analysis of three primary categories of compressible duct flow: isentropic flow in a duct of a changing area, adiabatic flow in a duct of a constant area (with friction), and frictionless flow in a constant area duct with heat transfer. When none of these simplifications can be made, the problem is much more complicated. Isothermal duct flow with friction is one case where there is heat transfer as well as frictional effects, but this can be analyzed.

For the case of adiabatic flow in a constant area duct with friction, the stagnation enthalpy of the fluid must remain constant since no energy is added and no work is done. This leads to the rather unique result that the Mach number always approaches unity toward the end of the duct. This applies to both subsonic flow (where the Mach number will increase toward one) and supersonic flow (where M will decrease toward one). Problems of this type are attacked by utilizing L^*, **the sonic length**, defined as the duct length required to develop from some initial Mach number to $M = 1$.

The dimensionless parameter $\dfrac{fL^*}{D}$ is tabulated as a function of the Mach number where f is the Darcy friction factor obtainable from the Moody Chart, and D is the diameter of a round duct or the hydraulic diameter of a nonround duct. For cases where the duct is not long enough to reach sonic conditions at its exit, the relationship between the duct length and the Mach numbers M_1 and M_2 at the inlet and outlet of the duct respectively is:

$$\frac{fL}{D} = \left(\frac{fL^*}{D}\right)_{M_1} - \left(\frac{fL^*}{D}\right)_{M_2}.$$

Constant area duct flow problems, where friction can be ignored but heat is added or subtracted, must be addressed using the integral (control volume) conservation laws of mass, momentum, and energy, where heat transfer rate $\dot{Q}$ appears in the energy equation. Ratios of temperatures, stagnation temperatures, pressures, stagnation pressures, and velocities can be found as functions of the Mach number and are tabulated for air and aid in the solution of problems.

The most common category of flows encountered is adiabatic, isentropic flow in a duct of a varying area. Thermodynamic relationships, combined with the integral conservation laws of mass and energy, lead to expressions of temperature, pressure, and density ratios as functions of the Mach number and the ratio of specific heats, k. These are tabulated in the form $\dfrac{T}{T_o}$, $\dfrac{p}{p_o}$, $\dfrac{\rho}{\rho_o}$, and $\dfrac{A}{A^*}$ as functions of M, where the subscript o denotes total properties and the asterisk denotes the value at $M = 1$. The only way to attain supersonic flow in a duct of this kind is by first passing through a converging section, then a throat, followed by a diverging section. The flow upstream of the throat will be subsonic, and the flow downstream may reach supersonic conditions if the pressure drop is sufficient. The condition $M = 1$ can only occur at the throat, and the throat area is then defined as A^*. If the flow remains isentropic, one can find all desired quantities for a given $\dfrac{A}{A^*}$ by using the isentropic tables (Tables 4 and 5)or equations to find M, and then using M to find all other quantities.

TABLE 4
BASIC EQUATIONS FOR
ISENTROPIC FLOW OF AN IDEAL GAS

Continuity: $\quad\quad\quad\quad \rho_1 v_1 A_1 = \rho_2 v_2 A_2 = \dot{m}$

Momentum: $\quad\quad\quad R_x + p_1 A_1 - p_2 A_2 = \dot{m} v_2 - \dot{m} v_1$

First Law: $\quad\quad\quad h_1 + \dfrac{v_1^2}{2} = h_2 + \dfrac{v_2^2}{2}$

Second Law: $\quad\quad\; s_1 = s_2$

Equation of State: $\quad p = \rho R T$

Process Equation: $\quad \dfrac{p}{\rho^k} = \text{constant}$

TABLE 5
ISENTROPIC FLOW RATIOS

Stagnation pressure: $\quad \dfrac{p_0}{p} = \left[1 + \dfrac{k-1}{2} M^2\right]^{\frac{k}{(k-1)}}$

Stagnation temperature: $\quad \dfrac{T_0}{T} = 1 + \dfrac{k-1}{2} M^2$

Stagnation density: $\quad \dfrac{\rho_0}{\rho} = \left[1 + \dfrac{k-1}{2} M^2\right]^{\frac{1}{(k-1)}}$

In addition, the ratio of gas velocity at some point to the sonic velocity in the throat is:

$$\frac{v}{a^*} = \left[\frac{\dfrac{(k+1)}{2} M^2}{\dfrac{(k-1)}{2} M^2 + 1}\right]^{\frac{1}{2}},$$

and the ratio $\dfrac{A}{A^*}$ is:

$$\frac{A}{A^*} = \frac{1}{M}\left[\frac{1 + \dfrac{k-1}{2}M^2}{1 + \dfrac{k-1}{2}}\right]^{\frac{(k+1)}{2(k-1)}}$$

since,

$$\rho A v = \text{constant.}$$

If the downstream pressure is not low enough to attain supersonic flow throughout the entire length of the diverging nozzle section, a normal shock wave will form in the diverging section. A normal shock leads to a sudden rise in temperature and pressure, and the flow abruptly changes from supersonic to subsonic. Tables are available for the ratios of temperature, pressure, etc., across a normal shock wave. These, combined with the isentropic tables, are used to find the Mach numbers upstream and downstream of the shock. The flow is assumed to be isentropic everywhere except across the shock where entropy increases significantly, resulting in a great loss of stagnation pressure.

EXAMPLE

An airflow ($k = 1.4$) is expanded isentropically in a nozzle from $M_1 = 0.3$, $A_1 = 1.0$ m², to a Mach number M_2 of 3.0. Determine (a) the minimum nozzle area, (b) A_2, (c) $\dfrac{p_2}{p_1}$, and (d) $\dfrac{T_2}{T_1}$ (see figure).

Figure 19. Airflow through nozzle

SOLUTION

(a) Since flow in the nozzle goes from subsonic to supersonic speeds, the flow must pass through a minimum area A^* at which $M = 1$. From Table 6, at $M_1 = 0.3$, $\dfrac{A_1}{A^*} = 2.0351$ so that the minimum area $= \dfrac{1}{2.0351} = 0.491$ m².

TABLE 6

$$\frac{p}{p_t} \text{ when } k = 1.4$$

M	$\frac{p}{p_t}$	$\frac{T}{T_1}$	$\frac{A}{A_0}$	M	$\frac{p}{p_t}$	$\frac{T}{T_1}$	$\frac{A}{A_0}$
0	1.0000	1.0000	∞	0.30	0.9395	0.9823	2.0351
.01	.9999	1.0000	57.8738	.31	.9355	.9811	1.9765
.02	.9997	.9999	28.9421	.32	.9315	.9799	1.9219
.03	.9994	.9998	19.3005	.33	.9274	.9787	1.8707
.04	.9989	.9997	14.4815	.34	.9231	.9774	1.8229
.05	.9983	.9995	11.5914	.35	.9188	.9761	1.7780
.06	.9975	.9993	9.6659	.36	.9143	.9747	1.7358
.07	.9966	.9990	8.2915	.37	.9098	.9733	1.6961
.08	.9955	.9987	7.2616	.38	.9052	.9719	1.6587
.09	.9944	.9984	6.4613	.39	.9004	.9705	1.6234
.10	.9930	.9980	5.8218	.40	.8956	.9690	1.5901
.11	.9916	.9976	5.2992	.41	.8907	.9675	1.5587
.12	.9900	.9971	4.8643	.42	.8857	.9659	1.5289
.13	.9883	.9966	4.4969	.43	.8807	.9643	1.5007
.14	.9864	.9961	4.1824	.44	.8755	.9627	1.4740

TABLE 7

$$\frac{T}{T_t} \text{ when } k = 1.4$$

M or M_1	$\frac{p}{p_t}$	$\frac{T}{T_1}$	$\frac{A}{A_0}$
2.90	0.3165^{-1}	0.3729	3.850
2.91	$.3118^{-1}$	.3712	3.887
2.92	3071^{-1}	.3696	3.924
2.93	$.3025^{-1}$	.3681	3.961
2.94	$.2980^{-1}$	.3665	3.999
2.95	$.2935^{-1}$	.3649	4.038
2.96	$.2891^{-1}$	.3633	4.076
2.97	$.2848^{-1}$	.3618	4.115
2.98	$.2805^{-1}$	.3602	4.155
2.99	$.2764^{-1}$	.3587	4.194
3.00	$.2722^{-1}$	.3571	4.235
3.01	$.2682^{-1}$	.3556	4.275
3.02	$.2642^{-1}$	.3541	4.316
3.03	$.2603^{-1}$	.3526	4.357
3.04	$.2564^{-1}$	.3511	4.399

(b) At $M_2 = 3.0$, $\dfrac{A_2}{A*} = 4.235$ so $A_2 = 2.08$ m².

(c) For this isentropic flow, T_t and p_t are constants.

$$\frac{p_2}{p_1} = \frac{\dfrac{p_2}{p_{t_2}}}{\dfrac{p_1}{p_{t_1}}} = \frac{0.0272}{0.9395} = 0.0290 \text{ (see the Table 6 for } \frac{p}{p_t})$$

d) $$\frac{T_2}{T_1} = \frac{\dfrac{T_2}{T_{t_2}}}{\dfrac{T_1}{T_{t_1}}} = \frac{0.3571}{0.9823} = 0.363 \text{ (see the Table 7 for } \frac{T}{T_t})$$

REVIEW PROBLEMS

PROBLEM 1

The specific weight of water at ordinary pressure and temperature is 62.4 lbf/ft³ (9.81 kN/m³). The specific gravity of mercury is 13.55. Compute the density of water and the specific weight and density of mercury.

SOLUTION

Knowing that density and specific weight of a fluid are related as follows:

$$\rho = \frac{\gamma}{g} \text{ or } \gamma = \rho g$$

and that specific gravity s of a liquid is the ratio of its density to that of pure water at a standard temperature, we can calculate:

$$\rho_{water} = \frac{\gamma_{water}}{g} = \frac{62.4 \text{ lbf/ft}^3}{32.2 \text{ ft/s}^2} = 1.94 \text{ slugs/ft}^3$$

$$\rho_{water} = \frac{9.81 \text{ kN/m}^3}{9.81 \text{ m/s}^2} = 1,000 \text{ kg/m}^3 = 1.00 \text{ g/cm}^3$$

$$\rho_{mercury} = s_{mercury}\rho_{water} = 13.55(1.94) = 26.3 \text{ slugs/ft}^3$$

$$\rho_{mercury} = 13.55(1,000) = 13,550 \text{ kg/m}^3$$

$$\gamma_{mercury} = \rho_{mercury}g = 26.3(32.2) = 846.9 \text{ lbf/ft}^3$$

$$\gamma_{mercury} = (13,550)(9.81) = 132.4 \text{ kN/m}^3$$

PROBLEM 2

Oil with a specific gravity of 0.80 is 3 ft (0.91 m) deep in an open tank that is otherwise filled with water. If the tank is 10 ft (3.05 m) deep, what is the pressure at the bottom of the tank?

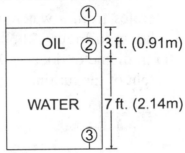

Figure 20. Tank schematic

SOLUTION

First determine the pressure at the oil-water interface staying within the oil, and then calculate the pressure at the bottom.

$$\frac{p_1}{\gamma} + z_1 = \frac{p_2}{\gamma} + z_2$$

where

p_1 = Pressure at free surface of oil

z_1 = Elevation of free surface of oil

p_2 = Pressure at interface between oil and water

z_2 = Elevation at interface between oil and water

For this example, $p_1 = 0$, $\gamma = 0.80 \times 62.4$ lbf/ft³, $z_1 = 10$ ft, and $z_2 = 7$ ft. Therefore,

$$p_2 = 3 \times 0.80 \times 62.4 = 150 \text{ psfg.}$$

Now, obtain p_3 from:

$$\frac{p_2}{\gamma} + z_2 = \frac{p_3}{\gamma} + z_3,$$

where p_2 has already been calculated and $\gamma = 62.4$ lbf/ft³ (or 9.81 kN/m³).

$$p_3 = 62.4\left(\frac{150}{62.4} + 7\right)$$
$$= 587 \text{ psfg}$$
$$= 4.07 \text{ psig} \left(\text{or } 28.6 \text{ kN}/\text{m}^3\right).$$

PROBLEM 3

A hydraulic turbine operates from a water supply with a 61 m head above the turbine inlet, as shown in Figure 21. It discharges the water to atmosphere through a 0.305 m diameter duct, with a velocity of 13.7 m/s. Calculate the horsepower output of the turbine.

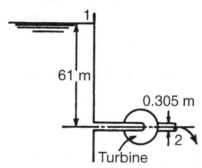

Figure 21. Hydraulic turbine

SOLUTION

If E is the energy extracted per pound of fluid flowing, then the energy equation may be written as

$$\frac{p_1}{\gamma} + \frac{v_1^2}{2g} + z_1 = E + \frac{p_2}{\gamma} + \frac{v_2^2}{2g} + z_2$$

where suffix 1 refers to a point upstream of the turbine and suffix 2 to a point downstream of the turbine.

If the exit from the turbine is defined as the potential datum, then $z_2 = 0$ and:

$$\frac{p_1}{\gamma} + \frac{v_1^2}{2g} + z_1 = 61 \text{ m}$$

where $p_1 = 0$ and $v_1 = 0$ at the surface.

Therefore:

$$61\,m = E + \frac{p_2}{\gamma} + \frac{v_2^2}{2g} + 0.$$

Now since the discharge is to atmosphere, $p_2 = 0$. Hence:

$$61 = E + \frac{13.7^2}{2g}$$

Thus:

$$E = 61 - 9.6 = 51.4\ m.$$

The rate of fluid flow is given by $Q = Av$ m³/s, and the weight of fluid flowing by $Q\gamma$ N/s. Therefore, the rate of work done on the turbine is $EQ\gamma$ Nm/s or:

$$51,326\,\text{Nm/s} \cong 675\ hp.$$

PROBLEM 4

Consider the steady flow of water ($\rho = 1.94$ kg/m³) through the device shown in the diagram. The areas are $A_1 = 0.3$ m², $A_2 = 0.5$ m², and $A_3 = A_4 = 0.4$ m². Mass flow out through section 3 is given as 3.88 kg/s. The volumetric flow rate in through section 4 is given as 1 m³/s, and $V_1 = 10\hat{\imath}$ m/s. If properties are assumed uniform across all inlet and outlet flow sections, determine the flow velocity at section 2.

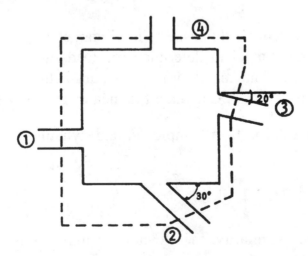

Figure 22. Control volume diagram

SOLUTION

The dashed lines in the figure represent a control volume. Equation (1) represents the control volume formulation of the conservation of mass.

$$O = \frac{\partial}{\partial t} \int_{CV} \rho \, dv + \int_{CS} \rho v \bullet dA \tag{1}$$

Since the flow is steady (not time dependent), equation (1) becomes

$$\int_{A_2} \rho v \bullet dA = 3.88 \frac{kg}{s}$$

Since $v \bullet dv$ is positive at section 2, the flow is out.

Evaluating the integral at section 2, v_2 can be found:

$$\rho v_2 A_2 = 3.88 \frac{kg}{s}$$

$$|v_2| = \left(3.88 \frac{kg}{s}\right)\left(\frac{m^3}{1.94 kg}\right)\left(\frac{1}{0.6 m^2}\right) = 3.33 \frac{m}{s}$$

$$v_2 = |v_2|(\sin \theta i - \cos \theta j)$$

$$v_2 = (1.66 i - 2.88 j)\frac{m}{s}$$

PROBLEM 5

A submarine-launched missile, 1 m in diameter by 5 m long, is to be studied in a water tunnel to determine the loads acting on it during its underwater launch. The maximum speed during this initial part of the missile's flight is 10 ms^{-1}. Calculate the mean water tunnel flow velocity if a $\frac{1}{20}$ scale model is to be employed and dynamic similarity is to be achieved.

SOLUTION

For dynamic similarity, the Reynolds number must be constant for the model and the prototype:

$$Re_m = Re_p,$$

$$\frac{v_m l_m \rho_m}{\mu_m} = \frac{v_p l_p \rho_p}{\mu_p}.$$

The model flow velocity is given by

$$v_m = v_p \left(\frac{l_p}{l_m}\right)\left(\frac{\rho_p}{\rho_m}\right)\left(\frac{\mu_m}{\mu_p}\right),$$

but $\rho_p = \rho_m$ and $\mu_p = \mu_m$. Therefore,

$$v_m = (10)(20)(1)(1) = 200 \text{ ms}^{-1}.$$

This is a high-flow velocity and illustrates the reason why a few model tests are made with completely equal Reynolds numbers. At high Re values, however, the divergences become of lesser importance.

PROBLEM 6

Water is discharged from a large reservoir through a straight pipe of 0.0762 m diameter and 366 m long at a rate of 0.0057 m³/s. The discharge end is open to the atmosphere. If the open end is 12.2 m below the surface level in the reservoir, what is the Darcy friction factor? Losses other than pipe friction may be ignored.

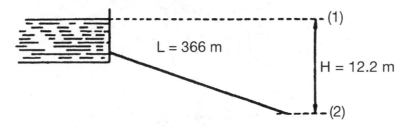

Figure 23. Flow into reservoir

SOLUTION

Applying the flow equation between levels 1 and 2, as shown in the figure,

$$z_1 + \frac{p_1}{\gamma} + \frac{v_1^2}{2g} = z_2 + \frac{p_2}{\gamma} + \frac{v_2^2}{2g} + h_f$$

Both ends of the system are open to the atmosphere, then:

$$p_1 = p_2.$$

Ignoring losses other than pipe friction, and using the Darcy equation:

$$h_f = 4f\left(\frac{L}{D}\right)\frac{v^2}{2g}$$

where v is the velocity in the pipe. It follows that $v_2 = v$ since

$$z_1 - z_2 = \frac{p_2}{\gamma} + \frac{v_2^2}{2g} + h_f - \frac{p_1}{\gamma} - \frac{v_1^2}{2g}$$

and

$$p_1 = p_2,$$

then

$$z_1 - z_2 = \frac{v_2^2}{2g} - \frac{v_1^2}{2g} + h_f.$$

As $v_1 = 0$ and $H = z_1 - z_2$:

$$H = \frac{v^2}{2g} + 4f\left(\frac{L}{D}\right)\frac{v^2}{2g}$$

$$H = \frac{v^2}{2g}\left(1 + 4f\frac{L}{D}\right)$$

$$A = D^2\frac{\pi}{4} = (0.0762)^2\frac{\pi}{4} = \frac{0.0058\pi}{4}\ \text{m}^2$$

$$v = \frac{Q}{A} = \frac{0.0057}{\dfrac{0.0058\pi}{4}} = \frac{3.93}{\pi}\ \text{m/s}$$

Substituting into the equation for H:

$$12.2 = \frac{(3.93)^2}{2(9.8)(\pi^2)}\left(1 + 4f\frac{366}{0.0762}\right)$$

from which:

$$f = 0.008.$$

PROBLEM 7

A 4 in. × 1 in. nozzle, shown in the figure, is attached to the end of a 4-in hose line. The velocity of the water leaving the nozzle is 96 fps, the coefficient of velocity, C_v, is 0.96 and the coefficient of contraction, C_c, is 0.80. Determine the necessary pressure at the base of the nozzle. Use English units and a specific weight of 62.3 lbf/ft³.

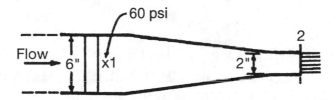

Figure 24. Flow in nozzle

SOLUTION

Figure 24 shows the nozzle attached to the 4-in. hose line. Since the coefficient of velocity, C_v, is $\frac{v_{actual}}{v_{ideal}}$,

$$v_{ideal} = \frac{96}{0.96} = 100 \text{ fps}.$$

The ratio of the area of the *vena contracta* to the area of the tip of the nozzle is called the coefficient of contraction. Incorporated with the continuity equation yields:

$$\frac{v_1}{v_2} = \frac{a_2}{a_1} = \frac{d_2^2}{d_1^2} = 0.8\frac{(1)^2}{4^2} = \frac{1}{20},$$

$$v_1 = \frac{100}{20} = 5 \text{ fps (ideal)}$$

Substituting these values into the Bernoulli equation, gives:

$$\frac{p_1}{\gamma} + z_1 + \frac{v_1^2}{2g} = \frac{p_2}{\gamma} + z_2 + \frac{v_2^2}{2g}$$

$$\frac{p_1}{62.3} + 0 + \frac{5^2}{64.4} = 0 + 0 + \frac{100^2}{64.4}$$

and

$$\frac{p_1}{62.3} = \frac{10,000 - 25}{64.4} = \frac{9,975}{64.4} = 155 \text{ ft}.$$

Therefore,

$$p_1 = 67.1 \text{ psi}.$$

PROBLEM 8

An aircraft is flying in level flight at a speed of 250 km/hr through air with standard conditions. The lift coefficient at this speed is 0.4, and the drag coefficient is 0.0065. The mass of the aircraft is 850 kg. Calculate the effective lift area for the craft.

SOLUTION

Apply the definition of the lift coefficient.

$$C_L = \frac{F_L}{\frac{1}{2}\rho v^2 A_p}$$

Assume lift equals weight in level flight. Then:

$$F_L = mg = C_L \frac{1}{2}\rho v^2 A_p.$$

Solving for A_p:

$$A_p = \frac{2mg}{C_L \rho v^2}$$

$$A_p = \left(\frac{2}{0.4}\right)(850 \text{ kg})\left(9.81 \frac{\text{m}}{\text{s}^2}\right)\left(\frac{\text{m}^3}{1.23 \text{ kg}}\right)\left(\frac{\text{hr}}{250 \times 10^3 \text{ m}} \times \frac{3,600 \text{ s}}{\text{hr}}\right)^2 = 7.03 \text{ m}^2$$

PROBLEM 9

Air flowing through a nozzle encounters a shock. The Mach number upstream of the shock is M_x = 1.8, and the static temperature downstream of the shock is T_y = 800°R. How much has the velocity changed across the shock? Assume k = 1.4.

TABLE 8

ONE-DIMENSIONAL NORMAL-SHOCK FUNCTIONS (FOR AN IDEAL GAS WITH CONSTANT SPECIFIC HEAT AND MOLECULAR WEIGHT, k = 1.4)

M_x	M_y	$\dfrac{P_y}{P_x}$	$\dfrac{\rho_y}{\rho_x}$	$\dfrac{T_y}{T_x}$	$\dfrac{P_{0y}}{P_{0x}}$
1.00	1.00000	1.00000	1.00000	1.00000	1.00000
1.05	0.95312	1.1196	1.08398	1.03284	0.99987
1.10	0.91177	1.2450	1.1691	1.06494	0.99892
1.15	0.87502	1.3762	1.2550	1.09657	0.99669
1.20	0.84217	1.5133	1.3416	1.1280	0.99280
1.25	0.81264	1.6562	1.4286	1.1594	0.98706
1.30	0.78596	1.8050	1.5157	1.1909	0.97935
1.35	0.76175	1.9596	1.6028	1.2226	0.96972
1.40	0.73971	2.1200	1.6896	1.2547	0.95819
1.45	0.71956	2.2862	1.7761	1.2872	0.94483
1.50	0.70109	2.4583	1.8621	1.3202	0.92978
1.55	0.68410	2.6363	1.9473	1.3538	0.91319
1.60	0.66844	2.8201	2.0317	1.3880	0.89520
1.65	0.65396	3.0096	2.1152	1.4228	0.87598
1.70	0.64055	3.2050	2.1977	1.4583	0.85573
1.75	0.62809	3.4062	2.2791	1.4946	0.83456
1.80	0.61650	3.6133	2.3592	1.5316	0.81268
1.85	0.60570	3.8262	2.4381	1.5694	0.79021
1.90	0.59562	4.0450	2.5157	1.6079	0.76735
1.95	0.58618	4.2696	2.5919	1.6473	0.74418
2.00	0.57735	4.5000	2.6666	1.6875	0.72088
2.05	0.56907	4.7363	2.7400	1.7286	0.69752
2.10	0.56128	4.9784	2.8119	1.7704	0.67422
2.15	0.55395	5.2262	2.8823	1.8132	0.65105
2.20	0.54706	5.4800	2.9512	1.8569	0.62812
2.25	0.54055	5.7396	3.0186	1.9014	0.60554
2.30	0.53441	6.0050	3.0846	1.9468	0.58331
2.35	0.52861	6.2762	3.1490	1.9931	0.56148
2.40	0.52312	6.5533	3.2119	2.0403	0.54015
2.45	0.51792	6.8362	3.2733	2.0885	0.51932
2.50	0.51299	7.1250	3.3333	2.1375	0.49902
2.55	0.50831	7.4196	3.3918	2.1875	0.47927
2.60	0.50387	7.7200	3.4489	2.2383	0.46012
2.65	0.49965	8.0262	3.5047	2.2901	0.44155
2.70	0.49563	8.3383	3.5590	2.3429	0.42359

SOLUTION

We seek $v_x - v_y$, which may be expressed as:

$$v_x - v_y = v_x\left(1 - \frac{v_y}{v_x}\right).$$

$\dfrac{v_y}{v_x}$ can be found from Table 8 because M_x is given.

From Table 8 and $M_x = 1.8$:

$$\frac{v_y}{v_x} = \frac{\rho_x}{\rho_y} = \frac{1}{\dfrac{\rho_y}{\rho_x}} = \frac{1}{2.36} = 0.425$$

$$\frac{T_x}{T_y} = \frac{1}{\dfrac{T_y}{T_x}} = \frac{1}{1.53} = 0.653$$

v_x can be determined from:

$$v_x = M_x a_x = M_x\sqrt{kRT_x} = M_x\sqrt{kR\left(\frac{T_x}{T_y}\right)}\sqrt{T_y},$$

where $\dfrac{T_y}{T_x}$ is known as a function of M_x:

$$v_x = \left(M_x\right)\left(49.02\sqrt{\frac{T_x}{T_y}}\sqrt{T_y}\right) = (1.8)\left(49.02\sqrt{0.653}\right)\left(\sqrt{800}\right)$$

$$= 2,020 \text{ m/s}$$

Therefore:

$$v_x - v_y = 2,020 \text{ m/s } (1 - 0.425) = 1,160 \text{ m/s}.$$

FE/EIT

Fundamentals of Engineering: AM Exam

CHAPTER 12

Material Science/ Structure of Matter

CHAPTER 12

MATERIAL SCIENCE/ STRUCTURE OF MATTER

The key to the success of technology over the past century lies in our ability to make better use of materials obtained from nature and to develop new materials with starting, useful properties. It is difficult for us to imagine a world without plastics, lightweight metals for planes, and medical equipment that makes techniques for the treatment of illness possible. Our learning how to make such materials lies in the area of Material Science. In this chapter we explore the main ideas of this field in eight sections. Chapter 12 begins with the atomic structure of materials. Here we explore the forces that bind materials together and the various phases in which these materials are found. Similarly, we classify materials on the basis of the structural arrangement of their molecules. In the next section, we examine structures and structural defects of materials, a subject forming the basis for such areas as metals and ceramics. The third section is devoted to the mechanical and thermal properties of materials, forming the basis for materials processing. In the fourth section, we turn to multicomponent materials and phase diagrams, describing the relationship between the composition of a material and its phase for a given temperature. We next turn to diffusion and reactions in materials. Here we look at such processes as the movement of the atoms of one material through the solid, crystalline phase of another with subsequent implications for the strength of the material. In sixth and seventh sections, we examine the processes of corrosion and radiation alteration of materials, while the eighth section concerns composite materials.

MATERIALS AND THEIR ATOMIC STRUCTURE

For our purposes the building blocks of all materials are the atoms of those elements making up the material. To understand the atom we must first recall the concept of electric charge. Forces exerted between bodies due to electrical effects are **electromagnetic forces**. Unlike gravity, which is always an attractive force tending to draw bodies nearer to each other, electromagnetic forces can be either attractive or repulsive, the latter driving the bodies further apart. We can focus only on **electrostatic forces**, which are those exerted between two electrically charged bodies at rest. The fact that both repulsive and attractive forces are involved leads us to postulate two kinds of charges: positive and negative. Bodies that are charged in the same way (both negative or both positive) will be repelled by each other, while oppositely charged bodies are attracted to each other. In 1909, American physicist Robert Millikan found that the magnitude of an electric charge always appears as an integer multiple of a fixed value Ne, $N = 1, 2, 3,...$ The fundamental charge "e" is that of a single fundamental charged particle, the electron. Electrical charge is given in terms of the **Coulomb**, which is the amount of charge flowing past a point in a wire in one second when the current in the wire is one Ampere. Denoting the Coulomb by "C," we have $1A = 1\frac{C}{s}$. The charge of an electron, which by convention is taken as negative, is equal to $e = -1.602 \times 10^{-19}$ C while its mass is 9.11×10^{-31} kg.

The atom is essentially composed of three kinds of particles: electrons, protons, and neutrons—the latter two constitute the **nucleus** of the atom. A **proton** is a positively charged particle, the magnitude of whose charge is equal to that of the electron. Its mass, however, is approximately 1,840 times as large: proton mass = 1.67×10^{-27} kg. Since they have equal and opposite charges, the proton and electron can be in electrical balance; together they compose the atom of hydrogen, the lightest element. For the hydrogen atom, the nucleus is comprised simply of the proton itself, while the single electron is viewed as rotating about the proton. The **neutron** is an electrically neutral particle (neither positively nor negatively charged) whose mass can be taken as equal to that of the proton. While the hydrogen atom has no neutrons in its nucleus, the nucleus of the helium atom has two protons and two neutrons, with two electrons rotating around it. Regarding the nucleus as a sphere, its diameter is of the order of 10^{-14} m and, at some distance from the nucleus, we find the electrons rotating about it. Normally the number of electrons in orbit is equal to the number of protons in the nucleus. In this case, the atom is electrically neutral. If one or more electrons are missing, then the resulting atomic structure is positively charged and is referred to as a **positive ion**. If, on the other hand, the atom has acquired one or more additional electrons, then it is called a **negative ion**.

All materials are composed of combinations of over 100 **elements**. Typical elements are hydrogen and helium, naturally occurring as gases; mercury, which we recognize readily in its liquid form in thermometers; and iron or aluminum, familiar to us in solid form. Some elements, such as radium and plutonium, are essentially not present in nature but can be created by means of suitable laboratory or industrial processes. An element is composed of atoms that uniquely correspond to it. The number of protons in the nucleus of an atom defines the **atomic number** of the element. Thus, the atomic numbers of hydrogen, helium, sodium, aluminum, and oxygen are, respectively, 1, 2, 11, 13, and 8, that is, the number of protons in any atom of the corresponding element. Elements are named (e.g., helium, hydrogen) and assigned symbols such as H (hydrogen), He (helium), Al (aluminum), O (oxygen), and Fe (iron). The number of neutrons for atoms of the same element may differ. Thus, uranium (U) with an atomic number 92 (the number of protons in the nucleus) may have atoms with 143 neutrons or 146 neutrons. The various forms of an element differing in the numbers of neutrons in their atoms are referred to as **isotopes** of the element. The **atomic weight** of an atom is its mass expressed in "Atomic Mass Units" (AMUs) where oxygen, with eight protons and eight neutrons, is taken to have a mass of exactly 16 Atomic Mass Units. The atomic **weight number** is the nearest natural number to the atomic weight in AMUs. Thus, the atomic weight number of normally occurring hydrogen is 1; an isotope of hydrogen is deuterium, with an atomic weight number of 2, corresponding to the appearance of a neutron in the atomic nucleus. Normally occurring carbon has an atomic number of 6 and a mass number of 12 (with six neutrons). Carbon also has an isotope whose mass number is 13 (with seven neutrons). The mass numbers of the two isotopes of uranium noted above are 235 and 238. Since the atomic weight and atomic weight number are very near in value, it is standard practice to use the rounded atomic weight number in place of the actual atomic weight, and to refer to it as the atomic weight of the element. This will be our practice as well (Figure 1).

THE PERIODIC TABLE

KEY

Atomic Number → 22

Group Classification

Ti

Symbol

Atomic Weight → 47.88

( ) indicates most stable or best known isotope

METALS ——————————————— NONMETALS ————

TRANSITIONAL METALS ———————————

1 IA IA																	18 VIII 0
1 H 1.008	2 IIA IIA											13 IIIB IIIA	14 IVB IVA	15 VB VA	16 VIB VIA	17 VIIB VIIA	2 He 4.003
3 LI 6.941	4 Be 9.012											5 B 10.811	6 C 12.011	7 N 14.007	8 O 15.999	9 F 18.998	10 Ne 20.180
11 Na 22.990	12 Mg 24.305	3 IIIA IIIB	4 IVA IVB	5 VA VB	6 VIA VIB	7 VIIA VIIB	8 VIIIA VIII	9 VIIIA VIII	10 VIIIA VIII	11 IB IB	12 IIB IIB	13 Al 26.982	14 SI 28.086	15 P 30.974	16 S 32.066	17 Cl 35.453	18 Ar 39.948
19 K 39.098	20 Ca 40.078	21 Sc 44.956	22 Ti 47.88	23 V 50.942	24 Cr 51.996	25 Mn 54.938	26 Fe 55.847	27 Co 58.933	28 Ni 58.693	29 Cu 63.546	30 Zn 65.39	31 Ga 69.723	32 Ge 72.61	33 As 74.922	34 Se 78.96	35 Br 79.904	36 Kr 83.8
37 Rb 85.468	38 Sr 87.62	39 Y 88.906	40 Zr 91.224	41 Nb 92.906	42 Mo 95.94	43 Tc (97.907)	44 Ru 101.07	45 Rh 102.906	46 Pd 106.4	47 Ag 107.868	48 Cd 112.411	49 In 114.818	50 Sn 118.710	51 Sb 121.757	52 Te 127.60	53 I 126.905	54 Xe 131.29
55 Cs 132.905	56 Ba 137.327	57 La 138.906	72 Hf 178.49	73 Ta 180.948	74 W 183.84	75 Re 186.207	76 Os 190.23	77 Ir 192.22	78 Pt 195.08	79 Au 196.967	80 Hg 200.59	81 Tl 204.383	82 Pb 207.2	83 BI 208.980	84 Po (208.982)	85 At (209.982)	86 Rn (222.018)
87 Fr (223.020)	88 Ra (226.025)	89 Ac (227.028)	104 Unq (261.11)	105 Unp (262.114)	106 Unh (263.118)	107 Uns (262.12)	108 Uno (265)	109 Une (266)	110 Uun (269)								

Alkali Metals | Alkaline Earth Metals

Halogens | Noble Gases

LANTHANIDE SERIES	58 Ce 140.115	59 Pr 140.908	60 Nd 144.24	61 Pm (144.913)	62 Sm 150.36	63 Eu 151.965	64 Gd 157.25	65 Tb 158.925	66 Dy 162.50	67 Ho 164.930	68 Er 167.26	69 Tm 168.934	70 Yb 173.04	71 Lu 174.967
ACTINIDE SERIES	90 Th 232.038	91 Pa 231.036	92 U 238.029	93 Np (237.048)	94 Pu (244.064)	95 Am (243.061)	96 Cm (247.070)	97 Bk (247.070)	98 Cf (251.080)	99 Es (252.083)	100 Fm (257.095)	101 Md (258.1)	102 No (259.101)	103 Lr (262.11)

Figure 1. The Periodic Table of Elements

The electrons in orbit around the nucleus of an atom have different energy levels. This has given rise to our viewing the atom as a nucleus surrounded by shells or groups of electrons having different energy levels. The lowest energy shell (**quantum shell**) has at most two electrons. The second shell has at most eight, the third 18, and the fourth 32. The maximum number of electrons in the nth shell is thus given by $2n^2$; n is called the **principal quantum number** of the shell. Thus, the hydrogen atom with atomic number 2 will have one electron rotating around its nucleus in the lowest energy shell, while oxygen, with atomic number 8, will have two electrons in its lowest energy shell and six in the next shell. It is important to note that the energies of electrons in different shells differ by fixed amounts. If an electron moves from a higher energy shell to the next lower energy shell, then an amount (quantum) of energy is released from the atom. This amount of energy is referred to as a **photon**. For reasons that are beyond the scope of this chapter, stability considerations favor the completion of the outer shell—that is, that there should be exactly $2n^2$ electrons in shell number n. We refer to electrons in the outer shell of an atom as **valence electrons**.

Shells are further subdivided into **orbitals** labeled, respectively, the s, p, d, and f orbitals. These will have maximum numbers of 2, 6, 10, and 14 electrons, respectively. The shell and orbital structures of some familiar elements are shown in Table 1:

TABLE 1 SHELL AND ORBITAL STRUCTURES														
Shell	1	2		3			4				5			
Element	s	s	p	s	p	d	s	p	d	f	s	p	d	f
Hydrogen	1													
Helium	2													
Carbon	2	2	2											
Nitrogen	2	2	3											
Oxygen	2	2	4											
Sodium	2	2	6	1										
Aluminum	2	2	6	2	1									
Chlorine	2	2	6	2	5									
Iron	2	2	6	2	6	6	2							
Copper	2	2	6	2	6	10	1							
Cadmium	2	2	6	2	6	10	2	6	10		2			
Xenon	2	2	6	2	6	10	2	6	10		2	6		
Gold	2	2	6	2	6	10	2	6	10	14	2	6	10	

When atoms of two or more elements bind together in definite proportions to form a substance, this substance is referred to as a **compound**. Examples are water (two atoms of hydrogen and one of oxygen, H_2O) and salt (one atom each of sodium and chlorine, NaCl).

A molecule is the smallest particle into which a material can be subdivided without changing its physical or chemical properties. It is composed of atoms that are bound together by "binding forces." These forces may be weak or strong, and determine the nature of the material. We will now examine the various kinds of binding forces maintaining a molecule of a material.

We begin with ionic binding which is based on attraction between oppositely charged particles. Let us consider ordinary table salt, whose molecules consist of atoms of sodium (Na), and chlorine (Cl). Their atomic numbers are, respectively, 11 and 17. The shell makeup of sodium is 2 + 8 + 1 (that is, two on the inner shell, eight on the next, and one on the outermost), while that of chlorine is 2 + 8 + 7. The two atoms would have an electrical propensity to "meld" together with the single outermost electron of sodium "leaving" the Na atom and "joining" the outermost shell of the Cl atom. The result is the formation of a positively charged Na ion being attracted to the negatively charged Cl ion, arising from the addition of the electron to its outer shell. **Ionic binding** is the binding stemming from mutual attraction of oppositely charged particles arising from the "sharing" of available electrons to complete shells in the atomic structure. Another example of ionic binding is that of magnesium chloride ($MgCl_2$). Magnesium, with an atomic number 12, has an electron structure 2 + 8 + 2; chlorine has the structure 2 + 8 + 7. Hence, the two magnesium electrons in the outer shell can move to two chlorine atoms, resulting in a positively charged Mg ion (charge = $+2e$) and two negatively charged Cl ions (charge = $-2e$) which then are bound to form magnesium chloride.

While ionic bonding is characterized by transfer of electrons from one atom to another, **covalent bonding** is that in which electrons are shared between the atoms. An example is that of the hydrogen molecule, consisting of two covalently bound hydrogen atoms (Figure 2). Roughly speaking, the two electrons available from the pair of atoms form a negatively charged "entity" binding the two positively charged nucleii. Another example of covalent binding is that of methane (CH_4) in which carbon (atomic number 6, shell structure 2 + 4) has each of its four outer electrons paired with the single orbital electron for each of the four hydrogen atoms to form a strong negatively charged link between the hydrogen nucleii and the carbon nucleus. Other familiar examples of covalently bonded molecules are the oxygen molecule (O_2) (atomic number 8, shell structure 2 + 6) in which a bridge of four electrons is formed, and the nitrogen molecule (N_2) (atomic number 7, shell structure 2 + 5) in which a bridge of six electrons is formed. A third binding force is the **metallic bond**. In this structure the valence electrons form a negatively charged "cloud" surrounding and moving through a positively charged "core" of positively charged particles.

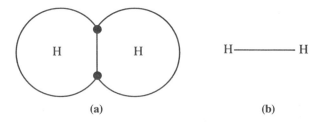

Figure 2. Simplified Representations of the Covalent Bond of Hydrogen

Ionic, covalent, and metallic bonds are the primary mechanisms through which materials form structures. Other, weaker binding mechanisms are also present. These arise primarily from assymetries in the electrical structures of atoms and molecules, and are generally referred to as **Van der Waals** forces. An example of Van der Waals forces is given by the binding forces maintaining the physical structure of water in its liquid and solid (ice) phases.

Material structure rests on the fact that atoms assume spatial arrangements as a result of interactions between them. These interactions are the result of a combination of the above attractive forces, tending to draw atoms together, and repulsive forces, arising from the interactions of electrons. The sum of the attractive and repulsive forces is the net force between two atoms. The energy arising from this net force is said to be the **bonding energy** between the atoms. This energy represents the potential energy of the atomic pair. The atomic distance for which it is minimum coincides with the distance for which the sum of attractive and repulsive forces is zero. The addition of energy, such as that due to heating, can serve to drive atoms apart and break the bonds maintaining structure, while removal of energy will lead the atoms to assume their equilibrium position.

The molecular weight of a molecule is the total sum of the molecular weights of its atoms. Thus, the molecular weight of water is determined by adding that of two atoms of hydrogen (2 × 1) to that of one atom of oxygen (1 × 16) yielding the value 18. A **gram-mole** or **mole** of a molecule is that amount of the material whose weight in grams is equal to the molecular weight of the molecule. The **gram-molecular weight** is the mass of one mole of a compound equal in grams to the molecular weight. The number of molecules per gram-molecular weight is a constant, referred to as **Avagadro's number**, and equal to 6.02×10^{23}. Similarly, every gram-atom contains Avagadro's number of atoms.

EXAMPLE

How many atoms are in 80 grams of aluminum?

SOLUTION

One gram-atom of aluminum contains the atomic weight of aluminum in grams, or 26.98 grams. Hence, 80 grams of aluminum is equal to $80 \div 26.98 = 2.965$ gram-atoms, which in turn contains

$$2.965 \times 6.02 \times 10^{23} = 17.849 \times 10^{23} \text{ atoms.}$$

Most materials may be categorized into three classes: **metals, ceramics**, and **polymers**. Metals are composed of elements that easily give up electrons to form the "electron cloud" of a metallic bond. These include iron, copper, aluminum, nickel, and alloys or combinations of metals. Metals are characterized by high thermal and electrical conductivity, high strength and ductility. These properties will be further explained later in the text. Iron is the most commonly used metal; iron oxides, or pig iron are extracted from the iron ore in a blast furnace. The pig iron, which contains carbon and other impurities, is further processed to reduce the carbon content and obtain various grades of steel. Examples of processes include **Bessemer** and **oxygen processes**, also known as the L-D or **Linz-Donawitz processes**. Carbon steels are the simple grades and have carbon as the major non-ferrous element. Nickel, copper, manganese, and other metals are alloyed with steel to obtain desirable properties. For example, adding chromium improves the steel and reduces corrosion, thus giving stainless steel.

Ceramics are materials containing compounds of both metals and nonmetals that are bound by both ionic and covalent bonds. Ceramics usually have high thermal and chemical resistances, and they are generally poor conductors of heat and electricity. Some simple examples include: magnesium oxide, beryllium oxide, silicon carbide, and silicon nitride. The structure may be a combination of highly ordered crystals and glassy regions. Ceramics may be roughly classified into four groups: **clays, refractories, cements**, and **glasses**. When wet, the clays can be easily blended and molded. Upon drying or **firing**, materials such as bricks, tiles, porcelain, and stoneware can be manufactured. The type of drying process alters the porosity and permeability of the substance. Refractories are designed to withstand high temperatures in industrial operations: gas-turbines, ram-jet engines, and nuclear reactors. Some examples include alumina-silica compositions, carbides, nitrides, carbon, and graphite. Cements are characterized by their ability to set and harden after being mixed with water; a common type is Portland cement. Finally glasses, mainly made of silica, are materials that have been cooled to a rigid condition but have not been crystallized. For economic reasons, metal oxides are usually added to the glass mixture to reduce the melting temperature. Commercial products include soda lime or lime glass, lead glasses, borosilicate glasses, and high-silica glasses.

To define polymers we must recall the notion of an organic compound, one made up of molecules containing carbon. Examples are methane (CH_4) and propane (C_3H_8). Compounds containing only hydrogen and carbon are **hydrocarbons**. Plastics consist of hydrocarbon molecules that are linked together, primarily through covalent bonds, to form giant molecular chains. To see how this is done consider the methane molecule CH_4. The four atoms of hydrogen and one of carbon are bound covalently through the sharing of one electron of each of the hydrogen atoms, with the outer shell of the carbon atom. The resulting molecule of methane can be visualized as shown in Figure 3:

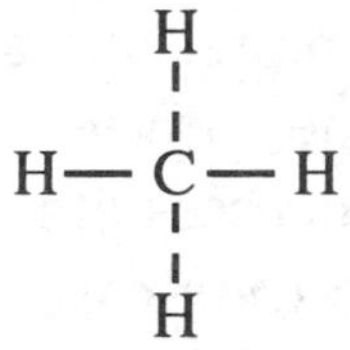

$$
\begin{array}{c}
H \\
| \\
H-C-H \\
| \\
H
\end{array}
$$

Figure 3. The Methane Molecule

The single line represents the covalent sharing of a single hydrogen electron. The molecule is electrically balanced with the four outer-shell vacancies in the carbon atom being compensated for by the "bridge" of four electrons. We can easily expand on our figure to a more complex hydrocarbon molecule by considering the case of two carbon atoms. For this case we can build a new hydrocarbon, bonded covalently, with the structure shown in Figure 4:

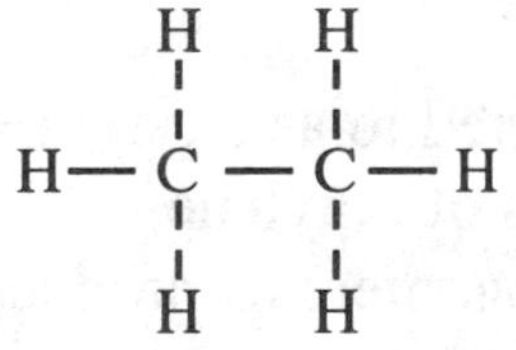

$$
\begin{array}{cc}
H & H \\
| & | \\
H-C- & C-H \\
| & | \\
H & H
\end{array}
$$

Figure 4. The Ethane Molecule

Figure 4 describes the bonding structure of a molecule of the hydrocarbon ethane. In the same way we can successively add triplets of a single carbon atom and two hydrogen atoms to build long chain molecules with a "backbone" of carbon atoms. Generally speaking, the extension of this structure to one of n carbon atoms contains $2n + 2$ hydrogen atoms and has the chemical formula $C_nH_{2n + 2}$; these compounds are referred to as **paraffins**. Since all electron shells of paraffins are filled, there is no way for a paraffin molecule to chemically combine with any additional hydrogen atom. Such a molecule is referred to as saturated. A molecule that can admit additional hydrogen atoms is unsaturated. An example of an unsaturated molecule having a "double bond" between carbon atoms is ethylene, whose binding structure is shown in Figure 5:

```
    H       H
    |       |
    |       |
    C   =   C
    |       |
    |       |
    H       H
```

Figure 5. The Ethylene Molecule

Here, as above, each line represents a covalent structural link of an electron pair; hence, between the carbon atoms we have a bridge of four electrons. Under appropriate processes ethylene molecules may be altered in such a way that the double carbon-carbon bond is replaced by a single carbon-carbon bond, and the now free remaining electrons can be used to create bonds with new carbon atoms in other former ethylene molecules, resulting in a structure of possibly enormous length, a typical segment of which would assume the following form:

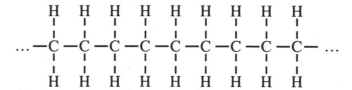

Figure 6. A Polymer Structure

Such a structure is referred to as a **polymer,** formed by the linking of two or more C_2H_4 molecules of ethylene, which constitute the **monomers** of our structure. Linking monomers to produce polymers is referred to as **polymerization**. The polymer chain structure may be altered by the formation of links tying the chains together. Such linking is referred to as **cross-linking,** occurring through connections between unsaturated carbon atoms within the chain. The result of cross-linking is to significantly restrict movement between adjacent chains and alter mechanical properties. One example is the aging of rubber. A second form of a polymer chain is branching. **Branching** occurs when a polymer chain bifurcates into two chains, resulting in a material with little movement possible between adjacent molecules.

EXAMPLE

Show the structure of a polyethylene monomer which incorporates a chlorine atom through substitution of a hydrogen atom, as well as the addition polymerization of this monomer.

SOLUTION

Substitution of a hydrogen atom by one of chlorine will produce the monomer with the following structure:

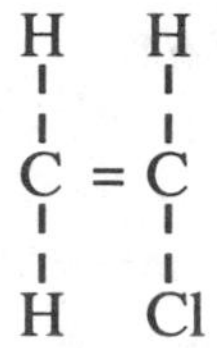

$$
\begin{array}{ccc}
\text{H} & & \text{H} \\
| & & | \\
\text{C} & = & \text{C} \\
| & & | \\
\text{H} & & \text{Cl}
\end{array}
$$

Figure 7. Substituted Monomer

Addition polymerization of this monomer yields the material vinyl chloride, with the structure:

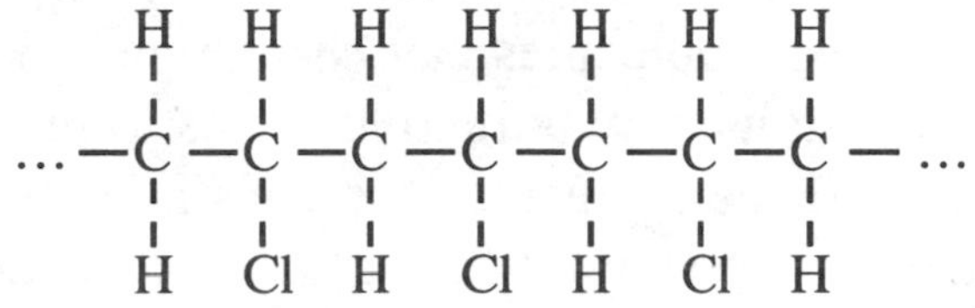

$$
\begin{array}{ccccccccccccc}
\text{H} & & \text{H} & & \text{H} & & \text{H} & & \text{H} & & \text{H} & & \text{H} \\
| & & | & & | & & | & & | & & | & & | \\
\cdots - \text{C} & - & \text{C} & - & \text{C} & - & \text{C} & - & \text{C} & - & \text{C} & - & \text{C} - \cdots \\
| & & | & & | & & | & & | & & | & & | \\
\text{H} & & \text{Cl} & & \text{H} & & \text{Cl} & & \text{H} & & \text{Cl} & & \text{H}
\end{array}
$$

Figure 8. Polymer of Chlorinated Monomer

Organic materials occur in nature (e.g., wood) and are artificially produced (e.g., plastics). Our manufactured organics are made by creating large molecules such as the above via polymerization. We define the **degree of polymerization** as the ratio of the molecular weight of the polymer to that of the monomer. For most commercial plastics, the degree of polymerization ranges from 75 to 750 mers per molecule. Polymerization is carried out by subjecting monomers to combinations of heat, pressure, light, or a catalyst, resulting in replacing the double carbon-carbon bond by a single one. The mechanisms for doing this are either **addition polymerization**, in which successive monomer bonds are broken down and the monomer is added to the molecule, or by **condensation polymerization** in which the polymer is a direct by-product of a batch-type process. The term **copolymerization** refers to the situation in which combinations of more than one monomer are used in producing the polymer.

The actual atomic arrangement of atoms in a molecule is not determined uniquely by the makeup of the molecule. Distinct structures of molecules having the same composition are referred to as **isomers**. Examples of two isomers of the compound H_8C_3O are given in Figure 9. The isomer on the left is normal propyl alcohol; the isomer on the right is isopropyl alcohol. Despite their identical composition these isomers have different physical properties.

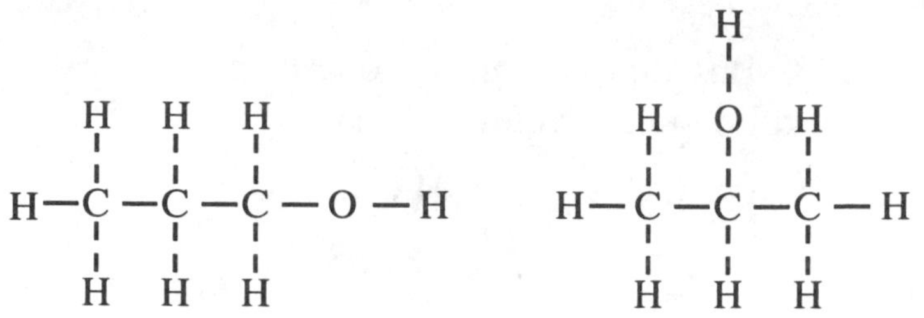

$$
\begin{array}{ccccc}
 & H & H & H & \\
 & | & | & | & \\
H- & C- & C- & C- & O-H \\
 & | & | & | & \\
 & H & H & H &
\end{array}
\qquad
\begin{array}{cccc}
 & & H & \\
 & & | & \\
 & H & O & H \\
 & | & | & | \\
H- & C- & C- & C-H \\
 & | & | & | \\
 & H & H & H
\end{array}
$$

Figure 9. Isomers

The way in which the molecules of a material are arranged relative to each other determines the phase of the material. Familiar phases are gas, liquid, and solid. A **gas** is a material whose molecules are free to move independently of each other. The material has no structure or form. A **liquid** is a material whose molecules can change their position relative to each other but are constrained by attractive forces to maintain a relatively fixed volume. In a **solid** the molecules are constrained to fixed positions relative to each other and essentially no change in shape or volume will occur. Solids, in turn, can be further categorized. In crystalline solids we find a periodic structure in any spatial direction on the atomic scale: molecules are arranged in a definite ordering relative to each other, much like the corner points on a stack of identical boxes. Amorphous materials (solid or liquid) have no such ordering, and on the atomic scale one will see little or no ordering. Examples of crystalline solids include common metals; window glass is an example of an amorphous material.

STRUCTURES AND STRUCTURAL DEFECTS OF MATERIALS

As noted, materials can be structured in either an ordered, periodic form, or at the other extreme, be totally disordered. In this section we turn to a more detailed examination of the physical structure of materials.

We may regard a molecule as a collection of a small number of atoms, which are strongly bound together but whose bonds with other similar atomic groups is much weaker. An example is that of the water molecule H_2O which is covalently bonded. The bonds between water molecules arise from Van der Waals forces and are significantly weaker than the internal bonding forces. The relative strengths of the internal and external binding forces for molecular compounds such as water are manifested in such effects as: a) relatively low melting and boiling temperatures (as compared, e.g., with metals); b) maintenance of molecular structure in the liquid and gaseous phases; and c) solids formed from compounds are relatively soft and can be made to move with the application of relatively small forces. We note that the "small" number of atoms in a molecule may nevertheless be several thousand in number—particularly in the case of hydrocarbons.

Most solid materials used in engineering are crystalline, with their molecules consisting of structured, periodic arrangements of atoms in all directions (Figure 10). The smallest unit, whose periodic repetition determines the solid, is called the **primitive lattice** or **unit cell** of the crystal. The geometric structure of the unit cell determines the categories of crystalline solids. A material composed of several or many crystals, in contrast to one composed of a single crystal, is said to be **polycrystalline**.

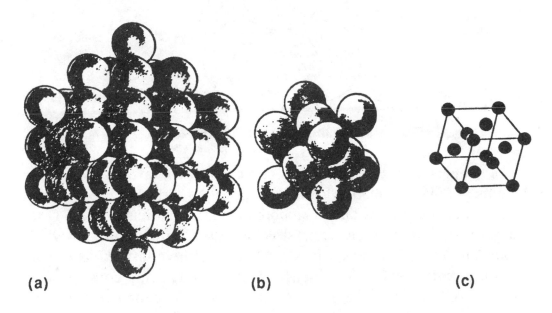

(a)   (b)   (c)

Figure 10. The Crystal Lattice of Copper.
Copper Ions are Shown as Spheres: (a) in the Lattice, (b) in the Unit Cell,
and (c) in the Representation of the Unit Cell.

Every atom has an **atomic radius** measured effectively at the radius of the electron cloud around the nucleus. The equilibrium distance between the centers of two adjacent atoms of a material can be regarded as the sum of their atomic radii, possibly increased by temperature or other factors. One such factor would be the presence of one or more additional atoms in their neighborhood. As more atoms are present, the repulsive forces between atoms grow as do their equilibrium distance. The **coordination number** for an atom is the number of closest neighbors that an atom may have. Consider three atoms of radius R placed next to each other as the vertices of a triangle (Figure 11). Between the three there is a gap in which an additional atom could be placed. The largest ratio r of this atom that could physically fit in this gap is found to be given by $r/R = 0.155$. For four atoms, this ratio is at most 0.225, while for six neighbors it would be 0.414. The ways in which these atoms are arranged in the solid determines the properties of the material. The density of atoms in the crystal is described by the **packing factor** and defined as the ratio of volume of atoms per unit cell to the volume of the unit cell. The volume of the unit cell is dependent on the crystal structure and is discussed below.

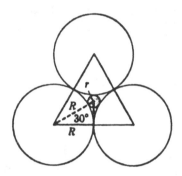

Figure 11. A Gap Between Three Atoms

The simplest structure is that of a **cubic primitive lattice**. In this case four atoms are placed, relative to each other, as the vertices of a cube, that is, at equal distances from three neighbors with perpendicular axes. Three lattice types are based on the cubic structure: the **simple cubic**, for which the atoms are located at the vertices and each primitive lattice has exactly eight atoms; **body-centered cubic**, for which eight atoms correspond to the vertices of a cube, while a ninth is located at the center of the cube; and **face-centered cubic**, in which in place of a single atom located at the cube center, we have six additional atoms located at the centers of the six faces of the cube. These structures are commonly referred to as "sc," "bcc," and "fcc" lattice structures, respectively. At room temperature the crystal lattice structure of iron is body-centered cubic. Similarly, copper atoms are arranged in a face-centered cubic lattice structure.

Moving from a cubic structure, we encounter the **tetragonal lattice structure**, whose primitive lattice has two of three axis lengths equal, and all three axes at right angles to each other. For this configuration we find both simple and body-centered lattice structures; unlike the cubic lattice we do not find face-centered lattice structures.

The classification of all primitive lattices is shown in Table 2. In it a, b, and c denote the axis lengths for the lattice, while α, β, and Γ denote the angles between the axis pairs (a, b), (b, c), and (c, a), respectively. Note that with this notation the cubic lattice corresponds to the case $a = b = c$, and $\alpha = \beta = \Gamma = 90°$. The "options" shown refer to "simple" (atoms only at vertices), body-centered (an additional atom at the center), face-centered (additional atoms located on each face), and base-centered (an additional atom located on one face).

	TABLE 2 PRIMITIVE LATTICE TYPES		
System Name	Axes	Angles	Options
Cubic	$a = b = c$	$\alpha = \beta = \Gamma = 90°$	simple face-centered body-centered
Tetragonal	$a = b \neq c$	$\alpha = \beta = \Gamma = 90°$	simple body-centered
Monoclinic	$a \neq b \neq c$	$\alpha = \beta = 90° \neq \Gamma$	simple base-centered
Hexagonal	$a = b \neq c$	$\alpha = \beta = 90°$ $\Gamma = 120°$	simple
Triclinic	$a \neq b \neq c$	$\alpha \neq \beta \neq \Gamma$	simple
Orthorhombic	$a \neq b \neq c$	$\alpha = \beta = \Gamma = 90°$	simple face-centered body-centered base-centered
Rhombohedral	$a = b = c$	$\alpha = \beta = \Gamma \neq 90°$	simple

The crystal structure of salt (NaCl) is cubic, with each sodium atom surrounded by four chlorine atoms, and each chlorine atom surrounded by four sodium atoms arranged like the vertices of a cube. Iron at room temperature has the body-centered cubic (bcc) crystal structure; at 910°C iron undergoes a phase transformation in which its crystal structure changes to face-centered cubic (fcc). Such a phase transformation is referred to as

recrystallization. At room temperature the crystal structure of copper is face-centered cubic (fcc), while that of sodium is body-centered cubic (bcc). Other metals having the fcc crystal structure include nickel and platinum.

The primitive lattice or unit cell of the hexagonal crystal can be considered as part of a structure in which we have three axes lying in a plane at angles of 120° from each other, in addition to a fourth axis perpendicular to the plane of the other three. Such a structure is found, for example, in magnesium, titanium, and zinc, and is referred to as **close-packed hexagonal (hcp)** (Figure 12).

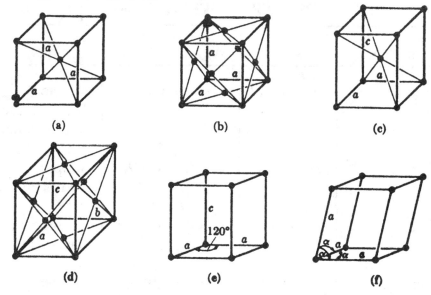

(a) Body-centered Cubic, (b) Face-centered Cubic, (c) Body-centered Tetrangonal, (d) Face-centered Othorhombic, (e) Simple Hexagonal, and (f) Rhombohedral

Figure 12. Unit cells

Directions and planes of a crystal are identified using a vector notation. Placing an origin at a vertex of the primitive lattice, the vector notation [*hkl*] indicates directions within the crystal, while (*hkl*) denotes crystal planes. The entities [100], [010], and [001] correspond to directions along the corresponding *a, b,* and *c* axes. Similarly [110] leads us to the diagonally opposite crystal vertex. On the other hand, face-centered atoms are indicated by the value two in the corresponding face, whence [112] indicates the center of the top face of the unit cell. Crystal planes are indicated by the Miller indices (after W. H. Miller; Figure 13). Here the convention is that if *h, k,* and *l* are the reciprocals of the intercepts of the plane with the *x, y,* and *z* axes, then the Miller index representation of the plane is (*hkl*). If the intercept is negative, then the minus sign is replaced by a bar above the corresponding value. Thus, the plane given by $(1\bar{1}1)$ cuts the *x, y,* and *z* axes at 1, –1, and 1.

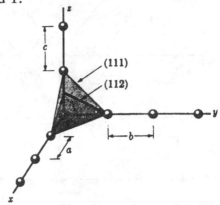

Figure 13. Miller Indices. The (112) Plane Intersects the Axes at Distances of 1, 1, and ½.

A material with the same composition may assume various crystal structures. These crystal structures are referred to as **polymorphs**. An example of polymorphism is iron, assuming both the bcc and fcc structures. As a result the density may well change, as it does in iron, since the packing of the crystal lattice by the material atoms will change with the change of the lattice.

Most metals in the solid phase assume crystal structures. The most convenient method for determining the structure is **x-ray diffraction**. Diffraction occurs because the wavelength of the x-ray is on the same order of magnitude as the distance between atoms in the crystal, about 0.1 to 0.2 nm. Consider three layers (or planes) of atoms (Figure 14). The difference between the paths *DEF* and *ABC* is *GEH*, and *GEH* = 2 *GE*. From trigonometry, we have *GE* = *EH* = *d* sin θ. Bragg discovered that *GE* is an integer if

$$n\lambda = 2d \sin \theta$$

with *n* = 1, 2, 3, ... (an integer) and λ = wavelength. This relationship can be combined with the Miller indices [*hkl*] to give:

$$\frac{(\lambda n)}{2 \sin \theta} = \frac{a}{\sqrt{(h^2 + k^2 + l^2)}}$$

where *a* is the lattice constant of the crystal.

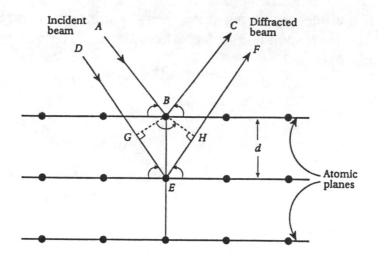

Figure 14. Diffraction From Planes of Atoms

The **density** of a crystal can be easily calculated if the structure is known. For a unit cell of a cubic crystal with side, a, and n atoms in the pattern, the weight of the unit cell is $\dfrac{nM}{N_A}$. M is the atomic weight, N_A is Avagadro's number. Density, ρ, is the weight divided by the volume, a^3.

$$\rho = \frac{nM}{a^3 N_A} = \frac{nM}{V N_A}$$

where V is the volume of the unit cell. Since for a face-centered cubic (fcc), the lattice constant, a, is related to the atomic radius, ρ, by $a = \dfrac{4\rho}{\sqrt{2}}$, then $V = \dfrac{32 r^3}{\sqrt{2}}$.

Ceramics are defined as compounds of metals and nonmetals. As for metals, ceramic structures are generally crystalline, but unlike the case of metals, these lattices are unaccompanied by clouds of free electrons. Ceramics generally have much higher melting temperatures than do metals; they are harder and resistant to chemical change. In addition, they are ordinarily electric insulators, and are poor heat conductors. Because of their rather complex crystal structure, the response of ceramics to thermal events is slow. For this reason, cooling of molten ceramics generally occurs too rapidly for crystal lattice structures to form; hence, the materials often solidify as **supercooled liquids** still containing their latent heat of melting.

Because polymer molecules can bind with each other only via the relatively weak Van der Waals forces, crystal structures are either imperfect or totally lacking. The actual structure of organics, which can serve to link neighboring organic chains, can be based on **cross-linking**, in which adjacent chains are bound together through a number of unsaturated atoms. An example of the use of cross-linking is in the rubber of an automobile tire, in which sulfur atoms are used for linking between neighboring chains. The addition of sulfur for this purpose is referred to as **vulcanization**.

By definition, **amorphous structures** are those that are not crystalline. These may be divided into a number of categories. Two examples of interest to us are liquids and glasses. A liquid, while not assuming a crystalline form, does nevertheless possess a local ordering for its molecules. To define a glass, let us examine the performance of a material as its temperature is reduced. Generally, with reduction in temperature, the energy of motion of the material molecules decreases; hence, the average density increases and the specific volume (reciprocal of the density) declines. During this process the crystalline structure is preserved. At the **fictive temperature**, representative of the material, the decline in specific volume may cease, corresponding to a maintenance of local ordering, and a breakdown in longer-range ordering of the material and of its crystal structure. The material is now said to be in its **glassy phase**.

Crystals express a long-range ordering of the molecules of a material. This ordering is ultimately marred on a scale that is macroscopic, by **crystal defects** which may be expressed as point defects, line defects, or boundaries (Figure 15). Let us now examine these concepts.

Point defects may arise when atoms in the crystal lattice are missing, displaced from their desired lattice locations, or when extra atoms appear in the lattice. A **vacancy** is a defect in which an atom is missing from where it should be in the crystal lattice. Vacancies occur because of imperfect packing of atoms when the crystal was formed or from vibrations at elevated temperatures. Similarly, they can be induced by bombardment by neutrons in situations involving radioactivity. **Schottky defects** are related to vacancies and involve the lack of a pair of oppositely charged ions from the lattice. Another kind of point defect is that of an **interstitialcy**, which occurs when an additional atom is found in the lattice structure. This may occur for a material of high specific volume and will generally result in a localized distortion of the lattice structure. Similarly, a **Frenkel defect** is one in which an atom is displaced from its site to a neighboring site where it constitutes an interstitialcy.

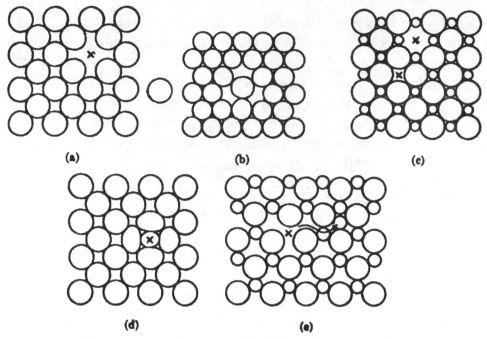

(a) Vacancy, (b) Di-vacancy (Two Missing Atoms), (c) Schottky Defect (d) Interstitialcy, (e) Frenkel Defect

Figure 15. Kinds of Defects

Line defects occur when an entire line of atoms is misplaced in the crystal lattice. An example is an **edge dislocation**, which arises from an edge or additional plane of atoms within the lattice. This, in turn, induces regions of compression and tension in the lattice. A **screw dislocation** is a special case of an edge dislocation in which the crystal lattice is placed much like a winding staircase corresponding to a dislocation (Burgers) vector. The dislocation appears very much like the steps of a screw located along the Burgers vector direction (Figures 16 and 17).

The **Burgers vector, b**, is parallel to the screw dislocation. It can be related to the shearing force, V, per unit length, L, and the shear stress, τ, by the equation:

$$\frac{V}{L} = \mathbf{b}\tau$$

These dislocations, when subjected to stress, can move, producing **slip** or **climb**. Slip refers to the motion of the dislocation, or **slip plane**, parallel to the crystalline plane. It is a plastic deformation. In climb, the edge dislocation moves perpendicularly to the slip plane. Climb occurs at much higher temperatures and is not as common as slip.

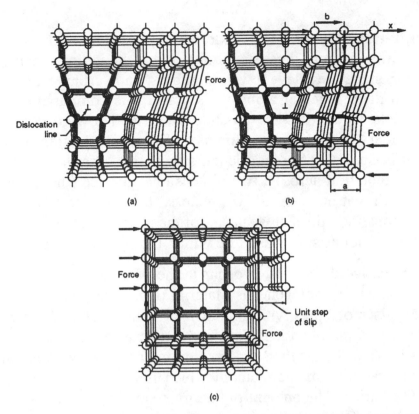

(a) Misplaced Atoms, (b) Compression and Tension in the Lattice, (c) Resultant Unit Step of Slip

Figure 16. Motion of an Edge Dislocation and Production of a Unit Slip Defect at a Crystal Surface

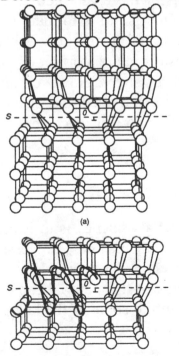

Figure 17. Production of a Screw Dislocation in a Crystal

Boundaries may appear as external surfaces. At such surfaces the atoms are different from those on the interior of the lattice. Their energies are different, since they have fewer neighbors, and surface tension effects tend to bind them together along the surface. The comparable effect for liquid droplets where flow is possible is to tend toward a spherically shaped boundary. A **grain boundary** is a planar imperfection. It separates crystals (or grains) of different orientations. In this case there is a jump in the lattice orientation across a two-dimensional surface (the grain boundary itself) such that on each side the material has a lattice structure. Grain boundaries constitute lines of weakness of the material since binding forces across them are not as strong as those within the lattice structure.

Crystal lattice defects often occur in the process of crystallization of liquid material. If a homogeneous material (e.g., liquid copper) is gradually cooled, its molecules will gradually align themselves in such a way that we find a common orientation in a lattice arrangement on an ever-growing spatial scale. At the solidification temperature, an amount of energy is withdrawn from the material which is large enough to "fix" the atoms in the lattice. The amount of energy needed to do this is the **latent heat of melting**. If the cooling is slow, then the alignment will take place with local attractive and repulsive forces controlling the alignment. If, on the other hand, the cooling is rapid, then time may be lacking for the proper alignment to take place. This, in turn, has a high probability of resulting in misalignments of the crystal lattice and the formation of the defects discussed above. Once solid is formed, it is generally subject to a variety of compressive and shear stresses. When these are sufficiently small, their application results in a distortion of the lattice whose extent is reversed upon removal of the stress. However, should the stress be sufficiently large, even when it is removed, the distortion remains permanent. Distortion of this kind may involve displacement of the lattice along planes, grains, or locally.

PROPERTIES OF MATERIALS

The chief aim of materials science is to learn how materials respond to processes being applied to them. These processes may be physical, such as compression or tension, electrical, thermal, or radioactive. As a result of these processes, the response of the material can be characterized quantitatively. In this section we turn to some of the key properties of materials in the light of applied processes.

We begin by examining **mechanical properties** of materials. The key properties of this type are strength, ductility, elasticity, creep, hardness, and toughness. Each of these properties measures some aspect of the response of the material to some form of mechanical force. The **tensile test** is performed on materials to determine their properties, for example: stiffness, elasticity, or fracture strength. Briefly, a specimen loaded with tension and elongation (or deformation) is measured as the load increases.

Stress is a force per unit area applied to the material. **Strain** is a measure of the deformation of the material. It is generally measured as the relative length of deformation of the material. An example of a stress-strain curve for a ductile sample is shown in Figure 18. From point O to P, Hooke's law applies and a linear relationship exists between stress and strain. The slope of the curve is an index of the **stiffness** of the material. Sometimes it is called the **modulus of elasticity** or **Young's modulus**. Point E is the **elastic limit** of the material. Up to this point, the material returns to its original state after the tension has been removed. However, beyond this point, all deformations are permanent and the material does not recover. Point Y, the **upper yield point** (or strength), is the stress necessary to free dislocations. The dislocations are moved through the lattice at the **lower yield point** L. The **ultimate strength** of the material is shown at point U. Point R represents the **breaking point** or **fracture strength**.

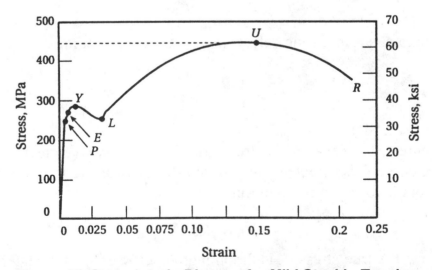

Figure 18. Stress-strain Diagram for Mild Steel in Tension

For plastics, the stress-strain curve has a slightly different shape as seen in Figure 19. After the yield point Y, the sample elongates and the diameter decreases. A phenomenon known as **necking** occurs when the deformation becomes concentrated, altering the shape of the curve. Brittle materials, such as glass, cast iron, and ceramics, can only support small stresses and approach failure (or fracture strength) rapidly.

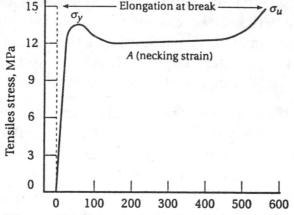

Figure 19. Stress-strain Curve for a Plastic

A stress-strain curve predicts a fracture stress that is lower than the ultimate strength of the material. This error is due to the fact that the stress is calculated on the basis of the original cross-sectional area. The **true stress-strain curve** calculates the instantaneous deformation. A differential strain element $d\varepsilon$ is the ratio of the instantaneous length, dl, to the original length, l.

$$d\varepsilon = \frac{dl}{l}$$

The total strain during deformation is then the integral

$$\varepsilon = \int_{l_o}^{l} \frac{dl}{l} = \ln\left(\frac{l}{l_o}\right).$$

Figure 20 compares the true stress-strain curve (corrected) to the nominal curve (uncorrected). In addition, the part of the true stress-strain curve from Y to R can be approximated by the **Power law equation**:

$$\sigma = K\varepsilon^n$$

where σ is the true stress, K is the strength coefficient of the material, and n is the strain hardening coefficient.

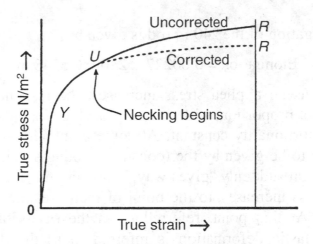

Figure 20. True Stress-strain Curve

For large deformation Young's modulus will be a small value, while for inelastic materials it will be large. Some typical values of Young's modulus are 6.89×10^{10} N/m^2 for aluminum, 2.07×10^{11} N/m^2 for steel down to values as low as 500 for certain rubbers.

EXAMPLE

For a steel with an average modulus of elasticity of 28,000,000 N/m^2, how much of an elongation will be induced in a wire which is 240 m long and 0.2 m in diameter under a load of 2,000 N?

SOLUTION

The amount of elongation will be found from the strain which is given by

$$\text{Strain} = \frac{\text{Stress}}{\text{Young's modulus}}$$

From our conditions

$$\text{Stress} = \frac{\text{load}}{\text{cross - sectional area}}$$

$$= \frac{2,000}{\left[\left(\frac{\pi}{4}\right)(0.2)^2\right]}$$

$$= 63,662 \text{ N/m}^2$$

whence

$$\text{Strain} = 63,662/28,000,000 = 0.00227 \text{ m/m}$$

and so the elongation of the 240 m rod is given by

$$\text{Elongation} = 0.00227 \times 240 = 0.5548 \text{ m}.$$

Normally as an applied stress increases, the responding strain will increase in direct proportion, with the reciprocal to Young's modulus serving as the proportionality constant. At some point (the **elastic limit**) the increase ceases to be given by the (constant) Young's modulus value, but rather the material suddenly "gives way," allowing much greater strains in response to stress increases, to the point of total breakdown of the cohesive structure. At this point, referred to as the **breaking point** of the material, the plastic deformation is referred to as the **ductility** of the material. **Ductility** is defined as the ratio of the ultimate failure strain to the yielding strain. The percent of elongation at failure is calculated by

$$\text{percent elongation} = \frac{\left(L_f - L_o\right)}{L_o} \times 100\%$$
$$= e_f \times 100\%$$

where L_o and L_f are the initial and final lengths of the sample, respectively, and e_f is the final elongation. Likewise, the reduction in area at the point of failure is expressed as:

$$\text{reduction in area} = \frac{\left(A_o - A_f\right)}{A_o} \times 100\%.$$

Typically ductile materials have reductions around 50% or greater, and for brittle materials, less than 10% reduction is expected.

Another term for the plastic deformation at the elastic limit is the **yield**. If we divide the stress inducing the elastic limit by the cross-sectional area of the body being deformed, then the result is the **yield strength** of the material. The yield strength indicates the ability of the material to resist plastic deformation. For certain materials there is a definite yield strength, to which we refer as the **yield point**. In others the transition is somewhat more gradual. Under elastic deformation arising from an applied stress, the strain is essentially proportional to the stress. A compression or elongation of a body in one direction due to the applied stress produces a change in the dimensions of the body in the direction perpendicular to the applied stress. Thus, generally, a compression in the stress direction will produce a broadening of the body in the normal direction, with the opposite holding for elongation. The negative of the ratio of the strain in the normal direction, or **lateral strain** to the strain in the stress direction, is **Poisson's ratio**. This value is normally between 0.25 and 0.5.

When a stress is applied to part of the surface of a body, a **shear stress** is created, producing a displacement of one plane of atoms relative to its neighboring plane. The **shear angle**, α, is the angular displacement produced in this way; for no displacement, this angle would be zero. Its tangent, $\Gamma = \tan(\alpha)$, defines the **elastic shear strain**. The **shear modulus** is the ratio G = Shear stress/G, which corresponds to Young's modulus for the induced strain in the direction of the applied stress. We find that Young's modulus E is related to the shear modulus G and the Poisson ratio v as:

$$E = 2G(1 + v).$$

An applied pressure δP to a body of volume V results in a change in volume δV. The **bulk modulus** of a material is defined as

$$K = \frac{V\delta P}{\delta V}.$$

This is related to the modulus of elasticity and the Poisson ratio as

$$K = \frac{E}{3(1 - 2v)}.$$

The maximum stress applied to a body before failure occurs is a known, measurable value. Dividing this by the original cross-sectional area of the body results in the **tensile strength** of the body. Dislocations in the crystal structure of a material make failure possible at reduced stresses, compared with the theoretical limits for perfect crystalline structures.

These concepts refer to the strength of the material arising from the molecular and atomic bonds of the body. We now turn to a property which relies partly on the surface nature of the body. We refer to the ability of a body to resist penetration by an indenting body as its **hardness**. Two standards for measuring hardness are the **Brinell hardness number** (BHN) and the **Rockwell hardness** (R). There is a linear correlation between the hardness and the tensile strength, as might be expected.

Energy, or work, is the product of force and distance. The ability of a body to withstand breaking under an imposed energy is its **toughness.** This property is found by using standard tests such as the **Charpy**. Another term for toughness is **impact strength**.

In general the Young's modulus of polymers is smaller than that of metals (by one or more orders of magnitude), corresponding to the fact that a given stress will induce a greater strain. A polymer with a substantial degree of elasticity is referred to as an **elastomer**.

Thermal properties of materials relate to their response to the injection or removal of thermal energy. These include the **density**, which normally decreases with increasing temperature; the **specific heat**, which is essentially the amount of heat needed to raise the temperature of the material through a single degree; and the **thermal conductivity** (measuring the ratio of the heat flux generated by a temperature gradient to the gradient itself). The **thermal diffusivity** is the ratio of the conductivity to the product of density and specific heat, and it represents the ratio of the rate of temperature increase to spatial change in the gradient. Normally, materials have a characteristic temperature at which they melt and at which they vaporize. The **heat of fusion** (latent heat) is the amount of heat inducing melting of the solid phase of the material at the melting temperature; similarly, the **heat of vaporization** is the amount of heat inducing the vaporization of the liquid material at the vaporization temperature. The **thermal expansion coefficient** is the relative change in volume of a material induced by a unit temperature rise. In SI units these properties are given by the following:

thermal conductivity	$\dfrac{kJ}{m-s-°C}$
specific heat	$\dfrac{kJ}{kg}$
density	$\dfrac{kg}{m^3}$
diffusivity	$\dfrac{m^2}{s}$
latent heat of fusion	$\dfrac{kJ}{kg}$
heat of vaporization	$\dfrac{kJ}{kg}$
expansion coefficient	$\dfrac{1}{°C}$

We recall that a voltage V (1 Volt = 1 Watt/A = 1 Joule/s – A) across a wire is equal to the product of the current I (A) through the wire and the resistance R (ohms), $V = IR$. The resistance of the wire is in turn equal to the product of the resistivity and the length of the wire, whence

$$\text{Resistivity} = \text{Resistance} \times \frac{\text{Area}}{\text{Length (ohm} - \text{m)}}.$$

EXAMPLE

The resistivity of copper is 1.7×10^{-6} ohm-cm. What is the resistance of a 200 meter length of wire whose diameter is 1 cm in diameter?

SOLUTION

By our relation,

$$\text{Resistance} = \text{Resistivity} \times \frac{\text{Length}}{\text{Area}}$$

$$= 1.7 \times 10^{-6} \, 200 \times \frac{10^2}{\pi(.5)^2}$$

$$= .022 \text{ ohms}$$

Electrical conductivity is the reciprocal of the resistivity. **Conductors** are materials with high conductivity such as copper and aluminum. A typical resistivity value is that of copper, which is 1.7×10^{-8} ohm-m. **Dielectrics** are electrical insulators having very low electrical conductivity. Certain materials lose all electrical resistance at a sufficiently low temperature at which point they become **superconductors**. In recent years certain ceramic materials have been found to go through this change of phase at relatively moderate temperatures.

Semiconductors are materials having resistivities lying between those of conductors and insulators. Examples are silicon, germanium, and diamond. While semiconductors are poor conductors of electricity, their conductivity can be enhanced by the addition of electronic imperfections. If, for example, in a silicon lattice a single silicon atom is replaced by an atom of another element for which an electron is missing which would otherwise be there if the atom of silicon were in place, then the resulting "hole" will tend to be filled by electrons coming from a negative side of an imposed electric current. Thus, the hole will migrate toward this negative source, effectively acting like a migrating positively charged particle.

Electric current in this case is referred to as **p-type semiconduction**. If, on the other hand, the electronic imperfection is due to the presence of an atom with a surplus valence electron, then this excess electron cannot fit into the usual bonding structure and will instead migrate to a positive source. This current flow is referred to as **n-semi-conduction**. Binding a semiconductor with an electron "hole" (p-type) to one with a surplus electron (n-type) results in a **p-n junction**.

Diffusion (or movement of atoms within a solid matrix due to random movements on an atomic scale) is the movement of atoms relative to each other in a homogeneous (single phase) body, and the movement of atoms of one material (solute) within a matrix of a second material (solvent). In each case the **diffusion coefficient** is the ratio of the flux of the diffusing material to its concentration gradient. The diffusion coefficient is generally a function of temperature as well as of the materials involved.

A number of metals including iron, cobalt, and nickel are magnetic, in the sense that in response to a magnetic field their atoms will become magnetically aligned, resulting in the material itself becoming magnetic. We refer to the magnetic properties in this case as **ferromagnetism**. If the magnetism is permanent, then the material is **magnetically hard**; if not, it is then **magnetically soft.**

Luminescence of a material is the capability of the electrons in the atoms of the material to be raised to higher energy levels in response to energy input; in certain cases, upon halting the energy input, the electrons move back to lower energy levels, releasing the excess energy in the form of photons and in this way emitting light.

Having examined the various properties of materials, we now turn to the manner in which a body will deform and mechanically fail, in the sense that it has been permanently damaged and is more likely to break apart. Permanent deformation is referred to as **plastic deformation**. The ability of a material to be permanently deformed without breaking apart is referred to as **plasticity**.

We define **slip** as the permanent displacement of the crystal planes relative to each other due to shear stress. The **critical shear stress** is that value of the shear stress which is sufficient to induce slip. Slip will be favored in certain directions over others, dependent on the crystal structure of the material. Solid solutions of metals, wherein one metal is dissolved in another, are less vulnerable to slip than are pure metals. Similarly, grain boundaries interfere with slip, so that materials having much reduced grain size (e.g., polycrystalline materials) are much less vulnerable to slip.

We refer to cold working as the shaping of a metal by mechanical operations while at moderate (room) temperature below the melting point. The term **cold work** is a measure of the distortion resulting from a decrease in cross-sectional area during plastic deformation,

$$\text{Cold Work} = 100 \times \frac{\delta A}{A_0}$$

for the original area A_0. One result of cold working is that small amounts of slip induce less ordering, and hence reduced vulnerability to additional slip and an increase in material hardness. The increase in hardness arising from plastic deformation is **strain hardening**. The dependence of properties on temperature for a cold-worked material is seen in Figure 21.

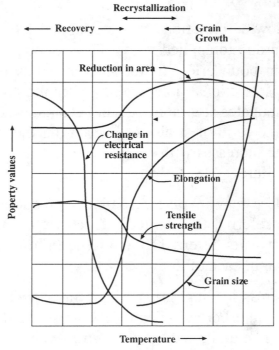

Figure 21. Property Variation with Temperature for a Cold-worked Metal

EXAMPLE

To have a tensile strength of more than 60,000 psi in its final form, we may subject a brass rod to cold work greater than 15%. What is the final diameter in English units of a brass rod with an initial diameter of 0.3 in. and cold work of 25% as its drawing process specification?

SOLUTION

From the definition of the cold work, if d is the final diameter of the rod, then

$$0.25 = \frac{\left[(0.3)^2 \, \frac{\pi}{4} - d^2 \, \frac{\pi}{4} \right]}{(0.3)^2 \, \frac{\pi}{4}}$$

$$d = 0.2598 \text{ in}$$

Annealing is the heating of a plastically deformed material to a temperature sufficient to move the lattice atoms into a crystalline array stronger than their original form, undergoing a process of **recrystallization**. **Quenching** and **tempering** are heat treatment methods for hardening and toughening materials. When applied to glass, tempering involves heating to a high temperature followed by immersion in oil to subject the surface to a permanent compression.

Creep is the slow deformation of a material under stress in the period of steady elongation due to applied stress. This period begins after initial adjustments of grain boundaries, flaws, etc., and ends when significant reduction in the cross-sectional area begins. After the area reduction begins, the material elongates at a rapid rate and eventually fails or ruptures. The **creep rate** is the ratio of strain to time during the period of steady creep. The creep rate increases with temperature and stress, which in turn, reduce the time to failure.

The actual failure may involve a continuous reduction of cross-sectional area to zero, referred to as **ductile fracture**, or separation of the material into distinct parts, referred to as **brittle failure**. **Fracture** is the failure of the material in each of these ways.

Under cyclic stress loading, a material is more vulnerable to failure than under static loading. For sufficiently low stress the number of cycles leading to failure will be unlimited. At some stress value, referred to as the **endurance limit**, this ceases to be the case, and for stresses beyond this value the number of cycles leading to failure decreases rapidly. We refer to the failure of a material under cyclic loading as **fatigue**.

The term "plastics" is used because these materials undergo plastic deformations and have a high degree of plasticity. This is manifested by the fact that one can subject them to pressure and high temperature, pour them into a mold, and upon "setting," cooling, and removal of the pressure, one will have a permanently shaped object. Materials whose plasticity increases with temperature are referred to as **thermoplastic resins**. In contrast, **thermosetting resins** set essentially as one large covalently bound molecule simply upon mechanical stress, with no slippage possible. Generally this type of resin is stronger than the thermoplastic type. The intermolecular forces of thermoplastic polymers are overcome at high temperatures while those of the thermosetting plastics are not.

MULTICOMPONENT MATERIALS AND PHASE DIAGRAMS

We now turn to the makeup and behavior of mixtures of pure materials. We refer to such mixtures as **solutions** or **alloys**. To gain an understanding of the behavior of a solution, we begin with two examples.

Consider a quantity of pure water at some temperature T_0. We know that should we reduce the temperature to $T_1 = 0°C$ the water will freeze and pure ice will form. Let us now add a small amount of salt to the water stirring the mixture. We know that the small amount of salt added should totally dissolve in the water, forming liquid **brine**. Should we now reduce the temperature of the brine, we would find that at some temperature $T_2 <$ T_1, which is less than the freezing temperature of pure water, we obtain a mixture of ice and brine; further reduction to a temperature of $-21°C$ results in a separation of salt from the brine, freezing of the water in the brine, and a mixture of ice and salt only. Adding more salt to our water at the initial temperature T_0 results in a brine solution, which upon cooling will produce ice and brine at yet a temperature below T_2 and whose further cooling to $-21°C$ results only in pure ice and salt. If we now successively add more and more salt to the water, we eventually obtain a solution which, upon reducing the temperature, remains a brine solution until we reach $-21°C$ at which point pure ice and salt, with no brine present, is formed. Adding additional salt to the water at T_0 results now in different behavior: if its temperature is reduced from this initial value, we obtain salt and brine, instead of ice and brine at some temperature which is now above $-21°C$! Further reduction of the temperature to $-21°C$ results again in ice and salt. We thus see that our mixture of water and salt can result in four distinct physical phases, depending on the amount (or concentration) of salt and the temperature. These phases can be listed as: a) brine (pure liquid consisting of water and dissolved salt); b) ice and brine (that is, liquid brine with salt crystals); c) salt and brine (that is, liquid brine with salt crystals); and d) ice and salt (that is, mutually exclusive bodies of salt and ice). The minimum temperature of $-21°C$ reached by the demarcation points between ice + brine and brine or salt + brine and brine is the **eutectic temperature** of a salt/water solution; the corresponding salt concentration is its **eutectic composition**. The diagram indicating the phase of the solution in the temperature/composition plane is referred to as a **phase diagram** for the solution (Figure 22). By means of the phase diagram, we know what is the physical state of the solution for any combination of values of salt concentration and temperature. The curves demarcating the brine state and those of salt + brine and ice + brine are the solubility curves for the solubility of ice in brine and salt in brine, respectively. We note that this phase diagram is an equilibrium phase diagram, in the sense that it reflects the phases that would be formed after a time which is long enough for our system to reach equilibrium and undergo no transient changes.

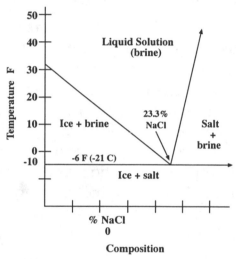

Figure 22. Phase Diagram for Water and Salt Mixture

An example of a metallic phase diagram is given by the solution of copper and nickel (Figure 23). It is found that the atoms of these metals occupy about the same volume, while in crystal form each has a face-centered cubic structure. Hence, each can physically replace the other in a crystal lattice. Pure nickel is known to melt at 1,455°C, while the melting point of pure copper is 1,083°C. Hence, if we begin with pure nickel at a temperature above 1,455°C and begin to reduce its temperature, the nickel will crystallize (freeze) at this temperature, and below it we will find solid nickel. Let us now add a small amount of copper to the liquid nickel at the initial temperature above 1,455°C. Reducing the temperature of this solution now produces, at a temperature T_1, which is less than 1,455°C, a semi-solid phase, comprised of intermixed solid and liquid particles; this phase is maintained as we reduce the temperature until we reach a value $T_2 < T_1$ at which point we find a solid solution of copper and nickel. The values of T_1 and T_2 depend on the relative concentrations of copper and nickel. As more copper is added and its concentration rises, their values decrease. Moreover, after an initial increase in their difference, we find that they tend to be closer to each other, agreeing at the value 1,083°C where we have pure copper only. The curve in the plane determined by temperature/copper composition obtained from the values of T_1, beyond which all compositions are liquid, is referred to as the **liquidus curve**; similarly that curve determined by T_2, beyond which all compositions are solid, is the **solidus curve**. The resulting phase diagram is again an equilibrium phase diagram corresponding to equilibrium conditions in which enough time has elapsed to allow movement of atoms and heat to produce uniform conditions in our sample. In an actual slow freezing or casting process for a copper/nickel alloy, we would expect to avoid the semi-solid state, obtaining, for uniform temperature, bodies of material at concentrations determined by the liquidus and solidus curves for that temperature. Equilibrium diagrams are often referred to as **constitutional diagrams**. The significance of the phase diagram is that it makes it possible for us to extract such information as what will be present and in what percentage for a given state. For the simple Cu-Ni phase diagram, any point below the solidus curve is a solid Cu-Ni alloy system. For a point in the semi-solid zone between solidus and liquidus curves, we have a mixture of solid and liquid phases whose compositions can be found from the so-called **Lever rule**; what we do is to find the points of intersection of a drawn through the point for constant temperature with the solidus and liquidus curves. These points of intersection determine the states of the two phases present.

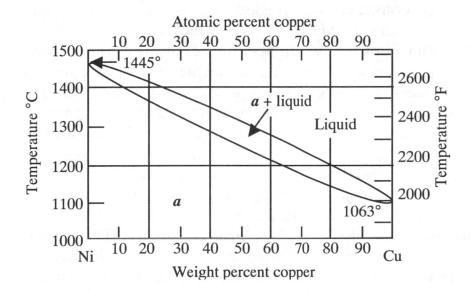

Figure 23. Copper-nickel Phase Diagram

For Figure 23, the fractions of solid and liquid at point A can be found by the lever rule and the definitions:

$$\text{fraction of solid} = \frac{s}{t} = 1 - \text{fraction of liquid}$$

$$\text{fraction of liquid} = \frac{l}{t} = 1 - \text{fraction of solid}$$

In this case, at a temperatue of 1,200°C and a 70 weight percent,

$$s = 70 - 60 = 10$$
$$l = 79 - 70 = 9$$
$$t = 79 - 60 = 19$$

$$\text{fraction of solid} = \frac{9}{19} = 0.47$$

$$\text{fraction of liquid} = \frac{10}{19} = 0.53$$

Probably the most important metallic alloy is steel, which is an alloy of iron and carbon. Pure iron undergoes recrystallization at the temperatures $T_0 = 910°C$ and $T_1 = 1,400°C$. Below T_0 it is body-centered; between T_0 and T_1 it is face-centered. Beyond T_1 it returns to the body-centered structure. The corresponding materials are respectively, ferrite (α-iron), austenite (Γ-iron), and δ-iron (Figure 24). **Ferrite** is familiar iron at room temperature. It is soft, ductile, and highly ferromagnetic. **Carbon** is essentially insoluble in ferrite which has no space available for accommodating carbon atoms. **Austenite** is soft and ductile, not ferromagnetic, but can accommodate dissolved carbon for forming steel. The δ-**iron**, like ferrite, is body-centered cubic in its lattice structure, but because of the high temperature at which we process it, it can accommodate substantially more carbon than ferrite. An additional carbon-iron alloy form is **cementite**, or **iron-oxide**, which arises when excess carbon atoms are bonded to iron atoms in an orthorhombic unit cell. Cementite is extremely hard and substantially strengthens steels in which it is present. A metallurgically important form of steel is **pearlite**, which results when slowly cooling steel undergoes a eutectic phase transformation at 723°C. It is composed of alternate sheets of iron and iron-carbide, Fe_2C. If steel is quenched rapidly enough to make it undergo a phase transformation at a low temperature, the product is referred to as **martensite**. Martensite is supersaturated with carbon atoms which could alloy with iron at a higher temperature but which, due to quenching, are literally "frozen" into place at the lower temperature (Figure 25).

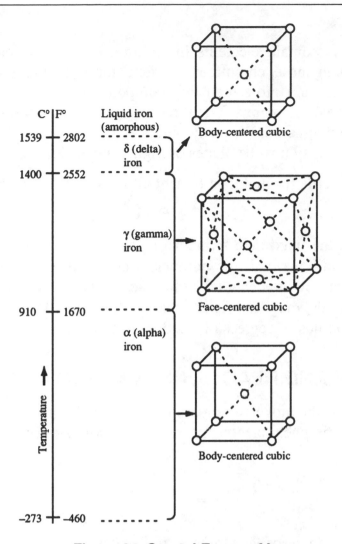

Figure 24. Crystal Forms of Iron

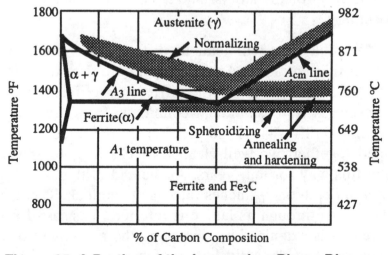

Figure 25. A Portion of the Iron-carbon Phase Diagram

Most steels contain elements in addition to iron and carbon; these may include manganese, chromium, or nickel for additional features. Such alloy systems contain more than two components, giving rise to **multi-component phase diagrams**. For three components we would thus find **ternary phase diagrams**. We again obtain eutectic compositions and temperatures, which may now be planes or higher dimensional surfaces.

The **phase rule** for multicomponent alloy systems takes the form

$$P = C + E - V.$$

Here P is the maximum number of phases that could coexist under equilibrium conditions; C is the number of components; E is the number of environmental factors being taken into account (e.g., temperature, pressure, electric fields, magnetic fields, composition); and V is the number of unassigned variables or degrees of freedom of the system.

DIFFUSION AND REACTIONS IN MATERIALS

Diffusion is the movement of atoms or molecules in a material. Fick's law describes this phenomenon; in one-dimension, steady-state diffusion is written as:

$$J = -D\frac{dC}{dx}$$

where J is the amount of the atoms or molecules moving per unit time, C is the concentration of the atoms, and x is the distance along which the diffusion occurs.

Atoms or molecules will tend to diffuse from points of higher to points of lower concentration. As the temperature rises the diffusion coefficient will tend to rise; similarly, the diffusion coefficient depends on the materials present as well as ambient conditions (pressure, etc.). An interesting example of diffusion is the case where the director of the British mint clamped together two well-cleaned blocks of gold and of lead and kept them in this way for four years. At the end of this period gold could be detected at a depth of $5/16$ inches into the lead block. The diffusion of a metal's own atoms through its lattice is referred to as **self-diffusion**. This form of diffusion is examined by observing the movement of radioactive isotopes of a metal in the solid lattice of nonradioactive isotopes of the same metal. An industrial process based on diffusion of carbon atoms in steel is that of **carburizing**. In this process a low carbon steel is exposed to carbon atoms at a high temperature; the small carbon atoms diffuse into the subsurface of the solid metal to form a high-carbon coating. If the body is then quenched, we obtain a hard, wear-resistant, martensite surface with a ferrite core; such materials are of particular use in machining processes. Atoms of gases can also diffuse in metals. One undesirable instance of such a process is that of **hydrogen embrittlement**, wherein atoms of hydrogen arising, for instance from radiation sources, penetrate steel, diffuse to regions of greater stress, and induce cracks and premature fracture. This is of particular concern in nuclear reactors.

A variety of reactions that produce new solid phases are of major engineering interest. The simplest such reaction is that of a **polymorphic transformation**. An example would be that of recrystallization of iron at its appropriate transition temperatures. As we have seen earlier, this is accompanied by changes of density and other material properties. In studying phase diagrams, we noted that upon cooling an alloy system at a slow rate, we may obtain two or more distinct materials whose concentrations experience jumps. Such reactions are referred to as **eutectic reactions**. An example of a eutectic reaction is the pearlite formation reaction referred to earlier. Eutectic reactions must proceed slowly, since they require diffusion of atoms of the component materials with respect to each other to achieve the demands of the phase diagrams.

Other reactions exist at different phases and states while a **eutectic reaction** describes a liquid cooled to another liquid A and a solid B. (When a solid is cooled to a liquid A and a solid B, the term eutectic is replaced by **eutectoid**.) However, if the liquid and a solid A is cooled to a solid B, the reaction is **peritectic**, and liquid cooled to liquid B and solid A is **monotectic**. Again, **peritectoid** and **monotectoid** are used for the cooling of the solids.

Of major importance is the rate of a reaction. If the reaction requires, for example, that we have simultaneous diffusion and heat transfer, then rapid cooling may prevent the needed diffusion from occurring, and hence the material will enter into a state which is not equilibrium and which from the point of view of least potential energy, is unstable. Such a state is referred to as **metastable**. An example of such a metastable state is that of supercooled water, obtained when water, in a clean beaker, is cooled to a temperature below 0°C without freezing. In the same sense, an alloy system in its liquid phase may be cooled so rapidly that diffusion to accommodate the demands of the phase diagram cannot take place. In this case the material may enter the metastable constitutionally supercooled state. In general, to move from a metastable to a stable state may require some additional input of energy, an example being vibration of supercooled water, which immediately initiates freezing. The martensitic phase of steel is another example of a metastable phase.

By altering the microstructure of materials, we can, in principle, incorporate desirable properties into the materials. These changes can be induced via plastic deformations, by recrystallization, by selection of appropriate solvent and trace components of our materials, and through appropriate crystal orientation. In turn, the microstructure determines the thermal and mechanical properties (e.g., density, thermal conductivity, hardness, etc.) that are of importance to use of these materials. Some typical heat treating processes are **annealing**, in which we heat the material to remove strains (for cold-worked materials and glass) and to soften (for steel); **quenching**, for hardening; **tempering** via quenching, to toughen materials such as steel and glass; **age-hardening**, in which we rapidly cool an alloy, reheat partly, and then cool again, for hardening of aluminum alloys; and **firing**, in which we heat a solid solution to form glassy bonds for producing bricks.

Treatments that help strengthen materials are of crucial importance. One approach is to reduce the grain size resulting in a reduced ability to encounter slip. For alloy systems, the low concentration (solute) atoms may tend to cluster around a dislocation in the high concentration (solvent) atoms raising the stress needed to cause failure. The hardening method based on this is referred to as **alloy hardening** and is found in all alloy systems. In some systems the method of **precipitation hardening** or **age-hardening**, occurring as a result of precipitation from a supersaturated solution, results in greatly improved material strength. Steel can be made particularly strong, as we have seen, as a result of the richness of hardening treatments such as the production of the martensitic state.

CORROSION AND RADIATION DAMAGE

Corrosion is the destructive attack of a metal by chemical or electrochemical reaction with its environment. This is in contrast with erosion, galling, or wear, which are physical processes. **Rusting** refers to the corrosion of iron or iron-based alloys. Thus, by definition, nonferrous metals may corrode but do not rust.

Corrosion generally occurs as the result of the processes of solution and oxidation. **Solution** is the process wherein a material dissolves in a solute. This may take the form of dissolving as molecules, as in the case of sugar in water, or as electrically charged ions, as in the case of salt, creating sodium and chloride ions. Generally, a solute dissolves more easily in a solvent if a) the solute molecules or ions are small; b) the solute and solvent are similar in structure; c) the temperature increases; and d) multiple solutes are present. **Oxidation** is the process of removing electrons from an atom. An example is the removal of electrons in two stages from an iron atom:

$$Fe \rightarrow Fe^{2+} + 2e^-$$

$$Fe^{2+} \rightarrow Fe^{3+} + e^-$$

The first reaction involves the oxidation of iron to form ferrous ions, while the second is the oxidation of ferrous ions to form ferric ions. In the presence of water and oxygen, rust, whose chemical formula is $4Fe(OH)_3$, can now be produced according to the reaction

$$4Fe + 3O_2 + 6H_2O \rightarrow 4Fe(OH)_3$$

which requires the initial dissolving of the iron in the water to produce iron ions. Thus, iron will not rust unless both water and oxygen are present. This form of corrosion is referred to as **solution corrosion**. A second type of corrosion is **galvanic corrosion**; if iron is placed in water, it will rapidly produce electrons and ions. The presence now of negatively charged electrons and positively charged ions results in an electrical potential, the **electrode potential**. Hydrogen atoms, too, will dissolve in water, producing an electron and the positively charged hydrogen ion. The potential difference between a source of hydrogen and a plate of iron in water will be 0.44 volts, promoting an electric current from the iron to the hydrogen source. The pair consisting of the hydrogen source and the iron plate constitutes a **galvanic couple** or **cell**. We refer to each as an **electrode**. In general, the electrode supplying electrons to the circuit is referred to as the **anode**, while the electrode receiving the electrons is the **cathode**. The flow of electrons to the cathode, or hydrogen source, results in the generation and release of hydrogen gas at the cathode, resulting in a greater tendency for oxidation of the iron at the anode to produce additional electrons. Hence, iron at the anode continues to dissolve into the solution, releasing additional electrons to the cathode, and hence promoting the process. The iron plate will, in this way, corrode through the process of **galvanic corrosion**. The removal of hydrogen from the water results in a greater concentration of hydroxide ions $(OH)^-$ whose presence now promotes the production of rust through the reaction

$$Fe^{3+} + 3(OH)^- \rightarrow Fe(OH)_3.$$

The rust is essentially insoluble in water, whence it precipitates, and allows the galvanic corrosion reaction to continue.

Galvanic cells may be formed between any two distinct materials. The material producing the greater flux of electrons (having the greater **electromotive potential**) will serve as the anode, while the second material will serve as the cathode. Examples include tools containing both steel and brass, steel pipes connected to copper plumbing, and others. Some methods for attempting to protect steel are based on this principle. Thus, galvanized steel is made by coating the steel with a zinc coating. So long as the latter is not scratched, the zinc will indeed protect the steel; if, however, the steel is exposed at a point, then this point can serve as the source of corrosion arising from the zinc/steel galvanic cell, with zinc acting as the anode and steel as the cathode.

Methods for protecting the surface of an object from corrosion are based on three approaches: a) isolation of electrodes via protective surfaces; b) avoidance of galvanic couples; and c) use of galvanic cells for protection. One approach to protecting steel by isolation is through the plating of the steel with ions of $(CrO_4)^{2-}$, with the chromium serving the role of introducing an electrically passive surface for the steel. Avoidance of galvanic couples is achieved, e.g., by the use of a single component. On the other hand, the galvanic reaction can be used to protect the material. An example is the use of zinc coating on a steel surface to serve as a sacrificial material for the galvanic reaction. Often corrosion can be inhibited by the formation of a protective oxide layer, an example being given by aluminum.

RADIATION ALTERATION OF MATERIALS

Radiation can be classified as **electromagnetic** and **particulate**. The former includes radio waves, infrared radiation, light, x-rays, and gamma-rays; the latter includes accelerated protons, electrons (β-rays), helium nuclei (α-rays), and neutrons. In the nuclear industry the principal particles are gamma-rays and neutrons.

Radiation results in transferring energy to the material on which it impacts, resulting in the breaking of bonds and the rearrangement of the atoms of the material. The nature of the impact depends on the particle. For charged particles such as α and β rays, proximity of the particle to the atoms of the material results in interraction and possible structural alteration. On the other hand, the neutron is a massive, uncharged particle that can only interract upon the occurrence of a collision. This collision will usually occur in the interior of the material and result in an interior vacancy. The displacement of an atom in a material can result in a number of possible changes: the material may become activated and available for further reactions; it may be degraded, resulting in loss of material strength; or it may become distorted via displacement. Some typical effects of neutron bombardment include coloring of glasses, loss of elasticity in natural and butyl rubber, hardening of natural rubber, loss of ductility of carbon steels, and rendering plastics unusable as structural materials, depending on the energy of the neutrons. A positive effect for certain stainless steels is an increase in tensile strength and hardness due to dislodging of atoms and restriction of slip. The effects of radiation damage can generally be repaired via annealing at temperatures which may be relatively moderate.

COMPOSITE MATERIALS

It is possible to prepare materials which are composites of various kinds of materials having desirable but complementary properties. An obvious example would be the coating of metal by glass to inhibit corrosion of the metal. Composite materials can be divided into three categories: agglomerated materials, surface coatings, and reinforced materials. We shall now examine each in turn. **Agglomerated materials** consist of a matrix material, "filler" material for the pore spaces in the matrix, and a "glue" to bind the rest of the structure together into the form of a single "brick." A typical glue or binding material would be water in a hydrated solid, linking together distinct molecules. Such is the case for concrete: **concrete** is gravel, with a mixture of sand to fill the pores of the gravel. The remaining space is then filled with a paste of cement and water. The cement hydrates to form a cement paste binding the agglomerate together. The actual chemical constitution of Portland cement is (before binding) a mixture of calcium aluminate and calcium silicate.

Sintering is a process of heating to agglomerate small particles into a large bulk structure. The exact relations may involve melting of a binding material, followed by its crystallization as part of a large, hardened structure. An example of this process is vitreous sintering which is used in brick manufacturing.

We often wish to coat a material surface with a hard surface for resisting wear. Methods for doing this include welding a hard metal coat onto the surface, spraying a special coating onto the surface, or alteration of the surface for this purpose. **Surface alteration** is done usually via heat treatment of the surface, using such techniques as **induction** and **flame hardening**, the former using high frequency currents at the metal surface, and the latter using localized heating. An alternative method of surface alteration rests on the diffusion of elements into the surface, an example being **nitriding**. Here suitable chemical reactions are used to produce a concentration of aluminum nitride at the surface, which forms a wear-resistant surface layer. An alternative approach is **carburizing**, wherein suitable processes result in a high-carbon "case" immersed in the surface of the material. Compressive forces can be applied to the surface of the material by suitable volume changes induced by thermal or compositional changes. These too can result in desired surface layer changes.

Reinforcement of materials can be carried out by introducing small particles into the material which are substantially harder than their surroundings. With this aim we develop a variety of dispersion-strengthened alloys which are substantially stronger than their original forms. In place of particles it is sometimes advantageous to introduce high temperature "whiskers" of, e.g., Al_2O_3 to add strength to a ductile metal which is maintained at elevated temperatures. The same concept is the basis for such materials as glass-reinforced plastics and steel-reinforced concrete.

Properties of composites are a reflection of their components and the purposes for which they have been designed. Thus, for glass-reinforced plastic, the glass provides tensile strength and dimensional stability while the plastic gives us coherency and is not porous. The determination of gross mechanical properties can be carried out in much the same manner as for noncomposite materials. Thus, for example, the determination of the heat transfer properties of a composite material would have to be found by means of standard heat flux and temperature experiments.

REVIEW PROBLEMS

PROBLEM 1

Discuss the difference between extensive and intensive properties and name the properties inherent to a given material.

SOLUTION

Any material properties can be described as either extensive or intensive. An extensive property is one that depends on the amount of material present. An intensive property is one that depends upon each specific material. Density, the yield point, Young's modulus, and Poisson's ratio are all intensive properties and are inherent to a given material. Flexural strength depends on the cross-section of the element and the direction in which the force is applied. Therefore, it is an extensive property and is not inherent to the material.

PROBLEM 2

Explain how the electrical conductivity of an *n*-type semiconductor crystal is dependent upon the number of donor atoms and the electron mobility.

SOLUTION

In an *n*-type semiconductor crystal, the density of electrons in the conduction band is essentially the density of donor atoms in the crystal, and hence the electrical conductivity is given by the relation:

$$\sigma_n = N_d q \mu_n$$

where

σ_n = Electrical conductivity of an *n*-type semiconductor

N_d = Number of donor atoms per cubic meter

μ_n = Electron mobility

q = Charge of an electron, which is constant

Hence, the conductivity closely depends on the number of donor atoms and the electron mobility.

PROBLEM 3

The measure of specific heat of a material relates to the quantity of heat required to change the temperature of a given mass of that material. At ordinary temperature ranges for a small temperature range, the specific heat, C, may be considered constant. Explain the significance of aluminum having a greater specific heat (0.217 cal/gm°C) than copper (0.093 cal/gm°C).

SOLUTION

For a solid:

$$q = C\Delta T$$

Rearranging,

$$\Delta T = \frac{q}{C}$$

For the same ΔT, as C decreases, q must decrease. Likewise, as C increases, q must increase. Thus, it takes more energy in the form of heat to change the temperature of aluminum than copper of equal mass.

PROBLEM 4

The viscoelastic behavior of an amorphous polymer will change with increasing temperature from its rigid structure at low temperatures. The polymer's behavior may proceed through the following stages: leathery, rubbery, and viscous. Explain the properties of these stages and their order.

SOLUTION

The polymer goes from a leathery stage, to a rubber and then a viscous stage. In the leathery stage the polymer can be deformed readily but it cannot regain its shape quickly if the stress is removed. In the rubbery stage the polymer can regain its original shape quickly. In the viscous stage the polymer deforms extensively by viscous flow.

PROBLEM 5

Molybdenum has a body-centered cubic lattice structure (shown in Fiugre 26). What are the number of atoms per unit cell?

SOLUTION

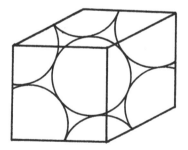

Figure 26. Body-centered Lattice Structure

$$1 \text{ atom centered} + 8 \times \left(\frac{1}{8} \text{ atoms in each corner} \right) = 2 \text{ atoms}$$

PROBLEM 6

Aluminum has a higher atomic packing factor than molybdenum by about 6%. What does this mean?

SOLUTION

Aluminum is heavier than molybdenum.

PROBLEM 7

Miller indices provide a system of notation for describing crystallographic planes and directions. Using Figure 27, write a set of indices that is parallel to (101).

SOLUTION

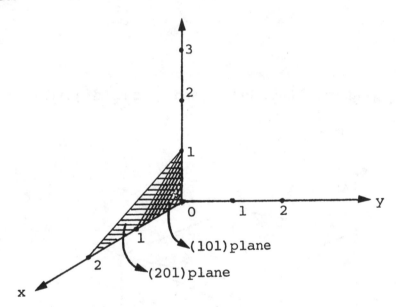

Figure 27. Parallel Miller Indices and Planes

Miller indices specify a plane by the integral common denominator of the values of the three coordinates of its location. The planes (101) and (201) overlap and thus are parallel.

PROBLEM 8

Using Miller indices and the lattice shown in Figure 28 describe the direction of [111].

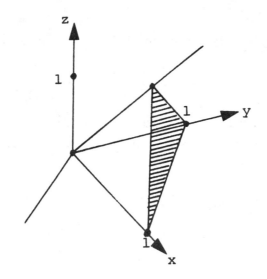

Figure 28. Miller Indices and Direction of [111]

SOLUTION

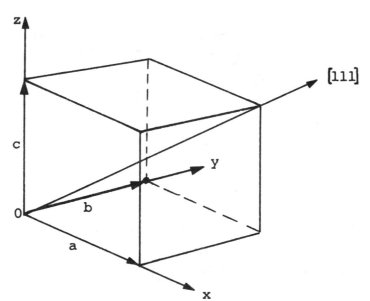

Figure 29. Plane (111) Perpendicular to [111]

The plane (111) is shown in Figure 29; it can be seen that the direction [111] is perpendicular to it. This is true in general for Miller indices. But Miller indices apply only to cubic lattice structures.

PROBLEM 9

Compare the planes shown in Figure 30.

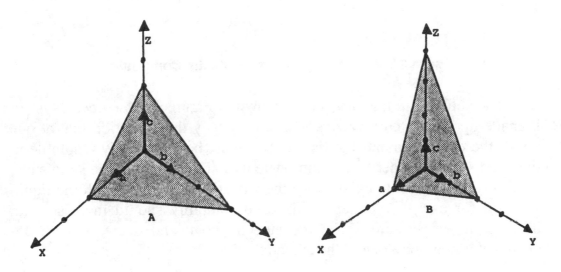

Figure 30. Miller Indices of Two Planes

SOLUTION

Miller indices for A and B, respectively, are (232) and (124). Since Miller indices apply to all cubic lattice structures, plane A does not represent only body-centered crystal lattice structures. The planes are not parallel, and the direction vector [232] is perpendicular to the plane (232).

PROBLEM 10

Draw a phase diagram for a eutectic system.

SOLUTION

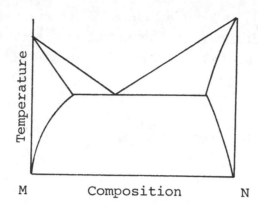

Figure 31. Phase Diagram of a Eutectic Composition

The solution to this problem is shown in Figure 31. A eutectic system is made up of two components and must satisfy the condition that at one point, the eutectic point, the liquid state must be completely insoluble in the solid state. In order to accommodate partial solubility in the solid state, a solid solution should exist above the eutectic point along with the liquid solution for each component. This solid solubility should increase with decreasing temperature above the eutectic point and decrease with decreasing temperature below the eutectic point.

FE/EIT

Fundamentals of Engineering: AM Exam

CHAPTER 13

Engineering Economics

CHAPTER 13

ENGINEERING ECONOMICS

INVESTMENT

Money invested generates more money, and engineering economics gives the basis for making a systematic evaluation of investment alternatives for economic decisions to allocate the corporation's capital for a maximum return on these investments. An economic evaluation of a proposed investment includes determining the expected profit and capital expenditures, and these alternatives can include construction of a new plant and expansion of existing facilities.

New plants, products, and technology require new capital, and most firms have limited resources. Consequently, investment decisions require capital budgeting. This is the evaluation and selection of the best investments from a set of options. Common methods for evaluating investments include net present value and rate of return for private companies and benefit-cost analysis for public projects.

Risk is also part of the decision process. The analysis of projects must incorporate the level of risk to be able to compare projects with high returns and high risks with those having lower returns and more certain outcomes.

Engineering economics provides the framework for the preparation of economic feasibility studies as part of a company's continual planning process. The fundamental concepts used in these evaluations include profit, capital, expenses, and cash flow. These require an understanding of the time value of money, which is discussed in the next section.

TIME VALUE OF MONEY

Investment means committing funds in the present with a certain amount of assurance for a greater return of this money in the future. This growth in money is called the **time value of money**.

Interest is the cost of borrowed money, or it is the reward for lending money. Also, interest is the return which can be obtained when money is put to productive use.

Simple interest means that only the principal, P, is used in calculation of interest, I, due. Thus:

$$I = iPn \tag{1}$$

where i is the interest rate and n is the number of interest periods. It is understood that n and i refer to the same unit of time (year, month, etc.).

If $1,000 is borrowed for five years at 8% simple interest rate, the total interest would be:

$$I = (0.08)(\$1,000)(5) = \$400$$

and the total amount, F, due at the end of the loan period is equal to:

$$F = P + I = \$1,000 + \$400 = \$1,400$$

Simple interest is rarely used, and usually interest is compounded. **Compound interest** means that interest which has been accrued over the interest period is also subject to the interest rate in the next period. If $1,000 was borrowed for five years at 8%, compounded annually, the amount of principle plus interest, F_1, due after the first year could be calculated just as simple interest, since there is no compounding in the first year.

$$F_1 = P + iP = P(1 + i)$$
$$F_1 = \$1,000(1 + 0.08) = \$1,080$$

In the second year, the interest rate i (= 8%) is then applied to F_1 (= $1,080) if no payment is made at the end of the first year:

$$F_2 = iF_1 + F_1$$
$$F_2 = iP(1 + i) + P(1 + i)$$
$$F_2 = P(i + 1)^2$$

$$F_2 = \$1,000(1 + 0.08)^2 = \$1,166$$

In the third year, the procedure is repeated:

$$F_3 = iF_2 + F_2$$
$$F_3 = iP(i + 1)^2 + P(1 + i)^2$$
$$F_3 = P(i + 1)^3$$
$$F_3 = \$1,000(1 + 0.08)^3 = \$1,260$$

The amount to be repaid in years four and five would be:

$$F_4 = P(i + 1)^4 = \$1,361$$
$$F_5 = P(i + 1)^5 = \$1,469$$

In general, the formula to compute the amount F_n to be paid at the end of n time periods with an interest rate of i is given by the following equation:

$$F_n = P(1 + i)^n \tag{2}$$

Compounding can be calculated more than once a year, e.g., quarterly, monthly, even daily. However, interest rates are usually quoted as an **annual nominal interest rate**, r. If m is the number of times the interest is compounded between payments, then the **annual effective interest rate**, i_e, is given by using equations (1) and (2), and the result is the following equation:

$$i_e = \left(1 + \frac{r}{k}\right)^k - 1 \tag{3}$$

For example, the effective interest rate is $i_e = 0.0824$ for a nominal interest rate $r = 0.08$ compounded quarterly ($k = 4$) using equation (3). The value of i_e is used in equation (2) to evaluate F_n given P; and for P equal to $\$1,000$, the value of F_5 is $\$1,486$ for five years.

As shown by equation (2), money, having an ability to earn interest, has its value increase over time, thus the term **time value of money**. The **future worth**, F_n, of an amount of money P is given by equation (2), and P is called the **present value** of an amount of money whose future worth is F_n available in n time periods at an interest rate of i. An amount of money F_n, available in n time periods in the future is worth less than the same amount of money available in the present. That the amount F_n decreases in value is shown by rearranging equation (2) to have:

$$P = \frac{F}{(1+i)^n} \tag{4}$$

In the example, \$1,469 received in five years is only worth \$1,000 if the interest rate available is 8%.

INFLATION

The cost of goods and services increases with time as a result of inflation. The inflation rate is usually given as a percentage that is compounded annually. For a constant inflation rate, f, expressed as a fraction over a period of n years the future cost of a commodity, F_c, increases in relation to the present cost, P_c, by the following equation:

$$F_c = P_c(i + f)^n \tag{5}$$

Also, the future worth, F, of money decreases in relation to the present value, P; and the devaluation is given by the following equation for a constant inflation rate for n years:

$$F = \frac{P}{(1+f)^n} \tag{6}$$

However, if P is invested at a constant interest rate i i, the future worth F would be given by the following equation using equations (2) and (6):

$$F = \frac{P(1+i)^n}{(1+f)^n} = P\left[\frac{1+i}{1+f}\right]^n$$

For example, if the inflation rate was 6% ($f = 0.06$) for the first five-year period ($n = 5$) when $P = \$1,000$ was invested at an interest rate of 8%, the future worth is only \$1,098 compared to \$1,469, not considering inflation.

TAXES

Interest earned in a given year is subject to taxes for that year. If the interest period is the same as the tax period, then the interest earned during this period is iP, and the tax due on this earned interest is tiP, where t is the tax rate. For companies, t can be as much as 0.38, and the net return after taxes is interest minus taxes, $I - T = iP - tiP = (1 - t)iP$. Consequently, the future worth, F, after one year, including taxes, is:

$$F = P + (1 - t)iP = [1+(1 - t)i]P$$

and if inflation proceeds at a rate f during this year, the above equation can be written as:

$$F = \left[\frac{1+(1-t)i}{1+f}\right]P \qquad F = \left[1+\frac{(1-t)i-f}{1+f}\right]P$$

Then, this equation can be put in the form of equation (2) by defining a composite interest rate that includes inflation and taxes as:

$$i_c = \frac{(1-t)i - f}{1+f} \tag{7}$$

Now, the effects of interest, inflation, and taxes can be included in the evaluation of the future worth, F, knowing the present value P by the following equation:

$$F = P(1 + i_c)^n \tag{8}$$

For a tax rate of 0.20 with an inflation rate of 0.06, the future worth of \$1,000 invested at an interest rate of 8% for five years is now only \$1,019 compared to \$1,469, not considering inflation and taxes.

The intervals for the interest, inflation, and tax rates in equation (8) must all be the same, and the rates must be constant. If this is not the case, the same procedure is used, but each interval has to be evaluated separately and sequentially.

RISK

The effect of risk can be approximated in this analysis by replacing the interest rate i in equation (7) with the sum $(i + i_r)$. Here i_r represents an addition to the cost of financing a project when there is more risk involved than is normally expected.

CASH FLOW

To this point, we have been discussing the results of investing a single sum of money. However, money received from the sale of products and spent on manufacturing costs by a company occurs on nearly a continuous basis, and income is reinvested daily by the company. To be able to analyze the income and expenditures for a company, it is convenient to select an interval, typically a year, to perform the evaluations. The **cash**

flow for the period is the difference between all of the funds received and all of the funds disbursed. It is convenient to represent this net annual cash flow on a diagram, and this is especially useful for project evaluations. A **cash flow diagram** will show what is expected to take place over the life of a project. The horizontal axis represents time intervals, and the vertical axis represents the amount of cash flow in each of the intervals. A simple cash flow diagram is shown in Figure 1, where the negative cash flows in the first two years represent a net loss for the project. After that, all flows are positive, meaning a net gain in each of those three years. This diagram could apply to a company that planned to purchase a new generator which would reduce utility bills by $4,000 per year for six years, and the generator would be purchased with two payments of $9,000 in the first two years. Then, at the end of the sixth year, the generator could be sold at a salvage value of $1,000, which is added to the income received in the sixth year.

This example illustrates the **end of year convention**, which assumes that income and disbursements are made at the end of each year. Although receipts and payments are usually made throughout the year, the end of year convention greatly simplifies calculation, and poses no problem, since it will not lead to errors in choices between alternatives.

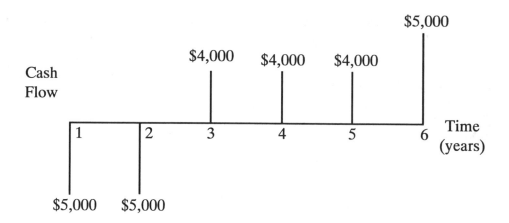

Figure 1. Simple Cash Flow Diagram

A more realistic cash flow diagram is shown in Figure 2 for a typical projection of the net annual income for the estimated life of a new plant. To construct this diagram many items must be estimated. These include demand for product, plant capacity to meet the demand for the company's planned penetration into the market, selling price, cost of raw materials, direct fixed capital for design and construction of the plant, allocated and working capital, land costs, and out-of-pocket expenses.

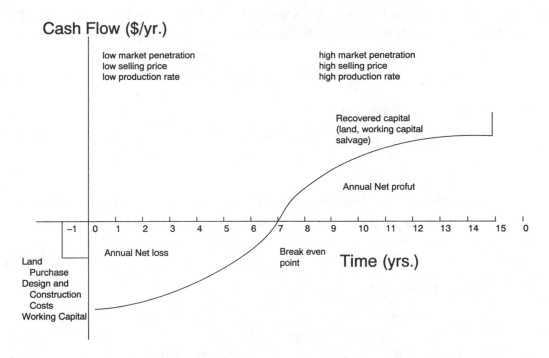

Figure 2. A Typical Diagram for the Economic Life of a Proposed Plant with a 15-Year Economic Life

As shown in the Figure 2, the new plant is in the negative cash position through the sixth year, and in the positive cash position from the eighth year through the end of the plant's planned life in the fifteenth year. The **break-even point** is shown at the seventh year when the firm's cumulative cash flow reaches zero. **Break-even capacity** is the production rate at which all of the costs, excluding depreciation, are equal to the sales realized.

The break-even point and the payback period (discussed later) are two ideas that are used in **break-even analysis** to compare different projects. Other methods used by companies to select the best alternative include determining the useful life for alternate pieces of equipment and the capacity utilization of alternative pieces of equipment in terms of time used per year.

INTEREST FACTORS

There are several interest factors that are routinely used in engineering economics calculations to evaluate the present value P, future worth F, uniform payment (receipt) A, and uniform gradient G. These equations require a constant interest rate i over a series of uniform time intervals n. Values for these factors can be found in tables of compound interest factors.

Also, some electronic calculators incorporate these calculations with special keys. The cash flow diagrams for these factors are shown in Figure 3.

Single-Payment, Compound-Amount Factor, $\dfrac{F}{P}$, is equation (2) written in the following form:

$$\frac{F}{P} = (1+i)^n \tag{9}$$

Values on the right-hand side of equation (9) can be computed by specifying i and n, and these can be used to multiply the present value P to give the future worth F. For example, with interest rate of 0.08 and five years, $n = 5$, the factor is $(1 + 0.08)^5 = 1.469$, and the future worth of $1,000 is $1,469.

There is a standard notation to represent the equations for these factors, and the notation $\left(\dfrac{F}{P}, i\%, n\right)$ is used to represent equation (9). Thus, for the example $\left(\dfrac{F}{P}, 8\%, 5\right) = 1.469$.

Single-Payment, Present-Worth Factor: This factor $\dfrac{P}{F}$ is the reciprocal of the single-payment, compound-amount factor and is given by the following equation:

$$\frac{P}{F} = (1+i)^{-n} \tag{10}$$

The quantity $(1 + i)^{-n}$ is also called the **discount factor**. The future worth F can be multiplied by this factor to determine the present value P. For example, with $i = 0.08$ and $n = 5$, the value of the factor is 0.68058, and the present value of $F = \$1,469$ is $1,000. Here $\left(\dfrac{F}{P}, 8\%, 5\right) = 0.68058$.

Uniform-Series, Compound-Amount Factor: This factor $\dfrac{F}{A}$ gives the future worth, F, of a uniform series of equal payments or receipts, A, that are made over n years earning an interest rate i. The equation for this factor is given below.

$$\frac{F}{A} = \frac{(1+i)^n - 1}{i} \tag{11}$$

A uniform annual series of payments can be multiplied by this factor to determine their future worth F. For example, if \$1,000 is invested annually for five years, $n = 5$, at an interest rate of $i = 0.08$, the value of this factor is 5.867; and the future worth of these funds is \$5,867. Here $\left(\dfrac{F}{P}, 8\%, 5\right) = 5.867$.

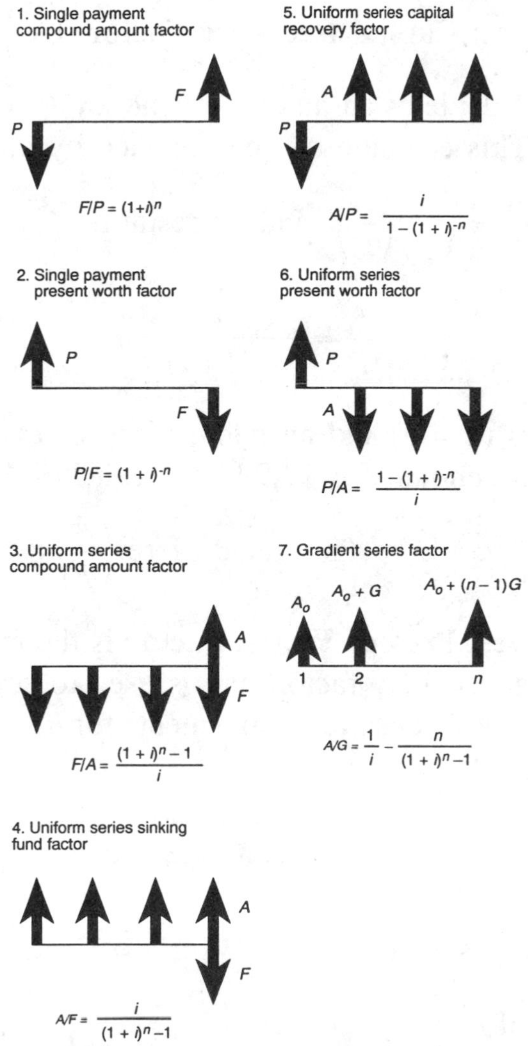

1. Single payment compound amount factor

$F/P = (1+i)^n$

2. Single payment present worth factor

$P/F = (1 + i)^{-n}$

3. Uniform series compound amount factor

$F/A = \dfrac{(1 + i)^n - 1}{i}$

4. Uniform series sinking fund factor

$A/F = \dfrac{i}{(1 + i)^n - 1}$

5. Uniform series capital recovery factor

$A/P = \dfrac{i}{1 - (1 + i)^{-n}}$

6. Uniform series present worth factor

$P/A = \dfrac{1 - (1 + i)^{-n}}{i}$

7. Gradient series factor

$A_o \qquad A_o + G \qquad A_o + (n-1)G$

$1 \qquad 2 \qquad n$

$A/G = \dfrac{1}{i} - \dfrac{n}{(1 + i)^n - 1}$

Figure 3. Cash Flow Diagrams for Interest Factors

Uniform-Series, Sinking-Fund Factor, $\left(\dfrac{A}{F}\right)$, is the reciprocal of the uniform-series, compound amount factor and is given by the following equation:

$$\frac{A}{F} = \frac{i}{(1+i)^n - 1} \tag{12}$$

This factor provides a means to compute the value of a uniform series, A, to have a total amount F accumulated after n years. For five years $(n = 5)$ and an interest rate of $i = 0.08$, the factor is 0.17045; and using $F = \$5,867$ from above, then $A = \$1,000$. Here $\left(\frac{A}{F}, 8\%, 5\right) = 0.17045$.

Uniform-Series, Capital-Recovery Factor, $\left(\frac{A}{P}\right)$, gives the uniform series value A that depletes an amount of money P over n years with an interest rate of i. This equation can be obtained by multiplying equations (9) and (12), i.e., $\frac{A}{P} = \left(\frac{F}{P}\right)\left(\frac{A}{F}\right)$, and the result is:

$$\frac{A}{P} = \frac{i}{1 - (1+i)^{-n}} \tag{13}$$

For five years $(n = 5)$ and an interest rate of $i = 0.08$, this factor is 0.25046, and for an amount $P = \$3,993$, the value of A is $\$1,000$, i.e., five payments of $\$1,000$ could be distributed. Here $\left(\frac{A}{P}, 8\%, 5\right) = 0.25046$.

Uniform-Series, Present Worth Factor is the reciprocal of the uniform-series, capital-recovery factor, and is used to compute the principal needed to assure a uniform series of payments for n years at interest rate i. The equation is:

$$\frac{P}{A} = \frac{1 - (1+i)^{-n}}{i} \tag{14}$$

This equation has a value of 3.993 for $n = 5$ and $i = 0.08$; and for $A = \$1,000$, the value of P is $\$3,993$. Here $\left(\frac{P}{A}, 8\%, 5\right) = 3.993$.

Gradient Series Factor is for an initial series value of A_O and each succeeding year A_O is increased, first by an amount G then $2G$ as shown in Figure 3. At year n the series value is $A_O + (n - 1)G$. The amount accumulated after n years is F, and that amount can be converted into a series of uniform payments A by the following equation:

$$\frac{A}{G} = \frac{1}{i} - \frac{n}{(1+i)^n - 1} \qquad (15)$$

This equation is used with the **gradient-series, present worth factor,** $\frac{P}{G}$ to determine the present worth of the series where $\frac{P}{G} = \left(\frac{A}{G}\right)\left(\frac{P}{A}\right)$,

and $\left(\frac{P}{A}\right)$ is given by equation (14). The use of these factors will be illustrated in a subsequent example.

MINIMUM ATTRACTIVE RATE OF RETURN (MARR)

Private corporations require a **minimum attractive rate of return** (MARR) before considering investing in a project. This is an interest rate that may be a project-specific number, but it usually reflects the average return on investment for a particular corporation. Determining the appropriate MARR is a corporate policy matter. However, in an economist's point of view, an investment is attractive as long as the marginal rate of return is equal to or greater than the marginal cost of borrowed capital. However, a corporation and their investors usually require a substantially higher return than that which could be obtained by simply investing in a bank account.

The source of funds is a consideration when choosing a value for MARR. A private corporation can use funds from the owners, usually through the sale of stock, or from profits which are fed back into the corporation, or from capital recovery. The **cost of equity capital** is related to a company's policy on debt financing. High leverage makes equity in a business more risky, since equity capital must sustain any losses first before debt capital. Hence, investors require a higher return to compensate for the risk. Also, the minimum attractive rate of return generally represents the opportunity cost of money, since funds expended in one project are unavailable for others.

METHODS OF PROJECT ANALYSIS

The present worth and annual worth methods of project analysis all assume estimations have been made regarding initial investment, cash flows, acceptable MARR, and the possibility of salvage value on equipment after the project has been completed. The equivalent uniform annual series equation used with these methods is described also.

Present-Worth Method

A method of economic decision analysis that converts cash flows into an equivalent present value for a certain minimum attractive rate of return as shown by equation (16) to evaluate the present worth (PW)

$$PW = \sum_{j=1}^{n} CF_j \left(\frac{P}{F}\right) \tag{16}$$

where $\left(\dfrac{P}{F}\right)$ is evaluated by equation (10) for the interest rate i and year j for the cash flow CF_j.

When a necessary expense is being planned (the installation of a new cooling system), then the present worth of costs is minimized. For maximizing profit, MARR is used, and the present worth has to be greater than zero. The following example illustrates the evaluation of present worth.

EXAMPLE

Consider the following series of payments and profits from ABC Pipes Inc.'s plan to institute a new product line of pipe fittings.

$150,000 initial cost for new equipment
$ 22,000 yearly after-tax cash flow
$ 40,000 maintenance of equipment in year 10
$ 30,000 salvage value of equipment in 20 years

SOLUTION

To find the present worth of this project at a 10% *MARR*, equation (16) gives:

$$PW = \$150{,}000 + \$22{,}000 \left(\frac{P}{A}, 10\%, 20\right) - \$40{,}000$$

$$\left(\frac{P}{F}, 10\%, 10\right) + \$30{,}000 \left(\frac{P}{F}, 10\%, 20\right) = \$9{,}238$$

The present worth is greater than zero, and this project would be acceptable to a corporation requiring a 10% rate of return. A modification of this example shows another option that can be considered.

EXAMPLE

Instead of manufacturing the pipe fittings, ABC Pipes Inc. is also considering expanding its existing product line of pipes with a new state-of-the art plastic. The cash flows for this project are

$72,000	initial investment
6,000	profit in year 1
6,500	profit in year 2, and the profit continues to increase $500 every year for 20 years

SOLUTION

Assuming zero maintenance and no salvage value, the present worth for this project is:

$$PW = -72,000 + 6,000 \left(\frac{P}{A}, 10\%, 20\right) + 500 \left(\frac{P}{G}, 10\%, 20\right)$$

$$= -72,000 + 6,000(8.514) + 500(55.407)$$

$$= -72,000 + 51,084 + 27,704$$

$$= \$6,787$$

Both courses of action would be acceptable to ABC, but if funds were not available for both, other considerations need to be addressed. The pipe fittings are more profitable; and, all things being equal, would be the clear choice. Yet all things are not equal. If the lower initial investment for the plastics would leave funds for another, even more profitable project, then that too must be evaluated. Another concern is competition. And what if the project lives of the two alternatives were unequal? The two would not be comparable if the equipment for plastics would have to be retired in 10 years. In instances when the analyst needs to compare projects with unequal lives, engineering judgment is required. In this instance, both could be considered over 10 years, or over 20 years, if additional new equipment would be purchased in year 10. The new plastics alternative would then look like this:

$$PW = 72,000 + 6,000 \left(\frac{P}{A}, 10\%, 20\right) + 500 \left(\frac{P}{G}, 10\%, 20\right) - 72,000$$

$$\left(\frac{P}{F}, 10\%, 10\right) = -\$20,969$$

An accurate approximation of project life is essential in economic analyses like these.

Annual-Worth Method

Also called equivalent uniform annual disbursements, the annual-worth method converts uneven cash flows into their equivalent uniform annual values using the equivalent uniform annual series as described below. The results are the same as in the present worth method; that is, the indicated best choice between alternatives will always be the same, but annual worth may be easier to grasp.

Equivalent Uniform Annual Series is an equation that converts the present value (present worth, *PW*) from a series of cash flows to a series of uniform annual payments. The present worth for the series of cash flows is computed using equation (16).

$$PW = \sum_{j=1}^{n} CF_j \left(\frac{P}{F} \right) \tag{16}$$

where $\left(\dfrac{P}{F} \right)$ is evaluated by equation (10) for the interest rate *i* and year *j* for the cash flow CF_j.

Then the present worth is converted to a uniform series (EUAS) using equation (13) for $\left(\dfrac{A}{P} \right)$, the uniform-series, capital-recovery factor, i.e.,

$$EUAS = PW \left(\frac{A}{P} \right) \tag{17}$$

The equivalent uniform annual series (EUAS) is also called the **annual worth** (AW). When the cash flows are negative, representing costs, then the above equation is called the **equivalent uniform annual cost** (EUAC) or **annual cost** (AC). The following example illustrates this procedure.

EXAMPLE

A company needs additional warehouse space for product as a result of plant expansion. The options include constructing a prefabricated steel building, a tilt-up concrete building, or renting space. The steel building has a cost of $150,000 and a service life of 25 years with annual maintenance and property taxes of $6,000 per year. The concrete building has a cost of $200,000 and a service life of 50 years with annual maintenance and property taxes of $4,000. Both buildings have no realizable salvage value, and the company uses a 15% minimum attractive rate of return. The company can rent suitable space for $32,000 per year. Basing the decision for additional warehouse space on the equivalent uniform annual cost, should the company construct the steel building, construct the concrete building, or rent warehouse space?

SOLUTION

The equivalent uniform annual cost (*EUAC*) for the building is given by:

$$EUAC = -P\left(\frac{A}{P}, i\%, n\right) - [\text{maintenance and taxes}]$$

where $\left(\frac{A}{P}, i\%, n\right)$ is the uniform-series, capital-recovery factor and P is the cost of the building.

Steel Building: $EUAC = -150,000\left(\frac{A}{P}, 15\%, 25\right) - 6,000$

$$EUAC = -150,000\,(0.15470) - 6,000 = -\$29,205$$

Concrete Building: $EUAC = -200,000\left(\frac{A}{P}, 15\%, 50\right) - 4,000$

$$EUAC = -200,000(0.15014) - 4,000 = -\$34,028$$

Comparing the above annual rates with renting at $32,000 per year, the best decision is to build the steel building for $29,205 equivalent uniform annual cost.

The following example illustrates another way to use the equivalent uniform annual cost to determine the best alternative for an investment decision.

EXAMPLE

Refractory bricks lining a furnace have an installed cost of $35,000 and last six years. The furnace must be partially relined at the end of three years at a cost of $12,000. A new high-temperature refractory material has been developed, and test results show that a lining with this material will last 15 years with no intermediate repair costs. What is the largest annual cost which can be justified economically for using this new material? The company uses a 25% minimum attractive rate of return.

SOLUTION

The equivalent uniform annual cost ($EUAC$) for the current and new refractory materials will be equated to determine the maximum initial cost of the new material using the company's minimum attractive rate of return of 25%.

current material: initial cost = $35,000 lasting 6 years

repair cost = $12,000 after 3 years

$$EUAC = 35,000\left(\frac{A}{P}, 25\%, 6\right) + 12,000\left(\frac{P}{F}, 25\%, 3\right)\left(\frac{A}{P}, 25\%, 6\right)$$

$$= 35,000(0.33882) + 12,000(0.51001)(0.33882) = \$13,941 \text{ per year}$$

new material: The maximum equivalent uniform annual cost for new material lasting 15 years = $13,941

Let P = initial cost of new material and

$$13,941 = P\left(\frac{A}{P}, 25\%, 15\right)$$

$$13.941 = P(0.25912)$$

$$P = \$53,801$$

Thus, $53,801 is the largest initial cost that can be justified for this material.

PROFITABILITY ANALYSIS

The two standard methods used for profitability analysis by private corporations are net present value (*NPV*) and rate of return (*ROR*). Projects are ranked by these measures of return on investment to compete for the limited capital for plant improvements and new processes. The **net present value** is the sum of all of the cash flows for the project discounted to the present value, usually using the company's minimum attractive rate of return, *MARR*, and the capital investment required. The **rate of return** is the interest rate in the net present value calculation that gives a zero net present value.

The net present value is an estimate of profitability of a project. It has the advantage that the net present value for several projects can be added to obtain the net present value for all the projects.

The rate of return is sometimes called the discounted cash flow rate of return (*DCFRR*) and the internal rate of return (*IRR*). The rate of return has the advantage of being used to compare directly with alternate uses of money that have rates of return, such as bonds and certificates of deposit.

There are numerous similar measures of profitability, but all of these are variations of net present value and rate of return, except the payback period or payout time which has the flaw of neglecting the time value of money. One example is the net rate of return (*NRR*) which is the net present value divided by the product of the capital investment at year zero and the product life expressed as a percentage.

Net Present Value

To evaluate the net present value (*NPV*), the net annual cash flows, CF_j, are needed.

These cash flows are used in the following equation to compute the net present value (*NPV*) where CF_O is the initial capital investment for the project.

$$NPV = -CF_O + \sum_{j=1}^{n} CF_j(1+i)^{-j}$$

To determine the net present value, the interest rate, i, usually the minimum attractive rate of return, and the number of years, n, for the project are specified. There is no assumption about the signs of the cash flows, CF_j, but the equation has the initial cash flow, CF_O, being negative to represent the initial capital investment.

Referring to Figure 2 and equation (18), the individual annual cash flows would be discounted to the present and combined with the capital investment to estimate the net present value for the proposed new plant. The following simple example illustrates the calculation of the net present value.

EXAMPLE

A straight-run fuel oil stream in a refinery can be converted to a high octane fuel for blending into premium gasoline using hydrocracking. A proposal has been made to add a $15,000 bbl/day unit at a capital cost of $71.0 million. The annual net profit in million dollars is given below for the estimated life of the hydrocracking unit. The net present value is to be evaluated for interest rates of 15% and 25%, and the profitability compared. These results are shown in the Table 1.

TABLE 1
ANNUAL NET PROFIT FOR ESTIMATED
LIFE OF HYDROCRACKING UNIT

End of Year n	Annual Net Profit, F	$\frac{P}{F}$ (15%) $(1.15)^{-n}$	Present Value	$\frac{P}{F}$ (25%) $(1.25)^{-n}$	Present Value
1	32.0	0.8695	27.83	0.8000	25.60
2	28.0	0.7561	21.17	0.6400	17.92
3	22.0	0.6575	14.47	0.5120	11.26
4	17.0	0.5718	9.72	0.4091	6.96
5	15.0	0.4972	7.46	0.3277	4.92
Total	114.0		80.64		66.66

SOLUTION

Computing the net present value gives:

$$NPV(15\%) = -71.0 + 80.84 = 9.64 \qquad NPV(25\%) = -71.0 + 66.66 = -4.34$$

The investment is marginally attractive with a positive net present value if funds are available at 15%, but the project is not considered with a negative net present value for funds available at 25%.

A convenient form of equation (18) is obtained if all of the cash flows, CF_j, are equal by using equation (14).

$$NPV = -CF_O + A\left[\frac{1-(1+i)^{-n}}{i}\right] \tag{18}$$

where A is the uniform cash flow in the equation.

The use of this form of the equation for net present value is illustrated by the following example which also shows the use of the gradient series factor, equation (15).

EXAMPLE

Two projects are competing for an oil company's capital improvement funds. One is an additional distillation column for improved product quality, and the other is a new lubricant packaging system to reduce product packaging costs. The capital investment is $110,000 for each one. The cash flow for the distillation column is $38,000 for the first year, and then it declines by $4,000 for each subsequent year for the 10 year life of the project. The cash flow for the packaging system is $5,000 for the first year, and then it increases by $4,000 for each subsequent year for the 10 year life of the project. For a 15% minimum attractive rate of return compute the net present value for each proposed project.

SOLUTION

For both of the oil company's projects:

Capital investment, $CF_O = \$110,000$; $i = 15\%$, and $n = 10$ years

Distillation column cash flows: Year 1 $CF_1 = \$38,000$
Year 2 – 10 – declines by $4,000
Packaging system cash flows: Year 1 $CF_1 = \$5,000$
Year 2 – 10 – increases by $4,000

The following equation gives the net present value (*NPV*) for these projects.

$$NPV = CF_O + CF_1\left(\frac{P}{A}, i\%, 10\right) + G\left(\frac{A}{G}, i\%, 10\right)\left(\frac{P}{A}, i\%, 10\right)$$

where G = Gradient of the cash flow

$$\left(\frac{A}{G}, i\%, n\right) = \text{Gradient series factor}$$

$$\left(\frac{P}{A}, i\%, n\right) = \text{Uniform series, present-worth factor}$$

For the distillation column:

$$NPV = -110,000 + 38,000\left(\frac{P}{A}, 15\%, 10\right) - 4,000\left(\frac{A}{G}, 15\%, 10\right)$$

$$\left(\frac{P}{A}, 15\%, 10\right)$$

$$= -110,000 + 38,000(5.0188) - 4,000(3.3832)(5.0188)$$

$$= -\$12,800$$

For the packaging system:

$$NPV = -110,000 + 5,000(5.0188) + 4,000(3.3832)(5.0188)$$
$$= -\$17,000$$

where compound interest factors were obtained from standard tables. The distillation column is a potentially attractive investment with a positive net present value, but the lubrication packaging system is not with a negative net present value.

Rate of Return

The rate of return (ROR) is the interest rate where the net present value is zero, i.e., from equation (18).

$$0 = -CF_O + \sum_{j=1}^{n} CF_j (1 + i)^{-j} \tag{19}$$

To determine this interest rate, it is usually necessary to interpolate between two known values of the net present value. In the example on page 724 the net present value was 9.64 at an interest rate of 15% and – 4.34 at 25%. Interpolating gives the rate of return for this case to be 21.9%. The following example gives an additional illustration of the evaluation of the rate of return.

EXAMPLE

A division of a company has been allocated $100,000 to invest at the start of the next fiscal year in cost-reduction projects. Three projects are under consideration and are summarized in Table 2.

	TABLE 2 SAMPLE COST = REDUCTION PROJECTS		
Project	Investment Required	Estimated Economic Life (years)	Net Annual Cash Flow
A	$50,000	9	$16,600
B	$50,000	8	$15,000
C	$100,000	6	$30,000

The minimum attractive rate of return for the company is 20% for projects with this economic life. Would recommendation based on the rate of return for these projects be (A) invest in A only, (B) invest in B only, (C) invest in A and B, (D) invest in C only, or (E) seek other alternatives?

SOLUTION

Alternatives are evaluated for investing $100,000 by comparing the rate of return for the projects with the minimum attractive rate of return of 20%. The rate of return (i) is the interest rate where the net present value is zero. For a uniform net annual cash flow (A), the equation for the net present value (NPV) is:

$$NPV = CF_O = A\left(\frac{P}{A}, i\%, n\right)$$

where CF_O is the capital investment and $\left(\frac{P}{A}, i\%, n\right) = \dfrac{\left[1 - (1+i)^{-n}\right]}{i}$ is the uniform series capital recovery factor.

For Project A:

$$0 = -50{,}000 + 16{,}600\left(\frac{P}{A}, i\%, 9\right) \text{ or } \left(\frac{P}{A}, i\%, 9\right) = 3.012$$

In addition to using tabulations of $\left(\frac{P}{A}, i\%, 9\right)$, from tables of compound interest factors in standard texts, gives $i = 30.0\%$.

For Project B:

$$0 = -50{,}000 + 15{,}000\left(\frac{P}{A}, i\%, 8\right) \text{ or } \left(\frac{P}{A}, i\%, 8\right) = 3.3333$$

Using standard tables of compound interest factors, gives $i = 25.0\%$.

For Project C:

$$0 = -100{,}000 + 30{,}000\left(\frac{P}{A}, i\%, 6\right) \text{ or } \left(\frac{P}{A}, i\%, 6\right) = 3.33$$

Using a standard table of compound interest factors, gives $i = 20.0\%$.

Summary:

Project	Rate of Return
A	30.0%
B	25.0%
C	20.0%

The investment decision is to select Projects A and B because their rate of return is greater than the minimum attractive rate of return; and all of the available capital is used.

It should be noted that the rate of return method is best when comparing independent alternatives. It is probably one of the most popular tools used in capital budgeting. Net present value is widely used to choose among dependent alternatives. A thorough economic analysis will use more than one method, and it will try to include as much information as can be made available.

The **Payback Period** is the time required to recover the capital investment from the net profit but neglecting the time value of money. The equation for the payback period is:

$$CF_O = \sum_{j=1}^{PBP} CF_j \tag{20}$$

and if the yearly net profits A are uniform, then the payback period (PBP) is given by the following equation.

$$PBP = \frac{CF_O}{A} \tag{21}$$

This is a simple and popular calculation, but it ignores the time value of money and should not be used for making economic decisions for that reason. It is sometimes called the **payout time**. However, there is a modification to the payout time called the **discounted payout time** that computes the number of years to have the cumulative discounted cash flows sum to zero, and this does include the time value of money.

To illustrate the calculation of the payback period using the example at the end of this chapter, the capital investment was to be $71.0 million, and the sum of the cash flows was $80.64 million for the five years. The payback period is determined by:

$$71.0 = 32.0 + 28.0 + 22.0(0.5) = 71$$

which gives a payback period of about 2.5 years. Although this time to recover the capital investment may sound attractive, it is not a good investment if the cost of money is at an interest rate of 25% as shown in the example.

Benefit-Cost Analysis

The benefit cost ratio (BCR) is used in municipal and government projects, and it is defined by the following equation:

$$BCR = \frac{B - D}{C} \tag{22}$$

The benefit-cost ratio is the difference between the benefits, *B,* and the disbenefits, *D,* divided by the costs, *C.* For example, in a project to build a hydroelectric dam, the benefits would be electric power generation and possibly flood protection; and the disbenefits would be loss of productive farmland. The costs would include the construction and maintenance of the dam.

Although benefits and costs can be estimated without too much difficulty, it is usually difficult to measure the cost of the loss of wildlife habitat, scenic rivers, and land loss downstream in coastal marshes from lack of replenishing sediments. For projects to be considered by the U.S. Army Corps of Engineers, BCR should be about 2.0 or larger.

EQUIVALENCE

In comparing investment opportunities, there are times when two or more plans give the same result, the same net present value, for example, even though plans involve different interest rates and times. A plan that has a uniform annual series value of $8,000 for 25 years at an interest rate of 6% has a present value of $102,264. Another plan that has equal quarterly deposits of $156.07 for 40 years at a nominal interest rate of 6.0% has the same net present value of $102,264. This illustrates the concept of **equivalence**, i.e., being of equal value. The interest factors presented previously are called equivalence factors, also. Other simple examples of equivalence include the following:

A uniform annual payment of $655.56 for 20 years at an interest rate of 8% is equivalent to a single payment of $30,000 in year 20.

A single payment today of $30,000 would be equivalent to an annual payment of $6,436.45 over 20 years at an 8% interest rate.

Investing $6,436.45 for 20 years at a 15% rate is equivalent to $105,342 today. A uniform series of payments of $1,028 for 20 years at a 15% rate is also equivalent to $105,342.

The first two examples show that, at 8%, $30,000 in 20 years is equal to $655.56 a year for 20 years, which is also equivalent to $6,436.45 in the present. The third example shows investing two different amounts of money are equivalent to $105,342.40 today.

TAXES AND DEPRECIATION

In any project analysis, it is important to distinguish between before tax cash flows and after tax cash flows (*BTCF* and *ATCF*). In general, project decisions are best made based on after tax cash flows, but before tax figures can often be used in the preliminary stages of analysis as an approximation for the desirability of a project. Typically, a corporation's first $75,000 to $100,000 in profits is tax exempt; but, in economic studies, it is usually assumed that this profit margin has been met, and that the corporation is operating and making decisions where marginal profits are taxed at the highest rate (currently about 38%). Although tax rates are constant for marginal profits, what makes after tax analysis more difficult than before tax analysis is the issue of depreciation.

To understand depreciation, you need to have an understanding of **capital**. Capital goods are those accumulated in order to produce other goods. Two kinds of capital can be distinguished, fixed and working. **Fixed capital** is that which cannot be readily converted into a different sort of asset. **Working capital** is the investment that puts the plant into production. It can be estimated to be a tenth to a fifth of fixed capital, or as a value of one month's worth of raw materials.

Total capital (fixed plus working) does not include the expenses of operation. These are other indirect expenses such as overhead, taxes, insurance, and **depreciation**. The amount of depreciation in any given year depends on the amount of **fixed** capital only. Furthermore, income taxes are a function of depreciation.

Depreciation exists because anything valuable will lose some or all of that value with time. Depreciation is a tax allowance and is considered a cost of operation. It is a measure of declining value, and a means of building a fund to finance plant replacement.

The accounting of depreciation is also a way to plan for replacing equipment, except actual **replacement** of obsolete equipment is rare. New technology and new methods of production will usually require totally new equipment.

Depreciation appears on a financial statement as a cost of operation, but this is equally misleading. Capital costs are depreciated, and in that way are translated into yearly operating costs, but the actual disbursement was made at the time of equipment purchase. The reason for depreciating the amount over time is this: capital equipment is an asset to the plant; each year, the value of that asset declines and even though there is no out-of-pocket cost, the declining value is a real cost to the plant. However, since capital costs are incurred at the inception, depreciation costs are calculated yearly only for the calculation of taxes.

Depreciation as a tax allowance is the most important consideration when planning a project. The depreciation entry in the cost column serves to lessen taxable income, and can make the crucial difference in profitability. This entry may have little to do with the actual physical depreciation of the asset, for tax laws have increasingly standardized the ways in which depreciation is calculated, thus making the depreciation entry less a measure of an individual piece of equipment's useful life. Still, the expense should be viewed as a measure of useful life.

To determine the amount of depreciation for tax purposes, a few values need to be known. The **depreciable base** consists of fixed capital only. Land, however, is excepted from the depreciable base, because it is always thought to retain all of its original value, and so cannot be considered a depreciable item. The **write-off life** is the hypothetical life of the asset. The IRS has guidelines for write-off life of equipment, and plant equipment is depreciable over about ten years. Computers have a life of about five years. Next, various methods of calculating depreciation will be explained.

There are three methods of computing depreciation: straight line, accelerated, and decelerated. Straight line assumes a steady loss of value over time, while accelerated depreciates more in the early years of the asset, while decelerated depreciates more in later years.

Straight-Line Method

With the Straight-Line Method, the annual depreciation is constant. To evaluate the depreciation charge for the rth year, it is computed as the difference between the original cost P and the estimated salvage value S divided by the estimated service life n in years, i.e.,

$$D_r = \frac{(P-S)}{n} \tag{23}$$

Then the book value at the end of the rth year, BV_r is obtained by subtracting r times the depreciation D_r obtained from equation (25) as shown below.

$$BV_r = P - rD_r \tag{26}$$

For example, the original cost is \$20,000; and the service or write-off life is 12 years for a piece of equipment. With no salvage value, the depreciation for year 1 ($r = 1$) is: $D_1 = \dfrac{(20,000-0)}{12} = \$1,667$; and the book value is: $BV_1 = 20,000 - (1)(1,667) = \$18,333$.

Sum-of-Years-Digits Method

The Sum-of-Years-Digits Method is an accelerated method using the sum-of-year-digits, SY, that depreciates about 75% of the cost in the first half of the service life. SY is given by the following equation.

$$SY = \sum j = 1 + 2 + \dots + n = n\frac{(n+1)}{2} \tag{27}$$

where n is the service life. The amount of depreciation D_r is computed as follows:

$$C = \frac{(P-S)}{SY} \tag{28}$$

and
$$D_r = (n + 1 - r)C \tag{29}$$

Then the book value is obtained from the following equation:

$$BV_r = P - C\left[SY - (n-r)\frac{(n-r+1)}{2}\right] \tag{30}$$

Using the information from the straight line method, the sum-of-year-digits is:

$$SY = \frac{12(12+1)}{2} = 78,$$

and the value of

$$C = \frac{(20,000 - 0)}{78} = \$256.$$

Evaluating equation (29): $D_1 = (12 + 1 - 1)256 = \$3,072$, and the book value from equation (30) is:

$$BV_1 = 20,000 - 256\left[\frac{78 - (12-1)(12-1+1)}{2}\right] = \$16,928.$$

Double-Rate Declining Balance Method

The Double-Rate Declining Balance Method computes the depreciation at double the straight line depreciation rate, and it is one way to do the declining balance method. If f is the double-declining balance rate given by:

$$f = \frac{2.0}{n} \tag{31}$$

then the book value is computed by the following equation:

$$BV_r = P(1 - f)^r \tag{32}$$

The depreciation at year r is given by the following equation:

$$D_r = (BV_{r-1} - BV_r) = fBV_{r-1} \tag{33}$$

Using information from the straight line method, the double-declining balance rate is $f = \frac{2.0}{12} = 0.167$ by equation (31). Then the book value for year 1 ($r = 1$) is: $BV_1 = (20,000)(1 - 0.167) = \$16,000$, and the depreciation is: $D_1 = (20,000 - 16,660) = \$3,340$.

In this method the net salvage value is not evaluated as part of the procedure. The method can have the book value become smaller than the net salvage value. However, IRS regulations require that the book value not be less than the salvage value, and the depreciation must stop at this point.

Sinking Fund Method

The Sinking Fund Method depreciates equipment with an imaginary sinking fund that is equivalent to the company making a series of equal annual deposits to have an amount equal to the cost of replacing the equipment at the end of its service life. The amount of depreciation in any given year is equal to the amount of the annual deposit into the sinking fund plus interest. This method is used when the replacement of the equipment is assumed to cost the same as the original. It is the only method in which depreciation increases in time. The accumulated depreciation in year r, AD_r, is given by the following equation:

$$AD_r = (P - S)\left(\frac{A}{F}, i\%, n\right)\left(\frac{F}{A}, i\%, r\right) \tag{34}$$

The depreciation for year r is computed by difference, i.e.:

$$D_r = AD_r - AD_{r-1} \tag{35}$$

Then the equation to evaluate the book value is:

$$BV_r = P - (P - S)\left(\frac{A}{F}, i\%, n\right)\left(\frac{F}{A}, i\%, n\right)\left(\frac{F}{A}, i\%, r\right) \tag{36}$$

Using the information from the straight line method and an interest rate of 8%, the accumulated depreciation for the first year is: $AD_1 = (20,000 - 0)(0.0527)(1) = \$1,054$ using equation (34), and the depreciation is: $D_1 = 1,054 - 0 = \$1,054$ using equation (35). Then the book value is $BV_r = 20,000 - 20,000 (0.0527) (1) = \$18,946$ from equation (36).

In this method the annual depreciation increases geometrically with time. Tax laws require that this method be used only with equipment that has to be replaced with equipment which cost at least as much as the original. This does not allow a company to take a total depreciation allowance that is greater than the equipment's current net adjusted cost.

Group Accounts

Often it will be more convenient to group assets, which are bought in the same year, for depreciation purposes. Items which have the same useful life can be pooled into a **group account**, regardless of whether they were bought in the beginning or the end of the year. A **classified account** groups items according to use, regardless of useful life, and a **composite account** includes items which have diverse lives and uses. With classified or composite accounts, the depreciation rate for any year is found by determining depreciation for each item or each group of similar items, and that total is divided by total cost. Any of the above depreciation methods will work.

Comparing the depreciation methods, the accelerated methods are those for which the accumulated depreciation exceeds the straight-line method. However, the sinking fund curve is below the straight-line, meaning it is decelerated. The amount of depreciation is ultimately the same for all, except in double declining balance, in which the depreciation total approaches, but never reaches, the full amount. In instances where the salvage value is significant, the double-declining rate's acceleration effect is enhanced, since salvage value is not considered in the calculation.

It might seem that, since the depreciation amount is ultimately the same, acceleration is simply a short-sighted way of grabbing tax credits in the shortest time possible. Not at all. The advantage of accelerated depreciation is very real. Because of money's value in time, the declining balance and sum-of-years-digits methods, because they are accelerated, yield a higher present worth for net income after taxes; the discount for the tax savings in earlier years is not as great as the discount in later years.

Sometimes, especially with an accelerated depreciation method, the depreciation charge exceeds the actual before tax cash flow in a given year. When this occurs, realize that, although each investment decision is treated separately in the economic study, the income generated and taxes paid are part of the cash flow for the entire firm. Hence, if the depreciation charge is $1,000 and income is $600 for that year, then the other $400 of depreciation is not lost, but is subtracted from the general before tax cash flow of the firm. For purposes of analysis, this extra benefit to the firm can be included in the economic study of the specific investment decision in the following manner, which shows an after tax profit greater than the actual before tax receipts.

Before Tax Cash Flow	$ 600
depreciation	1,000
taxable income	– 400
tax at 33%	– 132
After Tax Cash Flow	$ 732

Every year, regulations on depreciation are being revised, and less choice is given to the corporation (or individual) in how they may claim depreciation deductions. The methods outlined above are important to know, since next year or thereafter they may be the basis of the newest law. Since 1981, however, formulas for depreciation have been set by the Accelerated Cost Recovery System (ACRS). With the ACRS, all assets can be grouped into one of four categories, each with a corresponding recovery period, and depreciation percentages are set for each year. This greatly simplifies matters, being very amenable to **group asset** depreciation.

Note that equipment is not subject to depreciation prior to the year it has been placed in service, that is, when it is not yet ready for use. A plant that takes three years to build is not depreciable until it is completed and placed in service. However, it makes no difference to the yearly deduction if the equipment was placed in service during the beginning of the year or in late December.

A company can reduce operating costs by $16,300 per year for 12 years by automating a process with new digital control computer. The cost of the computer and control system is $78,000, and straight line depreciation over 12 years is used with zero salvage value. If the applicable income tax rate is 38%, determine the rate of return after taxes.

For the new control system:

operating cost is reduced by $16,300 per year for 12 years

equipment cost is $78,000

straight line depreciation for 12 years with no salvage value income tax rate is 38%

The equation for the net present value (*NPV*) for uniform annual cash flow (*A*) is:

$$NPV = CF_O + A\left(\frac{P}{A}, i\%, n\right)$$

where CF_O = $78,000, the capital investment for the control system.

Change in the net profit $= \$16,300 - \dfrac{(\$78,000 - 0)}{12} = \$9,800$ per year before taxes minus depreciation

Taxes on the change in net profit = $9,800 × 0.38 = $3,724

A = Change in net annual income after taxes = $16,300 − $3,724 = $12,576

Computing the rate of return (interest rate at zero net present value):

$$0 = -78,000 + 12,576\left(\frac{P}{A}, i\%, 12\right)$$

or

$$\left(\frac{P}{A}, i\%, 12\right) = 6.202$$

Using tables of compound interest factors at 12 years gives:

$$i = 12.0\%$$

which is the rate of return after taxes.

SENSITIVITY ANALYSIS

Sensitivity analysis is an important method of ensuring the reliability of the forecast. It will tell how "sensitive" a project is to some foreseeable change to any certain element that has been estimated, such as selling price, cost of materials, or the tax rate. A sensitive project is one whose desirability is highly affected by a small change in any certain variable. A project is insensitive to a variable if wide ranges of values do not alter the conclusions of the study. Typically, a base case is used, and the present value or rate of return is evaluated for variations in parameters such as product price, sales volume, plant cost and size, working capital, etc. For example, a plant design is based on a capacity that will produce 4,000 items per unit time with a net present value of $3.0 million based on a projected selling price of $0.50 per unit. The sensitivity of the net present value to selling price of $0.25 and $0.75 per unit is –$0.5 million and $4.2 million.

The sources of probable risk are any uncertainties, i.e., everything that is estimated: disbursements, receipts, the length of time the project will be in service, salvage value, and the tax rate. Again, a general rise in prices due to inflation is not a consideration in economic studies, since receipts should change along with disbursements. Differential price changes, however, when the price of a certain item varies in contrast to the general price level, should be included in analysis, if they can be foreseen. Differential prices may be foreseen if revenues rely on contract pricing which is not indexed for inflation, or if governmental price controls apply. Fluctuation in oil prices are another example.

Another source of differential price changes occurs regularly, because income tax deductions for depreciation are not indexed for current dollars. If a piece of equipment costing $100,000 is depreciated over a period when inflation is 10%, the costs and receipts will go up as well, but the deduction for tax purposes will not. Thus, the corporation will be taxed on a higher percentage of income than would occur if there were no inflation, or if depreciation was indeed indexed.

RISK ANALYSIS

Sensitivity analysis is linked to risk analysis, which seeks to give the probability of the occurrence of certain scenarios. If the probability was high that the plant would not be used at capacity, then the desirability of the project is severely lessened. Sensitivity analysis and probability analysis together try to quantify elements of uncertainty.

Risk analysis attempts to quantitatively evaluate risks associated with research, development, economics, politics, natural disasters, and other possible uncertainties. Probability estimates for these risks can be obtained from past experience, simulations, expert estimation and experimental data, among others.

The objective is to use risk-weighted expected values of the profit to maximize the income in selecting among projects accounting for risk associated with them. Risk-weighted expected values are the sum of the product of the probabilities and the associated profit for that outcome. The profit can be measured by the net present value, annual worth, or other appropriate economic values.

A simple risk assessment for economic decision analysis involves the following steps. For each project under consideration, determine the range of possible outcomes that would effect the profit, e.g., the range in product selling price. Evaluate the profit over this range of possible outcomes. Separately, estimate the probability of occurrences of the possible outcomes, e.g., the probability the selling price will be at the low value when the plant is constructed (a very unfavorable situation). Then evaluate the weighted average of the profit by computing the sum of the profit and associated probabilities. This weighted average profit is an estimate of the expected value of the profit. These expected values for the projects are used to rank them in order of economic potential with risk incorporated in the comparison.

A simple illustration of the separate determination of profit and probability is given in this example. Consider having the opportunity of paying for a chance to bet on the flip of a coin. Each toss costs a quarter, but the payoff is $1.00. The expected value of the game is the sum of the probabilities of the possible outcomes, both 0.5, times the payoff, either $1.00 or 0. Thus, the expected value is $(0.5 \times \$1.00 + 0.5 \times 0) = \$0.50$. Even though, for any one toss, you may not receive $0.50; this is a bargain at a quarter a game. However, if the price of playing the game was exactly fifty cents, then the odds would not be for you or against you.

Determining the expected value of any given project consists of summing the product of the probabilities of all possible events times their corresponding payoffs. For example, if it was determined that the supply of seafood is directly related to weather conditions, the probability that a seafood plant will be used to capacity in any one year could be predicted, using data from past years about what likely weather conditions will be and what the consequent seafood harvests will be. With this information, it is predicted that the probability of the plant being used at 75% capacity in any one year was 30%, the probability for a full capacity year was 45%, and the probability of usage of 125% of capacity was 25%. Using an estimate of the annual worth, calculations of expected worth are then simple to do (Table 3).

TABLE 3 CALCULATION OF EXPECTED WORTH			
% Capacity	Annual Worth	Probability	Expected Value
75%	$ 22,314	0.30	$ 6,694.20
100%	124,045	0.45	55,820.25
125%	212,151	0.25	53,037.75
		Expected Value (AW)	$115,552.75

Note that the sum of the probabilities is equal to one. This will always be the case. This example gives the expected value of the annual worth, but any of the methods of project evaluation could be used.

Sometimes, if the decision-maker does not know the probability of the success or failure of a specific scheme, risk analysis can still be used. For example, if an oil company is considering whether to invest in drilling a certain well, they might have these four alternatives

1. Drill the well with a 100% working interest (*WI*).

2. Drill with a 50% partner.

3. Farm out, but back in for a 50% working interest.

4. Do not drill the well and use the funds elsewhere.

Table 4 gives the payoffs for each alternative in the event of success or failure:

TABLE 4
PAYOFFS FOR EACH ALTERNATIVE

Possible Outcomes	Drill with 100% WI	Drill with 50% Partner	Farm Out	Don't Drill
Dry hole (failure)	−500	−250	0	0
Producer (success)	3,000	1,500	1,500	0

If there are only two possible outcomes (success or failure), and if the chance for success is simply not known, a value P_S can be assigned to show a linear relationship between the chance of success and the expected value (Figure 4). If NPV_S is the net present value in case of success, then $(1 - P_S)$ is the chance of failure with a net present value of NPV_S. The expected value becomes a function of the probability of success.

$$EV = P_S NPV_S + (1 - P_S) NPV_f$$

$$= P_S (NPV_S - NPV_f) + NPV_f$$

Substituting values for the net present values for the four cases gives us the following equation:

$$EV_{100\%WI} = \$3,500\,P_S - \$350$$
$$EV_{50\%partner} = \$1,750\,P_S - \$250$$
$$EV_{farm\ out} = \$1,500\,P_S$$
$$EV_{do\ not\ drill} = 0$$

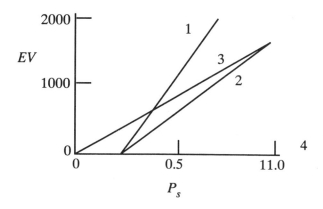

Figure 4. Expected Value

These are linear equations, and the $EV_{100\%WI}$ is greater than the other two for values of P_S of more than 25%. If the analyst would hesitate to put a specific value to the probability of success, these relationships can at least illustrate how much latitude his estimates can contain. For any probability of success less than 25%, farming out would be the best alternative.

There are times when expected value is an inappropriate tool for decision making. Expected values are **long-run** values. If immediate outcome is crucial, such that any risk is unpalatable, then expected value is not a true measure of project worth. One common example is health insurance. People do not buy health insurance with the hope of making money. Rather, they are paying for the prevention of a financial disaster in case they are faced with a debilitating or long-term illness. The value of being sure about preventing financial disaster is more important to them than the risk of losing money in the transaction. That the expected value of health insurance is lower than the price paid for it is evidenced by the fact that insurance companies are profit-making businesses. To them, expected values and probability of illness are pertinent information; to the insurance policy holder, the knowledge that he is at risk is more important than knowing he's probably losing money.

What does this say to the engineering economist? When all risk is unacceptable, expected values should not be used. If an investment of $5,000 would yield an 8% return, or $400 a year, and a competing investment of $5,000 would yield a 75% return, but with only a 15% likelihood of occurrence, the investors would have to choose between a sure $400, or an expected value of $562.50. The smart choice, that is, the economically sound choice, is the second investment, unless the chance of failure would mean disaster for the investor.

One Final Note about *MARR* (Minimum Attractive Rate of Return)

The concept of risk can add to a full comprehension of what the choice of an *MARR* entails. Three major elements can be seen to theoretically sum up the designated *MARR*. The first is pure interest, which is the amount an investor could make if he were to place his money in the bank to earn interest. Add to that an amount that represents the compensation for management, that is, whatever value the investor or company places on its involvement in the economy. A risk factor can then be added, which compensates implicitly for the level of risk the company or investor is willing to take.

REVIEW PROBLEMS

PROBLEM 1

What amount of money would have to be invested to have $4,000 at the end of three years at a 10% compound interest rate?

SOLUTION

$$P = \frac{F}{(1+i)^n}$$

$$= \frac{4,000}{(1+0.10)^3}$$

$$= \$3,005$$

PROBLEM 2

If the inflation rate is 8%, and you invest $20,000 at an 11% simple interest rate, will you have retained your buying power at the end of a) 5 years? b) 10 years?

SOLUTION

a) The principal will grow to:

$$F = \$20,000[1 + 5(0.11)] = \$31,000$$

To see if the buying power is the same, the future amount must be discounted for inflation, so that $1.00 in the future can be converted to an equivalent amount today.

$$F_I = \frac{P_I}{(1+r)^n}$$

where F_I is the future worth, measured in today's dollars P_I, and where r is equal to the rate of inflation. Notice that discounting for inflation is the reverse of compound interest problems.

$$F_I = \frac{31,000}{(1+0.08)^5}$$

$$F_I = \$21,098$$

Buying power is retained, plus a little extra.

b) $$F = \$20,000[1 + 10.11]$$
$$= \$42,000$$
$$F_I = \frac{42,000}{(1 + 0.08)^{10}}$$
$$F_I = \$19,454 < \$20,000$$

With an increase in time, buying power diminishes because of the compounding nature of inflation.

PROBLEM 3

Five hundred thousand dollars is borrowed at a nominal rate of 8%, compounded quarterly. If no payments are made in the first three years, how much will be owed? How much would the amount be if interest was compounded annually? Daily?

SOLUTION

For quarterly compounding, first find the effective interest rate from equation (3).

$$\left(1 + \frac{0.08}{4}\right)^4 - 1 = 8.24\%$$

$$F = \$500,000 \left(\frac{F}{P}, 8.24\%, 12\right)$$

$$= \$636,064$$

Compounded annually

$$F = \$500,000 \left(\frac{F}{P}, 8\%, 3\right)$$

$$= \$629,856$$

Compounded daily

$$F = \$500,000 \left(\frac{F}{P}, \frac{8}{365\%}, 1,095\right)$$

$$= \$635,608$$

PROBLEM 4

If you are 25 years old now and want to retire at age 50 with an annuity account that would give you $5,000 a year for 30 years, how much do you need to deposit each month at 6% to be able to have enough in the account?

SOLUTION

First, find the present value of the annuity:

$$P = \$5,000 \left(\frac{P}{A}, 6\%, 30 \right)$$

$$= \$68,824$$

This is the future target amount. To get the annual deposit required:

$$A = \$68,824 \left(\frac{A}{P}, 6\%, 25 \right)$$

$$= \$1,254$$

PROBLEM 5

A company needs to decide whether to use some of their undistributed profits to automate certain procedures. The initial investment would cost $60,000 and the system would have a seven-year lifetime savings. Savings from the automation are estimated at $18,000. Calculate the *AW*, the *PW*, and the *ROR* at 10%.

SOLUTION

$$PW = \$27,631$$

$$AW = \$5,676$$

$$ROR = 22.92\%$$

PROBLEM 6

Manufacturers of motors for small household equipment wonder if they should close one of their two plants (Plant A) and expand operations at Plant B. It seems there is not enough business to keep both plants running at capacity, yet expansion of Plant B would have to occur for it to handle double the usual load. Net income has been a steady $800,000 at Plant A and $840,000 at Plant B. Due to savings in overhead costs, it is thought that, with the same level of business, net income from an upgraded Plant B alone would equal $1,780,000. Salvage value of Plant A and sale of the land is estimated at $120,000. The investment to expand Plant B would cost $1.1 million, and it would take three years before the level of production could be increased.

a) If the company has a required *MARR* of 11%, and operations are thought to be steady for the next 15 years, how desirable would this course of action be, if disassembly of Plant A were to begin immediately and the total cost of upgrading was incurred at time zero?

b) If disassembling Plant A was to occur at the end of year three, when the expansion is completed?

c) If the disbursement for upgrading was spread evenly over the first three years of construction?

SOLUTION

a) The first task is to separate all factors unique to the proposed course of action. If disassembling the plant were to occur immediately, that is, at time zero, a cost of $980,000 would be incurred, which is the expenditure for upgrading minus the income from sale and salvage of Plant A. The first three years of the project would incur a loss of $800,000 from Plant A, with no changes in income from Plant B. The next 15 years would see a positive cash flow of $140,000, which is the change in income caused by the project.

The internal rate of return is a negative 4.65%, and the return on investment is –2,198,866, clearly unacceptable.

b) If disassembling is delayed until the third year, the cost in year zero is $1.1 million, no income change occurs in years one and two, with a positive cash flow in year three from sale of land and Plant A. Income of $140,000 is then constant for 15 years. Delaying the plant disassembly is clearly the more practical choice, yet return on investment at 7.4% still does not meet the requirement of the company. Net present value is –$276,150.

c) If the disbursements for upgrading were spread evenly over the three years, instead of a lump sum at time zero, then at the close of years one and two, –$366,667 is incurred, –246,667 at year three (366,667 – 120,000), and $140,000 for the 15 years thereafter. This makes the investment more attractive at a return on investment of 9.6%, but this is still not sufficient to meet an *MARR* of 11%. The net present value is –$72,180.

PROBLEM 7

A corporation has $225,000 in its capital budget to invest this year. There are several proposals for projects under consideration to either reduce costs or raise profits.

<table>
<tr><td colspan="5" align="center">TABLE 5
PROPOSAL COMPARISON</td></tr>
<tr><td>Project</td><td>Investment
Required</td><td>Estimated
Economic
Life (Years)</td><td>Estimated
Salvage Value</td><td>Annual After
Tax Cash Flow</td></tr>
<tr><td>1</td><td>$18,000</td><td>5</td><td>$ 2,000</td><td>$ 4,000</td></tr>
<tr><td>2</td><td>70,000</td><td>8</td><td>10,000</td><td>12,000</td></tr>
<tr><td>3</td><td>60,000</td><td>12</td><td>0</td><td>14,000</td></tr>
<tr><td>4</td><td>45,000</td><td>10</td><td>2,000</td><td>4,800</td></tr>
<tr><td>5</td><td>52,000</td><td>8</td><td>5,000</td><td>18,000</td></tr>
<tr><td>6</td><td>10,000</td><td>5</td><td>1,000</td><td>3,400</td></tr>
<tr><td>7</td><td>85,000</td><td>15</td><td>5,000</td><td>1,800</td></tr>
</table>

a) Calculate the prospective return on investment for each project, and rank the projects accordingly. Which projects should be undertaken, if you were not to consider any other matter? What should be the company's *MARR* this year?

b) Suppose management is averse to the risk inherent in a long-term-investment and wants to consider profitability over only an eight year period. How would the choice of projects, and the *MARR*, change?

SOLUTION

a) The choice of projects would occur in this order: 5, 6, 3, 7; and the *MARR* would correspond to the *ROR* of the last project chosen, i.e., 19.9%.

b) The *ROR* for projects 3, 4, and 7 change, and the choice of projects becomes 5, 6, 3, and 4. The *MARR* is lowered to 14.3%, and the

$58,000 left of funds is either saved until another project can be found that meets that *MARR*, or some is invested in project 1, if the rate that can be earned in by investing in a highly liquid bank account is less than 6.6%.

PROBLEM 8

A paper company is building a paper mill, but is uncertain as yet how large to make it. The greater the capacity of the plant, the greater their income, but whether the extra investment will meet the company's *MARR* of 17% is unsure. The seven alternatives are outlined below.

TABLE 6 PAPER MILL ALTERNATIVES							
	1	2	3	4	5	6	7
Investment	$50,000	55,000	60,000	65,000	70,000	75,000	88,000
After tax cash flow	10,000	15,000	18,000	20,000	21,000	22,000	25,000

a) Compute the return on investment for each alternative.

b) Calculate the marginal return on each increment of investment.

c) Which alternative is the best?

SOLUTION

	1	2	3	4	5	6	7
a) *ROR*	5.47	16.19	19.91	20.93	19.91	19.01	17.75
b) Marginal *ROR*		98.36	55.81	32.66	5.47	5.47	8.16

c) Alternative four is best, because the marginal return on investment for alternative five is less than 17% and none of the successive alternatives can produce a marginal *ROR* of 17% or greater, when compared with alternative four.

PROBLEM 9

There are several models of a piece of equipment which would cut costs for a company. If their *MARR* is 20% before taxes, which of the six models should they choose if there is no salvage value and the equipment will last eight years?

TABLE 7		
COST-CUTTING MODELS		
Model	Investment	Cost Reduction(annual)
1	$ 82,500	$18,010
2	93,200	22,020
3	98,066	22,252
4	104,400	30,003
5	110,110	32,580
6	112,000	33,008

SOLUTION

TABLE 8			
COMPARISON OF MODELS			
ROR	Increment of Investment	Increment of Cost Reduction	Before Tax *ROR* on Increment of Investment
1 14.38%			
2 16.81%			
3 19.6%			
4 23.39%			
5 24.44%	$5,710	$2,577	42.47%
6 24.3%	$1,890	$428	15.49%

Models 1, 2, and 3 do meet the *MARR*, so there is no need to calculate the marginal return on investment. Model four becomes the base case, by which model five is compared, and comes out ahead, becoming the new base case. Model six does not have a high enough marginal return on investment, so model five is best.

PROBLEM 10

If the tax rate is 33% and the equipment is depreciated as five-year property under *ACRS*, and if the company's after-tax *MARR* is 15%,

a) find the after-tax cash flows for each model and calculate the *ROI*.

b) do an incremental analysis of cash flows and *ROI*, and decide which model is the best.

SOLUTION

a)

	TABLE 9 AFTER-TAX FLOWS		
	Model 1	**Model 2**	**Model 3**
Year	*ATCF*	*ATCF*	*ATCF*
1	$17,512	$20,905	$23,395
2	20,779	24,595	27,275
3	18,601	22,368	24,686
4	17,579	19,674	22,097
5	14,245	17,214	19,508
6	12,067	14,753	16,919
7	12,067	14,753	16,919
8	12,067	14,753	16,919
	ROR = 11.48%	*ROR* = 13.13%	*ROR* = 15.23%

	TABLE 10 AFTER-TAX FLOWS		
	Model 4	**Model 5**	**Model 6**
Year	*ATCF*	*ATCF*	*ATCF*
1	$26,992	$29,096	$29,507
2	31,127	33,456	33,943
3	25,056	30,549	30,986
4	25,614	27,643	28,029
5	22,858	24,736	25,072
6	20,102	21,829	22,115
7	20,102	21,829	22,115
8	20,102	21,829	22,115
	ROR = 17.47%	*ROR* = 18.94%	*ROR* = 18.85%

b)

	TABLE 11 INCREMENTAL ANALYSIS		
Year	Comparison of Models 3 and 4	Comparison of Models 4 and 5	Comparison of Models 5 and 6
1	$3,601	$2,104	$411
2	3,852	2,329	487
3	370	5,493	437
4	3,517	2,029	386
5	3,350	1,878	336
6	3,183	1,727	286
7	3,183	1,727	286
8	3,183	1,727	286
	Increment of investment = $6,334	Increment of investment = $5,710	Increment of investment = $1,890
	After-tax incremental *ROR* = 46.34%	After-tax incremental *ROR* = 43.18%	After-tax incremental *ROR* = 12.03%

* Model 5 is the choice in after-tax analysis.

FE/EIT

Fundamentals of Engineering: AM Exam

CHAPTER 14

Ethics

CHAPTER 14

ETHICS

Engineers' moral responsibility extends well beyond that which they owe their employers to society as a whole, as underscored in the closing years of the 20th century by high-profile cases of engineering-related failures, including the *Challenger* disaster, the Kansas City Hyatt Regency Hotel walkways collapse, and the Exxon oil spill in Prince William Sound. As a response to this concern, a new discipline—engineering ethics—has emerged on campuses across the United States.

ENGINEERING ETHICS

Engineering ethics is (1) the study of moral issues and decisions confronting individuals and organizations involved in engineering and (2) the study of related questions about moral conduct, character, ideals, and relationships of peoples and organizations involved in technological development (Martin and Schinzinger, *Ethics in Engineering*).

NATIONAL SOCIETY OF PROFESSIONAL ENGINEERS BOARD OF ETHICAL REVIEW

The National Society of Professional Engineers (NSPE) Board of Ethical Review was established in the 1950s to review factual situations involving ethical dilemmas submitted by engineers, public officials, and members of the public. These anonymous dilemma situations are reviewed by the members of the Board and considered in light of the language of the NSPE Code of Ethics, Board of Ethical Review precedents, and the practical experiences of professional engineers who represent each of NSPE's seven geographical regions.

Following extensive deliberation, the Board issues written opinions which contain a description of the facts, pertinent Code citations, relevant questions, detailed discussions, and conclusions. Some opinions also include dissents.

NSPE CODE OF ETHICS FOR ENGINEERS

PREAMBLE

Engineering is an important and learned profession. The members of the profession recognize that their work has a direct and vital impact on the quality of life for all people. Accordingly, the services provided by engineers require honesty, impartiality, fairness, and equity, and must be dedicated to the protection of the public health, safety, and welfare. In the practice of their profession, engineers must perform under a standard of professional behavior which requires adherence to the highest principles of ethical conduct on behalf of the public, clients, employers, and the profession.

I. FUNDAMENTAL CANONS

Engineers, in the fulfillment of their professional duties, shall:

1. Hold paramount the safety, health, and welfare of the public in the performance of their professional duties.

2. Perform services only in the areas of their competence.

3. Issue public statements only in an objective and truthful manner.

4. Act in professional matters for each employer or client as faithful agents or trustees.

5. Avoid deceptive acts in the solicitation of professional employment.

II. RULES OF PRACTICE

1. Engineers shall hold paramount the safety, health, and welfare of the public in the performance of their professional duties.

    a. Engineers shall at all times recognize that their primary obligation is to protect the safety, health, property, and welfare of the public. If their professional judgment is overruled under circumstances where the safety, health, property, or welfare of the public are endangered, they shall notify their employer or client and such authority as may be appropriate.

b.   Engineers shall approve only those engineering documents which are safe for public health, property, and welfare in conformity with accepted standards.

c.   Engineers shall not reveal facts, data, or information obtained in a professional capacity without the prior consent of the client or employer except as authorized or required by law or this Code.

d.   Engineers shall not permit the use of their name or firm name nor associate in business ventures with any person or firm which they have reason to believe is engaging in fraudulent or dishonest business or professional practices.

e.   Engineers having knowledge of any alleged violation of this Code shall cooperate with the proper authorities in furnishing such information or assistance as may be required.

2.   Engineers shall perform services only in the areas of their competence:

a.   Engineers shall undertake assignments only when qualified by education or experience in the specific technical fields involved.

b.   Engineers shall not affix their signatures to any plans or documents dealing with subject matter in which they lack competence, nor to any plan or document not prepared under their direction and control.

c.   Engineers may accept assignments and assume responsibility for coordination of an entire project and sign and seal the engineering documents for the entire project, provided that each technical segment is signed and sealed only by the qualified engineers who prepared the segment.

3.   Engineers shall issue public statements only in an objective and truthful manner.

a.   Engineers shall be objective and truthful in professional reports, statements, or testimony. They shall include all relevant and pertinent information in such reports, statements, or testimony.

b. Engineers may express publicly a professional opinion on technical subjects only when that opinion is founded upon adequate knowledge of the facts and competence in the subject matter.

c. Engineers shall issue no statements, criticisms, or arguments on technical matters which are inspired or paid for by interested parties, unless they have prefaced the comments by explicitly identifying the interested parties on whose behalf they are speaking, and by revealing the existence of any interest the engineers may have in the matters.

4. Engineers shall act in professional matters for each employer or client as faithful agents or trustees.

a. Engineers shall disclose all known or potential conflicts of interest to their employers or clients by promptly informing them of any business association, interest, or other circumstances which could influence or appear to influence their judgment or the quality of their services.

b. Engineers shall not accept compensation, financial or otherwise, from more than one party for services on the same project, or for services pertaining to the same project, unless the circumstances are fully disclosed to, and agreed to by, all interested parties.

c. Engineers shall not solicit or accept financial or other valuable consideration, directly or indirectly, from contractors, their agents, or other parties in connection with work for employers or clients for which they are responsible.

d. Engineers in public service as members, advisors, or employees of a governmental or quasi-governmental body or department shall not participate in decisions with respect to professional services solicited or provided by them or their organization in private or public engineering practice.

e. Engineers shall not solicit or accept a professional contract from a governmental body on which a principal or officer of their organization serves as a member.

5. Engineers shall avoid deceptive acts in the solicitation of professional employment.

a. Engineers shall not falsify or permit misrepresentation of their, or their associates', academic or professional qualifications. They shall not misrepresent or exaggerate their degree of responsibility in or for the subject matter of prior assignments. Brochures or other presentations incidental to the solicitation of employment shall not misrepresent pertinent facts concerning employers, employees, associates, joint ventures, or past accomplishments with the intent and purpose of enhancing their qualifications and their work.

b. Engineers shall not offer, give, solicit, or receive, either directly or indirectly, any political contribution in an amount intended to influence the award of a contract by public authority, or which may be reasonably construed by the public of having the effect or intent to influence the award of a contract. They shall not offer any gift or other valuable consideration in order to secure work. They shall not pay a commission, percentage, or brokerage fee in order to secure work except to a bona fide employee or bona fide established commercial or marketing agency retained by them.

III. PROFESSIONAL OBLIGATIONS

1. Engineers shall be guided in all their professional relations by the highest standards of integrity.

    a. Engineers shall admit and accept their own errors when proven wrong and refrain from distorting or altering the facts in an attempt to justify their decisions.

    b. Engineers shall advise their clients or employers when they believe a project will not be successful.

    c. Engineers shall not accept outside employment to the detriment of their regular work or interest. Before accepting any outside employment, they will notify their employers.

    d. Engineers shall not attempt to attract an engineer from another employer by false or misleading pretenses.

    e. Engineers shall not actively participate in strikes, picket lines, or other collective coercive action.

    f. Engineers shall avoid any act tending to promote their own interest at the expense of the dignity and integrity of the profession.

2. Engineers shall at all times strive to serve the public interest.

    a. Engineers shall seek opportunities to be of constructive service in civic affairs and work for the advancement of safety, health, and well-being of their community.

    b. Engineers shall not complete, sign, or seal plans and/or specifications that are not of a design safe to the public safety, health, and welfare and in conformity with accepted engineering standards. If the client or employer insists on such unprofessional conduct, they shall notify the proper authorities and withdraw from further service on the project.

    c. Engineers shall endeavor to extend public knowledge and appreciation of engineering and its achievements and to protect the engineering profession from misrepresentation and misunderstanding.

3. Engineers shall avoid all conduct or practice which is likely to discredit the profession or deceive the public.

    a. Engineers shall avoid the use of statements containing a material misrepresentation of fact or omitting a material fact necessary to keep statements from being misleading or intended or likely to create an unjustified expectation, or statements containing prediction of future success.

    b. Consistent with the foregoing, Engineers may advertise for recruitment of personnel.

    c. Consistent with the foregoing, Engineers may prepare articles for the lay or technical press, but such articles shall not imply credit to the author for work performed by others.

4. Engineers shall not disclose confidential information concerning the business affairs or technical processes of any present or former client or employer without his consent.

    a. Engineers in the employ of others shall not, without the consent of all interested parties, enter promotional efforts or negotiations for work or make arrangements for other employment as a principal or to practice in connection with a specific project for which the Engineer has gained particular and specialized knowledge.

b. Engineers shall not, without the consent of all interested parties, participate in or represent an adversary interest in connection with a specific project or proceeding in which the Engineer has gained particular specialized knowledge on behalf of a former client or employer.

5. Engineers shall not be influenced in their professional duties by conflicting interests.

   a. Engineers shall not accept financial or other considerations, including free engineering designs, from material or equipment suppliers for specifying their product.

   b. Engineers shall not accept commissions or allowances, directly or indirectly, from contractors or other parties dealing with clients or employers of the Engineer in connection with work for which the Engineer is responsible.

6. Engineers shall uphold the principle of appropriate and adequate compensation for those engaged in engineering work.

   a. Engineers shall not accept remuneration from either an employee or employment agency for giving employment.

   b. Engineers, when employing other engineers, shall offer salary according to professional qualifications.

7. Engineers shall not attempt to obtain employment or advancement or professional engagements by untruthfully criticizing other engineers, or by other improper or questionable methods.

   a. Engineers shall not request, propose, or accept a professional commission on a contingent basis under circumstances in which their professional judgment may be compromised.

   b. Engineers in salaried positions shall accept part-time engineering work only to the extent consistent with policies of the employer and in accordance with ethical considerations.

   c. Engineers shall not use equipment, supplies, laboratory, or office facilities of an employer to carry on outside private practice without consent.

8. Engineers shall not attempt to injure, maliciously or falsely, directly or indirectly, the professional reputation, prospects, practice, or employment of other engineers, nor untruthfully criticize other engineers' work. Engineers who believe others are guilty

of unethical or illegal practice shall present such information to the proper authority for action.

    a.   Engineers in private practice shall not review the work of another engineer for the same client, except with the knowledge of such engineer, or unless the connection of such engineer with the work has been terminated.

    b.   Engineers in governmental, industrial, or educational employ are entitled to review and evaluate the work of other engineers when so required by their employment duties.

    c.   Engineers in sales or industrial employ are entitled to make engineering comparisons of represented products with products of other suppliers.

9.   Engineers shall accept responsibility for their professional activities; provided, however, that Engineers may seek indemnification for professional services arising out of their practice for other than gross negligence, where the Engineer's interest cannot otherwise be protected.

    a.   Engineers shall conform with state registration laws in the practice of engineering.

    b.   Engineers shall not use association with a nonengineer, a corporation, or partnership as a "cloak" for unethical acts, but must accept personal responsibility for all professional acts.

10.   Engineers shall give credit for engineering work to those to whom credit is due, and will recognize the proprietary interests of others.

    a.   Engineers shall, whenever possible, name the person or persons who may be individually responsible for designs, inventions, writings, or other accomplishments.

    b.   Engineers using designs supplied by a client recognize that the designs remain the property of the client and may not be duplicated by the Engineer for others without express permission.

    c.   Engineers, before undertaking work for others in connection with which the Engineer may make improvements, plans, designs, inventions, or other records which may justify copyrights or patents, should enter into a positive agreement regarding ownership.

d.   Engineers' designs, data, records, and notes referring exclusively to an employer's work are the employer's property.

11. Engineers shall cooperate in extending the effectiveness of the profession by interchanging information and experience with other engineers and students, and will endeavor to provide opportunity for the professional development and advancement of engineers under their supervision.

a.   Engineers shall encourage engineering employees' efforts to improve their education.

b.   Engineers shall encourage engineering employees to attend and present papers at professional and technical society meetings.

c.   Engineers shall urge engineering employees to become registered at the earliest possible date.

d.   Engineers shall assign a professional engineer duties of a nature to utilize full training and experience, insofar as possible, and delegate lesser functions to subprofessionals or to technicians.

e.   Engineers shall provide a prospective engineering employee with complete information on working conditions and proposed status of employment, and after employment will keep employees informed of changes.

CASES AND JUDGEMENTS

The following cases and judgments have been adapted from the NSPE Board of Ethical Review.

NSPE Case 76-4

Public Welfare - Knowledge of Information Damaging to Client's Interest

Facts

The XYZ Corporation has been advised by a State Pollution Control Authority that it has 60 days to apply for a permit to discharge manufacturing wastes into a receiving body of water. XYZ is also advised of the minimum standard that must be met.

In an effort to convince the authority that the receiving body of water after receiving the manufacturing wastes will still meet established environmental standards, the corporation employs Engineer Doe to perform consulting engineering services and submit a detailed report.

After completion of his studies but before completion of any written report, Doe concludes that the discharge from the plant will lower the quality of the receiving body of water below established standards. He further concludes that corrective action will be very costly. Doe verbally advises the XYZ Corporation of his findings. Subsequently, the corporation terminates the contract with Doe with full payment for services performed, and instructs Doe not to render a written report to the corporation.

Thereafter, Doe learns that the authority has called a public hearing and that the XYZ Corporation has presented data to support its view that the present discharge meets minimum standards.

Question

> *Does Doe have an ethical obligation to report his findings to the authority upon learning of the hearing?*

References

Code of Ethics - Section 1 - "The Engineer will be guided in all his professional relations by the highest standards of integrity, and will act in professional matters for each client or employer as a faithful agent or trustee."

Section 1(c) - "He will advise his client or employer when he believes a project will not be successful."

Section 2 - "The Engineer will have proper regard for the safety, health, and welfare of the public in the performance of his professional duties. If his engineering judgment is overruled by nontechnical authority, he will clearly point out the consequences. He will notify the proper authority of any observed conditions which endanger public safety and health."

Section 2(a) - "He will regard his duty to the public welfare as paramount."

Section 2(c) - "He will not complete, sign, or seal plans and/or specifications that are not of a design safe to the public health and welfare and in conformity with accepted engineering standards. If the client or employer insists on such unprofessional conduct, he shall notify the proper authorities and withdraw from further service on the project."

Section 7 - "The Engineer will not disclose confidential information concerning the business affairs or technical processes of any present or former client or employer without his consent."

Discussion

Section 1 of the Code is clear in providing that the engineer "will act in professional matters for each client or employer as a faithful agent or trustee." In this spirit Engineer Doe has advised the XYZ Corporation that the results of his studies indicate that the established standards will in his opinion be violated. His verbal advice to the corporation would seem to meet the letter and spirit of Section 1 and 1(c).

The termination of Doe's contract with full payment for services rendered is a business decision which we will presume is permitted by the terms of the engineering services contract between Doe and his client. Doe, however, has reason to question why the corporation specifically stipulates that he not render a written report. Upon learning of the hearing, he is squarely confronted with his obligations to the public concerning its safety, health, and welfare. Section 2(a) requires that his duty to the public be paramount. In this case, it is presumed that a failure to meet the minimum standards established by law is detrimental to the public health and safety.

Prior to this case, the Board has not had occasion to interpret Section 2(c) of the Code. That portion of Section 2(c) which requires the engineer to report any request for "unprofessional" conduct to "proper authorities" is particularly pertinent in this situation. The client's action instructing Doe to not render a written report, when coupled with XYZ's testimony at the hearing, raises the question of Doe's obligation under Section 2(c). The Board interprets the language in the context of the facts to mean that it would now be "unprofessional conduct" for Doe to not take further action to protect the public interest.

It is not material, in the Board's view, that the subject matter does not involve plans and specifications as stipulated in Section 2(c). The Board interprets "plans and specifications" in this section to include all engineering instruments of service. That particular reference must be read in light of the overall thrust of Sections 2 and 2(a), both of which indicate clearly that the paramount duty of the engineer is to protect the public safety, health, and welfare in a broad context. As has been noted in a prior case, even though involving unrelated facts and circumstances, "It is basic to the entire concept of a profession that its members will devote their interests to the public welfare, as is made abundantly clear in Section 2 and Section 2(a) of the Code."

Section 7 of the Code does not give the Board pause because the action of the engineer in advising the proper authority of the apparent danger to the public interest will not in this case be disclosing the technical processes or business affairs of the client.

Conclusion

Doe has an ethical obligation to report his findings to the authority upon learning of the hearing.

Note: This opinion is based on data submitted to the Board of Ethical Review and does not necessarily represent all of the pertinent facts when applied to a specific case. This opinion is for educational purposes only and should not be construed as expressing any opinion on the ethics of specific individuals. This opinion may be reprinted without further permission, provided that this statement is included before or after the text of the case.

NSPE Case No. 88-5

Signing of Drawings by Engineer in Industry

Facts

Engineer A is employed by a computer manufacturing company. She was responsible for the design of certain computer equipment several years ago. She signed off on the drawings for the equipment at that time. Although Engineer A's design was properly prepared, the equipment manufacturing process was faulty and, as a result, the equipment became too costly and suffered mechanical breakdown. The manufacturing division made a number of recommended modifications to her design, which it believed would help reduce costs in the manufacturing process. Engineer A's analysis of the manufacturing division's recommendations revealed that they would reduce the reliability of the product and greatly increase the downstream costs to the company through warranty claims. Engineer A's supervisor, who is not an engineer, asks Engineer A to sign off on the changes for the new computer equipment. There is nothing to suggest that the equipment would pose a danger to the public health and safety. Engineer A raises her concerns to her supervisor but nevertheless agrees to sign off on the changes without further protest.

Question

Did Engineer A fulfill her ethical obligation by signing off on the changes without further action?

References

Code of Ethics - Section II.1 .: "Engineers shall hold paramount the safety, health, and welfare of the public in the performance of their professional duties."

Section II.1.a.: "Engineers shall at all times recognize that their primary obligation is to protect the safety, health, property, and welfare of the public. If their professional judgment is overruled under circumstances where the safety, health, property, or welfare of the public are endangered, they shall notify their employer or client and such other authority as may be appropriate."

Section II.1.b.: "Engineers shall approve only those engineering documents that are safe for public health, property, and welfare in conformity with accepted standards."

Section II.2.b.: "Engineers shall not affix their signatures to any plans or documents dealing with subject matter in which they lack competence, nor to any plan or document not prepared under their direction and control."

Section II.4.: "Engineers shall act in professional matters for each employer or client as faithful agents or trustees."

Section III.2.b.: "Engineers shall not complete, sign, or seal plans and/or specifications that are not of a design safe to the public health and welfare and in conformity with accepted engineering standards. If the client or employer insists on such unprofessional conduct, they shall notify the proper authorities and withdraw from further service on the project."

Discussion

This case raises a fundamental issue concerning the professional integrity of engineers and the ethical obligations engineers owe to their employers, clients, and others. How far must engineers go in stating concerns in matters which directly involve their judgment as professional engineers but do not directly impact upon the public health and safety?

It is clear from the Code of Ethics and from previous Board of Ethical Review opinions that in matters involving the public health and safety, the engineer has an ethical obligation to "stand firm" and take action to protect the interest of the public. The Code is replete with provisions which reinforce the view that engineers have a fundamental obligation to the public welfare; and if their judgment is overruled under circumstances which endanger the public, the engineers should notify employers, clients, or such other authority as may be appropriate.

In addition, it should be noted at this juncture that the NSPE Code of Ethics makes it clear that the engineer has an ethical obligation to act in professional matters for her employer as a "faithful agent and trustee." In this regard, to what extent would this provision in the Code of Ethics impact upon any obligation which an engineer might have to "stand firm," in a difference of opinion, with an employer on a matter which does not have a direct impact upon the public health and safety?

These seemingly conflicting provisions of the Code of Ethics can be reconciled. While it is clear that the engineer should act consistently with the interests of her employer and not act disloyally by impinging the motives of her employer in any way, it is vitally important for an engineer whose professional judgment is overruled to clearly explain the reasons for her position and vigorously engage those persons who disagree with her judgments in a serious debate as to the technical issues involved. Here, Engineer A was asked to approve modifications which she believed, based upon her technical knowledge, would not be in the long-term interests of her employer. Since she possessed the engineering expertise, experience, and background to make these determinations and was presumably hired to provide that input to the company, it would seem that she would clearly be performing as a "faithful agent and trustee" if she were to make her concerns known to those in management who were most directly concerned with the long-term interests of the company. An engineer could not be said to be acting as a "faithful agent or trustee" by silently assenting to a course of action which will have serious long-term ramifications for an employer.

Engineers should be vocal on technical issues in which they possess knowledge and should not merely serve as a "rubber stamp" on engineering matters. Section II.4. should not be used as a "crutch" for engineers to avoid confronting difficult professional decisions, but instead as a basis for providing their employers and clients with critical engineering judgments and determinations.

Finally, it should be added that since Engineer A's immediate supervisor was not receptive to her concerns, Engineer A had an ethical obligation to bring this matter to the attention of those in management at a higher level than her immediate supervisor. Prior to taking this action, Engineer A should explain to her immediate supervisor her professional and ethical obligations under the circumstances and disclose her course of action.

Conclusion

Engineer A did not fulfill her ethical obligation by signing off on the changes without further action.

NSPE Case No. 77-5

Use of Another's Project Study

Facts

A state agency contacted Firm A and requested preliminary data regarding the possibility of designing a facility of a somewhat unique nature and which required special expertise in the field of solar energy. Firm A had previously proposed the concept for that special type of facility to a federal agency, which apparently was made known by the federal agency to the state agency. Firm A submitted the requested preliminary information to the state agency, which in turn made the information available to a private foundation in the form of a proposal to secure additional funds for the project. During this process the state agency and representatives of Firm A engaged in a series of informal discussions on the contemplated project, leading Firm A to believe it had been assured it would be awarded the design of the project if it went ahead.

Some months later the state agency advised Firm A that it had received both public and private funds for the project, but not in sufficient amount for the full scope of the facility. Firm A was requested to then evaluate whether a more limited facility could be provided for the limited funds. Firm A then made subsequent investigations, including out-of-state visits, at its own expense, upon its belief that it would be awarded the design contract. Based upon the further studies, Firm A submitted a revised proposal to the state agency. Firm A estimated it expended approximately $3,000 in its endeavors.

Subsequently, the chief engineer of the state agency advised Firm A that he had turned over all the data furnished by Firm A to Firm B for its use. This was followed by a notice from the state agency that it was conducting initial negotiations with Firm B, and that if these negotiations were not successful it would contact Firm A for negotiations for the project assignment. Firm B was aware of the involvement of Firm A prior to its initial negotiations. During the course of these developments, Firm B did not contact Firm A for any discussion of the project or the earlier submissions of Firm A to the state agency. Firm A has protested to the state agency, alleging that the procedure followed by the agency and the action of Firm B violated the Code of Ethics.

Questions

1. *Was it ethical for Firm A to expend approximately $3,000 under the circumstances?*

2. *Was it ethical for the chief engineer of the state agency to turn over the studies, reports, and data provided by Firm A to other firms?*

3. *Was it ethical for Firm B to enter into negotiations for the project under these circumstances?*

References

Code of Ethics - Section 7 - "The Engineer will not disclose confidential information concerning the business affairs or technical processes of any present or former client or employer without his consent."

Section 9 - "The Engineer will uphold the principle of appropriate and adequate compensation for those engaged in engineering work."

Section 11 - "The Engineer will not compete unfairly with another engineer by attempting to obtain employment or advancement or professional engagements by competitive bidding, by taking advantage of a salaried position, by criticizing other engineers, or by other improper or questionable methods."

Section 11(a) - "The Engineer will not attempt to supplant another engineer in a particular employment after becoming aware that definite steps have been taken toward the other's employment."

Section 11(g) - "An Engineer will not use "free engineering" as a device to solicit or otherwise secure subsequent paid engineering assignments."

Section 14 - "The Engineer will give credit for engineering work to those to whom credit is due, and will recognize the proprietary interests of others."

Discussion

The problem posed by the first question is similar to the problem that confronted the Board in another case. In the previous case, an engineer provided free engineering services with the knowledge that he had not yet been selected and was then still in competition with other firms. In the discussion in that case, the Board acknowledged the practical difficulties faced by engineers in this phase of negotiations. "On balance," the Board concluded it was not ethical to provide the services described in that case. In this case, Firm A was under the impression, as mistaken as subsequent events found the impression to be, that it was going to be awarded the design of the project if the project went ahead. So the situation anticipated by Section 11(g) did not really exist since Firm A thought it already had the assignment.

Turning now to the actions of the chief engineer of the state agency, the Board did not find a section of the Code that deals directly with the question his actions pose. However, Section 7 states in part, "The Engineer will not disclose confidential information concerning...technical processes of any present...employer without his consent." The facts in this case indicate that Firm A had special expertise in a narrow field. Despite this expertise, Firm A had to make investigations at considerable expense in order to submit a proposal to the agency. It seems logical to assume that Firm A's proposal contained much highly specialized technical information.

Although the chief engineer did not violate the letter of any part of the Code in turning over the data to Firm B, he skirted the spirit of several Code provisions which are generally intended to protect engineers from improper use of their technical accomplishments (see Sections 7, 9, and 14).

The Board could not find any specific provision of the Code that deals either directly or indirectly with the ethical obligations of an engineer on behalf of or as an agent of the owner to avoid taking advantage of another engineer who has, in good faith, provided substantial valuable information for a proposed project on an understanding (even if an imperfect one) that the engineer providing the assistance will receive the commission for it. However, engineers in private practice who are tempted to expend substantial time, effort, and funds to secure a commission should be alert to the danger they run when that expenditure exceeds a nominal investment.

Under the stated facts it cannot be said that Section 11(a) has been offended on the part of Firm B because there is no showing that "definite steps" had been taken to retain Firm A. The Board noted as to Firm B under these facts, that while it did not apparently initiate the contact with the agency to secure the work, it did have actual knowledge of the previous services provided to the agency by Firm A. The practice of professional courtesy should have dictated that Firm B contact Firm A to discuss Firm B's involvement.

At this point the Board gratuitously noted that some of the difficulties that developed would have been avoided if Firm A had not relied upon its belief that it would be awarded the contract.

Conclusions

1. It was ethical for Firm A to expend approximately $3,000 under the circumstances.

2. It was not unethical for the chief engineer of the state agency to turn over the studies, reports, and data provided by Firm A to other firms.

3. It was ethical for Firm B to enter into negotiations for the project under these circumstances.

NSPE Case No. 84-4

Engineer's Dispute with Client Over Design

Facts

Client hires Engineer A to design a particular project. Engineer A develops what he believes to be the best design and meets with the client to discuss the design. After discussing the design plans and specifications, the client and Engineer A are involved in a dispute concerning the ultimate success of the project. The client believes Engineer A's design is too large and complex and seeks a simpler solution to the project. Engineer A believes a simpler solution will not achieve the result and could endanger the public. The client demands that Engineer A deliver over to him the drawings so that he can present them to Engineer B to assist Engineer B in completing the project to his liking. The client is willing to pay for the drawings, plans, specifications, and preparation, but will not pay until Engineer A hands over the drawings. Engineer A refuses to deliver the drawings.

Question

Would it be ethical for Engineer A to hand over the plans and specifications to the client?

References

Code of Ethics - Section II.1.a.: "Engineers shall at all times recognize that their primary obligation is to protect the safety, health, property, and welfare of the public. If their professional judgment is overruled under circumstances where the safety, health, property, or welfare of the public are endangered, they shall notify their employer or client and such other authority as may be appropriate."

Section II.1.e.: "Engineers having knowledge of any alleged violation of this Code shall cooperate with the proper authorities in furnishing such information or assistance as may be required." **b.:** "Engineers shall advise their clients or employers when they believe a project will not be successful."

Discussion

The facts of the case presented to the Board, at first glance, appear to be fairly straightforward and easily addressed by the Code of Ethics. On its face, we are presented with an engineer who has been retained by a client to design a project. However, both parties cannot agree as to the ultimate success of the project as developed by Engineer A. Thus, the client seeks to terminate the services of Engineer A, but wishes to obtain the drawings, plans, and specifications from Engineer A for a fee. Our discussion will be limited to the ethical rather than the contractual considerations of this case.

Much of the language contained in the Code relates to the engineer's obligation to protect the public health, property, and welfare (Section II.1.a.). In the present case, it appears that Engineer A had a strong concern for the protection of the public health and welfare. Nevertheless, it is the view of the Board that Engineer A could have given the drawings to the client and his conduct would have been ethically proper.

While it is true that Engineer A has an ethical obligation under Section II.1.a., that obligation assumes that Engineer A is in possession of verifiable facts or evidence which would substantiate a charge that an actual danger to the public health or safety exists.

In the instant case, Engineer A makes the overly broad assumption that if he were to give the client the drawings so that the client can present them to Engineer B to assist Engineer B in completing the project to the client's liking, Engineer B would develop a set of plans that would endanger the public health and safety. Such an assumption is ill-founded and is not based upon anything more than a supposition by Engineer A. Therefore, Engineer A should not have withheld the drawings on the basis of Section II.1.a. In reviewing the conduct of Engineer A up until his refusal to give the drawings to the client, Engineer A went as far as he was ethically required to go in preparing what he believed was the best design for the project and in informing the client of the dangers of proceeding with the client's simplified solution. Section III.1.b. is very clear in stating an "Engineer shall advise [his] client...when [he] believes a project will not be successful." By conferring with the client and explaining his concerns over a proposed simplified solution, Engineer A met his ethical responsibility.

In the event, however, that Engineer A does give the client the plans so that the client can present them to Engineer B for completion of the project to the client's liking, and thereafter Engineer A discovers that Engineer B developed plans that constitute a danger to the public, certain actions would then be required by Engineer A under the Code. Any verifiable conduct on the part of Engineer B that indicates that Engineer B's plans are a danger to the public should be brought to the attention of the proper authorities, i.e., the responsible professional societies or the state engineering registration board.

Conclusion

It would be ethical under the above circumstances for Engineer A to give the plans and specifications to the client.

NSPE Case No. 80-4

Participation of Engineer with Competing Firms for Same Contract

Facts

Engineer Able, on behalf of the firm of which he is a principal, submitted a statement of qualifications to a governmental agency for a project. In due course, he was notified that his firm was on the "short list" for consideration along with several other firms, but it was indicated to him that his firm did not appear to have qualifications in some specialized aspects of the requirements, and that it might be advisable for the firm to consider a joint venture with another firm with such capabilities. Engineer Able thereupon contacted Engineer Baker, a principal of a firm with the background required for the specialized requirements, and inquired if the Baker firm would be interested in a joint venture if Able was awarded the job. The Baker firm responded in the affirmative.

Thereafter, Engineer Carlson, a principal in a firm that was also on the "short list," contacted Engineer Baker and indicated the same requirement for a joint venture for specialized services, and also asked if the Baker firm would be willing to engage in a joint venture if the Carlson firm was selected for the assignment. Baker also responded in the affirmative to Carlson but did not notify Able of his response to Carlson.

Question

Is it ethical for Engineer Baker to agree to participate in a joint venture arrangement with more than one of the firms since he did not make a full disclosure to all of the firms?

References

Code of Ethics - Section 1 - "The Engineer will be guided in all his professional relations by the highest standards of integrity, and will act in professional matters for each client or employer as a faithful agent or trustee."

Section 8 - "The Engineer shall disclose all known or potential conflicts of interest to his employer or client by promptly informing them of any business connections, interests, or other circumstances which could influence his judgment or the quality of his services, or which might reasonably be construed by others as constituting a conflict of interest."

Discussion

As is often the case in a particularized set of facts, the Code does not specifically address the question, but we have the latitude to read related sections of the Code to apply within reasonable limits. On that basis, Section 8 on conflicts of interest and Section 1 on professional integrity are stated broadly enough to provide a basis for an opinion.

The thrust of Section 8 is to require full and complete disclosure of known or potential conflicts of interest, but it does not necessarily rule out such conflicts if they exist. If there was objection by any party, the ethical question would have to be determined under the pertinent facts of that case.

The Board did not have to reach that question in this case, however, because there is not a conflict of interest under the facts before us. The Code does not define "conflict of interest." At the very least, however, it means that "a professional person may not take action or make decisions which would divide his loyalties or interests from those of his employer or client."

In this case there is no potential or actual division of loyalty as to either the Able or Carlson firm on the part of Baker. Assuming that Baker is willing to work out a joint venture agreement with either firm which might secure the contract, his loyalty would be centered only with the one selected firm. As a joint venturer, in fact, he would be a party to a single legal entity (the joint venture) for the one contract.

Technically, the disclosure requirement of Section 8 would not mandate that Baker advise Able of the contact from Carlson or advise Carlson that he had talked to Able because at this point Baker does not have a "client," as such.

However, the requirement of Section 1 for highest standards of integrity makes it ethically necessary for Baker to contact both of the firms and advise each that he had indicated his willingness to participate in a joint venture with either. In this connection we consider that the agreement of Baker to work with Able constitutes a relationship of trust which should not be diluted by establishing a similar and possibly competitive relationship with Carlson unless disclosure is made to all concerned.

Conclusion

It is unethical for Engineer Baker to agree to participate in a joint venture agreement with more than one of several firms being considered for an engineering engagement since he did not make a disclosure to all of the firms.

NSPE Case No. 69-13

Engineer's Disclosure of Potential Conflict of Interest

Facts

Engineer A is retained by the state to perform certain feasibility studies relating to a possible highway spur. The state is considering the possibility of constructing the highway spur through an area that is adjacent to a residential community in which Engineer A's residence is located. After learning of the proposed location for the spur, Engineer A discloses to the state the fact that his residential property may be affected by the new spur and fully discloses the potential conflict with the state. The state does not object to Engineer A performing the work. Engineer A proceeds with his feasibility study and ultimately recommends that the spur be constructed. The highway spur is constructed.

Question

> *Was it ethical for Engineer A to perform the feasibility study despite the fact that his land may be affected thereby?*

References

Code of Ethics - Section II.4.: "Engineers shall act in professional matters for each employer or client as faithful agents or trustees."

Section II.4.a.: "Engineers shall disclose all known or potential conflicts of interest to their employers or clients by promptly informing them of any business association, interest, or other circumstances which could influence or appear to influence their judgment or the quality of their services."

Discussion

The Board has noted on numerous occasions that the ethical duty of the engineer in areas of conflict of interest is to inform the client of those business connections or interests that may influence the judgment and quality of the engineering services. Those decisions have been consistent with the provisions of Section Il.4.a. of the NSPE Code of Ethics cited above.

While that provision of the Code has been interpreted many times over the years, it is, as are all Code provisions, subject to constant examination and reinterpretation. For any code of ethics to have meaning, it must be a living, breathing document which responds to situations that evolve and develop.

This Board has generally interpreted that Code provision in a strict manner. Previously, the Board reviewed a situation where an engineer was an officer in an incorporated engineering consulting firm that was engaged primarily in civil engineering projects for clients. Early in the engineer's life, he had acquired a tract of land by inheritance, which was in an area being developed for residential and industrial use. The engineer's firm had been retained to study and recommend a water and sewer system in the general area of his land interest. The question faced by the Board under those facts was, "May the engineer ethically design a water and sewer system in the general area of his land interest?" The Board ruled that the engineer could not ethically design the system under those circumstances.

The Board acknowledged that the question was a difficult one to resolve, pointing to the fact that there was no conflict of interest when the engineer entered his practice but that the conflict developed in the normal course of his practice when it became apparent that his study and recommendation could lead to the location of a water and sewer system that might cause a considerable appreciation in the value of his land depending upon the exact location of certain system elements in proximity to his land. The Board stated that while the engineer must make full disclosure of his personal interest to his client before proceeding with the project, such disclosure was not enough under the Code. The Board stated, "He can avoid such a conflict under these facts either by disposing of his land holdings prior to undertaking the commission or by declining to perform the services if it is not feasible or desirable for him to dispose of his land at the particular time." The Board concluded by saying: "This is a harsh result, but so long as men are in their motivations somewhat 'lower than angels,' it is a necessary conclusion to achieve compliance with both the letter and the spirit of the Code of Ethics. The real test of ethical conduct is not when compliance with the Code comports with the interests of those it is intended to govern, but when compliance is adverse to personal interests."

In its reading of the Code of Ethics, the Board took a strict view of the meaning of the Code provisions then in force, which stated:

> "*8. The Engineer will endeavor to avoid a conflict of interest with his employer or client, but when unavoidable, the Engineer shall fully disclose the circumstances to his employer or client.*"

> "*8 (a). The Engineer will inform his client or employer of any business connections, interests, or circumstances which may be deemed as influencing his judgment or the quality of his services to his client or employer.*"

It is clear from a reading of that case that the Board focused its attention on the first clause of Section 8 stating that "The engineer will endeavor to avoid a conflict of interest with his employer or client." Undoubtedly, the Board reasoned that this was the basic obligation of the engineer in this context, and that any qualification of that obligation would dilute the essential meaning and intent of that obligation. Therefore, the Board did not choose to rely upon the remaining provisions contained in Sections 8 and 8(a) in reaching its decision. Instead, the Board determined that under the facts it would not be sufficient for the engineer to make full disclosure of his personal interest to the client in order to properly address the potential conflict-of-interest question.

While the reasoning of the Board is extremely important in understanding the ethical dimensions of the instant case, the decision becomes less significant in view of the fact that the Code provisions under which the decision was rendered have been crucially altered. (See Code Sections II.4. and II.4.a., the successor provisions to Section 8.)

As one can readily see, the phrase "engineer will endeavor to avoid a conflict of interest with his employer or client..." is no longer contained in the applicable Code provision. Clearly, the reason for that omission is certainly not out of a lack of desire within the engineering profession for an ethical proscription relating to conflicts of interest. Truly, ethical dilemmas relating to conflicts of interest are some of the most significant issues facing the engineering profession today.

Nevertheless, the provision in the Code relating to conflicts of interest was amended and those changes impact upon the manner in which this Board regards the previous case, as well as the manner in which the Board interprets the Code. It is evident that had Sections II.4. and II.4.a. been in effect at the time the Board decided the prior case, the Board may well have reached a different result.

While it is not the Board's role to speculate upon the intent of this significant change in the NSPE Code of Ethics, the Board does think that some expression in that regard would assist readers in understanding the basis for the change. In no sense should this change be interpreted in any way to suggest a retreat by this Board or the Code of Ethics from a deep concern for dilemmas relating to conflicts of interest. Rather, it is the modifications in the Code that reflect recognition of the fact that conflicts of interest emerge in a multitude of degrees and circumstances and that a blanket, unqualified expression prohibiting engineers to avoid all activities that raise the shadow of a conflict of interest is not a workable approach.

It is often a question of degree as to what does and does not constitute a significant conflict of interest. Obvious and significant conflicts of interest are easily identifiable and should always be avoided. These difficult, multifaceted situations require discussion and consideration as they are complex and sometimes irresolvable. A code should address and provide guidance for these kinds of conflicts of interest. The new Code provisions sought to establish the ethical obligation to engage in dialogue with a client or employer on the difficult questions relating to conflicts of interest. It was for this reason that the Code provisions were altered.

Turning to the facts of the instant case, the ethical obligations contained in Section II.4.a. do not require the engineer to "avoid" any and all situations that may or may not raise the specter of a conflict of interest. Such an interpretation of the Code would leave engineers with neither any real understanding of the ethical issues nor any guidance as to how to deal with the problem. The basic purpose of a code of ethics is to provide the engineering profession with a better awareness and understanding of ethical issues that impact upon the public. Only through interacting with the public and clients will engineers be able to comprehend the true dimensions of ethical issues.

The Board assumes that, under the facts of this case, the state agency involved has a fully qualified staff which will ultimately review the recommendation of the engineer. Therefore, Engineer A's discussion with the client prior to performing the services and disclosing the possible conflict of interest came within the ethical guidelines of the Code and was a proper course to take in dealing with the conflict. In this case the Board did not state that the engineer can only avoid such a conflict either by "disposing of his land and holdings prior to undertaking the commission or by declining to perform the services if it is not feasible or desirable for him to dispose of his land at the particular time."

Conclusion

It was not unethical for Engineer A to perform the feasibility study despite the fact that his land may be affected thereby.

NSPE Case No. 78-7

Commission Basis of Payment Under Marketing Agreement

Facts

John Doe, P.E., has been engaged extensively in recent years in a variety of engineering activities in the international market. He determines that on the basis of his experience, familiarity with the special requirements of engineering work in other countries, and personal contacts with officials of certain foreign countries he could better serve the interests of the engineering profession, as well as his own economic interests, by representing United States firms that wish to engage in international engineering and lack a background in the special fields of knowledge required for that purpose, or which do not have the resources to develop the necessary skills to successfully enter that field.

Recognizing the inability of many U.S. firms to commit themselves to a substantial capital outlay to develop their potential in the international market pending the award of a contract, Doe drafts a plan, called a "Marketing Agreement," under which he offers his services to represent U.S. firms interested in obtaining international work. The agreement calls for Doe to provide information and develop contacts within stated geographical areas, to evaluate potential projects for the firms he represents, to coordinate project development, arrange contract terms between the client and the represented firm, and provide such other special services as the represented firms may authorize.

For these services Doe is to be paid a basic fee, the amount of which is to be negotiated on an individual firm basis, a monthly retainer fee of a negotiated amount on an individual firm basis, and a "marketing fee" of a negotiated percentage of the fees actually collected by the firm he represents for projects that were "marketed" by Doe.

Question

Is it ethical for an engineering firm to enter into such a "Marketing Agreement" with Doe?

Reference

Code of Ethics - Section 11(b) - "He will not pay, or offer to pay, either directly or indirectly, any commission, political contribution, or a gift, or other consideration in order to secure work, exclusive of securing salaried positions through employment agencies."

Discussion

It is presumed that the case does not violate federal laws or laws of the country involved. It is clear that the "commercial marketing firm" involved is an individual professional engineer offering his services on a commission basis, in part.

In an earlier Board decision, a paramount factor was that a sales representative of an engineering firm to be paid on a combined salary-commission basis was not an engineer. In that case it was concluded that the firm could utilize the sales promotion of a nonengineer, provided he did not discuss engineering aspects of the project, and only commented on the commission payment issue that "...this method of compensation is undesirable since it could lead to loss of confidence by the public in the professional nature of engineering services."

Extending that comment however, the Board said that the use of a commercial marketing firm would offend the Code of Ethics because "...the engineering firm has control over the conduct of an employee, whereas it has little or no control over the conduct of an outside marketing firm which operates on a commercial basis. The danger is thus much enhanced that a commercial marketing firm may more readily in its zeal to earn its compensation engage in conduct which may adversely reflect upon the dignity or honor of the profession."

Three members of the Board of Ethical Review, while signing that opinion, expressed "additional views" to the effect that "...in the context of modern business practices as required by our complex society and the increasing number of U.S. firms exporting their technical expertise on a global basis, there is a serious question as to whether the present language of the code is unduly restrictive while offering at best a limited measure of protection of the public interest." The members of the BER subscribing to the additional views suggested that the issue should be reviewed for a possible change in the pertinent code language or concept. To date, however, Section II(b) of the code has not been revised.

When the prohibition of commission fees as a basis to secure work is read in conjunction with other parts of Section II(b), i.e., political contributions or gifts, it would appear that the original purpose and intent were to foreclose circumstances which might arouse doubt or suspicion of impropriety in securing engineering assignments.

It is clear, however, that Section II(b) prohibits the payment of "any" commission in order to secure work (other than salaried positions), thereby ruling out the permissibility of a commission basis coupled with definite sums as a retainer fee or basic fee.

Conclusion

It is not ethical for an engineering firm to enter into such a "marketing agreement" with Doe.

NSPE Case No. 92-1

Credit for Engineering Work Design Competition

Facts

Engineer A is retained by a city to design a bridge as part of an elevated highway system. Engineer A then retains the services of Engineer B, a structural engineer with expertise in horizontal geometry, superstructure design, and elevations to perform certain aspects of the design services. Engineer B designs the bridge's three curved welded plate girder spans, which were critical elements of the bridge design.

Several months following completion of the bridge, Engineer A enters the bridge design into a national organization's bridge design competition. The bridge design wins a prize. However, the entry fails to credit Engineer B for his part of the design.

Question

Was it ethical for Engineer A to fail to give credit to Engineer B for his part in the design?

References

Section I.3.: "Issue public statements only in an objective and truthful manner."

Section II.3.a.: "Engineers shall be objective and truthful in professional reports, statements, or testimony. They shall include all relevant and pertinent information in such reports, statements, or testimony."

Section III.3.: "Engineers shall avoid all conduct or practice which is likely to discredit the profession or deceive the public."

Section III.5.a.: "Engineers shall not accept financial or other considerations, including free engineering designs, from material or equipment suppliers for specifying their product."

Section III.10.a.: "Engineers shall, whenever possible, name the person or persons who may be individually responsible for designs, inventions, writings, or other accomplishments."

Discussion

Basic to engineering ethics is the responsibility to issue statements in an objective and truthful manner (Section I.3.). The concept of providing credit for engineering work to those to whom credit is due is fundamental to that responsibility. This is particularly the case where an engineer retains the services of other individuals because the engineer may not possess the education, experience, and expertise to perform the required services for a client. The engineer has an obligation to the client to make this information known (Section II.3.a.). The principle is not only fair and in the best interests of the profession, but it also recognizes that the professional engineer must assume personal responsibility for his decisions and actions.

In another case, city department of public works retained Firm A to prepare plans and specifications for a water extension project. Engineer B, chief engineer of the department having authority in such matters, instructed Firm A to submit its plans and specifications without showing the name of the firm on the cover sheets but permitted the firm to show the name of the firm on the working drawings. It was also the policy of the department not to show the name of the design firm in the advertisements for construction bids; in fact, the advertisements stated "plans and specifications as prepared by the city department of public works."

The Board noted that the policy of the department is, at best, rather unusual in normal engineering practices and relationships between retained design firms and clients. The Board surmised on the basis of the submitted facts that the department policy was intended to reflect the idea that the plans and specifications, when put out to construction bid, are those of the department. In concluding that Engineer B acted unethically in adopting and implementing a policy which prohibited the identification of the design firm on the cover sheets for plans and specification, the Board noted that Engineer B, in carrying out the department policy, denied credit to Firm A for its work. The Code of Ethics Section III.10.a. states that engineers shall, whenever possible, name the person or persons who may be individually responsible for designs, inventions, writings, or other accomplishments. The Board concluded that under the circumstances, it was possible for Engineer B to name the persons responsible for the design.

While each individual case must be understood based upon the particular facts involved, Engineer A had an ethical obligation to his client, to Engineer B, and to the public to take reasonable steps to identify all parties responsible for the design of the bridge.

Conclusion

It was unethical for Engineer A to fail to give credit to Engineer B for his part in the design.

NSPE Case No. 92-9

Use of Disadvantaged Firm After Learning of Impropriety

Facts

Engineer A is a principal in a large consulting engineering firm specializing in civil and structural engineering. Engineer A's firm does a large percentage of its engineering work for public agencies at the state, federal, and local level. Engineer A is frequently encouraged by representatives of those agencies to consider retaining the services of small, minority, or women-owned design firms as sub-consultants to the firm, particularly on publicly funded projects.

For about a year, Engineer A's firm has retained the services of Engineer B's firm, a disadvantaged firm of a type described above, on several public and private projects. Engineer A's firm has gotten a good deal of public relations benefit as a result of its retention of Engineer B's firm, particularly among its public and private clients. The work of Engineer B's firm is adequate but not of high quality. In addition, Engineer B suddenly began charging Engineer A much higher charges and fees in recent months, particularly after an article appeared in a local publication that was very complementary of Engineer A's efforts to retain disadvantaged firms.

Question

What would be the proper action for Engineer A to take under the circumstances?

References

Preamble: "Engineering is an important and learned profession. The members of the profession recognize that their work has a direct and vital impact on the quality of life for all people. Accordingly, the services provided by engineers require honesty, impartiality, fairness, and equity, and must be dedicated to the protection of the public health, safety and welfare. In the practice of their profession, engineers must perform under a standard of professional behavior which requires adherence to the highest principles of ethical conduct on behalf of the public, clients, employers, and the profession."

Section II.2.a.: "Engineers shall undertake assignments only when qualified by education or experience in the specific technical fields involved."

Section III.6.: "Engineers shall uphold the principle of appropriate and adequate compensation for those engaged in engineering work."

Discussion

Over the past several years a significant amount of socioeconomic legislation and regulation has been enacted at the federal, state, and local levels to promote the retention of businesses that had been heretofore underrepresented in the procurement process. As a result, many engineering firms have been encouraged both by public and private clients to establish goals to retain qualified employees and consultants representative of such underrepresented groups.

This Board has never had occasion to examine a case in the context of such a program. As a general proposition, the Board believes the Code of Ethics is generally supportive of the establishment of voluntary programs that provide engineers with the opportunity to be of constructive service in community affairs and to work for its advancement and well-being. Many governmental and private procurement procedures take into account such factors consistent with their procurement requirements and standards.

Having made these general observations, we turn to the case before us. It appears that while the philosophy of establishing voluntary targets or goals for the retention of disadvantaged firms is not inconsistent with the objective of the Code of Ethics, the continued retention of a firm that is abusing its relationship with its client may be at odds with the intent of the Code. In order for an engineer to ethically engage in a joint venture, the engineer must maintain a careful scrutiny of the operation of the firm of the other engineer to assure itself to the extent possible that unethical conduct will not develop during and with respect to the joint venture. If an engineer's scrutiny of the operation of the firm reveals improper action, the engineer has an ethical obligation to disassociate with that firm in a manner that would not be prejudicial to his client.

Regarding Engineer B's unjustified escalation of his firm's fees and charges, the key to avoiding a misunderstanding in this area is through careful negotiation and discussion and through a "give and take" procedure. In the context of the present case, this type of negotiation was lacking. As it appears under the facts, Engineer B unilaterally imposed an escalation of his firm's fees and charges. Instead, Engineer B had an obligation to negotiate any future increases in his fees and charges with Engineer A's firm.

Conclusion

Engineer A has an obligation to discuss and negotiate with Engineer B in an effort to improve the quality and relative value of Engineer B's services. If a mutual agreement cannot be reached concerning the terms and conditions of service, Engineer A should terminate his relationship with Engineer B and in the future continue to strive to retain qualified employees and consultants representative of such under-represented groups.

NSPE Case No. 75-11

Credit for Engineering Work Research Data

Facts

The XYZ Company headed by Engineer A offered to provide funding to professors in the chemistry department of a major university for research on removing poisonous heavy metals (copper, lead, nickel, zinc, chromium) from waste streams. The university then agreed to contract with XYZ Company to give the company exclusive use of the technology developed in the field of water treatment and waste water stream treatment. Under the agreement, XYZ Company will provide a royalty to the university from profits derived from the use of the technology. Also, a group of the university professors organized QRS, a separate company to exploit applications of the technology other than the treatment of water and waste water. At the same time that the university research was being conducted, XYZ continued to conduct research in the same area. Performance figures and conclusions were developed. XYZ freely shared the figures and conclusions with QRS.

At the university, Engineer B, a professor of civil engineering, wanted to conduct research and develop a paper relating to the use of the technology to treat sewage. Engineer B contacted the professors in the university's chemistry department. The chemistry professors provided XYZ's data to Engineer B for use in the research and paper. The professors did not reveal to Engineer B that the data was generated by Engineer A and XYZ Company.

Engineer B's paper was published in a major journal. Engineer A's data was displayed prominently in the paper, and the work of XYZ constituted a major portion of the journal. The paper credits two of the chemistry professors as major authors along with Engineer B. No credit was given to Engineer A or XYZ as the source of the data, the funds that supported the research. After publication, Engineer B learns about the actual source of the data and its finding.

Question

Does Engineer B have an obligation under the Code of Ethics to clarify the source of the data contained in the paper?

References

Section III.10.: "Engineers shall give credit for engineering work to those to whom credit is due, and will recognize the proprietary interests of others."

Section III.10.a.: "Engineers shall, whenever possible, name the person or persons who may be individually responsible for designs, inventions, writings, or other accomplishments."

Discussion

The issue of providing credit for research work performed by others is a vital matter in this day and age. Its importance is more than merely crediting contributions of individuals who have performed work in an area of engineering and scientific research. In actual fact, funding decisions for research and development of various technologies are vitally affected by the credit and acknowledgments.

Engineer B did not knowingly fail to credit Engineer A or XYZ Company for its contributions to the research which formed the basis of his paper. Instead, Engineer B assumed that the material he received from the other professors was developed solely by those professors.

The Board concluded that Engineer B did not knowingly and deliberately fail to credit Engineer A or XYZ for its contributions to the research. However, had Engineer B made more of an effort to substantiate the sources contained in his paper, he may have been able to identify those sources. Also of concern is the conduct of the chemistry professors, who, for whatever reason(s), misled Engineer B by failing to reveal the sources of the data. While not technically covered by this Code, the conduct of the chemistry professors is clearly deplorable and is unacceptable under the philosophical standards embodied in the Code of Ethics.

Finally, the Board suggested Engineer B prepare and request that the journal publish a clarification of the matter explaining how the matter occurred along with an apology for any misunderstanding which may have arisen as a result of the publication of the paper.

Conclusion

Engineer B has an obligation to request that the journal publish a clarification of the matter explaining how the matter occurred along with an apology for any misunderstanding which may have arisen as a result of the publication of the paper.

ENGINEERS' CREED

The Engineers' Creed was developed in response to a desire for a short statement of philosophy of service, similar to the Hippocratic Oath for medical practitioners or similar oaths of the legal profession, that can be used in ceremonies or in recognition of individuals. Approved in June 1954, the Creed is used widely in NSPE, state society, and local chapter officer installation ceremonies, licensure certificate presentations, and engineering school graduations.

ENGINEERS' CREED

As a Professional Engineer, I dedicate my professional knowledge and skill to the advancement and betterment of human welfare. I pledge: To give the utmost of performance;

To participate in none but honest enterprise;

To live and work according to the laws of man and the highest standards of professional conduct;

To place service before profit, the honor and standing of the profession before personal advantage, and the public welfare above all other considerations.

In humility and with need for Divine Guidance, I make this pledge.

Adopted by National Society of Professional Engineers, June 1954

MORAL VISION AND THE LANDSCAPE OF ENGINEERING PROFESSIONALISM

Part I

Too often engineering, or any profession, is true to the adage: "It is not one thing after another; it is the same thing over and over." This adage can be applied to many professional circumstances, but particularly to the ethical domain of engineering.

Engineering is a profession in transition. Many changes have occurred in recent years, and they are self-evident. But those changes have transformed the public image of engineering, its scope of practice, the way it is taught, and often the very nature of the profession's activities. The future and well-being of the profession rests upon private views of responsibility; and in turn, a collective willingness to make a difference. There is truth in the adage cited a moment ago. Repetition, "the same thing over and over," plagues the practice of our professions. Too commonly, that practice is limited to recurrent naggings of routine and convention, habits of seeing, habits of feeling, and habits of doing that understandably drain professionals of their spontaneity. As a result, we may become indiscriminate, immune to the unique circumstances and conditions of the situation at hand. Patterns of behavior may begin to predominate as responses emerge from a type of "ethical auto-pilot."

Preoccupation with daily routine and work patterns causes professionals to lose touch with their profession, its ideas, and its ideals. This circumstance gives rise to doubt about the model—its legitimacy, validity, teachability, and most dangerously, its importance.

We must begin to ask why certain things occur. Why do so many engineers begin their careers on a bright note, only to find themselves bored and unchallenged in a matter of a few years? Why do some engineering students think there is no more to ethics than obeying the law? Why, in so many cases, is profit put before the best interests of the client? Has the profession fundamentally changed? Has the way we think about ethics and teach ethics changed? It could be that the complexity of our professional lives has forced us into daily conventions that become ruts, ruts so deep that we no longer are aware of the ethical dilemmas and opportunities for choice that present themselves every day.

Obviously though, not everyone for whom engineering is a source of livelihood is bored, stoic, and passive. Robert Bellah points out in his landmark book *Habits of the Heart* that work can be a source of self-esteem. It may provide new challenges and pathways to social standing and power. Yet many professionals miss a sense of calling that, in Bellah's words, "not only links a person to his or her fellow workers," but "links a person to the larger community as a whole in which the calling of each is a contribution to the good of all."

Yet, indifference and even cynicism can be found in the professions. Cynicism arises when options are limited, when possibilities for choosing are lost. Lines become blurred and difficult to draw, and standards seem out of reach. Deception begins to dominate, leading many to place self-interest above societal interest.

We cannot be both cynical and honest to ourselves. We cannot be both cynical and consciously moral, because to be moral, we act by what we truthfully see as right and wrong.

Genuine ethical autonomy is the product of reflective and honest choice. It is the freedom to gauge meaning, to browse among one's meditations, to turn a thought around here, then there, changing one's perspective. To be morally alert is to be conscious of the complexities that ethical dilemmas impose. It is to see differences in the landscapes of one moral problem contrasted with another. It is to weigh self-interest against the interest of others.

Morally autonomous engineers are truly free to see and to act upon their ideas and intentions. The way in which one exercises this autonomy lies at the core of a person's conception of him or herself. Naturally, this liberty implies the availability of resources and freedom of movement. And this is not all: there must be a prodding of will, a tightening of control, a building of resolve, because many times the choices will be difficult, and perhaps painful.

The professional capacity for full moral discourse is presently hampered by several factors. One is that engineers cannot avoid the fact that they deal in a marketplace economy, where competition, cost, and profit motives seem to be the bottom line. And as you well know, many times what it takes to please the boss, the stockholders, the client, and your conscience are not the same. Clearly, the demands and conflicts of capitalism inherent in the engineering profession present the difficult dilemma of balancing many interests.

It is no wonder that many face a discussion of these dilemmas with apprehension. But we can no longer allow profit motives and self-interest, however "legal" these strategies might be, to substitute for common sense, courtesy, and morality. The fact is this: engineers must address their ethical problems before they become legal issues, scandals, and rip-offs. All too often, the media and the legal profession become the watchdogs of public interest. In fact, the law and the media should be the last and only the last groups that address the issues confronting the engineering profession.

Part II

The development of professional codes of ethics is often discussed in response to issues of professional integrity. Clearly, there are ways in which these standards contribute to the professional's ethical integrity.

They bring focus and force to ethical predicaments that otherwise might go unattended. Codes of ethics provide a means of participating in the moral life of the professional community and sharing in the professional consensus concerning courtesy, responsibility, and competency. They relieve some of the extraordinary psychological burden and moral aggravation that professionals otherwise would face. And, to an important degree, these standards distinguish the professional's obligations that are role-specific from those of ordinary persons.

However, in his book *The Moral Foundation of Professional Ethics* (1980), Arthur H. Goldman chides doctors, lawyers, business leaders, and engineers who contrive their own codes of ethics—codes that can serve to excuse us from personal morality. Even more troubling is law professor Tom Shaffer's concern that ethical codes and rules can be used as a tool for avoiding morality. And in some cases, codes of ethics are designed merely to avoid outside regulation of a profession.

True ethical discourse involves freedom to question and autonomy to act on the complexities of the moral choice at hand. Codes can stifle true ethical discourse by providing ready-made solutions to complex moral choices. In their ideal sense, codes of ethics should help define the relationship and responsibility of the professional to society. But blind devotion to ethical codes will not address the ethical concerns of the engineering profession. The final burden is upon the individual's conscience and values. In the end, codes of ethics can never be an engineer's voice, except as he or she chooses to recite the rules or struggles with the ideas that shaped them.

Of course, there are engineers who do not fall victim to indifference. There are engineers who surmount it, who do not sink into static conditions and cynicism. What makes them different? What do they do that their colleagues do not?

Those who fully realize their ethical and truth-seeking potential engage in a two-fold activity.

First, they talk honestly with themselves. They compose mental essays and then edit, critique, and revise them with bright red ink. They feed the life of the mind outside of conventional discourse, not as a means of enlitisting amusement, but as a source of self-enablement. They read, they think, and they ponder ideas. Engineers who do not talk to themselves are setting themselves up for self-deception, for false self-justification. To avoid this fate, they must engage in a second activity, which I call "moral vision." They must move beyond rules, procedures, or even logical analysis, to the broadest configuration of life. They must make a "larger sense" out of their existence that goes beyond their own experience. While moral vision entails rule following and formal reasoning, it also encompasses imagination, emotion, and insight. It is that secret room that traps and releases our many and various moral thoughts and deeds. Moral vision takes into account our recollections of being treated fairly or shabbily; it considers examples set by moral mentors, and remembers details of a particular person's inner strength that touched us. It recalls past habits of moral choice and our disposition to think and behave rightly or wrongly.

Vision is also the circumstance of our culture and ethical history. It embodies more than commonly held moral principles, political frameworks, and procedural habits. Engineers must recognize and cultivate the social and cultural architecture that has formed them. They must begin to understand T. S. Elliot's dictum: "We are nothing without a knowledge of the traditions that made us." Engineers who are willing to examine those traditions in the context of what it means to be human will better understand the struggle and moral dilemmas that have plagued us from the beginning of time.

There are three avenues to follow in cultivating moral vision. First, the process must be ongoing and dynamic. Vision must sweep back and forth between historical and contemporary perspectives. It must encompass problems of the past when addressing engineers' current conflicts in their relations among themselves, between themselves and their clients, and between themselves and the public.

The technological advances of our rapidly changing society present new dilemmas on a daily basis for all of you, whether you are biomedical, environmental, industrial, civil, or software engineers. Vision will require a historical as well as a future perspective to address these issues. By shifting between the past and the present, we must seek order and constancy in the chaotic appearances of our human differences.

The second avenue toward moral vision entails movement between abstract and concrete knowledge. Vision favors abstraction, but also must accommodate specificity. A new vision necessarily implies new ways of knowing, and then integrating new forms of knowledge with the values and procedures of our society. Moral vision is an important act of ordering that tests the relevance of particular elements to the overall concept. In this sense, advances in many areas, such as genetic or environmental engineering, will need to be examined in terms of the effects new technologies will have on our social and moral fabric.

As a third avenue toward moral vision, we must constantly shift between public and private spheres. This requires integrating one's personal history with a cultural literature. We must not only ponder ideas in our own minds, we must also talk with each other, sharing ideas and perspectives. Moral vision does not operate in a vacuum. We must be aware of the values of other cultures and societies in order to be effective world citizens. Here we acquire the richness of overview that must inform basic human values. We thus acquire what the theologian Paul recognized as "the courage to be oneself and the courage to be as a part."

To what extent are educational institutions and professional schools to blame for lack of moral vision, for disillusionment, for shoddiness? Insofar as they fail to encourage students to reflect critically upon their own thoughts and upon their participation in life, our schools and other education enterprises are responsible.

Yet the burden must be shared by the individual, too. As former IBM Chairman John F. Akers noted: "If an M.B.A. candidate doesn't know the difference between honesty and crime, between lying and telling the truth, then business school, in all probability, will not produce a convert." Likewise, Mortimer Adler once said, during an interview on teaching ethics, that there are two kinds of ethical skills: the skill of the will and the skill of the intellect. If the student has no will, then all the ethical analysis in the world isn't going to go very far.

As a step toward greater ethical discourse, the education of engineering students can and should be a part of the solution. Indeed, it must be part of the solution. Our educational institutions and schools of engineering should give greater attention to the arts and humanities as a way to enable individual and collective vision across all professions. Through the arts and humanities—through a novel, a story, or a play—our existence is expanded, our vision extended. That is the value of the arts and humanities. They enrich our professions as classroom teaching cannot. They transcend professional education.

The arts are relevant for another reason. Often they depict and celebrate moral vision. They prompt us to answer humanly and honestly to life. Students, whether in colleges of engineering or other educational settings, must be given opportunities to enhance their self-understanding. The moral life and the satisfying life begin with reflection, a sense of self-identity. This is particularly important in today's educational climate, which gives significantly greater weight to mastering quantities of facts and information. We must return to the ideals of our professions, of our calling.

Engineering education and the engineering profession must increase recognition and awareness among their constituencies of the dimensions of competency and ethics that are not covered by formal standards. The engineer's sense of identity and ethical responsibility demands critical reflection upon the multiple avenues of professional conduct, rather than blind adherence to codes.

Moral vision is, as we have seen, an extension of the best within us. It is intrinsically introspective. In a practical sense, it causes us to assume responsibility for our own profession. We must assume responsibility for our professions; the burden must not be passed on to others.

Where do we start? We can support and stimulate each other within our professional communities. There should be more opportunities for reflection, more opportunities for mentoring, more opportunities for the experienced to share their moral vision with engineering newcomers. Engineering professors, and employers or supervisors of other engineers, must assume professional responsibility of exploring ethical conflicts with their employees. Increased attention must also be given to the character and ethical consequences of our own behavior, not only as it relates to clients, but also colleagues. To reduce internal competition, companies will need to begin to evaluate the manner in which employees are recognized and rewarded for a team effort.

As a further measure, management must expand its values beyond the profit motive and encourage more flexible employee/employer relationships. There is no denying that when the company loses money, everyone loses. But clearly the profit motive can be more balanced with sound business practices.

The engineering profession and schools of engineering should also consider developing opportunities in which they can collectively discuss difficult dilemmas, mutual ethical commitments, and agendas for action.

More workshops or conferences with ethical concerns might provide greater opportunities for engineers to receive instruction on important issues of professional conduct.

We also need companion materials to the growing body of literature that addresses the ethical professional concerns. We need a new literature that discusses current problems, their complexity, and their impact on the engineer's responsibility. Such literature would take into account moral vision and its proper role in our everyday life.

The call for vision is usually associated with ideals with long-range aspirations and integrity. And moral vision requires moral resolve. At times we will be called upon to make painful decisions in response to ethical dilemmas. These decisions will affect not only ourselves, but our families, our work, and our society.

Through the exercise of moral vision, we will define what we are and what we are not; what being an engineer promises, and what it does not; what it means to have the "courage to be oneself and the courage to be as a part." Once we accept this challenge, professionalism will then become clearly a joining of the best within us, and among us.

REVIEW PROBLEMS

PROBLEM 1

You are hired as an engineering consultant to investigate the effects of a plant's discharge stream on the environment. You find that the discharge is entering into a nearby lake and appears to be killing many of the small fish. You write the information in your report. You submit your report, and are paid fairly for your work, not knowing what action, if any, the company plans to take.

Several months later a news reporter approaches you and says that he is doing an investigation on the company. He further tells you that the company is still discharging its waste stream and the fish are being killed. The reporter asks you to comment on the situation. What should you say?

SOLUTION

This problem brings up two issues: the obligation to the client and public welfare. Engineers shall act in professional matters for each employer of client as faithful agents or trustees. Also engineers shall hold paramount the safety, health, and welfare of the public in performance of the professional duties, Since you acted as an employee of the company, you should not disclose any of the information in your findings to the news reporter. Thus, the best answer to the news person is either "No comment," or "I cannot discuss this matter."

However, if the company's actions are endangering the public welfare, then the obligation to society supercedes the obligation to the client. You should discuss your concerns with the appropriate regulatory or government agency, perhaps the EPA. Discussing this matter with the news media is inappropriate.

PROBLEM 2

You are submitting a paper to a journal for publication. Your boss helped you in that he read the final manscript and suggested some minor stylistic changes. Now your boss feels that he should be included as an author. Should you give your boss co-authorship?

SOLUTION

According to the ethics code: Engineers shall avoid the use of statements containing material misrepresentation of fact or omitting a fact necessary to keep statements from being misleading or intended or likely to create an unjustified expectation, or statements containing prediction of future success. Consistent with the foregoing, engineers may prepare articles for the lay or technical press but such articles shall not imply credit to the author for work performed by others.

Authorship on a publication implies that all the authors made significant contributions to the work being reported. Reviewing the manuscript does not automatically warrant authorship. If the minor changes that your boss suggested were not integral to the entire document, then your boss's contribution does not warrant authorship. To include him/her as an author would be misrepresenting your work. However, you may include your boss's name as an acknowledgement, thanking him for reviewing the work.

PROBLEM 3

The president of an engineering firm is elected to the board of trustees of a local private university. After sitting on the board for a year, the engineer discovers that his company is planning to bid on a project to be contracted by the university. What should he do?

SOLUTION

Engineers shall act in professional matters for each employers or client as faithful agents or trustees. Engineers shall disclose all known or potential conflicts of interest to their employers or clients by promptly informing them of any business association, interest, or other circumstances which could influence their judgement or quality of their services.

Since the president of the engineering company is also on the board of trustees, a potential conflict of interest arises. The president should disclose this information to the university and the board to trustees. The simplest action would be for the engineering company not to bid for the contract. However, this may not be in the best interest of the company. The president could also remove himself from the board of trustees. Another option is for the company president to inform the university of this dilemma. In most universities the actual awarding of contracts is done by other offices and this situation should not affect the process. But, the engineering company president should not try to influence the building process so that his company is awarded the contract.

PROBLEM 4

Engineer A works for a consulting firm in Town 1 and is also employed by the municipality in Town 2 on a part-time basis. This arrangement never introduced a conflict of interest. Now Engineer A is given the opportunity to advance in his company, but this change in jobs also includes taking a new position in Town 2 and possibly working for the municipality of Town 2. Should Engineer A accept the new position while continuing his current work for the municipality of Town 2?

SOLUTION

The opportunity for advancement introduces a possible conflict of interest if the municipality of Town 2 employs the engineering firm. Engineer A should disclose his situation to both his company and Town 2. An arrangement may be made to avoid future conflicts of interest, such as, if Town 2 employs the company, another engineer will provide the professional services. According to the code of ethics, Engineers in public service as members, advisors, or employees of a governmental or quasi-governmental bodies or departments shall not participate in decisions with respect to professional services elicited or provided by them or their organizations in private or public engineering practice.

PROBLEM 5

Engineer Smith, after a briefing session and an interview, submitted a proposal to the state government concerning a new project. The proposal included technical information and assessments that the state had requested. Engineer Smith was fairly paid for his work. A state agent then gave Engineer Doe the report prepared by Engineer Smith. Engineer Doe used Smith's data and assessments for a proposal for another project without referencing Smith's report. Should Engineer Doe have cited Engineer Smith's contribution of the date and assessments in Doe's report?

SOLUTION

According to the ethics code, engineers shall give credit for engineering work to those whom the credit is due, and will recognize the propriety interests of others. Since the state projects were apparently different, there was no competition between the engineers Smith and Doe. However, since the data from Smith's report was used by Doe, Doe had an obligation to cite the sources. It is unethical to present Smith's work as Doe's own. All contributions to Doe's report which were not his own work should have been properly cited, and in some cases the proper permission may have been needed.

PROBLEM 6

Engineer A is contracted by a development company to assess the feasibility of two plots of land for building a shopping mall. Site 1 is not ideal due to drainage problems. Site 2 is a better choice for the mall. However, Engineer A's mother lives near Site 2, and she and her neighbors are against the building of the mall since they feel that it will hurt their property value. Engineer A recommends Site 1 as the better site, omitting the drainage concerns, in his report to the development company. Was Engineer A's recommendation correct?

SOLUTION

This is a case of misrepresentation. Engineers shall avoid the use of statements containing a material misrepresentation of fact or omitting a material fact necessary to keep statements from being misleading, or intended or likely to create an unjustified expectation, or statements containing prediction of future success.

Engineer A did not disclose the potential drainage problems with Site 1. If his mother and her neighbors were against building the mall, they should take their concerns to the local government or zoning board. Since the building of the mall does not appear to endanger the welfare of the public, Engineer A has no obligation to the public in this case. The engineer should make a fair assessment of both sites, unbiased by outside or personal influences.

PROBLEM 7

A manufacturer of construction materials has invited several engineers, including Engineer Miller, to a one-day symposium which includes free lunch and dinner. The symposium is aimed at educating the engineers about new building materials and applications for these materials. Engineer Miller attends the symposium. During the course of the day, Engineer Miller realizes that one of the new materials would be ideal to use in one of her current projects.

The next week Engineer Miller describes this new product to her engineering team, and all agree that the new material will be the best material for the project. They recommend this new product instead of an older one. Was it ethical for Engineer Miller to use this new product, considering that she obtained information about it at a company-sponsored symposium, or should she have continued to recommend the older product?

SOLUTION

The ethics code states: Engineers shall not accept commissions or allowances directly or indirectly from contractors or other parties dealing with clients or employers of the engineer in connection with work for which the engineer is responsible. In this case, Engineer Miller was given lunch and dinner at the symposium. However, the main goal of the symposium was education. It was serendipitous that one of the new products was a better alternative for a certain project. The meals were not considered gifts, but rather they were appropriate for the symposium. In addition, the engineering team at her company decided to use the new product. The decision to use the new product was based on the merit of the product, not on incentive from the manufacturer. In was ethical for Engineer Miller to use the new product.

PROBLEM 8

Engineer A was hired to confirm the structural integrity of a building. Her report states that the building is structurally sound. Her boss, Engineer

B, hears from an outside source that the building was originally constructed with an inferior grade of steel, which could possibly compromise the structural integrity of the building. Engineer A did not state this information in her report, and, when asked, she was unaware of this problem and could find no supporting evidence to this claim. Engineer B, in his report to the client, stated that the building was not structurally sound, citing the steel problem and indicating it was found by Engineer A. Did Engineer B act in an ethical manner?

SOLUTION

Again, this is a problem of misrepresentation. Engineers shall avoid the use of statements containing a material misrepresentation of fact or omitting a material fact necessary to keep statements from being misleading or intended or likely to create an unjustified expectation, or statements containing prediction of future success. Engineer B credited Engineer A with the information about the steel. Secondly, Engineer B did not confirm the statements about the steel. When Engineer A was asked, she could not provide the supporting evidence for the claim. If Engineer B was concerned, another evaluation of the building could have been performed. By stating that the findings were made by Engineer A, Engineer B demonstrated a misrepresentation of the facts.

PROBLEM 9

Smith, an electrical engineer, is considering changing jobs. The new job is in a chemical engineering firm and will involve managing a group of other chemical engineers. The new job will involve very little, if any, technical work. Smith has no experience in the chemical engineering field and has spent the last 15 years designing computer circuits. Should Smith take the new job?

SOLUTION

If the new job does not require Smith to handle the technical aspects of the chemical engineering work and only work on the managerial level, then Smith may accept the new position. While an engineer should only practice within his/her own discipline, this constraint in only valid with respect to technical matters, not managerial or business matters.

PROBLEM 10

John has been asked by his boss to evaluate the strengths of two different materials. The boss says that material A should be stronger than material B. After the tests are performed, the results show that B is the stronger of the two materials. However, his boss has already published that A is stronger without providing the data. Since John's data are contrary, the boss asks to see the lab notebooks and does not return them. One year later, John sees that the data have been published in a journal, but the data have been reversed to show that material A is stronger. What action, if any, should John take?

SOLUTION

This is a case of misrepresentation. John should bring the error to the attention of his boss and possibly other superiors. If the boss recognizes that the data have been reversed, then the boss should correct the error in the journal by submitting an erratum. If the boss does not recognize the error, or refuses to take action to correct it, then John should write a letter to the editor of the journal explaining the error.

PROBLEM 11

Mark is evaluating emissions from a stack of a plant. The laboratory tests show a high level of a non-toxic compound A. Mark knows that compound A is easily converted in the air to compounds B and C, and that compound C is highly toxic to humans. Mark notifies his superiors of the possible problems with compound C. He is told that since only compound A is being released from the stack, the company is not responsible for compound C. Mark then is assigned to another project. Should Mark take any further action with regards to the stack emissions?

SOLUTION

Engineers should hold paramount the safety, health, and welfare of the public in the performance of their professional duties. While Mark's superiors may be correct in saying that since only compound A is being emitted, and thus the company is within regulations. The potential risk to the public welfare obligates Mark to notify the proper authorities. Since compound C is highly toxic and thus a potential dange to the public, he cannot ignore this problem.

PROBLEM 12

Several engineers employed by a consulting firm are unhappy with their current wages. After several meetings, the engineers feel that the only way to get paid at the level they feel they deserve is to strike starting

Monday if their demands are not met. The next Monday, after several more meetings, the engineers start picketing outside the firm. The management terminates their positions and starts the hiring process to find replacements. Was is correct for the engineers to have picketed?

SOLUTION

According to the code of ethics, engineers should not participate in strikes, picket lines, or other collective coercive actions. Thus, issues such as salary should be negotiated by other means. The engineers were wrong to have picketed.

FE/EIT

Fundamentals of Engineering: AM Exam

Practice Test 1

FUNDAMENTALS OF ENGINEERING - MORNING SESSION
Test 1

(Answer sheets appear in the back of this book.)

TIME: 4 Hours
120 Questions

DIRECTIONS: For each of the following questions and incomplete statements, choose the best answer from the four answer choices.

---

1. Given the following set of simultaneous linear equations

$$4x + 6y = 10$$
$$2x + 3y = 7$$

the solution is

(A) $x = 2, y = 1.$

(B) indefinite.

(C) nonexistent.

(D) $x = -2, y = 1.$

2. The velocity of two bodies is given by

Body A: $V_A = 2t^2 - 12, t > 0$

Body B: $V_B = -t, t > 0$

The velocity of Body A is twice that of Body B for time $t > 0$ at $t =$

(A) $-3.$

(B) $2.$

(C) $\dfrac{\left(-1 + \sqrt{97}\right)}{2}.$

(D) $-1 + \sqrt{97}.$

3. The solution to the differential equation

$$\frac{dy}{dt} + 2y = 1, \ y(0) = 1, \text{ is}$$

(A) $\frac{1}{2} + \frac{1}{2} e^{2t}$.

(C) $\frac{1}{2} + e^{-2t}$.

(B) $\frac{1}{2} + \frac{1}{2} e^{-2t}$.

(D) $\frac{1}{2} + e^{2t}$.

4. The sample standard deviation of the following data 2, 8, 3, 10 is close to

(A) 3.345.

(C) 44.75.

(B) 3.862.

(D) 0.

5. The inner surface area in square meters of a closed (both ends) cylinder 2 meters in height and 3 meters in diameter is

(A) $10\frac{1}{2} \pi$.

(C) 6π.

(B) $3\frac{3}{4} \pi$.

(D) 30π.

6. Given the following three ordinary differential equations, where x is the dependent variable and t is the independent variable,

I. $\quad 2\frac{d^2x}{dt^2} + 2x\frac{dx}{dt} = 0$

II. $\quad 2\frac{d^2x}{dt^2} + 2x\frac{dx}{dt} + t^2 = e^{-t}$

III. $\quad 2\frac{d^2x}{dt^2} + 2t\frac{dx}{dt} = 0$

(A) I and II are linear.

(C) Only III is linear.

(B) I and III are linear.

(D) II and III are linear.

7. Given the function

$$f(x) = x^3 - 3x - 5,$$

the minimum value of the function in the domain $-5 < x < 5$ is

(A) –1.

(C) – 3.

(B) –7.

(D) 0.

8. In an unbiased coin toss, the probability of getting heads or tails is exactly $1/2$. A coin is tossed and one gets heads. If the coin is tossed again, the probability of getting heads is

(A) $\dfrac{1}{3}$.

(C) 0.

(B) 1.

(D) $\dfrac{1}{2}$.

9. Given two square matrices $[A]$ and $[B]$ of the same order, if $[C] = [A] + [B]$, then

(A) det $[C] =$ det $[A] +$ det $[B]$.

(B) det $[C] =$ det $[A] -$ det $[B]$.

(C) det $[C] = 0$.

(D) none of the above

10. The shortest distance between two points $(0, 3)$ and $(5, - 6)$ on an x-y graph is

(A) 34.

(C) $\sqrt{106}$.

(B) 106.

(D) 14.

11. The series $\displaystyle\sum_{k=1}^{\infty} \frac{\left[(-1)^n\right]}{k}$

(A) diverges if $n = 2$.

(C) converges if $n = k$.

(B) converges if $n = 1$.

(D) both (A) and (C)

12. The inflection point of the function

$$f(x) = 3x^{\frac{5}{3}} \text{ is}$$

(A) 0.

(C) ∞.

(B) nonexistent.

(D) –1.

13. If $f(x)$ is a real function, then the equation $f(x) = 0$ has at least one real root in the interval $[a, b]$ if

(A) $f(a) f(b) < 0$.

(B) $f(a) f(b) < 0$ and $f(x)$ is continuous.

(C) $f(a) f(b) > 0$ and $f(x)$ is piecewise continuous.

(D) $f(a) f(b) > 0$ and $f(x)$ is continuous.

14. $\lim\limits_{x \to 0} \dfrac{\sin(5x) - 2x}{x}$

(A) not defined.

(C) 3.

(B) ∞.

(D) 0.

15. The acute angle between the two straight lines

$$y = 3x + 2$$
$$y = 4x + 7$$

is close to

(A) 90°.

(C) 28.30°.

(B) 4.399°.

(D) 5.194°.

16. A bag contains four red balls, three green balls, and five blue balls. The probability of not getting a red ball in the first draw is

(A) $\dfrac{1}{3}$.

(C) 0.

(B) $\dfrac{2}{3}$.

(D) 2.

17. The integral

$$\iint_R xy\,dA,$$

where the region R is $0 \le x \le 1$, $1 \le y \le 2$, is given by

(A) $\dfrac{3}{4}$.

(C) 0.

(B) $\dfrac{1}{4}$.

(D) $-\dfrac{3}{4}$.

18. The equation of a circle on the x-y plane is given by

$$x^2 - 2x + y^2 + 2y = 0.$$

The center and the radius of the circle are respectively

(A) $(1, -1), \sqrt{2}$.

(C) $(1, -1), 2$.

(B) $(-1, 1), 2$.

(D) $(0, 0), \sqrt{2}$.

19. The intercept of a straight line on the y-axis is -3. If $(5, 2)$ is a point on the straight line, the slope of the straight line is

(A) -3.

(C) 0.

(B) 1.

(D) 0.2.

20. The velocity of a body is given by $v(t) = \sin(\pi t)$, where the velocity is given in meters/seconds and t is given in seconds. The distance covered in meters between $t = {}^1\!/_4$ and ${}^1\!/_2$ seconds is close to

(A) -0.2251.

(C) 8.971×10^{-5}.

(B) 0.2251.

(D) 1.

21. Which of the following is true for the electric resistance of a cable?

(A) It is proportional to the diameter of the cable.

(B) It is proportional to the square root of the diameter of the cable.

(C) It is inversely proportional to the diameter of the cable.

(D) It is inversely proportional to the square of the diameter of the cable.

22. In the circuit shown here, the voltage across the 3 Ω resistance is given by

    (A) 6.4 V.

    (B) 13.7 V.

    (C) 10.8 V.

    (D) 5.9 V.

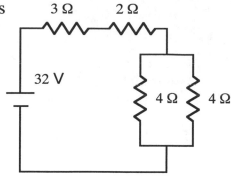

23. For the circuit shown here, the resistance between terminals *ab* is equal to

    (A) 8 Ω.

    (B) 4 Ω.

    (C) 2 Ω.

    (D) 10 Ω.

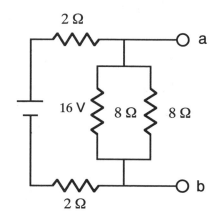

24. For the circuit shown, the Thevenin equivalent voltage between terminals *ab* is

    (A) 12 V.

    (B) 16 V.

    (C) 4 V.

    (D) 2 V.

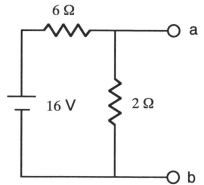

25. For the circuit shown, the current through the 2 Ω resistor is

    (A) 3.2 A.

    (B) 4.0 A.

    (C) 8.0 A.

    (D) 2.0 A.

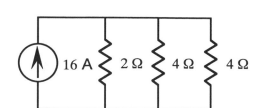

26. In the circuit shown, the 0.1 Ω resistor is connected by an ideal transformer with a turn ratio of 1:10 to a 100 V AC voltage source. The current I is given by

    (A) 9.1 A.

    (B) 50 A.

    (C) 99.01 A.

    (D) 9.33 A.

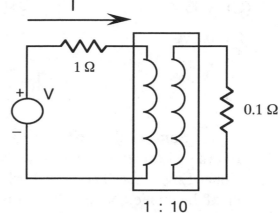

27. The magnetic field at a distance r from a long straight wire carrying a current i and close to the middle of the wire is proportional to

    (A) $\dfrac{i^2}{r}$.

    (C) $\dfrac{r}{i}$.

    (B) $\dfrac{i}{r^2}$.

    (D) $\dfrac{i}{r}$.

28. In the circuit shown, a constant voltage and a constant current source are connected in series. The current through the 3 Ω resistors is given by

    (A) 5 A.

    (B) 10 A.

    (C) 1.25 A.

    (D) 2.5 A.

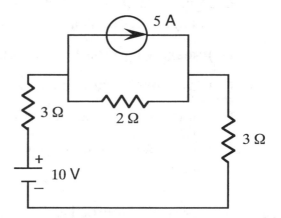

29. In the circuit shown, an independent voltage source of 24 V is connected in series with a dependent voltage source of value 0.5 V_R, where V_R is the voltage across the 3 Ω resistor. The current i is given by

(A) 1.6 A.

(B) 1.78 A.

(C) 1.45 A.

(D) 0.8 A.

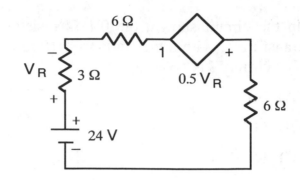

Some of the questions that follow were based on the Board of Ethical Review of the National Society of Professional Engineers. The Board asks that the following statement be made. Note: These opinions are based on data submitted to the Board of Ethical Review and do not necessarily represent all of the pertinent facts when applied to a specific case. This opinion is for educational purposes only and should not be construed as expressing any opinion on the ethics of specific individuals. This opinion may be reprinted without further permission, provided that this statement is included before or after the text of the case.

30. As an engineering consultant, you are hired by a company to investigate possible environmental effects resulting from their plant discharge. Your investigation reveals that severe environmental damage is being done. You should

(A) make your report to your client and consider the matter closed.

(B) ask your client to make a full disclosure of your findings.

(C) inform the proper authorities of the dangers you discovered.

(D) make no mention of your findings, since your first obligation is to your client.

31. The 24 V DC source has been connected to the circuit shown for a long time. The voltage across the terminals of the capacitor is

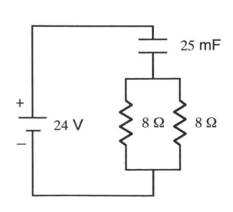

(A) 24 V.

(B) 0 V.

(C) 12 V.

(D) 9.09 V.

32. In the circuit shown here, the capacitor has been connected to the 36 V source for many hours. The voltage across the capacitor is

    (A) 27 V.

    (B) 9 V.

    (C) 18 V.

    (D) 3 V.

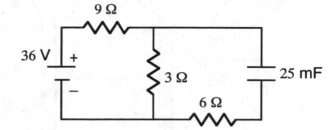

33. For the circuit shown here, the expression for the current in the 50 mF capacitor for time t greater than zero is given by

    (A) $8e^{-0.1t}$

    (B) $8 - 8e^{-10t}$

    (C) $8 - 8e^{-0.1t}$

    (D) $8e^{-10t}$

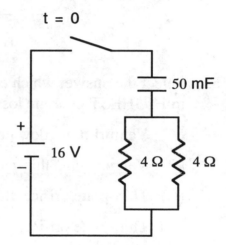

34. The AND circuit shown below will result in what binary output?

    (A) 00000

    (B) 11111

    (C) 10001

    (D) 01110

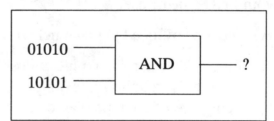

35. In the following diagram, which point has the highest pressure?

    (A) *A*   (C) *C*

    (B) *B*   (D) *D*

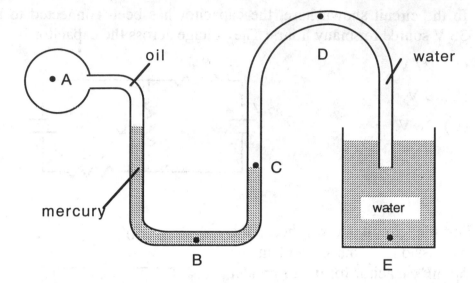

36. Select the answer which correctly ranks fluid meters from LOWEST to HIGHEST pressure loss (i.e., low loss, medium loss, high loss).

    (A) Venturi tube, flow nozzle, thin-plate orifice

    (B) Venturi tube, thin-plate orifice, flow nozzle

    (C) Thin-plate orifice, flow nozzle, Venturi tube

    (D) Thin-plate orifice, Venturi tube, flow nozzle

37. Identify one of the following problems for which the Moody chart would NOT be of use.

    (A) Flow of oil in a long channel with square cross section

    (B) Flow of water in a pipe whose inner wall is corroded and extremely rough (for example, the average roughness height being 4% of the pipe diameter)

    (C) Flow in a subsonic diffuser

    (D) Flow of water in a pipe at very high speeds, where the flow is extremely turbulent

Problems 38 and 39 deal with the following two sketches. The geometry and upstream conditions are identical. Neglect friction, and assume adiabatic, one-dimensional flow.

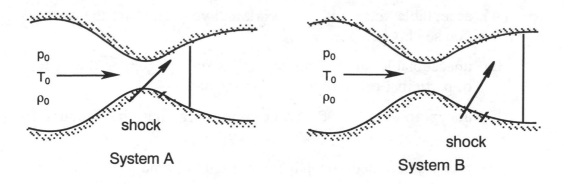

38. Choose the correct statement.

    (A) The shock in system A is STRONGER than the one in system B.

    (B) The mass flow rate in system A is LOWER than that in system B.

    (C) The pressure just UPSTREAM of the shock in system A is HIGHER than the pressure just UPSTREAM of the shock in system B.

    (D) The Mach number just DOWNSTREAM of the shock in system A is HIGHER than the Mach number just DOWNSTREAM of the shock in system B.

39. Choose the correct statement.

    (A) The pressure at the exit plane in system A is HIGHER than the pressure at the exit plane in system B.

    (B) The stagnation temperature at the exit plane in system A is LOWER than that at the exit plane in system B.

    (C) The flow downstream of the shock in system A is SUBSONIC, but for system B, if the shock is close to the exit plane, the flow downstream of the shock (but still INSIDE the duct) may be SUPERSONIC.

    (D) If P_0 were increased in either system, keeping everything else the same, the shock would remain in the same location since the flow is choked.

40. You are submitting a paper for a publication for which your best friend has made only minimal contributions. You decide to include him as a co-author. According to the NCEES Rules of Professional Conduct, this action is

(A) acceptable since it is your work and you can share the credit if you so choose.

(B) unacceptable since it misrepresents or exaggerates the degree of participation of your friend in the paper.

(C) acceptable and a fairly common practice that occurs in academia.

(D) acceptable since you put your friend's name second and not first.

41. For steady, incompressible, inviscid flow, with no shaft work or heat transfer, Bernoulli's equation can be written

$$\frac{p}{\rho} + \frac{V^2}{2} + gz = \text{constant}.$$

This form of the equation is valid

(A) for rotational flow, but ONLY along streamlines.

(B) for irrotational flow, but ONLY along streamlines.

(C) for rotational flow EVERYWHERE.

(D) ONLY for irrotational flow (i.e., it is NEVER valid if the flow is rotational).

Questions 42 – 44 refer to the following: In the figure below, 6 m³/hour of water is pumped from the lake to a reservoir whose surface is 17 m above the lake surface. The total frictional head losses are estimated to be 2.5 m of water.

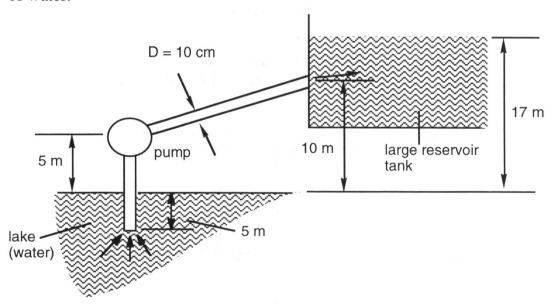

42. The difference in atmospheric pressure between the reservoir surface and the surface of the lake is typically neglected. For air at a constant density of 1.2 kg/m³, this difference in pressure is closest to

(A) 200 Pascals.

(C) 657 Pascals.

(B) 350 Pascals.

(D) 3,400 Pascals.

43. The power delivered by the pump to the water is closest to

(A) 128 Watts.

(C) 1,048 Watts.

(B) 319 Watts.

(D) 2,096 Watts.

44. If the pump is only 65% efficient, how much electrical power is required to pump 6 m³/hr of water?

(A) 83.2 Watts

(C) 491 Watts

(B) 207 Watts

(D) 681 Watts

45. The simplified continuity equation $\nabla \cdot \mathbf{V} = 0$ is NOT valid for

(A) steady incompressible flow.

(B) steady compressible flow.

(C) unsteady incompressible flow.

(D) steady rotational incompressible flow.

46. In the following diagram, high pressure air is released from the large tank into ambient air at atmospheric pressure, p_a. If the flow is SUPERSONIC at the exit plane of the duct, which one of the following statements is correct? (Isentropic flow may be assumed except across a shock wave.)

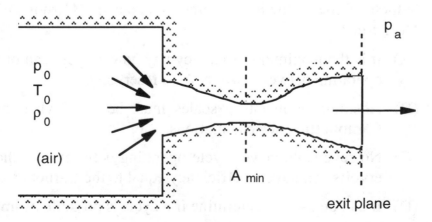

(A) The pressure at the exit plane will be HIGHER than the pressure at the throat (i.e., at A_{min}).

(B) A normal shock wave is likely to exist somewhere inside the DIVERGING section of the duct.

(C) A normal shock wave is likely to exist somewhere inside the CONVERGING section of the duct.

(D) The density at the exit plane will be LOWER than the density at the throat (i.e., at A_{min}).

47. The binary representation of a number is 101000. What is the value of this number in octal (base 8)?

(A) 28   (C) 50

(B) 40   (D) 65

48. What is the function of a macro in a spreadsheet?

(A) Does repetitive operations

(B) Required for large spreadsheets

(C) Must precede any table larger than 10×10

(D) Is not used in a spreadsheet

49. An adiabatic process is characterized by which of the following?

(A) The entropy change is zero.

(B) The heat transfer is zero.

(C) It is isothermal.

(D) It is reversible.

50. Which of the following statements about the Carnot efficiency is NOT true?

(A) It is the maximum efficiency any power cycle can obtain while operating between two thermal reservoirs.

(B) Absolute temperature scales must be used when performing Carnot efficiency calculations.

(C) No reversible power cycle operating between two thermal reservoirs can have an efficiency equal to the Carnot efficiency.

(D) It can be used to determine if a cycle is possible or impossible.

51. A rigid container is heated by the sun. There is no shaft work associated with the container. From the First Law of Thermodynamics, you determine the resulting work to be

    (A) equal to the heat transfer.

    (B) equal to the change in internal energy.

    (C) equal to the volume times the change in pressure.

    (D) equal to zero.

52. An inventor claims to have built an engine which will revolutionize the automotive industry. Which of the following would be the best test to determine if the inventor's claims are true?

    (A) Conservation of Mass

    (B) Zeroth Law of Thermodynamics

    (C) First Law of Thermodynamics

    (D) Second Law of Thermodynamics

53. An engineering professor, who is also a registered professional engineer, accepts a job from a company to investigate the potential for a piece of property. After accepting the job, the professor learns that the property is owned by his school. The professor should

    (A) notify both parties of the potential conflict of interest and ask permission to continue.

    (B) continue with the project to see if a conflict of interest arises.

    (C) ask the local NCEES board for a ruling.

    (D) say nothing and try to act as impartially as possible in the matter.

54. Two independent intensive properties are required to fix the state of a pure, simple compressible substance. People often attempt to fix the state of a medium using heat and/or work, which are not properties. Which of the following statements about heat and work is not true?

    (A) Heat and work are transient phenomena.

    (B) Heat and work are forms of energy.

    (C) Heat and work are associated with processes.

    (D) Heat and work are point functions.

55. An ideal vapor compression refrigeration cycle requires 2.5 kW to power the compressor. You have found the following data for the cycle:

 – the enthalpy at the condenser entrance is 203 kJ/kg

 – the enthalpy at the condenser exit is 55 kJ/kg

 – the enthalpy at the evaporator entrance is 55 kJ/kg

 – the enthalpy at the evaporator exit is 178 kJ/kg

If the mass flow rate of the refrigerant is 0.10 kg/s, then the coefficient of performance of this refrigerator is most nearly

(A) 49.2.   (C) 5.92.

(B) 59.2.   (D) 4.92.

56. The isentropic (process) efficiency is used to compare actual devices such as turbines, compressors, nozzles, and diffusers to ideal ones. Which statement is true?

(A) Only the ideal device is considered adiabatic.

(B) The inlet state and exit pressure are the same for both the ideal and actual device.

(C) The efficiency can be greater than one.

(D) Neither device is adiabatic.

57. Referring to the diagrams below for the ideal compression ignition cycle, which of the statements is false?

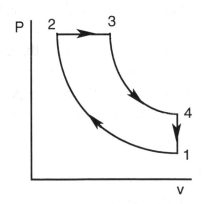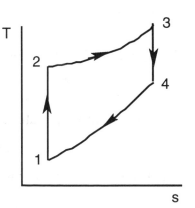

(A) $W_{cycle} = W_{23} + W_{34} - W_{12}$

(B) $Q_{cycle} = Q_{23} - Q_{41}$

(C) $n_{th} = \dfrac{W_{cycle}}{Q_{cycle}}$

(D) $W_{cycle} = Q_{23} - Q_{41}$

58. Which of the following can be the contents of a cell in a spread-sheet?

(A) A numerial value

(C) A formula

(B) A label

(D) All of the above.

59. A steam power cycle is modeled by the ideal cycle known as the

(A) Otto cycle.

(C) Rankine cycle.

(B) Diesel cycle.

(D) Brayton cycle.

60. In an ideal refrigeration cycle, liquid leaves the condenser and is expanded in such a manner that the enthalpy of the liquid is equal to the enthalpy of the resulting saturated mixture. This type of expansion is known as

(A) a throttling process.

(C) a compression process.

(B) an isothermal process.

(D) an isochoric process.

61. Engineer A works for a consulting firm that employs other design professionals. Engineer A is also retained on a part-time basis by a municipality to furnish limited advice. His agreement with the municipality states that when Engineer A's firm is employed as a client to provide professional services, other professionals in his firm, and not Engineer A, will be used. Would it be ethical for Engineer A to provide engineering services under the conditions herein described?

(A) Only if approved by the local NCEES board

(B) It would not be unethical for Engineer A to provide engineering services under the circumstances herein described.

(C) No, since this is clearly a case of conflict of interest.

(D) No, since working for the opposing team is never allowed under the code.

62. Engineer A is employed by a company and his assigned duties relate to the work of subcontractors, including review of the adequacy and acceptability of the plans for material provided by subcontractors. In the course of this work, Engineer A advised his superiors of problems he found with certain submissions of one of the subcontractors and urged management to reject such work. Management rejected the comments of Engineer A, owing to excessive cost and time delays that would occur. Does Engineer A have an ethical obligation to continue his efforts to secure change in the policy of his employer?

(A) Yes, Engineer A does have an ethical obligation to continue his effort since engineers shall at all times recognize that their primary obligation is to protect the safety, health, property, and welfare of the public.

(B) No, Engineer A does not have an ethical obligation to continue his effort since there is no clear-cut danger to the welfare of the public.

(C) No, Engineer A does not have an ethical obligation to continue his effort since it is contrary to the wishes of his employer.

(D) Yes, Engineer A has an ethical obligation to continue his efforts since, in his opinion, a wrong has occurred.

63. Given the following acceleration-time curve for a particle, find the distance between points A and B.

Note that for t = 0, $\frac{ds}{dt} = 0$.

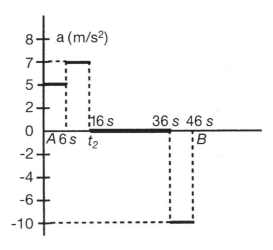

(A) 3,240 m

(B) 4,100 m

(C) 2,250 m

(D) 3,100 m

64. A 40 kg missile moves with a velocity of 150 m/s. It is intercepted by a laser beam which causes it to explode into two fragments, A and B, which weigh 25 kg and 15 kg respectively. If the fragments travel as shown immediately after explosion, find the magnitude of velocity of fragment A.

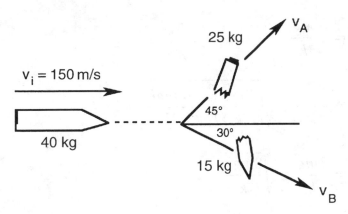

(A) 101.25 m/s   (C) 36.01 m/s

(B) 73.21 m/s   (D) 43.92 m/s

65. A 20 kg box is released from rest at point *A*. It travels down a slope of 35°. If the coefficient of friction, μ, is 0.3, what will be the velocity of the box at point *B*?

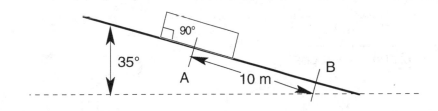

(A) 8.02 m/s   (C) 7.32 m/s

(B) 10.60 m/s   (D) 9.11 m/s

66. A block of mass *m*, initially at rest, is dropped from a height *h* onto a spring whose force constant is *k*. Find the maximum distance *y* that the spring will be compressed.

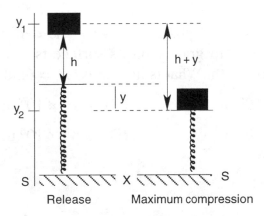

Release   Maximum compression

The total fall of the block is h + y.

(A) $y = \pm \dfrac{mg}{k}$

(B) $y = \dfrac{2mg}{k} \pm \sqrt{\left(\dfrac{2mg}{k}\right)^2 + \dfrac{8mgh}{k}}$

(C) $y = \dfrac{2mg}{k} \pm \sqrt{\dfrac{8mgh}{k}}$

(D) $y = \dfrac{1}{2}\left[\dfrac{2mg}{k} + \sqrt{\left(\dfrac{2mg}{k}\right)^2 + \left(\dfrac{8mgh}{k}\right)}\right]$

67. A body of mass m has an initial velocity v_0 directed up a plane that is at an inclination angle θ to the horizontal. The coefficient of sliding friction between the mass and the plane is μ. What distance d will the body slide up the plane before coming to rest?

(A) $\dfrac{V_0^2}{2g(\sin\theta - \mu\cos\theta)}$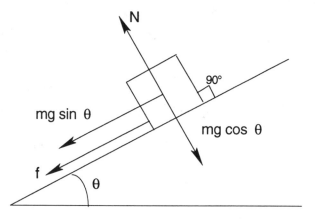

(B) $\dfrac{V_0^2}{2g(\mu\cos\theta + \sin\theta)}$

(C) $\dfrac{V_0^2}{2g(\mu\sin\theta + \cos\theta)}$

(D) $\dfrac{V_0^2}{2g\sin\theta}$

68. A newly discovered planet has twice the density of earth, but the acceleration due to gravity on its surface is exactly the same as on the surface of earth. What is its radius? $R_e = 6.38 \times 10^6$ m.

(A) 6.38×10^6 m   (C) 3.19×10^6 m

(B) 1.60×10^6 m   (D) 3.84×10^6 m

69. A car, with its door open and free to swing on its hinges, is accelerating with a constant acceleration a. Determine the angular acceleration of the door, relative to the car, as a function of the acceleration of the automobile.

(A) $\dfrac{ma\, l\cos\theta}{I_A}$

(B) $\dfrac{ma\, l\sin\theta}{I_A}$

(C) $\dfrac{ma\, l\cos\theta}{2I_A}$

(D) $\dfrac{2ma\, l\sin\theta}{I_A}$

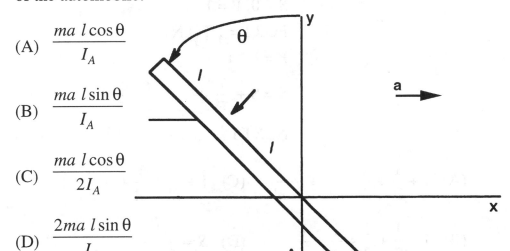

70. Two cars, A and B, are traveling along the same route. Car A is traveling at 4.5 m/s and has a mass of 1,150 kg. Car B is traveling at 6.7 m/s and has a mass of 1,300 kg. If car B gently bumps into car A and their bumpers lock together, what will be their common velocity?

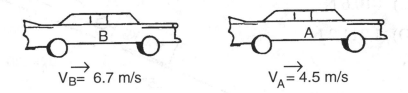

$V_B = 6.7$ m/s $V_A = 4.5$ m/s

(A) 5.53 m/s   (C) 5.67 m/s

(B) 11.33 m/s   (D) 5.60 m/s

71. A wheel of radius .5 m rolls to the right (without slipping) with its center C having a velocity of 2.5 m/s. Find the velocity of point B.

(A) 2.5$\mathbf{i}$ m/s

(B) (3.56$\mathbf{i}$ – 1.06$\mathbf{j}$) m/s

(C) (– 1.06$\mathbf{i}$ – 3.56$\mathbf{j}$) m/s

(D) (– 2.5$\mathbf{i}$ + 1.5$\mathbf{i}$) m/s

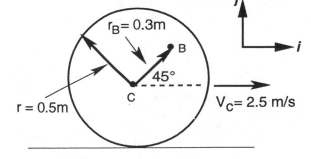

$r_B = 0.3$m

$r = 0.5$m

$V_C = 2.5$ m/s

72. For the following programming segment, the value of S will be equal to:

INPUT N
S = 0; P = 1
FOR I = 1 TO N
P = P * I
$$S = S + \frac{1}{P}$$
NEXT I

(A) $1 + \dfrac{1}{1!} + \dfrac{1}{2!} + \dfrac{1}{3!} + \cdots \dfrac{1}{n!}$

(C) $1 + \dfrac{1}{2!} + \dfrac{1}{3!} + \cdots \dfrac{1}{n!}$

(B) $1 + \dfrac{1}{2} + \dfrac{1}{3} + \dfrac{1}{4} \cdots \dfrac{1}{n}$

(D) $S = \dfrac{1}{1-n}$

73. Determine the tension, T, in the cable which will give the 150 kg block a steady acceleration of 4 m/s² up the slope.

(A) 547.3 N

(B) 844.4 N

(C) 810.6 N

(D) 1,211.2 N

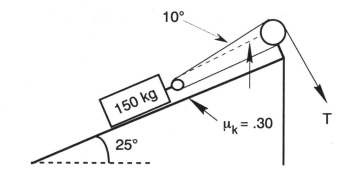

74. In an ideal transformer, the voltage ratio is proportional to the

(A) loss ratio.

(C) current ratio.

(B) turns ratio.

(D) impedance ratio.

75. The Laplace transform of the depicted pulse is:

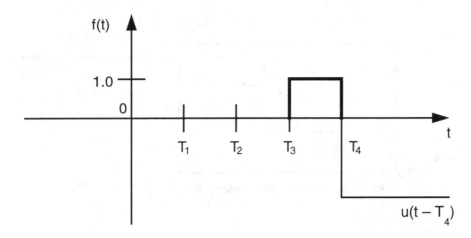

(A) $\dfrac{\varepsilon^{-sT_3}}{S} - \dfrac{\varepsilon^{-sT_4}}{S}$

(B) $\dfrac{\varepsilon^{-sT_1}}{S}$

(C) $\varepsilon^{-sT_4} + \varepsilon^{-sT_3}$

(D) $\varepsilon^{-sT_1} + \varepsilon^{-sT_2} - \varepsilon^{-sT_3} - \varepsilon^{-sT_4}$

76. Determine the rope tension force for the pulley system.

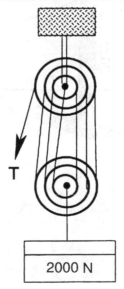

2000 N

(A) 1000 N   (C) 333 N

(B) 167 N   (D) 500 N

77. Determine the reaction at point *B*.

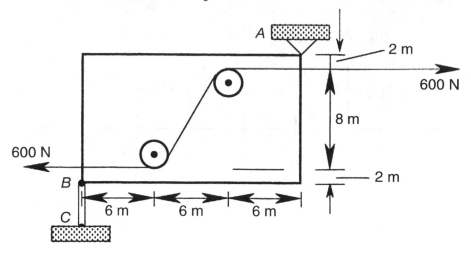

(A) 267 N   (C) 300 N

(B) 600 N   (D) 534 N

78. Determine the moment about line *AB* in units of in-lbs. Hint: Use vector mathematics with the triple scalar product.

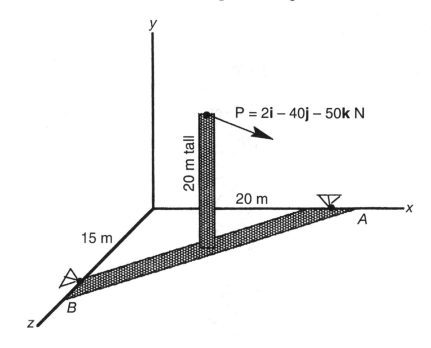

(A) 667 Nm   (C) 776 Nm

(B) 336 Nm   (D) 846 Nm

79. Write the 3,000 N force T_{BD} in vector form with the vector pointing from B to D.

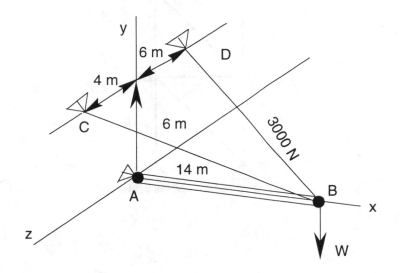

(A) $-1,100\mathbf{i} + 850\mathbf{j} + 606\mathbf{k}$

(B) $+1,100\mathbf{i} - 850\mathbf{j} - 606\mathbf{k}$

(C) $-2,566\mathbf{i} + 1,100\mathbf{j} + 1,100\mathbf{k}$

(D) $-2,566\mathbf{i} + 1,100\mathbf{j} - 1,100\mathbf{k}$

80. Determine the reaction at point A.

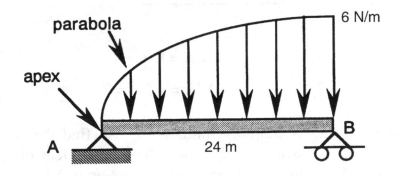

(A) 48 N   (C) 38 N

(B) 96 N   (D) 58 N

81. Determine the force in truss member *CD*.

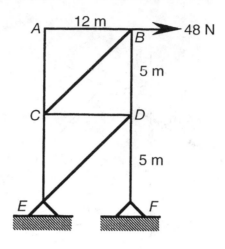

(A) 24 N (C) 60 N

(B) 36 N (D) 48 N

82. Find the centroid of the four 2 × 2 areas for both the *x* and *y*–direction.

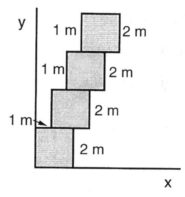

(A) $x = 4, y = 2.5$ (C) $x = 8, y = 4$

(B) $x = 2, y = 2.5$ (D) $x = 2.5, y = 4$

83. Assuming the 250 N weight is initially at rest, find the force required to start it moving up the plane. The coefficient of kinetic friction is 0.30, and the coefficient of static friction is 0.40.

(A) 75 N

(B) 50 N

(C) 212 N

(D) 190 N

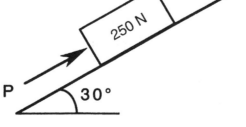

84. Find the vertical reaction at point *F*.

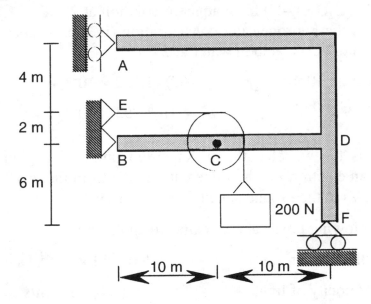

(A) 100 N   (C) 120 N

(B) 200 N   (D) 400 N

85. Assume that the friction is large enough that the cylinder will not slide. Find the tensile force in the rope.

(A) 200

(B) 36

(C) 63

(D) 84

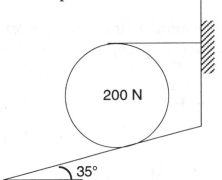

86. Avogadro's Number (6.023×10^{23}) represents

(A) the number of molecules in 1 gram of any compound.

(B) the number of molecules in 1 liter of any gas at 1 atm pressure and 0° C.

(C) the number of molecules in 1 gram mole of any compound.

(D) the number of valence electrons in a mole of any element.

87. The ionization equilibrium constant for the acidic hydrogen of acetic acid ($C_2H_3O_2$–H) in an aqueous solution at 25° C is 1.753×10^{-5}. What is the hydrogen ion concentration (in moles/liter) in a 0.1 M solution of acetic acid in water at 25° C?

(A) 1.32×10^{-3}

(C) 1.753×10^{-5}

(B) 4.19×10^{-3}

(D) 1.753×10^{-6}

88. What is the wavelength, in Angstrom units, of a photon emitted when an electron in a hydrogen atom falls from the $n = 2$ state ($E_2 = -3.4$ eV) to the ground state ($E_1 = -13.6$ eV)?

The following physical constants are applicable:

| Plank's constant | $h = 6.63 \times 10^{-34}$ J s |
| Velocity of light | $c = 3.0 \times 10^8$ m/s |

$$1 \text{ eV} = 1.602 \times 10^{-19} \text{ J}$$

$$1 \text{ Å} = 1 \times 10^{-10} \text{ m}$$

(A) 3,651 Å

(C) 4,868 Å

(B) 1,217 Å

(D) 730 Å

89. The chemical formula of the most common compound formed from beryllium (a Group IIa element) and iodine (a Group VIIa element) is

(A) Be_2I_7.

(C) BeI_2.

(B) BeI.

(D) Be_7I_2.

90. The chemical formula of the salt formed from the neutralization of potassium hydroxide and sulfuric acid is

(A) NaCl.

(C) PSO_4.

(B) KSO_4.

(D) K_2SO_4.

91. Aluminum hydroxide, $Al(OH)_3$, is called an amphoteric hydroxide because

(A) it contains three hydroxyl groups.

(B) it has limited solubility in water.

(C) either one, two, or all three hydroxyl groups can ionize in water.

(D) it can react as either an acid or a base.

92. Which of the following characteristics of the alkaline earth elements is unique to this group of elements?

(A) They have two "s" electrons in the outer orbit.

(B) They exhibit a valence of +2.

(C) They are in Group IIa of the Periodic Table.

(D) They form hydroxides which are alkaline in aqueous solution.

93. The presence of calcium and magnesium ions makes water "hard" because

(A) they raise the freezing point so that ice crystals form much more easily.

(B) insoluble carbonates precipitate and form a "hard" scale on pipe walls and elsewhere.

(C) they precipitate soap rendering it useless for cleaning purposes.

(D) Both (B) and (C)

94. Which of the following reactions is NOT an oxidation-reduction reaction?

(A) $Cu^{++} + SO_4^{-} \rightarrow CuSO_4 \downarrow$

(B) $5H_2O_2 + 2KMnO_4 + 6HCl \rightarrow 2MnCl_2 + 5O_2 \uparrow + 8H_2O + 2KCl$

(C) $H_2S + O_2 \rightarrow 3/2 \, SO_2 + H_2O$

(D) $CH_4 + H_2O \rightarrow 3H_2 + CO$

95. The Principle of LaChatelier permits qualitative predictions of

(A) how equilibrium compositions will shift when the temperature changes.

(B) how equilibrium compositions will shift when pressure changes.

(C) how equilibrium compositions will shift when the concentration of reacting species changes.

(D) All of the above.

96. From the following Table of Heats of Formation, which statement about the water-gas reaction ($CH_4 + H_2O \rightarrow 3H_2 + CO$) is correct?

Table 1 — Heats of Formation

$(\Delta H_f)_{298°K}$ (Kcal/mole)	
CH_4	−17.899
$H_2O_{(g)}$	−57.798
CO	−26.416

(A) The reaction is exothermic at 298 K.

(B) The reaction is endothermic at 298 K.

(C) The reaction may be either exothermic or endothermic depending on the pressure at which the reaction occurs.

(D) It is impossible to determine because the value of $(\Delta H)_{f298}K$ for H_2 is missing from the table.

97. Find the normal stress on section ① − ①, if the member has a constant cross-section area of 0.1 m².

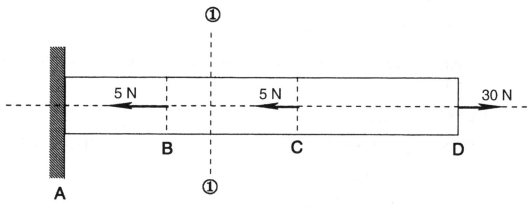

(A) 250 N/m² (tension)   (C) 50 N/m² (tension)

(B) 250 N/m² (compression) (D) 50 N/m² (compression)

98. Find the maximum tensile stress of the given beam.

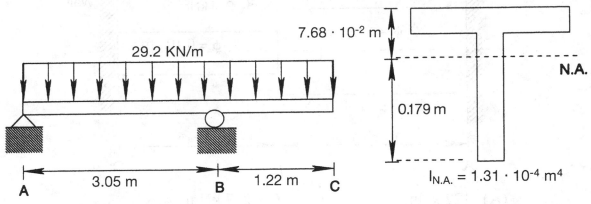

(A) $1.38 \cdot 10^4 \text{ kN/m}^2$

(C) $5.51 \cdot 10^4 \text{ kN/m}^2$

(B) $3.45 \cdot 10^4 \text{ kN/m}^2$

(D) $8.27 \cdot 10^4 \text{ kN/m}^2$

99. Determine the elongation of member '*EC*'.

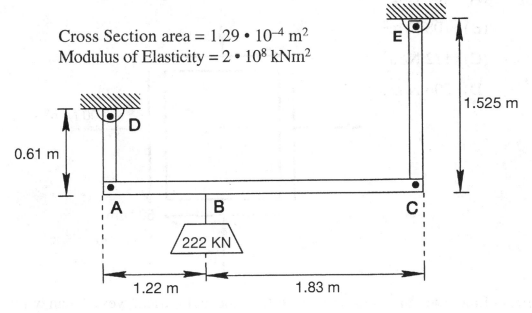

(A) $5.1 \cdot 10^{-4}$ m

(C) $5.2 \cdot 10^{-3}$ m

(B) $1.02 \cdot 10^{-3}$ m

(D) $7.87 \cdot 10^{-3}$ m

100. '*AB*' and '*BC*' are circular shafts made from the same material. A twisting moment, or torque, of 271 kNm is applied at the connection '*B*'. Determine the reaction at '*A*'.

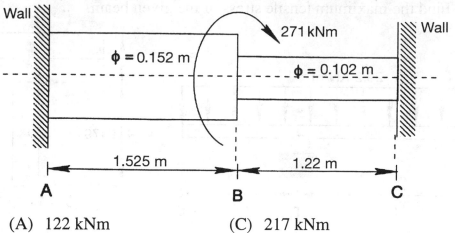

(A) 122 kNm   (C) 217 kNm

(B) 136 kNm   (D) 272 kNm

101. Find the maximum tensile stress.

(A) 100 N/m²

(B) 108 N/m²

(C) 112 N/m²

(D) 206 N/m²

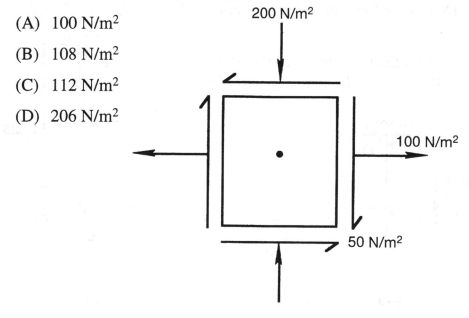

102. Find the maximum pressure that the cylindrical vessel can withstand.

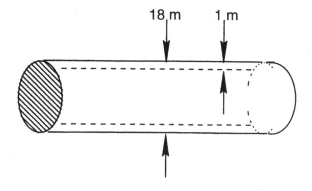

Given: The longitudinal stress cannot exceed 20 N/m^2.

The circumferential (tangential) stress cannot exceed 8 N/m^2.

The wall thickness is 1 m.

The diameter of the vessel is 18 m.

(A) 445 N/m^2

(C) 1,780 N/m^2

(B) 890 N/m^2

(D) 2,220 N/m^2

103. What is the maximum load, *P*, that can be applied to the connection shown if the shear stress in the rivets is limited to 14 N/m^2?

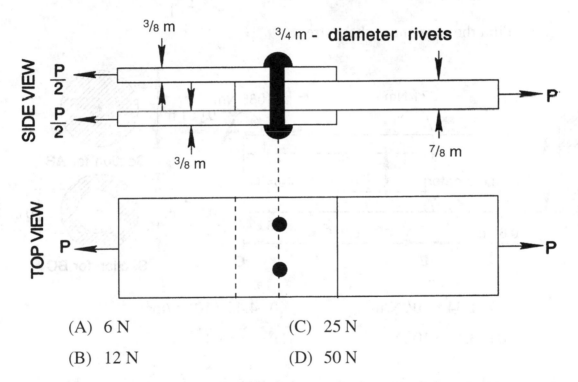

(A) 6 N

(C) 25 N

(B) 12 N

(D) 50 N

104. Find the maximum shear stress on the given section due to the vertical shear force of 50 N. (See following figure.)

(A) 1,250 N/m^2

(C) 3,210 N/m^2

(B) 2,639 N/m^2

(D) 4,860 N/m^2

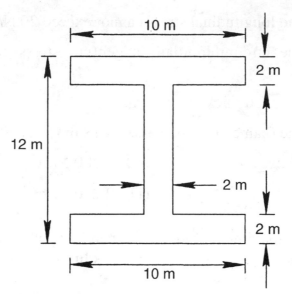

105. Find the maximum shear stress.

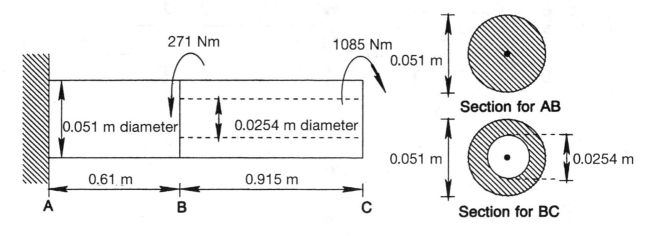

(A) $1.34 \cdot 10^7 \text{ N/m}^2$ (C) $4.42 \cdot 10^7 \text{ N/m}^2$

(B) $3.16 \cdot 10^7 \text{ N/m}^2$ (D) $7.65 \cdot 10^7 \text{ N/m}^2$

106. Find the maximum compressive stress in concrete. Given the moment at the section is 1,000,000 Nm.

Modulus of Elasticity

Concrete $E_c = 3 \cdot 10^6 \text{ N/m}^2$

Steel $E_s = 30 \cdot 10^6 \text{ N/m}^2$

(A) 750 N/m^2 (C) $1,660 \text{ N/m}^2$

(B) $1,500 \text{ N/m}^2$ (D) $3,220 \text{ N/m}^2$

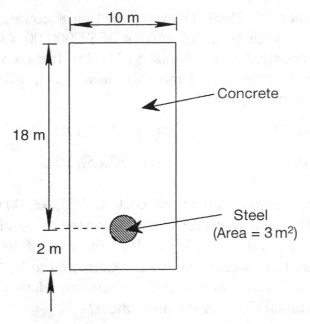

107. Find the maximum axial load that the column can carry without yielding or buckling.

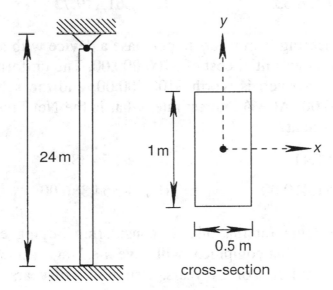

cross-section

Modulus of Elasticity:

$$E = 30 \cdot 10^8 \text{ N/m}^2$$

Stress at yield point:

$$\sigma_{yp} = 30 \text{ N/m}^2$$

(A) 4 N   (C) 11 N

(B) 5 N   (D) 26 N

108. On December 20, 1989, Dixon opened an account at the Eastman Credit Union with an initial deposit of $1,000.00. On February 20, 1990, he deposited an additional $1,000.00. If the credit union pays 12% interest compounded monthly, how much will be in the account on March 20, 1990?

(A) $1,030.20

(B) $1,010.10

(C) $2,040.30

(D) $3,050.50

109. A company requires an initial cost of $75,000.00 to purchase a minicomputer whose useful life is estimated to be eight years. The computer will sell for $15,000.00 at the end of its useful life. If operating and maintenance costs are estimated to be $10,000.00 per year, and the interest rate is 25% per annum, what is the Equivalent Uniform Annual Cost for the investment?

(A) $31,773.91

(B) $50,438.33

(C) $30,046.15

(D) $61,119.73

110. An engineering firm wants to purchase a device with a useful life of 10 years, at an initial cost of $700,000.00. The uniform annual benefit to be derived is worth $100,000.00, and the salvage value is $180,000.00. At 8% interest rate, what is the Net Present Worth of the investment?

(A) – $51.41

(B) – $51,410.00

(C) + $54.38

(D) + $54,386.00

111. Ozok Systems International is considering buying equipment for $50,000.00. This equipment will have a salvage value of $8,000.00 after a useful life of 14 years. Using sum-of-years-digit (SOYD) method of depreciation, compute the depreciation charge on the equipment for the third year of its useful life.

(A) $16,400.00

(B) $4,800.00

(C) $8,200.00

(D) $9,600.00

112. Which of the following statements is true?

(A) The capitalized cost is always greater than the present worth of the costs for a project of finite life.

(B) The payback period analysis technique ignores time value of money.

(C) The payback formula: "Payback period = First cost/Annual Benefits" is always valid.

(D) Both (A) and (B)

113. Which of the following statements about the free carrier concentration associated with intrinsic semiconductors at room temperature is valid?

(A) It increases with increasing values of energy gap.

(B) It decreases with increasing values of energy gap.

(C) It decreases with increasing carrier mobility.

(D) It is independent of both energy gap and carrier mobility.

114. At absolute zero temperature (0 K), all the valence electrons in an intrinsic semiconductor

(A) are in the valence band.

(B) are in the conduction band.

(C) are free electrons.

(D) are equally distributed between the valence band and the conduction band.

115. Carrier mobility depends on

(A) resistivity.

(B) conductivity.

(C) recombination rate.

(D) temperature and the regularity of the crystal structure.

116. The movement of charges from an area of high carrier concentration to an area of lower carrier concentration is called

(A) gradient. (C) diffusion.

(B) recombination. (D) mobility.

117. Which term describes a material whose properties depend on the direction of stress?

(A) Anisotropic

(C) Symmetrical

(B) Isotropic

(D) Endotropic

118. A heat sink will dissipate heat more rapidly if

(A) its surface area is increased.

(B) it is covered with a material having a high thermal resistance.

(C) it is kept away from air currents.

(D) its temperature is lower than the temperature of the surrounding air.

119. Materials that emit light in the absence of high heat and continue to emit light after the energy source has been removed are called

(A) phosphorescent.

(C) semiconductor-laser diodes.

(B) fluorescent.

(D) light-emitting diodes.

120. Which of the following statements about the two crystalline forms of carbon, graphite, and diamond is NOT correct?

(A) The properties of the two crystals are, in fact, more similar than dissimilar.

(B) The diamond crystalline lattice permits little or no relative atomic motion while the graphite lattice offers little resistance to relative atomic motion.

(C) The diamond lattice is transparent to visible light, graphite is not.

(D) At high temperatures diamond is a semiconductor; graphite is a conductor.

TEST 1

ANSWER KEY

1.	(C)	16.	(B)	31.	(A)	46.	(D)
2.	(B)	17.	(A)	32.	(B)	47.	(C)
3.	(B)	18.	(A)	33.	(D)	48.	(A)
4.	(B)	19.	(B)	34.	(A)	49.	(B)
5.	(A)	20.	(B)	35.	(B)	50.	(C)
6.	(C)	21.	(D)	36.	(A)	51.	(D)
7.	(B)	22.	(B)	37.	(C)	52.	(D)
8.	(D)	23.	(C)	38.	(D)	53.	(A)
9.	(D)	24.	(C)	39.	(A)	54.	(D)
10.	(C)	25.	(C)	40.	(B)	55.	(D)
11.	(D)	26.	(A)	41.	(A)	56.	(B)
12.	(A)	27.	(D)	42.	(A)	57.	(C)
13.	(B)	28.	(D)	43.	(B)	58.	(D)
14.	(C)	29.	(B)	44.	(C)	59.	(C)
15.	(B)	30.	(C)	45.	(B)	60.	(A)

61.	(B)	76.	(C)	91.	(D)	106.	(C)
62.	(B)	77.	(A)	92.	(C)	107.	(C)
63.	(A)	78.	(C)	93.	(D)	108.	(C)
64.	(D)	79.	(D)	94.	(A)	109.	(A)
65.	(A)	80.	(C)	95.	(D)	110.	(D)
66.	(D)	81.	(D)	96.	(B)	111.	(B)
67.	(B)	82.	(D)	97.	(A)	112.	(D)
68.	(C)	83.	(C)	98.	(B)	113.	(B)
69.	(A)	84.	(A)	99.	(C)	114.	(A)
70.	(C)	85.	(C)	100.	(C)	115.	(D)
71.	(B)	86.	(C)	101.	(B)	116.	(C)
72.	(C)	87.	(A)	102.	(B)	117.	(A)
73.	(B)	88.	(B)	103.	(C)	118.	(A)
74.	(B)	89.	(C)	104.	(B)	119.	(A)
75.	(A)	90.	(D)	105.	(C)	120.	(A)

DETAILED EXPLANATIONS
OF ANSWERS

Test 1

1. **(C)** A set of equations does not have a unique solution if the determinant of the coefficient matrix is zero. The determinant of the coefficient matrix is

$$\det \begin{vmatrix} 4 & 6 \\ 2 & 3 \end{vmatrix} = 4 \times 3 - 2 \times 6 = 0$$

Since the determinant is zero, (B) and (C) are the possible answers. But since one equation is not an exact multiple of the other, infinite numbers of solutions do not exist. This would have been the case if the right-hand side of the second equation had been 5 instead of 7.

2. **(B)** Since the velocity of Body A is double that of Body B,

$$V_A = 2V_B,$$
$$2t^2 - 12 = -2t$$
$$t^2 + t - 6 = 0$$
$$(t + 3)(t - 2) = 0$$
$$t = -3, t = 2$$

Since the solution sought is for time $t > 0$, the correct answer is $t = 2$. $t = -3$ is not a solution within the domain of required time, $t > 0$.

3. **(B)** The characteristic equation is

$$s + 2 = 0$$
$$s = -2$$

and the homogeneous part of the solution is

$$y_h = Ke^{-2t}$$

The particular part of the solution is of the form $y_p = A$, which gives $A = {}^1/_2$ by inspection.

The complete solution is

$$y = y_h + y_p = Ke^{-2t} + \tfrac{1}{2}$$

Applying the initial condition, $y(0) = 1$, $y = \tfrac{1}{2} e^{-2t} + \tfrac{1}{2}$

Common mistakes: Choice (A) may be chosen if the characteristic equation root is taken as +2. Choice (C) may be chosen by applying the initial condition on only the homogeneous part. Choice (D) may be chosen if mistakes, both in parts (A) and (C), are committed.

4.　**(B)**　The mean of the sample is 5.75.

$$S_t = (2 - 5.75)^2 + (8 - 5.75)^2 + (3 - 5.75)^2 + (10 - 5.75)^2$$

$$= 44.75$$

Standard deviation

$$= \sqrt{\frac{S_t}{(n-1)}}$$

$$= \sqrt{\frac{44.75}{(4-1)}}$$

$$= 3.862$$

Note that the sample standard deviation formula includes division by $(n-1)$ and not (n). Common mistakes: Choice (A) may be chosen if $(n-1)$ is replaced by (n). Sample standard deviation is the measure of the spread of the sample about the mean. One reason that division is made by $(n-1)$, and not (n), is that there is no such thing as the spread of a single data point. For the case of $n = 1$, the formula for sample standard deviation gives a result of infinity.

5.　**(A)**　In calculating the inner surface area of a cylinder, the surface area is given by

$$\text{Surface Area} = \pi \frac{D^2}{4} \times 2 \text{ ends} + \pi DL$$

$$= \pi \frac{3^2}{4} \times 2 \text{ ends} + \pi \times 3 \times 2$$

$$= 10\frac{1}{2} \pi$$

Common mistakes: Choice (B) may be chosen as the correct answer if one closed end is not accounted for. Choice (C) may be chosen if both the ends are not accounted for. Choice (D) may be chosen if the formula for the surface is chosen as $\pi D_2 \times 2$ ends $+ 2\pi DL$, that is, by mistake, substituting the diameter for the radius.

6. **(C)** An ordinary differential equation is linear if the coefficients of the dependent variable x and its derivatives are constants or are functions of the independent variable t. Only equation (III) meets this requirement. Common mistakes: The coefficients of the dependent variable terms in a linear differential equation need not be a constant. If all the coefficients are all constants, it is only a special case of linear ordinary differential equations called fixed coefficient linear ordinary differential equations.

7. **(B)** $f(x) = x^3 - 3x - 5$

$$f'(x) = 3x^2 - 3$$

Hence, the extremes are at $f'(x) = 0$, that is, $x = \pm 1$. Since $f''(x) = 6x$, the minimum occurs at $x = +1$ ($f''(x) > 0$). The value of the function at this point is

$$f(1) = 1 - 3(1) - 5$$
$$= -7$$

8. **(D)** Since each toss is independent and one can get heads or tails with the same probability in the next toss, the probability is still $1/2$. Common mistakes: Since heads was the result in the earlier try, the probability of getting heads on the next toss may be thought to be zero in the next toss. Also, the probability of the event of getting two heads in consecutive tosses is $1/4$.

9. **(D)** det $[C] \neq$ det $[A]$ + det $[B]$. Unlike matrices, determinants of matrices do not follow the addition law. For example

$$[A] = \begin{bmatrix} 2 & 1 \\ 1 & 0 \end{bmatrix}, [B] = \begin{bmatrix} -1 & -1 \\ 2 & 3 \end{bmatrix}, \text{ then } [C] = \begin{bmatrix} 1 & 0 \\ 3 & 3 \end{bmatrix}, \text{ then}$$

$$\det [A] = -1, \det [B] = -1, \det [C] = 3.$$

In mathematics, in order to prove that a statement is true, one needs to prove it for all cases. If the statement is to be proven to be false, one needs to find only one example which shows that it is false.

10. **(C)**   The shortest distance between two points (x_1, y_1) and (x_2, y_2) is given by the straight line distance between two points.

$$\text{Shortest Distance} = \sqrt{(x_1 - x_2)^2 + (y_1 - y_2)^2}$$
$$= \sqrt{(5 - 0)^2 + (-6 - 3)^2}$$
$$= \sqrt{106}$$

11. **(D)**   Although

$$\lim_{k \to \infty} |a_k| = 0,$$

the series may diverge because the condition

$$\lim_{k \to \infty} |a_k| = 0$$

is only a necessary condition for a series to converge. However, if $n = k$, that is, the series is an alternating series, the condition

$$\lim_{k \to \infty} |a_k| = 0$$

becomes a necessary, as well as a sufficient, condition for convergence of a series.

12. **(A)** $f'(x) = 5x^{2/3}$,   and $f''(x) = {}^{10}/_3 x^{-1/3}$.

The second derivative does not exist at $x = 0$ and the second derivative is never zero. So $x = 0$ is the only possibility of an inflection point. $f''(x) > 0$ for $x > 0$ and $f''(x) < 0$ for $x < 0$. This implies f is concave down on $(-\infty, 0]$ and concave up for $[0, \infty)$. Hence, $f(x)$ has an inflection point at $x = 0$.

Common mistakes: Choice (B) may be chosen if points where $f''(x) = 0$ are considered to be the only possible points of inflection.

13. **(B)**   For a function $f(x)$, if $f(a)\, f(b) < 0$, there is at least one root in $a < x < b$. However, the function also needs to be continuous in $a < x < b$. For example,

$$f(x) = 1 \quad \text{if } 1 < x \leq 2$$
$$f(x) = -1 \quad \text{if } 2 < x < 3$$

satisfies the condition $f(1)\, f(3) < 0$ but does not have a root in the interval $1 < x < 3$ because the function is piecewise continuous.

14. **(C)**   Since the expression is of 0/0 (indeterminate) form at $x = 0$ and the functions on the numerator and the denominator are differentiable, one can apply L'Hôpital's rule to find the limit.

$$\lim_{x \to 0} \frac{\sin(5x) - 2x}{x} = \lim_{x \to 0} \frac{5\cos(5x) - 2}{1} = 3$$

Identical results can be also found by expanding $\sin(5x)$ in terms of a Maclaurin Series and then take the limit.

15. **(B)**   The angle between the two lines can be found by finding the slope of the two lines. The slope of the first line is 3 and the second line 4. Hence, the angle between the two lines is

$$| \tan^{-1} 4 - \tan^{-1} 3 | = 4.399°.$$

16. **(B)**   The probability of getting a red ball is

$$p\{red\} = \frac{\{no.\ of\ red\ balls\}}{\{total\ balls\}}$$

$$= \frac{4}{(4 + 3 + 5)}$$

$$= \frac{1}{3}$$

Hence,

$$p\{not\ red\} = 1 - p\{red\}$$

$$= 1 - \frac{1}{3}$$

$$= \frac{2}{3}$$

17. **(A)** $\iint\limits_{R} xy\,dA = \int_1^2 \int_0^1 xy\,dx\,dy$

$$= \int_1^2 \frac{y}{2}\,dy$$

$$= \frac{3}{4}$$

The integral is found by integrating over y and then over x. Since the region R is a rectangle, the order of integration can be interchanged to get the same answer.

18. **(A)**   The given equation can be rewritten as follows

$$(x-1)^2 + (y+1)^2 = \left(\sqrt{2}\right)^2,$$

which shows that the equation is of a circle with radius of $\sqrt{2}$ and center at $(1, -1)$.

19. **(B)**   Since the intercept is on the y-axis at $x = 0$, one of the points on the straight line is $(0, -3)$. The other point $(5, 2)$ is already given. The slope between two points (x_1, y_1) and (x_2, y_2) is given by

$$m = \frac{(y_1 - y_2)}{(x_1 - x_2)}$$

$$= \frac{[2 - (-3)]}{[5 - 0]}$$

$$= 1$$

20. **(B)**   The distance covered between $t = {}^1/_4$ and ${}^1/_2$ seconds is

$$\int_{1/4}^{1/2} \sin(\pi t)\, dt = \frac{1}{\pi}\left[-\cos(\pi t)\right]_{1/4}^{1/2}$$

$$= \frac{1}{\left(\pi\sqrt{2}\right)}$$

$$= 0.2251$$

Common mistakes are not including the negative sign in the integral of sin (πt). Also, be sure that you change the angle mode in the calculator to the radian mode from the default degree mode. If the mode of angle is kept at degrees, you will get an answer of approximately zero, choice (C).

21. **(D)**   The resistance R of a cable is given by

$$R = \frac{\rho L}{A},$$

where ρ is the resistivity of the cable, L the length of the cable, and A its cross section, which is given by

$$A = \frac{D^2\pi}{4}.$$

The resistance of the cable is therefore inversely proportional to the square of the diameter of the cable.

22. **(B)** The two 4 Ω resistors are connected in parallel and therefore are equivalent to:

$$\frac{1}{R_{eq}} = \frac{1}{R_1} + \frac{1}{R_2}$$
$$= \frac{1}{4} + \frac{1}{4}$$
$$= \frac{1}{2}$$
$$R_{eq} = 2\ \Omega$$

The circuit has been reduced to three resistances in series as shown in the figure below.

The equivalent resistance is therefore equal to

$$R_{eq} = R_1 + R_2 + R_3$$
$$= 2 + 2 + 3$$
$$= 7\ \Omega$$

By Ohm's Law the current in the circuit is given by

$$i = \frac{V}{R_{eq}}$$
$$= \frac{32}{7}$$
$$= 4.57\ A$$

and the voltage across the 3 Ω resistor is given by Ohm's Law

$$V = i\,R_3$$
$$= 4.57 \times 3$$
$$= 13.7\ \text{V}$$

23. **(C)** The 16 V voltage source has no resistance. Therefore, if one connects an Ohm-meter between terminals *ab*, the device will measure the combinations of R_s shown in Figure (a) below.

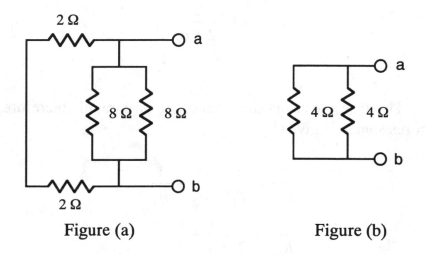

Figure (a)   Figure (b)

The two 8 Ω resistances are in parallel and are therefore equivalent to

$$\frac{1}{R_{eq}} = \frac{1}{R_1} + \frac{1}{R_2}$$
$$= \frac{1}{8} + \frac{1}{8}$$
$$= \frac{1}{4}$$
$$R_{eq} = 4\Omega$$

The two 2 Ω resistances are connected in series and therefore are equivalent to

$$R_{eq} = R_1 + R_2$$
$$= 2\,\Omega + 2\,\Omega$$
$$= 4\ \Omega$$

The circuit has been simplified to the parallel combinations of R_s shown in Figure (b) above.

Following the procedure shown to combine two resistances in parallel, the resistance between terminal ab is $R_{ab} = 2\ \Omega$.

24. **(C)** By the voltage divider rule the voltage between terminals ab is given by

$$V_{ab} = V \frac{R_1}{R_1 + R_2}$$
$$= 16 \frac{2}{2 + 6}$$
$$= 4\ V$$

25. **(C)** The three resistors are connected in parallel; therefore, their equivalent resistance is given by

$$\frac{1}{R_{eq}} = \frac{1}{R_1} + \frac{1}{R_2} + \frac{1}{R_3}$$
$$\frac{1}{R_{eq}} = \frac{1}{2} + \frac{1}{4} + \frac{1}{4}$$
$$R_{eq} = 1.0\ \Omega$$

The voltage between nodes ab is therefore by Ohm's Law:

$$V_{ab} = R_{eq} \times i$$
$$= 1.0 \times 16$$
$$= 16.0\ V$$

and by Ohm's Law the current i' through the 2 Ω resistor is

$$i' = \frac{V_{ab}}{R}$$
$$= \frac{16.0}{2}$$
$$= 8.0\ A$$

26. **(A)** The 0.1 Ω resistor is connected to the secondary of an ideal transformer with a turn ratio of 1:10. It therefore is equivalent to a 0.1 $\times$ $10^2 = 10\ \Omega$ resistor connected to the primary of the transformer. The total

resistance seen by the 100 V AC source is therefore $1 + 10 = 11\ \Omega$ and the primary current I is by Ohm's Law

$$\frac{100}{11} = 9.1\ \text{A}$$

27. **(D)**   Because we are examining the magnetic field in the middle of a long wire, the wire can be considered infinite. Therefore by Biot-Savart's Law the magnetic field B at a distance r of an infinite straight long wire carrying a current i is given by

$$B(r) = \frac{\mu_0 i}{2\pi r},$$

where μ_0 is the permeability constant.

The magnetic field is therefore proportional to $\dfrac{i}{r}$.

28. **(D)**   A 5 A current source in parallel with a 2 Ω resistor can be transformed into a voltage source with $V = RI$ in series with an R resistor. The circuit can therefore be transformed into the circuit shown here.

Kirchhoff's voltage law around the loop establishes that

$$- 10 + 3i + 2i - 10 + 3i = 0.$$

Therefore,

$$i = \frac{20}{8}$$
$$= 2.5\ \text{A}$$

29. **(B)**   Kirchhoff's voltage law (KVL) around the loop establishes that

$$- 24 + 3i + 6i - 0.5\, V_R + 6i = 0,$$

where by Ohm's Law

$$V_R = 3i.$$

Therefore, KVL can be written as

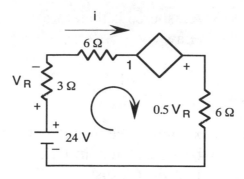

$$-24 + 3i + 6i - (0.5 \times 3i) + 6i = 0, \text{ or } 24 = 13.5i.$$

The current is therefore 1.78 A.

30. **(C)**   Engineers shall hold paramount the safety, health, and welfare of the public in the performance of their professional duties. If their professional judgment is overruled under circumstances where the safety, health, property, or welfare of the public are endangered, they shall notify their employer or client and such authority as may be appropriate. Hence the obligation of the engineer to society supersedes the obligation to a client. (A) and (B) are not correct since they rely on someone who has a vested interest to right the wrong. (D) would be correct if the public safety were not involved in the problem.

31. **(A)**   After the DC voltage source has been connected for a long time to the circuit, the capacitor becomes charged and no more current flows through the capacitor. The capacitor can therefore be modeled as an open circuit as shown here.

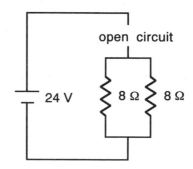

The voltage across the terminals of the capacitor is therefore 24 V.

32. **(B)**   Since the capacitor has been connected to the circuit for many hours, it has been charged and no more current flows through it. The circuit has an open branch as shown below:

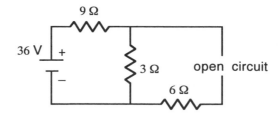

and

$$R_{eq} = R_1 + R_2$$
$$= 9 + 3$$
$$= 12 \text{ ohm}$$

By Ohm's Law the current is given by

$$i = \frac{V}{R_{eq}}$$
$$= \frac{36}{12}$$
$$= 3 \text{ A,}$$

and by Ohm's Law

$$V_{ac} = R\,i$$
$$= 3 \times 3$$
$$= 9 \text{ V}$$

Since no current flows through the 6 ohm resistor, $V_b = V_c$, and therefore $V_{ab} = V_{ac}$.

$$V_{ad} = 9 \text{ V}$$

33. **(D)** The two 4 Ω resistors are connected in parallel and can therefore be substituted by an equivalent resistance of 2 Ω. The time constant τ is given by

$$\tau = RC$$
$$= 2 \times 0.050$$
$$= 0.1 \text{ s}$$

and

$$\frac{1}{\tau} = 10.$$

Immediately after the breaker is closed, the capacitor is not charged and therefore can be modeled by a short circuit as shown here:

By Ohm's Law the initial current is given by

$$i = \frac{V}{R_{eq}}$$
$$= \frac{16}{2}$$
$$= 8 \text{ A}$$

After the capacitor has been charged, no more current flows through the circuit. The final current is therefore equal to zero and the expression for the current in the capacitor is given by

$$i(t) = 8e^{-10t},$$

where the response of a discharging RC circuit is given by

$$i(t) = I_o e^{-t/RC}.$$

34. **(A)**   The AND operation returns a 1 if both corresponding items are 1s. In this example, since no corresponding values are 1s, the results will be all 0s. If this had been an OR circuit, then a 1 is returned if either corresponding input is a 1. In that case, the correct result would have been **(B)**.

35. **(B)**

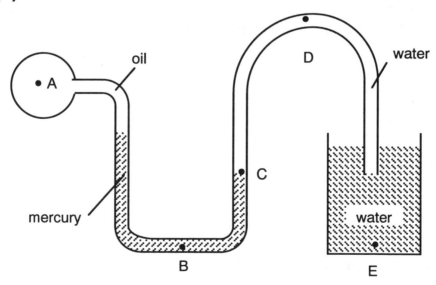

In the horizontal plane cutting through point C, the pressure through any of the three sections must be constant. Then, since mercury is denser than water, the pressure at B will be greater than that at E. All other pressures are lower.

36. **(A)**   The three fluid metering devices are sketched below.

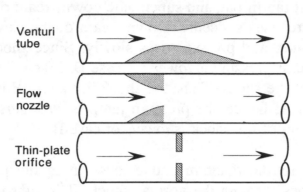

Venturi tube

Flow nozzle

Thin-plate orifice

All three devices serve the same purpose: to measure volumetric flow rate in a pipe. Because of its smooth design, the Venturi tube has the lowest pressure loss. The thin-plate orifice, which is not smooth on either side, has the highest pressure loss. The flow nozzle is in between.

37. **(C)**   The Moody chart is designed for use with long, straight sections of pipe. The flow in the pipe may be laminar or turbulent, and the walls may be smooth or rough. The only restriction is that the pipe must have constant cross-sectional shape. Even if the cross section is not circular, the Moody chart is still fairly accurate when hydraulic diameter is substituted for pipe diameter.

A subsonic diffuser is an expanding pipe, which does not have constant cross section; hence, the Moody chart is of no use.

38. **(D)**   For a converging diverging nozzle without friction or heat addition, the pressure ratio p/p_0 is plotted against downstream distance x:

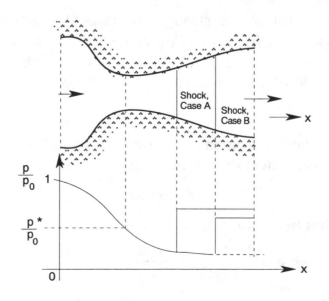

The pressure decreases continuously with x. The flow is subsonic before the throat, sonic at the throat, and supersonic downstream of the throat. At the shock, pressure rises suddenly. Downstream of the shock, the flow is once again *subsonic*, and pressure rises slowly. Since shock B is further downstream, the exit pressure is *lower* for case B. Mach number increases with x upstream of the shock. Thus, the shock in system B is *stronger* than the one in system A; hence, the pressure jump is *stronger*, and the Mach number downstream of the shock is *lower* for case B.

39. **(A)**   Refer to the diagram and discussion in the problem above. Once the flow goes through the normal shock, it is *subsonic* and cannot become supersonic again unless another throat would be added downstream. Choice (D) is incorrect because even though the flow is *choked*, changing stagnation pressure will still have an effect on the flow. Remember that it is the ratio of exit pressure to stagnation pressure that determines the shock location.

40. **(B)**   Engineers shall avoid the use of statements containing a material misrepresentation of fact or omitting a material fact necessary to keep statements from being misleading or intended or likely to create an unjustified expectation, or statements containing prediction of future success. Consistent with the foregoing, engineers may prepare articles for the lay or technical press, but such articles shall not imply credit to the author for work performed by another. While (A) may be thought of as commendable, it is not appropriate under the Engineering Code. Whether or not statement (C) is true does not make it ethical. (D) is incorrect since it still represents a material misrepresentation.

41. **(A)**   This form of the steady incompressible Bernoulli equation is valid everywhere for *irrotational* flow; but if the flow is *rotational*, it is valid only along streamlines of the flow. In other words, the constant in the right-hand side of the equation may be different for each streamline in a rotational flow field.

42. **(A)**   For static conditions, a close approximation for variation of atmospheric pressure over short height differences is

$$\Delta p = \rho g \, \Delta z$$

where density has been assumed to be constant.

Here, $\Delta z = 17m$, $\rho = \dfrac{1.2 \text{ kg}}{m^3}$, $g = \dfrac{9.8m}{s^2}$.

Thus

$$\Delta p = \left(\frac{1.2\,kg}{m^3}\right)\left(\frac{9.8\,m}{s^2}\right)(17\,m)\left(\frac{Ns^2}{\dfrac{kg}{m}}\right) = 200\,\frac{N}{m^2}$$

43. **(B)**   Use the one-dimensional energy equation (in terms of head) from point ① to point ②, which are on the surface of the lake and the surface of the reservoir tank, respectively.

$$\frac{p_1}{\rho g} + \alpha_1\frac{V_1^2}{2g} + z_1 = \frac{p_2}{\rho g} + \alpha_2\frac{V_2^2}{2g} + z_2 + h_f + h_s - h_q \qquad (1)$$

Here h_s = shaft work head done by the fluid (to be solved for)

h_q = heat transfer head (neglect this term)

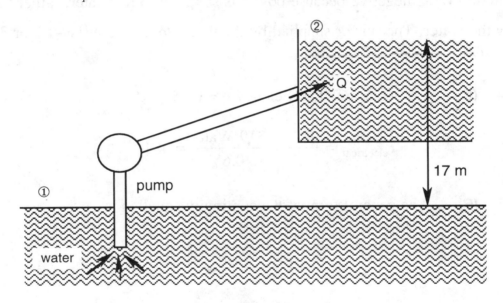

h_f = frictional head loss (given at 2.5 m of water)

$V_1 = V_2$ = average velocities (≈ 0 on the surfaces)

$p_1 \approx p_2 = p_a$ = atmospheric pressure on the surfaces. (Note that from above, $p_2 - p_a$ is negligible.)

(1) becomes $h_z = z_1 - z_2 - h_f = -17\,m - 2.5\,m = -19.5\,m$ (h_z is negative because work is being done *on* the fluid).

Finally,

$$h_s = \frac{\dot{W}_s}{\dot{m}g}$$

where $\dot{W}_s$ = shaft power done by the water and $\dot{m}$ = mass flow rate = ρQ where Q = volume flow rate. Hence,

$$
\begin{aligned}
W_s &= \rho Q g h_s \\
&= \left(\frac{100 \text{ kg}}{\text{m}^3}\right)\left(\frac{6 \text{ m}^3}{\text{hr}}\right)\left(\frac{1 \text{ hr}}{60 \text{ min}}\right)\left(\frac{1 \text{ min}}{60 \text{ s}}\right)\left(\frac{9.8 \text{ m}}{\text{s}^2}\right)(-19.5 \text{ m}) \\
&= -\left(\frac{319 \text{ kg m}^2}{\text{s}^3}\right)\left(\frac{\text{N s}^2}{\text{kg m}}\right)\left(\frac{\text{W s}}{\text{N} \times \text{m}}\right) \\
&= -319 \text{ Watts}
\end{aligned}
$$

Finally $\dot{W}_s$ is negative because power is supplied *to* the water, rather than *by* the water. The power supplied by the pump *to* the water is $-\dot{W}_s$ or 319 Watts.

44. **(C)**   For a pump with efficiency $\eta = 0.65$,

$$P_{\text{electrical}} = \frac{-\dot{W}_s}{\eta} = \frac{319 \text{ Watts}}{0.65} = 491 \text{ Watts}$$

45. **(B)**   The general form of the continuity equation is

$$\frac{\partial \rho}{\partial t} + \nabla(\rho \cdot \mathbf{V}) = 0$$

(1)

which is valid for steady or unsteady, compressible or incompressible, rotational or irrotational flow. Only when ρ = constant (i.e., only for *incompressible* flow) does (1) reduce to

$$\nabla \cdot \mathbf{V} = 0.$$

Thus, choices (A), (C), and (D) are valid, but (B) is not.

46. **(D)**   This is a standard converging-diverging nozzle. In the converging section (upstream of $A_{\min}$), the flow is *subsonic*. Hence, the velocity increases, pressure decreases, and density decreases in the flow

direction. Downstream of the throat (i.e., in the diverging section of the duct) the flow must be everywhere supersonic. Note that if a normal shock were to appear in the duct, the flow would change suddenly from super-sonic to subsonic. We know this is not the case since the flow was given as *supersonic* at the exit plane. In the converging section then, the velocity increases, pressure decreases, and density decreases. Hence, the density at the exit plane must be *less than* the density at A_{min}.

47. **(C)** To convert binary numbers to octal, the digits are grouped in 3s, starting at the right-hand side. In this case, we would have {101} and {000}. The octal number will consist of two digits. The last digit corresponding to {000} is found as follows:

$$0 * 2^2 + 0 * 2^1 + 0 * 2^0 = 0$$

The first digit corresponding to {101} is found as follows:

$$1 * 2^2 + 0 * 2^1 + 1 * 2^0 = 5$$

$$101000_2 = 50_8$$

The hexadecimal, or base 16, is found in a similar manner with the grouping of numbers being 4 instead of 3. This will give {10} and {1000} for the groupings. The resulting number to base 16 is 28. The decimal (base 10) representation is found from:

$$1 * 2^5 + 0 * 2^4 + 1 * 2^3 + 0 * 2^2 + 0 * 2^1 + 0 * 2^0 = 32 + 8 = 40$$

48. **(A)** In a spreadsheet, a macro is a grouping and recording of in-structions that the user executes manually. (B) and (C) make no sense. (D) implies that macros exist in other applications, but not in a spreadsheet.

49. **(B)** An adiabatic process has no associated heat transfer; the heat transfer is zero. An adiabatic process can be isothermal, and an isothermal process can be adiabatic; however, neither is the precondition for the other. A word about entropy; if the process occurs, the entropy must change, unless the process is reversible and is then adiabatic and revers-ible. The last case is referred to as an isentropic process.

50. **(C)** The Carnot efficiency is the standard against which we mea-sure the cycle efficiency of other cycles. If the efficiency of other cycles exceeds that of Carnot, then they are not possible. The Carnot efficiency is expressed in equation form as

$$n_{th,rev} = 1 - \frac{T_c}{T_h} \quad \text{or} \quad n_{th,rev} = \frac{(T_h - T_c)}{T_h}$$

where T_c and T_h are the absolute temperatures of the cold and hot thermal reservoirs, respectively. Only another reversible cycle operating between the same thermal reservoirs can have an efficiency EQUAL to the Carnot efficiency.

51. **(D)**   For the rigid container, a closed system, there are two work modes: work associated with a rotating shaft, and expansion and compression work. Since the container is rigid, the latter is zero. Thus, the work associated with the heating process is zero.

52. **(D)**   The Second Law of Thermodynamics provides the mechanism to test the applicability of solutions provided by the other laws. The direction of processes, the theoretical performances of cycles, relationships of properties, and the definition of the absolute temperature scale are important aspects of the Second Law. Often the First Law will be satisfied, but if the Second Law is not satisfied, the process/cycle fails the critical test.

53. **(A)**   Engineers shall act in professional matters for each employer or client as faithful agents or trustees. Engineers shall disclose all known or potential conflicts of interest to their employers or clients by promptly informing them of any business association, interest, or other circumstances which could influence or appear to influence their judgment or the quality of their services. (B) and (D) are both incorrect. When a conflict of interest is discovered, the parties should be immediately informed. (C) is incorrect since the circumstances in this case are quite clear.

54. **(D)**   Properties are point functions while heat and work are path functions, depending on both the end points and the path followed. Only properties can be used to fix the state of the medium. Heat and work can be used to evaluate properties.

55. **(D)**   The coefficient of performance of a refrigerator is defined as the cooling capacity divided by the work required to make the refrigerator operate. The cooling effect is associated with the evaporator. The work is associated with the compressor. In this problem, units must be converted to either kW or kJ/kg for each device. The mass flow rate is provided for this reason. Choice (A) is obtained if the units are not changed. (B) and (C) would be obtained if the device was analyzed as a heat pump, with (C) being correct in such a case and (B) reflecting a failure to change units.

56. **(B)**   The isentropic (process) efficiency is a comparison of the adiabatic actual device with the adiabatic reversible (ideal) device, operating between the same inlet state point and exit pressure. The efficiency must be less than one unless the actual device is adiabatic and reversible.

57. **(C)**   The efficiency of the compression ignition cycle is calculated by dividing the work of the cycle by the heat added. The heat is added during the constant pressure process and is labeled Q_{23}. For a cycle the work equals the heat transfer, thus the efficiency in choice (C) would be 100%. This is totally impossible to obtain.

58. **(D)**   (A), (B), and (C) represent valid contents for the cells of a spreadsheet.

59. **(C)**   The Rankine cycle is the ideal cycle used to model the steam power cycle. The others are: Otto-spark ignition cycle, Diesel-compression ignition cycle, Brayton-gas turbine cycle, and Stirling (like the Carnot cycle with the two isentropic processes replaced by two constant-volume regeneration processes).

60. **(A)**   The expansion process in an ideal refrigeration cycle is modeled as an adiabatic process with no work, and no change in potential or kinetic energy. Although the enthalpy is probably not constant throughout the process, the end state enthalpies are the same. This can be easily verified by applying the first law for a control volume. The strongly irreversible process which takes place is known as throttling.

61. **(B)**   Engineers in public service as members, advisors, or employees of a governmental or quasi-governmental body or department shall not participate in decisions with respect to professional services solicited or provided by them or their organizations in private or public engineering practice. Engineers shall not solicit or accept a professional contract from a governmental body on which a principal or officer of their organization serves as a member (1) where an engineer acts in some capacity as an advisor to a public agency and also provides professional services to the public agency and (2) where an engineer is part of the decision-making group within a public agency and also providing professional services to the public agency. The former will generally, in the absence of other circumstances and factors, be found acceptable under the code while the latter, on its face, will be found to be unacceptable under the code. (A) would be incorrect because this is not the function of the local board.

While there is an apparent conflict of interest, (C) is incorrect due to the mitigating circumstances. (D) is incorrect because of the word *never*. While there are many instances that would prohibit this sort of relationship, there are circumstances that allow them.

62. **(B)**   If their professional judgment is overruled under circumstances where the safety, health, property, or welfare of the public are endangered, they shall notify their employer or client and such other authority as may be appropriate. However, in this case, the issue does not allege a danger to public health or safety. (A) is incorrect since no clear-cut danger to the public has been established. (C) is incorrect since conforming to client's wishes is not sufficient reason to suppress the information. (B) is incorrect since, at most, the engineer has an ethical right as a matter of personal conscience to notify the proper authorities.

63. **(A)**   First, find the velocity-time curve for the particle. Since the acceleration is either constant or zero, and velocity is the integral of acceleration, the velocity curve consists of straight lines connecting points whose abscissa are the times when the acceleration changes ($t = 0$, 6, 16, 36, 46s) and whose ordinates are the total area under the $a - t$ curve up to that value of t.

$$t = 0 \quad v = 0 \hspace{6cm} (0, 0)$$

$$t = 6, \quad v = (5)\,(6) \hspace{5cm} (6, 30)$$

$$t = 16, \quad v = (5)\,(6) + (7)\,(10) \hspace{3.5cm} (16, 100)$$

$$t = 36, \quad v = (5)\,(6) + (7)\,(10) \hspace{3.5cm} (36, 100)$$

$$t = 46, \quad v = (5)\,(6) + (7)\,(10) + (-10)\,(10) \hspace{1.5cm} (46, 0)$$

This curve is shown in Figure 1.

Now find the position-time curve for the particle. Position is the integral of velocity, and the points to be connected on the $x\text{-}t$ curve will be determined by the same method as those on the $v\text{-}t$ curve. However, now the velocity is constant only between $t = 16s$ and $t = 36s$. The only straight line segment will be present over this interval of the $x\text{-}t$ curve. The other sections will have parabolic curves, turning upward for $t < 16s$, and downward for $t > 36s$. The defining points are:

$$t = 0 \quad x = 0 \hspace{6cm} (0, 0)$$

$$t = 6 \quad x = \frac{1}{2}\,(6)\,(30) \hspace{4.5cm} (6, 90)$$

$$t = 16, \quad x = \frac{1}{2}(6)(30) + \frac{1}{2}(10)(30 + 100) \qquad (16, 740)$$

$$t = 36, \quad x = 740 + (20)(100) \qquad (36, 2740)$$

$$t = 46, \quad x = 2740 + \frac{1}{2}(10)(100) \qquad (46, 3240)$$

This curve is shown in Figure 2. Also, the result of $x(t = 46s) = 3,240$ m yields the distance between points A and B.

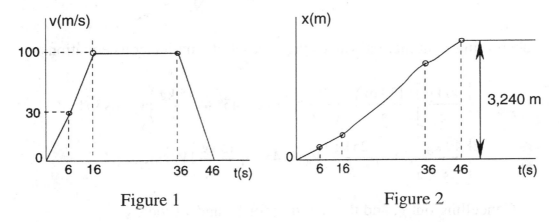

Figure 1   Figure 2

64. **(D)** There are no external forces in this system since the explosion is caused by an internal force. Therefore, linear momentum of the system is conserved.

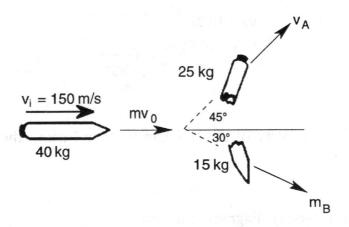

Momentum before = Momentum after

$$(m_A + m_B)\, v_0 = m_A\, v_A + m_B\, v_B$$

This equation can be broken into components. In the x-direction

$$(m_A + m_B)\, v_0 = m_A\, v_A \cos 45° + m_B\, v_B \cos 30°$$

and in the y-direction

$$(m_A + m_B)\,(0) = m_A\,v_A \sin 45° - m_B\,v_B \sin 30°$$

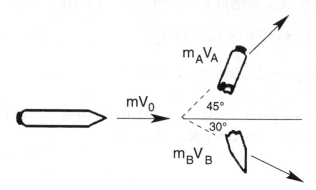

Substituting in numerical values yields a set of simultaneous equations.

$$\left[\frac{40\ \text{kg}}{g}\right]\left(\frac{150\ \text{m}}{\text{s}}\right) = \left(\frac{25\ \text{kg}}{g}\right)V_A \cos 45° + \left(\frac{15\ \text{kg}}{g}\right)V_B \cos 30°$$

$$\left[\frac{40\ \text{kg}}{g}\right](0) = \left(\frac{25\ \text{kg}}{g}\right)V_A \sin 45° - \left(\frac{15\ \text{kg}}{g}\right)V_B \sin 30°$$

Cancelling out g, and then solving for V_A and V_B yields

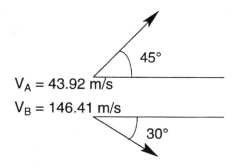

$V_A = 43.92$ m/s
$V_B = 146.41$ m/s

65. **(A)** The velocity of the box can be found using the work-kinetic energy relation:

$$W = \Delta KE$$

First, draw a free-body diagram of the box:

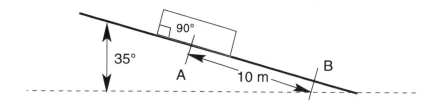

$$W = (20 \text{ kg}) (9.8 \text{ m/s}^2) = 196 \text{ } N$$

Using the equation of equilibrium in the y-direction,

$$\Sigma F_y = 0$$
$$(196 \text{ N}) \cos 35° + N = 0$$
$$N = 166.5 \text{ } N$$
$$f = \mu N$$
$$f = .3 (160.5) = 48.2 \text{ } N$$

The work done in the x-direction is equal to $\Sigma F_x \times$ displacement.

$$\Sigma F_x = W \sin 35° - f = (196 \text{ N}) \sin 35° - 48.2 \text{ N} = 64.3 \text{ N}$$
$$\text{Work} = (64.3 \text{ N}) (10 \text{ m}) = 642.5 \text{ Nm} = 642.5 \text{ J}$$
$$\text{Work} = \Delta KE = \frac{1}{2} m V_b^2 - \frac{1}{2} m V_a^2$$
$$V_a = 0$$
$$m = 20 \text{ kg}$$
$$647.5 \text{ N} \times m = \frac{1}{2} (20 \text{ kg}) (V_a)^2$$
$$V_b = 8.02 \text{ m/s}$$

66. **(D)**   The general procedure used in solving any problem in mechanics is to calculate all the forces acting on the system and then derive the equation of motion of the system.

An easier way to do mechanics problems involves the use of conservation principles. These laws are not applicable to all problems, but when they are, they simplify the calculation of the solution tremendously.

In this problem, we may use the principle of conservation of energy. We relate the energy of the block before it was released to the block's energy at the point of maximum compression (see figure in question). At the moment of release, the kinetic energy is zero. At the moment when maximum compression occurs, there is also no kinetic energy.

As shown in the figure in the question, the reference level for gravitational potential energy is the surface S. The initial gravitational potential energy of m is mgy_1. At the point of maximum compression, the potential energy of m is mgy_2. However, at this point, the spring is compressed a distance y and also has elastic potential energy $\frac{1}{2} ky^2$. Hence, equating the energy at the point of release to the energy at the point of maximum compression,

$$mgy_1 = mgy_2 + \frac{1}{2}\,ky^2$$

$$mg(y_1 - y_2) = \frac{1}{2}\,ky^2$$

But $y_1 - y_2 = h + y$ and

$$mg(h + y) = \frac{1}{2}\,ky^2$$

$$y^2 = \frac{2\,mg}{k}(h + y)$$

$$y^2 - \left(\frac{2\,mg}{k}\right)y - \frac{2\,mgh}{k} = 0$$

Therefore, using the quadratic formula to solve for y,

$$y = \frac{1}{2}\left(\frac{2\,mg}{k} + \sqrt{\left(\frac{2\,mg}{k}\right)^2 + \left(\frac{8\,mgh}{m}\right)}\,\right).$$

67. **(B)**   The forces on the body, resolved in the plane and perpendicular to the plane, are shown in the following figure.

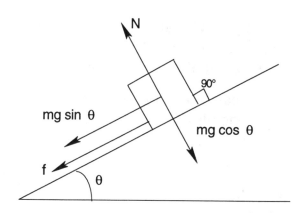

The motion is perpendicular to the normal force N and the $mg\cos\theta$ component of gravity: they do not work on the block. The other two forces $mg\sin\theta$ and $f = \mu N = \mu\,mg\cos\theta$ are along the path of motion and do work. The amount of which is equal to their magnitudes, which are constant, times the distance d the body travels:

$$W = -(mg\sin\theta)\,d - (\mu\,mg\cos\theta)\,d.$$

This quantity of work is equal to the energy loss, from the body's initial kinetic energy,

$$\Delta KE = -\frac{1}{2}\,mv_0^2$$

$$-\frac{1}{2} mv_0^2 = -(mg \sin \theta)\, d - \mu\, (mg \cos \theta)\, d \qquad (1)$$

$$d = \frac{v_0^2}{2g(\mu \cos \theta + \sin \theta)}.$$

The purist may say this analysis misleadingly puts the non-conservative force, friction, on equal footing with the conservative force, gravity. The results, however, are identical. Using the most general energy conservation law,

$$W_{nc} = \Delta E + \Delta V$$

yields equation (1) again. $W_{nc} = -\mu mgd \cos \theta$, $\Delta E = -\frac{1}{2} mv_0^2$ and $\Delta V = mg\Delta h = mgd\sin \theta$ so

$$-\mu mgd \cos \theta = -\frac{1}{2} mv_0^2 + mgd \sin \theta$$

$$\theta = \frac{v_0^2}{2g(\mu \cos \theta + \sin \theta)}$$

68. **(C)** This problem must be approached carefully. We must express the acceleration due to gravity in terms of the density and the radius of the planet. If the radius is R and the mass of the planet M, then the acceleration due to gravity on its surface is found from Newton's Second Law, $F = ma$. Consider an object of mass m on the surface of the planet. Then the only force on m is the gravitational force F, and

$$F = \frac{GMm}{R^2}$$

But a is the acceleration of m due to the planet's gravitational field, or g_p. Then

$$g_v = \frac{GM}{R^2}$$

Assuming the planet is spherical, its volume is the volume of a sphere of radius R:

$$V = \frac{4}{3}\pi R^3$$

Since Mass = Volume × Density.

$$M = \frac{4\pi R^3 \rho}{3}$$

where ρ (the Greek letter rho) is the density of the planet. Therefore,

$$g_v = \frac{G \frac{4}{3} \pi R^3 \rho}{R^2}$$

$$= \frac{4\pi}{3} GR\rho$$

Similarly, the acceleration due to gravity on the surface of the earth is

$$g = \frac{4}{3} \pi GR_e \rho_e$$

where ρ_e is the density of the earth, and R_e is its radius. If

$$g_v = g$$

Then

$$\frac{4}{3} \pi GR\rho = \frac{4}{3} \pi GR_e \rho_e$$

Canceling $^4/_3 \pi G$ on both sides

$$R\rho = R_e \rho_e .$$

If the density of the planet is twice that of the earth,

$$\rho = 2 \rho_e$$

So

$$R 2\rho_e = R_e \rho_e$$

whence

$$R = \frac{1}{2} R_e$$

$$= \frac{1}{2} \times 6.38 \times 10^6 \text{ m}$$

$$= 3.19 \times 10^6 \text{ m}$$

The radius of the planet is one-half of the radius of the earth, or 3.19×10^6 meters.

69. **(A)**   Shown is a free-body diagram of the door, of mass m and length $2l$. Not shown is the fictitious force ma acting at the center of mass of the door. In the car's frame of reference we consider this force to be real and use it in developing a solution.

The forces A_x and A_y are unknown. When one takes moments about A, these two unknown forces passing through point A would not appear in the moment equation. The moment equation then is

$$ma \cdot y = I_A \, \alpha$$

$$(ma) \ l \cos \theta = I_A \alpha \ (\text{since } y = l \cos \theta)$$

Solving for the angular acceleration of the door,

$$\alpha = \frac{ma \ l \cos \theta}{I_A}.$$

70. **(C)**   This is a conservation of linear momentum problem. The common velocity can be found by equating the momentum of the system (cars $A + B$) before they locked together to the momentum of the system *after* they locked together.

With

$$M_A : \text{ mass of car } A = 1{,}150 \text{ kg}$$

$$M_B : \text{ mass of car } B = 1{,}300 \text{ kg}$$

$$V_A : \text{ speed of car } A = 4.5 \text{ m/s}$$

$$V_B : \text{ speed of car } B = 6.7 \text{ m/s}$$

$$V_C : \text{ common speed}$$

$$\underbrace{M_A V_A + M_B V_B}_{\substack{\text{momentum before} \\ \text{collision}}} \ = \ \underbrace{(M_A + M_B) V_C}_{\substack{\text{momentum after} \\ \text{collision}}}$$

$$(1{,}150 \text{ kg}) \ (4.5 \text{ m/s}) + (1{,}300 \text{ kg}) \ (6.7 \text{ m/s}) = (1{,}150 \text{ kg} + 1{,}300 \text{ kg}) \, V_C$$

$$V_C = \frac{13.885 \ \text{kgm/s}}{2{,}450 \text{ kg}}$$

$$V_C = 5.67 \text{ m/s}$$

71. **(B)**   To find the velocity of point *B* we will use the following equation:

$$V_B = V_C + V_{B/C}$$

where V_B = velocity of point *B*

V_C = velocity of point *C*

$V_{B/C}$ = velocity of point *B* relative to point *C*

In addition, we know that

$$V_{B/C} = \omega \times r_B$$

or $$V_B = V_C + (\omega \times r_B)$$

where $w = (-V_C / r)\,k = (-2.5 \text{ m/s} / 0.5m)\,k = -5k \text{ rad/s}$

Note: The vector ω is directed into the paper by the right-hand rule, hence the negative sign.

$$r_B = 0.3\ m\ (\cos 45°i + \sin 45°j)\ m = (0.212\,i + 0.212\,j)\ m$$

$$V_C = 2.5i \text{ m/s}$$

Now, by solving the vector equation, we find V_B:

$$V_B = 2.5i \text{ m/s} + [-5k \text{ rad/s} \times (0.212i + 0.212j)m]$$

$$V_B = 2.5i \text{ m/s} + [-1.06j \text{ m/s} + 1.06i \text{ m/s}]$$

$$V_B = (3.56i - 1.06j) \text{ m/s}$$

72. **(C)**   (A) would have been the correct response if S = 1 instead of S = 0 in line 2. (B) is incorrect since n! and not n is being evaluated. (D) gives the wrong sum to the series.

73. **(B)**   First, draw a free-body diagram of the block.

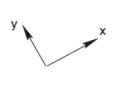

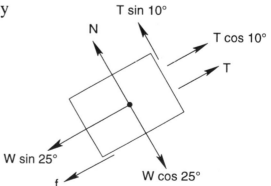

Using Newton's Law,

$$\left.\begin{array}{l} \Sigma F_y = ma_y \\ \Sigma F_y = 0 \end{array}\right\} \text{There is no acceleration in the } y \text{ direction.}$$

$$\Sigma F_y = N + T \sin 10° - W \cos 25° = 0$$

$$N = W \cos 25° - T \sin 10° \qquad (1)$$

From Newton's Law

$$\Sigma F_x = ma$$

$$\Sigma F_x = T \cos 10° + T - W \sin 25° - f = ma_x \qquad (2)$$

Since $f = \mu_k N$,

$$f = .30\,(W \cos 25° - T \sin 10°).$$

Substituting into equation (2),

$$T \cos 10° + T - W \sin 25° - .30\,(W \cos 25° - T \sin 10°) = ma_x$$

with

$$W = (150 \text{ kg})(9.8 \text{ m/s}^2) = 1{,}470 \text{ N}$$

$$a_x = 4 \text{ m/s}^2$$

$$m = 150 \text{ kg}$$

$$T(1 + \cos 10°) - 1{,}470 \text{ N} \sin 25° - .30\,(1{,}470 \text{ N} \cos 25°$$

$$- T \sin 10°) = (150 \text{ kg})(4 \text{ m/s}^2)$$

$$T(1.866) - 621.2 \text{ N} - 400 \text{ N} + .052\,T = 600 \text{ N}$$

$$192\,T = 1{,}621.2 \text{ N}$$

$$T = 844.4 \text{ N}$$

74. **(B)**   The equations for an ideal transformer are:

$$\frac{V_2}{V_1} = \frac{N_2}{N_1}$$

$$\frac{V_2}{V_1} = \frac{I_2}{I_1}$$

$$\frac{V_2}{V_1} = sqrt\left(\frac{Z_2}{Z_1}\right)$$

Therefore, since the voltage ratio is equal to the turns ratio, N_2/N_1, choice (B) is correct. Choice (A) is incorrect since an ideal transformer is assumed to have no losses, and a loss ratio does not exist. Choice (C) is incorrect since the voltage ratio is the inverse of the current ratio. Choice (D) is incorrect since the voltage ratio is equal to the square root of the impedance ratio.

75. **(A)**   The pulse shown is comprised of two delayed unit steps. Therefore, the following expression can be written to describe the pulse:

$$\text{pulse} = u(t - T_3) - u(t - T_4)$$

The Laplace transform of the pulse is then

$$L(\text{pulse}) = L\big\{u(t - T_3)\big\} - L\big\{u(t - T_4)\big\}$$

and

$$Lu(t - T) = \frac{\varepsilon^{-sT}}{s}$$

Therefore, $L(\text{pulse}) = \dfrac{\varepsilon^{-sT_3}}{s} - \dfrac{\varepsilon^{-sT_4}}{s}$ which is choice (A).

76. **(C)**   Six ropes are connecting the lower pulley to the upper pulley; therefore, the force in the rope is

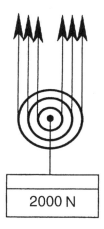

$$\text{Tension} = \frac{2,000}{6} = 333 \text{ N}$$

77. **(A)**   A reactive couple results at reactions A and B from the applied couple of $600 \text{ N} \times 8\text{m}$.

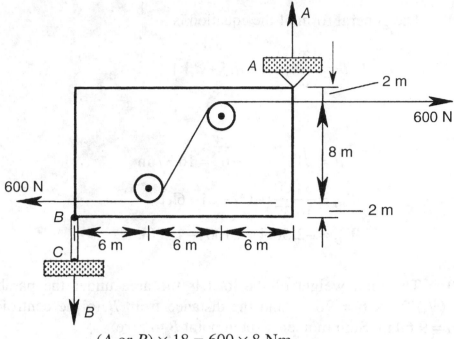

$$(A \text{ or } B) \times 18 = 600 \times 8 \text{ Nm}$$

$$A = B = 600 \times \frac{8}{18} = 267 \text{ N}$$

A second approach would be to sum moments about point A.

$$\Sigma M_a = 0$$

$$600 \times 8 - 18 \times B = 0$$

$$B = 600 \times \frac{8}{18} = 267 \text{ N}$$

78. **(C)**   The moment about the line AB results in a vector triple scalar product.

$$\lambda_{AB} = \frac{-20\mathbf{i} + 15\mathbf{k}}{25}$$

$$M_{AB} = \lambda_{AB} \cdot \mathbf{r} \times \mathbf{P}$$

$$M_{AB} = \begin{vmatrix} -0.8 & 0 & 0.6 \\ 0 & 20 & 0 \\ 2 & -40 & -50 \end{vmatrix} = 0.8 \times 20 \times 50 - 0.6 \times 20 \times 2$$

$$M_{AB} = 776 \text{ Nm}$$

79. (D)   The general form of the equation is

$$T = \frac{|\mathbf{T}|}{d}\left(d_x\mathbf{i} + d_y\mathbf{j} + d_z\mathbf{k}\right)$$

where

$$d = \sqrt{14^2 + 6^2 + 6^2} = 16.37 \text{ m}$$

$$\mathbf{T}_{BD} = \frac{3,000}{16.37}\left(-14\mathbf{i} + 6\mathbf{j} - 6\mathbf{k}\right)$$

$$\mathbf{T}_{BD} = -2,566\mathbf{i} + 1,100\mathbf{j} - 1,100\mathbf{k} \text{ N}$$

80. (C)   The total weight of the load is the area under the parabola $^2/_3bh = (^2/_3)\,24 \times 6 = 96$ N, and the distance from B to the centroid is $0.4 \times 24 = 9.60$ m. Sum moments about point B to give

$$\Sigma M_B = 0$$

$$24 \times R_A - 96 \times 9.6 = 0$$

$$R_A = 9.6 \times \frac{96}{24} = 38.4 \text{ N (See figure below)}$$

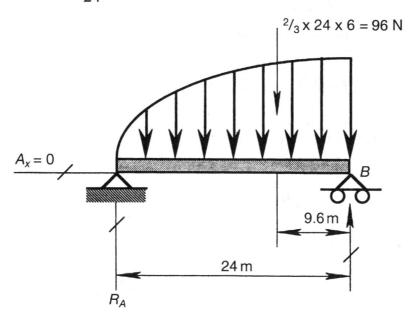

81. (D)   There are two general methods of solution for trusses. The method of joints can be used to solve for two member unknowns at each joint in sequence until all members' forces are found or the desired member force is found. The method of sections is used to find the force of a single member unknown.

Method of Sections:

Draw the free-body diagram and sum forces $F_x = 0$

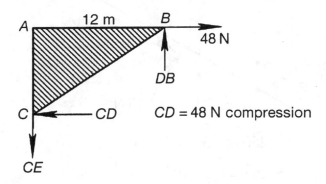

$CD = 48$ N compression

Method of Joints:

Make a larger drawing of the truss. Sum forces at each joint in sequence starting at a joint with only two unknown members. For this truss only joints *A*, *B*, and *C* have been considered. Draw a circle around the joint and sum forces within the circle in the *x*- and *y*-direction. Use the slope relationship to help find the horizontal or vertical components.

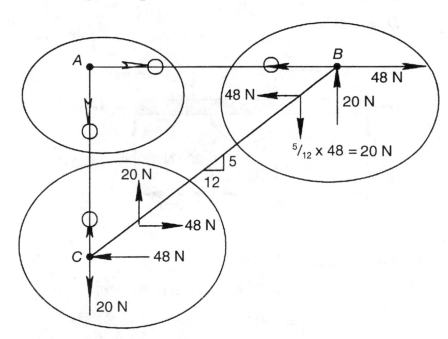

82. **(D)**   By observation $\bar{x} = 2.5$ m and $\bar{y} = 4.0$ m.

83. **(C)**   Static friction governs since the weight is not moving. Draw the free-body diagram and sum forces along the surface.

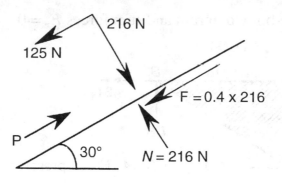

$$N = 250 \cos 30° = 216 \text{ N}$$

$$\text{Friction} = 0.4 \times N$$

$$\Sigma F = 0 : P - 125 - 0.4 \times 216 = 0$$

$$P = 212 \text{ N}$$

84. **(A)**   This problem must be worked in stages using at least two free-body diagrams. First, working with *BD*, find D_y.

$$\Sigma M_B = 0 : 200 \times 12 - 200 \times 2 - 20D_y = 0$$

$$D_y = 100 \text{ N}$$

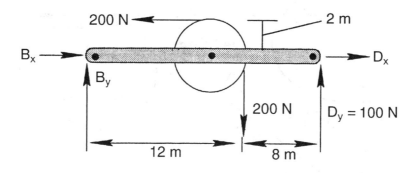

Next, working with *ADF*, find F_y.

$$\Sigma F_y = 0 : F_y - 100 = 0$$

$$F_y = 100 \text{ N}$$

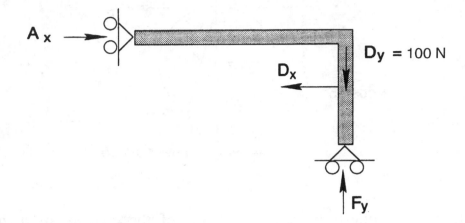

85. **(C)**   Two procedures may be used. The forces of a three force system must either intersect at a point or be parallel. For this problem, the weight, tensile force, and the reaction intersect at the top of the cylindrical weight. The tensile force can be found by drawing the three force polygon as shown.

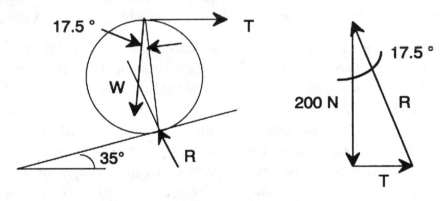

A second procedure is to sum moments about the point of contact with the inclined surface.

$$\Sigma M = 0$$

$$T \cdot r(1 + \cos 35°) - 200\, r \sin 35° = 0$$

$$T = 63 \text{ N}$$

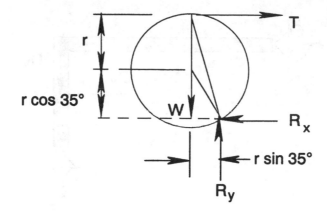

86. **(C)** This question tests knowledge of the concept of a gram mole—the key to understanding the gas law, Avogadro's Law, equivalent weight, and many other concepts.

The correct answer is (C). The number of molecules in a gram mole (the mass equal to the molecular weight in grams) of a compound is the same for all compounds. That number (6.023×10^{23}) is called Avogadro's Number in honor of the Italian Renaissance physicist, Amedeo Avogadro.

Choice (A) is incorrect because the number of molecules in a gram depends on the mass (or molecular weight) of the molecule, and it is different for each species. Choice (B) is incorrect. The volume of 1 mole (which contains 6.023×10^{23} molecules) of any gas at standard conditions is 22.4 liters. One liter of a gas at standard conditions will contain only $(6.023 \times 10^{23})/22.4$ molecules. Choice (D) is incorrect. Avogadro's Number of valence electrons exists in one gram equivalent weight of a species. The equivalent weight and molecular weight are equal only when the valence is ±1.

87. **(A)** This question tests knowledge of equilibrium calculations and ionization. The calculation is essentially identical to that used in calculating other kinds of equilibria (e.g., solubility equilibria, chemical equilibria, etc.). {An alternative question might be to determine the pH of the solution [pH = $- \log_{10}(C_{H+})$].}

The correct answer is (A).

If the acetate radical $(C_2H_3O_2)^{-1}$ is abbreviated as Ac-, then the ionization of acetic acid can be expressed by the following chemical equation:

$$HAc \leftrightarrow H^+ + Ac-$$

The ionization equilibrium constant is defined as

$$K = \frac{\left[a_{H^+}\right]\left[a_{Ac^-}\right]}{\left[a_{HAc}\right]}$$

where (a_i) represents the chemical activity of species i. In dilute solutions, the activity is equal to the concentration. For each mole of H+ formed, one mole of Ac^- is also formed and one mole of acetic acid is consumed. The concentrations of H^+ and Ac^- are, therefore, equal (let that concentration = x), and the concentration of HAc, diminished by the amount of H^+ or Ac^- formed, is $(0.1 - x)$.

$$K = \frac{x^2}{(0.1 - x)}$$

If $x << 0.1$, the equation becomes $0.1\ K = x^2$ or $x = 1.32 \times 10^{-3}$. [Answer (A)]

(Note that the assumption that $x << 0.1$ is justified.)

Choice (B) is obtained if the effect of the initial concentration of HAc is neglected. Choice (C) is obtained if both the error leading to choice (B) and the error leading to choice (D) are made. Choice (D) is obtained if the equation $x = 0.1\ K$ is used rather than $x^2 = 0.1\ K$.

88. **(B)** This equation tests knowledge of the structure of electronic energy states in matter and the quantum theory of matter and energy which predicts the frequency or wavelength associated with quanta of radiated energy.

$$E = h\nu = \frac{hc}{\lambda}$$

where E is the energy, h is Plank's constant, ν is the frequency of the radiation, c is the velocity of light, and λ is the wavelength.

$$E = E_2 - E_1 = (-3.4) - (-13.6) = 10.2\ eV$$

$$E = 10.2eV = \frac{\left(6.63 \times 10^{-34}\ Js\right)\left(3 \times 10^8\ m/s\right)}{\left(\lambda \times 1.602 \times 10^{-19}\ \frac{J}{e}\ V\right)}$$

$$\lambda = 1.2172 \times 10^{-7}\ m = 1{,}217\ \text{Å}$$

Therefore, the correct answer is (B).

Choices (A), (C), and (D) might be obtained by making one of a number of somewhat obvious errors. Choice (A) is three times the correct answer and may be obtained if the correct value of C is not used. Choice (C) is four times the correct answer. Choice (D) is obtained if the energy of the photon is mistakenly calculated as 17 eV (3.4 eV + 13.6 eV).

89. **(C)** This question tests knowledge of chemical formulas, valence, and the Periodic Table. It also tests knowledge of the chemical symbol for iodine.

The correct answer is (C). Beryllium has, as do all Group IIa elements, a valence of +2, meaning that it can donate two electrons in a reaction. The only negative valence of iodine (and all other Group VIIa elements) is −1, meaning it can accept 1 electron in a reaction. Since the algebraic sum of the valences of all elements in a compound will be zero (i.e., the electrons donated by one element must be accepted by some other element), two iodine atoms are required to react with one beryllium atom.

Choice (A) is incorrect. It may be selected if the examinee confuses the numbers assigned to groups in the Periodic Table with the number of valence electrons of elements in the group. Choice (B) is incorrect because all Group IIa elements, including beryllium, donate two electrons in a reaction and a single iodine atom can accept only one. Choice (D) is incorrect. It, like choice (A), may be selected if the examinee confuses the numbers assigned to groups in the Periodic Table with the number of valence electrons of elements in the group.

90. **(D)** This question tests knowledge that sulfate, $(SO_4)^{-2}$, is the anion in sulfuric acid (the most common mineral acid), knowledge of the valence of the sulfate radical, $(SO_4)^{-2}$, and of potassium, the chemical symbol for potassium, and that any product of acid-based neutralization is called a salt.

The correct answer is (D). Two molecules of potassium hydroxide (KOH) are required to neutralize one molecule of sulfuric acid (H_2SO_4).

Choice (A) is incorrect. The chemical formula for common table salt is NaCl, but the product of any acid-base neutralization reaction is also called a salt. NaCl is the product of the neutralization of sodium hydroxide (NaOH) and hydrochloric acid (HCl). Choice (B) is incorrect because two atoms of potassium, which has a valence of +1, are required to react with one sulfate radical, which has a valence of −2. Choice (C) is incorrect for the same reason that choice (A) is incorrect.

91. **(D)**   This question tests knowledge of amphoteric hydroxides which can provide either an H^+ ion or an OH^- ion and react as either an acid or a base.

The correct answer is (D). Aluminum hydroxide, like many other metal hydroxides, can provide either an H^+ ion or an OH^- ion in reaction. The circumstances of the reaction determine whether it behaves as an acid or base.

Choice (A) is incorrect. Although an amphoteric hydroxide may contain three hydroxyl groups, that is not what makes it amphoteric. Choice (B) is incorrect. The solubility is immaterial in determining whether or not the material is amphoteric. Choice (C) is incorrect. The number of hydroxyl groups which ionize is immaterial in determining whether or not the material is amphoteric.

92. **(C)**   This question tests knowledge of the Periodic Table and the names of the groups in the Periodic Table.

The correct answer is (C). The alkaline earth metals are those in Group IIa.

Choice (A) is incorrect. Only the Group Ia elements do not have two "s" electrons in the outer orbit. Choice (B) is incorrect. Many other elements also exhibit a valence of +2. Choice (D) is incorrect. Most metal hydroxides form alkaline solutions in water.

93. **(D)**   This question tests knowledge of what makes water "hard" and the chemistry associated with hard water.

The correct answer is (D).

Choice (A) is incorrect. Solutes tend to lower, not raise, the freezing point. Although the high school (or perhaps junior high school) riddle, "How do you spell 'hard water' with three letters?" (ice) is still oft repeated, it is not ice crystals that make water hard. Choices (B) and (C) are both correct statements, hence the correct answer is (D).

94. **(A)**   This question tests knowledge of the class of reactions known as oxidation-reduction reactions. These reactions result in a change in the oxidation or valence states of at least two of the elements in the reaction. The total of the oxidations states of all elements must add to zero for each neutral species in the reaction.

The correct answer is (A). There is no change in the oxidation state of any of the elements in this reaction. It is simply the precipitation of copper sulfate from copper and sulfate ions.

Choice (B) is incorrect. Mn is reduced from a valence of +7 to +2. Oxygen (in H_2O_2) is oxidized from a valence of −1 to 0. Choice (C) is incorrect. Sulfur is oxidized from −2 to +4. Oxygen is reduced from a valence state of 0 to −2. Choice (D) is incorrect. Carbon is oxidized from a valence of −4 to +2. Hydrogen is reduced from a valence of +1 to 0.

95. **(D)**   This question tests knowledge of the Principle of Le Chatelier, which states that a system in equilibrium will shift to offset any imposed change or stress. Therefore, the system will tend to shift to offset changes in temperature, pressure, or concentration (of which pH is simply a special case).

The correct answer is, therefore, (D).

96. **(B)**   This question tests knowledge of heats of formation and how to calculate the heat of reaction from data on heats of formation.

The heat of formation of a species is defined as the heat of reaction to make the species from the elements. Since the elements are conserved in a chemical reaction, the First Law of Thermodynamics dictates that the heat of reaction is the sum of the heats of formation of the products minus the sum of the heats of formation of the reactants. Note that from the definition, the heat of formation of an element is zero.

For this case (at 298 K):

$$(\Delta H)_r = 3(\Delta H)_{fH_2} + (\Delta H)_{fCO} - (\Delta H)_{fCH_4} - (\Delta H)_{fH_2O}$$

Since $(\Delta H)_{fH_2}$ is zero by definition, $(\Delta H)_r = 49.281$ Kcal/mole.

Since $(\Delta H)_r > 0$, the reaction is endothermic. The correct answer is (B).

Choice (A) is incorrect. If $(\Delta H)_r$ were negative, the reaction would be exothermic. Choice (C) is incorrect. The pressure does not affect $(\Delta H)_r$ for ideal gases. Even at extreme pressures where departure from ideal behavior is significant, the effect is insufficient to change this reaction from being endothermic to exothermic. Choice (D) is incorrect. $(\Delta H)_f$ for the elements is zero by definition and is frequently not tabulated in tables.

97. **(A)**   **Step 1.** Cut the section at section ① – ① and draw a free-body diagram. There are two possible free-body diagrams, one on the left and

one on the right. If the left part is chosen, the reaction at *A* must be determined first. It is easier in this problem to use the right part as a free-body diagram. The free-body diagram is shown below with the unknown internal reaction at the section.

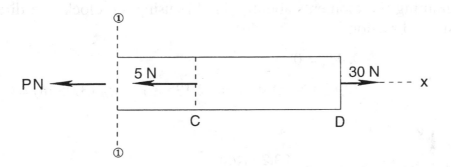

Step 2. To determine the unknown internal reaction *P*, a static equilibrium equation is used. To maintain the equilibrium in the horizontal direction (*x*-axis), the sum of forces along the *x*-axis must be zero. To be consistent among forces in the equation, forces pointing to the right are considered as positive forces.

$$\Sigma F_x = 0 \text{ (to the right is positive)}$$

$$-P - 5\,\text{N} + 30\,\text{N} = 0$$

$$\text{Therefore, } P = +\,25\,\text{N}$$

The positive value of the result indicates that the assumed direction of "*P*" is correct. Since the force "*P*" is acting away from the section (pulling the section), the internal reaction is in tension.

Step 3. Assuming that all forces act through the centroidal axis of the member, the axial stress is distributed uniformly across the cross section. The normal (axial) stress is then computed using the following equation:

$$\sigma = \frac{P}{A}$$

where σ =   normal stress (N/m^2)

P =   normal force (N)

A =   area (m^2)

Thus, $\sigma = \dfrac{(25\,\text{N})}{(0.1\,\text{m}^2)} = 250\,\text{N/m}^2$ (tension).

98. **(B)** **Step 1.** Support reactions are determined using equilibrium equations. To maintain the equilibrium, the sum of moments about any point must be zero, and the sum of forces in any direction must also be zero.

Summing the moments about point "A" using the clockwise direction as positive direction:

$$\Sigma M_A = 0$$

$$(29.2 \text{ kN/m})(4.27 \text{ m})(2.135 \text{ m}) - (R_B)(3.05 \text{ m}) = 0$$

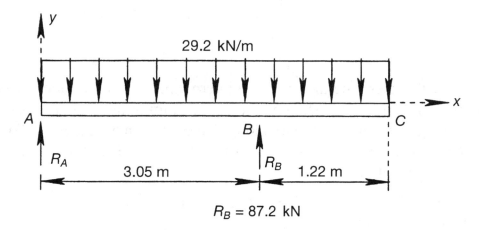

$$R_B = 87.2 \text{ kN}$$

Summing the forces in the vertical direction (y-axis) using upward direction as positive direction:

$$\Sigma F_y = 0$$

$$(R_A) + (87.2 \text{ kN}) - (29.2 \text{ kN/m})(4.27 \text{ m}) = 0$$

$$R_A = 37.5 \text{ kN}$$

Step 2. Sketch the shear and moment diagrams to determine critical sections for bending moment.

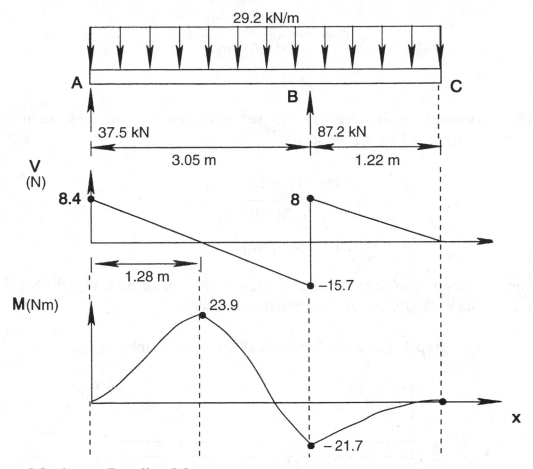

Maximum Bending Moments:

Positive Moment = 23.9 kNm

Negative Moment = 21.7 kNm

Step 3. Bending stresses can be computed using the following equation:

$$\sigma = \frac{My}{I}$$

where σ = bending stress (N/m²)

y = distance from the neutral axis (N.A.) to the point of interest (m)

I = moment of interia (I) with respect to the neutral axis (m⁴)

M = bending moment (Nm)

The maximum tensile stress at the maximum positive moment section occurs on the bottom fiber of the section.

$$\sigma = \frac{(23.9 \text{ kNm})(0.179 \text{ m})}{(1.31 \cdot 10^{-4} \text{ m}^4)}$$

$$= 3.26 \cdot 10^4 \text{ kN/m}^2$$

The maximum tensile stress at the maximum negative moment section occurs on the top fiber of the section.

$$\sigma = \frac{(21.7 \text{ kNm})(7.68 \cdot 10^{-2} \text{ m})}{(1.31 \cdot 10^{-4} \text{ m}^4)}$$

$$= 1.27 \cdot 10^4 \text{ kN/m}^2$$

The maximum tensile stress of the entire beam is then $3.26 \cdot 10^{-4}$ kN/m² and occurs at the maximum positive moment section.

99. **(C)**   **Step 1.** Draw the free-body diagram of member *ABC*.

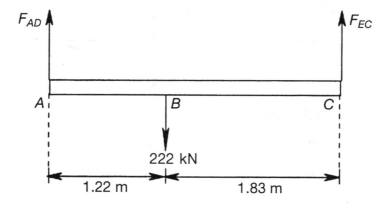

Step 2. Determine the force in member EC using an equilibrium equation.

Summing the moments about point "*A*" using the closewise direction as positive direction:

$$\Sigma M_A = 0$$

$$(220 \text{ kN})(1.22 \text{ m}) - (F_{EC} \text{ kN})(3.05 \text{ m}) = 0$$

$$F_{EC} = 88 \text{ kN}$$

Step 3. Calculate the elongation of member "*EC*" using the following equation:

$$\delta = \frac{PL}{AE}$$

where δ = elongation (m)

    P = force (kN)

    L = member length (m)

    A = cross-section area (m^2)

    E = modulus of elasticity (kN/m^2)

Thus,

$$\delta_{EC} = \frac{(88\text{ kN})(1.525\text{ m})}{(1.29 \bullet 10^{-4}\text{ m}^2)(2 \bullet 10^8\text{ kN/m}^2)}$$

$$= 5.2 \bullet 10^{-3}\text{ m}$$

100. **(C)** In the following solution, double-headed arrows are used to represent the twisting moments or torques. The direction of a double-headed arrow is determined using the right-hand rule, where the fingers represent the direction of the twisting moment and the thumb represents the direction of the double-headed arrow.

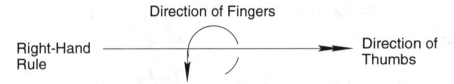

Direction of Fingers

Right-Hand Rule

Direction of Thumbs

Step 1. Draw the free-body diagram of the whole structure.

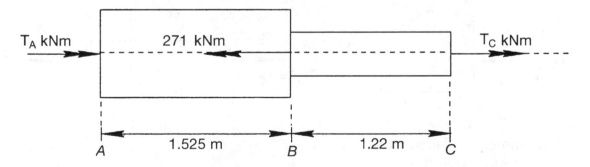

T_A kNm   271 kNm T_C kNm

1.525 m   1.22 m

A   B   C

Step 2. Write an equilibrium equation by summing the twisting moments using the double-headed arrow to the right as positive direction.

$$\Sigma T = 0$$

$$(T_A\text{ kNm}) + (T_C\text{ kNm}) - (271\text{ kNm}) = 0$$

which can be simplified to:

$$T_A + T_C = 271 \text{ kNm} \tag{1}$$

Step 3. Write a compatibility equation using the condition that the total angle of twist from A to C is zero.

$$\theta_{AC} = 0$$

$$\theta_{AB} + \theta_{BC} = 0$$

The angle of twist in a member can be determined from:

$$\theta = \frac{TL}{JG}$$

where

θ = angle of twist (radian)

T = twisting moment (kNm)

L = length (m)

G = shear modulus (kN/m²)

J = polar moment of inertia (m⁴) = $(\pi/2)\, r^4$ for circular section (r = radius)

Therefore,

$$\theta_{AB} + \theta_{BC} = 0 \Rightarrow \frac{T_{AB}L_{AB}}{J_{AB}G} + \frac{T_{BC}L_{BC}}{J_{AB}G} = 0$$

Free-body diagrams showing internal twisting moments of AB and BC are:

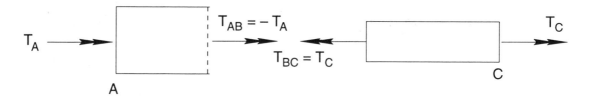

Polar moment of inertias are:

$$J_{AB} = \frac{\pi(0.076\,\text{m})^4}{2} = 5.24 \bullet 10^{-5}\,\text{m}^4$$

$$J_{BC} = \frac{\pi(0.051\,\text{m})^4}{2} = 1.06 \bullet 10^{-5}\,\text{m}^4$$

Therefore, the compatibility equation becomes (G was cancelled out from the equation):

$$\frac{(-T_A \text{ kNm})(1.525 \text{ m})}{(5.24 \cdot 10^{-5} \text{ m}^4)} + \frac{(T_C \text{ kNm})(1.22 \text{ m})}{(1.06 \cdot 10^{-5} \text{ m}^4)} = 0$$

which can be simplified to:

$$T_C = 0.25 \, T_A \tag{2}$$

Step 4. Solve the unknown (T_A) by substituting T_C from equation (2) into equation (1).

$$T_A + 0.25 \, T_A = 271 \text{ kNm}$$

$$T_A = 217 \text{ kNm}$$

101. **(B)** Problem 101 may be found by sketching Mohr's Circle or by using the principal stress equations.

Solution 1 (Mohr's Circle)

Step 1. Sketch the Mohr's Circle

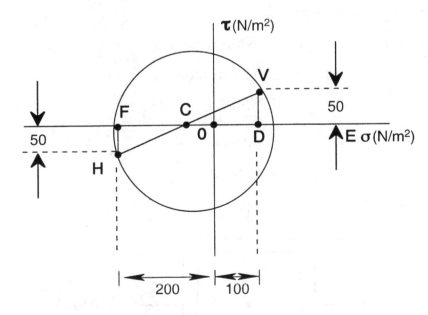

H = horizontal plane

V = vertical plane

τ = shear stress (clockwise is positive)

σ = normal stress (tension is positive)

C = center of the Mohr's Circle

Step 2. Calculation based on geometry.

$$CD = \frac{DF}{2} = \frac{(OD+OF)}{2} = \frac{\left(100 \text{ N/m}^2 + 200 \text{ N/m}^2\right)}{2} = 150 \text{ N/m}^2$$

Radius of the Mohr's Circle = R

$$R = CV = \sqrt{CD^2 + DV^2} = \sqrt{150^2 + 50^2} = 158 \text{ N/m}^2$$

$$CO = CD - OD = 150 \text{ N/m}^2 - 100 \text{ N/m}^2 = 50 \text{ N/m}^2$$

Maximum Tensile Stress = $OE = R - CO = 158 \text{ N/m}^2 - 50 \text{ N/m}^2 = 108 \text{ N/m}^2$

Solution 2 (Principal Stress Equations)

The maximum tensile stress or the positive principal stress may be found with the following equation:

$$\sigma_{1,2} = \frac{\sigma_x + \sigma_y}{2} \pm \sqrt{\left(\frac{\sigma_x - \sigma_y}{2}\right)^2 + \tau_{xy}^2}$$

From the problem statement

$$\sigma_x = 100 \text{ N/m}^2 \text{ (tension)}$$

$$\sigma_y = -200 \text{ N/m}^2 \text{ (compression)}$$

$$\tau_{xy} = 50 \text{ N/m}^2$$

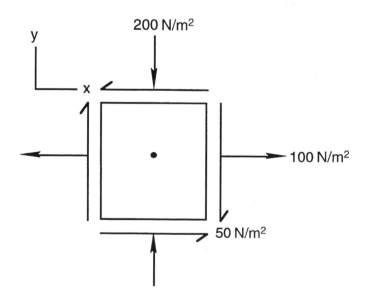

Substituting into the above equation

$$\sigma_{1,2} = \frac{100 - 200}{2} \pm \sqrt{\left(\frac{100 + 200}{2}\right)^2 + (50)^2}$$

$$\sigma_{1,2} = -50 \pm \sqrt{25,000}$$

$$\sigma_1 = -50 + 158 = 108 \text{ N/m}^2 \text{ (tension)}$$

$$\sigma_2 = -50 - 158 = -208 \text{ N/m}^2 \text{ (compression)}$$

Since we're looking for maximum *tensile* stress, we choose σ_1 or 108 N/m^2 as our answer.

102. **(B)** **Step 1.** The longitudinal stress in the cylindrical vessel can be computed from

$$\sigma_{\text{long.}} = \frac{pD}{4t}$$

where

p = pressure in the vessel (kN/m^2)

D = diameter of the vessel (m)

t = thickness of the vessel (m)

$\sigma_{\text{long.}}$ = longitudinal stress (kN/m^2)

Therefore,

$$\sigma_{\text{long.}} = \frac{\left(p \text{ kN/m}^2\right)(18 \text{ m})}{(4)(1 \text{ m})} \leq 20 \text{ kN/m}^2$$

$$p \leq 4.44 \text{ kN/m}^2$$

Step 2. The circumferential (tangential) stress can be computed from

$$\sigma_{\text{tang.}} = \frac{pD}{2t}$$

Therefore,

$$\sigma_{\text{long.}} = \frac{\left(p \text{ N/m}^2\right)(18 \text{ m})}{(2)(1 \text{ m})} \leq 8 \text{ kN/m}^2$$

$$p \leq 0.89 \text{ kN/m}^2$$

Step 3. From Step 1 and Step 2, the critical p is 0.89 kN/m². Therefore, the maximum pressure in the vessel is 0.89 kN/m² or 890 N/m².

103. **(C)** **Step 1**. Find the maximum force that a rivet can carry. The free-body diagram of a rivet is drawn. There are two shear planes, the rivet is therefore under the double-shear situation.

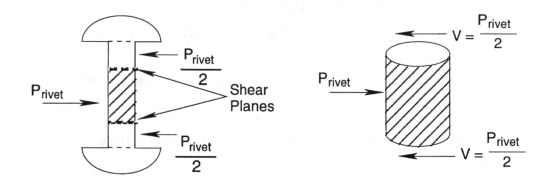

The area of the rivet is

$$A = \frac{\pi}{4}d^2 = \frac{\pi}{4}\left(\frac{3}{4}\ \text{m}\right)^2 = 0.44\ \text{m}^2$$

The shear stress can be computed from

$$\tau = \frac{V}{A}$$

where
τ = shear stress (N/m²)
V = shear force (N)
A = area (m²)

Therefore,

$$\tau = \frac{V}{A} = \frac{(P_{\text{rivet}}/2\ \text{N})}{(0.44\ \text{m}^2)} \leq 14\ \text{N/m}^2$$

$$P_{\text{rivet}} \leq 12.32\ \text{N}$$

Step 2. Since we have two rivets at the connection, the applied P is then the capacity of two rivets.

$$P = (2\ \text{rivets})\ (12.32\ \text{N/rivet}) = 24.64\ \text{N} \approx 25\ \text{N}$$

104. **(B)** **Step 1.** The centroid is at half-depth of the section due to symmetry. The moment of inertia about the neutral axis can be computed by

$$I \text{ n.a.} = I \text{ n.a.}_{ABCD} - 2\left[I \text{ n.a.}_{EFGH}\right]$$

$$= \frac{1}{12}(10 \text{ m})(12 \text{ m})^3 - 2\left[\frac{1}{12}(4 \text{ m})(8 \text{ m})^3\right]$$

$$= 1{,}099 \text{ m}^4$$

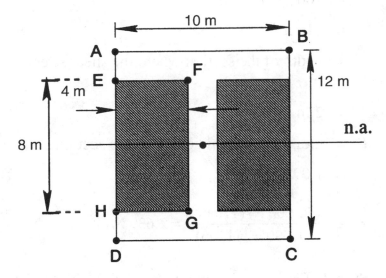

Step 2. The maximum stress for *I*-sections occurs at the neutral axis and can be computed from

$$\tau = \frac{VQ}{It}$$

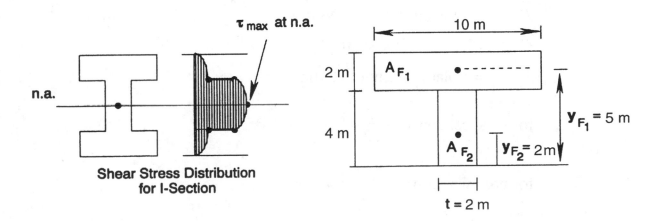

Shear Stress Distribution
for I-Section

where $\quad \tau \quad =$ shear stress (N/m^2)

$\quad V \quad =$ vertical shear force (N)

$\quad Q \quad =$ moment of area (m^3)

$\quad\quad\quad = \quad A_{F_1} y_{F_1} + A_{F_2} y_{F_2}$

$\quad\quad\quad = \quad (10 \times 2\ \text{m}^2)(5\ \text{m}) + (4 \times 2\ \text{m}^2)(2\ \text{m})$

$\quad\quad\quad = \quad 100\ \text{m}^3 + 16\ \text{m}^3$

$\quad\quad\quad = \quad 116\ \text{m}^3$

$\quad t \quad =$ width of the section where the shear stress is considered (m)

$\quad\quad\quad = \quad 2\ \text{m}$

$\quad I \quad =$ moment of inertia of the entire section about n.a.

$\quad\quad\quad = \quad 1{,}099\ \text{m}^4$

Thus, $\quad \tau \quad = \dfrac{(50{,}000\ \text{N})(116\ \text{m}^3)}{(1{,}099\ \text{m}^4)(2\ \text{m})} = 2{,}639\ \text{N/m}^2$

105. **(C)** **Step 1.** Find the maximum shear stress in *AB*. The maximum shear stress occurs on the outermost fiber of the shaft and can be computed from

$$\tau_{max} = \frac{T \cdot C}{J}$$

where $\quad \tau_{max} \quad =$ maximum shear stress (N/m^2)

$\quad T \quad\quad =$ twisting moment (Nm)

$\quad C \quad\quad =$ radius of the shaft (m)

$\quad J \quad\quad =$ polar moment of inertia (m^4)

for solid section $J = \dfrac{\pi}{32} d^4$

for hollow section $J = \dfrac{\pi}{32}\left(d_0^4 - d_i^4\right)$

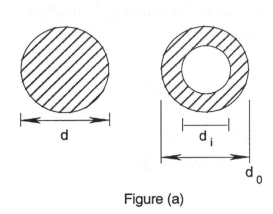

Figure (a)

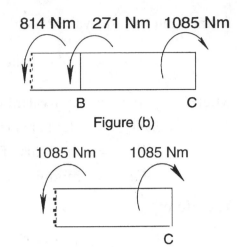

814 Nm 271 Nm 1085 Nm

B C

Figure (b)

1085 Nm 1085 Nm

C

Figure (c)

For *AB*, $T = 1085 \text{ Nm} - 271 \text{ Nm} = 814 \text{ Nm}$

$$J = \frac{\pi}{32}(0.051)^4 = 6.64 \cdot 10^{-7} \text{ m}^4$$

Thus,

$$\tau_{max} = \frac{(814 \text{ Nm}) \, (0.0254 \text{ m})}{(6.64 \cdot 10^{-7} \text{ m}^4)} = 3.11 \cdot 10^7 \text{ N/m}^2$$

Step 2. Find the maximum shear stress in *BC*. (See Figure (c).)

$$T = 1085 \text{ Nm}$$

$$J = \frac{\pi}{32}\left[(0.051 \text{ m})^4 - (0.0254 \text{ m})^4\right] = 6.23 \cdot 10^{-7} \text{ m}^4$$

Thus,

$$\tau_{max} = \frac{(1085 \text{ Nm}) \, (0.0254 \text{ m})}{(6.23 \cdot 10^{-7} \text{ m}^4)} = 4.42 \cdot 10^7 \text{ N/m}^2$$

Step 3. Compare the maximum stresses from Step 1 and Step 2. The maximum shear stress = $4.5 \cdot 10^7 \text{ N/m}^2$.

106. **(C)** **Step 1.** When there is more than one material, the transformed section method is normally utilized. In this method, the section is transformed into an equivalent section of only one material. All materials are transformed into one material. In this case, the steel area can be trans-

formed into an equivalent area of concrete using the following equations:

$$Acs = n\,As \quad \text{and} \quad n = \frac{Es}{Ec}$$

where Acs = equivalent concrete area for steel (m^2)

As = steel area (m^2)

Es = modulus of elasticity of steel (N/m^2)

Ec = modulus of elasticity of concrete (N/m^2)

Therefore,

$$n = \frac{\left(30 \times 10^6 \text{ N/m}^2\right)}{\left(3 \times 10^6 \text{ N/m}^2\right)} = 10$$

$$Acs = (10)\,(3 \text{ m}^2) = 30 \text{ m}^2$$

The transformed section becomes as shown in the following figure.

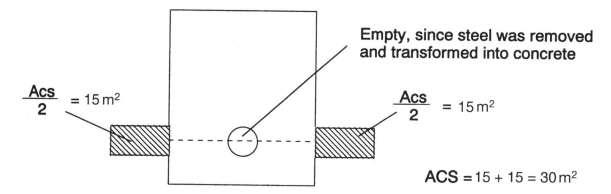

In reinforced concrete bending members, the concrete on the tension side is cracked at a very low stress (200–400 N/m^2), while the concrete in the compression side can withstand much higher (about 10 times of the tensile strength). The steel can even withstand higher stress (about 30,000 N/m^2 to 60,000 N/m^2). It is therefore very common to neglect the concrete in the tension side, since once cracked it cannot transfer the stress. The transformed section is then changed to the concrete on the compression side, and the steel which has been transformed to an equivalent concrete area. The section becomes:

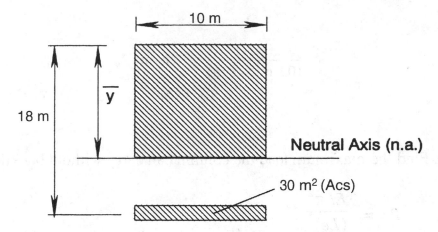

Step 2. Find the neutral axis of the transformed section after taking out the unusable concrete in the tension side. The neutral axis passes through the centroid of the section. The summation of the moments of the areas about the centroidal axis must be zero.

Thus,

$$(10\,\bar{y}\ \text{m}^2)\left(\frac{\bar{y}}{2}\ \text{m}\right) - (30\ \text{m}^2)\,(18 - \bar{y}\ \text{m}) = 0$$

$$\bar{y}^2 + 6\,\bar{y} - 108 = 0$$

$$\bar{y} = 7.82\ \text{m}\ \text{(Ignore the negative value of }\bar{y}.)$$

Step 3. Find the moment of inertia of the transformed section about the neutral axis.

$$I_{NA} = {}^1\!/_3\,(10\ \text{m})\,(7.82\ \text{m})^3 + (30\ \text{m}^2)\,(18\ \text{m} - 7.82\ \text{m})^2 = 4{,}703\ \text{m}^4$$

Step 4. Find the stress on the top of the beam (maximum compressive stress in concrete).

$$\sigma = \frac{Mc}{I} = \frac{(1{,}000{,}000\ \text{Nm})\,(7.82\ \text{m})}{\left(4{,}703\ \text{m}^4\right)} = 1{,}663\ \text{N/m}^2 \approx 1{,}660\ \text{N/m}^2.$$

107. **(C)** **Step 1.** Find the maximum load the column can carry without yielding.

$$\sigma = \frac{P}{A} \le \sigma_{yp}$$

where P = axial load, and A = cross-sectional area.

Thus,

$$\frac{(P \text{ N})}{(0.5 \text{ m} \times 1 \text{ m})} \le 30 \text{ N/m}^2$$

$$P \le 15 \text{ N}$$

Step 2. Find the maximum load the column can carry without buckling.

$$P = \frac{EI \pi^2}{(Le)^2}$$

where $\quad E$ = modulus of elasticity = $30 \cdot 10^3 \text{ N/m}^2$

I = moment of inertia = $I_y = \frac{1}{12}(1)(0.5)^3 = 0.0104 \text{ m}^4$

Le = effective length = 0.7 (length of column)

= 0.7 (24 m) = 16.8 m

Note: Effective length is dependent on column's end conditions, i.e., fixed, pinned, free, etc.

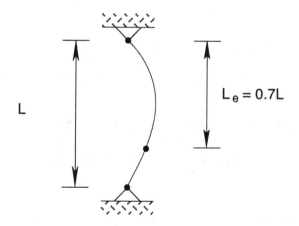

Thus,

$$P = \frac{\left(30 \times 10^3 \text{ N/m}^2\right)\left(0.0104 \text{ m}^4\right)\pi^2}{(16.8 \text{ m})^2} = 10.9 \text{ N}$$

Step 3. Compare P from Step 1 and Step 2.

$$P = 10.9 \text{ N} \approx 11 \text{ N}$$

108. **(C)** Given: Effective Interest / Future Worth / Equivalence Problem.

    (i) Two deposits of $1,000. One at zero time, P_0, and one at the end of one second month, P_2.

    (ii) Interest rate is 12% compounded monthly, i.e., interest rate per interest period of one month

$$= \frac{12\% \text{ nominal rate}}{12 \text{ interest periods}}$$

$$= 1\% \text{ per month}$$

Required to Find: Future amount (accrual) at the end of the third month.

Cash Flow Diagram:

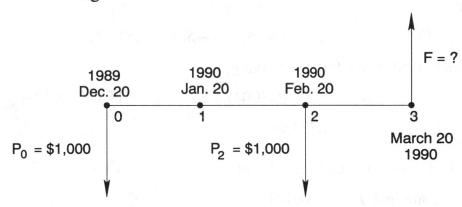

Equation:

$$F = \$P_0\,(F/P,\,1\%,\,3) + \$P_2(F/P,\,1\%,\,1)$$

Use tables to find above factors. Solving,

$$= \$1,000\,(1.030301) + \$1,000\,(1.01)$$

$$= \$2,040.30$$

109. **(A)** Given: Annual Cost Problem

    (i) Principal (initial cost), $P = \$75,000$

    (ii) Salvage value, S, after 8 years $= \$15,000$

    (iii) Operating and Maintenance costs, $A = \$10,000$ per year

    (iv) Interest rate $= 25\%$

Required to Find: Equivalent Uniform Annual Cost, EUAC

Cash Flow Diagram:

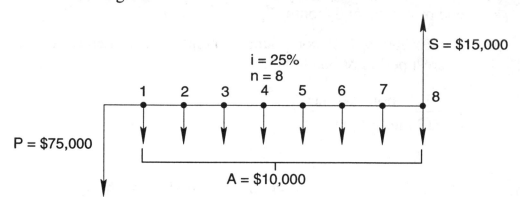

Equation:

$$EUAC = P(A/P, 25\%, 8) + A - S(A/F, 25\%, 8)$$

Use tables to find above factors. Solving,

$$= \$75,000 (0.3004) + \$10,000 - \$15,000 (.0504)$$

$$= \$31,773.91$$

110. **(D)** Given: Present Worth Problem

   (i)   Principal, $P = \$700,000$

   (ii) Salvage value, $S = \$180,000$

   (iii) Uniform Annual Benefit (UAB), $A = \$100,000$

   (iv) Interest rate = 8% per annum and $n = 10$ years

Required to Find: Net Present Worth, NPW

Cash Flow Diagram:

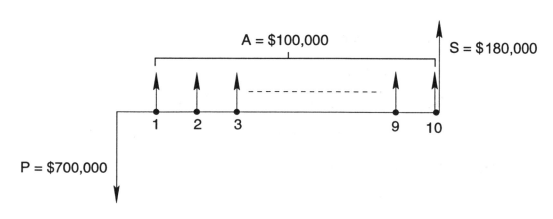

Equation:

$$NPW\,(8\%) \,=\, -P + A\,(P/A,\, 8\%,\, 10) + S(P/F,\, 8\%,\, 10)$$

Use tables to find the above factors. Solving,

$$= -\$700{,}000 + \$100{,}000\,(6.7101)$$

$$+ \$180{,}000\,(0.4632)$$

$$= -\$700{,}000 + \$671{,}010 + \$83{,}376$$

$$= +\$54{,}386$$

111. **(B)** Given: Depreciation Problem

    (i)   Principal, $P = \$50{,}000$

    (ii)   Salvage, $S = \$8{,}000$

    (iii) Useful life, $n = 14$ years

Required to Compute: The depreciation during the third year, using Sum of Years Digit (*SOYD*) method.

Solution: Sum of Years Digit,

$$SOYD = \frac{n}{2}(n+1)$$

$$= \frac{14}{2}(14+1) = 105$$

Now *SOYD* depreciation for k^{th} year

$$= \frac{\left(\begin{array}{c}\text{Remaining Life}\\[2pt]\text{beginning of } k^{\text{th}}\text{ year}\end{array}\right)}{(SOYD)}(P-S)$$

Substituting,

$$= \left(\frac{14-3+1}{105}\right)(\$50{,}000 - \$8{,}000)$$

$$= \$4{,}800$$

112. **(D)** Given: Capitalized cost / Payback period analysis technique questions.

Answer:

(i) (A) and (B) are statements of facts and need no further explanation.

(ii) (C) is false. The formula is valid only when: (a) There is a single first cost at time zero and (b) Annual Benefits = Net Annual Benefits after subtracting any annual costs. Hence, the true statements are (A) and (B).

113. **(B)** (A) is incorrect because it is the exact opposite of the answer. (B) is correct because for an intrinsic semiconductor the concentration of free electrons (n) must equal the concentration of free holes (p) to satisfy charge neutrality.

$$n = p = n_i\ \alpha e^{-E_G / 2kT}$$

As E_G increases, n_i decreases. (C) is incorrect because free carrier concentration has little to do with mobility. (D) is incorrect because it is not independent of the energy gap.

114. **(A)** No free electrons exist at 0 K temperature. They are located at their lowest energy levels — the valence band.

115. **(D)** (A) is wrong because resistance of a crystal will not impede the movement of a carrier, only free electrons. (B) is wrong for the same reason; conductivity is the opposite of resistance. (C) recombination rate will not affect the movement of a carrier in a crystal. (D) is correct because mobility is defined as the ease with which carriers can be made to move through the crystal. Consequently, it only depends on temperature and the regularity of the crystal structure.

116. **(C)** (A) A gradient is what the charges move through in this question. (B) Recombination can destroy charges. (C) is correct because this is simply the definition of diffusion. (D) Mobility is the movement through a crystal.

117. **(A)** (A) is correct because this is simply the definition of anisotropic. (B) Isotropic is just the opposite of anisotropic; the properties of the material are the same in all directions. (C) refers to geometric structure, not physical properties.

118. **(A)** (A) is correct because the purpose of a heat sink is to increase the flow of heat away from the source of heat. Thermal resistance can be likened to electrical resistance ($R = rl/A$). The thermal resistance can be reduced with a heat sink having a larger surface area to allow more rapid heat dissipation. (B) This will keep heat from radiating away from it, thus lowering its efficiency. (C) Lack of air currents will also make it less capable of taking heat away.

119. **(A)** For this to be correct the question would have to state that these materials continue to emit light for up to several seconds after the energy source has been removed; this is simply the definition of phosphorescent. (B) is correct if the light is emitted only for a few milliseconds after the energy source is removed; (C) and (D) only emit light when an energy source is connected to them, not after it is removed.

120. **(A)** This question tests knowledge of the crystalline structure of diamond and graphite—two very important crystalline forms of carbon. The correct answer (i.e., the statement that is not correct) is (A). The two crystalline forms of carbon are very different. Each of the other statements is correct. Choice (B) is correct. The tetrahedral structure of diamond permits little relative atomic motion. The hexagonal structure of graphite, on the other hand, permits slipping along the crystalline planes; hence, graphite is an excellent lubricant. Choice (C) is also correct. Diamonds are transparent to visible light with a large angle of internal refraction which causes gems to sparkle. Graphite, on the other hand, is opaque and has a characteristic gray color. Choice (D) is also correct. Diamond is an excellent high-temperature semiconductor because of the large band gap or Fermi level. Graphite is a conductor with the unusual property that the resistivity decreases with increasing temperatures.

FE/EIT

Fundamentals of Engineering: AM Exam

Practice Test 2

FUNDAMENTALS
OF ENGINEERING -
MORNING SESSION
Test 2

(Answer sheets appear in the back of this book.)

TIME: 4   Hours
          120   Questions

> **DIRECTIONS**: For each of the following questions and incomplete statements, choose the best answer from the four answer choices.

1. Find the area bounded by the parabola $y = 4 - x^2$ and the straight line $y = 2$.

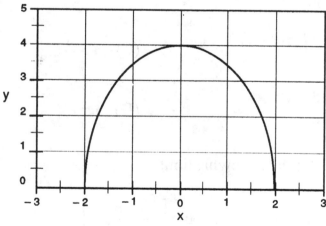

   (A) $\dfrac{7\sqrt{2}}{3}$ (C) $3\sqrt{2}$

   (B) $\dfrac{8\sqrt{2}}{3}$ (D) 4

2. Suppose the curve represented by $y = x^2$ from $(0, 0)$ to $(1, 1)$ is rotated about the x-axis. The total volume is then calculated as

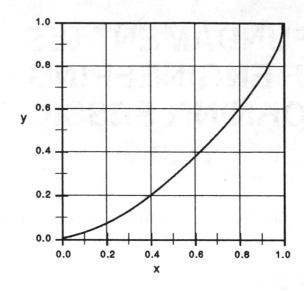

(A) $\dfrac{1}{3}$.

(C) $\dfrac{2}{3}$.

(B) $\dfrac{\pi}{3}$.

(D) $\dfrac{\pi}{5}$.

3.   Find $\int_0^x 3xe^{2x^2}\,dx$.

(A) $\dfrac{3}{4}\left(e^{2x^2}-1\right)$

(C) $3e^{2x^2}-1$

(B) $\dfrac{3}{4}e^{2x^2}$

(D) $3e^{2x}$

4.   Consider the following limit:

$$\lim_{x\to 0}\left[\frac{\pi \sin x}{\log(1+x)}\right]$$

Its value is equal to

(A) 1.

(C) $\dfrac{\pi}{e}$.

(B) $\dfrac{\pi}{\log 2}$.

(D) π.

5. A square sheet of metal 18 meters on a side is to be used to make an open-top box by cutting a small square from each corner as shown below, then bending up the sides. What should the value of y be so that the volume of the box is maximized?

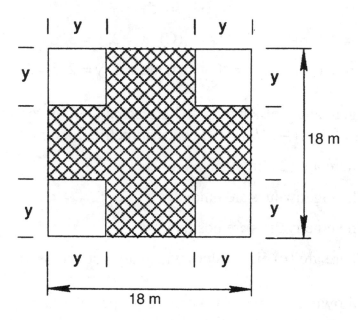

(A) 3 m   (C) 2 m

(B) 6 m   (D) 4 m

6. Find the slope of $y = x^{1.5} + \cos(\pi x)$ at $x = 0.25$.

(A) 1   (C) 0.71

(B) π (D) –0.5

7. Find d^2y / dx^2 if $x = 3 - 2z$ and $y = z^2 - 3z^3$.

(A) $0.5 + 9z$ (C) $0.5 - 4.5z$

(B) $1 - 9z$ (D) $-1 + \dfrac{3z^2}{2}$

8. The equation of a straight line passing through point (2, 3) and (3, 2) is given by

(A) $x + 2y = 7$.   (C) $x + y = 5$.

(B) $x - y = 3$.   (D) $2x + y = 7$.

9.   Solve the following set of linear algebraic equations for x, y, and z.

$$x - y = -1$$
$$x + y - 2z = -3$$
$$y + z = 5$$

(A) $x = 3, y = 4, z = 1$ (C) $x = 2, y = 3, z = 2$

(B) $x = -4, y = -3, z = 8$ (D) $x = 1, y = 2, z = 3$

10.   The eigenvalues of a matrix $[A]$ are calculated by forcing the determinant of $|[A] - \lambda[I]| = 0$. For a symmetric $n \times n$ matrix.

(A) There are $(2 \times n)$ eigenvalues.

(B) The eigenvalues are unique.

(C) The eigenvalues are positive.

(D) There are (n) eigenvalues which are not necessarily unique.

11.   The following matrix $[A]$ has a very special property in that it is equal to its own inverse. Find the determinant of the matrix $2[A]^{10}$.

$$[A] = \begin{bmatrix} 17 & -20 & 8 \\ 40 & -49 & 20 \\ 64 & -80 & 33 \end{bmatrix}$$

(A) 2   (C) 8

(B) -8 (D) -2

12.   Find the standard deviation of 9, 3, 6, 2, and 10.

(A) $5\sqrt{2}$ (C) -0.5

(B) $0.5\sqrt{2}$ (D) $\dfrac{\sqrt{50}}{2}$

13.   How many different groups of six passengers can fit into a four-passenger vehicle?

(A) 30   (C) 15

(B) 60   (D) 360

14. Consider ten throws of an ordinary coin. The probability for heads or tails is equal to 1/2. What is the probability that exactly five heads will turn up?

(A) 0.25

(C) 1.000

(B) 0.50

(D) 0.35

15. In the circuit below, what is the number of turns in transformer #2?

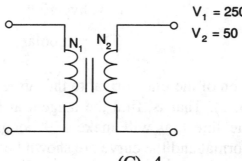

$V_1 = 250$
$V_2 = 50$

(A) 3

(C) 4

(B) 5

(D) 1

16. Solve the differential equation

$$\frac{d^2y}{dt^2} - 7\frac{dy}{dt} = 0, \; y(0) = 1, \text{ and } \frac{dy(0)}{dt} = 1$$

(A) $\dfrac{e^{3.5t}}{7} + \dfrac{6}{7}$

(C) $\dfrac{e^{-3.5t}}{7} + \dfrac{6}{7}$

(B) $\dfrac{e^{7t}}{7} + \dfrac{6}{7}$

(D) $\dfrac{e^{-7t}}{7} + \dfrac{6}{7}$

17. Given the differential equation

$$\frac{dy}{dx} - 5\frac{x}{e^y} = 0$$

with $y(1) = 0$, find $y\left(\sqrt{2}\right)$.

(A) $e^{2.5}\left(e^{2.5} - \sqrt{2}\right)$

(C) $e^5 + 2$

(B) $e^3 + 5$

(D) $e^5 - e^{2.5}$

18. Find the center of the circle given by the equation $x^2 + y^2 - 8x + 2y = 9$.

   (A) $(-4, 2)$ (C) $(4, -1)$

   (B) $(-4, -1)$ (D) $(8, -2)$

19. The equation $3x^2 + 6xy + 2y^2 - 4y = 10$ represents which conic section?

   (A) ellipse   (C) hyperbola

   (B) circle   (D) parabola

20. Find the equation of the line normal to the curve $y^2 - 4x + 2y - 3 = 0$ at the point $(3, 3)$. That is, find the tangent at $(3, 3)$, then find the equation of the line that will make a 90 degree angle with that tangent. The normal and the curve are shown below.

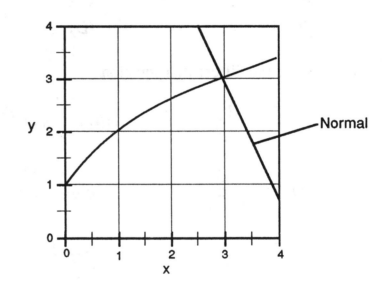

   (A) $y = 7 - 2x$

   (B) $y = 10 - 3x$

   (C) $y = 8 + 3x$

   (D) $y = 9 - 2x$

21. Given the DC circuit shown below, which of the following is true?

   (A) $V_1 = -V_2$

   (B) $V_1 = V_2$

   (C) $V_1 = 2 V_2$

   (D) $V_1 = \dfrac{V_2}{2}$

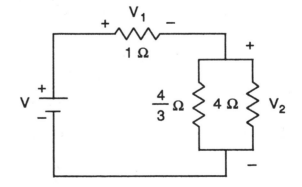

22. What should be the values of the capacitor C and the resistor R in order for the circuits (a) and (b) to be equivalent at the frequency of 15.9 MHz?

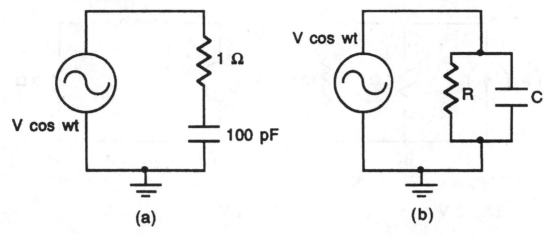

(a) (b)

(A) $R = 1\,\Omega$, $C = 100\,pF$

(B) $R = 10\,k\,\Omega$, $C = 100\,pF$

(C) $R = 10\,\Omega$, $C = 1\,pF$

(D) $R = 10\,k\,\Omega$, $C = 1\,pF$

23. An electromagnetic wave travels in medium 1 with frequency f, velocity v, and wavelength λ. If the same wave enters a new medium 2, which parameters remain unchanged?

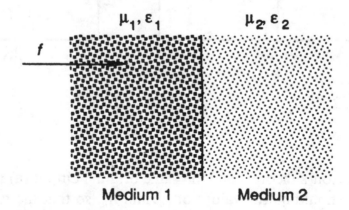

Medium 1   Medium 2

(A) Frequency f

(B) Velocity v

(C) Wavelength λ

(D) All parameters (f, v, and λ) will change.

24. Given the two circuits shown below, what should be the value of V_s so that they are equivalent?

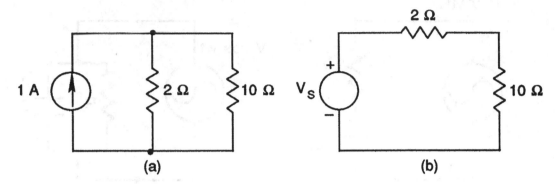

(a)   (b)

(A) 2 V   (C) 1 V

(B) 0.5 V   (D) 10 V

25. Using Thevenin's theorem, what should be the values of V_{th} and R_{th} so that the two circuits are equivalent?

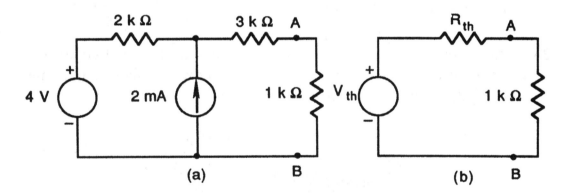

(a)   B   (b)   B

(A) 5 V, 2 KΩ   (C) 8 V, 5 KΩ

(B) 8 V, 3 KΩ   (D) 5 V, 1.2 KΩ

26. Using Norton's theorem and the same original circuit (a) in Problem 25, what should be the values of I_{nr} and R_{nr} so that the two circuits are equivalent?

(A) 4 mA, 5 KΩ

(B) 1.6 mA, 1.2 KΩ

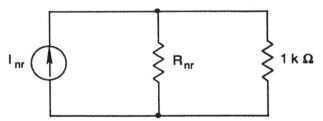

(C) 4 mA, 1.2 KΩ

(D) 1.6 mA, 5 KΩ

27. Given the passive circuit shown, which of the following relations is true?

(A) $V_1 = 2V_2$

(B) $V_1 = \dfrac{V_2}{2}$

(C) $V_1 = V_2$

(D) $V_1 = -V_2$

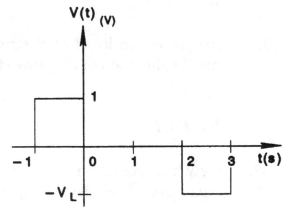

28. For the same circuit in Problem 27, which of the following relations is true?

(A) $I_1 = 2I_2$

(C) $I_1 = I_2$

(B) $I_1 = \dfrac{I_2}{2}$

(D) $I_1 = -I_2$

29. The current $i(t)$ is flowing through an inductor L. The voltage across this inductor is given by $v(t)$ as shown below. What is the value of L, knowing that

$$v(t) = L\frac{di}{dt}?$$

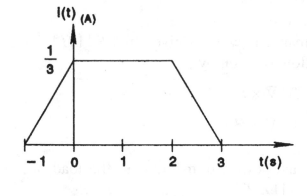

(A) $\dfrac{1}{3}$ H

(C) 3 H

(B) 2 H

(D) 0.667 H

30. Electric flux lines and equipotential surfaces intersect at right angles. This follows from

(A) $V = \nabla \times E$.

(C) $E = \nabla \times (\nabla V)$.

(B) $V = \nabla(\nabla \times E)$.

(D) $E = -\nabla V$.

31. The Hall voltage polarity, in a Hall effect experiment, can be used as an indicator of the polarity of the carrier of I in a semiconductor material. Thus, using a semiconductor slab we can find out if it is

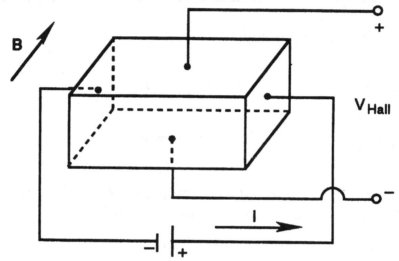

(A) P-type.

(C) P-type or N-type.

(B) N-type.

(D) insulator.

32. The power density of an electromagnetic wave is given by $|E||H|$, then the direction of the power flow is given by

(A) E.

(C) $\nabla \times E$.

(B) $E \times H$.

(D) $\nabla \times H$.

33. For which condition is the average power, transferred to the load, maximized, given the load $Z_L = Z_1 \,||\, Z_2$?

(A) $Z = \dfrac{Z_1 + Z_2}{2}$

(B) $Z^* = Z_1 + Z_2$

(C) $Z^* = Z_1 \,||\, Z_2$

(D) $Z \times Z^* = Z_1 \times Z_2$

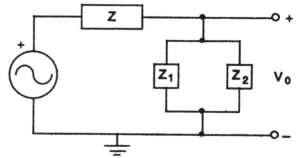

34. Considering the following waveform:

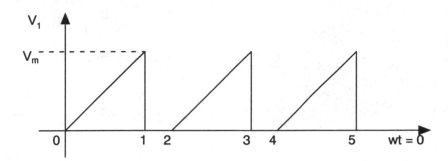

the waveform does not satisfy any of the symmetry conditions; therefore, the average value of the function will be

(A) V_m.

(C) $2V_m$.

(B) $\dfrac{V_m}{2}$.

(D) 0.

35. A round, flat disk is sliding on a thin film of oil at a velocity $V = 10$ m/s. The disk is 15 cm in diameter, and the viscosity of the oil is 0.1 N-s/m². (See figure below.) The drag force of the oil on the plate is

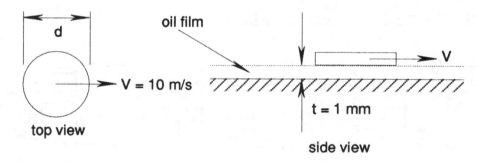

(A) 17.7 N.

(C) 118 N.

(B) 70.8 N.

(D) 0.118 N.

36. A reference frame which remains *fixed* while fluid flows through it is called

(A) Eulerian.

(C) Stokesian.

(B) Lagrangian.

(D) Bernoullian.

37. Consider a very large tank filled with water ($\rho = 1{,}000$ kg/m³) as shown on the next page.

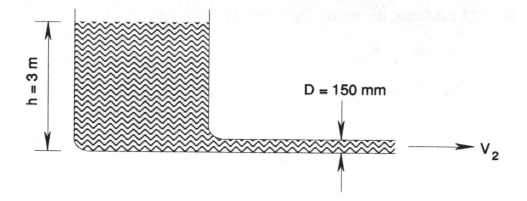

Neglecting friction, what is the steady-state velocity V_2 at the pipe exit, if we neglect the change of water height with time (the tank is extremely large)?

(A) 13.9 m/s

(B) Infinite, since no friction

(C) 2.31 m/s

(D) 7.67 m/s

QUESTIONS 38–39 refer to the following:

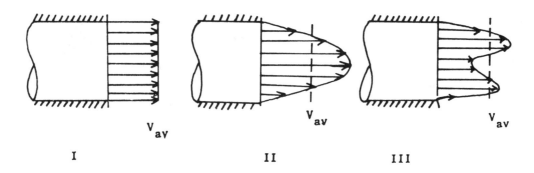

Consider the steady, incompressible flow of water exiting a round pipe. Shown above are three outlet velocity profiles. For all three cases, average velocity, V_{av}, is the same.

38.   The volume flow rates, Q_I, Q_{II}, and Q_{III}, are related as

(A) $Q_I = Q_{II} = Q_{III}$.

(C) $Q_I > Q_{II}$, $Q_{II} = Q_{III}$.

(B) $Q_I > Q_{II} > Q_{III}$.

(D) $Q_I < Q_{II} < Q_{III}$.

39. What can be said about momentum flux correction factor, β?

(A) Since V_{av} is the same in all three cases, momentum flux correction factor β is also the same for all three cases.

(B) Since only case III is non-symmetric, β_{III} is non-zero, but β_I and β_{II} are both zero.

(C) Only $\beta_I = 0$, while β_{II} and β_{III} are greater than zero.

(D) $\beta_I = 1.0$, but β_{II} and β_{III} are greater than 1.0.

QUESTIONS 40–41 refer to the diagram below, which represents steady, incompressible flow over a two-dimensional body; a boundary layer coordinate system is sketched on the upper surface:

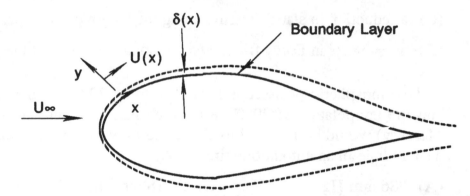

40. Which one of the following statements about the boundary layer approximation is correct?

(A) The rate of change of velocity in the x-direction is much larger than the rate of change of velocity in the y-direction.

(B) The boundary layer approximation is only valid for very low Reynolds numbers.

(C) Normal velocity, v, is much smaller than tangential velocity, U, in the boundary layer.

(D) Boundary layer thickness, δ, does not change in the x-direction unless the boundary layer goes turbulent.

41. If, over a section of the body, pressure, p, increases in the x-direction (i.e., $dp/dx > 0$) in the inviscid flow region outside of the boundary layer, which one of the following statements is correct?

(A) This condition is called a favorable pressure gradient.

(B) This condition can be either a favorable or an adverse pressure gradient, depending on the geometry of the body.

(C) The velocity $U(x)$ just outside of the boundary layer would be decreasing under these conditions.

(D) In order for dp/dx to be positive, the boundary layer must have separated off the body somewhere upstream.

42. For steady, incompressible fully-developed flow in a constant-area pipe, friction along the walls of the pipe causes

(A) a reduction in mass flow rate along the length of the pipe.

(B) a reduction in velocity along the length of the pipe.

(C) a reduction in static pressure along the length of the pipe.

(D) an *increase* in Darcy friction factor along the length of the pipe.

43. If the atmospheric pressure is measured to be 732 mm of mercury, and the temperature is 20°C, how much gage pressure (in mm of Mercury) would be required to choke the flow of air escaping from a small hole in an automobile tire?

(A) 386 mm Hg   (C) 2,118 mm Hg

(B) 1,386 mm Hg   (D) 654 mm Hg

44. In an ionic crystalline solid, the defect which occurs when vacant cation and anion sites are present is known as

(A) n-type.   (C) Frenckel.

(B) Schottky.   (D) Farbe.

45. When a member is subjected to two loads, such as axial and flexural loads, the problem is solved using all of the following EXCEPT:

(A) superposition for the combined stresses.

(B) Mohr's circle.

(C) assumption of failure of the material.

(D) principle of maximum stress.

46. $(\frac{1}{3}) \times 3$ yields a value of 0.99999999 on a computer which is capable of storing data to eight significant figures. Could this present problems in engineering computations?

(A) No, since three significant figures is the acceptable accuracy of most engineering calculations.

(B) No, since most modern computers are programmed to spot this kind of problem and would correctly return the value of 1.0000000.

(C) Yes, since most engineering calculations require at least eight significant figures.

(D) Yes, if the computer is being used to perform iterations, the errors will become cumulative and could become quite significant.

47. Cells A1...A5 of a spreadsheet contain the values of 1, 2, 3, 4, and 5, respectively, which represent the value of variable x. Cells B1...B5 are to contain the values of variable $y = x^2 - 1$. Which of the following would be the correct content for cell B3?

(A) $x^2 - 1$ (C) A1^2 – 1

(B) $y = x^2 - 1$ (D) A3 × A3 – 1

48. Engineer B submitted a proposal to a city council following an interview concerning a project. The proposal included technical information and data that the council requested as a basis for the selection. Smith, a staff member of the council, made Engineer B's proposal available to Engineer A. Engineer A used Engineer B's proposal, without Engineer B's consent, in developing another proposal, which was subsequently submitted to the council. Was it unethical for Engineer A to use Engineer B's proposal without Engineer B's consent in order for Engineer A to develop a proposal which Engineer A subsequently submitted to the council?

(A) No, since this was a public project, any work that Engineer B submits becomes part of the public record and as such is available to all.

(B) No, since the material was given to Engineer A by a third party, this relinquished any responsibility of A to B.

(C) Yes, since Engineer A should have asked permission or provided compensation to Engineer B.

(D) Yes, since a proposal must only contain work that you personally generated.

49. The vapor dome for water is shown below. Water initially at state point 1 undergoes a process to reach state point 2. All of the following are true EXCEPT:

(A) State 1 is a saturated liquid.

(B) The quality of the mixture decreases from state 1 to state 2.

(C) The temperature is constant.

(D) The pressure is constant from state 1 to state 2.

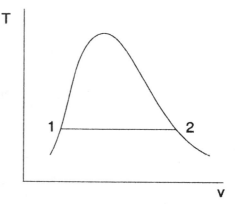

50. A closed system experiences a reversible process where heat rejection is the only energy transfer. The entropy change

(A) must be zero.

(B) must be positive.

(C) must be negative.

(D) cannot be negative due to Second Law requirements.

51. Consider an air-water vapor mixture similar to the atmosphere. If the dry-bulb temperature equals the dew point temperature, the relative humidity will be

(A) 0%.   (C) 75%.

(B) 25%.   (D) 100%.

52. For the reaction

$$CH_4 + (1.5)(2)(O_2 + 3.76N_2) \rightarrow CO_2 + 2H_2O + O_2 + 11.28N_2$$

more air has been supplied than is necessary for complete combustion. The percentage of theoretical air is most nearly

(A) 300%.   (C) 50%.

(B) 100%.   (D) 150%.

53. If the temperature of a medium is 0°C, what will the temperature be if it is doubled?

(A) 0°C   (C) 273°C

(B) 524 R   (D) 64°F

54. A compression ignition cycle is modeled by which ideal cycle?

(A) Otto cycle   (C) Rankine cycle

(B) Diesel cycle   (D) Brayton cycle

55. An ideal gas is contained in a rigid container. There is no work of a rotating shaft associated with the container. Any heat transfer is a function of

(A) pressure only.

(B) volume only.

(C) temperature only.

(D) There cannot be any heat transfer.

56. In a combustion chamber, fuel is burned to raise the temperature of the medium prior to production of work through an expansion process. The heat generated during the combustion reaction is the

(A) heat of vaporization.   (C) heat of reaction.

(B) heat of formation.   (D) heat of fusion.

57. There are many types of work associated with energy transfer across a boundary. One form of work is flow work, which is described by all of the following EXCEPT:

(A) it is the work which pushes mass into or out of a device.

(B) it is necessary to maintain a continuous flow.

(C) it is added to the internal energy to obtain enthalpy in the First Law for a control volume.

(D) it is associated with a closed system.

58. An open system First Law should be utilized for all the following EXCEPT:

   (A) a turbine.

   (B) a piston-cylinder device with no inlet/exhaust values.

   (C) a compressor.

   (D) a pump.

59. A piston-cylinder device provides 8 kJ of work to an external device. Two kg of air are contained inside the cylinder. If the internal energy of the air increases by 2 kJ/kg during the process, the heat transfer is

   (A) 12 kJ added.   (C) 4 kJ rejected.

   (B) 4 kJ added.   (D) 12 kJ rejected.

60. Engineer A is retained by the county to make recommendations concerning the location of a new landfill in the county. Two parcels of land located on a river have been identified by the county as the "candidates" for the sites. The first parcel is undeveloped and owned by an individual who plans to build a recreational home for his family. The second parcel, owned by Engineer A, is developed. Engineer A discloses that he is the owner of the second parcel of land and recommends that the county build the facility on the undeveloped parcel of land because (1) it is a better location for the facility from an engineering standpoint, and (2) it would be less costly for the county to acquire. The county did not object to having Engineer A perform the feasibility study. Was it ethical for Engineer A to perform a feasibility study and make recommendations concerning the location of a new facility in the county?

   (A) Yes, because he made full disclosure to the county of his situation and thus circumvented any potential conflict of interest.

   (B) Yes, because no conflict of interest was present.

   (C) No, since this is a clear case of conflict of interest and as such, Engineer A did not act in an ethical manner.

   (D) No, since the NCEES Board was not notified.

61. The flowchart for a computer program contains the following segment:

    $X = -1$

    $Y = -2$

    $Z = X \times Y$

    IF $Z < 0$ THEN $Z = Z + 1$

    RETURN

    What will be the value of Z returned by this program segment?

    (A) -1 (C) 2

    (B) 0   (D) 3

62. The binary number 110.011_2 is equivalent to what decimal value?

    (A) 6.375   (C) 6.875

    (B) 6.3   (D) 6.03

63. A stone is thrown from the top of a 200 m building with an initial velocity of 150 m/s at an angle of 30° with the horizontal line. Neglecting the air resistance, determine the maximum height above the ground reached by the stone.

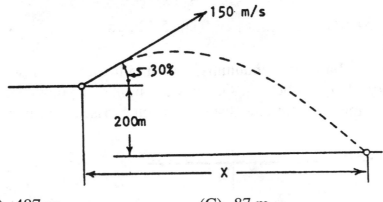

    (A) 487 m   (C) 87 m

    (B) 287 m   (D) 861 m

64. The outside curve on a highway forms an arc whose radius is 45.75 m. If the roadbed is 9.15 m wide and its outer edge is 1.22 m higher than the inner edge, for what speed is it ideally banked?

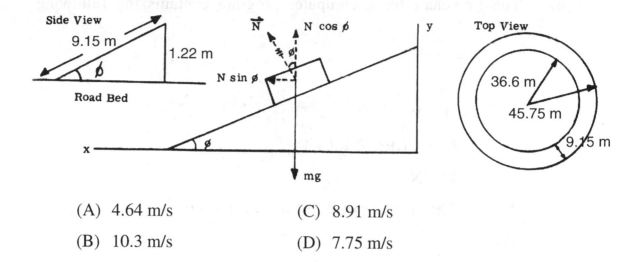

(A) 4.64 m/s   (C) 8.91 m/s

(B) 10.3 m/s   (D) 7.75 m/s

65.   A railway gun, initially at rest, whose mass is 70,000 kg fires a 500-kg artillery shell at an angle of 45° and with a muzzle velocity of 200 m/s. Calculate the recoil velocity of the gun.

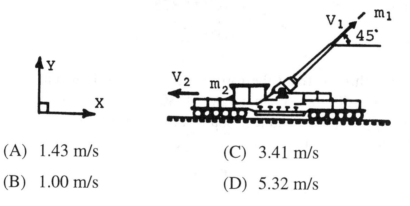

(A) 1.43 m/s   (C) 3.41 m/s

(B) 1.00 m/s   (D) 5.32 m/s

66.   Given the ballistic pendulum problem illustrated below, find the velocity of the bullet, v_1. Given are a bullet of known mass m_1, a block of mass m_2, and the distance the block rises after impact h.

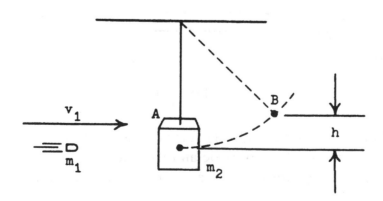

(A) $v_1 = \left[\dfrac{m_1}{m_1 + m_2}\right] 2\,gh$ (C) $v_1 = \left[\dfrac{m_1}{m_1 + m_2}\right]\sqrt{2\,gh}$

(B) $v_1 = \left[\dfrac{m_1 + m_2}{m_1}\right]\sqrt{2\,gh}$ (D) $v_1 = \left[\dfrac{m_1 + m_2}{m_1}\right] 2\,gh$

67. A horizontal rod $A'B'$ rotates freely about the vertical with a counter-clockwise angular velocity of 8 rad/sec. Two solid spheres of radius 0.127 m, weighing 1.36 kg each, are held in place at A and B by a cord which is suddenly cut. Knowing that the centroidal moment of inertia of the rod and pivot is $\mathbf{I}_r = 0.34$ Nms^2, determine the angular velocity of the rod after the spheres have moved to positions A' and B'.

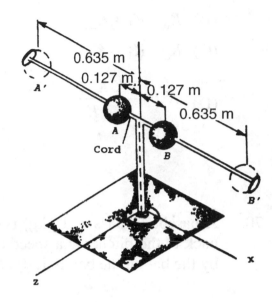

(A) 1.6 rad/s   (C) 2.47 rad/s

(B) 8.00 rad/s   (D) 2.21 rad/s

68. The system of A and B and two pulleys C and D is assembled as shown in the figure. Neglecting friction and the mass of the pulleys, and assuming that the whole system is initially at rest, determine the acceleration of block A.

(A) 9.81 m/s^2

(B) 3.92 m/s^2

(C) 392 m/s^2

(D) 784 m/s^2

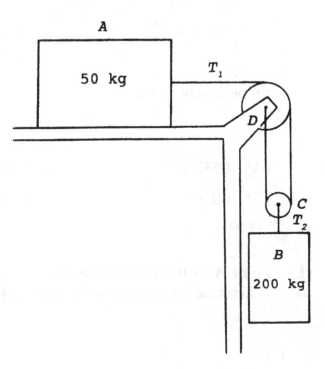

69. Two springs, S_1 and S_2, of negligible mass, with spring constants K_1 and K_2, respectively, are arranged to support a body A. In the diagram below, the springs are coupled in "parallel." Determine the equivalent spring constant, k_e, for parallel coupling of springs.

(A) $K_e = \dfrac{K_1 + K_2}{K_1 K_2}$

(B) $K_e = K_1 + K_2$

(C) $K_e = K_1 - K_2$

(D) $K_e = \dfrac{K_1 K_2}{K_1 + K_2}$

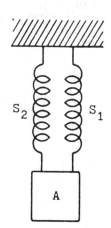

70. A baseball (mass = .16 kg) is moving 25 m/s when it is hit directly back to the pitcher at a speed of 45 m/s. If the average force exerted by the bat on the ball is 1,200 N, how long did the collision last?

immediately before:

bat   ball   ⟵———— 25 m/s

immediately after:

bat   ball   ————⟶ 45 m/s

(A) .0583 s   (C) .00933 s

(B) .00267 s   (D) .0167 s

71. Point A of the link shown below has an upward velocity of 3 m/s. Determine the angular velocity ω of AB when $\theta = 20°$.

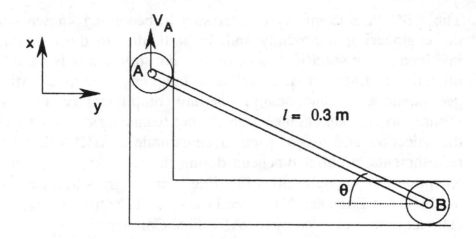

(A) 9.40 k rad/s

(C) −10.64 k rad/s

(B) 10.64 k rad/s

(D) −9.40 k rad/s

72. A particle of mass m is attached to the end of a string and moves in a circle of radius r_o with angular velocity ω_0, on a frictionless hortizontal table. The string passes through a frictionless hole in the table and, initially, the other end is fixed. If the string is pulled so that the radius of the circular orbit decreases to a radius, r, what is the final angular velocity, ω_f?

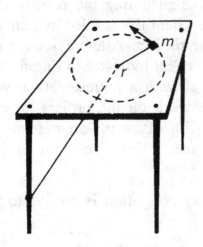

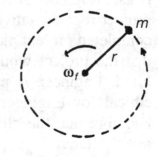

(A) $\omega_f = \dfrac{r_0}{r} \omega_0$

(C) $\omega_f = \left(\dfrac{r_0}{r}\right)^2 \omega_0$

(B) $\omega_f = \dfrac{r}{r_0} \omega_0$

(D) $\omega_f = \left(\dfrac{r}{r_0}\right)^2 \omega_0$

73. The ABC Pipe Company is interested in becoming known within the engineering community and, in particular, to those engineers involved in the specification of pipe in construction. ABC sends an invitation to Engineer A, as well as to other engineers in a particular geographic area, announcing a one-day complimentary educational seminar to educate engineers on current technological advances in the selection and use of pipe in construction. ABC will host all refreshments, a buffet luncheon during the seminar, and a cocktail reception immediately following. Engineer A agrees to attend. Was it ethical for Engineer A to attend the one-day complimentary educational seminar hosted by the ABC Pipe Company?

    (A) No, the acceptance of gifts in the context of any business operation is always unethical.

    (B) Yes, the level of gifts in this situation fall under the umbrella of acceptability.

    (C) Yes, but only if the Engineer pays for the food and refreshments.

    (D) No, because this could create a subsequent conflict of interest.

74. A client plans a project and hires Engineer A to furnish complete engineering services for the project. Because of the potentially dangerous nature of implementing the design during the construction phase, Engineer A recommends to the client that a full-time, on-site project representative be hired for the project. After reviewing the completed project plans and costs, the client indicates to Engineer A that the project would be too costly if such a representative were hired. Engineer A proceeds with his work on the project. Was it ethical for Engineer A to proceed with his work on the project knowing that the client would not agree to hire a full-time project representative.

    (A) Yes, since the Engineer's primary obligation is always to his client or employer.

    (B) Yes, since the requirement of the on-site representative was not the responsibility of the Engineer.

    (C) No, since the preservation of the public interest is the primary obligation of the Engineer.

    (D) Yes, since this was not a public project.

75. At this instant, car A is turning the circular curve at a speed of 25 m/s and is slowing down at a rate of 3 m/s². Car B is speeding up at a rate of 2 m/s². Determine the acceleration car B appears to have to an observer in car A.

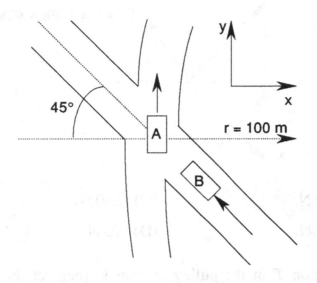

(A) $(-7.66\,\mathbf{i} + 4.41\,\mathbf{j})$ m/s²   (C) $(-1.41\,\mathbf{i} + 4.41\,\mathbf{j})$ m/s²

(B) $(4.84\,\mathbf{i} - 1.59\,\mathbf{j})$ m/s²   (D) $(7.66\,\mathbf{i} - 4.41\,\mathbf{j})$ m/s²

76. Micena, an engineer, is hired to confirm the structural integrity of an apartment building that Micena's client, Jones, is going to sell. Micena is to keep the report confidential. Micena determines that the building is structurally sound, but Jones confides to Micena that there are electrical code violations. While Micena is not an electrical engineer, he realizes that the problems could result in injury and informs Jones of this fact. In the report, Micena briefly mentions the conversation with Jones about these deficiencies, but does not report the violations to a third party. Was it ethical for Micena not to report the safety violations to the appropriate public authorities?

(A) Yes, since Micena's primary responsibility was to his client.

(B) Yes, since Micena was a structural and not an electrical engineer, he is only required to report violations in his field.

(C) Yes, since there was no conflict of interest in this situation.

(D) No, since the public interest is of paramount importance in the engineering code.

77. The magnitude of the resultant of the force system is

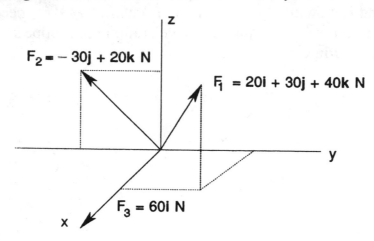

$F_2 = -30j + 20k$ N

$F_1 = 20i + 30j + 40k$ N

$F_3 = 60i$ N

(A) 140 N.   (C) 280 N.

(B) 100 N.   (D) 70 N.

78. The tension T in the pulley system is (neglect the friction of the pulley)

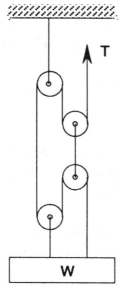

(A) $W/2$.   (C) $W/3$.

(B) $W/6$.   (D) $W/8$.

79. The tension in the cable *BC* is

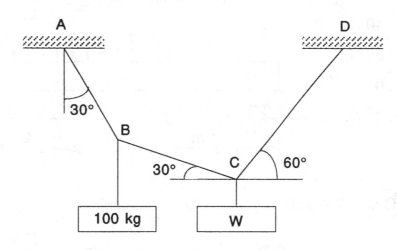

(A) 50 N. (C) 981 N.

(B) 100 N. (D) 490 N.

80. The vertical reaction at support *B* is

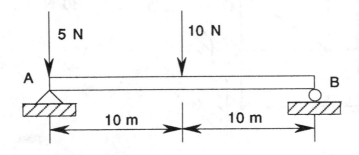

(A) 15 N. (C) 7.5 N.

(B) 10 N. (D) 5 N.

81. The maximum moment in the beam is

(A) 1,000 N-m.

(B) 500 N-m.

(C) 1,500 N-m.

(D) 200 N-m.

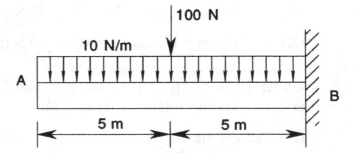

82. The vertical reaction at support *A* is

    (A) 40 N.

    (B) 80 N.

    (C) 0.

    (D) 20 N.

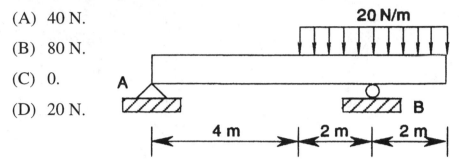

QUESTIONS 83-84 relate to the coplanar truss below.

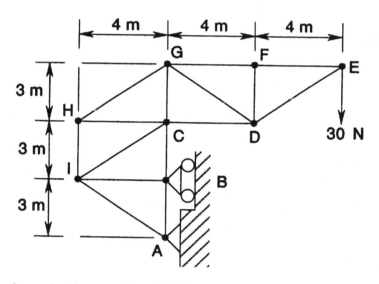

83. The force in the member *GD* is

    (A) 30 N (compression).   (C) 50 N (compression).

    (B) 40 N (tension).   (D) 50 N (tension).

84. The force in the member *DC* is

    (A) 30 N (compression).   (C) 30 N (tension).

    (B) 80 N (compression).   (D) 80 N (tension).

85. Under what circumstances would a conflict of interest between an engineer and his client be acceptable?

    (A) According to the NPSE code, a conflict of interest is never justified and the project should be terminated immediately.

(B) If the engineer makes a full disclosure to the client of the potential conflict of interest before continuing with the project

(C) If the conflict of interest is not discovered until after the project is started

(D) Only if approved by the local NPSE Board

86. The moment of inertia about the centroidal x-axis of the composite area is

(A) 4,275 m^4.

(B) 8,875 m^4.

(C) 1,440 m^4.

(D) 7,100 m^4.

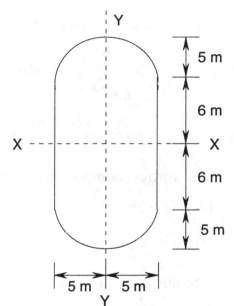

87. The force P which will result in impending motion down the slope is

(A) 736 N.

(B) 981 N.

(C) 638 N.

(D) 392 N.

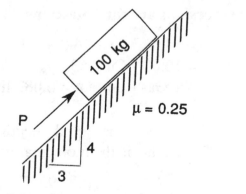

QUESTIONS 88-89 relate to the coplanar frame below.

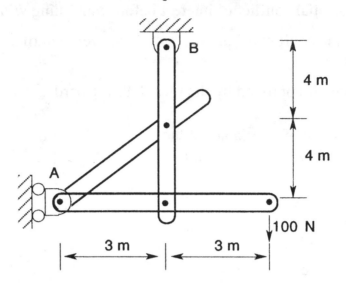

88. The vertical component of the reaction at support *B* is

    (A) 200 N.   (C) 150 N.

    (B) 50 N.   (D) 100 N.

89. The horizontal reaction at support *A* is

    (A) 75 N.   (C) 37.5 N.

    (B) 50 N.   (D) 100 N.

The following conversions are for Questions 90–92.

Atomic Weights: N = 14.0   Fe = 56.0
                      O = 16.0   Cu = 63.5
                      R, the Gas Constant = 0.082 lit. atm./deg. K mole

90. A 0.40 g sample of a volatile liquid occupies 107.0 ml at 1.00 atm. pressure and 27°C. What is the molecular weight of the liquid?

    (A) 137   (C) 92

    (B) 575   (D) 2,232

91. A 2.86 g sample of an alloy of gold (Au) and copper (Cu) upon reaction with excess nitric acid (HNO_3) formed 3.75 g of cupric nitrate, $Cu(NO_3)_2$. What is the percent of Au by mass in the alloy?

$$Cu + 4HNO_3 \rightarrow Cu(NO_3)_2 + 2H_2O + 2NO_2$$

(A) 4.44   (C) 44.4

(B) 55.6   (D) 95.56

92. Calculate the dipole moment of methylene dibromide (CH_2Br_2) assuming that the C–H bond is perfectly non-polar, the C–Br bond movement is 1.38 D, and the angle between two C–Br bonds is 112°.

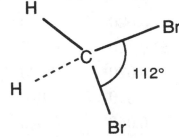

(A) 6.04 D

(B) 1.63 D

(C) 0.44 D

(D) 1.54 D

93. A 5.0 amp current is passed for 3 hours and 30 minutes through this electrolytic cell in which iron metal is deposited on the cathode. If the efficiency of the process is 68%, how many g of iron are deposited?

$$Fe^{+3} \xrightarrow{+3e} Fe^0$$

(A) 8.26 g   (C) 1.66 g

(B) 12.19 g   (D) 2.44 g

94. Trinitrotoluene (TNT) is a high explosive. The explosion of TNT can be represented by the equation:

$$2\,C_7H_5(NO_2)_{3(s)} \rightarrow 7C_{(s)} + 7CO_{(g)} + 3N_{2(g)} + 5H_2O_{(g)}$$

How much heat in Kcal will be generated by detonating 3.00 lbs of TNT?

Given: Heats of formation (H_f) of:

$$C_7H_5(NO_2)_{3(g)} = -87.1\ \text{Kcal/mole}$$

$$CO_{(g)} = -26.4\ \text{Kcal/mole}$$

$$H_2O_{(g)} = -57.8\ \text{Kcal/mole}$$

Note: Heat of formation of any element by itself is zero.

(A) −299.6   (C) −473.8

(B) −898.8   (D) +174.2

95. From the following data regarding decomposition of A to form B and C, which metal(s) act(s) as a catalyst(s)?

	Conc. of A	Conc. Metal X	Conc. Metal Y	Conc. Metal Z	Rate of Decomposition of A (moles/lit.sec)
Expt. #1	0.020	0.020	0.020	0.020	1.6×10^{-2}
Expt. #2	0.020	0.020	0.040	0.020	1.6×10^{-2}
Expt. #3	0.030	0.020	0.020	0.020	2.4×10^{-2}
Expt. #4	0.030	0.020	0.020	0.030	3.6×10^{-2}
Expt. #5	0.020	0.040	0.040	0.020	1.6×10^{-2}

(A) Metal X

(B) Metal Y

(C) Metal Z

(D) All three metals

96. A 0.5 mole of $CO_{(g)}$ and 1.0 mole of $H_2O_{(g)}$ were placed in a 5.0 lit. steel container at 127°C. When equilibrium was reached, 0.3 mole of CO_2 was formed.

$$CO_{(g)} + H_2O_{(g)} \rightarrow CO_{2(g)} + H_{2(g)}$$

What is the K_c for the reaction?

(A) 1.6

(B) 0.45

(C) 0.64

(D) 0.18

97. Ammonia is prepared by Haber's process:

$$N_{2(g)} + 3H_{2(g)} \rightarrow 2NH_{3(g)} \quad \Delta H = -5.3 \text{ kJ}$$

In order to maximize the yield of ammonia, one can

(A) increase concentrations of hydrogen and ammonia, and decrease the temperature.

(B) increase concentrations of hydrogen and nitrogen, and decrease the temperature.

(C) increase concentrations of hydrogen and nitrogen, and increase the temperature.

(D) increase concentrations of all three gases, and increase the temperature.

98. What is the actual e.m.f. (E_{actual}) of the cell

$$Cu^0 / Cu^{+2} // Ag^+ / Ag^0$$

at 25°C if $[Cu^{+2}] = 0.1$ M and $[Ag^+] = 0.1$ M? The standard reduction potentials of Cu and Ag are as follows:

$$Cu^{+2} + 2e \rightarrow Cu^0 + 0.34 \text{ volts}$$

$$Ag^+ + 1e \rightarrow Ag^+ + 0.80 \text{ volts}$$

(A) 0.53 volts   (C) 0.40 volts

(B) 0.46 volts   (D) 0.50 volts

99. A 222,400 N load is supported by two 0.0254 m diameter aluminum rods and a 0.051 m diameter steel rod as shown in the figure below. The length of all three rods is 0.254 m before the load is placed. The load is placed in such a fashion that the deformation of all three rods is the same. Young's Modulus for steel and aluminum is $E_S = 2.07 \cdot 10^{11}$ N/m² and $E_A = 6.89 \cdot 10^{10}$ N/m², respectively. The approximate load carried by the steel rod is

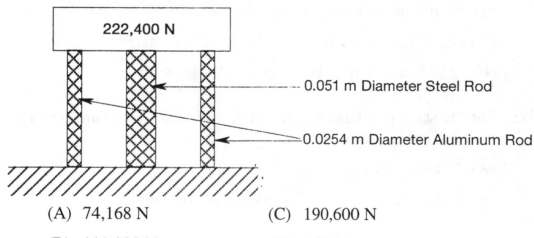

(A) 74,168 N   (C) 190,600 N

(B) 111,000 N   (D) 148,340 N

100. The beams shown in Figures (a) and (b) below have identical cross section and length. The beam in Figure (a) has hinge joint at A and roller support at B. The beam in Figure (b) has both ends A and B fixed. For both beams, the concentrated load P is applied at the center.

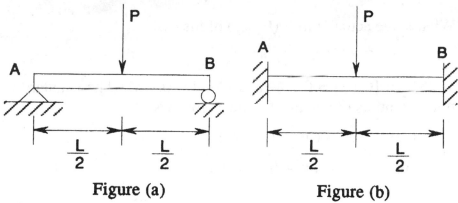

Figure (a)   **Figure (b)**

The load carrying capacity of the beam in Figure (b) compared to the beam in Figure (a) is

(A) 50% more.   (C) 200% more.

(B) 100% more.   (D) 100% less.

101. The gap between two 30 ft railroad tracks laid at 60°F is 0.1 in. On a hot day after the train has passed, the temperature of the rail rises to 140°F. The coefficient of expansion is $\alpha = 6.5 \times 10^{-6}$ in/in/°F and Young's Modulus is $E = 30 \cdot 10^6$ psi. If the rails do not bend or buckle, the approximate stress in English units is

(A) 7,266 psi compression   (C) 7,266 psi tension

(B) 8,337 psi compression   (D) 8,337 psi tension

102. For the same problem as stated in Problem 101, the actual strain in the 30 ft rail is approximately

(A) 0.000277 in/in.   (C) 0.003324 in/in.

(B) 0.000520 in/in.   (D) 0.002900 in/in.

103. For a 10 m long, simply supported beam, the shear diagram is shown. The maximum bending moment is approximately

(A) 152 Nm.

(B) 112 Nm.

(C) 102 Nm.

(D) 205 Nm.

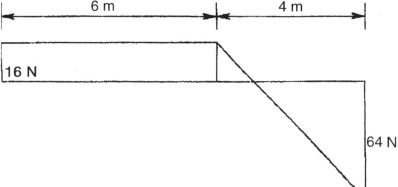

104. A 0.152 m diameter, 0.91 m long steel rod is subjected to an axial tensile force of 2.22 • 10^5 N. The modulus of elasticity of the material is $E = 2.07 • 10^{11}$ N/m^2 and Poisson ratio is $v = 0.3$. The actual change in volume of the steel rod is

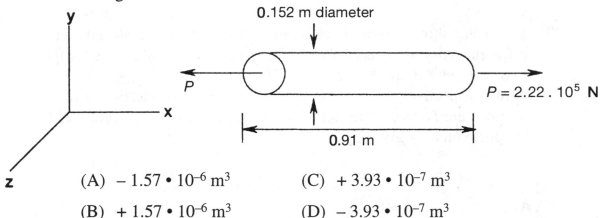

(A) $-1.57 • 10^{-6}$ m^3 (C) $+3.93 • 10^{-7}$ m^3

(B) $+1.57 • 10^{-6}$ m^3 (D) $-3.93 • 10^{-7}$ m^3

QUESTIONS 105–106 refer to the following diagram.

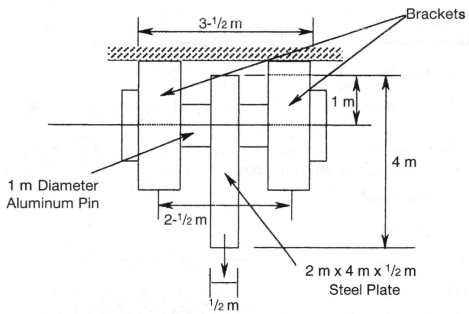

A steel plate of ½ m thickness and 2 m × 4 m dimension carries a load $P = 5,000$ N. The plate is attached to a pair of brackets by a round aluminum pin of 1 m diameter. The yield stress for tension and shear for steel are 80,000 N/m^2 and 50,000 N/m^2, respectively, and for aluminum they are 40,000 N/m^2 and 20,000 N/m^2, respectively.

105. The average shear stress in the aluminum pin is approximately

(A) 2,500 N/m^2 (C) 3,185 N/m^2

(B) 6,370 N/m^2 (D) 5,000 N/m^2

106. The maximum tensile stress in the steel plate is

    (A) 10,000 N/m²   (C) 15,000 N/m²

    (B) 5,000 N/m²   (D) 2,500 N/m²

107. The beam shown below is made up of two different materials with different cross sections at AB and BC. The Young's Modulus for the two sections AB and BC are $E_{AB} = 20 \bullet 10^6$ N/m² and $E_{BC} = 30 \bullet 10^6$ N/m², respectively. The cross-sectional moment of inertia for these sections are $I_{AB} = 0.67$ m⁴ and $I_{BC} = 0.083$ m⁴. Beam deflection at C is approximately given by

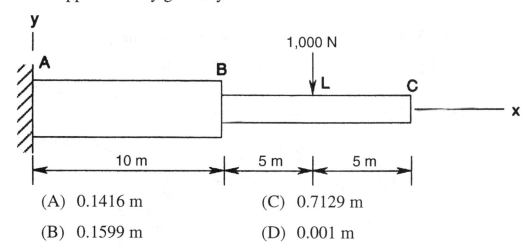

    (A) 0.1416 m   (C) 0.7129 m

    (B) 0.1599 m   (D) 0.001 m

108. The cross section of a beam subjected to a moment of $M = 10,000$ Nm is shown. The stress at point A is given by

    (A) 196 N/m²

    (B) 306 N/m²

    (C) 208 N/m²

    (D) 266 N/m²

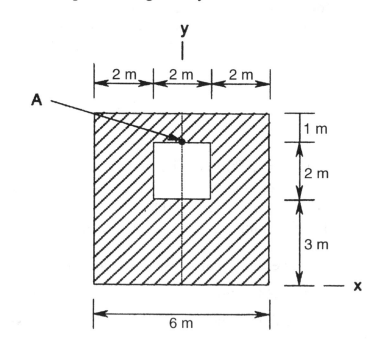

109. Given a nominal interest rate per year of 10% and two compounding subperiods per year, what is the effective rate per compounding subperiod?

   (A) 0.1%   (C) 2.5%

   (B) 20%   (D) 5%

110. During inflationary time, which one of the following statements describes best the loan payments of a fixed amount?

   (A) Future payments are worth more in year 0 dollars.

   (B) Future payments in year 0 dollars are not constant in amount.

   (C) In actual dollars, the amount of future payments decreases.

   (D) Year 0 dollars are worth less than future dollars.

111. A large profitable corporation has purchased a jet plane for use by its executives. The cost of the plane is $76 million. It has a useful life of five years. The estimated resale value at the end of five years is six million dollars. Using the sum-of-years-digit method of depreciation, what is the book value of the jet plane at the end of three years?

   (A) $14 million   (C) $34 million

   (B) $20 million   (D) $48 million

112. You purchased a lot for building your house four years ago for $20,000. Each year you paid $220 in property taxes. Each year you spent $80 in maintaining the lot, because the town requires that a lot be mowed periodically to keep grass and weeds less than 10" in height. Now you are selling the lot and will get $25,000 after deducting selling expense. What is the rate of return you receive on your investment? Assume that the interest is compounded annually.

   (A) 10%   (C) 4%

   (B) 8%   (D) 2%

113. Two different fork lift trucks are being considered for a warehouse. One of the two should be bought to realize savings in material handling operations. The cost and benefit estimates are as follows:

	Truck A	Truck B
Initial Cost	$15,900	$32,100
Uniform Annual Savings	$5,400	$6,300
Useful Lives in Years	5	6

Use a nominal annual interest rate of 10%. Neglecting taxes, what is the annual net benefit advantage of truck A over truck B?

(A) $135

(B) $1,070

(C) $4,973

(D) $6,043

114. The Miller indices of the plane shown in the accompanying figure are

(A) 112.

(B) 221.

(C) 111.

(D) 010.

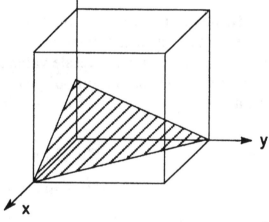

115. A polyester with an elastic modulus of 400,000 N/m² is reinforced by the addition of 20 percent (by volume) of glass fibers with a modulus of 10 million N/m². The elastic modulus of the composite when it is loaded parallel to the glass fibers is

(A) 10 million N/m²

(B) 5.26 million N/m²

(C) 2.32 million N/m²

(D) 8.08 million N/m²

116. Which of the following material properties is adversely affected by grain refinement?

(A) Tensile strength

(B) Creep resistance

(C) Elastic modulus

(D) Yield strength

117. Which of the following classes of materials exhibits a decreasing electrical conductivity with increasing temperature?

(A) Pure ionic materials
(C) Metals

(B) Intrinsic semiconductors
(D) p-type semiconductors

118. How many atoms are in a body centered cubic unit cell?

(A) 2
(C) 4

(B) 1
(D) 9

119. The property that characterizes a material's ability to be drawn into a wire is its

(A) tensile strength.
(C) thermal conductivity.

(B) fatigue endurance limit.
(D) ductility.

120. The flowchart for a computer program contains the following segment:

N = 7
S = 1; K = 0
FOR I = 3 TO N STEP 2
K = K + 1
S = S + 1/I * (− 1) ^ K
NEXT N

Which expression represents the resulting value of S?

(A) $1 - \dfrac{1}{3} + \dfrac{1}{5} - \dfrac{1}{7}$

(C) $1 + \dfrac{1}{3^2} + \dfrac{1}{5^2} + \dfrac{1}{7^2}$

(B) $1 + \dfrac{1}{3} + \dfrac{1}{5} + \dfrac{1}{7}$

(D) $1 - \dfrac{1}{3^2} + \dfrac{1}{5^2} - \dfrac{1}{7^2}$

TEST 2

ANSWER KEY

1.	(B)	16.	(B)	31.	(C)	46.	(D)
2.	(D)	17.	(D)	32.	(B)	47.	(D)
3.	(A)	18.	(C)	33.	(C)	48.	(C)
4.	(D)	19.	(C)	34.	(B)	49.	(B)
5.	(A)	20.	(D)	35.	(A)	50.	(C)
6.	(C)	21.	(B)	36.	(A)	51.	(D)
7.	(C)	22.	(B)	37.	(D)	52.	(D)
8.	(C)	23.	(A)	38.	(A)	53.	(C)
9.	(D)	24.	(A)	39.	(D)	54.	(B)
10.	(D)	25.	(C)	40.	(C)	55.	(C)
11.	(C)	26.	(D)	41.	(C)	56.	(C)
12.	(D)	27.	(C)	42.	(C)	57.	(D)
13.	(C)	28.	(B)	43.	(D)	58.	(B)
14.	(A)	29.	(C)	44.	(B)	59.	(A)
15.	(C)	30.	(D)	45.	(C)	60.	(C)

61.	(C)	76.	(D)	91.	(B)	106.	(A)
62.	(A)	77.	(B)	92.	(D)	107.	(B)
63.	(A)	78.	(C)	93.	(A)	108.	(C)
64.	(D)	79.	(C)	94.	(B)	109.	(D)
65.	(B)	80.	(D)	95.	(C)	110.	(B)
66.	(B)	81.	(A)	96.	(C)	111.	(B)
67.	(D)	82.	(C)	97.	(B)	112.	(C)
68.	(A)	83.	(D)	98.	(A)	113.	(D)
69.	(B)	84.	(B)	99.	(C)	114.	(A)
70.	(C)	85.	(B)	100.	(B)	115.	(C)
71.	(C)	86.	(D)	101.	(A)	116.	(B)
72.	(C)	87.	(C)	102.	(A)	117.	(C)
73.	(B)	88.	(D)	103.	(C)	118.	(A)
74.	(C)	89.	(C)	104.	(C)	119.	(D)
75.	(A)	90.	(C)	105.	(C)	120.	(A)

DETAILED EXPLANATIONS
OF ANSWERS

Test 2

1. **(B)** Find the points of intersection between the parabola and the horizontal line. This is accomplished by equating the two equations

$$4 - x^2 = 2$$

Solving for the unknown x-values gives the upper and lower limits of integration. Thus,

$$x = -\sqrt{2} \quad \text{and} \quad x = +\sqrt{2}$$

The shaded area is calculated by integrating the vertical strip from the lower to the upper limit. The width of the strip is dx and its height is $h = 4 - x^2 - 2 = 2 - x^2$.

$$\text{Area} = \int_{-\sqrt{2}}^{\sqrt{2}} h\,dx$$

$$= 2\int_0^{\sqrt{2}} h\,dx$$

$$= 2\int_0^{\sqrt{2}} (2 - x^2)\,dx$$

$$= 2\left[2x - \frac{x^3}{3} \Big|_0^{\sqrt{2}} \right]$$

$$= \frac{8\sqrt{2}}{3}$$

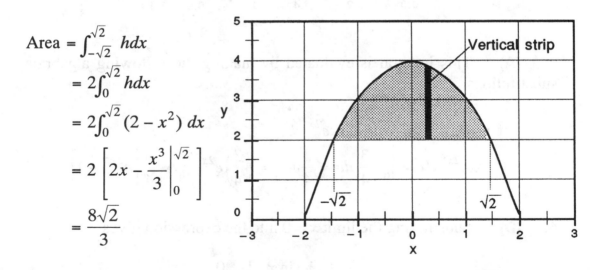

Note that because of symmetry of the shaded area, it is possible to evaluate $\frac{1}{2}$ the area, then multiply the results by 2.

2. **(D)** The volume is calculated by rotating the vertical strip with a radius equal to r as shown in the figure below about the x-axis. Note that the disc has a width of dx. The volume of a disk is given by

$$dv = \pi\, r^2\, dx = \pi\, y^2 dx = \pi[x^2]^2\, dx = \pi\, x^4\, dx$$

The total volume is then given by integrating from 0 to 1.0 as follows:

$$\text{Volume} = v = \int_0^1 \pi x^4 dx = \frac{\pi x^5}{5}\bigg|_0^1 = \frac{\pi}{5}$$

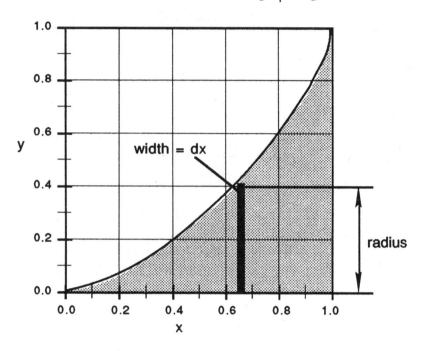

3. **(A)** This integral is evaluated by making the following algebraic substitutions:

$$\text{if } u = e^{2x^2} \quad\Rightarrow\quad du = 4xe^{2x^2}\, dx$$

$$\int_0^x 3xe^{2x^2}\, dx = \int_0^x \frac{3}{4}\, du = \frac{3}{4}\, u\bigg|_0^x = \left(\frac{3}{4}\right)e^{2x^2}\bigg|_0^x = \frac{3}{4}\left[e^{2x^2} - 1\right]$$

4. **(D)** Substituting the limit $x = 0$ into the expression gives

$$\lim_{x\to 0}\left[\frac{\pi \sin x}{\log(1 + x)}\right] = \frac{0}{0}$$

When $\%$ occurs, the limit may be defined using L'Hopital's rule. This rule stipulates that the limit may be found by differentiating the numerator and the denominator which gives

$$\frac{d}{dx}(\pi \sin x) = \pi \cos x \qquad \frac{d}{dx}(\log(1+x)) = \frac{1}{1+x}$$

$$\lim_{x \to 0}\left[\frac{\pi \sin x}{\log(1+x)}\right] = \lim_{x \to 0}\left[\frac{\pi \cos x}{\frac{1}{(1+x)}}\right] = \left[\frac{\pi \cos 0}{\frac{1}{(1+0)}}\right] = \frac{\pi}{1} = \pi$$

Note that $(\pi \sin x)$ and $\log(1+x)$ are differentiated separately.

5. **(A)**   Clearly, the volume of the box is computed as the product of the area $(18 - 2y)(18 - 2y)$ and the height y. That is

$$V = (18 - 2y)^2\, y = 324y - 72y^2 + 4y^3$$

The maximum and minimum of a function is determined by setting the first derivative equal to zero. Thus,

$$\frac{dV}{dy} = 324 - 144y + 12y^2 = 0 = 27 - 12y + y^2$$

$$(y - 9)(y - 3) = 0$$

which implies that $y = 9$ or 3. However, if $y = 9$, then the volume will be zero. Thus, $y = 3$ is the correct answer. Note that this fact can be verified using the second derivative as follows:

$$\frac{d^2V}{dy^2} = -144 + 24y \quad \Rightarrow \quad \frac{d^2V}{dy^2}\bigg|_9 = 72 \quad \frac{d^2V}{dy^2}\bigg|_3 = -72$$

Since the second derivative is positive for $y = 9$, it implies a minimum and since for $y = 3$ the second derivative is negative, it implies a maximum.

6. **(C)**   Applying basic rules of differentiation

$$\frac{dy}{dx} = 1.5x^{0.5} - \pi \sin x\pi$$

$$\frac{dy}{dx} = 1.5(0.25)^{0.5} - \pi \sin(0.25\pi)$$

$$\frac{dy}{dx} = 0.75 - \pi \sin \frac{\pi}{4}$$

$$\frac{dy}{dx} = 0.71$$

7. **(C)** The required derivatives are evaluated using the following notation:

$$\frac{dy}{dx} = y' = \frac{dy/dz}{dx/dz}$$

$$\frac{d^2y}{dx^2} = y'' = \frac{dy'}{dx} = \frac{dy'/dz}{dx/dz}$$

$$y' = \frac{dy/dz}{dx/dz} = \frac{2z - 9z^2}{-2} = -z + \frac{9}{2}z^2$$

$$y'' = \frac{dy'/dz}{dx/dz} = \frac{\frac{d}{dz}\left(-z + \frac{9}{2}z^2\right)}{-2} = \frac{-1 + 9z}{-2} = 0.5 - 4.5z$$

8. **(C)** The equation of a straight line is given as $y = a + mx$, where a is the intercept and m is the slope. Therefore, substituting the two points through which the straight line is supposed to pass into the equation gives two equations in two unknowns.

$$3 = a + 2m$$

$$2 = a + 3m$$

Solving for the unknowns using Cramer's rule gives

$$a = \frac{\begin{vmatrix} 3 & 2 \\ 2 & 3 \end{vmatrix}}{\begin{vmatrix} 1 & 2 \\ 1 & 3 \end{vmatrix}} = \frac{5}{1} = 5 \text{ and } m = \frac{\begin{vmatrix} 1 & 3 \\ 1 & 2 \end{vmatrix}}{1} = \frac{-1}{1} = -1$$

The equation of the line is then given by $y = 5 - x$ or $y + x = 5$.

9. **(D)** The set of linear algebraic equations can be solved easily using the Gauss elimination method. Using R to refer to a row, we have

$$\begin{bmatrix} 1 & -1 & 0 & : & -1 \\ 1 & 1 & -2 & : & -3 \\ 0 & 1 & 1 & : & 5 \end{bmatrix} \xrightarrow{-R_1 + R_2} \begin{bmatrix} 1 & -1 & 0 & : & -1 \\ 0 & 2 & -2 & : & -2 \\ 0 & 1 & 1 & : & 5 \end{bmatrix} \xrightarrow{R_2/2}$$

$$\begin{bmatrix} 1 & -1 & 0 & : & -1 \\ 0 & 1 & -1 & : & -1 \\ 0 & 1 & 1 & : & 5 \end{bmatrix} \xrightarrow{\ -R_2+R_3\ } \begin{bmatrix} 1 & -1 & 0 & : & -1 \\ 0 & 1 & -1 & : & -1 \\ 0 & 0 & 2 & : & 6 \end{bmatrix}$$

Using back substitutions gives

$$\left. \begin{array}{l} x-y = -1 \\ y-z = -1 \\ 2z = 6 \end{array} \right\} \Rightarrow \quad \begin{array}{l} x = -1+2 = 1 \\ y = -1+3 = 2 \\ z = \dfrac{6}{2} = 3 \end{array}$$

10. **(D)**   The eigenvalues are a property of any square matrix. For an $n \times n$ matrix, there are n eigenvalues. It makes no difference whether the matrix is symmetrical or asymmetrical, the corresponding eigenvalues are generally unique. However, in some cases, the eigenvalues may not be unique. For the special case described by the determinant

$$\left| [A] - 1[I] \right| = 0,$$

the eigenvalues are not unique. Consequently, the correct answer is (D).

11. **(C)**   Since the matrix is equal to its own inverse, then $[A][A] = [I]$, where $[I]$ is the identity matrix. Therefore, raising the matrix to the power of 10 gives the identity matrix as well. The determinant is given by

$$\text{determinant} = 2\,[A]^{10} = 2 \begin{bmatrix} 1 & 0 & 0 \\ 0 & 1 & 0 \\ 0 & 0 & 1 \end{bmatrix} = \begin{bmatrix} 2 & 0 & 0 \\ 0 & 2 & 0 \\ 0 & 0 & 2 \end{bmatrix} = 2 \times 2 \times 2 = 8$$

12. **(D)**   The standard deviation is calculated in terms of the average value of the given data as follows:

$$\text{Mean} = \bar{x} = \frac{\displaystyle\sum_{i=1}^{n} x_i}{n} = \frac{\displaystyle\sum_{i=1}^{5} x_i}{5} = \frac{9+3+6+2+10}{5} = 6$$

$$\text{Standard Deviation} = \sigma = \sqrt{\frac{\displaystyle\sum_{i=1}^{n}(x_i-\bar{x})^2}{n-1}} = \sqrt{\frac{\displaystyle\sum_{i=1}^{5}(x_i-\bar{x})^2}{4}}$$

$$\sigma = \left[\frac{(9-6)^2 + (3-6)^2 + (6-6)^2 + (2-6)^2 + (10-6)^2}{4} \right]^{1/2} = \frac{\sqrt{50}}{2}$$

13. **(C)** This is a combination problem in which $n = 6$ and $r = 4$ where

$$C(n,r) = \frac{n!}{(n-r)! \, r!} = \frac{6!}{(6-4)! \, 4!} = \frac{6 \times 5 \times 4!}{2! \, 4!} = \frac{30}{2 \times 1} = 15$$

Therefore, there are 15 different groups that can be fitted into the four-passenger car.

14. **(A)** Although one may assume that the answer is 0.50, it is not. In an independent-trials process with two outcomes, the probability of exactly "r" successes in "n" experiments is given by the following binomial probability expression:

$$b(r;n,p) = \frac{n!}{r! \, (n-r)!} P^r (1-P)^{n-r}$$

For $P = 0.5$, $n = 10$, and $r = 5$, then

$$b\left(5;10,\frac{1}{2}\right) = \frac{10!}{5! \, (10-5)!} \left(\frac{1}{2}\right)^5 \left(1 - \frac{1}{2}\right)^{10-5}$$

$$b\left(5;10,\frac{1}{2}\right) = \frac{10 \times 9 \times 8 \times 7 \times 6 \times 5!}{(5 \times 4 \times 3 \times 2 \times 1) \, 5!} \left(\frac{1}{2}\right)^{10} = \frac{30,240}{120} (0.00097656)$$

$$b\left(5;10,\frac{1}{2}\right) = 0.246 \approx 0.25$$

15. **(C)** Using the relationship: $\frac{V_2}{V_1} = \frac{N_2}{N_1}$, $V_1 = 250$, $V_2 = 50$, and $N_1 = 20$. Solving for N_2,

$$N_2 = \frac{V_2 \times N_1}{V_1} = \frac{50 \times 20}{250} = 4.$$

Fourier and Laplace transforms –1.

16. **(B)** This differential equation is integrated by assuming a solution of the form:

$$y = Ge^{st} \quad \Rightarrow \quad \dot{y} = s\,Ge^{st} \quad \Rightarrow \quad \ddot{y} = s^2 Ge^{st}$$

Substituting into the differential equation and simplifying gives

$$s^2 - 7s = 0 \quad \Rightarrow \quad s = 0 \quad \text{and} \quad s = 7$$

The solution is of the form

$$y = C_1 + C_2\, e^{7t}$$

The constant C_1 and C_2 are evaluated using the given initial conditions. That is

$$\left. \begin{array}{l} y(0) = 1 = C_1 + C_2 \\ \dot{y}(0) = 1 = 7C_2 \end{array} \right\} \quad \Rightarrow \quad C_1 = \frac{6}{7} \quad \text{and} \quad C_2 = \frac{1}{7}$$

The solution to the differential equation is then given by

$$y = \frac{6}{7} + \frac{e^{7t}}{7}$$

17. **(D)** This differential equation is solved by separating the variables then integrating as follows:

$$e^y\, dy = 5x\, dx \quad \Rightarrow \quad e^y = 2.5x^2 + c'$$

Or more simply

$$y = ln(2.5x^2 + c)$$

Introducing the initial condition at $x = 1$, we have $y(1) = 0$:

$$y(1) = 0 = ln(2.5(1) + c) \quad \Rightarrow \quad c = -1.5$$

The solution is then given as

$$y(x) = ln(2.5x^2 - 1.5) \quad \Rightarrow \quad y\left(\sqrt{2}\right) = ln(5 - 1.5) = ln\, 3.5 = 1.253$$

18. **(C)** The equation of a circle with a center at $(-k, -c)$ and a radius r has the following form:

$$(x + k)^2 + (y + c)^2 = r^2$$

"Complete the squares" to convert the given equation

$$x^2 + y^2 - 8x + 2y = 9$$

into the above form.

After grouping the variables:

$$(x^2 - 8x) + (y^2 + 2y) = 9$$

By squaring the half of each coefficient in front of x and y and adding to each side of the equation

$$(x^2 - 8x + 16) + (y^2 + 2y + 1) = 9 + 16 + 1$$

Rewriting the above equation

$$(x - 4)^2 + (y + 1)^2 = 26$$

we see that

$$-k = -4 \quad -c = 1$$

Therefore, the center of the circle is at $(4, -1)$.

19. **(C)** Algebraic equations of the form $Ax^2 + Bxy + Cy^2 + Dx + Ey + F = 0$ are classified as follows:

$$\text{Ellipse:} \quad B^2 - 4AC < 0$$

$$\text{Parabola:} \quad B^2 - 4AC = 0$$

$$\text{Hyperbola:} \quad B^2 - 4AC > 0$$

In this problem, the term $A = 3$, $B = 6$, and $C = 2$

$$36 - 4(3)(2) = 12 > 0$$

Therefore, the equation represents a hyperbola.

20. **(D)** Differentiate both sides of the equation with respect to x, then solve for dy/dx, which gives

$$2y \frac{dy}{dx} - 4 + 2\frac{dy}{dx} = 0 \quad \Rightarrow \quad \frac{dy}{dx} = \frac{2}{1 + y}$$

The slope at $(3, 3)$ is computed as

$$\left.\frac{dy}{dx}\right|_{(3,3)} = \frac{2}{1 + 3} = \frac{1}{2} = m_1$$

The normal will have a slope equal to $m_2 = -1/m_1 = -2$. The equation of the normal is a straight line of the form $y = a + m_2 x$. The value of a is determined from the point $(3, 3)$ as follows:

$$y = a - 2x \quad \Rightarrow \quad 3 = a - 2(3) \quad \Rightarrow \quad a = 9$$

The equation of the normal is then given as $y = 9 - 2x$.

21. **(B)** The parallel combination of 4 Ω and $^4/_3$ Ω is 1 Ω. Therefore, the voltage source V will split equally, and $V_1 = V_2 = ^V/_2$.

22. **(B)** The two circuits will be equivalent if the impedances, as seen by the AC voltage source in both circuits and at the specified frequency, are the same.

Thus, the series combination of the $R_s = 1$ Ω resistor and $C_s = 100$ pF capacitor, should be the same as the parellel combination of the resistor $R = R_p$ and the capacitor $C = C_p$ at $f = 15.9$ MHz.

After setting up the equations, we solve for R_p and C_p, and find

$$R_p = \frac{R_s^2 + (\omega \times C_s)^2}{R_s} = 10\,k\Omega; \quad C_p = \frac{\dfrac{1}{\omega^2 \times C_s}}{R_s^2 + \dfrac{1}{(\omega \times C_s)^2}} = 100\,pF$$

with $\omega = 2 \times \pi \times f$.

23. **(A)** In any medium of permittivity constant ε and permeability constant μ, the velocity of any electromagnetic wave in the same medium is given by

$$v = \frac{1}{\sqrt{\mu \times \varepsilon}}\ (\text{m/sec})$$

So, if the medium is changed, so does the velocity.

On the other hand, we have a relation that links the three specified parameters, f, v, λ, which is

$$\lambda = \frac{v}{f}$$

The wave cannot be packed on one side of medium 1, but it has to flow evenly. The only way this can happen is if the frequency stays constant and the wavelength changes in such a way that the previous equation is verified.

24. **(A)** Using the transformation of a current source in parallel with a resistance into a voltage source in series with a resistance, as shown in the figure, we find that V_s should equal 1 A $\times$ 2 Ω = 2 V.

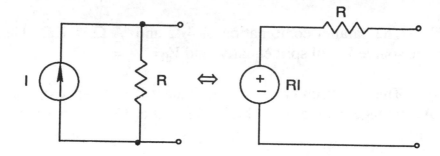

25. **(C)** Apply Thevenin's theorem, which says that *any linear circuit seen from two points can be reduced into a voltage source in series with a resistance. The voltage source is obtained by open-circuiting the two considered points and computing the voltage between them; the resistance is found by short-circuiting voltage sources and open-circuiting current sources and then grouping all resistances between the two points into a single resistance.*

Thus, open-circuiting A and B we see a voltage of

$$V_{th} = 4 \text{ V} + 2 \text{ mA} \times 2 \text{ K}\Omega = 8 \text{ V}$$

and, short-circuiting the 4 V voltage source and open-circuiting the 2 mA current source, we see in series a resistance of

$$R_{th} = 2 \text{ K}\Omega + 3 \text{ K}\Omega = 5 \text{ K}\Omega$$

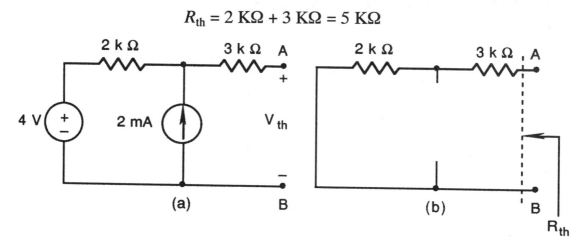

26. **(D)** Apply Norton's theorem, which says that *any linear circuit seen from two points can be reduced into a current source in parallel with a resistance. The current source is obtained by short-circuiting the two considered points and computing the current that flows through them. The resistance is found in exactly the same way as in Thevenin's theorem.*

Thus, short-circuiting A and B, we see a current

$$I_{nr} = \left(2\,\text{mA} + \frac{4\,\text{V}}{2\,\text{K}\Omega}\right) \times \left(\frac{3\,\text{K}\Omega}{3\,\text{K}\Omega + 2\,\text{K}\Omega}\right) = 1.6\,\text{mA}$$

and

$$R_{nr} = 5\,\text{K}\Omega$$

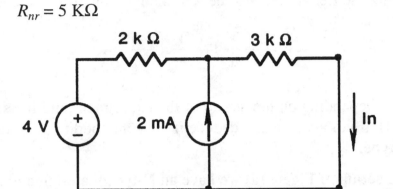

27. **(C)**   Since the two resistances of 6 Ω and 3 Ω are in parallel, the voltages V_1 and V_2 across them are equal.

28. **(B)**   From Problem 27 and the fact that $I = V/R$, we see that

$$I_1 = \frac{V_1}{6\Omega} = \frac{V_2}{2 \cdot 3\Omega} = \frac{I_2}{2}$$

29. **(C)**   Using the equation given, we deduce that the inductor L will be given by

$$L = \frac{v(t)}{\frac{di}{dt}}$$

In the intervals $(-1, 0)$ and $(2, 3)$, we see that di/dt is constant and equal respectively to $1/3$ and $-1/3$, and the respective values of $v(t)$ in those intervals are 1 and -1.

Thus,

$$L = \frac{1}{1/3} = \frac{-1}{-1/3} = 3\,\text{H}.$$

30. **(D)**   The gradient of any surface F is given by $-\nabla F$. Since, the electric flux lines **E** are perpendicular to the equipotential surface V, then we have $\mathbf{E} = -\nabla V$.

Another reason is that the electric intensity at any point is just the negative of the potential gradient at that point; the direction of the electric field is the direction in which the gradient is greatest, or in which the potential changes most rapidly.

The electric field **E** can also be written in terms of the potential *V* as

$$\mathbf{E} = -\frac{\partial V}{\partial x}\,\mathbf{i} - \frac{\partial V}{\partial y}\,\mathbf{j} - \frac{\partial V}{\partial z}\,\mathbf{k}$$

31. **(C)**   Depending on the set-up of the experiment and the sign of the measured Hall voltage, we can deduce if the semiconductor material is N-type or P-type.

In the set-up of Figure (a) we have an N-type material, and in the set-up of Figure (b) we have a P-type material.

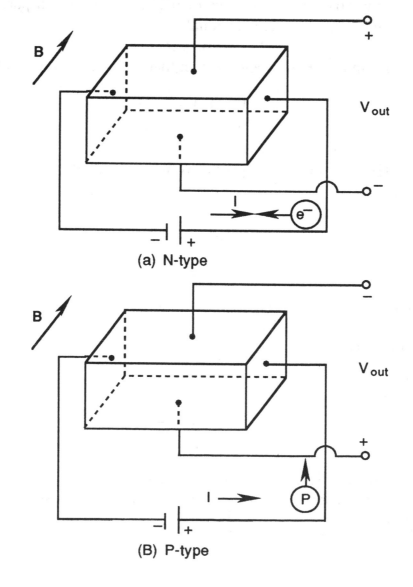

(a) N-type

(B) P-type

32. **(B)** From electromagnetism courses, we know that the integral of $E \times H$ over any closed surface gives the rate of energy flow through the surface. It is seen that the vector

$$P = E \times H$$

has the dimensions of watts per square meter. It is Poynting's theorem that the vector product $P = E \times H$ at any point is a measure of the rate of energy flow per unit area at that point. The direction of flow is perpendicular to E and H in the direction of the vector $E \times H$.

33. **(C)** The condition for maximum power transfer in a series circuit, as shown here, is

$$Z_L = Z_s{}^*$$

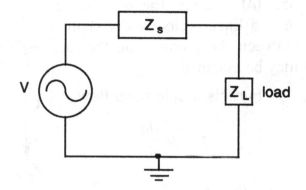

In our case, we have

$$Z_L = Z_1 || Z_2 \quad \text{and} \quad Z_s = Z.$$

34. **(B)** The average value can be found by evaluating the equation:

$$a_n = \frac{1}{\pi}\int_0^{2\pi} f(\theta)\cos n\theta \, d\theta = \frac{2}{T}\int_0^T f(t)\cos nwt \, dt$$

$$n = 0, 1, 2, 3, \ldots$$

And for this function:

$$n = 0,$$

$$\text{and } v(\theta) = \frac{V_m}{\pi}\theta, \ 0 \le \theta \le \pi$$

$$v(\theta) = 0, \quad \pi \le \theta \le 2\pi$$

Therefore,

$$a_0 = \frac{1}{\pi}\int_0^{2\pi} f(\theta)d\theta = \frac{1}{\pi}\int_0^{\pi}\frac{V_m}{\pi}\theta d\theta$$

$$= \frac{V_m}{2\pi^2}\left[\theta^2\right]_0^{\pi}$$

$$= \frac{V_m}{2}$$

$$\frac{a_0}{2} = \frac{V_m}{4}$$

Also, by inspection, the function (wave) area is

$$\frac{V_m}{2}$$

and therefore the average value would be

$$\frac{\frac{V_m}{2}}{2} = \frac{V_m}{4}$$

35. **(A)**   Since the oil layer is *thin*, a linear velocity distribution between the ground and the disk may be assumed.

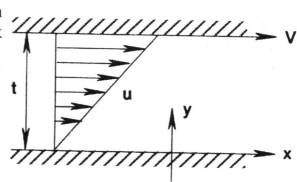

For this simple shear flow,

$$\tau = \mu \frac{du}{dy}$$

where $\frac{du}{dy} = \frac{v}{t}$ Hence, $\tau = \mu \frac{v}{t}$.

The total drag (friction) of the oil on the plate is $D = \tau \times A$, where A is the surface area of the plate which is in contact with the oil.

$$D = \mu \frac{V}{t} A = \mu \frac{V}{t} \frac{\pi d^2}{4}$$

$$\therefore \quad = \left(0.1 \frac{N \times s}{m^2}\right)\left(10 \frac{m}{s}\right)\left(\frac{1}{1\,mm}\right)\left(\frac{1,000\ mm}{m}\right)\left(\frac{\pi}{4}(0.15\ m)^2\right)$$

$$D = 17.7\ N$$

36. **(A)**   The Lagrangian reference frame, choice (B), is one where individual fluid particles are "tagged" and followed. In the Eulerian reference frame, individual particles are not followed; rather, fluid particles flow through the control surface. The two other choices (C) and (D) are undefined.

37. **(D)**   Since there is no friction, we can use Bernoulli's steady-state equation

$$\frac{p_1}{\rho} + \frac{V_1^2}{2} + gz_1 = \frac{p_2}{\rho} + \frac{V_2^2}{2} + gz_2 \tag{1}$$

Let point 1 be at the surface of the tank and let point 2 be at the exit plane of the pipe.

Then, $p_1 = p_2 = p_a$ = atmospheric pressure.

Also, $V_1 \approx 0$ since the tank is very large and the surface will move down very slowly.

Thus (1) reduces to

$$V_2 = \sqrt{2g(z_1 - z_2)}$$
$$V_2 = \sqrt{(2)(9.8 \text{ m/s}^2)\,(3 \text{ m})}$$
$$V_2 = 7.67 \text{ m/s}$$

38. **(A)** By definition, the average velocity, $V_{av} = Q/A$, where Q = volume flow rate and A = cross-sectional area. Here, it is known that

$$V_{av_I} = V_{av_{II}} = V_{av_{III}}$$

Also, the cross-sectional areas are identical for the three cases. Hence, it follows that

$$Q_I = Q_{II} = Q_{III}$$

39. **(D)** Momentum flux correction factor, β, is defined for cases where the velocity over a cross-section is non-uniform. β is defined as

$$\beta = \frac{1}{A} \iint_A \left(\frac{u}{V_{av}}\right)^2 dA$$

From this definition, $\beta = 1.0$ for uniform flow, as in case I. For cases II and III, $\beta > 1.0$, since the velocity profiles are non-uniform. Note that β is always ≥ 1.0.

40. **(C)** Choices (A), (B), and (D) are invalid for the following reasons:

(A) The opposite is true; for example

$$\frac{\partial u}{\partial x} << \frac{\partial u}{\partial y}.$$

In other words, changes of velocity in the x-direction can be completely neglected with respect to changes in the y-direction.

(B) The opposite is true; the boundary layer approximation is only valid for the very *high* Reynolds numbers.

(D) Boundary layer thickness, δ, is a function of *x*, (typically δ increases with *x*).

41. **(C)**   In the inviscid flow outside of the boundary layer, Bernoulli's equation is valid.

$$\frac{p}{\rho} + \frac{1}{2}U^2 + gz = \text{constant}$$

Neglecting gravitational effects, as *p* increases, *U* must decrease. Choices (A), (B), and (D) are incorrect for the following reasons:

(A) This condition is not favorable because increasing pressure usually leads to boundary layer separation.

(B) When $dp/dx > 0$, the pressure gradient is unfavorable (i.e., adverse) regardless of the body geometry.

(D) If $dp/dx > 0$, separation is more likely to occur; however, it is possible for the boundary layer to remain attached for small values of dp/dx.

42. **(C)**   By definition, "fully developed" pipe flow implies that the velocity profile shape or magnitude does not change with downstream distance along the pipe. Mass flow rate cannot change either since mass must be conserved. Darcy friction factor *f* is constant along the entire length of a fully developed pipe flow. Of all the parameters listed in the choices, static pressure is the only one that changes. In other words, a pressure drop is required to "push" the fluid through the pipe as it has to overcome friction.

43. **(D)**   This problem can be represented by a large tank discharging air into the atmosphere.

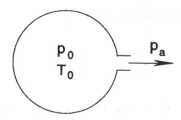

The mass flow of air becomes "choked" when $\dfrac{p_a}{p_0} \approx 0.5283$, regardless of the hole size, for standard temperatures.

Here, then

$$p_0 = \frac{p_a}{0.5283} = \frac{(732 \text{ mm Hg})}{0.5283} = 1,386 \text{ mm Hg}$$

However, the *gage* pressure is equal to $p_0 - p_a$, i.e.,

$$p_0 - p_a = 1,386 - 732 = 654 \text{ mm Hg}.$$

44. **(B)** A Schottky defect occurs when vacant cation and anion sites exist in proportion to the stochiometry of the compound, and thus leave equal numbers of vacancies. NaCl crystals commonly have Schottky defects. A Frenckel defect (choice (C)) occurs when an ion occupies a space which is normally open; these defects are most common in crystals where the cation is much smaller than the anion. In a Farbe defect, the stochiometry of the crystal is changed and fewer anion sites are occupied, leaving a greater number of cation sites. In some cases, a Farbe defect leads to a color change. An n-type defect is used to describe a replacement from one atom to another, especially in semi-conductors. An n-type semiconductor is a negatively charged material usually doped with arsenic.

45. **(C)** All of the other choices are part of the solution problem. Mohr's circle is used to determine the direction and magnitude of the stress. The principles of maximum stress and superposition can only be applied if the assumption that the material will **not** fail is made. Therefore, (C) is the correct choice; the problem does not use this assumption.

46. **(D)** While (A) is true, the accumulative error of roundoff could make the answer incorrect to three significant figures. (B) Most computers will perform as stated in the problem with no correction for the roundoff error. (C) is incorrect since seldom, if ever, is an engineering problem worked to eight significant figures.

47. **(D)** (A) and (B) are incorrect since the spreadsheet would interpret them as labels and formulae. (C) would give the value corresponding to y_1 when the value corresponding to y_3 is required. $A3 * A3 - 1$ means that the contents of cell $B3$ are the contents of cell $A3$ times the contents of cell $A3$ minus 1, which is the required result.

48. **(C)**   Engineers shall give credit for engineering work to those to whom credit is due, and will recognize the proprietary interests of others. It was unethical for Engineer A to use Engineer B's proposal without Engineer B's consent in order to develop a proposal that was subsequently submitted to the council. (A) and (B) are incorrect since credit should have been given for Engineer A's work. (D) is incorrect since a proposal can contain work from other sources, provided proper credit is given.

49. **(B)**   The quality of a saturated liquid (state 1) is 0.0. The quality of a saturated vapor (state 2) is 1.0. As the process proceeds from state 1 to state 2 the quality will increase. Under the vapor dome, temperature and pressure are not independent and both remain constant unless acted upon by some outside force.

50. **(C)**   In the reversible process there is no entropy generation. Since entropy is a function of absolute temperature (always positive) and the heat transfer, then, if the heat transfer is negative (rejected), the entropy change will be negative. This does not violate the Second Law since the entropy of the universe must be considered to complete the Second Law analysis.

51. **(D)**   On the saturated vapor curve of the Psychrometric chart, the dew point temperature and the dry-bulb temperature are identical. It is at this point that the relative humidity is 100%. The pressure of the vapor mixture, p_v, and the saturation pressure, p_{sat} or p_g, are equal. The ratio of these pressures produces the relative humidity.

52. **(D)**   A stoichiometric relationship would require 100% theoretical air, or exactly the amount needed for complete combustion with no excess. Fifty percent theoretical air would cause incomplete combustion resulting in unburned hydrogen and/or carbon monoxide. One hundred fifty percent theoretical air indicates that there is 50% more oxygen (along with the appropriate amounts of nitrogen) present. It is readily apparent that $2O_2$ are required for complete combustion and that $3O_2$ are present. Thus, there is 50% excess or 150% theoretical air.

53. **(C)**   When temperatures are multiplied, an absolute scale must be utilized. Two times 273 K equals 546 K or 273°C. The other choices were obtained by multiplying temperatures in either °F or °C without converting first to an absolute scale.

54. **(B)** The Diesel cycle is used to model the ideal compression ignition cycle. The others are: Otto-spark ignition cycle, Rankine-steam power cycle, and Brayton-gas turbine cycle.

55. **(C)** According to the First Law for a closed system, in the absence of work, the heat transfer will be equal to the change in internal energy. Since internal energy is a function of temperature only for an ideal gas, the heat transfer will be a function of temperature only.

56. **(C)** In exothermic reactions, some amount of energy is liberated in the form of heat. This is known as the heat of reaction and is normally associated with combustion processes. The heat of formation is related to the energy absorbed or released as the compound is formed.

57. **(D)** Flow work is associated with open systems, flow processes, or control volume problems. Flow work is included via pressure and volume terms where their product is added to the internal energy to obtain a new property, enthalpy. In equation form:

$$h = u + pv.$$

Flow work cannot occur in closed systems since no mass enters or leaves the boundaries of the system.

58. **(B)** The piston-cylinder device is a closed system since no mass flow crosses the boundary. All the other devices are flow devices and are analyzed using a control volume across which mass can flow.

59. **(A)** To increase the internal energy of 2 kg of air by 2 kJ/kg, 4 kJ of energy are required. Since the work produced is 8 kJ, the total amount of heat required is the sum, or 12 kJ. In equation form from the First Law for a closed system

$$Q_{12} = m(u_2 - u_1) + W_{12}, \text{ where } (u_2 - u_1) = 2 \text{ kJ/kg}$$
$$Q_{12} = 2 \text{ kg}(2 \text{ kJ/kg}) + 8 \text{ kJ} = 12 \text{ kJ}$$

60. **(C)** It was unethical for Engineer A to perform a feasibility study and make recommendations concerning the location of a new facility in the county. While Engineer A made full disclosure, he had too great an interest in the proceedings to act impartially. (A) would be correct if he had a lesser interest in the proceedings. (B) is incorrect, since there was a clear conflict of interest. (D) is incorrect, since this is not the function of the NCEES Board.

61. **(C)** Z becomes 2 and, as such, the conditional statement $Z < 0$ is false, which means that the statement $Z = Z + 1$ will *not* be executed. (A) would be the correct response if $Z = -2$, since the conditional statement would apply in this case. (D) would be the correct response if the conditional statement was "$Z > 0$," in which case the 2 would be incremented by 1.

62. **(A)** The whole number is found from $110_2 = 1 * 2^2 + 1 * 2^1 + 0 * 2^0 = 6$. The fractional part is found in a similar manner: $0 * 2^{-1} + 1 * 2^{-2} + 1 * 2^{-3} = 0 + 0.250 + 0.125 = 0.375$. (B) and (D) are based on the incorrect premise that $011_2 = 3_{10}$. (C) would be correct if the number was 110.111.

63. **(A)** The best way to solve projectile problems is to consider the horizontal and vertical motions separately. The initial velocity given may be decomposed as such:

$$v_{0x} = v_0 \cos \theta$$
$$v_{0x} = 150 \text{ m/s } (\cos 30°) = + 129.9 \text{ m/s}$$
$$v_{0y} = v_0 \sin \theta$$
$$v_{0y} = 150 \text{ m/s } (\sin 30°) = + 75 \text{ m/s}$$

The vertical motion is uniformly accelerated motion. The horizontal motion is uniform motion.

The projectile reaches the maximum height at the moment when $v_y = 0$. Applying the equation

$$v_y = v_{0y} + at$$

yields $0 = + 75 \text{ m/s} - 9.8 \text{ m/s}^2 \, t$

or

$$t = \frac{-75}{-9.8} s = 7.7s.$$

Now, substituting this value into the vertical motion equation to solve for y_{max} yields

$$y = v_{0y} + \frac{1}{2} a_y t^2$$
$$y_{max} = + 75 \text{ m/s } (7.7 \text{ } s) - 4.9 \text{ m/s}^2 (7.7 \text{ } s)^2 = 287 \text{ m}$$

However, this describes the distance above the roof which the stone reaches rather than its elevation from the ground. The elevation above the ground is found by adding to y_{max} the height of the building. Hence, the greatest elevation

$$= 200 \text{ m} + 287 \text{ m} = 487 \text{ m}.$$

64. **(D)** We wish to relate the velocity of the car to ϕ, the banking angle. Note that the car is undergoing circular motion; hence, its acceleration in the x-direction is

$$a = \frac{v^2}{R},$$

where R is its distance from the center of the circle (see figure). Applying Newton's Second Law, $F = ma$, to the x component of motion,

$$ma = N \sin \phi$$

But $a = v^2 / R$ and

$$\frac{mv^2}{R} = N \sin \phi \qquad (1)$$

The acceleration of the car in the y-direction is zero, since it remains on the road. Applying the Second Law to this component of motion,

$$N \cos \phi = mg \qquad (2)$$

Dividing (1) by (2),

$$\frac{\dfrac{mv^2}{R}}{mg} = \frac{N \sin \phi}{N \cos \phi} = \tan \phi$$

Hence, $v = \sqrt{Rg \tan \phi}$

Now, note that the width of the road bed is much smaller than the inner radius of the road. Hence, we may approximate R as the inner radius.

$$R \approx 45.75 \text{ m}$$

$$v = \sqrt{(45.75 \text{ m}) (9.8 \text{ m/s}^2) \tan \phi}$$

From the figure,

$$\sin \phi = \frac{1.22}{9.15} = 0.133$$

$$\cos^2 \phi = 1 - \sin^2 \phi = 1 - 0.133^2 = 0.982$$

Hence,

$$\cos \phi = 0.99$$

and

$$\tan \phi = \frac{0.133}{0.99} = 0.1345$$

Therefore,

$$v = \sqrt{(45.75 \text{ m}) (9.81 \text{ m/s}^2) (0.1345)}$$
$$v = \sqrt{60.36}$$
$$v = 7.75 \text{ m/s}$$

65. **(B)** Designate the shell with subscript 1 and the gun with subscript 2.

Since there are no external forces acting on the system (gun + shell) in the x-direction, p_x (before) = p_x (after) = p_{1x} (after) + p_{2x} (after). Since p_x (before) = 0, p_{1x} (after) − p_{2x} (after) = 0, because the gun will move to the left.

$$0 = m_1 v'_{1x} - m_2 (v'_{2x}).$$

So,

$$m_2 v'_{2x} = m_1 v'_{1x}.$$

But,

$$v'_{1x} = v'_1 \cos 45°.$$

Therefore, express p_{1x} (after) as

$$p_{1x} \text{ (after)} = m_1 v'_1 \cos 45°$$

$$p_{1x} \text{ (after)} = (500 \text{ kg}) (200 \text{ m/s}) (0.707)$$

$$= 7.07 \times 10^4 \text{ kg-m/s.}$$

This must be numerically equal, but oppositely directed to p_{2x} (after) from equation (1). So, p_{2x} (after) = $m_2 v'_{2x}$ = − 7.07×10^4 kg-m/sec.

And

$$v'_{2x} = \frac{-7.07 \times 10^4 \text{ kg-m/sec}}{7 \times 10^4 \text{ kg}}$$

$$v'_{2x} \approx 1 \text{ m/s}$$

Ignore the vertical component of the recoil momentum due to the extremely large value of the earth's mass compared to the railway gun.

66. **(B)** The ballistic pendulum problem naturally divides into two parts of analysis: The totally inelastic collision when the bullet imbeds itself into the block, and the rise of the bullet and the block together due to the velocity imparted by the collision.

The collision is inelastic, so we are restricted to the always-applicable conservation of momentum equation.

$$\begin{array}{ccc} m_1 v_1 + m_2 v_2 & & m_1 V_1 + m_2 V_2 \\ \text{(before collision)} & = & \text{(after collision)} \end{array}$$

For the ballistic pendulum, $v_2 = 0$ and $v_1 = v_2$ since the bullet imbeds itself in the block. So

$$m_1 v_1 = (m_1 + m_2) V. \tag{1}$$

Now we must determine V by consideration of the rise of the pendulum. The equation used now is conservation of energy

$$KE_i + PE_i = KE_f + PE_f.$$

At the top of the rise, the system is not moving, so $KE_f = 0$. We use the available arbitrariness to set $PE_i = 0$. Therefore, we have

$$\tfrac{1}{2} (m_1 + m_2)V^2 = (m_1 + m_2) gh. \tag{2}$$

Equations (1) and (2) contain all the analyses needed for this problem. Solving for v_1 yields

$$v_1 = \left(\frac{m_1 + m_2}{m_1} \right) \sqrt{2gh}. \tag{3}$$

Just to put some perspective on this highly practical equation, we will provide some pertinent data: m_1 weighs 0.045 kg, m_2 weighs 11.34 kg, and $h = 0.102$ m.

$$v_1 = \left(\frac{\frac{0.045}{9.8} + \frac{11.34}{9.8}}{\frac{0.045}{9.8}} \right) \sqrt{2(9.8)(0.102)}$$

$$= \left(\frac{11.385}{0.045} \right) \sqrt{1.999} = 357 \text{ m/s}$$

67. **(D)**   It is clear that the final angular velocity may be found by using conservation of total angular momentum since there are no external forces involved. The total angular momentum is

$$L = I_{\text{rod}}\, \omega + 2I_{\text{sphere}}\, \omega + 2\,(m_{\text{sphere}}\, r^2)\, \omega.$$

The last two terms follow from the parallel axis theorem. Setting $L_i = L_f$,

$$I_r\omega_i + 2I_s\omega_i + 2m_s\, r_i^2\, \omega_i = I_r\omega_f + 2I_s\omega_f + 2m_s r_f^2 \omega_f$$

$$(I_r + 2I_s + 2m_s r_i^2)\, \omega_i = (I_r + 2I_s + 2m_s r_f^2)\omega_f \tag{1}$$

We are given $I_r = 0.34 \text{ N} \cdot \text{m} \cdot \sec^2$, $m_s = 13.34 \text{ N}$, $r_i = 0.127$ m, and $r_f = 0.635$ m. We compute

$$I_s = \frac{2}{5}\, m_s a^2 = \frac{2}{5} \left(\frac{13.34 \text{ N}}{(9.8 \text{ m/sec}^2)} \right) (0.127)^2$$

$$= 0.00875 \text{ Nm} \cdot \sec^2,$$

and

$$m_s r_i^2 = \left(\frac{13.34}{9.8} \right) (0.127)^2 = 0.0219 \text{ Nm} \cdot \sec^2$$

$$m_s r_f^2 = \left(\frac{13.34}{9.8} \right) (0.635)^2 = 0.549 \text{ Nm} \cdot \sec^2$$

Substituting these values into equation (1) yields:

$$[0.34 + 2\,(0.00875) + 2\,(0.0219)]\omega_i$$

$$= [0.34 + 2\,(0.00875) + 2\,(0.549)]\omega_f$$

$$\omega_f = \frac{0.4013}{1.4555}\, \omega_i = 0.2757(8 \text{ rad/sec}) = 2.21 \text{ rad/sec}$$

68. **(A)**   Since the pulleys are massless, the cord *ACD* has the same tension throughout, say T_1. The tension in cord *BC* can be called T_2. The effect of having the cord double back around pully *C* produces

$$d_B = \tfrac{1}{2} d_A, \tag{1}$$

where d_B and d_A are the distances moved, respectively, by blocks *B* and *A*. Then differentiating twice

$$a_B = \tfrac{1}{2} a_A \tag{2}$$

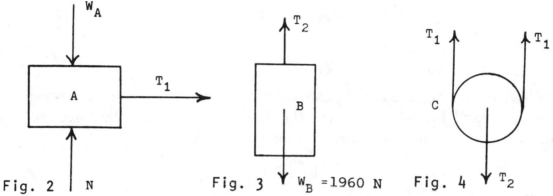

Fig. 2   N   Fig. 3 W_B =1960 N   Fig. 4 T_2

Now we shall analyze blocks *A, B,* and pulley *C* as free bodies. The free-body diagram of block *A* is given in Figure 2. W_A and N, the weight and normal force, respectively, cancel, so from Newton's Second Law we have

$$T_1 = 50 \, a_A. \tag{3}$$

The free-body diagram of block *B* is in Figure 2.

$$W_B = mg = (200 \text{ kg}) (9.8 \text{ m/s}^2) = 1{,}960 \text{ N}.$$

Again using Newton's Law

$$W_B - T_2 = 1{,}960 \text{ N} - T_2 = (200 \text{ kg}) \, a_B \tag{4}$$

Pulley *C* (Figure 3) is massless; therefore, the sum of the forces on it must be zero.

$$2T_1 - T_2 = 0 \tag{5}$$

Equations (2), (3), (4), and (5) now form a system of four equations.

Substituting for a_A from (2) into (3) yields $T_1 = (100 \text{ kg}) \, a_B$. Using this and equation (4) to substitute into (5) yields

$$(200 \text{ kg}) \, a_B - (1{,}960 \text{ N} - (200 \text{ kg}) \, a_B) = 0$$

$$(200 \text{ kg}) \, a_B + (200 \text{ kg}) \, a_B = 1{,}960 \text{ N}$$

$$a_B = \frac{1{,}960 \text{ N}}{400 \text{ kg}} = 4.9 \text{ m/s}^2 \tag{6}$$

Putting (6) back into (2) gives us

$$a_A = 9.8 \text{ m/s}^2 \tag{7}$$

69. **(B)** In a parallel coupling, the extensions of the two springs are the same:

$$x_1 = x_2 = x.$$

Body *A* is now acted upon by three forces, the weight and the two spring forces, F_1 and F_2, as illustrated in the figure below, where the forces on the other parts of the system are also shown. We now have the relations

$$F_1 + F_2 = Mg,$$

and $\qquad\qquad F_1 = K_1 x, \quad F_2 = K_2 x.$

The condition for equilibrium of *A* then becomes

$$x(K_1 + K_2) = Mg,$$

$$x = \frac{Mg}{K_1 + K_2}.$$

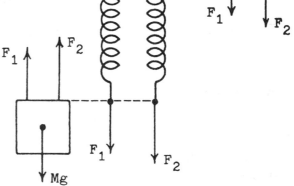

Consequently, the equivalent spring constant in this case becomes

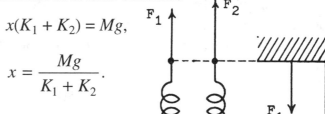

$$K_e = K_1 + K_2.$$

In the special case when $K_1 = K_2 = K$, $K_e = 2K$.

70. **(C)** The true length of the collision can be found using the impulse-momentum theorem. Where

$$\Delta p = F \Delta t$$

or

$$\Delta t = \frac{\Delta p}{F}$$

Since we are working in one direction, the vector notation may be dropped:

$$\Delta t = \frac{\Delta p}{F} = \frac{0.16 \text{ kg}[45 \text{ m/s} - (-25 \text{ m/s})]}{1,200 \text{ N}}$$

$$\Delta t = 0.00933 \text{ s}$$

71. **(C)** To find ω_{AB}, use the equation of relative velocity between ends A and B:

$$V_A = V_B + V_{A/B}.$$

We know that

$$V_{A/B} = \omega_{AB} \times r_{A/B} = \omega_{AB} \, k \times (-0.3 \cos 20° \, i + 0.3 \sin 20° \, j) \text{m}$$
$$V_B = -V_B \, i$$
$$V_A = 3 \, j \text{ m/s}$$

Therefore,

$$3 \, j \text{ m/s} = -V_B \, i + \omega_{AB} \, k\text{x} \, (-0.282 \, i + 0.103 \, j) \text{m}$$
$$3 \, j \text{ m/s} = -V_B \, i - 0.282 \, \omega_{AB} \, j \text{ M} - 0.103 \, \omega_{AB} \, i \text{ m}$$

Matching coefficients of the respective i and j terms, we get

$$3 \text{ m/s} = -0.282 \, \omega_{AB} \text{ m}$$
$$\omega_{AB} = -10.64 \text{ rad/s}$$

or
$$\omega_{AB} = -10.64 \, k \text{ rad/s}$$

72. **(C)** In this problem, no external torques act on the particle; therefore, angular momentum is conserved. Angular momentum, L, equals $r \times mv$ and, for this problem, $L = mr^2\omega$ since the motion is circular and $r\omega = v$.

If the string's length is altered from r_0 to r, the angular rotation changes from ω_0 to ω.

However, $L = L_0$ (angular momentum is conserved) and it follows that $mr^2\omega = mr_0^2 \, \omega_0$.

Rearranging the above expression and dividing by m yields

$$\omega_f = \frac{r_0^2 \omega_0}{r^2} = \left(\frac{r_0}{r}\right)^2 \omega_0 .$$

73. **(B)**   Engineers shall not accept commissions or allowances, directly or indirectly, from contractors or other parties dealing with clients or employers of the Engineer in connection with work for which the Engineer is responsible. However, in this case, the gift was of an appropriate nature. Therefore, it was ethical for Engineer A to attend the one-day complimentary educational seminar hosted by the ABC Pipe Company. (A) is incorrect because acceptance of small gifts is ethical. (C) is incorrect since the refreshments constitute an acceptable business gift. (D) is incorrect since the amount of the gift would not contribute to a conflict of interest.

74. **(C)**   Engineers shall at all times recognize that their primary obligation is to protect the safety, health, property, and welfare of the public. It was unethical for Engineer A to proceed with work on the project knowing that the client would not agree to hire a full-time, on-site project representative. (A) is incorrect since an engineer has a higher obligation to public safety than to his client. (B) is incorrect since the engineer's decision ultimately affects the public safety. (D) is incorrect since an engineer's obligations are the same for both public and non-public projects.

75. **(A)**   To find the acceleration of car B as observed by car A, we use the relative acceleration equation

$$a_B = a_A + a_{B/A}$$

From the problem statement, the acceleration of car B is

$$a_B = 2 \, (- \cos 45° \, i + \sin 45° \, j) \text{ m/s}^2$$
$$a_B = (- 1.41 \, i + 1.41 \, j) \text{ m/s}^2$$

The acceleration of car A is

$$a_A = \frac{(25 \text{ m/s})^2}{100 \text{ m}} i - 3 \text{ m/s}^2 \, j$$
$$a_A = (6.25 \, i - 3 \, j) \text{ m/s}^2$$

Solving for $a_{B/A}$,

$$a_{B/A} = a_B - a_A$$
$$a_{B/A} = (- 1.41 \, i + 1.41 \, j) \text{ m/s}^2 - (6.25 \, i - 3 \, j) \text{ m/s}^2$$
$$a_{B/A} = (- 7.66 \, i + 4.41 \, j) \text{ m/s}^2$$

76. **(D)** The facts presented in this case raise a conflict between two basic ethical obligations of an engineer: The obligation of the engineer to be faithful to the client and not to disclose confidential information concerning the business affairs of a client without that client's consent, and the obligation of the engineer to hold paramount the public health and safety. It was unethical for engineer A not to report the safety violations to the appropriate public authorities since the latter takes precedence over the former. (A) is incorrect since public safety takes precedence. (B) is incorrect since an engineer should report all known violations. (C) is incorrect since there was no conflict in this example.

77. **(B)** The resultant vector, $R = \Sigma F_i$

$$R = (20\,\boldsymbol{i} + 30\,\boldsymbol{j} + 40\,\boldsymbol{k})\text{N} + (\cong 30\,\boldsymbol{j} + 20\,\boldsymbol{k})\text{N} + (60\,\boldsymbol{i})\ \text{N}$$
$$R = (80\,\boldsymbol{i} + 60\,\boldsymbol{k})\ \text{N}$$

Magnitude of $R = \sqrt{(80)^2 + (60)^2} = 100\ \text{N}$.

78. **(C)** The tension T in the main cable is the same at any section. If we take a section below the top pulley, then

$$\Sigma F_y = 0, \quad T + T + T \cong W = 0$$

$$T = \frac{W}{3}.$$

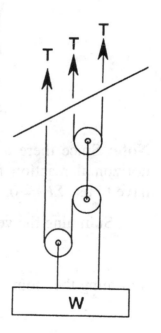

79. **(C)** Weight of 100 kg mass

$$= 100\ \text{kg} \times 9.81\ \text{m/s}^2 = 981\ \text{N}$$

By analyzing joint B:

$$\Sigma F_x = 0, \cong T_{AB} \cos 60° + T_{BC} \cos 30° = 0$$
$$T_{AB} = 1.732\ T_{BC}$$
$$\Sigma F_y = 0, +T_{AB} \sin 60° - T_{BC} \sin 30° - 981\ \text{N} = 0$$

$$(1.732\ T_{BC})\ (0.866) - 0.5\ T_{BC} - 981\ N = 0$$

$$T_{BC} = 981\ N$$

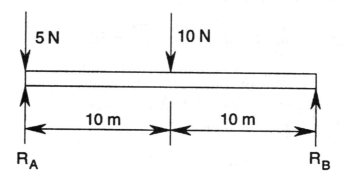

80. **(D)** Use the fundamental equations of equilibrium

$$\Sigma F_x = 0 \quad \Sigma F_y = 0 \quad \Sigma M = 0$$

to find reaction force at B.

5 N   10 N

10 m   10 m

R_A R_B

Note: Since there are no horizontal external forces acting on the beam, horizontal reaction forces at A and B equal zero. Otherwise, we would have to use $\Sigma F_x = 0$.

Summing the vertical forces,

$$R_A - 5\ N - 10\ N + R_B = 0$$

Summing the moments about A (counterclockwise direction is positive),

$$-(10\ N \times 10\ M) + (R_B \times 20\ M) = 0$$

$$R_B = 5\ N$$

Note: Since there are only two unknown forces and one may be eliminated by taking the sum of the moments about A, the last equation alone was sufficient to solve the problem. However, this may not always be the case.

81. **(A)** The bending moment diagram for the loaded beam is:

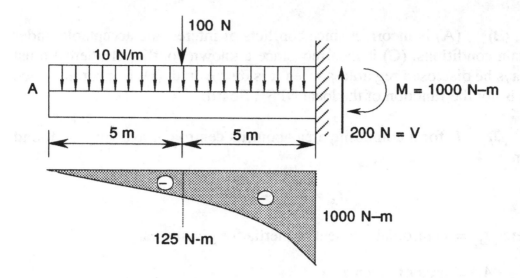

From the bending moment diagram, the maximum bending moment is 1,000 N/M.

82. **(C)**   The load 20 N/M is equally distributed to the right and to the left of the support at *B*. So, support *B* will take care of all the load. The reaction at *A* will be zero.

83. **(D)**   If we take a vertical section passing through the member *GD* and consider the left side of the section,

$$\Sigma F_y = 0, \quad {}^3/_5\, F_{GD} - 30\,\text{N} = 0$$

$$F_{GD} = 50\,\text{N (tension)}$$

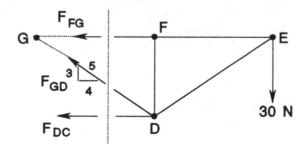

84. **(B)**   By taking moment about the point *G*, considering clockwise positive,

$$F_{DC} * 3 + 30 * 8 = 0$$

$$F_{DC} = -80\,\text{N}$$

Force in the member *DC* is compressive and of magnitude of 80 N.

85. (B) (A) is incorrect since conflicts of interest are acceptable under certain conditions. (C) is incorrect since a known conflict of interest must always be disclosed regardless when it is discovered. (D) is incorrect since this is not the function of the local NPSE Board.

86. (D) I_x for a composite area about its centroidal axis may be found from

$$I_x = \Sigma I_{x_i} + \Sigma A_i d_i^2$$

where I_{x_i} = centroidal moment of inertia for given area

   A_i = area of given area

   d_i = distance between centroid of given area and centroidal axis of composite area

Redraw the composite area and divide into separate areas:

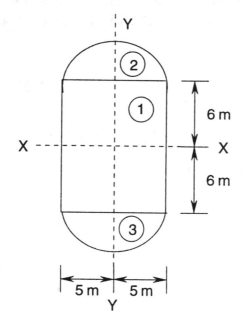

For area ①

$$I_{x_i} = \frac{bh^3}{12} = \frac{(10 \text{ m})(12 \text{ m})^3}{12} = 1,440 \text{ m}^4$$

$A_1 = (12 \text{ m})(10 \text{ m}) = 120 \text{ m}$

$d_1 = 0 \text{ M (centroid of area ① coincides with centroidal axis)}$

For area ②

$$I_{x_2} = \frac{\pi r^4}{8} = \frac{\pi (5 \text{ m})^4}{8} = 245.44 \text{ m}^4$$

$$A_2 = \frac{\pi (5 \text{ m})^2}{2} = 39.27 \text{ m}^2$$

$$d_2 = \frac{4r}{3\pi} + 6 \text{ m} = \frac{4(5 \text{ m})}{3\pi} + 6 \text{ m} = 8.12 \text{ m}$$

For area ③

Since area ① and ③ are identical

$$I_{x_3} = 245.44 \text{ m}^4$$

$$A_3 = 39.27 \text{ m}^2$$

$$d_3 = 8.12 \text{ m}$$

Therefore, $I_x = [1{,}440 \text{ m}^4 + 0] + 2[245.44 \text{ m}^4 + 39.27 \text{ m}^2 (8.12\text{m})^2] = 7{,}100 \text{ m}^4$.

87. **(C)** The weight of the block = 100 kg × 9.81 m/s² = 981 N acting in the downward direction. By taking sum of all forces along the x-direction equal to zero,

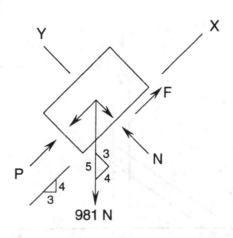

$$\Sigma F_x = 0.$$

$$P + F - \frac{4}{5} * 981 \text{ N} = 0 \qquad (1)$$

and $\qquad \Sigma F_y = 0, \quad N - \frac{3}{5} \times 981 \text{ N} = 0$

$$N = 588.6 \text{ N}$$

The frictional force, $F = \mu N = 0.25 * 588.6 \text{ N}$, $F = 147.15$ N. Using equation (1),

$$P = \frac{4}{5} * 981 \text{ N} - F = \frac{4}{5} \times 981 \text{ N} - 147.15 \text{ N}$$

$$P = 637.65 \text{ N}$$

88. **(D)** Support A has only one horizontal reaction, and the vertical at B has two reactive components: at B (H_B) a horizontal reaction, and a vertical reaction at B (V_B). Now,

$$\Sigma F_V = 0, \uparrow +,$$

$$V_A - 100 = 0$$

$$V_A = 100 \text{ N} \uparrow +.$$

89. **(C)** By looking at the free-body diagram the summation of moments about $B = 0$,

$$\Sigma M_B = 0$$

$$100 \text{ N} \times 3_m - R_A \times 8 = 0$$

$$R_A = 37.5 \leftarrow +$$

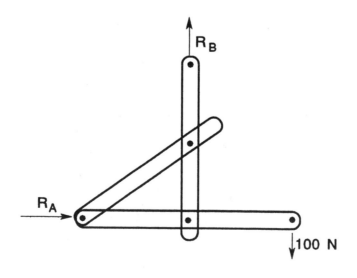

90. **(C)**   The General Gas Equation can be used to solve this problem

$$PV = nRT$$

where P = pressure in atm

V = volume in lit

n = no. of moles

R = the gas constant

= 0.082 lit atm./K · mole

T = temperature in K

Since n, the no. of moles

$$= \frac{\text{mass in g}}{\text{molecular wt.}},$$

the above equation can be written as

$$PV = \frac{gRT}{\text{M.W.}}$$

Substituting,

$$(1.0 \text{ atm}) (0.107 \text{ lit}) = \frac{(0.4 \text{ g}) (0.082 \text{ lit atm/K mole}) (300 \text{ K})}{\text{M.W.}}$$

M.W. = 92.0 g/mole

91. **(B)**   Gold is a noble metal. Even concentrated acids, such as nitric, hydrochloric or sulfuric, do not attack it. Only a mixture of conc. hydrochloric and conc. nitric acids in a 3 : 1 ratio (called "aqua-regia") can dissolve gold.

In solving this problem, therefore, the assumption is that only copper metal from the alloy is reacted upon by nitric acid.

$$Cu + 4 HNO_3 \rightarrow Cu(NO_3)_2 + 2H_2O + 2NO_2$$

Using atomic weights, the molecular weight of $Cu(NO_3)_2$ is calculated to be 187.5 g/mole. By setting the stoichiometric ratio between Cu and $Cu(NO_3)_2$, the mass of copper in the sample of alloy can be calculated as follows:

$$3.75 \text{ g Cu(NO}_3)_2 \times \frac{63.5 \text{ g Cu}}{187.5 \text{ g Cu(NO}_3)_2} = 1.27 \text{ g Cu}$$

Therefore, the mass of gold in the sample is

$$2.86 \text{ g alloy} - 1.27 \text{ g Cu} = 1.59 \text{ g Au}$$

Percent of Au in alloy

$$= \frac{1.59 \text{ g Au}}{2.86 \text{ g alloy}} \times 100$$

$$= 55.6\% \text{ Au}$$

92. **(D)** By convention, the direction of dipole is from $\delta+$ to $\delta-$. The resultant of two C–Br moments is exactly in the middle of two C–Br bonds, at an angle of 56° from each C–Br bond. The contribution of each C–Br bond to the resultant can be calculated by using vector analysis. Contribution of each C–Br bond to the resultant

$$= \text{bond moment of C–Br bond} \times \cos 56°$$

$$= 1.38 \text{ D} \times 0.56 = 0.77 \text{ D}$$

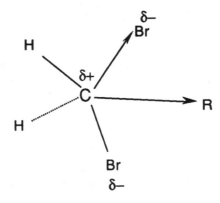

Contribution of the other C–Br bond to the resultant is also 0.77 D in the same direction.

Therefore, the total resultant, which is the (total) dipole moment of CH_2Br_2 is $0.77 \text{ D} + 0.77 \text{ D} = 1.54 \text{ D}$.

93. **(A)** Let us first express the amount of electricity passed in Faradays.

Coulombs passed = amp × sec = 5.0 amp × 12,600 secs = 63,000

$$63{,}000 \text{ coulombs} \times \frac{1 \text{ Faraday}}{96{,}500 \text{ coulombs}} = 0.65 \text{ Faraday}$$

$$Fe^{+3} + 3 \text{ e} \rightarrow Fe°$$

One mole of Fe^{+3} with 3 moles of electrons (or 3 moles of Faraday) forms one mole of Fe metal. Therefore, the equivalent weight of Fe° in this reaction

$$= \frac{\text{Atomic weight of Fe}}{3 \text{ Faraday}} = \frac{56}{3} = 18.67 \text{ g/Faraday}$$

That is, one Faraday of electricity will theoretically deposit 18.67 g of Fe metal.

0.65 Faraday will deposit 12.14 g of Fe metal at 100% efficiency.

At 66% efficiency, 68% of 12.14 g = 8.26 g of Fe metal will be deposited.

94. **(B)** The Heat of Reaction (ΔH), also called the Change in Enthalpy, is equal to the total enthalpy of all the products minus the total enthalpy of all the reactants.

$$
\begin{aligned}
\Delta H_{\text{reaction}} &= H_{\text{products}} - H_{\text{reactants}} \\
&= [7\, H_f\, C_{(s)} + 7\, H_f\, CO_{(g)} + 3\, H_f\, N_{2(g)} + 5\, H_f\, H_2O_{(g)}] \\
&\quad - [2\, H_f\, TNT_{9(s)}] \\
&= [7\,(\text{zero}) + 7\,(-26.4) + 3\,(\text{zero}) + 5(-57.8)] \\
&\quad - [2(-87.1)] \\
&= -299.6 \text{ Kcal per two moles of TNT}
\end{aligned}
$$

Now solve for H of 3.00 lbs of TNT.

$$\frac{-299.6 \text{ Kcal}}{2} \times \frac{1}{227} \times \frac{1,362}{3 \text{ lb}}$$

$$= -898.8 \text{ Kcal}$$

Note: Negative sign indicates an exothermic reaction.

95. **(C)** When the conc. of a metal is changed, there should be a change in the rate of reaction if the metal is acting as a catalyst. If changing the conc. of a metal does not change the rate of reaction, it is not acting as a catalyst.

In order to determine if a metal is acting as a catalyst, for comparison select two experiments in which the only difference is different concentrations of a given metal. If the rate is higher, with higher conc. of the metal, it is acting as a catalyst.

To evaluate the effect of metal Y, compare expt. Nos. 1 and 2. There is a higher conc. of metal Y in expt. 2 than in expt. 1, but the reaction rates for both experiments are the same. Therefore, metal Y does not act as a catalyst. In the same manner, comparing expt. Nos. 2 and 5, we find that metal X does not act as a catalyst. Comparing expt. Nos. 3 and 4, we find that metal Z does act as a catalyst.

96. **(C)** The K_c for a reaction is its equilibrium constant involving concentration in moles/lit or Molarity (M). In order to calculate K_c, we must know the M of all reactants and products at equilibrium.

$$CO_{(g)} + H_2O_{(g)} \rightleftharpoons CO_{2(g)} + H_{2(g)}$$

From the equation, we see that one mole of CO reacts with one mole of H_2O to form one mole of CO_2 and one mole of H_2. Therefore, if 0.3 mole of CO_2 is present at equilibrium, the moles of CO at equilibrium are

$$(0.5 - 0.3) = 0.2 \text{ mole,}$$

moles of H_2O at equilibrium are

$$(1.0 - 0.3) = 0.7$$

and moles of H_2 at equilibrium are 0.3.

Now let's calculate equilibrium concentrations of each.

$$[CO] = \frac{0.2 \text{ mole}}{5.0 \text{ lit}} = 0.04 \text{ M}$$

$$[H_2O] = \frac{0.7 \text{ mole}}{5.0 \text{ lit}} = 0.14 \text{ M}$$

$$[CO_2] = \frac{0.3 \text{ mole}}{5.0 \text{ lit}} = 0.06 \text{ M}$$

$$[H_2] = \frac{0.3 \text{ mole}}{5.0 \text{ lit}} = 0.06 \text{ M}$$

The expression for K_c for this reaction is

$$K_c = \frac{[CO_2][H_2]}{[CO][H_2O]} = \frac{(0.06)(0.06)}{(0.04)(0.14)} = 0.64$$

97. **(B)** Conditions for this equilibrium are concentration, pressure (because we have 4 moles of gases on the left and 2 moles of gases on the right), and temperature (because the reaction is exothermic).

The correct choice, therefore, is (B): in order to maximize the yield of NH_3, increase concentrations of H_2 and N_2 and decrease the temperature.

98. **(A)** The standard reduction potential for

$$Ag^+ + 1\, e \rightarrow Ag^\circ$$

is more positive (+0.80 volts) than for

$$Cu^{+2} + 2\, e \rightarrow Cu^\circ$$

(+0.34 volts). This means that silver has greater tendency for reduction than copper. Therefore, in this galvanic cell, copper will be oxidized and silver will be reduced.

$$Cu^\circ + 2\, e \rightarrow Cu^{+2} \quad \text{Half equation for oxidation.}$$

$$Ag^+ + 1\, e \rightarrow Ag^\circ \quad \text{Half equation for reduction.}$$

Using the electron balance method, we get the balanced equation:

$$Cu^\circ + 2\, e \rightarrow Cu^{+2}$$

$$2\, Ag^+ - 2\, e \rightarrow 2\, Ag^\circ$$

$$Cu_{(s)}^\circ + 2\, Ag^+_{(aq)} \rightarrow Cu^{+2}_{(aq)} + Ag_{(s)}^\circ \tag{1}$$

The standard electrode potential,

$$E^\circ = E_{reduction} - E_{oxidation}$$

$$= (+0.80 \text{ volts}) - (+0.34 \text{ volts}) = 0.46 \text{ volts}$$

The actual e.m.f. (E_{actual}) can be calculated using the Nearnst Equation.

$$E_{actual} = E^\circ - RT \ln K,$$

where R = gas constant, T = temperature in K, and K = equilibrium expression for the reaction.

Looking at balanced equation (1),

$$K = \frac{[Cu^{+2}]}{[Ag^+]^2}$$

At 25°C and using log to the base of 10, the Nearnst Equation can be written as:

$$E_{actual} = E° - \frac{0.0592}{n} \log K,$$

where n = number of moles of electrons transferred in a balanced equation.

In this reaction $n = 2$. Substituting in the equation,

$$E_{actual} = E° - \frac{0.0592}{n} \log \frac{[Cu^{+2}]}{[Ag^+]^2}$$

$$= 0.56 - \frac{0.0592}{2} \log \frac{[0.1]}{[0.1]^2}$$

$$= 0.53 \text{ v}$$

99. **(C)** P_1 and P_3 are forces generated by two aluminum rods with corresponding deformation, Δ_1 and Δ_3.

P_2 is the force generated by the steel rod in the middle with corresponding deformation, Δ_2.

From equilibrium equation:

$$P_1 + P_2 + P_3 = 222,400 \tag{1}$$

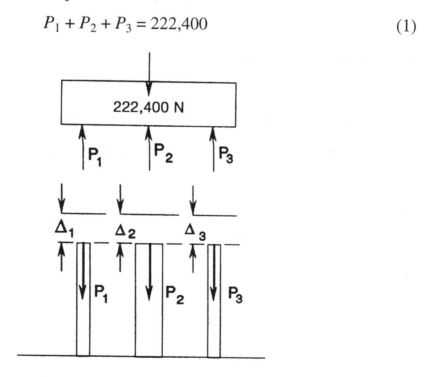

Deformations

This is a statistically indeterminate problem since the equilibrium equation has too many unknowns. Therefore, deformation must be considered.

$$\Delta_1 = \Delta_2 = \Delta_3;$$

since $\qquad \sigma = \dfrac{P}{A}; \varepsilon = \dfrac{\Delta}{L}$ and $\sigma = E\varepsilon$ gives

$$\frac{P}{A} = E\frac{\Delta}{L} \quad \text{or} \quad \Delta = \frac{PL}{AE}$$

We have

$$L_1 = L_2 = L_3 = 0.254 \text{ m}$$

$$A_1 = A_3 = \pi(0.0127)^2 \text{ and } A_2 = \pi(0.0254)^2$$

$$E_1 = E_3 = E_{AL} = 6.89 \cdot 10^{10} \text{ N/m}^2 \text{ and } E_2 = E_s = 2.07 \cdot 10^{11} \text{ N/m}^2$$

Considering $\Delta_1 = \Delta_3$ and substituting the above values,

$$\frac{P_1(0.254 \text{ m})}{\pi(0.0127)^2 \times (6.89 \times 10^{10} \text{ N/m}^2)} = \frac{P_3(0.254 \text{ m})}{\pi(0.0127)^2 \times (6.89 \times 10^{10} \text{ N/m}^2)}$$

gives $\qquad\qquad\qquad P_1 = P_3 \qquad\qquad\qquad$ (2)

This could also have been obtained by observing symmetry.

Consider $\Delta_1 = \Delta_2$ and substituting values of A, E, and L,

$$\frac{P_1(0.254 \text{ m})}{\pi(0.0127)^2 \times (6.89 \times 10^{10} \text{ N/m}^2)} = \frac{P_2(0.254 \text{ m})}{\pi(0.0254)^2 \times (2.07 \times 10^{11} \text{ N/m}^2)}$$

gives $\qquad\qquad\qquad P_2 = 12P_1 \qquad\qquad\qquad$ (3)

Substituting (2) and (3) in (1), we get

$$P_1 + 12P_1 + P_1 = 14P_1 = 222,400 \text{ N}$$

$$P_1 = 15,900 \text{ N}; \text{ so } P_2 = 12P_1 = 12(15,900) = 190,600 \text{ N}$$

100. **(B)**

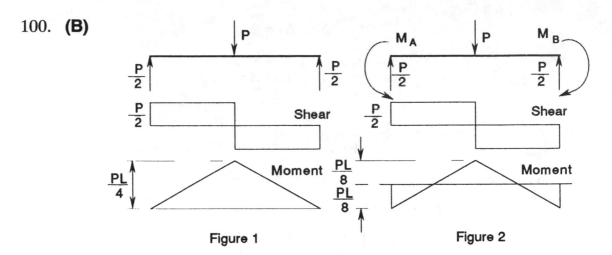

Figure 1   Figure 2

For Beam in Figure 1:

Between $x = 0$ to $L/2$ (left side)

$$V_x = \frac{P}{2} \text{ ;since } \frac{dM}{dx} = V$$

$$M = \int V dx = \frac{P}{2} x + c$$

at $x = 0$, $M = 0$ giving $c = 0$ so

$$M = \frac{P}{2} x,$$

giving maximum moment at $x = L/2$

$$M_{max} = \frac{P}{2}\left(\frac{L}{2}\right) = \frac{PL}{4}$$

For Beam in Figure 2:

Between $x = 0$ to $L/2$ (left side)

$$V_x = \frac{P}{2} \text{ giving } M = \frac{P}{2} x + c$$

at $x = 0$, $M = M_A$ giving $c = -M_A$ so

$$M = \frac{P}{2} x - M_A .$$

In this moment equation, the slope of moment line is $P/2$ and the intercept is $-M_A$. Maximum moment is at $x = 0$ and $x = L/2$.

$$M_{max}\Big|_{x=0} = -\frac{PL}{8}$$

$$M_{max}\Big|_{x=\frac{L}{2}} = \frac{PL}{8}$$

Since maximum moment of Case 2 is half that of Case 1, the beam in Case 2 will support twice the load, hence, 100% more.

101. **(A)** If the 30 ft long rail was allowed to expand freely, then total elongation would be

$$\Delta = \alpha\,(\Delta T)\,L = 6.5 \times 10^{-6}\ \text{in/in}\,°\text{F}\ (140°\text{F} - 60°\text{F})\ (30\ \text{ft} \times 12\ \text{in/ft})$$

$$= 0.1872\ \text{in}$$

Since the rail can grow freely up to 0.1 in, no stress will develop up to that growth.

Compressive stress will develop due to restriction of $(0.1872 - 0.1) = 0.0872$ in growth. The equivalent stress for this growth is:

corresponding strain is $\varepsilon = \frac{\Delta}{L} = 0.0872\ \text{in}\ /\ (30\ \text{ft} \times 12\ \text{in/ft})$

$$= 0.0002422$$

$$\sigma = E\varepsilon = 30 \times 10^6\ \text{psi} \times 0.0002422\ /\ (30\ \text{ft} \times 12\ \text{in/ft})$$

$$= 7{,}266\ \text{(compression)}$$

102. **(A)** The actual elongation is 0.1 in. So the actual strain is

$$\varepsilon = \frac{\Delta}{L} = 0.1\ \text{in}\ /\ (30\ \text{ft} \times 12\ \text{in/ft}) = 0.000277.$$

Note: In thermal stress problems, the formula $\sigma = E\varepsilon$ does not use actual strain. As, for example, in the previous problem, it used an equivalent strain of 0.0002422, which resulted from restricting the growth of 0.0872 in. A rod that grows freely has zero stress but finite strain. Similarly, a rod that is totally restricted to grow has zero strain but finite stress.

103. **(C)** The beam is simply supported, so the bending moment at the ends are zero. Since

$$\frac{dM}{dx} = V,\ M \text{ is maximum where } \frac{dM}{dx} = 0 \ \text{ or }\ V = 0.$$

So we locate the zero shear point as follows:

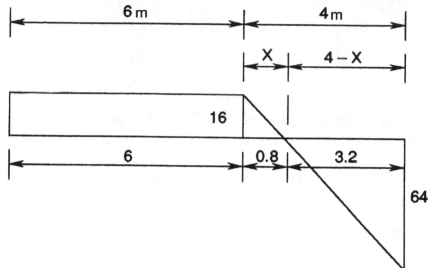

From similar triangles:

$$\frac{x}{16} = \frac{4-x}{64}$$
$$64x = 64 - 16x$$
$$x = \frac{64}{80} = 0.8$$
$$(\text{so, } 4 - x = 3.2).$$

Since moment is zero at the ends, the moment at zero shear point is given by the area of the shear diagram to the left (or to the right) of the zero shear point. Note:

$$dM = Vdx; \int_0^M dM = \int_0^x Vdx;$$

hence, increase in moment = area of shear diagram.

Area of shear diagram to the left

$$= (16\text{ N}) (6\text{ m}) + \tfrac{1}{2} (16\text{ N}) (0.8\text{ m}) = 102.4\text{ Nm or}$$

Area of shear diagram to the right

$$= \tfrac{1}{2} (64\text{ N}) (3.2\text{ m}) = 102.4\text{ Nm.}$$

104. **(C)** Original volume of rod

$$V_0 = \pi R^2 L = \pi (0.076)^2 (0.91) = 0.0165\text{ m}^3$$

Axial Strain

$$\varepsilon_{xx} = \frac{\sigma_{xx}}{E} = \frac{P}{AE} = \frac{222,410 \text{ N}}{\pi(0.076)^2(2.07\times10^{11}\text{N/m}^2)} = 5.92\times10^{-5}$$

There is no stress in y and z direction. Hence,

$$\varepsilon_{yy} = \varepsilon_{zz} = -v\varepsilon_{xx} = -0.3\,(5.92\times10^{-5}) = -17.76\times10^{-6}.$$

Changes in dimensions are obtained from the definition of strain as follows:

$$\varepsilon_{xx} = \frac{\Delta L}{L} = \frac{\Delta L}{0.91 \text{ m}} = 5.92\times10^{-5}; \Delta L = 5.39\bullet10^{-5} \text{ m}$$

(+ indicates increase in length due to tension.)

$$\varepsilon_{yy} = \varepsilon_{zz} = \frac{\Delta D}{D} = -17.76\times10^{-6}; \; D = 0.152 \text{ m}$$

Therefore, change in diameter

$$\Delta D = (-17.76\times10^{-6})\,(0.152 \text{ m}) = -2.69\bullet10^{-6} \text{ m}.$$

(– indicates decrease in diameter due to Poisson Ratio effect.)

New length $L' = L + \Delta L = 0.9100539$ m

New diameter $= 0.152 - 2.69\bullet10^{-6} = 0.151997$ m

New volume $V' = \pi\left(\dfrac{D'}{2}\right)^2 (L') = 0.016513 \text{ m}^3$

Change in volume $= V' - V_0 = 0.016513 - 0.0165 = +0.000013$ m

(+ indicates increase in volume.)

Note: For Poisson Ratio $v = 0.5$, there is no change in volume.

105. **(C)** The pin shear stress may be obtained by two methods:

1. The total load of 5,000 N is supported by two cross-sectional areas a and b as shown in Figure (a).

Net shear area $= 2\left[\dfrac{\pi}{4}d^2\right] = 2\left[\dfrac{\pi}{4}(1\text{ m})^2\right] = 1.57 \text{ m}^3$

Pin shear stress $\tau = \dfrac{5,000 \text{ N}}{1.57 \text{ m}^2} = 3,185 \text{ N/m}^2$

2. The approximate free-body diagram of the pin is shown in Figure (b). From symmetry, R on both the left and right end of the pin is 2,500 N. Considering the pin as a beam, maximum shear force is 2,500 N. Hence, maximum shear stress is

$$\frac{2,500 \text{ N}}{\left(\frac{\pi}{4}\right)(1 \text{ m})^2} = 3,185 \text{ N/m}^2$$

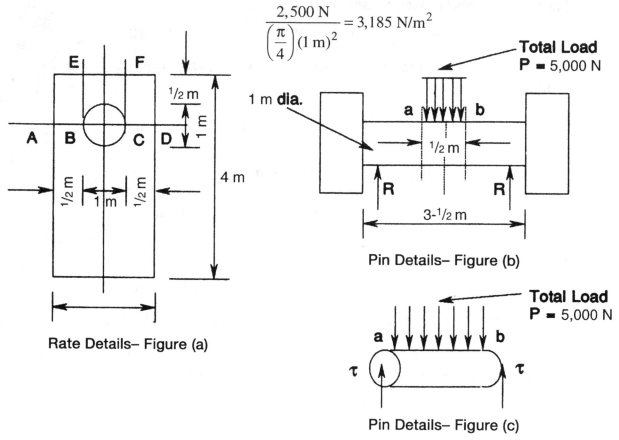

Rate Details– Figure (a)

Pin Details– Figure (b)

Pin Details– Figure (c)

106. **(A)** Maximum tensile stress will be acting at minimum plate area (section *AB* and *CD* at Figure (A) in Answer 105).

Max Plate Tensile Stress

$$= \frac{5,000 \text{ N}}{2\left(\frac{1}{2} \text{ m} \times \frac{1}{2} \text{ m}\right)} = 10,000 \text{ N/m}^2$$

107. **(B)** Since *EI* is variable along the length, the "Moment-Area" method is employed.

$$y_c = \text{Deflection at } C = A_{EI}\,\overline{X}_c,$$

where A_{EI} = Area of $M/_{EI}$ vs. x diagram left of point C

$\overline{X}_c$ = Distance of centroid of A_{EI} measured from C.

Moment Diagram

$$E_{AB}\, I_{AB} = 20 \times 10^6 \text{ N/m}^2 \times 0.67 \text{ m}^4$$

$$= 13.4 \times 10^6 \text{ Nm}^2$$

$$E_{BC}\, I_{BC} = 30 \times 10^6 \text{ N/m}^2 \times 0.083 \text{ m}^4$$

$$= 2.49 \times 10^6 \text{ Nm}^2$$

M/EI Diagram

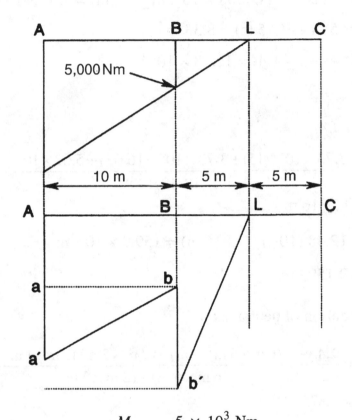

$$\frac{M}{E_{AB}I_{AB}} = \frac{5 \times 10^3 \text{ Nm}}{13.4 \times 10^6 \text{ Nm}^2}$$

$$= 0.373 \times 10^{-3}\,\text{m}^{-1}$$

$$\frac{M}{E_{AB}I_{AB}} = \frac{15 \times 10^3 \text{ Nm}}{13.4 \times 10^6 \text{ Nm}^2}$$

$$= 1.119 \times 10^{-3}\,\text{m}^{-1}$$

$$\frac{M}{E_{BC}I_{BC}} = \frac{5 \times 10^3 \text{ Nm}}{2.49 \times 10^6 \text{ Nm}^2}$$

$$= 2.008 \times 10^{-3}\,\text{m}^{-1}$$

A_{EI} and $\overline{X}_c$ is determined from the above diagram as follows:

A_1 = $ABba = 0.373 \times 10^{-3}$ m$^{-1} \times 10$ m $= 3.73 \times 10^{-3}$

x_1 = 10 m + 5 m = 15 m

A_2 = $aba' = \frac{1}{2}(1.119 - 0.373) \times 10^{-3}(10$ m$) = 3.73 \times 10^{-3}$

x_2 = 10 m + $\frac{2}{3}(10$ m$) = 16.67$ m

A_3 = $BLb' = \frac{1}{2}(2.008 \times 10^{-3}$ m$^{-1})(5$ m$) = 5.02 \times 10^{-3}$

x_3 = 5 m + $\frac{2}{3}(5$ m$) = 8.33$ m

A_{EI} = $A_1 + A_2 + A_3 = 12.48 \times 10^{-3}$

$$\overline{X}_c = \frac{\Sigma A_i X_i}{\Sigma A_i}$$

$$= \frac{3.73 \times 10^{-3}(15) + 3.73 \times 10^{-3}(16.67) + 5.02 \times 10^{-3}(8.33)}{12.48 \times 10^{-3}}$$

$$= 12.816 \text{ m}$$

$$\overline{Y}_c = 12.48(10^{-3})(12.816 \text{ m}) = 159.9 \times 10^{-3} \text{ m}$$

$$= 0.1599 \text{ m}$$

108. **(C)** Location of neutral axis

$$\overline{y} = \frac{\Sigma A_i y_i}{\Sigma A_i} = \frac{(6 \text{ m} \times 6 \text{ m})(3 \text{ m}) - (2 \text{ m} \times 2 \text{ m})(3 \text{ m} + 1 \text{ m})}{(6 \text{ m} \times 6 \text{ m}) - (2 \text{ m} \times 2 \text{ m})}$$

$$= 2.875 \text{ m}$$

NA is located 2.87 m from the bottom surface.

Y_A (distance between *NA* and Point *A*) = 5 m − 2.875 m = 2.125 m

I_{NA} = $\frac{1}{12}(6$ m $\times 6$ m$^3) + (6$ m $\times 6$ m$)(3$ m $- 2.875$ m$)^2$

$- [\frac{1}{12}(2$ m $\times 2$ m$^3) + (2$ m $\times 2$ m$)(4$ m $- 2.875$ m$)^2]$

= 102.163 m^4

$$\sigma_A = \frac{MY_A}{I} = \frac{(10,000 \text{ Nm})(2.125 \text{ m})}{102.163 \text{ m}^4} = 208 \text{ N/m}^2$$

109. **(D)** Effective interest rate per compounding subperiod is

$$i = \frac{r}{m}$$

Here $r = 10\%$ and $m = 2$. Therefore, $i = {}^{10\%}/_2 = 5\%$.

110. **(B)** The inflation may vary. Therefore, the future payments in year 0 dollars will not be constant and will change with changes in inflation.

111. **(B)**

Year	Book Value Before Depreciation Change	SOYD Depreciation for the Year	Book Value After Depreciation Change
1	76.00	${}^{5}/_{15}\,(76\text{--}6) = 23.33$	52.67
2	52.67	${}^{4}/_{15}\,(76 - 6) = 18.67$	34.00
3	34.00	${}^{3}/_{15}\,(76 - 6) = 14.00$	20.00
4	20.00	${}^{2}/_{15}\,(76 - 6) = 9.33$	10.67
5	10.67	${}^{1}/_{15}\,(76 - 6) = 4.67$	6.00

Note: The book values and depreciation in the above table are in millions of dollars.

112. **(C)** Draw the cash-flow diagram.

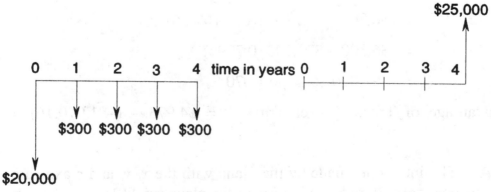

i = interest rate per year compounded annually

The rate of return must be found by a trial-and-error process as shown below. If the rate of return is $i\%$, then the present worth of revenue should equal the present worth of expenses.

$$\underbrace{\$20,000 + \$300\ (P/A,\ i\%, 4)}_{\text{Present worth of expenses}} = \underbrace{\$25,000(P/F,\ i\%, 4)}_{\text{Present worth of revenue}}$$

Compute the left-hand side (LHS) and right-hand side (RHS) of the above equation for different values of i using interest tables for annual compounding. The value of i that makes LHS = RHS is the rate of return on the investment.

Interest Rate (%)	LHS ($)	RHS ($)	RHS– LHS ($)
3	21,115.00	22,212.50	1,097.50
4	21,088.00	21,370.00	282.00
5	21,063,00	20,567.00	– 496.00

The rate of return is about 4%.

113. **(D)** *EUAB*: Equivalent Annual Benefit
     EUAC: Equivalent Annual Cost

Truck A:

$$
\begin{aligned}
EUAB - EUAC &= \$5,400 - \$15,900\ (A/P,\ 10\%,\ 5) \\
&= \$5,400 - \$15,900\ (0.02683) \\
&= \$4,973.40 \approx \$4,973
\end{aligned}
$$

Truck B:

$$
\begin{aligned}
EUAB - EUAC &= \$6,300 - \$32,100\ (A/P,\ 10\%,\ 6) \\
&= \$6,300 - \$32,100\ (0.2296) \\
&= -\$1,070.16 \approx -\$1,070
\end{aligned}
$$

Advantage of Truck A over Truck B = $\$4,973 - (-\$1,070.16) = \$6,043$.

114. **(A)** The intercepts made by the plane with the x, y, and z axes are 1, 1, $^1/_2$, respectively. Hence, the indices of the plane are 112.

115. **(C)** In a fiber reinforced material which is loaded in a direction parallel to that of the fibers, the elastic modulus of the composite is given by the rule of mixtures as $E_c = (1 - f)E_m + fE_f$, where f is the volume fraction of the fibers, E_m is the elastic modulus of the matrix, and E_f is the elastic modulus of the fibers. Application of this formula yields for the elastic modulus of the composite a value of 2.32 million N/m^2.

$$E_c = (1 - 0.2) \ 400{,}000 \ \text{N/m}^2 + 0.2 \ (10{,}000{,}000 \ \text{N/m}^2) = 2.32 \bullet 10^6 \ \text{N/m}^2$$

116. **(B)** Tensile and yield strengths increase with decreasing grain size according to the Hall-Petch relationship. Impact strength also increases with grain refinement. Creep resistance decreases with decreasing grain size due to increased diffusion flow contributing to several mechanisms of creep.

117. **(C)** In metals, the electrical conductivity decreases with increasing temperature due to increased resistance to electron flow by the phonons. In ionic materials, electrical conductivity is due to diffusional migration of ions which is accelerated by increasing the temperature. Thus, the conductivity increases with increasing temperature. In semiconductors of all types, one obtains an increase in the number of charge carriers with an increase in the temperature due to the increased thermal activation. Since conductivity is proportional to the product of number of charge carriers per unit volume and the velocity of charge carriers, one obtains, again, an increase in the conductivity.

118. **(A)** The unit cell of the body centered cubic crystal has eight atoms in the corners of the unit cell (each being shared by eight unit cells) and one atom at the center of the cube which belongs entirely to the unit cell. Thus, the total number of atoms belonging to one unit cell is $1 + {}^8/_8 = 2$.

119. **(D)** In wire drawing, the material is plastically deformed to obtain a reduction in the cross-sectional area. The material property that characterizes this is the ductility. None of the other properties in the list relate to this.

120. **(A)** This program segment gives a 4-term series with alternating signs. (B) is incorrect since the signs do not alternate. (C) and (D) are incorrect since the whole denominator is not raised to the $-K$ power, only the (-1) portion is $(-1)^K$.

FE/EIT

Fundamentals of Engineering: AM Exam

Practice Test 3

FUNDAMENTALS OF ENGINEERING - MORNING SESSION
Test 3

(Answer sheets appear in the back of this book.)

TIME: 4 Hours
120 Questions

> **DIRECTIONS**: For each of the following questions and incomplete statements, choose the best answer from the four answer choices.

1. $A = i + 2j$ is a two-component vector. Another vector B, which is perpendicular to A and whose component in the i direction is -6.2 is

   (A) $-62i - 4.7j$.

   (B) $-6.2i - 1.8j$.

   (C) $-6.2i + 3.1j$.

   (D) $-6.2i + 4.7j$.

2. The differential equation

   $$3\frac{d^2y}{dt^2} + t\frac{dy}{dt} - 4y = \sin(2t) \text{ is}$$

   (A) first-order, linear, and homogeneous.

   (B) second-order, linear, and homogeneous.

   (C) first-order, nonlinear, and homogeneous

   (D) second-order, linear, and nonhomogeneous.

3. The value of the limit

   $$\lim_{x \to 0} \frac{x + \tan x}{\sin 3x} \text{ is}$$

(A) 1.

(C) $\frac{1}{2}$.

(B) 2.

(D) $\frac{2}{3}$.

4. The length of each side of a regular pentagon inscribed in a unit circle is

(A) 0.26.

(C) 0.78.

(B) 0.59.

(D) 1.18.

5. The product of the complex numbers $(2 + 4i)$ and $(1 - 7i)$ is

(A) $30 - 10i$.

(C) $17 + 24i$.

(B) $22 + 8i$.

(D) $10 - 24i$.

6. Jones, a registered mechanical engineer, is hired by an old friend to act as chief engineer for a bridge construction project. The old friend is hiring Jones primarily for his managerial abilities and plans to provide Jones with a fully competent technical staff. Is it ethical for Jones to accept this position?

(A) No, since this project is out of his field of expertise.

(B) Yes, since Jones is not directly handling the technical aspects of the problem.

(C) No, since there could be a conflict of interest.

(D) Yes, since a registered engineer should be able to handle any type of project.

7. Let $x = 2$ be an initial approximation of the root to the expression

$$x^3 + 4x^2 + 2x - 2 = 0.$$

The next approximation of the root as calculated by Newton's method is

(A) 4.77.

(C) 0.92.

(B) 2.04.

(D) 1.13.

8. The concentration of a particular pesticide decays exponentially. One-half of the initial amount of the pesticide decomposes in 30 years. How many years are required for 90% of the pesticide to decompose?

   (A) 21   (C) 48

   (B) 37   (D) 100

9. The value of

$$\int_1^3 \frac{4x\,dx}{6+x^2} \text{ is}$$

   (A) 0.16.   (C) 1.20.

   (B) 0.58.   (D) 1.52.

10. The total differential of

$$F(x, y, z) = (1 + e^{xz}) \sin 4y \text{ is}$$

   (A) $z \sin(4y)\,dx + 2\cos(4y)e^{xz}\,dy + x\,e^{xz}\sin(4y)\,dz$.

   (B) $z\,e^{xz}\sin(4y)\,dx + 4\cos(4y)(1 + e^{xz})\,dy + x\,e^{xz}\sin(4y)\,dz$.

   (C) $x\,e^{xz}\cos(4y)\,dx + 16\cos(4y)(1 + e^{xz})\,dy + 4x\,e^{xz}\sin(4y)\,dz$.

   (D) $2z\,e^{xz}\cos(4y)\,dx + 2\cos(4y)(1 + 2e^{xz})\,dy + y\,e^{xz}\sin(4y)\,dz$.

11. The partial fraction expansion of

$$\frac{s-3}{(s+2)(s+3)(s+4)} \text{ is } \frac{A}{s+3} + \frac{B}{s+2} + \frac{C}{s+4}.$$

   The values of A, B, and C are

   (A) $-3, -\dfrac{5}{2}, 7$.   (C) $6, -\dfrac{5}{2}, -\dfrac{7}{2}$.

   (B) $2, -5, 7$.   (D) $-6, 6, -3$.

12. Measurements X have a normal distribution, which has a mean of 16 and a standard deviation of 2. The probability of measuring a value of X between 15 and 19 is

(A) $\dfrac{1}{\sqrt{2\pi}} \displaystyle\int_{0.5}^{1.5} e^{-Z^2/2}\, dZ$. (C) $\dfrac{1}{\sqrt{2\pi}} \displaystyle\int_{15}^{19} e^{-Z^2/2}\, dZ$.

(B) $\dfrac{1}{\sqrt{2\pi}} \displaystyle\int_{-0.5}^{1.5} e^{-Z^2/2}\, dZ$. (D) $\dfrac{1}{\sqrt{2\pi}} \displaystyle\int_{0}^{16} e^{-Z^2/2}\, dZ$.

13. Mary's boss is an acknowledged expert in the field of catalysis. Mary is the leader of a group that has been charged with developing a new catalyst system, and the search has narrowed to two possibilities, Catalyst A and Catalyst B. The boss is certain that the best choice is A, but he directs that tests be run on both, "just for the record." Owing to inexperienced help, the tests take longer than expected and the results show that B is the preferred material. The boss, therefore, directs Mary to work the math backwards and come up with phony data to substantiate the choice of Catalyst A. Mary writes the report. Was it ethical for Mary to write the report under these circumstances?

(A) Yes, since she was following the order of her immediate superior.

(B) No, since misrepresentation of data is a violation of the Code of Ethics.

(C) Yes, since their was no harm to the public welfare.

(D) Yes, since this data was not being published in a referenced journal.

14. Dale is a chemical engineer who changed employment from Company A to Company B. Before leaving Company A, his manager asked him to sign a document in which he agreed to keep confidential any proprietary information which he acquired at Company A. Soon after he arrives at Company B, Dale is assigned to solve a problem involving a new emission, Compound X, which is not regulated by the EPA. Dale's new manager does not know whether to be concerned about Compound X or not. However, Dale realizes that some of the proprietary information he acquired at Company A might enable him to modify the manufacturing process at Company B so that the suspicious new product would not be produced in the first place. This information would be used in an entirely different way than it was used by Company A and would not harm the competitive position of Company A with respect to Company B. Should

Dale approach his new manager with a proposal that requires the use of this information?

(A) No, since the document that he signed forbids him from making the revelation.

(B) No, since this would lead to a possible conflict of interest.

(C) Yes, since he has no obligations to his former employer.

(D) Yes, since this falls under the umbrella of public welfare, Dale should make the revelation.

15. Forty electrical engineers, 20 chemical engineers, 30 mechanical engineers, and 10 civil engineers attend a banquet. A television station randomly selects four engineers to interview. What is the probability that someone from all four disciplines will be interviewed?

(A) 4 / 100

(C) 240,000 / 94,109,400

(B) 198,360 / 94,109,400

(D) 224,120 / 100,000,000

16. Rotate the curve defined by $x^2 + y^2 = 1$ around the y-axis. The volume is

(A) $\dfrac{\pi}{6}$.

(C) $\dfrac{\pi}{2}$.

(B) $\dfrac{\pi}{3}$.

(D) $\dfrac{4\pi}{3}$.

17. A set of linear equations is written as

$$Ax = b$$

where A is the matrix of constant coefficients

x is the vector of unknown values

b is the vector of known constants

Let A^T represent the transpose of A

A^{-1} represent the inverse of A

The vector x can be determined by

(A) $x = A^{-1} b$ (C) $x = b A^{-1}$

(B) $x = A^{\mathrm{T}} b$ (D) $x = b A^{\mathrm{T}}$

18. What is the radius of the circle described by

$$x^2 - 4x + y^2 - 2y - 4 = 0?$$

(A) 1   (C) 3

(B) 2.7   (D) 4.2

19. Find the area of the region bounded by

$$x = 0$$
$$y = x + 1$$
$$y = .5 \, x^2$$

(A) 0.48   (C) 1.25

(B) 0.99   (D) 3.07

20. The tangent to the curve

$$y = x \, e^x \text{ at } x = 0.8 \text{ is}$$

(A) 1.8.   (C) 4.0.

(B) 3.6.   (D) 5.2.

21. In the circuit shown here, the capacitor had been charged to a voltage of 100 V before it was connected to a 100 K resistor to discharge. The voltage decreased to 36.8 V in 0.2 sec. The value of the capacitance is

(A) $2 \, \mu F.$

(B) $1 \, \mu F.$

(C) $4 \, \mu F.$

(D) $0.5 \, \mu F.$

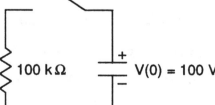

t = 0

100 kΩ   V(0) = 100 V

22. In the circuit shown below, before the switch is closed at time $t = 0$, no energy was stored either in the capacitor or in the inductor. Immediately after closing the switch, the current in the 3 Ω resistor is given by

    (A) 2.4 A

    (B) 4.0 A

    (C) 10.0 A

    (D) 3.3 A

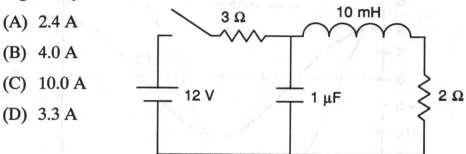

23. A resistor, an inductor, and a capacitor are connected in parallel to an AC source, and the values of the inductance L and the capacitance C have been adjusted so that the circuit is in resonance. The current i is

    (A) a maximum.   (C) lags the voltage by 90°.

    (B) a minimum.   (D) leads the voltage by 90°.

24. In the circuit shown here the voltage across the 4 Ω resistor is given by

    (A) 80 |53°.

    (B) 80 |–37°.

    (C) 18.71 |53°.

    (D) 18.71 |–53°.

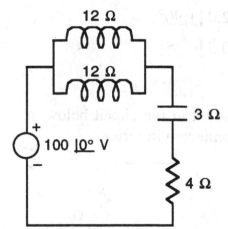

25. The voltage $v(t)$ and current $i(t)$ at the two terminals of a passive element have been recorded and are shown below. The impedance of this element is

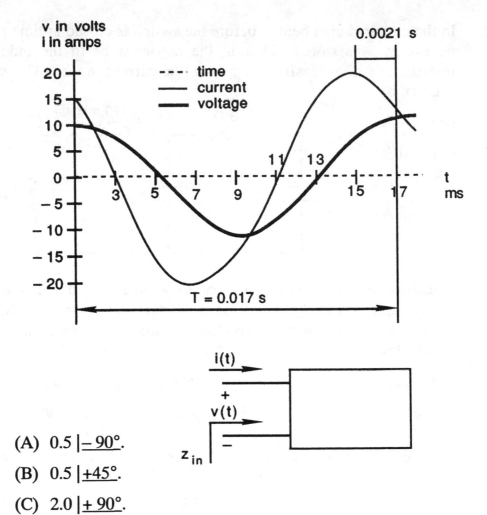

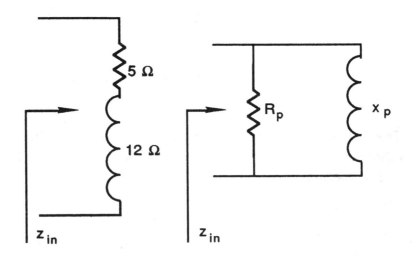

(A) $0.5 \underline{|-90°}$.

(B) $0.5 \underline{|+45°}$.

(C) $2.0 \underline{|+90°}$.

(D) $0.5 \underline{|-45°}$.

26. As shown in the circuit below, a 5 Ω resistor and a 12 Ω inductor are connected in series.

The value of the resistor R_p in a parallel combination shown above with the same input impedance is

(A) 12.0 Ω. (C) 33.8 Ω.

(B) 13.5 Ω. (D) 14.1 Ω.

27. An AC voltage of variable frequency is applied to the circuit shown below:

$v(t) = 120 \cos \omega t$

$R = 10 \text{ k}\Omega$

$L = 10 \text{ mH}$

$C = 50 \text{ μF}$

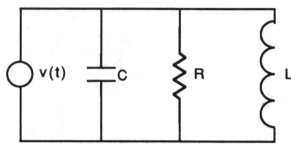

The angular frequency ω at which this circuit is resonant is given by:

(A) $1000s^{-1}$. (C) $14.14s^{-1}$.

(B) $1414s^{-1}$. (D) $700s^{-1}$.

28. In the circuit shown below the switch is closed at $t = 0$. The transient component of the current after the switch closes has a frequency of oscillation of

(A) 497 Hz.

(B) 6,240 Hz.

(C) 1,000 Hz.

(D) 159 Hz.

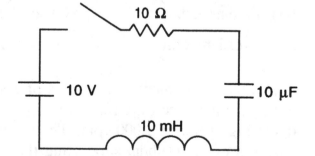

29. Two one phase loads, a 5 KW resistor, and a 10 KVA load with a 0.707 lagging power factor are connected in parallel to a 120 V source. The power factor of the current supplied to the two loads by the source is

(A) 0.71.   (C) 0.46.

(B) 0.67.   (D) 0.86.

30. Consider the diagram below. If the vibration is damped with the characteristic equation:

$$m\ddot{y} + c\dot{y} + ky = 0$$

or

$$m\frac{d^2y}{dt^2} + c\frac{dy}{dt} + ky = 0$$

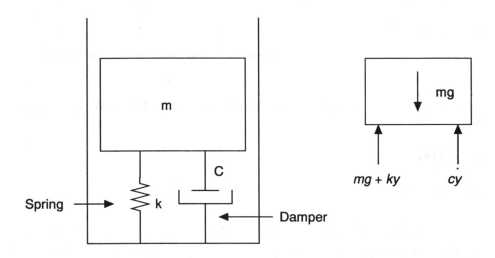

then the value of $c > c_{crit}$, then the system is said to be

(A) no damped.   (C) critically damped.

(B) overdamped.   (D) underdamped.

31. A piece of equipment with a mass of 100 lb has a rotating element with an imbalance (m_1e times gravity is 182 in/sec² 3 lb/in and an operating speed of 1,000 rpm. There are four springs, each with a stiffness of 1,500 lb/in, supporting the machine, whose frame may translate vertically. The damping ratio is 0.2. What is the effective external force amplitude?

(A) 300 lb   (C) 180 lb

(B) 50 lb   (D) 100 lb

32. To the three wire, three phase network shown here with an unbalanced load, a balanced three line 220 V voltage of positive sequence is applied. The current in line b, I_b is given by

(A) 75.5 A.

(B) 55.5A.

(C) 105.7 A.

(D) 104.6 A.

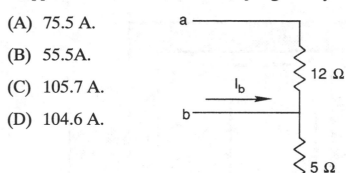

33. The crank shaft of an automobile may be subjected to the following combined stresses:

(A) torsional.

(C) flexural and axial.

(B) flexural.

(D) torsional and flexural.

34. The bonding in copper is referred to as

(A) sigma.

(C) ionic.

(B) covalent.

(D) metallic.

35. The resistance of a *Newtonian* fluid to a constant shearing force shows what general characteristics?

(A) Rate of deformation decreases with time.

(B) Rate of deformation is independent of shear force.

(C) Rate of deformation is directly proportional to shear force.

(D) Rate of deformation decreases with increasing shear force.

36. In the figure below, water is flowing out of the tank through the tube. Gravity is acting downward. Set up in this fashion, liquid will flow out of the tube because

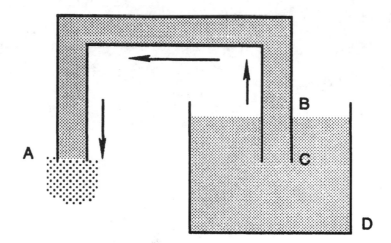

(A) the pressure at point *A* is higher than the pressure at point *C*.

(B) the pressure at point *A* is higher than the pressure at point *B*.

(C) the pressure at point *C* is higher than the pressure at point *A*.

(D) the pipe at point *C* is above point *D*.

QUESTIONS 37 and 38 refer to the following figure:

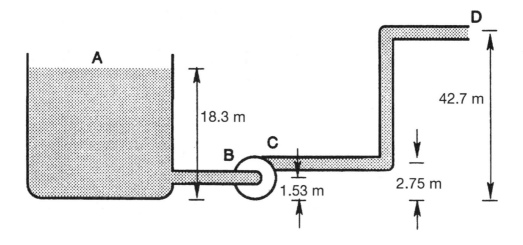

Note: The density of water is 997.5 kg/m³. All piping diameters are 0.305 m.

37. If the pump in the figure provides 30.5 m of head, what is the discharge velocity at point D in m/sec? Neglect friction losses in the piping.

(A) 0.55 m/s   (C) 16.5 m/s

(B) 10.9 m/s   (D) 22.6 m/s

38. What is the pressure at the inlet to the pump if the discharge velocity is measured at 15.2 m/s?

(A) $-1.013 \cdot 10^5$ N/m^{2}g   (C) $2.07 \cdot 10^3$ N/m^{2}g

(B) $-1.013 \cdot 10^4$ N/m^{2}g   (D) $4.83 \cdot 10^4$ N/m^{2}g

39. A Pitot-static tube is placed into an air duct and the deflection of the gage is 0.041 m of water. What is the velocity of air in the duct? Assume that the density of air is 1.2 kg/m^3.

(A) 81 m/s   (C) 73.5 m/s

(B) 94.3 m/s   (D) 19.5 m/s

40. Consider the hydraulic jump which exists at the outflow of a dam. The outflow is controlled so that the depth of the fluid at the outflow is constant. An increase in the volumetric flow rate through the dam will have what effect on the hydraulic jump?

(A) Increase the height difference across the jump and move its location upstream.

(B) Decrease the height difference across the jump and move its location upstream.

(C) Increase the height difference across the jump and move its location downstream.

(D) Decrease the height difference across the jump and move its location downstream.

41. Which of the following instruments for measuring fluid velocities does not need to be calibrated?

(A) Orifice meter   (C) Hot-wire anemometer

(B) Pitot-static tube   (D) Venturi tube

42. A submarine whose length is 120 m is to be towed at 3.5 m/sec. A model submarine (length 4 m) is towed in a towing tank and requires a force of 200 N to pull it at a dynamically similar velocity. Using the Reynolds number, estimate what force will be required to tow the full-size submarine.

   (A) 84 N
   (B) 309.2 N
   (C) 1,133 N
   (D) 200 N

43. A stream of water 2.54 cm with a 60.96 cm diameter (density = 1000 kg/m^3) impinges on a bathroom scale which measures a force of 1112 N. What is the approximate velocity of the stream?

   (A) 45 m/sec
   (B) 10 m/sec
   (C) 60 m/sec
   (D) 25 m/sec

44. What is the binary equivalent of 137_{10}?

   (A) 10001001
   (B) 89
   (C) 211
   (D) 111111

45. Capillarity, or the rise or fall of a liquid in a thin tube, is primarily controlled by which fluid property?

   (A) Density
   (B) Viscosity
   (C) Surface tension
   (D) Temperature

46. Cells A1...A10 of a spreadsheet contain the numbers 1 through 10. Cell B1 contains the formula 2 + A1 * A1. If this formula is now copied to cells B2...B10, what will be the value in cell B10?

   (A) 0
   (B) 3
   (C) 102
   (D) 120

47. Cell A1 of a spreadsheet contains the value 5. Cell B1 of the same spreadsheet contains the formula A1 + 2, where the $ indicates absolute cell reference. Cell B1 is now copied to cells C1 and D1. What will be the value in cell D1?

   (A) 2
   (B) 7
   (C) 9
   (D) 11

48. The significant part of Register A of a computer CPU contains 0011, while the significant part of Register B contains 0101. A NAND operation is performed on the two registers and the results are stored in Register C. Which of the following represents the contents of Register C?

(A) 0001   (C) 0111

(B) 1110   (D) 0112

49. A polytropic process is one in which the functional relationship between pressure P and volume V is given by the equation

$$PV^n = \text{Const.}$$

The exponent n may possibly be any value from $-\infty$ to $+\infty$ depending on the particular process. A constant-volume process is represented by n equals

(A) zero.   (C) 3.0.

(B) 2.0.   (D) ∞.

50. An ideal gas ($k = 1.4$) is expanded in a nozzle from $P_0 = 1.5$ MPa, $T_0 = 150°C$ ($V_0 = 0$), to $P_2 = 0.3$ MPa. Assuming reversible adiabatic process, the nozzle should be

(A) diverging.   (C) convergent-divergent.

(B) converging.   (D) constant cross-section.

51. A large class of devices (such as turbines, centrifugal compressors, and pumps) involve work. Assuming reversible steady-state, steady-flow process with negligible changes in kinetic and potential energy, the elementary work is

(A) $P\,dV$.   (C) $-V\,dP$.

(B) $V\,dP + P\,dV$.   (D) $P\,dV - V\,dP$.

QUESTIONS 52 – 54 refer to the following diagram.

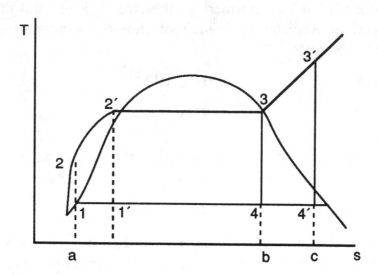

The Ideal Rankine Cycle and Reversible Carnot Cycle

52. If changes in kinetic and potential energy are negligible, heat transfer and work may be represented by various areas on the $T - S$ diagram. The thermal efficiency of the Rankine cycle with superheated steam is defined by the relation of areas

   (A) $\dfrac{1 - 2 - 2' - 3 - 3' - 4' - 1}{a - 2 - 2' - 3 - 3' - c - a}.$

   (B) $\dfrac{1' - 2' - 3 - 3' - 4' - 1'}{a - 2 - 2' - 3 - 3' - c - a}.$

   (C) $\dfrac{a - 2 - 2' - 3 - 3' - c - a}{1 - 2 - 2' - 3 - 3' - 4' - 1}.$

   (D) $\dfrac{1 - 2 - 2' - 3 - 4 - 1}{a - 2 - 2' - 3 - b - a}.$

53. Superheating the steam in the reversible Carnot cycle will cause

   (A) increase in thermal efficiency of the Carnot cycle.

   (B) decrease in thermal efficiency of the Carnot cycle.

   (C) no change in thermal efficiency of the Carnot cycle.

   (D) increase in maximum pressure of the Carnot cycle.

54. Change in entropy for the reversible Carnot cycle is

   (A) $dS > 0$.
   (C) $dS = 0$.

   (B) $ds = \dfrac{dQ}{T}$.
   (D) $dS < 0$.

55. Heat is transferred at constant volume process to the thermodynamic system of a fixed mass. The thermodynamic system will produce

   (A) a small amount of work.
   (C) a large amount of work.

   (B) zero work.
   (D) positive work.

56. In manufacturing process 1,000 kw of waste heat at temperature 327° C is available for utilization purposes. If ambient temperature is 27° C, the designed heat engine producing 510 kw of net power output will be

   (A) irreversible.
   (C) adiabatic.

   (B) reversible.
   (D) impossible.

57. Various thermodynamic processes are shown in the figure below.

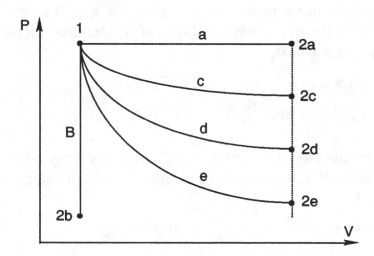

P = Const	PV^r = Const	T = Const
V = Const	PV^k = Const	

During expansion process (1 – 2) the maximum work done by the thermodynamic system will be obtained in the process

(A) P = Const. (C) PV^n = Const.

(B) V = Const. (D) PV^k = Const.

58. The reheat Rankine cycle is proposed to decrease

(A) volumetric flow rate of the working fluid.

(B) mass flow rate of cooling water in condenser.

(C) maximum temperature of the cycle restricted by the boiler working conditions.

(D) moisture content in the low-pressure stages of the turbine.

59. Compressibility factor Z is a measure of the deviation of the actual gas behavior from ideal gas. An actual gas behavior may be assumed close to the ideal gas when compressibility factor Z approaches

(A) zero. (C) 0.75.

(B) 0.50. (D) 1.0.

60. Let's assume that gas can be heated either at constant pressure or at constant volume processes. The amounts of heat q_p and q_v are transferred to the gas correspondingly. If temperature increment per unit mass ΔT = Const,

(A) $q_p > q_v$. (C) $q_p = q_v$.

(B) $q_p = q_v - \Delta u$. (D) $q_v = q_p + h$.

61. A certain computer system uses 2 bytes of storage to store an integer variable. What would be the largest positive number that can be stored.

(A) 3 (C) 65535

(B) 32767 (D) 127

62. The value of e, the base of the natural logarithm, is 2.7182. Which of the following is the best representation of the value in binary?

(A) 10.101101111110 (C) 2.B7E1

(B) 2.5576 (D) 100.0101

63. A particle moves from rest at point O in a straight line with a velocity whose square increases linearly with displacement. It reaches point A which is 600 m from O with velocity 60 **i** m/sec. The acceleration of the particle is near to

(A) 1 **i** m/sec².   (C) 3 **i** m/sec².

(B) 2 **i** m/sec².   (D) 6 **i** m/sec².

64. A car moves in a circular road of radius 201 m with a constant speed of 83 km/hr. At the shown position, the acceleration of the car is near to

(A) 0 m/s²

(B) –1 **i** m/s²

(C) 2.0 **i** m/s²

(D) –2.6 **i** m/s²

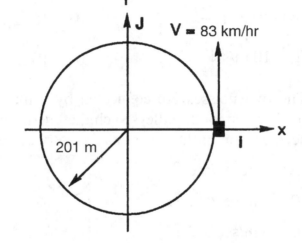

65. The shown disk rotates about a fixed axis O with a constant angular velocity of 12 **k** rad/sec. The particle p is moving with a relative velocity to the straight slot of 5.1 cm/sec. The absolute acceleration of the particle as it passes through O is near to

(A) 0.61 m/s².

(B) – 0.61 m/s².

(C) 1.22 m/s².

(D) – 1.22 m/s².

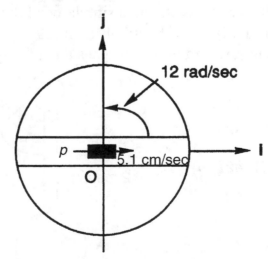

66. The figure shows a uniform thin disk of radius 1 m and rolls without slipping on a smooth surface. Its geometric center O has a constant velocity of 10 **i** m/sec. In the configuration shown, the line connecting points O and B is horizontal. The velocity of point B is near to

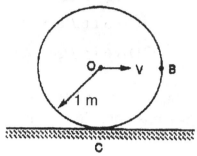

(A) 10 m/s →.

(B) 10 m/s ↓.

(C) $10\sqrt{2}$ m/sec ⟋ 45°.

(D) $10\sqrt{2}$ m/sec ⟍ 45°.

67. The two masses are connected by a massless string which passes over two smooth pulleys such that the friction can be neglected. The acceleration of the 10-kg mass is very close to

(A) 1 m/sec/sec ↑.

(B) 2 m/sec/sec ↑.

(C) 3 m/sec/sec ↑.

(D) 4 m/sec/sec ↑.

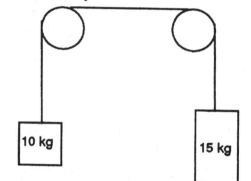

68. The mass M is carried by a massless rod of length 2 meters which is allowed to swing as a simple pendulum about the frictionless bearing O. If the velocity of the mass in position A is 2.3 m/sec, then it can move up until it reaches a maximum position B which makes an angle θ close to

(A) 15°.

(B) 30°.

(C) 45°.

(D) 60°.

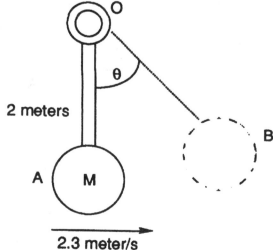

69. The static and kinetic coefficients of friction between mass m and the flat-bed of the truck are 0.3 and 0.2, respectively. If the speed of the truck is 48 km/hr, the smallest stopping distance of the truck without allowing the mass to slip is near to

(A) 15.25 m

(B) 30.5 m

(C) 45.75 m

(D) 61 m

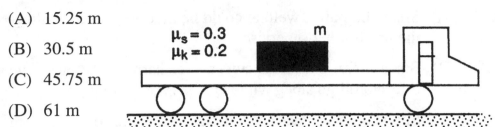

70. A steel ball is dropped from 2 meters height onto a smooth floor. If the coefficient of restitution between the ball and floor is 0.87, the ball will bound to a height h_1 near to

(A) 1.0 meter.

(B) 1.25 meters.

(C) 1.5 meters.

(D) 2.0 meters.

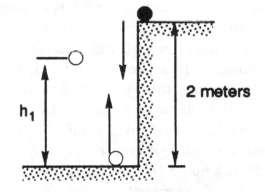

71. Sue has a problem. A compound emitted from the stack of the plant where she is employed has been linked by several studies to respiratory problems which can be severe in a small percentage of the population. The compound has not been regulated by the EPA, perhaps because it is relatively rare in industrial processes. Its elimination will be expensive, and it may force the elimination of the product line that produces the questionable compound. This would lead to the elimination of a number of jobs in a small community which is heavily dependent on the plant for employment for its citizens. An added dimension is that the product line could become very successful in the future, thus adding jobs in the community, which is in need of more sources of employment. Sue's supervisor instructs her not to bring up the issue in hearings with EPA officials. He believes he has a good chance of delaying any final action on the issue for several years at least, and by that time a modification in the process may eliminate the compound. He argues that the evidence for the

health problems supposedly produced by the compound is questionable, and that the health problems are not fatal, in any case. "I'm going to fight them as long as I can on this one," he says. How should Sue respond?

(A) Since the public welfare could be involved, Sue should go over the head of her supervisor.

(B) Since there is no clear evidence of harm to the public welfare, Sue should go along with her supervisor's request.

(C) Sue should contact her local NSPE Board and ask them what she should do.

(D) Sue should contact the local newspaper and inform them of the situation.

72. The Slug Corporation has been advised by a State Pollution Control Authority that it has 60 days to apply for a permit to discharge wastes into a receiving body of water. Slug is also advised of the minimum standard that must be met. In an effort to convince the authority that the receiving body of water, after receiving the wastes, will still meet established environmental standards, the corporation employs Engineer Ray to perform consulting engineering services and submit a detailed report. After completion of his studies, but before completion of any written report, Ray concludes that the discharge from the plant will lower the quality of the receiving body of water below established standards. He further concludes that corrective action will be very costly. Ray verbally advises the Slug Corporation of his findings. Subsequently, the corporation terminates the contract with Ray with full payment for services performed, and instructs Ray not to render a written report to the corporation. Thereafter, Ray learns that the authority has called a public hearing and that the Slug Corporation has presented data to support its view that the present discharge meets minimum standards. Does Ray have an ethical obligation to report his findings to the authority upon learning of the hearing?

(A) Ray should not report the results since this information would not have been known if XYZ did not hire Ray.

(B) No, since Ray has a responsibility to his client.

(C) Yes, since danger to the public welfare is involved.

(D) Yes, since there is a conflict of interest.

73. Block *A* weighs 82 lb and rod *BC* of length 8 ft weighs 46 lb. The rod is welded to block *A* at *B*. The combined system is restricted to move up vertically under the action of an applied force of magnitude 160 lb. The bending moment exerted by the weld on the rod at *B* is near to

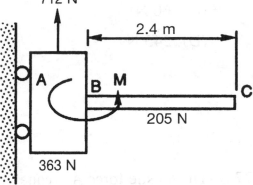

(A) 6.24 Nm counterclockwise.

(B) 18.71 Nm clockwise.

(C) 249 Nm clockwise.

(D) 308 Nm counterclockwise.

74. A thin uniform disk of mass 2 kg and radius 0.5 meter spins about an axis through its geometric center *O* with a constant angular velocity of 10 rad/sec. The axle *O* is mounted on a rigid frame that is restricted to move horizontally with a constant velocity of 2.5 meters/s. The kinetic energy of the disc is near to

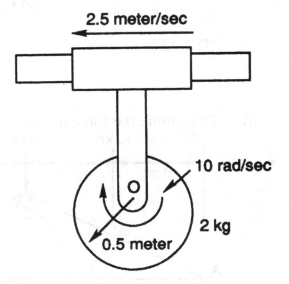

(A) 6 Joules.

(B) 12.5 Joules.

(C) 19 Joules.

(D) 31 Joules.

75. Find the weight *W* required for equilibrium.

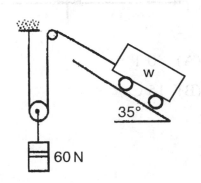

(A) 30 N

(B) 60 N

(C) 42.8 N

(D) 52.3 N

76. Determine the tensile force T_1.

    (A) 65 N

    (B) 185 N

    (C) 60 N

    (D) 245 N

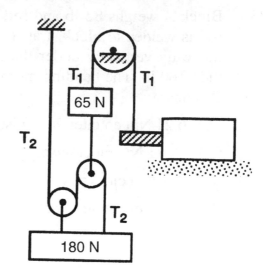

77. The tensile force A is equal to

    (A) 60 N

    (B) 73 N

    (C) 115 N

    (D) 42 N

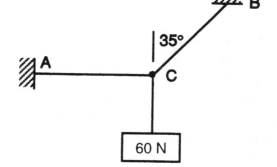

78. Determine the force in truss member AF.

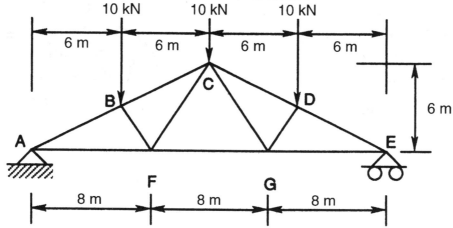

    (A) 30 T   (C) 33 T

    (B) 15 C   (D) 28 C

79. Find the shear force in the hinge at point *C*.

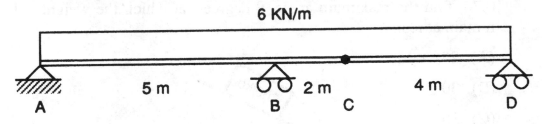

6 KN/m

5 m 2 m 4 m

A B C D

(A) 15   (C) 12

(B) 24   (D) 16

80. Find the force in truss member *BG*.

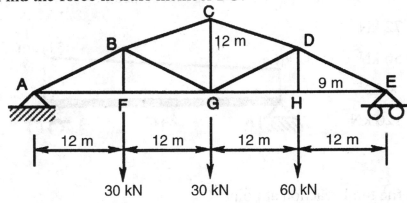

(A) 70 T   (C) 22 C

(B) 6 C   (D) 6 T

81. For the structure shown, determine the horizontal reactive force at joint *E*.

(A) 400

(B) 1,200

(C) 2,400

(D) 1,600

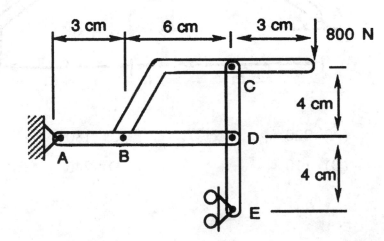

82. A 600 kilogram box rests on a slope. If the coefficient of friction is 0.70, find the maximum angle, θ degrees, at which the weight will remain at rest.

    (A) 25

    (B) 30

    (C) 35

    (D) 40

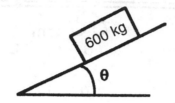

83. Find the reaction at point *A* for the loaded beam.

    (A) 72 kN

    (B) 56 kN

    (C) 64 kN

    (D) 120 kN

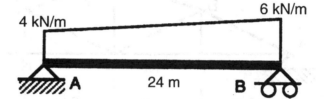

84. Find the total reaction at point *B*.

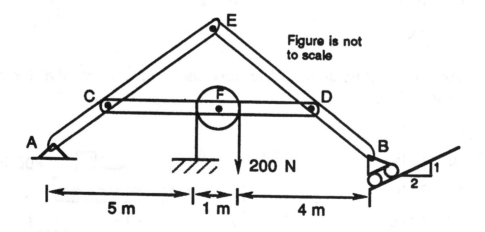

    (A) 220   (C) 180

    (B) 110   (D) 246

85. Add the three forces by using vector mathematics.

    (A) $51i + 61j$

    (B) $75i - 130j$

    (C) $326i - 69j$

    (D) $326i + 69j$

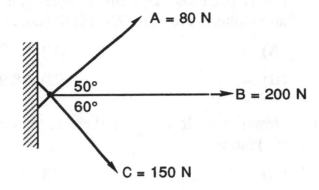

A = 80 N

50°

60°

B = 200 N

C = 150 N

QUESTIONS 86–87 refer to this information.

ATOMIC MASSES:

H = 1.0	S = 32.0
C = 12.0	Cu = 63.5
Na = 23.0	O = 16.0

86. How many moles are represented by 6.38 g of $CuSO_4$?

    (A) 0.04   (C) 0.06

    (B) 1,018   (D) 711

87. $Cu + 2AgNO_3 \rightarrow Cu(NO_3)_2 + 2\,Ag$

    The above reaction is an example of a

    (A) decomposition reaction.

    (B) combination reaction.

    (C) single displacement reaction.

    (D) double displacement reaction.

88. What is the freezing point (in °C) of a solution containing 93.0 g of ethylene glycol ($C_2H_6O_2$) dissolved in 750.0 g of water? The freezing point constant (K_f) of water = 0.81 deg C Kg/mole.

    (A) $-56.5°$ C   (C) $-1.07°$ C

    (B) $+1.62°$ C   (D) $-1.62°$ C

89. 0.180 g of a metal upon reaction with excess hydrochloric acid (HCl) produced 24.6 ml of hydrogen gas (H_2) at 27° C and 1.0 atmospheric pressure. What is the equivalent weight of the metal?

   (A) 3.60   (C) 9.00

   (B) 4.50   (D) 18.00

90. How many electrons are there in the outermost octate of a chlorine (Cl) atom?

   (A) 1   (C) 5

   (B) 3   (D) 7

91. 15.0 ml of a 0.15 N NaOH solution requires 12.0 ml of sulfuric acid (H_2SO_4) solution for neutralization. What is the molarity of the acid solution?

   (A) 0.94   (C) 0.38

   (B) 0.094   (D) 3.8

92. Balance the equation:

$$Fe_2O_3 + C \longrightarrow Fe + CO_2$$

   The coefficient of CO_2 in the balanced equation is

   (A) 1.   (C) 3.

   (B) 2.   (D) 4.

93. Balance the red-ox equation:

$$MnO_2 + HCl \longrightarrow MnCl_2 + H_2O + Cl_2$$

   The coefficient of HCl in the balanced equation is

   (A) 1.   (C) 3.

   (B) 2.   (D) 4.

94. The half-life (λ 1/2) of a radioactive isotope is 4.3 days. How long will it take for a soil sample contaminated with the isotope to reduce its radioactivity by 99%?

   (A) 6.65 days   (C) 23.0 days

   (B) 28.6 days   (D) 4.26 days

95. What is the missing particle in the following nuclear reaction?

$$^9_4\text{Be}-\ ?\ \rightarrow ^9_5\text{Be}$$

(A) $^0_{+1}\beta$

(C) ^1_1H

(B) $^0_{-1}\beta$

(D) ^1_0n

96. An isotopic species of lithium hydride ($^6\text{Li}\ ^2\text{H}$) is a potential nuclear fuel.

$$^6\text{Li}^2\text{H} \rightarrow 2\ ^4\text{He} + \text{Energy}$$

What is the expected energy production in KJ with the consumption of 1.00 g of the fuel per day at 70% efficiency?

$\bar{c}$, the velocity of light = 3.0×10^{10} cm/sec

Atomic Masses: $^6\text{Li} = 6.0151$ $^2\text{H} = 2.0141$
$^4\text{He} = 4.0026$

(A) 2.70×10^{11} KJ

(C) 1.89×10^{11} KJ

(B) 1.89×10^8 KJ

(D) 2.70×10^8 KJ

97. The torque required to produce 2 degrees twist at the end of a hollow rod shown below is given by (Assume shear modulus $G = 40,000$ N/m²):

(A) 9,802 Nm

(B) 171 Nm

(C) 183 Nm

(D) 2,052 Nm

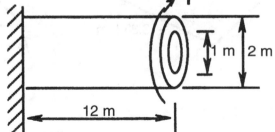

QUESTIONS 98–99 refer to the following figure.

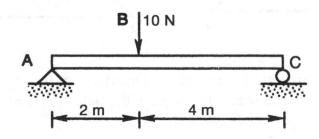

98. Which of the following is the correct shear force diagram for the beam?

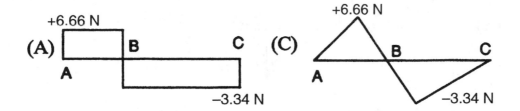

99. For the same beam of Problem 98, which of the following is the correct bending moment diagram?

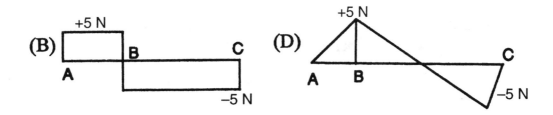

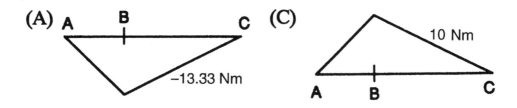

100. The simply supported beam is subjected to uniformly distributed load W N/m as shown. The correct bending moment diagram is given by

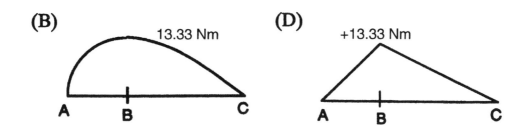

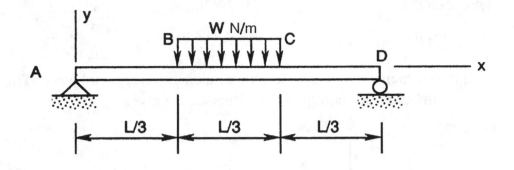

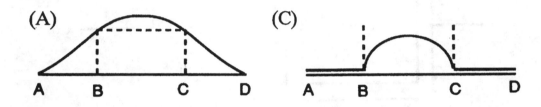

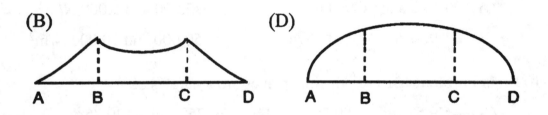

101. For a steel beam shown below, with a factor of safety = 3, find the maximum allowable load F using English units. (The yield stress for steel for both tension and compression is $\delta y = 60,000$ psi.)

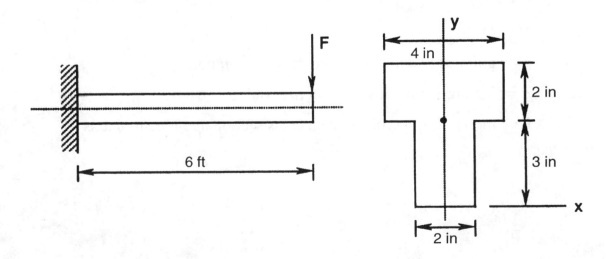

(A) 226 lbs　　　　　　　　(C) 1,920 lbs

(B) 160 lbs　　　　　　　　(D) 2,713 lbs

102.　The two dimensional stress field in an element is shown below. The maximum and minimum principal stresses are given as:

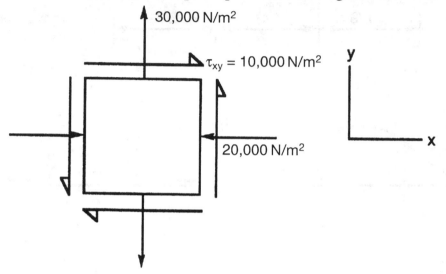

(A) 31,900 and 26,900 N/m²　　　(C) 25,000 and 5,000 N/m²

(B) 31,900 and –21,900 N/m²　　　(D) 50,000 and 10,000 N/m²

103.　In Problem 102 the principal planes are at angles of

(A) – 79.5° and – 259.5°.　　　(C) – 39.75° and – 129.75°.

(B) – 47° and – 227°.　　　　　(D) – 23.5° and – 113.5°.

104.　The deflection of a simply supported beam at the point of loading is given by:

$P =$　load

$a =$　point of loading measured from left support

$E =$　Young's modulus of beam material

$I =$　moment of inertia of beam cross section about neutral axis

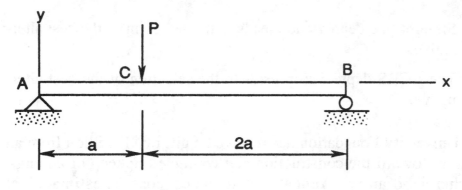

(A) $Y = -\dfrac{8Pa^3}{3EI}$.

(C) $Y = -\dfrac{4Pa^3}{9EI}$.

(B) $Y = -\dfrac{27Pa^3}{48EI}$.

(D) $Y = -\dfrac{27Pa^3}{2EI}$.

105. A credit card company compounds monthly and charges an interest of $1^1/_2\%$ per month. What is the effective interest rate per year?

(A) 18%

(C) 4.35%

(B) 19.56%

(D) 1.015%

106. If nominal interest rate per year is 12%, and compounding is continuous, what is the effective interest rate per year?

(A) 1.000%

(C) 11.275%

(B) 1.500%

(D) 12.75%

107. A large profitable corporation has purchased a jet plane for use by its executives. The cost of the plane is $76 million. It has a useful life of five years. The estimated resale value at the end of five years is six million dollars. Using straight-line depreciation, what is the book value of the jet plane at the end of three years?

(A) $14 million

(C) $34 million

(B) $15.2 million

(D) $48 million

108. In a before-tax comparison of alternatives, what effect does the method of depreciation have on which alternative is preferred?

(A) The method of depreciation has no effect on the alternative selected.

(B) The method of depreciation determines the alternative to be selected.

(C) Straight line depreciation leads to the selection of the best alternative.

(D) The ACRS depreciation leads to the selection of the best alternative.

109. The University Foundation has received a gift of $1 million from an alumnus toward the construction and continued upkeep of an engineering laboratory. Annual maintenance cost is estimated at $30,000. In addition, $50,000 will be needed every 10 years for major repairs. How much will be left for initial construction after funds are allocated for perpetual upkeep? The foundation invests the funds and earns a nominal interest rate of 10%.

(A) $331,350   (C) $1 million

(B) $668,650   (D) $1.3373 million

110. What type of bonds exists predominantly in a sodium chloride crystal?

(A) Metallic bond   (C) Covalent bond

(B) Ionic bond   (D) Polar bond

111. The Miller indices of the direction of the arrow in the accompanying figure of a unit cell of a cubic lattice is

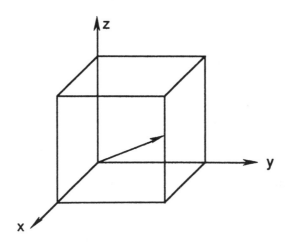

(A) 110.   (C) 221.

(B) 211.   (D) 112.

112. Pure metal *A* undergoes an isothermal transformation in which its crystal structure changes from face centered cubic (fcc) to body centered cubic (bcc). As a result, the volume of a piece of metal *A*

    (A) increases.

    (B) decreases.

    (C) decreases up to the midpoint of the transformation and then asymptotically reaches its original value.

    (D) increases up to the midpoint of the transformation and then asymptotically reaches its original value.

113. Which of the following leads to a reduction in the electrical resistivity of a pure metal?

    (A) Cold working

    (C) Grain refinement

    (B) Annealing

    (D) Addition of alloying elements

114. The ridigity of polymer can be increased by

    (A) increasing the degree of polymerization.

    (B) increasing the extent of cross linking.

    (C) crystallization.

    (D) all of the above.

115. Which of the following properties of a metal is insensitive to the micro-structure?

    (A) Tensile strength

    (C) Modulus of elasticity

    (B) Ductility

    (D) Hardness

116. The dominant charge carriers in a phosphorus-doped silicon crystal at room temperature are

    (A) protons.

    (C) silicon ions.

    (B) phosphorus ions.

    (D) electrons.

117. Metals are conductive because

    (A) they have a characteristic metallic luster.

(B) they have extra electrons as exhibited by normally positive valence states.

(C) the electrons are loosely bound to the nuclei and, therefore, mobile.

(D) they are on the left side of the Periodic Table.

118. Group Ia elements are easily ionized because

(A) they have a single "s" electron in the outer orbit.

(B) they are metals and, therefore, conductive.

(C) they react violently with water to liberate hydrogen.

(D) they have relatively low melting points for metals.

119. The rare earth metals all have very similar chemical properties because

(A) the reason is not known, but is observed experimentally.

(B) they melt at extreme temperatures, hence are nearly inert.

(C) successive members of the series are formed by adding 4f electrons which have little effect on reactivity.

(D) they are in a separate row at the bottom of the Periodic Table.

120. An electron volt is

(A) a voltage unit commonly used when measuring the voltage of electrons.

(B) the unit of electrical charge of one electron.

(C) a unit of energy equal to the energy possessed by an electron accelerating through a potential of one volt.

(D) any of the above depending on the context.

TEST 3

ANSWER KEY

1.	(C)	16.	(D)	31.	(C)	46.	(C)
2.	(D)	17.	(A)	32.	(B)	47.	(B)
3.	(D)	18.	(C)	33.	(D)	48.	(B)
4.	(D)	19.	(D)	34.	(D)	49.	(D)
5.	(A)	20.	(C)	35.	(C)	50.	(C)
6.	(B)	21.	(A)	36.	(C)	51.	(C)
7.	(D)	22.	(B)	37.	(B)	52.	(A)
8.	(D)	23.	(B)	38.	(D)	53.	(C)
9.	(D)	24.	(B)	39.	(A)	54.	(C)
10.	(B)	25.	(D)	40.	(C)	55.	(B)
11.	(C)	26.	(C)	41.	(B)	56.	(D)
12.	(B)	27.	(B)	42.	(D)	57.	(A)
13.	(B)	28.	(A)	43.	(A)	58.	(D)
14.	(D)	29.	(D)	44.	(A)	59.	(D)
15.	(C)	30.	(B)	45.	(C)	60.	(A)
61.	(B)	76.	(B)	91.	(B)	106.	(D)
62.	(A)	77.	(D)	92.	(C)	107.	(C)
63.	(C)	78.	(A)	93.	(D)	108.	(A)
64.	(D)	79.	(C)	94.	(B)	109.	(B)
65.	(C)	80.	(D)	95.	(B)	110.	(B)
66.	(D)	81.	(C)	96.	(A)	111.	(C)
67.	(B)	82.	(C)	97.	(B)	112.	(A)
68.	(B)	83.	(B)	98.	(A)	113.	(B)
69.	(B)	84.	(D)	99.	(D)	114.	(D)
70.	(C)	85.	(C)	100.	(A)	115.	(C)
71.	(B)	86.	(A)	101.	(D)	116.	(D)
72.	(C)	87.	(C)	102.	(B)	117.	(C)
73.	(D)	88.	(D)	103.	(D)	118.	(A)
74.	(C)	89.	(C)	104.	(C)	119.	(C)
75.	(D)	90.	(D)	105.	(B)	120.	(C)

DETAILED EXPLANATIONS
OF ANSWERS

Test 3

1. **(C)** The dot product of perpendicular vectors is zero. A is the known vector. B represents the unknown vector.

$$A \cdot B = (a_1 i + a_2 j) \cdot (b_1 i + b_2 j) = a_1 \cdot b_1 + a_2 \cdot b_2 = 0$$

The values of a_1 and a_2 are specified as

$$a_1 = 1 \quad \text{and} \quad a_2 = 2$$

Thus, $\qquad\qquad\qquad 1 \cdot b_1 + 2 \cdot b_2 = 0$

The value of b_1 is given as -6.2

Thus, $\qquad\qquad\qquad 2b_2 = 6.2 \quad \text{or} \quad b_2 = 3.1.$

2. **(D)** In this differential equation, t is the independent variable, and y is the dependent variable. The order of a differential equation is defined by the highest order derivative of the dependent variable. This equation contains the second derivative of y and is thus a second order equation. A differential equation is homogeneous if all terms contain the dependent variable or a derivative of the dependent variable. This equation contains a term containing only a function of t, $\sin(2t)$, which makes it non-homogeneous. A differential equation is linear if the coefficients of the dependent variable and its derivatives are not functions of the dependent variable. The coefficients of y and its derivatives in the problem equation are 3, t, and -4, none of which are functions of y. This equation is linear. One of the coefficients is t, the independent variable. In most applications, t represents time, and this equation would describe a "time-varying-parameter system."

3. **(D)** When the value of 0 is substituted into the function, the result is 0/0, which is indeterminate. L'Hopital's Rule is useful for indeterminate forms.

$$\lim_{x \to a} \frac{F(x)}{G(x)} = \lim_{x \to a} \frac{F'(x)}{G'(x)}$$

where $F'(x) = \dfrac{dF}{dx}$ and $G'(x) = \dfrac{dG}{dx}$.

L'Hopital's Rule is valid only if the right-hand side exists.

When the numerator and denominator of the given function are differentiated, the result is

$$\frac{d}{dx}(x + \tan x) = 1 + \sec^2 x$$

$$\frac{d}{dx}(\sin 3x) = 3\cos 3x$$

$$\lim_{x \to 0} \frac{x + \tan x}{\sin 3x} = \lim_{x \to 0} \frac{1 + (\sec x)^2}{3\cos 3x} = \frac{1 + 1^2}{3 \cdot 1} = \frac{2}{3}.$$

4. **(D)** A regular pentagon has five sides of equal lengths. The unit circle has a radius of 1 unit. Each side of the pentagon shown in the figure has a length of $2a$. The chord of length $2a$ subtends an angle of $^{360}\!/_5 = 72°$. The radius of the circle is 1.

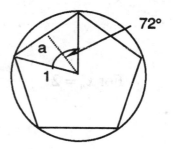

$$\frac{a}{1} = \sin\left(\frac{72°}{2}\right) = 0.588$$

The length of the side is $2a$ or 1.18.

5. **(A)** The imaginary number i is defined as $\sqrt{-1}$. Thus, $i^2 = -1$. The two factors are multiplied algebraically.

$$
\begin{aligned}
(2 + 4i) \cdot (1 - 7i) &= 2 - 14i + 4i - 28i^2 \\
&= 2 - 10i - 28 \cdot (-1) \\
&= 30 - 10i
\end{aligned}
$$

6. **(B)** (A) is incorrect. Although the project is outside his technical expertise, he is providing managerial skills, which is acceptable. (C) is incorrect since there is no conflict of interest involved in this problem. (D) is incorrect since an engineer should only practice in his own discipline when technical matters are involved.

7. **(D)** Newton's method is an iterative procedure to find the root of an equation

$$f(x) = 0$$

An initial approximation is assumed and successive approximations are calculated by

$$x_{n+1} = x_n - \frac{f(x_n)}{f'(x_n)}$$

where

$$f'(x_n) = \frac{df}{dx} \quad \text{at} \quad x = x_n.$$

For the given function

$$f(x) = x^3 + 4x^2 + 2x - 2$$
$$f'(x) = 3x^2 + 8x + 2$$

For $x_n = 2$

$$f(x_n) = f(2) = 26$$
$$f'(x_n) = f'(2) = 30$$

Thus,

$$x_{n+1} = 2 - \frac{26}{30} = 1.13$$

which is choice (D).

8. **(D)** This is an exponential decay problem in which a quantity decreases at a rate proportional to the amount present.

$$\frac{dQ}{dq} = -\frac{1}{\theta} Q \qquad Q_{(t=0)} = Q_0$$

where Q = quantity of material

t = time

θ = time constant of decay

The solution to this equation is

$$Q = Q_0 e^{-t/\theta}$$

The value of θ is determined from the problem statement

$$Q = \tfrac{1}{2} Q_0 \quad \text{for} \quad t = 30 \text{ yrs}$$

$$\tfrac{1}{2} Q_0 = Q_0 e^{-30 \text{ yrs}/\theta}$$

$$\tfrac{1}{2} = e^{-30 \text{ yrs}/\theta}$$

$$\ln 0.5 = -0.693 = \ln(e^{-30/\theta}) = \frac{-30}{\theta}$$

Thus, $\theta = \dfrac{+30 \text{ years}}{-(0.693)} = 43.3 \text{ years.}$

If 90% had decomposed then

$$\frac{Q}{Q_0} = 0.1 = e^{-t/43.3} \qquad\qquad Q = 0.10 Q_0$$

or
$$\ln (0.1) = \frac{-t}{43.3}$$

from which $t = 99.7$ years, which corresponds to choice (D).

9. **(D)** Note that the derivative of the denominator $(6 + x^2)$ is $2x\,dx$, and there is an $x\,dx$ in the numerator. When the numerator contains the derivative of the denominator, the antiderivative has the form of the logarithm of the denominator,

$$\int \frac{du}{u} = \ln u$$

Evaluate the antiderivative at the limits to find the result.

$$2 \int_1^3 \frac{2x\,dx}{6 + x^2} = 2 \left[\ln (6 + x^2)\right]_1^3$$

$$= 2 \left[\ln (6 + 3^2) - \ln(6 + 1^2)\right]$$

$$= 1.52$$

10. **(B)**   The problem requires the evaluation of

$$dF = \frac{\partial F}{\partial x} \, dx + \frac{\partial F}{\partial y} \, dy + \frac{\partial F}{\partial z} \, dz$$

where $\frac{\partial F}{\partial x}$ is the partial derivative of $F(x, y, z)$ with respect to x, which defines how F changes with x while y and z are held constant. The three partial derivatives are evaluated as follows:

$$\frac{\partial F}{\partial x} = 0 + ze^{xz} \sin(4y)$$

$$\frac{\partial F}{\partial y} = (1 + e^{xz})4 \cos(4y)$$

$$\frac{\partial F}{\partial z} = 0 + xe^{xz} \sin(4y)$$

These derivatives are substituted into the definition to give

$$dF = z \, e^{xz} \sin (4y) \, dx + 4 \cos (4y) (1 + e^{xz}) \, dy$$
$$+ x \, e^{xz} \sin (4y) \, d z$$

which is choice (B).

11. **(C)**   The simplest way to determine the constants A, B, and C is to multiply the equation by the denominator of the left-hand side.

$$s - 3 = A(s + 2)(s + 4) + B(s + 3)(s + 4) + C(s + 2)(s + 3)$$

By choosing appropriate values of s, the three constants can be determined.

If $s = -3$, the coefficients of B and C are zero and

$$-3 - 3 = A(-3 + 2)(-3 + 4) + 0 + 0$$

or
$$A = \frac{-6}{(-1)(1)} = 6$$

If $s = -2$, the coefficients of A and C are zero and

$$-2 - 3 = 0 + B(-2 + 3)(-2 + 4) + 0$$

or
$$B = \frac{-5}{(1)(2)} = -\frac{5}{2}$$

If $s = -4$, the coefficients of A and B are zero and

$$-4 - 3 = 0 + 0 + C(-4 + 3)(-4 + 2)$$

or

$$C = \frac{-7}{(-1)(-2)} = -\frac{7}{2}$$

12. **(B)**   The probability density function for a normal distribution is

$$f(Z) = \frac{1}{\sqrt{2\pi}} e^{-Z^2/2}$$

where

$$Z = \frac{X - \text{Mean}}{\text{Standard Deviation}}$$

The probability of measuring values between Z_1 and Z_2 is obtained by integrating the density function between these two limits.

$$\int_{Z_1}^{Z_2} f(Z) \, dZ$$

In problem 12, Z_1 is $\dfrac{(15 - 16)}{2}$, and Z_2 is $\dfrac{(19 - 16)}{2}$.

13. **(B)**   Engineers shall avoid the use of statements containing a material misrepressentation of fact or omitting a material fact necessary to keep statements from being misleading or intended or likely to create an unjustified expectation, or statements containing prediction of future success. It would be unethical for Mary to misrepresent the data. (A) is incorrect since "following orders" does not correct an improper activity. (C) is wrong because the public welfare was not an issue in the case. (D) is incorrect since application of the above section of the code extends to a wide range of activities.

14. **(D)**   Since the public welfare is concerned, Dale should make the revelations to his new employer. (A) is incorrect since the public safety takes precedent over the agreement. (B) is incorrect since there is no conflict of interest in this case. (C) is incorrect only because the public welfare was involved. If the public welfare was not involved then it would be unethical to make the revelations. Dale would have a responsibility to his former employer.

15. **(C)** There are a total of 100 engineers at the banquet. The probability that representatives from all disciplines are selected is the product of the probabilities of selecting someone from each discipline. Note that after each representative is selected, the pool from which to select decreases by one.

$$\frac{40}{100} \times \frac{20}{99} \times \frac{30}{98} \times \frac{10}{97} = \frac{240,000}{94,109,400} .$$

16. **(D)** The volume can be determined by defining a circular slice of thickness dy and radius x.

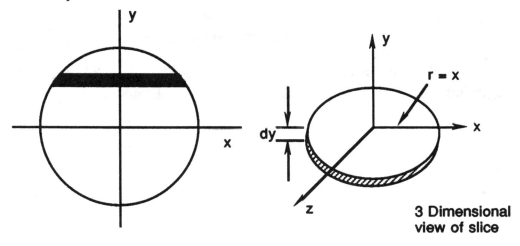

The volume of this slice is $\pi x^2 \, dy$. The total volume is found by integration or accumulating the volumes of the slices.

$$\text{Volume} = 2\int_0^1 \pi x^2 \, dy$$
$$x^2 + y^2 = 1 \qquad x^2 = 1 - y^2$$
$$= 2\pi \int_0^1 (1 - y^2) \, dy$$
$$= 2\pi \left[y - \frac{y^3}{3} \right]_0^1$$
$$= \frac{4\pi}{3}$$

Note that this is the volume of the unit sphere, which is the volume obtained by rotating the unit circle.

17. **(A)** Both sides of the equation are multiplied by $\mathbf{A}^{-1}$.

$$\mathbf{A}^{-1}\,\mathbf{A}x = \mathbf{A}^{-1}b$$

The product of $\mathbf{A}$ inverse and $\mathbf{A}$ is the unit matrix, which when multiplied by x gives x.

$$x = \mathbf{A}^{-1}b$$

18. **(C)** The equation needs to be converted to standard form

$$(x - x_0)^2 + (y - y_0)^2 = r^2$$

x_0, y_0 define the location of the center, r is the radius.

This is done by forming quadratic terms, which are squares.

$$x^2 - 4x + y^2 - 2y - 4 = 0$$
$$x^2 - 4x + y^2 - 2y = 4$$

Add the squares of $^1/_2$ the x and y coefficients to both sides of the equation

$$(x^2 - 4x + 4) + (y^2 - 2y + 1) = 4 + 4 + 1$$
$$(x^2 - 2)^2 + (y - 1)^2 = 9$$

This circle is centered at

$$x = 2 \quad y = 1$$

and has a radius of 3.

19. **(D)**

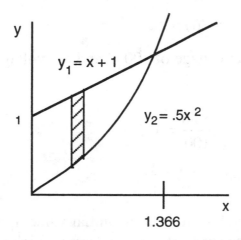

The intersection of the two functions is found by

$$y_1 = x + 1 = 0.5x^2 = y_2$$

$$0.5x^2 - x - 1 = 0$$

This has a positive root at $x = 2.732$.

The area is found by integrating the difference between the functions for x between 0 and the intersection

$$\int_0^{2.732} (y_1 - y_2)\, dx = \int_0^{2.732} (x + 1 - 0.5x^2)\, dx$$

$$= \left[\frac{x^2}{2} + x - 0.5\left(\frac{1}{3}\right)x^3 \right]_0^{2.732}$$

$$= \frac{(2.732)^2}{2} + 2.732 - \frac{0.5}{3}(2.732)^2$$

$$= 3.7319 + 2.732 - 3.3985 = 3.0654$$

20. **(C)** The tangent to the curve is the derivative of the function for y

$$\frac{dy}{dx} = xe^x + e^x$$

When $x = 0.8$, the derivative is

$$0.8e^{0.8} + e^{0.8} = 4.0,$$

which is choice (C).

21. **(A)** The voltage response of a discharging RC circuit is

$$V(t) = V_0 e^{-\frac{t}{RC}}$$

The ratio between the initial voltage of 100 V and the voltage after 0.2 sec is

$$\frac{36.8}{100} = 0.368$$

$$= \frac{1}{e}$$

As the voltage decreased in 0.2 s to $\frac{1}{e}$ of its initial value, the elapsed time is therefore equal to the time constant τ of the circuit which is given by

$$\tau = RC$$
$$C = \frac{0.2}{100 \cdot 10^3}$$
$$C = .000002\,\text{F}$$
$$= 2\mu\,\text{F}$$

22. **(B)**   The voltage across a capacitor cannot change instantaneously, and as the initial voltage was zero, immediately after closing the switch, it still is zero. Therefore, the capacitor can be modeled as a short circuit. The current through an inductor cannot change instantaneously, and as its initial value was zero, initially the inductor will be modeled as an open circuit. The model of the circuit immediately after closing the switch is shown below.

By Ohm's Law the current is

$$i = \frac{V}{R}$$
$$= \frac{12}{3}$$
$$= 4.0\,\text{A}$$

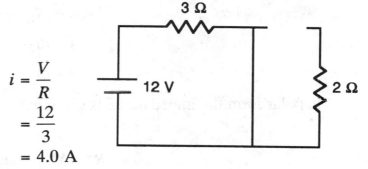

23. **(B)**   For a parallel circuit the admittance is given by:

$$Y = G + jB_C - jB_L$$

where Y is the admittance, in general a complex number, G the conductance, B_C the capacitive suceptance, and B_L the inductive suceptance. Under resonance

$$B_C = B_L$$

and therefore

$$Y = G$$

and the admittance is a minimum and as the current phasor I is given by:

$$I = V \cdot Y$$

where V is the voltage phasor, the current will be a minimum under resonance conditions.

24. **(B)** The two 12 Ω inductors are connected in parallel and therefore their equivalent reactance X_{eq} is given by:

$$\frac{1}{X_{eq}} = \frac{1}{X_1} + \frac{1}{X_2}$$

$$\frac{1}{X_{eq}} = \frac{1}{12} + \frac{1}{12}$$

$$X_{eq} = 6 \ \Omega$$

This equivalent reactance and the two other elements of the circuit are all connected in parallel and therefore the impedance Z, a complex number is given by:

$$Z = R + jX_L - jX_C$$

$$= 4 + j6 - j3$$

$$= 4 + j3$$

in polar form the impedance Z is given by:

$$Z = \sqrt{R^2 + X^2} \ \lfloor a \tan X/R$$

$$= \sqrt{4^2 + 3^2} \ \lfloor a \tan 3/4$$

$$= 5 \lfloor 37° \ \Omega$$

the current phasor I is therefore given by:

$$I = \frac{V}{Z}$$

$$= \frac{100 \lfloor 0°}{5 \lfloor 37°}$$

$$= 20 \lfloor -37° \ \text{amp}$$

and the voltage phasor V_R across the 4W resistor is given by:

$$V_R = I \cdot R$$

$$= 20 \lfloor -37° \ 4 \lfloor 0°$$

$$= 80 \lfloor -37° \ V$$

25. **(D)**   By definition the impedance is a complex number. Its magnitude is the ratio of the amplitude of the voltage to the amplitude of the current, and its angle is the lead angle of the voltage with relation to the current. From the graph shown in the problem, the voltage amplitude is 10 and the current amplitude 20; therefore, the magnitude of the impedance is $^{10}/_{20} = 0.5\ \Omega$. The voltage lags the current by 0.0021s, as the period of the signal is 0.017s and the ratio between the lag time and the period is $^{0.0021}/_{0.017} = \frac{1}{8}$. The phase angle is therefore $\frac{1}{8} \cdot 360° = 45°$. This angle is negative, as the voltage lags the current. The impedance is therefore $0.5\ \lfloor -45°$.

26. **(C)**   The series combination has an input impedance Z_{in} given by:

$$Z_{in} = R + jX$$
$$= 5 + j12$$

or in polar form:

$$= \sqrt{5^2 + 12^2}\ \lfloor a\tan X/R$$
$$= 13\ \lfloor 67.38°\ \Omega$$

The parallel combination has an input admittance Y_{in} given by:

$$Y_{in} = G_p - jB_p$$

The series and parallel combinations will have the same input impedance if:

$$Y_{in} = \frac{1}{Z_{in}}$$

therefore,

$$G_p - jB_p = \frac{1}{13\ \lfloor 67.38°}$$

$$= 0.0296 - j0.0711\ \text{mhos}$$

$$G_p = 0.0296\ \text{mhos}$$

$$B_p = 0.0711\ \text{mhos}$$

Thus,

$$R_p = \frac{1}{G_p}$$

$$= \frac{1}{0.0296}\ \Omega$$

$$= 33.78\ \Omega$$

$$X_p = \frac{1}{B_p}$$

$$= \frac{1}{0.0711}\ \Omega$$

$$= 14.06\ \Omega$$

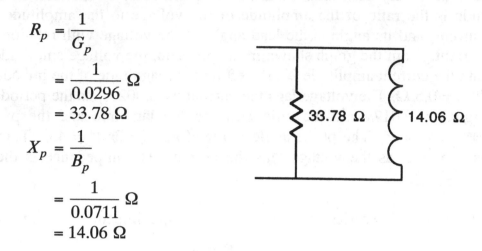

The equivalent parallel circuit is shown here.

27. **(B)**   A circuit is resonant if its input impedance or admittance is a real number.

As the elements are connected in series, it is easier to work with the admittance:

$$Y_{in} = \frac{1}{R} + j\omega X - j\frac{1}{\omega L}$$

The circuit would be in resonance if the imaginary part of the input admittance is zero:

$$j\omega C - j\frac{1}{\omega L} = 0$$

$$\frac{\omega^2 LC - 1}{L} = 0$$

$$\omega^2 LC - 1 = 0$$

$$\omega = \sqrt{\frac{1}{LC}}$$

$$= \sqrt{\frac{1}{50 \cdot 10^{-3} \cdot 10 \cdot 10^{-6}}}$$

$$= 1414 s^{-1}$$

28. **(A)**   To find the frequency of oscillation of the transient response, the characteristic equation of the circuit has to be found. In the "s" domain, the impedances of the three elements in the circuit are given by

$$Z_R = R$$

$$Z_L = SL$$

$$Z_C = \frac{1}{sC}$$

In the "s" domain the circuit diagram would be:

The complex impedance $Z(s)$ is therefore:

$$Z(s) = R + sL + \frac{1}{sC}$$

and the current $I(s)$ in the complex domain will be:

$$I(s) = \frac{V(s)}{R + sL + \dfrac{1}{sC}}$$

$$= \frac{sCV(s)}{s^2LC + sRC + 1}$$

The characteristic equation is the denominator of the above expression; the roots of this equation determine the nature of the transient behavior. We therefore set:

$$s^2LC + sRC + 1 = 0$$

$$s^2 + s\frac{R}{L} + \frac{1}{LC} = 0$$

and the roots are given by:

$$s_{1,2} = \frac{-\dfrac{R}{L} \pm \sqrt{\left(\dfrac{R}{L}\right)^2 - \dfrac{4}{LC}}}{2}$$

$$s_{1,2} = \frac{-\dfrac{10}{0.01} \pm \sqrt{\left(\dfrac{10}{0.01}\right)^2 - \dfrac{4}{0.01 \cdot 10 \cdot 10^{-6}}}}{2}$$

$$s_{1,2} = -500 \pm j3122.5$$

As the roots of the characteristic equation are complex,

$$S_{1,2} = -\alpha \pm j\omega_d,$$

the transient response is under-damped, therefore, oscillatory with an angular frequency, $\omega_d = 3122.5s^{-1}$ or a frequency:

$$f = \frac{\omega}{2\pi}$$

$$= \frac{3122.5}{2\pi}$$

$$= 497.5 \text{ Hz}$$

29. **(D)** The power diagram shows a real load of 5 KW and lagging load of 10 KVA; as cos 45° = 0.707 the angle between the two loads is 45°.

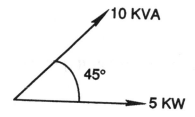

For the 10 KVA load the real power P_1 and the reactive power Q_1 are given by

$$P_1 = S_1 \cdot \cos 45°$$

$$= 10 \cdot 0.707$$

$$= 7.07 \text{ KW}$$

$$Q_1 = S_1 \cdot \sin 45°$$

$$= 10 \cdot 0.707$$

$$= 7.07 \text{ KVAR}$$

The 5 KW load has only a real component P_2

$$P_2 = 5 \text{ KW}$$

$$Q_2 = 0 \text{ KVA}$$

The total real P and reactive Q powers are therefore

$$P = P_1 + P_2$$

$$= 5 + 7.07$$

$$= 12.07 \text{ KW}$$

$$Q = Q_1$$

$$= 7.07 \text{ KVAR}$$

and the power factor of the two loads combined will be

$$\text{power factor} = \frac{P}{\sqrt{P^2 + Q^2}}$$

$$= \frac{12.07}{\sqrt{12.07^2 + 7.07^2}}$$

$$= 0.863$$

Because the total reactive power of the two loads is positive, the power factor is lagging.

30. **(B)** The roots of the characteristic equation are

$$\gamma = -\frac{c}{2m} \pm \sqrt{\left(\frac{c}{2m}\right)^2 - \frac{k}{m}}$$

and

$$c_{crit} = 2\sqrt{km}$$

The value of c is used as an indication of the damping. When the system is overdamped, the roots are both real and negative. If $c = 0$, the system is not damped, choice (A). A critically damped system occurs when $c = c_{crit}$, choice (C), and an underdamped system is characterized by $c < c_{crit}$.

31. **(C)** The effective external force amplitude can be found with the following equation:

$$P = m_1 e \ w^2 \qquad k = 4(1,500) = 6,000 \text{ lb/in}$$

and

$$w^2 = \frac{k}{\text{mass}}$$

$$w^2 = \frac{\dfrac{6,000}{100}}{182}$$

$$w^2 = 10,920\left(\frac{\text{rad}}{\text{sec}}\right)^2$$

Therefore, $P = \left(\dfrac{3}{182}\right)(10,920) = 180$ lb, choice (C).

32. **(B)** Given their positive sequence, the line voltages are:

$$V_{ab} = 220 \,\underline{|0°}\ V$$

$$V_{bc} = 220 \,\underline{|-150°}\ V$$

$$V_{ca} = 220 \,\underline{|+150°}$$

The currents through the two resistive loads as shown in the circuit diagram are therefore

$$
\begin{aligned}
I_{ab} &= \frac{V_{ab}}{R_1} \\
&= \frac{220\,\underline{|0°}}{12\,\underline{|0°}} \\
&= 18.3\,\underline{|0°}\ A
\end{aligned}
$$

and

$$
\begin{aligned}
I_{bc} &= \frac{V_{bc}}{R_2} \\
&= \frac{220\,\underline{|-150°}}{5\,\underline{|0°}} \\
&= 44.0\,\underline{|-150°}\ A
\end{aligned}
$$

Applying Kirchoff's current law to the node shown in the diagram,

$$
\begin{aligned}
I_b &= I_{bc} - I_{ab} \\
&= 44.0\,\underline{|-150°} - 18.3\,\underline{|0°} \\
&= -22 - j\,38.10 - 18.3 \\
&= -40.3 - j\,38.10
\end{aligned}
$$

or in polar form

$$= 55.5\,\underline{|-136.7°}\ A$$

33. **(D)**   Combined stresses implies that more than one type of stress is applied at the same time; hence, choices (A) and (B) are incorrect. A crank shaft may be twisted, or subjected to torsional stress, and may be bent, which implies flexural stress. Axial stress is used to describe pushing, or direct shear. Axial stress is usually not encountered by the crank shaft, and thus choice (C) is incorrect. Therefore, choice (D), torsional and flexural, is the correct choice.

34. **(D)**   Copper is a metal and has a high coordination number (8 or 12 nearest neighbors) and is therefore held together by metallic bonds. Ionic bonds (C) do not exist, and covalent bonds (B) are impossible, as there are too many electrons. Sigma (A) describes an electron shell and not a bond type.

35. **(C)**   A Newtonian fluid behaves according to the following stress/ strain rate relationship:

$$\tau = \mu \left(\frac{du}{dy} \right)$$

where τ is the shear stress acting on a fluid body, μ is the absolute viscosity of the fluid, and $\frac{du}{dy}$ is a velocity gradient of the fluid (or the shear strain rate). All real fluids show some resistance of motion to an imposed shear force. Fluids showing a non-linear proportionality between shear force and shearing motion are called "non-Newtonian" fluids. If the shear rate decreases with time, the fluid would be called "shear thickening."

36. **(C)**   Incompressible flow, like that of water, always leaves an exit of a pipe at atmospheric pressure. Therefore, the pressure at point *A* is atmospheric, so is the pressure at point *B*. The pressure at point *C* can be determined using a hydrostatic assumption such that:

$$P_C = \rho g z + P_A$$

where ρ is the density of water, g is the acceleration of gravity, and z is the vertical distance between points *C* and *A*. Therefore, the pressure at *C* is greater than that at *A* and therefore flow will result. This device is commonly referred to as a syphon. Flow will continue until the water level (*B*) reaches the entrance of the pipe (*C*).

37. **(B)**   The solution is arrived at by an energy balance, usually between points where something is known. In this case, the pressure and

velocity are known at point A ($P = 0$ N/m^2, $V = 0$ m/sec) and point D, as well as their elevations. The energy following a streamline can be determined by using Bernoulli's equation which can be written:

$$\frac{P}{\rho g} + \frac{V^2}{2g} + z + h_p = \text{constant}$$

where P is the pressure, V is the velocity, z is the vertical position with respect to some datum, and h_p is an energy addition or loss term which could represent either frictional dissipation or energy input through a pump. Using Bernoulli's equation between points, A and D yields:

$$\frac{P_A}{\rho g} + \frac{V_A^2}{2g} + z_A + h_p = \frac{P_D}{\rho g} + \frac{V_D^2}{2g} + z_D$$

In this case, the kinetic energy (and therefore the velocity) can be ignored at A. Also, the pressure at both points will be atmospheric (0 N/m^2). Therefore,

$$V_D = \sqrt{2g*(z_A - z_D + h_p)} = \sqrt{2(9.81 \text{ m/sec}^2)(6.1 \text{ m})} = 10.9 \text{ m/sec}$$

38. **(D)**   The velocity at discharge will be the same as the velocity at the entrance to the pump because of continuity of mass. The energy of a fluid following a streamline can be determined by using Bernoulli's equation which can be written:

$$\frac{P}{\rho g} + \frac{V^2}{2g} + z = \text{constant}$$

where P is the pressure, V is the velocity, and z is the vertical position with respect to some datum. Therefore, information can be gained using Bernoulli's equation between points A and B. This would be

$$\frac{P_A}{\rho g} + \frac{V_A^2}{2g} + z_A = \frac{P_B}{\rho g} + \frac{V_B^2}{2g} + z_B$$

Again, P_A will be 0 N/m^2, and $V_A = 0$ m/sec. Note that the power input by the pump does not enter into the equation because the pump is not between the two points in question. The velocity at the pump is known to be 15.2 m/sec. Therefore, solving for the pressure yields:

$$P_B = \rho g * \{(z_A - z_B) - \frac{V_B^2}{2g}\} = (984)\,(9.81)\,(18.3 - 1.53 - 11.77) = 4.83 \bullet 10^4 \text{ N/m}^2$$

Note that the pressure is still above atmospheric.

39. **(A)** The Pitot-static tube measures the difference between static and dynamic pressure. Using Bernoulli's equation then yields:

$$\frac{V_{\text{duct}}^2}{2g_c} = \frac{P_d}{\rho} - \frac{P_s}{\rho}$$

where P_d is the dynamic pressure and P_s is the static pressure. To determine the change in pressure from the Pitot-static tube, it is necessary to consider the weight of the water.

$$P_d - P_s = \rho_{\text{water}} \times \frac{g}{g_c} \times 0.041\,\text{m}$$

$$= 997.5\,\text{kg/m}^3 (9.81)(0.041\text{m})$$

$$= 401\,\text{N/m}^2$$

and therefore:

$$V_{\text{duct}} = \sqrt{2(9.81)\left(\frac{401\,\text{N/m}^2}{1.2\,\text{kg/m}^3}\right)} = 81\,\text{m/sec}$$

40. **(C)** A hydraulic jump occurs in open channel flow when the fluid velocity goes from supercritical to subcritical, resulting in a sharp increase in the depth of the fluid. All flows will eventually become subcritical because viscosity will slow the flow. Therefore, an increase in volumetric flow rate will push the point at which the hydraulic jump occurs downstream. Also, the size of the jump can be derived as:

$$q^2 = \frac{h^3 \cdot g}{2}(r + r^2)$$

where q is the volumetric flow rate, h is the depth of the fluid before the jump, and r is the ratio of the depth after the jump to before the jump. It is clear from the equation that if q increases while keeping h constant, then r must increase. Therefore, the height difference across the jump will increase with increased volumetric flow rate.

41. **(B)** Most flow measuring devices need to be calibrated. Both the venturi meter and the orifice meter depend on frictional head losses to produce a pressure drop which is related to velocity so they need to be calibrated. A hot-wire anemometer depends on matching heat transfer from a hot wire to a flow with a pre-determined calibration curve. A wire, while accurate after calibration, needs to have an experimentally determined calibration factor. Only the Pitot-static tube, based on Bernoulli's equation, can provide velocity information without having to be calibrated.

42. **(D)** To maintain dynamic similarity, the Reynolds number of the prototype must match the Reynolds number of the full-size vessel. The Reynolds number is defined as:

$$R_e = \frac{VL}{v}$$

where V is the velocity of the body, L is a length scale associated with the body, and v is the kinematic viscosity of the fluid. The Reynolds number represents the ratio of inertial to viscous forces. For dynamic similarity, the Reynolds numbers should be the same. Since the viscosity will be the same for the submarine and the model, this results in:

$$V_s L_s = V_m L_m$$

and

$$V_m = \frac{120\,\text{ft}}{4\,\text{ft}} \times 3.5\,\text{ft/sec} = 122.5\,\text{ft/sec}$$

But, the drag coefficients on the two bodies must also be the same:

$$C_{fm} = \frac{F_m}{\rho_m V_s^2 L_s^2} = C_{fs} = \frac{F_s}{\rho_s V_s^2 L_s^2}$$

so that the force needed to move the full-scale submarine will be (noting that the density of water falls out of the equation):

$$F_s = \frac{3.5^2 \times 12^2}{122.5^2 \times 4^2} \times 200 \, \text{lbf} = 146.9 \, \text{lbf}$$

43. **(A)**   Impulse-momentum equations for incompressible liquids (such as water) indicate that a jet impacting on a plate will transfer its momentum such that:

$$F = MV = \rho VA \times V = \rho A V^2$$

so

$$V = \sqrt{\frac{F}{\rho A}} = \sqrt{\frac{250 \times g_c}{62.4 \, \text{lbm/ft}^3 \times \left(\frac{1}{24}\right)^2 \times \pi}} = 153.7 \, \text{ft/sec}$$

44. **(A)**   Decimal numbers can be converted to binary numbers using the following:

Division	Quotient	Remainder
$^{137}/_2$	68	1
$^{68}/_2$	34	0
$^{34}/_2$	17	0
$^{17}/_2$	8	1
$^{8}/_2$	4	0
$^{4}/_2$	2	0
$^{2}/_2$	1	0
$^{1}/_2$	0	1

Copying the remainder column, starting from the bottom, yields 10001001_2 as the correct result. (B) and (C) are incorrect since they are not binary numbers. (D) is the combination of the binary equivalents of 1 + 3 + 7, which is incorrect.

45. **(C)**   The surface tension of a liquid is the dominant property in determining the behavior of a fluid in a thin capillary tube. The surface

tension is related both to the cohesive forces within the liquid as well as the adhesive forces of the liquid to the tube. Motion is usually slow, so the other parameters listed will have small effects.

46. **(C)** Due to relative addressing of the spreadsheet copy statement, the resulting formula in cell B10 would be 2 + A10 * A10. Since multiplication is performed before addition, a value of 102 would appear in cell B10. (A) makes no sense. (B) would be the answer if an absolute reference was made to cell A1 (2 + A1 * A1). (D) would be the correct answer if cell B1 contained (2 + A1) * A1.

47. **(B)** Because of absolute referencing, the same value in cell B1 will appear in cells C1 and D1. (A) and (C) are incorrect. (D) would be correct if cell B1 referenced cell A1 relatively (A1 + 2). In that case, 9 would appear in cell C1 and 11 would appear in cell D1.

48. **(B)** A NAND operation is an AND + NOT operation. The result of the AND operation is 0001. The NOT operation switched the 0s and 1s, resulting in 1110. (A) is incorrect since it represents the result of an AND operation. (C) is incorrect since it represents the result of an OR operation. (D) is incorrect since there is no way to store the digit 2.

49. **(D)** Equation $PV^n = \text{Const}$ can be rearranged:

$$P^{1/n} \cdot V = \text{Const}$$

At $n = \infty$ $P^{1/n} = 1$ and $V = \text{Const}$.

50. **(C)** The critical pressure ratio for our conditions can be determined:

$$\frac{P^*}{P_0} = \left(\frac{2}{K+1}\right)^{\frac{K}{K-1}} = \left(\frac{2}{1.4+1}\right)^{\frac{1.4}{1.4-1}} = 0.5283$$

where P_0 = stagnation pressure at the nozzle inlet (1.5 MPa)

   P^* = critical pressure at the throat of the nozzle

Then $P^* = 0.6283 P_0 = 0.5283 \times 1.5 \text{ MPa} = 0.792 \text{ MPa}$.

At pressure $P^* = 0.792$ MPa critical velocity is reached at the throat of the nozzle (Mach number $M = 1$) and further expansion takes place outside the converging nozzle.

Therefore, combined convergent-divergent nozzle should be used to utilize pressure difference $\Delta P = P^* - P_2 = 0.792 - 0.3 = 0.492$ MPa with supercritical velocity achieved at the nozzle exit.

51. **(C)**   Turbines, compressors, and pumps are well insulated devices ($q = 0$). Then from the first law of thermodynamics at $V_1 = V_2$ and $Z_1 = Z_2$

$$W = h_1 - h_2 \quad \text{or} \quad dw = -dh$$

it follows from the property relation

$$T \cdot dS = dh - v \cdot dP \quad \text{at} \quad dq = T \cdot dS = 0 \text{ that } dh = V \cdot \text{dp}.$$

Substituting dh we have

$$dW = V \cdot dP$$

52. **(A)**   The heat transfer q_{in} to the working fluid in process $2 - 2' - 3 - 3'$ is represented by area $a - 2 - 2' - 3 - 3' - c - a$, and the heat transferred from the working fluid q_{out} in process $4' - 1$ is represented by area $a - 1 - 4' - c - a$. According to the second law of thermodynamics, the thermal efficiency of any cycle is defined as

$$2_t = \frac{W_{net}}{q} = \frac{q_{in} - q_{out}}{q_{in}}$$

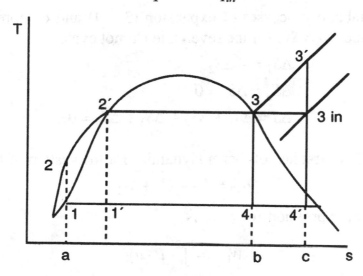

The net work of the cycle $W_{net} = q_{in} - q_{out} = $ AREA $1 - 2 - 2' - 3 - 3' - 4' - 1$ and

$$2_t = \frac{1 - 2 - 2' - 3 - 3' - 4' - 1}{a - 2 - 2' - 3 - 3' - c - a}$$

53. **(C)** The thermal efficiency of the reversible Carnot cycle does not depend on the nature of working fluid and is a function of maximum and minimum temperatures of the hot and cold sources only:

$$2_t = 1 - \frac{T_{min}}{T_{max}}$$

Therefore, using the figure presented in the question, superheating the steam (process $3 - 3''$) in the reversible Carnot cycle $1' - 2' - 3'' - 4' - 1'$ causes no change in thermal efficiency of the Carnot cycle since T_{max} and T_{min} remain constant.

54. **(C)** Consider reversible Carnot cycle $1' - 2' - 3 - 4 - 1'$ (see figure above). Change in entropy during heat transfer to the working fluid in isothermal process $2' - 3$ is:

$$\Delta S_1 = S_3 - S_{2'}$$

Change in entropy during heat transfer from the working fluid in isothermal process $4 - 1'$ is

$$\Delta S_2 = S_{1'} - S_4$$
$$\Delta S_3 = S_{2'} - S_{1'}$$
$$\Delta S_4 = S_4 - S_3$$

Since in adiabatic processes of expansion $(3 - 4)$ and compression $(1' - 2')$ $S_4 = S_3$ and $S_{1'} = S_{2'}$, for the reversible Carnot cycle

$$\Delta S_1 = -\Delta S_2$$
$$\Delta S_3 = \Delta S_4 = 0$$
$$\Delta S = \Delta S_1 + \Delta S_2 + \Delta S_3 + \Delta S_4 = 0$$

55. **(B)** The first law of thermodynamics for the system of fixed mass:

$$Q_{1-2} = U_2 - U_1 + W_{1-2}$$

where general expression for work is

$$W_{1-2} = \int_1^2 P \cdot dV.$$

Heat transfer at constant volume process will change only the internal energy of the system between states 1 and 2.

56. **(D)** If available waste heat $\overline{Q}_1$, = 1,000 kw and designed heat engine has net power output $\overline{W}$ = 510 kw, thermal efficiency of the

proposed engine can be determined:

$$2_t^e = \frac{\overline{W}}{\overline{Q}} = \frac{510}{1,000} = 0.51$$

$$2_t^e = 51.0\%$$

Thermal efficiency of the reversible Carnot cycle at a given temperature range can be also calculated:

$$2_t^c = 1 - \frac{T_{min}}{T_{max}} = 1 - \frac{(27 + 273)}{(327 + 273)} = 1 - \frac{300}{600} = 0.50$$

$$2_t^c = 50.0\%$$

2_t^c is maximum possible thermal efficiency of any reversible and irreversible cycle at a given temperature difference. $\Delta T = T_{max} - T_{min}$.

Since $2_t^e > 2_t^c$, such a heat engine is impossible.

57. **(A)** There is a graphical solution to determine work done ON or BY the thermodynamic system during the process. Since

$$W_{1-2} = \int_1^2 P \cdot dV$$

work is represented by area under the process on $P - V$ diagram, as shown below.

Therefore, during expansion $1 - 2$ (work is done **BY** the system and is positive) the most desirable process is constant pressure process $1 - 2a$ (maximum area under the process).

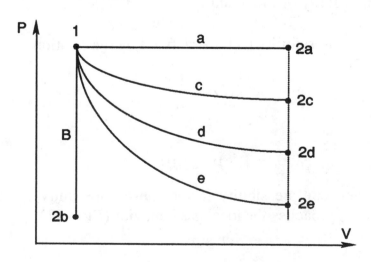

58. **(D)**   The quality of the steam in the low-pressure stage of the turbine affects significantly internal turbine efficiency and, as a result, thermal efficiency of the Rankine cycle. Also, increased moisture content can cause erosion of the last turbine stages. The basic Rankine cycle $1 - 2 - 3 - 4' - 1$ and the reheat cycle $1 - 2 - 3 - 4 - 5 - 6$ are represented in the following figure.

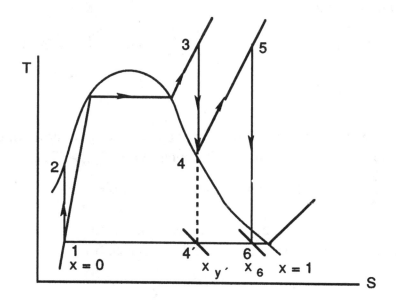

It follows from T–S diagram that the main advantage of the reheat cycle is in decreasing the moisture content of the working fluid in the low-pressure stages of the turbine:

$$(1 - X)_6 < (1 - X)_{4'}$$

where X is the quality of the steam.

59. **(D)**   Compressibility factor is defined by the relation

$$Z = \frac{Pv}{RT}$$

and

$$Pv = ZRT$$

Therefore, when compressibility factor approaches unity, actual gas behavior closely approaches the ideal gas behavior ($Pv = RT$).

60. **(A)** Heat transfer at $P = $ Const and $V = $ Const can be calculated as

$$dq_p = C_p \cdot dT \quad \text{and} \quad dq_v = C_v \cdot dT$$

For an ideal gas $C_p - C_v = R$ and $C_p > C_v$. Therefore,

$$dq_p > dq_v$$

Also, $\quad dq_p = dU + dW.$ However,

$dq_v = dU$ (since $dw = 0$). As a result,

$dq_p > dq_v.$

61. **(B)** By convention, there are 8 bits in a byte, therefore, 2 bytes are equivalent to 16 bits. One of the bits is used to store the sign of the number, leaving 15 bits available for the value. Fifteen 1s in binary is equivalent to 32,767. (A) is incorrect. (C) would be correct if a bit was not required for the sign. (D) would be correct if 8 bits were available for the number and sign.

62. **(A)** (B) and (C) are incorrect since they are not binary numbers. (B) is the octal representation of e and (C) is the hexadecimal representation of e. (D) is incorrect since the whole number part of e is 2, which is 10_2. The first six digits of the decimal binary part of e is found as follows:

0.7182	0.1
−0.5000	
0.2182	0.00
−0.000	
0.2182	0.001
−0.1250	
0.0932	0.0001
−0.0625	
0.0307	0.0000
−0.0000	
0.0307	0.00001
−0.015625	
0.15075	

63. **(C)** We know that

$$V^2 = cS.$$

c is the constant of proportionality. Find the relationship between velocity and acceleration:

$$V = \frac{dS}{dt} \cdot \frac{dV}{dt} \frac{dt}{dV}$$

$$V = a \cdot \frac{dS}{dV}$$

$$\int_0^v V \, dV = \int_0^S a \, dS$$

or $V^2 = 2aS$, thus $c = 2a$.

$$a = \left(\frac{(60)^2}{2 \cdot 600} \right) = 3 \, \mathbf{i} \, \text{m/sec}^2.$$

64. **(D)**   Convert velocity to m/sec.

$$V = 83(1,000/3,600) = 23 \, \text{m/sec}$$

Because the car's speed is constant, it only has a normal component of acceleration

$$a_n = V^2 \, / \, r = (23)^2/201 = -2.63 \, \mathbf{i} \, \text{m/sec}^2.$$

The negative sign is there because the acceleration is directed toward the center of curvature.

65. **(C)**   Using relative motion analysis applied to rotating axes, the following relationship is attained:

$$a_p = a_0 + \dot{\omega} \times (\omega \times r) + 2\omega \times V_{\text{rel}} + a_{\text{rel}}$$

The terms a_0, $\dot{\omega} \times (\omega \times r)$, and a_{rel} zeros because the disc is rotating about a fixed axis at a constant angular velocity, the slot is straight and the relative velocity is constant, thus

$$a_p = 2\omega \times V_{\text{rel}}$$

$$= \frac{2(12\mathbf{k}) \times (5.1\mathbf{i})}{100} = 1.22\mathbf{j} \, \text{m/sec}^2$$

66. **(D)**   At the instant we are calculating, assume the wheel is pinned at point C and point B rotates around it.

$$V_B = \omega \times CB$$

$$CB = \sqrt{1^2 + 1^2} = \sqrt{2} \text{ m}$$

$$V_B = \left(\frac{10}{1}\right)\sqrt{2} \quad \searrow 45°$$

67. **(B)** Equations of motion of the two masses

$$10a = T - 10g \;\uparrow$$
$$15a = 15g - T \;\downarrow$$

Adding the two equations gives

$$25a = 5g$$

or $a = \frac{8}{5} = 1.962$, or 2 m/sec/sec $\uparrow$ for the 10 kg mass.

68. **(B)** Using conservation of energy,

$$K_1 + U_1 = K_2 + U_2$$
$$\tfrac{1}{2} MV^2 = MgH$$
$$0.5 \, M(2.3)^2 = Mg \, 2(1 - \cos\theta).$$

Solving gives $\theta = 30°$.

69. **(B)** $V = 48\left(\dfrac{10}{36}\right) = 13.4$ m/sec

Equate forces on the mass m in the x direction:

$$ma = \mu_s mg$$
$$a = 9.81(0.3) = -2.94 \text{ m/sec}^2$$

As in problem 63, find the relationship between velocity and acceleration:

$$\int_v^0 V \, dV = \int_0^S a \, dS$$
$$\frac{-(13.4)^2}{2} = -2.94S$$
$$S = 30.5 \text{ m}$$

70. **(C)**   From the definition, the velocity of the particle just before it hits the floor:

$$V_a = \sqrt{2\,gh}\,\sqrt{2(9.81)\,2} = 6.26 \text{ meter/sec}$$

$$e = \frac{\text{rel. vel. of rebound}}{-\text{rel. vel. of approach}}$$

$$0.87 = \frac{-V_r}{(-V_a)}$$

$$V_r = 0.87(6.26) = 5.45 \text{ meter/sec}$$

$$= \sqrt{2\,gh_1}$$

which gives $h_1 = 1.5$ meters.

71. **(B)**   Since danger to the public welfare has not been established, Sue should go along with the wishes of her superiors. (A) is not correct in this situation since danger to the public welfare has not been established. (C) is not correct since this is not the function of the board. (D) is not correct since in this case there was not sufficient evidence and secondly, this is not the proper channel to address the problem if one arose.

72. **(C)**   (A) is incorrect since any information uncovered that endangers the public welfare must be revealed to proper authorities. (B) is incorrect since the responsibility to the public welfare takes precedence over responsibility to the client. (D) is incorrect since there was not conflict of interest in this case.

73. **(D)** $ma = \Sigma F$

$$\left[\frac{(363+205)}{9.81}\right]a = 712 - (363 + 205)$$

$$a = 2.49 \text{ m/sec}^2$$

Moments about *B:*

$$mad = \Sigma M_B$$

$$\left(\frac{205}{9.81}\right) 2.49(1.2) = M_B - 205(1.2)$$

$$M_B = 62 + 246 = 308 \text{ Nm CCW}$$

74. **(C)** $K = 0.5I\omega^2 + 0.5mV^2$

$$= 0.5\left(\frac{2}{2}\right)(0.5)^2\,(10)^2 + 0.5(2)\,(2.5)^2$$

$$= 12.5 + 6.25 = 18.75 \text{ joules}$$

75. **(D)**   Tension force in the rope is 30 N. Next, determine the weight of the block. Draw a free-body diagram and sum forces along the plane.

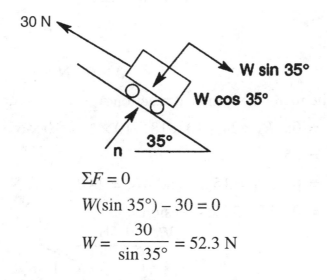

$$\Sigma F = 0$$

$$W(\sin 35°) - 30 = 0$$

$$W = \frac{30}{\sin 35°} = 52.3 \text{ N}$$

76. **(B)**   Two free-body diagrams are needed to find the forces in all ropes. Draw a free-body diagram for the 180 N weight, and next draw the free-body diagram for the 65 N weight.

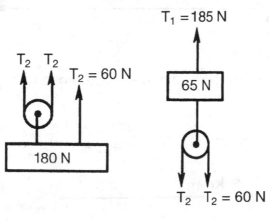

$$T_1 = 2T_2 + 65 \text{ N} = 185 \text{ N}.$$

77. **(D)** Draw the free-body diagram of point *C* and sum forces.

$$\Sigma F_y = 0: \quad B_y = 60 \text{ N}$$

$$B_x = B_y (\tan 35°) = 42 \text{ N}$$

$$\Sigma F_x = 0: \quad 42 - A = 0$$

$$A = 42 \text{ N}$$

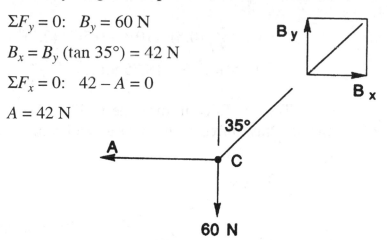

78. **(A)** Use the method of joints at reaction *A*

$$\Sigma M_B = 0: \quad R_A \times 24 - 10 \times 18 - 10 \times 12 - 10 \times 6 = 0$$

$$R_A = 15$$

$$\Sigma F_y = 0: \quad AB_y = 15 \text{ kN and } AB_x = 2AB_y = 30 \text{ kN}$$

$$\Sigma F_x = 0: \quad AF = 30 \text{ kN tension}$$

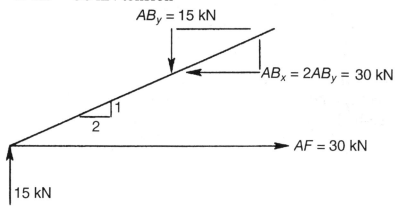

79. **(C)** Draw two free-body diagrams and work with portion *CD*. Because of symmetry

$$C_y = D_y = \frac{6 \times 4}{2} = 12 \text{ kN}$$

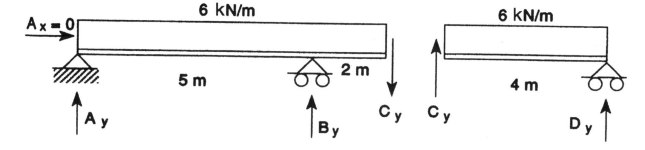

80. **(D)**   Find the reaction at A.

$$\Sigma M_E = 0:\quad 60 \times 12 + 30 \times 24 + 30 \times 36 - R_A(48) = 0$$

$$R_A = 232 \text{ KN}$$

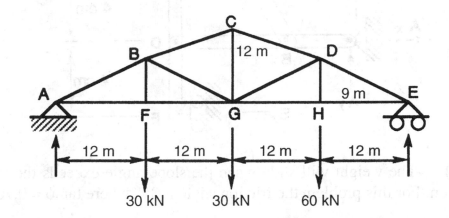

Then solve the force BG by the method of sections. Find the intersection at point O of the other two unknowns BC and FG. Sum moments about point O.

$$\Sigma M_0 = 0:\quad 36 \times 30 + 48BG_y - 24 \times 52.5 = 0$$

$$BG_y = 3.75 \text{ k and } BG = \left(\frac{5}{3}\right) 3.75 = 6.25 \text{ kN tension}$$

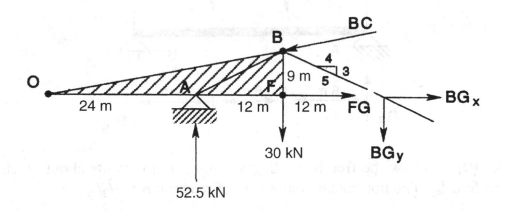

81. **(C)**   Draw the free-body diagram and sum moments about reactions A.

$$\Sigma M_A = 0:\quad 12 \times 800 - 4\,E_x = 0$$

$$E_x = 2,400 \text{ N}$$

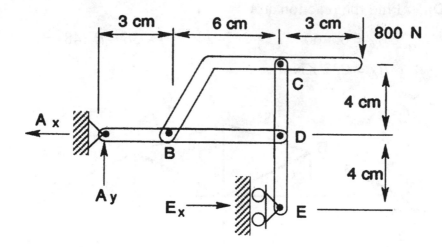

82. (C) The weight will slide when the slope angle exceeds the angle of friction. For this problem the friction angle is 35° where tan $\phi = 0.70$.

83. (B) The distributed load is broken into two parts. Total load is found for each part, and moments are summed about reaction B.

$$\Sigma M_B = 0: \quad 24R_A - 72 \times 8 - 48 \times 16 = 0$$

$$R_A = 56 \text{ kN}$$

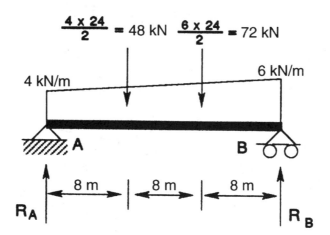

84. (D) Draw the free-body diagram and sum moments about reaction A to find B_y. The horizontal component of reaction B is $^1/_2 B_y$.

$$\Sigma M_a = 0: \quad 200 \times 5 + 200 \times 6 - 10B_y = 0$$

$$B_y = 220 \text{ N and } B_x = (^1/_2) B_y = 110 \text{ N}$$

$$B = \sqrt{220^2 + 110^2} = 246 \text{ N}$$

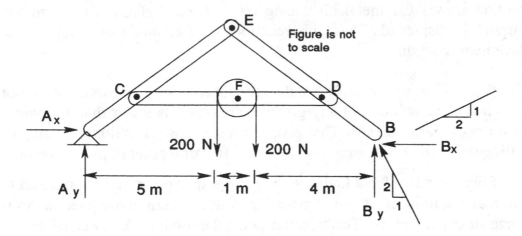

85. (C) Find the rectangular components of the three vectors and add each of the components.

$$A = 51.4i + 61.3j \quad N$$
$$B = 200\,i \quad\quad\quad N$$
$$C = 75Ii - 129.9j \quad N$$
$$\overline{R = 326.4i - 68.6j \quad N}$$

86. (A) One mole of a substance is equal to its molecular weight expressed in g. First find the molecular weight of $CuSO_4$ using atomic weights of respective elements. A molecule of $CuSO_4$ contains one atom of copper, one atom of sulfur, and four atoms of oxygen.

$$1 \times Cu = 1 \times 63.5 = 63.5$$
$$1 \times S \;\; = 1 \times 32.0 = 32.0$$
$$4 \times O \;\; = 4 \times 16.0 = \underline{64.0}$$
$$159.5$$

Thus, the molecular weight of $CuSO_4$ is 159.5 g/mole. Now convert 6.38 g to moles.

$$6.38 \text{ g} \times \frac{1 \text{ mole}}{159.5 \text{ g}} = 0.04 \text{ mole}$$

87. (C) $AgNO_3$ and $Cu(NO_3)_2$ are ionic substances. In $AgNO_3$, silver ion (Ag^+) is the positive ion or cation, and nitrate ion (NO^-_3) is the negative ion or anion. Cu by itself, and Ag by itself, are in metallic form. The reaction shows Cu metal displacing NO_3^- from $AgNO_3$. Only one ion (nitrate) is displaced. Thus, this reaction is an example of a single displacement reaction.

88. **(D)**   If a non-volatile solute is dissolved in a solvent, the vapor pressure of the solution at any given temperature is lower than the vapor pressure of pure solvent. This property results in elevation (raising) of boiling point and depression (lowering) of freezing point of pure solvent.

Ethylene glycol is a liquid of very low vapor pressure as compared to water. A solution of ethylene glycol in water is commonly used as antifreeze in car radiators. The freezing point depression (Δ^f) is equal to the freezing point constant of the solvent (K_f) times the molality (μ) of the solution.

$$\Delta^f = K_f \cdot m \tag{1}$$

Molality is defined as moles of solute per Kg of solvent. Using atomic weights, the molecular weight of ethylene glycol ($C_2H_6O_2$) is found to be 62.0 g/mole. Therefore, 93.0 g of ethylene glycol represents

$$93.0 \text{ g} \times \frac{1 \text{ mole}}{62.0 \text{ g}} = 1.50$$

moles of ethylene glycol. The molality of the solution is:

$$\frac{1.50 \text{ mole solute}}{0.750 \text{ Kg solvent}} = 2.00 \text{ mole/Kg}$$

(Remember that the mass of solvent is expressed in Kg in calculating molality.)

Now, using equation (1) shown above,

$$\Delta^f = 0.81 \frac{\text{deg C kg}}{\text{mole}} \times 2.00 \frac{\text{mole}}{\text{kg}} = 1.62 \text{ deg C}.$$

Thus, the freezing point depression is 1.62° C. The freezing point of pure water is 0.00° C. Therefore, the freezing point of the solution is $-1.62°$ C.

89. **(C)**   The equivalent weight of an element is defined as that weight which reacts with, or generates, 1.00 g of hydrogen, 16.00 g of oxygen, 32.00 g of sulfur, 35.5 g of chlorine, etc.

Let us first find the mass of hydrogen evolved, using the General Gas Equation, which is

$$PV = nRT$$

or

$$Pv = \frac{mRT}{M.W.}$$

Where

P = pressure of gas in atm

V = volume of gas in lit

m = mass of gas in g

R = the Gas Constant = 0.082 lit atm/deg mole

M.W. = Molecular weight of gas in g/mole

Rearranging the above equation,

$$m = \frac{(P)\,(V)\,(M.W.)}{(R)\,(T)}$$

$$= \frac{(1.0 \text{ atm})\,(0.0246 \text{ lit})\,(2.00 \text{ g/mole})}{(0.082 \text{ lit atm/deg mole})\,(300 \text{ deg})}$$

$$= 0.002 \text{ g}$$

This amount of hydrogen is produced by 0.180 g of the metal. Find the mass of the metal which would produce 1.00 g of hydrogen.

$$\frac{0.180 \text{ g metal}}{0.002 \text{ g hydrogen}} = 90.0 \text{ g metal per g of } H_2$$

Therefore, the equivalent weight of the metal is 90.0.

90. **(D)**   The K shell (the lowest energy shell) octate consists of a capacity for two electrons. Octates of other shells represent a capacity for eight electrons. Elements are placed in various groups according to the number of electrons present in the outermost octates of their atoms. Atoms of Group VIII (also called group O) elements contain complete outermost octates.

Chlorine (Cl) belongs to Group VII A. Therefore, an atom of Cl contains seven electrons in its outermost octate.

91. **(B)** Normality (N) of H_2SO_4 can be found using the equation:

$$(N_A)(V_A) = (N_B)(V_B)$$

where, N_A = Normality of acid

V_A = Volume of acid

N_b = Normality of base

V_b = Volume of base

Make sure to use same unit for volume on both sides of the equation.

Substituting,

$$(N_A)(12.0 \text{ ml}) = (0.15 \text{ N})(15.0 \text{ ml})$$

$$N_A = 0.187$$

The normality (N) and molarity (M) are two different ways of expressing concentration. For HCl, HNO_3, NaOH, or KOH, the normality is the same as the molarity, because each of these provide one mole of H^+ or one mole of OH^- per mole of the acid or base. Sulfuric acid (H_2SO_4) however provides 2 moles of H^+ per mole of the acid ($H_2SO_4 \rightarrow 2H^+ + SO_4^{-2}$). Therefore, the molarity of H_2SO_4 is half its normality.

Thus, M of

$$H_2SO_4 = \frac{0.187}{2} = 0.094$$

92. **(C)** A chemical equation is balanced if both sides of the equation show the same number of atoms of each element. During the process of balancing an equation, one can change the coefficient (i.e., the number before the formula) of a given substance in the reaction; but cannot change its formula.

In the present equation, there are two Fe atoms on the left; therefore, we can change the coefficient of Fe on the right side to 2.

On the left side, we have 3 oxygen atoms which go to form CO_2. From 3 oxygen atoms, we get 1.5 molecules of CO_2. So, the coefficient of CO_2 becomes 1.5. For 1.5 molecules of CO_2, we require 1.5 atoms of C; thus the coefficient of C becomes 1.5 atoms of C, thus the coefficient of C becomes 1.5.

$$Fe_2O_3 + 1.5 \text{ C} \rightarrow 2Fe + 1.5 \text{ CO}_2$$

Traditionally, a balanced equation is written using the smallest ratio of molecules in whole numbers. Therefore, the above equation will have to be doubled.

$$2 \, Fe_2O_3 + 3C \rightarrow 4Fe + 3CO_2$$

The coefficient of CO_2 in the balanced equation is 3.

93. **(D)** This is a simple red-ox equation which can be balanced by inspection. However, red-ox equations are easier to balance by using the "electron-balance method." The procedure is as follows:

First write the oxidation numbers of each element on both sides of the equation. A knowledge of oxidation numbers of common elements is extremely useful. It is also very helpful to know that the total oxidation number of a molecule or the formula is zero. The oxidation number of an element by itself is also zero.

$$Mn^{+4} \, O_2^{-4} + H^{+1} \, Cl^{-1} \rightarrow Mn^{+2} \, Cl_2 + H_2^{+2} \, O^{-2} + Cl_2^{0}$$

Inspect the oxidation number of each element *per atom* on both sides of the equation. Which elements have changed their oxidation numbers? Those elements that have changed the oxidation numbers have taken part in the reduction and oxidation.

$$Mn^{+4} \xrightarrow{+2e} Mn^{+2} \qquad \text{Half equation for reduction}$$

$$2 \, Cl^- \xrightarrow{-2e} Cl_2^{0} \qquad \text{Half equation for oxidation}$$

(Note: reduction is defined as gain of electron(s), while oxidation is defined as loss of electron(s).)

We can multiply each of the above half equations by any factor so that the total number of electrons lost is equal to the total number of electrons gained.

In the above half equations, we already have two electrons gained and two electrons lost. Now adding both equations, we get:

$$Mn^{+4} + 2Cl^- \rightarrow Mn^{+2} + Cl_2^{0}$$

This completes the balancing of the red-ox part of the equation. The rest of the equation must be balanced by inspection.

We need two more Cl^- ions from the left to form $MnCl_2$ on the right.

$$MnO_2 + 2Cl^- + 2Cl^- \rightarrow MnCl_2 + Cl_2^{0}$$

Total of four Cl^- come from four HCl:

$$MnO_2 + 4\ HCl \rightarrow MnCl_2 + Cl_2$$

How many H_2O molecules are formed? We have two O atoms and four H atoms on the left side. These form $2\ H_2O$.

Therefore, the complete balanced equation is:

$$MnO_2 + 4\ HCl \rightarrow MnCl_2 + Cl_2 + 2\ H_2O$$

The coefficient of HCl in the balanced equation is 4.

94. **(B)** The amount of a radioactive isotope can be expressed in terms of its mass (such as mg or ng) or in terms of its activity (such as counts/min). The half-life of a radioactive isotope is defined as the time it takes to reduce the original amount or activity by half. Thus, each half-life cycle reduces the amount by half.

The following equation can be used:

$$\text{Remaining amount or activity} = \frac{\text{Original amount or activity}}{2^n}$$

where n = the number of half-life cycles. To find out how many half-life cycles are needed to reduce the original amount or activity to 1%, we substitute in the above equation.

$$1 = \frac{100}{2^n} \quad \text{or} \quad 2^n = 100$$
$$n = 6.65$$

That is, it takes 6.65 half-life cycles to reduce the original amount or activity by 99%.

Each half-life cycle is 4.3 days.

$$6.65 \text{ cycles} \times \frac{4.3 \text{ days}}{1 \text{ cycle}} = 28.6 \text{ days}$$

is the required elapsed time.

95. **(B)** First let us look at some fundamental subatomic particles.

	Mass	**Charge**
Proton (H)	1.00 amu	+ 1
Neutron (N)	1.00 amu	0
Electron ($_{-1}{}^0\beta$)	$\frac{1}{1,800}$ amu	– 1
Positron ($_{+1}{}^0\beta$)	$\frac{1}{1,800}$ amu	+ 1

Now looking at the equation,

$$_4^9\text{Be} - ? \rightarrow {}_5^9\text{Be}$$

We find that the mass of the nucleus has remained the same (i.e., 9). However, the atomic number (which is the number of protons in the nucleus) is changed from four to five. The original nucleus has four protons and five neutrons. The nucleus produced has five protons and four neutrons. Obviously, the number of protons has increased by one, while the number of neutrons has decreased by one. What subatomic particle must be removed from a neutron to convert it to a proton? An electron. The answer is $_{-1}{}^0\beta$.

96. **(A)** Nuclear reactions often involve loss in mass as the reactants form products. This loss in mass is called the "mass defect." According to Einstein's theory of relativity, energy is produced at the cost of the mass lost.

Let us first find what the mass defect is. Using atomic weights which are given, the total mass on the left side of the equation is 6.0151 + 2.0141 = 8.0292. On the right side, we have two atoms of ^{4}He. The total mass on the right = 2 × 4.0026 = 8.0052. The mass defect = 8.0292 – 8.0052 = 0.0240 g per 8.0292 g of the fuel. Therefore, per 1.00 g of the fuel, the mass defect is 0.0030 g.

Now substituting in Einstein's famous equation,

$$E = mc^2$$

where m = mass defect in g

c = the velocity of light

= 3.0×10^{10} cm/sec

E = $(0.0030 \text{ g}) (3.0 \times 10^{10} \text{ cm/sec})^2$

= 2.7×10^{18} gcm^2/sec^2 = 2.7×10^{18} ergs

(Note that the units gcm²/sec² is the same as the unit erg.)

Now convert ergs to KJ

$$(2.7 \times 10^{18} \text{ ergs}) \left(\frac{1 \text{ J}}{1.0 \times 10^7 \text{ ergs}} \right) \left(\frac{1.0 \text{ kJ}}{1.0 \times 10^3 \text{ J}} \right) = 2.7 \times 10^8 \text{ KJ}$$

97. **(B)**   The twist angle is converted to radians:

$$\phi = 2° = 2 \left(\frac{2\pi}{360} \right) = 0.03489 \text{ rad}$$

$r_1 = 0.0127$ m; $r_2 = 0.0254$ m

Polar Moment of Inertia:

$$J = \frac{\pi}{2} \left(r_2^4 - r_1^4 \right)$$

$$J = \frac{\pi}{2} \left((1\,\text{m})^4 - (0.5\,\text{m})^4 \right) = 1.47\,\text{m}^4$$

$$T = \frac{GJ}{L}\phi = \frac{(40,000\,\text{N/m}^2)(1.47\,\text{m}^4)}{12\,\text{m}} (0.03489)$$

$$= 171\,\text{Nm}$$

98. **(A)** $\Sigma M_c = 0$; R_A (6 m) – 10 N (4 m) = 0 gives $R_A = 6.66$ N

Hence, $R_c = 10$ N – 6.66 N = 3.34 N

Starting from the left, upward force is positive shear. Hence, between A and B shear is +6.66 N. At B, shear drops by 10 N; hence, from B to C shear is 6.66 – 10 = – 3.34 N.

Also, since there is no external force between A and B, shear must remain constant at + 6.66 N. For similar reason constant shear – 3.34 N acts between B and C.

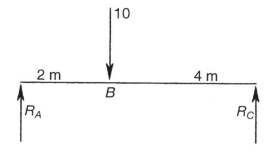

99. **(D)** $V = \dfrac{dM}{dx}$,

where $\quad V$ = shear force

$\quad M$ = bending moment

$\quad dM = V\,dx$

$\quad \oint M = V\,dx$

means increase of moment is equal to V vs. x diagram. Also, since V is constant (problem 98), moment would change linearly along x. This rejects (B) and (C).

$M = 0$ at A (due to hinge support); hence, moment at B is area of shear diagram (problem 98) up to $B = (6.66\ \text{N})\ (2\ \text{m}) = 13.33$ Nm. Furthermore, moment at $C = 0$ (roller support). This makes the correct answer (D).

Note:

The relation of + and – moment with curvature is shown.

Alternate Method: Moment from A to B;

$$M_{AB} = R_A X;$$

a straight line with a value of 0 at $x = 0$ (Point A) and a value of (6.66 N) (2 m) = 13.33 Nm at $x = 2$ (Point B).

Moment from B to C:

$$M_{BC} = R_A x - 10(x - 2)$$
$$M_{BC} = -3.34\,x + 20;$$

a straight line with negative slope as shown in (D).

100. **(A)** BM (bending moment) diagrams are understood well with a good understanding of SF (shear force) diagrams.

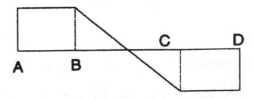

From symmetry, end reaction

$$\uparrow R_A = \uparrow R_B = \frac{1}{2}\left[\omega \cdot \frac{L}{3}\right] = \frac{\omega L}{6} = \text{constant}$$

The shear force diagram on the right suggests

1)   Linear variation of moment from A to B *and* C to D (Note: BM is obtained by integration of *SF*). Hence, reject (C) and (D).

2)   BM is maximum when

$$\frac{dM}{dx} = 0; \text{ but } \frac{dM}{dx} = V$$

From SF diagram, maximum BM will be halfway between B and C. Hence, (A) is the right choice.

Note: BM equation from B to C:

$$M = R_A x - \omega\left(x - \frac{L}{3}\right)\left[\frac{1}{2}\left(x - \frac{L}{3}\right)\right]$$

BM equation from A to B does not contain the second term making the variation linear up to B. The second term (quadratic in x) makes the variation parabolic from B to C.

101. **(D)**   Location of Neutral Axis:

$$\overline{Y} = \frac{\Sigma A_i y_i}{\Sigma A_i} = \frac{(3\,\text{in} \times 2\,\text{in})(1.5\,\text{in}) + (2\,\text{in} \times 4\,\text{in})(3\,\text{in} + 1\,\text{in})}{(3\,\text{in} \times 2\,\text{in}) + (2\,\text{in} \times 4\,\text{in})}$$
$$= 2.928\,\text{in}$$

N.A. is located 2.928 m from the bottom and (5 in − 2.928 in) = 2.072 in from the top.

Stress Equation:

$$\sigma_{mx} = \frac{M_{mx} C_{mx}}{I};$$

$$M_{mx} = (6\,\text{ft} \times 12\,\text{in/ft})\,F = 72\,F\,\text{lb} \bullet \text{in}$$

and $C_{mx} = Y_{mx}$

(on compression side, i.e., bottom surface of beam) = 2.928 in.

Moment of Inertia about N.A.:

$$= \frac{1}{12} (4 \text{ in} \times (2 \text{ in})^3) + (4 \text{ in} \times 2 \text{ in}) (2.072 - 1 \text{ in} - 1 \text{ in})^2$$

$$+ \frac{1}{12} (2 \text{ in} \times (3 \text{ in})^3) + (2 \text{ in} \times 3 \text{ in}) (2.928 - 1.5)^2$$

$$= 28.595 \text{ in}^4$$

$$\sigma_{mx} = \sigma_{allowable} = \frac{\sigma_y}{K} = \frac{60,000 \text{ psi}}{3} = 20,000 \text{ psi} = \frac{72 \, F(2.928)}{28.595}$$

$$F = 2,713 \text{ lbs}$$

102. **(B)** The Principal Stresses are given by:

$$\sigma_{mx.min} = \left[\frac{\sigma_x + \sigma_y}{2}\right] \pm \sqrt{\left(\frac{\sigma_x - \sigma_y}{2}\right)^2 + \tau_{xy}^2}$$

$$= \left[\frac{-20,000 + 30,000}{2}\right] \pm \sqrt{\left(\frac{-20,000 - 30,000}{2}\right)^2 + (10,000)^2}$$

$$= 5,000 \pm 26,900$$

$$= 31,900 \text{ N}/\text{m}^2 \text{ and } -21,900 \text{ N}/\text{m}^2$$

Note:

$$\tau_{mx} = \sqrt{\left(\frac{\sigma_x - \sigma_y}{2}\right)^2 + \tau_{xy}^2} = 26,900 \text{ N}/\text{m}^2$$

103. **(D)** Principal planes are at angle q_p where

$$\tan 2\theta_p = \frac{2\tau_{mx}}{\sigma_x - \sigma_y}.$$

From Problem 102;

$$\tan 2\theta_p = \frac{2(26,900)}{-20,000 - 30,000} = -1.076$$

$$2\theta_p = \tan^{-1}(-1.076) = -47° \text{ and } -227°$$

Hence, $\theta_p = -23.5°$ and $-113.5°$

Note:

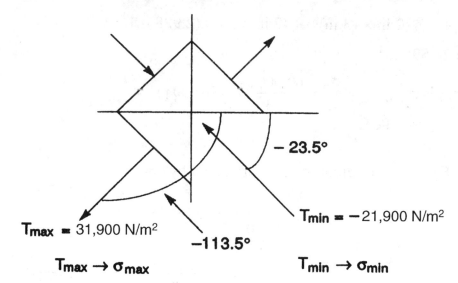

T_{max} = 31,900 N/m²

T_{min} = −21,900 N/m²

− 23.5°

−113.5°

$T_{max} \rightarrow \sigma_{max}$ $T_{min} \rightarrow \sigma_{min}$

104. **(C)** Reaction at A:

$$\Sigma M_B = 0; \quad R_A (3a) - P(2a) = 0; \quad \uparrow R_A = \tfrac{2}{3} P$$

Between 0 x a $(A$ to $C)$ $M = \tfrac{2}{3} Px$; hence,

$$EI \frac{d^2 y}{dx^2} = \frac{2}{3} Px$$

Integrating,

$$EI \frac{dy}{dx} = \frac{Px^2}{3} + C_1 \qquad (1)$$

Integrating again

$$EIy = \frac{Px^3}{9} + C_1 x + C_2 \qquad (2)$$

Between a x $3a$ $(C$ to $B)$; $M = \tfrac{2}{3} Px - P(x - a)$; hence,

$$EI \frac{d^2 y}{dx^2} = \frac{-P}{3} x + Pa$$

Integrating,

$$EI \frac{dy}{dx} = -\frac{Px^2}{6} + Pax + C_3 \qquad (3)$$

Integrating again

$$EIy = -\frac{Px^3}{18} + \frac{Pax^2}{2} + C_3x + C_4 \qquad (4)$$

The four constants of integration in equations (1) – (4) are determined from the following boundary conditions:

1. At $x = 0$; $y = 0$ is applied at equation (2) giving $C_2 = 0$

2. At $x = a$ (point C) y is the same if approached from right or left. Using equation (2) and equation (4)

$$\frac{Pa^3}{9} + C_1a = -\frac{Pa^3}{18} + \frac{Pa^3}{2} + C_3a + C_4$$

giving
$$C_1a - C_3a - C_4 = \frac{Pa^3}{3} \qquad (5)$$

3. Applying similar equality in slope ($\frac{dy}{dx}$) in equations (1) and (3)

$$\frac{Pa^2}{3} + C_1 = -\frac{Pa^2}{6} + Pa^2 + C_3$$

giving
$$C_1 - C_3 = \frac{Pa^2}{2} \qquad (6)$$

4. At $x = 3a$ (Point B) $y = 0$ is applied at equation (4) giving

$$-\frac{27Pa^3}{18} + \frac{9Pa^3}{2} + 3C_3a + C_4 = 0$$

giving
$$3C_3a + C_4 = -3Pa^3 \qquad (7)$$

Three unknowns C_1, C_3, and C_4 are solved from (5), (6), and (7) as:

$$C_1 = -\frac{5Pa^2}{9}$$

$$C_3 = -\frac{19Pa^2}{18}$$

$$C_4 = \frac{Pa^3}{6}$$

Substituting C_1 in equation (2)

$$EIy = \frac{Px^3}{9} - \frac{5Pa^2}{9}x$$

at Load Point $x = a$;

$$y = \frac{1}{EI}\left[\frac{Pa^3}{9} - \frac{5Pa^3}{9}\right] = -\frac{4Pa^3}{9EI}.$$

105. **(B)**   The effective interest rate per year

$= (1 + i)^m - 1$

$= (1 + 0.015)^{12} - 1 = 0.1956$ or 19.56 %

106. **(D)**   If r is the nominal interest rate per year, the effective interest rate per year with continuous compounding (i) is given by

$i = e^r - 1$

Here, $r = 0.12$. Therefore,

$i = e^{0.12} - 1$

$= 0.1275$ or 12.75%

107. **(C)**

Year	Book Value Before Depreciation Charge	Straight line Depreciation For the Year	Book Value After Depreciation Charge
1	76.00	$\frac{76 - 6}{5} = 14$	62.00
2	62.00	14	48.00
3	48.00	14	34.00
4	34.00	14	20.00
5	20.00	14	6.00

Note: The book values and depreciation in the above table are in millions of dollars.

108. **(A)** In a before-tax comparison of alternatives, depreciation is not taken into account.

109. **(B)** First consider the following cash flow and find the equivalent uniform annual cash flow A.

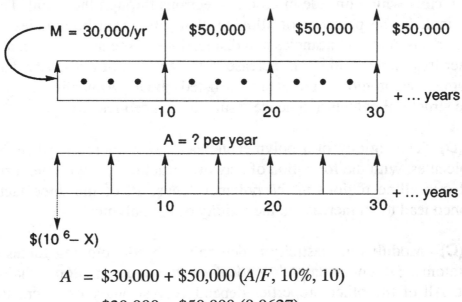

$$A = \$30,000 + \$50,000 \, (A/F, \, 10\%, \, 10)$$

$$= \$30,000 + \$50,000 \, (0.0627)$$

$$= \$33,135$$

Let X be the cost of construction.

$$\$(10^6 - X) = \frac{A}{i} = \frac{\$33,135}{0.1} = \$331,350$$

$$X = \$668,650$$

110. **(B)** In a sodium chloride crystal, sodium and chlorine are present as sodium and chloride ions, respectively. These ions are arranged in a periodic pattern to form the crystal. The electrostatic attraction between the positive sodium ion and the negative chloride ion forms the basis of the ionic bond that exists in a sodium chloride crystal.

111. **(C)** The direction vector begins at the origin and the coordinates of the position where it ends are 1, 1, 1/2. Thus, the direction represented by the arrow is 221.

112. **(A)** The change in crystal structure occurs isothermally and hence there are no thermally induced volume changes occurring. The volume

change is entirely due to the transformation. The bcc structure is less densely packed than the fcc structure and hence the transformation from fcc to bcc structure is accompanied by an increase in the volume.

113. **(B)** Electrical resistivity of a metal increases with increasing extent of factors which impede motion of electrons through the metal. These factors include the presence of alloying elements, grain boundaries, and crystal defects such as vacancies and dislocations. Except annealing, all of the other treatments lead to an increase in the amount of resistivity due to increasing one or more of the factors listed above. Annealing helps to remove structural defects and hence results in reduced resistivity.

114. **(D)** The rigidity of a polymer increases with increasing length of the molecules, with the formation of network structure and with the formation of crystalline regions in the polymer. Thus, all of the three factors mentioned lead to an increase in the rigidity of the polymer.

115. **(C)** Modulus of elasticity is determined by the binding forces between atoms, which is only dependent on the type of atoms that are present. All of the other properties depend very strongly on microstructural features such as grain size, dislocation density, and texture.

116. **(D)** A phosphorus doped silicon crystal is a n-type semiconductor. Phosphorus has five outer shell electrons of which four are used up in bonding. The extra electron is normally present in the donor level which is very close to the conduction band of the semiconductor. The thermal activation present at room temperature can elevate these electrons into the conduction band and these electrons are the major charge carriers in this material.

117. **(C)** This question tests knowledge of the mechanism of conductivity in metals. The correct answer is (C). Choice (A) is incorrect. Luster does not effect conductivity even though some feel that the characteristic luster and high conductivity both result from free electrons. Choice (B) is incorrect. "Extra" electrons must be carefully defined. Electrical neutrality requirements dictate that all atoms will have equal numbers of protons and electrons. Positive valence does not mean "extra" electrons. Choice (D) is incorrect. Position in the Periodic Table is quite arbitrary and not the cause of any physical or chemical property; but rather the converse — properties are organized in the table to reflect their periodically recurring nature.

118. **(A)** This question tests knowledge of Group Ia elements and their low values of electronegativity. The correct answer is (A). The Group Ia elements have a single "s" electron which is easily lost to form an alkali metal ion.

Choice (B) is incorrect. Conductivity is not related to the tendency of a metal to become ionized. The most conductive metal, silver, is not ionized nearly as easily as many less conductive metals. Choice (C) is incorrect. The violent reaction of the alkali metals with water to liberate hydrogen results from the position of the alkali metals on the emf series as does their ability to be ionized. But the reaction with water does not affect their ability to be ionized. Choice (D) is incorrect. The tendency of a metal to be ionized and the melting point are not related.

119. **(C)** This question tests knowledge of the electronic configuration of the rare earth metals and how it relates to their chemical properties. The correct answer is (C). The valence, or reactive, electrons are the same for each of the rare earth metals. They are $6s^2$ electrons. Each successive member of the series is made by adding a 4f electron which is two orbits down from the reactive $6s^2$ electrons and has a minimal effect on the chemical properties.

Choice (A) is incorrect. The reason is well known. Choice (B) is incorrect. The melting points of the rate earth metals are not particularly high or low, but typical of that of other metals in the Periodic Table. Choice (D) is incorrect. The position of the rare earth metals in the Periodic Table is arbitrary and cannot effect properties.

120. **(C)** This question tests knowledge of the electron volt — an important unit of energy that is commonly used in the quantum mechanical descriptions of the structure of matter and energy. The correct answer is (C). An electron volt (abbreviated eV) is an energy unit. It is the energy possessed by an electron after it has accelerated through an electrical potential of one volt. The common conversion factors are:

$$1 \text{ Joule} = 6.24 \times 10^{18} \text{ eV}$$

$$1 \text{ calorie} = 2.61 \times 10^{19} \text{ eV}$$

$$1 \text{ erg} = 6.24 \times 10^{11} \text{ eV}$$

Choice (A) is incorrect; an electron volt is not a voltage unit. Choice (B) is incorrect; an electron volt is not a unit of charge. Choice (D) is incorrect; an electron volt is a precisely defined unit of energy, and its definition does not depend on the context.

FE/EIT

Fundamentals of Engineering: AM Exam

Answer Sheets

FUNDAMENTALS OF ENGINEERING - MORNING SESSION
Test 1
ANSWER SHEET

1.	Ⓐ Ⓑ Ⓒ Ⓓ	31.	Ⓐ Ⓑ Ⓒ Ⓓ	61. Ⓐ Ⓑ Ⓒ Ⓓ
2.	Ⓐ Ⓑ Ⓒ Ⓓ	32.	Ⓐ Ⓑ Ⓒ Ⓓ	62. Ⓐ Ⓑ Ⓒ Ⓓ
3.	Ⓐ Ⓑ Ⓒ Ⓓ	33.	Ⓐ Ⓑ Ⓒ Ⓓ	63. Ⓐ Ⓑ Ⓒ Ⓓ
4.	Ⓐ Ⓑ Ⓒ Ⓓ	34.	Ⓐ Ⓑ Ⓒ Ⓓ	64. Ⓐ Ⓑ Ⓒ Ⓓ
5.	Ⓐ Ⓑ Ⓒ Ⓓ	35.	Ⓐ Ⓑ Ⓒ Ⓓ	65. Ⓐ Ⓑ Ⓒ Ⓓ
6.	Ⓐ Ⓑ Ⓒ Ⓓ	36.	Ⓐ Ⓑ Ⓒ Ⓓ	66. Ⓐ Ⓑ Ⓒ Ⓓ
7.	Ⓐ Ⓑ Ⓒ Ⓓ	37.	Ⓐ Ⓑ Ⓒ Ⓓ	67. Ⓐ Ⓑ Ⓒ Ⓓ
8.	Ⓐ Ⓑ Ⓒ Ⓓ	38.	Ⓐ Ⓑ Ⓒ Ⓓ	68. Ⓐ Ⓑ Ⓒ Ⓓ
9.	Ⓐ Ⓑ Ⓒ Ⓓ	39.	Ⓐ Ⓑ Ⓒ Ⓓ	69. Ⓐ Ⓑ Ⓒ Ⓓ
10.	Ⓐ Ⓑ Ⓒ Ⓓ	40.	Ⓐ Ⓑ Ⓒ Ⓓ	70. Ⓐ Ⓑ Ⓒ Ⓓ
11.	Ⓐ Ⓑ Ⓒ Ⓓ	41.	Ⓐ Ⓑ Ⓒ Ⓓ	71. Ⓐ Ⓑ Ⓒ Ⓓ
12.	Ⓐ Ⓑ Ⓒ Ⓓ	42.	Ⓐ Ⓑ Ⓒ Ⓓ	72. Ⓐ Ⓑ Ⓒ Ⓓ
13.	Ⓐ Ⓑ Ⓒ Ⓓ	43.	Ⓐ Ⓑ Ⓒ Ⓓ	73. Ⓐ Ⓑ Ⓒ Ⓓ
14.	Ⓐ Ⓑ Ⓒ Ⓓ	44.	Ⓐ Ⓑ Ⓒ Ⓓ	74. Ⓐ Ⓑ Ⓒ Ⓓ
15.	Ⓐ Ⓑ Ⓒ Ⓓ	45.	Ⓐ Ⓑ Ⓒ Ⓓ	75. Ⓐ Ⓑ Ⓒ Ⓓ
16.	Ⓐ Ⓑ Ⓒ Ⓓ	46.	Ⓐ Ⓑ Ⓒ Ⓓ	76. Ⓐ Ⓑ Ⓒ Ⓓ
17.	Ⓐ Ⓑ Ⓒ Ⓓ	47.	Ⓐ Ⓑ Ⓒ Ⓓ	77. Ⓐ Ⓑ Ⓒ Ⓓ
18.	Ⓐ Ⓑ Ⓒ Ⓓ	48.	Ⓐ Ⓑ Ⓒ Ⓓ	78. Ⓐ Ⓑ Ⓒ Ⓓ
19.	Ⓐ Ⓑ Ⓒ Ⓓ	49.	Ⓐ Ⓑ Ⓒ Ⓓ	79. Ⓐ Ⓑ Ⓒ Ⓓ
20.	Ⓐ Ⓑ Ⓒ Ⓓ	50.	Ⓐ Ⓑ Ⓒ Ⓓ	80. Ⓐ Ⓑ Ⓒ Ⓓ
21.	Ⓐ Ⓑ Ⓒ Ⓓ	51.	Ⓐ Ⓑ Ⓒ Ⓓ	81. Ⓐ Ⓑ Ⓒ Ⓓ
22.	Ⓐ Ⓑ Ⓒ Ⓓ	52.	Ⓐ Ⓑ Ⓒ Ⓓ	82. Ⓐ Ⓑ Ⓒ Ⓓ
23.	Ⓐ Ⓑ Ⓒ Ⓓ	53.	Ⓐ Ⓑ Ⓒ Ⓓ	83. Ⓐ Ⓑ Ⓒ Ⓓ
24.	Ⓐ Ⓑ Ⓒ Ⓓ	54.	Ⓐ Ⓑ Ⓒ Ⓓ	84. Ⓐ Ⓑ Ⓒ Ⓓ
25.	Ⓐ Ⓑ Ⓒ Ⓓ	55.	Ⓐ Ⓑ Ⓒ Ⓓ	85. Ⓐ Ⓑ Ⓒ Ⓓ
26.	Ⓐ Ⓑ Ⓒ Ⓓ	56.	Ⓐ Ⓑ Ⓒ Ⓓ	86. Ⓐ Ⓑ Ⓒ Ⓓ
27.	Ⓐ Ⓑ Ⓒ Ⓓ	57.	Ⓐ Ⓑ Ⓒ Ⓓ	87. Ⓐ Ⓑ Ⓒ Ⓓ
28.	Ⓐ Ⓑ Ⓒ Ⓓ	58.	Ⓐ Ⓑ Ⓒ Ⓓ	88. Ⓐ Ⓑ Ⓒ Ⓓ
29.	Ⓐ Ⓑ Ⓒ Ⓓ	59.	Ⓐ Ⓑ Ⓒ Ⓓ	89. Ⓐ Ⓑ Ⓒ Ⓓ
30.	Ⓐ Ⓑ Ⓒ Ⓓ	60.	Ⓐ Ⓑ Ⓒ Ⓓ	90. Ⓐ Ⓑ Ⓒ Ⓓ

91. Ⓐ Ⓑ Ⓒ Ⓓ 101. Ⓐ Ⓑ Ⓒ Ⓓ 111. Ⓐ Ⓑ Ⓒ Ⓓ
92. Ⓐ Ⓑ Ⓒ Ⓓ 102. Ⓐ Ⓑ Ⓒ Ⓓ 112. Ⓐ Ⓑ Ⓒ Ⓓ
93. Ⓐ Ⓑ Ⓒ Ⓓ 103. Ⓐ Ⓑ Ⓒ Ⓓ 113. Ⓐ Ⓑ Ⓒ Ⓓ
94. Ⓐ Ⓑ Ⓒ Ⓓ 104. Ⓐ Ⓑ Ⓒ Ⓓ 114. Ⓐ Ⓑ Ⓒ Ⓓ
95. Ⓐ Ⓑ Ⓒ Ⓓ 105. Ⓐ Ⓑ Ⓒ Ⓓ 115. Ⓐ Ⓑ Ⓒ Ⓓ
96. Ⓐ Ⓑ Ⓒ Ⓓ 106. Ⓐ Ⓑ Ⓒ Ⓓ 116. Ⓐ Ⓑ Ⓒ Ⓓ
97. Ⓐ Ⓑ Ⓒ Ⓓ 107. Ⓐ Ⓑ Ⓒ Ⓓ 117. Ⓐ Ⓑ Ⓒ Ⓓ
98. Ⓐ Ⓑ Ⓒ Ⓓ 108. Ⓐ Ⓑ Ⓒ Ⓓ 118. Ⓐ Ⓑ Ⓒ Ⓓ
99. Ⓐ Ⓑ Ⓒ Ⓓ 109. Ⓐ Ⓑ Ⓒ Ⓓ 119. Ⓐ Ⓑ Ⓒ Ⓓ
100. Ⓐ Ⓑ Ⓒ Ⓓ 110. Ⓐ Ⓑ Ⓒ Ⓓ 120. Ⓐ Ⓑ Ⓒ Ⓓ

FUNDAMENTALS OF ENGINEERING - MORNING SESSION
Test 2
ANSWER SHEET

1. Ⓐ Ⓑ Ⓒ Ⓓ
2. Ⓐ Ⓑ Ⓒ Ⓓ
3. Ⓐ Ⓑ Ⓒ Ⓓ
4. Ⓐ Ⓑ Ⓒ Ⓓ
5. Ⓐ Ⓑ Ⓒ Ⓓ
6. Ⓐ Ⓑ Ⓒ Ⓓ
7. Ⓐ Ⓑ Ⓒ Ⓓ
8. Ⓐ Ⓑ Ⓒ Ⓓ
9. Ⓐ Ⓑ Ⓒ Ⓓ
10. Ⓐ Ⓑ Ⓒ Ⓓ
11. Ⓐ Ⓑ Ⓒ Ⓓ
12. Ⓐ Ⓑ Ⓒ Ⓓ
13. Ⓐ Ⓑ Ⓒ Ⓓ
14. Ⓐ Ⓑ Ⓒ Ⓓ
15. Ⓐ Ⓑ Ⓒ Ⓓ
16. Ⓐ Ⓑ Ⓒ Ⓓ
17. Ⓐ Ⓑ Ⓒ Ⓓ
18. Ⓐ Ⓑ Ⓒ Ⓓ
19. Ⓐ Ⓑ Ⓒ Ⓓ
20. Ⓐ Ⓑ Ⓒ Ⓓ
21. Ⓐ Ⓑ Ⓒ Ⓓ
22. Ⓐ Ⓑ Ⓒ Ⓓ
23. Ⓐ Ⓑ Ⓒ Ⓓ
24. Ⓐ Ⓑ Ⓒ Ⓓ
25. Ⓐ Ⓑ Ⓒ Ⓓ
26. Ⓐ Ⓑ Ⓒ Ⓓ
27. Ⓐ Ⓑ Ⓒ Ⓓ
28. Ⓐ Ⓑ Ⓒ Ⓓ
29. Ⓐ Ⓑ Ⓒ Ⓓ
30. Ⓐ Ⓑ Ⓒ Ⓓ

31. Ⓐ Ⓑ Ⓒ Ⓓ
32. Ⓐ Ⓑ Ⓒ Ⓓ
33. Ⓐ Ⓑ Ⓒ Ⓓ
34. Ⓐ Ⓑ Ⓒ Ⓓ
35. Ⓐ Ⓑ Ⓒ Ⓓ
36. Ⓐ Ⓑ Ⓒ Ⓓ
37. Ⓐ Ⓑ Ⓒ Ⓓ
38. Ⓐ Ⓑ Ⓒ Ⓓ
39. Ⓐ Ⓑ Ⓒ Ⓓ
40. Ⓐ Ⓑ Ⓒ Ⓓ
41. Ⓐ Ⓑ Ⓒ Ⓓ
42. Ⓐ Ⓑ Ⓒ Ⓓ
43. Ⓐ Ⓑ Ⓒ Ⓓ
44. Ⓐ Ⓑ Ⓒ Ⓓ
45. Ⓐ Ⓑ Ⓒ Ⓓ
46. Ⓐ Ⓑ Ⓒ Ⓓ
47. Ⓐ Ⓑ Ⓒ Ⓓ
48. Ⓐ Ⓑ Ⓒ Ⓓ
49. Ⓐ Ⓑ Ⓒ Ⓓ
50. Ⓐ Ⓑ Ⓒ Ⓓ
51. Ⓐ Ⓑ Ⓒ Ⓓ
52. Ⓐ Ⓑ Ⓒ Ⓓ
53. Ⓐ Ⓑ Ⓒ Ⓓ
54. Ⓐ Ⓑ Ⓒ Ⓓ
55. Ⓐ Ⓑ Ⓒ Ⓓ
56. Ⓐ Ⓑ Ⓒ Ⓓ
57. Ⓐ Ⓑ Ⓒ Ⓓ
58. Ⓐ Ⓑ Ⓒ Ⓓ
59. Ⓐ Ⓑ Ⓒ Ⓓ
60. Ⓐ Ⓑ Ⓒ Ⓓ

61. Ⓐ Ⓑ Ⓒ Ⓓ
62. Ⓐ Ⓑ Ⓒ Ⓓ
63. Ⓐ Ⓑ Ⓒ Ⓓ
64. Ⓐ Ⓑ Ⓒ Ⓓ
65. Ⓐ Ⓑ Ⓒ Ⓓ
66. Ⓐ Ⓑ Ⓒ Ⓓ
67. Ⓐ Ⓑ Ⓒ Ⓓ
68. Ⓐ Ⓑ Ⓒ Ⓓ
69. Ⓐ Ⓑ Ⓒ Ⓓ
70. Ⓐ Ⓑ Ⓒ Ⓓ
71. Ⓐ Ⓑ Ⓒ Ⓓ
72. Ⓐ Ⓑ Ⓒ Ⓓ
73. Ⓐ Ⓑ Ⓒ Ⓓ
74. Ⓐ Ⓑ Ⓒ Ⓓ
75. Ⓐ Ⓑ Ⓒ Ⓓ
76. Ⓐ Ⓑ Ⓒ Ⓓ
77. Ⓐ Ⓑ Ⓒ Ⓓ
78. Ⓐ Ⓑ Ⓒ Ⓓ
79. Ⓐ Ⓑ Ⓒ Ⓓ
80. Ⓐ Ⓑ Ⓒ Ⓓ
81. Ⓐ Ⓑ Ⓒ Ⓓ
82. Ⓐ Ⓑ Ⓒ Ⓓ
83. Ⓐ Ⓑ Ⓒ Ⓓ
84. Ⓐ Ⓑ Ⓒ Ⓓ
85. Ⓐ Ⓑ Ⓒ Ⓓ
86. Ⓐ Ⓑ Ⓒ Ⓓ
87. Ⓐ Ⓑ Ⓒ Ⓓ
88. Ⓐ Ⓑ Ⓒ Ⓓ
89. Ⓐ Ⓑ Ⓒ Ⓓ
90. Ⓐ Ⓑ Ⓒ Ⓓ

91. Ⓐ Ⓑ Ⓒ Ⓓ   101. Ⓐ Ⓑ Ⓒ Ⓓ   111. Ⓐ Ⓑ Ⓒ Ⓓ
92. Ⓐ Ⓑ Ⓒ Ⓓ   102. Ⓐ Ⓑ Ⓒ Ⓓ   112. Ⓐ Ⓑ Ⓒ Ⓓ
93. Ⓐ Ⓑ Ⓒ Ⓓ   103. Ⓐ Ⓑ Ⓒ Ⓓ   113. Ⓐ Ⓑ Ⓒ Ⓓ
94. Ⓐ Ⓑ Ⓒ Ⓓ   104. Ⓐ Ⓑ Ⓒ Ⓓ   114. Ⓐ Ⓑ Ⓒ Ⓓ
95. Ⓐ Ⓑ Ⓒ Ⓓ   105. Ⓐ Ⓑ Ⓒ Ⓓ   115. Ⓐ Ⓑ Ⓒ Ⓓ
96. Ⓐ Ⓑ Ⓒ Ⓓ   106. Ⓐ Ⓑ Ⓒ Ⓓ   116. Ⓐ Ⓑ Ⓒ Ⓓ
97. Ⓐ Ⓑ Ⓒ Ⓓ   107. Ⓐ Ⓑ Ⓒ Ⓓ   117. Ⓐ Ⓑ Ⓒ Ⓓ
98. Ⓐ Ⓑ Ⓒ Ⓓ   108. Ⓐ Ⓑ Ⓒ Ⓓ   118. Ⓐ Ⓑ Ⓒ Ⓓ
99. Ⓐ Ⓑ Ⓒ Ⓓ   109. Ⓐ Ⓑ Ⓒ Ⓓ   119. Ⓐ Ⓑ Ⓒ Ⓓ
100. Ⓐ Ⓑ Ⓒ Ⓓ   110. Ⓐ Ⓑ Ⓒ Ⓓ   120. Ⓐ Ⓑ Ⓒ Ⓓ

FUNDAMENTALS OF ENGINEERING - MORNING SESSION
Test 3
ANSWER SHEET

1. Ⓐ Ⓑ Ⓒ Ⓓ	31. Ⓐ Ⓑ Ⓒ Ⓓ	61. Ⓐ Ⓑ Ⓒ Ⓓ
2. Ⓐ Ⓑ Ⓒ Ⓓ	32. Ⓐ Ⓑ Ⓒ Ⓓ	62. Ⓐ Ⓑ Ⓒ Ⓓ
3. Ⓐ Ⓑ Ⓒ Ⓓ	33. Ⓐ Ⓑ Ⓒ Ⓓ	63. Ⓐ Ⓑ Ⓒ Ⓓ
4. Ⓐ Ⓑ Ⓒ Ⓓ	34. Ⓐ Ⓑ Ⓒ Ⓓ	64. Ⓐ Ⓑ Ⓒ Ⓓ
5. Ⓐ Ⓑ Ⓒ Ⓓ	35. Ⓐ Ⓑ Ⓒ Ⓓ	65. Ⓐ Ⓑ Ⓒ Ⓓ
6. Ⓐ Ⓑ Ⓒ Ⓓ	36. Ⓐ Ⓑ Ⓒ Ⓓ	66. Ⓐ Ⓑ Ⓒ Ⓓ
7. Ⓐ Ⓑ Ⓒ Ⓓ	37. Ⓐ Ⓑ Ⓒ Ⓓ	67. Ⓐ Ⓑ Ⓒ Ⓓ
8. Ⓐ Ⓑ Ⓒ Ⓓ	38. Ⓐ Ⓑ Ⓒ Ⓓ	68. Ⓐ Ⓑ Ⓒ Ⓓ
9. Ⓐ Ⓑ Ⓒ Ⓓ	39. Ⓐ Ⓑ Ⓒ Ⓓ	69. Ⓐ Ⓑ Ⓒ Ⓓ
10. Ⓐ Ⓑ Ⓒ Ⓓ	40. Ⓐ Ⓑ Ⓒ Ⓓ	70. Ⓐ Ⓑ Ⓒ Ⓓ
11. Ⓐ Ⓑ Ⓒ Ⓓ	41. Ⓐ Ⓑ Ⓒ Ⓓ	71. Ⓐ Ⓑ Ⓒ Ⓓ
12. Ⓐ Ⓑ Ⓒ Ⓓ	42. Ⓐ Ⓑ Ⓒ Ⓓ	72. Ⓐ Ⓑ Ⓒ Ⓓ
13. Ⓐ Ⓑ Ⓒ Ⓓ	43. Ⓐ Ⓑ Ⓒ Ⓓ	73. Ⓐ Ⓑ Ⓒ Ⓓ
14. Ⓐ Ⓑ Ⓒ Ⓓ	44. Ⓐ Ⓑ Ⓒ Ⓓ	74. Ⓐ Ⓑ Ⓒ Ⓓ
15. Ⓐ Ⓑ Ⓒ Ⓓ	45. Ⓐ Ⓑ Ⓒ Ⓓ	75. Ⓐ Ⓑ Ⓒ Ⓓ
16. Ⓐ Ⓑ Ⓒ Ⓓ	46. Ⓐ Ⓑ Ⓒ Ⓓ	76. Ⓐ Ⓑ Ⓒ Ⓓ
17. Ⓐ Ⓑ Ⓒ Ⓓ	47. Ⓐ Ⓑ Ⓒ Ⓓ	77. Ⓐ Ⓑ Ⓒ Ⓓ
18. Ⓐ Ⓑ Ⓒ Ⓓ	48. Ⓐ Ⓑ Ⓒ Ⓓ	78. Ⓐ Ⓑ Ⓒ Ⓓ
19. Ⓐ Ⓑ Ⓒ Ⓓ	49. Ⓐ Ⓑ Ⓒ Ⓓ	79. Ⓐ Ⓑ Ⓒ Ⓓ
20. Ⓐ Ⓑ Ⓒ Ⓓ	50. Ⓐ Ⓑ Ⓒ Ⓓ	80. Ⓐ Ⓑ Ⓒ Ⓓ
21. Ⓐ Ⓑ Ⓒ Ⓓ	51. Ⓐ Ⓑ Ⓒ Ⓓ	81. Ⓐ Ⓑ Ⓒ Ⓓ
22. Ⓐ Ⓑ Ⓒ Ⓓ	52. Ⓐ Ⓑ Ⓒ Ⓓ	82. Ⓐ Ⓑ Ⓒ Ⓓ
23. Ⓐ Ⓑ Ⓒ Ⓓ	53. Ⓐ Ⓑ Ⓒ Ⓓ	83. Ⓐ Ⓑ Ⓒ Ⓓ
24. Ⓐ Ⓑ Ⓒ Ⓓ	54. Ⓐ Ⓑ Ⓒ Ⓓ	84. Ⓐ Ⓑ Ⓒ Ⓓ
25. Ⓐ Ⓑ Ⓒ Ⓓ	55. Ⓐ Ⓑ Ⓒ Ⓓ	85. Ⓐ Ⓑ Ⓒ Ⓓ
26. Ⓐ Ⓑ Ⓒ Ⓓ	56. Ⓐ Ⓑ Ⓒ Ⓓ	86. Ⓐ Ⓑ Ⓒ Ⓓ
27. Ⓐ Ⓑ Ⓒ Ⓓ	57. Ⓐ Ⓑ Ⓒ Ⓓ	87. Ⓐ Ⓑ Ⓒ Ⓓ
28. Ⓐ Ⓑ Ⓒ Ⓓ	58. Ⓐ Ⓑ Ⓒ Ⓓ	88. Ⓐ Ⓑ Ⓒ Ⓓ
29. Ⓐ Ⓑ Ⓒ Ⓓ	59. Ⓐ Ⓑ Ⓒ Ⓓ	89. Ⓐ Ⓑ Ⓒ Ⓓ
30. Ⓐ Ⓑ Ⓒ Ⓓ	60. Ⓐ Ⓑ Ⓒ Ⓓ	90. Ⓐ Ⓑ Ⓒ Ⓓ

91. Ⓐ Ⓑ Ⓒ Ⓓ   101. Ⓐ Ⓑ Ⓒ Ⓓ   111. Ⓐ Ⓑ Ⓒ Ⓓ
92. Ⓐ Ⓑ Ⓒ Ⓓ   102. Ⓐ Ⓑ Ⓒ Ⓓ   112. Ⓐ Ⓑ Ⓒ Ⓓ
93. Ⓐ Ⓑ Ⓒ Ⓓ   103. Ⓐ Ⓑ Ⓒ Ⓓ   113. Ⓐ Ⓑ Ⓒ Ⓓ
94. Ⓐ Ⓑ Ⓒ Ⓓ   104. Ⓐ Ⓑ Ⓒ Ⓓ   114. Ⓐ Ⓑ Ⓒ Ⓓ
95. Ⓐ Ⓑ Ⓒ Ⓓ   105. Ⓐ Ⓑ Ⓒ Ⓓ   115. Ⓐ Ⓑ Ⓒ Ⓓ
96. Ⓐ Ⓑ Ⓒ Ⓓ   106. Ⓐ Ⓑ Ⓒ Ⓓ   116. Ⓐ Ⓑ Ⓒ Ⓓ
97. Ⓐ Ⓑ Ⓒ Ⓓ   107. Ⓐ Ⓑ Ⓒ Ⓓ   117. Ⓐ Ⓑ Ⓒ Ⓓ
98. Ⓐ Ⓑ Ⓒ Ⓓ   108. Ⓐ Ⓑ Ⓒ Ⓓ   118. Ⓐ Ⓑ Ⓒ Ⓓ
99. Ⓐ Ⓑ Ⓒ Ⓓ   109. Ⓐ Ⓑ Ⓒ Ⓓ   119. Ⓐ Ⓑ Ⓒ Ⓓ
100. Ⓐ Ⓑ Ⓒ Ⓓ   110. Ⓐ Ⓑ Ⓒ Ⓓ   120. Ⓐ Ⓑ Ⓒ Ⓓ

FE/EIT

Fundamentals of Engineering: AM Exam

Appendix

VARIABLES

a	=	acceleration
a_t	=	tangential acceleration
a_r	=	radial acceleration
d	=	distance
e	=	coefficient of restitution
f	=	frequency
F	=	force
g	=	gravity = 32.2 ft/sec^2 or 9.81 m/sec^2
h	=	height
I	=	mass inertia
k	=	spring constant, radius of gyration
KE	=	kinetic energy
m	=	mass
M	=	moment
PE	=	potential energy
r	=	radius
s	=	position
t	=	time
T	=	tension, torsion, period
v	=	velocity
w	=	weight
x	=	horizontal position
y	=	vertical position
α	=	angular acceleration
ω	=	angular velocity
θ	=	angle
μ	=	coefficient of friction

EQUATIONS

Kinematics

Linear Particle Motion

Constant velocity

$$s = s_o + vt$$

Constant acceleration

$$v = v_o + at$$

$$s = s_o + v_o t + \left(\frac{1}{2}\right) at^2$$

$$v^2 = v_o^2 + 2a(s - s_o)$$

Projectile Motion

$$x = x_o + v_x t$$

$$v_y = v_{yo} - gt$$

$$y = y_o + v_{yo}t - \left(\frac{1}{2}\right) gt^2$$

$$v_y^2 = v_{yo}^2 - 2g\,(y - y_o)$$

Rotational Motion

Constant rotational velocity

$$\theta = \theta_o + \omega t$$

Constant angular acceleration

$$\omega = \omega_o + \alpha t$$

$$\theta = \theta_o + \omega_o t + \left(\frac{1}{2}\right) \alpha t^2$$

$$\omega^2 = \omega_o^2 + 2\alpha\,(\theta - \theta_o)$$

Tangential velocity

$$v_t = r\omega$$

Tangential acceleration

$$a_t = r\alpha$$

Radial acceleration

$$a_r = r\omega^2 = \frac{v_t^2}{r}$$

Polar coordinates

$$a_r = \frac{d^2 r}{dt^2} - r\left(\frac{d\theta}{dt}\right)^2 = \frac{d^2 r}{dt^2} - r\omega^2$$

$$a_\theta = r\left(\frac{d^2\theta}{dt^2}\right) + 2\left(\frac{dr}{dt}\right)\left(\frac{d\theta}{dt}\right) = r\alpha + 2\left(\frac{dr}{dt}\right)\omega$$

$$v_r = \frac{dr}{dt}$$

$$v_\theta = r\left(\frac{d\theta}{dt}\right) = r\omega$$

Relative and Related Motion

Acceleration

$$a_A = a_B + a_{A/B}$$

Velocity

$$v_A = v_B + v_{A/B}$$

Position

$$x_A = x_B + x_{A/B}$$

Kinetics

$$w = mg$$
$$F = ma$$

$$F_c = ma_n = \frac{mv_t^2}{r}$$
$$F_f = \mu N$$

Kinetic Energy

$$KE = \left(\frac{1}{2}\right) mv^2$$

Work of a force $= \int F ds$

$$KE_1 + \text{Work}_{1-2} = KE_2$$

Potential Energy

Spring $PE = \left(\frac{1}{2}\right) kx^2$

Weight $PE = wy$

$$KE_1 + PE_1 = KE_2 + PE_2$$

Power

Linear power $P = Fv$

Torsional or rotational power $P = T\omega$

Impulse-Momentum

$$mv_1 + \int F dt = mv_2$$

Impact

$$m_A v_{A1} + m_B v_{B1} = m_A v_{A2} + m_B v_{B2}$$

$$e = \frac{v_{B2} - v_{A2}}{v_{A1} - v_{B1}}$$

Perfectly plastic impact ($e = 0$)

$$m_A v_{A1} + m_B v_{B1} = (m_A + m_B)v'$$

One mass is infinite

$$v_2 = ev_1$$

Inertia

Beam $\quad I_A = \left(\frac{1}{12}\right)ml^2 + m\left(\frac{1}{2}\right)^2 = \left(\frac{1}{3}\right)ml^2$

Plate

$$I_A = \left(\frac{1}{12}\right)m\left(a^2 + b^2\right) + m\left[\left(\frac{a}{2}\right)^2 + \left(\frac{b}{2}\right)^2\right] = \left(\frac{1}{3}\right)m\left(a^2 + b^2\right)$$

Wheel $\quad I_A = mk^2 + mr^2$

Two-Dimensional Rigid Body Motion

$$F_x = ma_x$$
$$F_y = ma_y$$
$$M_A = I_A\alpha = I_{cg}\,\alpha + m(a)d$$

Rolling Resistance

$$F_r = \frac{mga}{r}$$

Energy Methods for Rigid Body Motion

$$KE_1 + \text{Work}_{1-2} = KE_2$$

$$\text{Work} = \int F ds + \int M d\theta$$

Mechanical Vibration

Differential equation

$$\frac{md^2x}{dt^2} + kx = 0$$

Position

$$x = x_m \sin\left[\sqrt{\frac{k}{m}}\,t + \theta\right]$$

Velocity

$$v = \frac{dx}{dt} = x_m \sqrt{\frac{k}{m}} \cos\left[\sqrt{\frac{k}{m}}\,t + \theta\right]$$

Acceleration

$$a = \frac{d^2x}{dt^2} = -x_m \left(\frac{k}{m} \right) \sin \left[\sqrt{\frac{k}{m}} \, t + \theta \right]$$

Maximum values

$$x = x_m, \, v = x_m \sqrt{\frac{k}{m}}, \, a = x_m \left(\frac{k}{m} \right)$$

Period

$$T = \frac{2\pi}{\left(\sqrt{\frac{k}{m}} \right)}$$

Frequency

$$f = \frac{1}{T} = \frac{\sqrt{\frac{k}{m}}}{2\pi}$$

Springs in parallel

$$k = k_1 + k_2$$

Springs in series

$$\frac{1}{k} = \frac{1}{k_1} + \frac{1}{k_2}$$

AREA UNDER NORMAL CURVE

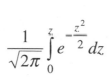

$$\frac{1}{\sqrt{2\pi}} \int_0^z e^{-\frac{z^2}{2}} dz$$

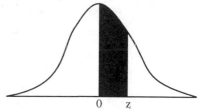

Z	0	1	2	3	4	5	6	7	8	9
0.0	.0000	.0040	.0080	.0120	.0160	.0199	0239	.0279	.0319	.0359
0.1	.0398	.0438	.0478	.0517	.0557	.0596	.0636	.0675	.0714	.0754
0.2	.0793	.0832	.0871	.0910	.0948	.0987	.1026	.1064	.1103	.1141
0.3	.1179	.1217	.1255	.1293	.1331	.1368	.1406	.1443	.1480	.1517
0.4	.1554	.1591	.1628	.1664	.1700	.1736	.1772	.1808	.1844	.1879
0.5	.1915	.1950	.1985	.2019	.2054	.2088	.2123	.2157	.2190	.2224
0.6	.2258	.2291	.2324	.2357	.2389	.2422	.2454	.2486	.2518	.2549
0.7	.2580	.2612	.2642	.2673	.2704	.2734	.2764	.2794	.2823	.2852
0.8	.2881	.2910	.2939	.2967	.2996	.3023	.3051	.3078	.3106	.3133
0.9	.3159	.3186	.3212	.3238	.3264	.3289	.3315	.3340	.3365	.3389
1.0	.3413	.3438	.3461	.3485	.3508	.3531	.3554	.3577	.3599	.3621
1.1	.3643	.3665	.3686	.3708	.3729	.3749	.3770	.3790	.3810	.3830
1.2	.3849	.3869	.3888	.3907	.3925	.3944	.3962	.3980	.3997	.4015
1.3	.4032	.4049	.4066	.4082	.4099	.4115	.4131	.4147	.4162	.4177
1.4	.4192	.4207	.4222	.4236	.4251	.4265	.4279	.4292	.4306	.4319
1.5	.4332	.4345	.4357	.4370	.4382	.4394	.4406	.4418	.4429	.4441
1.6	.4452	.4463	.4474	.4484	.4495	.4505	.4515	.4525	.4535	.4545
1.7	.4554	.4564	.4573	.4582	.4591	.4599	.4608	.4616	.4625	.4633
1.8	.4641	.4649	.4656	.4664	.4671	.4678	.4686	.4693	.4699	.4706
1.9	.4713	.4719	.4726	.4732	.4738	.4744	.4750	.4756	.4761	.4767
2.0	.4772	.4778	.4783	.4788	.4793	.4798	.4803	.4808	.4812	.4817
2.1	.4821	.4826	.4830	.4834	.4838	.4842	.4846	.4850	.4854	.4857
2.2	.4861	.4864	.4868	.4871	.4875	.4878	.4881	.4884	.4887	.4890
2.3	.4893	.4896	.4898	.4901	.4904	.4906	.4909	.4911	.4913	.4916
2.4	.4918	.4920	.4922	.4925	.4927	.4929	.4931	.4932	.4934	.4936
2.5	.4938	.4940	.4941	.4943	.4945	.4946	.4948	.4949	.4951	.4952
2.6	.4953	.4955	.4956	.4957	.4959	.4960	.4961	.4962	.4963	.4964
2.7	.4965	.4966	.4967	.4968	.4969	.4970	.4971	.4972	.4973	.4974
2.8	.4974	.4975	.4976	.4977	.4977	.4978	.4979	.4979	.4980	.4981
2.9	.4981	.4982	.4982	.4983	.4984	.4984	.4985	.4985	.4986	.4986
3.0	.4987	.4987	.4987	.4988	.4988	.4989	.4989	.4989	.4990	.4990
3.1	.4990	.4991	.4991	.4991	.4992	.4992	.4992	.4992	.4993	.4993
3.2	.4993	.4993	.4994	.4994	.4994	.4994	.4994	.4995	.4995	.4995
3.3	.4995	.4995	.4995	.4996	.4996	.4996	.4996	.4996	.4996	.4997
3.4	.4997	.4997	.4997	.4997	.4997	.4997	.4997	.4997	.4997	.4998
3.5	.4998	.4998	.4998	.4998	.4998	.4998	.4998	.4998	.4998	.4998
3.6	.4998	.4998	.4999	.4999	.4999	.4999	.4999	.4999	.4999	.4999
3.7	.4999	.4999	.4999	.4999	.4999	.4999	.4999	.4999	.4999	.4999
3.8	.4999	.4999	.4999	.4999	.4999	.4999	.4999	.4999	.4999	.4999
3.9	.5000	.5000	.5000	.5000	.5000	.5000	.5000	.5000	.5000	.5000

POWER SERIES FOR ELEMENTARY FUNCTIONS

$$\frac{1}{x} = 1 - (x-1) + (x-1)^2 - (x-1)^3 + (x-1)^4 - \ldots + (-1)^n (x-1)^n + \ldots,$$
$$0 < x < 2$$

$$\frac{1}{1+x} = 1 - x + x^2 - x^3 + x^4 - x^5 + \ldots + (-1)^n x^n + \ldots, \qquad -1 < x < 1$$

$$\ln x = (x-1) - \frac{(x-1)^2}{2} + \frac{(x-1)^3}{3} - \frac{(x-1)^4}{4} + \ldots + \frac{(-1)^{n-1}(x-1)^n}{n} + \ldots,$$
$$0 < x \le 2$$

$$e^x = 1 + x + \frac{x^2}{2!} + \frac{x^3}{3!} + \frac{x^4}{4!} + \frac{x^5}{5!} + \ldots + \frac{x^n}{n!} + \ldots, \qquad -\infty < x < \infty$$

$$\sin x = x - \frac{x^3}{3!} + \frac{x^5}{5!} - \frac{x^7}{7!} + \frac{x^9}{9!} - \ldots + \frac{(-1)^n x^{2n+1}}{(2n+1)!} + \ldots, \qquad -\infty < x < \infty$$

$$\cos x = 1 - \frac{x^2}{2!} + \frac{x^4}{4!} - \frac{x^6}{6!} + \frac{x^8}{8!} - \ldots + \frac{(-1)^n x^{2n}}{(2n)!} + \ldots, \qquad -\infty < x < \infty$$

$$\arctan x = x - \frac{x^3}{3} + \frac{x^5}{5} - \frac{x^7}{7} + \frac{x^9}{9} - \ldots + \frac{(-1)^n x^{2n+1}}{2n+1} + \ldots, \qquad -1 \le x \le 1$$

$$(1+x)^k = 1 + kx + \frac{k(k-1)x^2}{2!} + \frac{k(k-1)(k-2)x^3}{3!}$$
$$+ \frac{k(k-1)(k-2)(k-3)x^4}{4!} + \ldots, \qquad -1 < x < 1$$

$$(1+x)^{-k} = 1 - kx + \frac{k(k+1)x^2}{2!} - \frac{k(k+1)(k+2)x^3}{3!}$$
$$+ \frac{k(k+1)(k+2)(k+3)x^4}{4!} - \ldots, \qquad -1 < x < 1$$

TABLE OF MORE COMMON LAPLACE TRANSFORMS

$f(t) = L^{-1}\{F(s)\}$	$F(s) = L\{f(t)\}$
1	$\dfrac{1}{s}$
t	$\dfrac{1}{s^2}$
$\dfrac{t^{n-1}}{(n-1)!}; n = 1, 2, \ldots$	$\dfrac{1}{s^n}$
e^{at}	$\dfrac{1}{s-a}$
$t\,e^{at}$	$\dfrac{1}{(s-a)^2}$
$\dfrac{t^{n-1}e^{-at}}{(n-1)!}$	$\dfrac{1}{(s+a)^n}; n = 1, 2, \ldots$
$\dfrac{e^{-at} - e^{-bt}}{b-a}; a \neq b$	$\dfrac{1}{(s+a)(s+b)}$
$\dfrac{a\,e^{-at} - b\,e^{-bt}}{a-b}; a \neq b$	$\dfrac{s}{(s+a)(s+b)}$
$\sin at$	$\dfrac{a}{s^2 + a^2}$
$\cos at$	$\dfrac{s}{s^2 + a^2}$
$\sinh at$	$\dfrac{a}{s^2 - a^2}$

$f(t) = L^{-1}\{F(s)\}$	$F(s) = L\{f(t)\}$
$\cosh at$	$\dfrac{s}{s^2 - a^2}$
$\dfrac{1}{a^2}(1 - \cos at)$	$\dfrac{1}{s\left(s^2 + a^2\right)}$
$\dfrac{1}{a^3}(at - \sin at)$	$\dfrac{1}{s\left(s^2 + a^2\right)}$
$\dfrac{t}{2a}\sin at$	$\dfrac{s}{\left(s^2 + a^2\right)^2}$
$\dfrac{1}{b}e^{-at}\sin bt$	$\dfrac{1}{(s+a)^2 + b^2}$
$e^{-at}\cos bt$	$\dfrac{s+a}{(s+a)^2 + b^2}$
$h_1(t-a)$	$\dfrac{1}{s}e^{-as}$
$h_1(t) - h_1(t-a)$	$\dfrac{1 - e^{-as}}{s}$
$\dfrac{1}{t}\sin kt$	$\arctan\dfrac{k}{s}$

HANDBOOK of MATHEMATICAL, SCIENTIFIC, & ENGINEERING FORMULAS, FUNCTIONS, GRAPHS, TABLES, & TRANSFORMS

RESEARCH & EDUCATION ASSOCIATION

A particularly useful reference for those in math, science, engineering and other technical fields. Includes the most-often used formulas, tables, transforms, functions, and graphs which are needed as tools in solving problems. The entire field of special functions is also covered. A large amount of scientific data which is often of interest to scientists and engineers has been included.

Available at your local bookstore or order directly from us by sending in coupon below.

"The ESSENTIALS"
of Math & Science

Each book in the ESSENTIALS series offers all essential information of the field it covers. It summarizes what every textbook in the particular field must include, and is designed to help students in preparing for exams and doing homework. The ESSENTIALS are excellent supplements to any class text.

The ESSENTIALS are complete and concise with quick access to needed information. They serve as a handy reference source at all times. The ESSENTIALS are prepared with REA's customary concern for high professional quality and student needs.

Available in the following titles:

Advanced Calculus I & II
Algebra & Trigonometry I & II
Anatomy & Physiology
Anthropology
Astronomy
Automatic Control Systems /
   Robotics I & II
Biology I & II
Boolean Algebra
Calculus I, II, & III
Chemistry
Complex Variables I & II
Computer Science I & II
Data Structures I & II
Differential Equations I & II
Electric Circuits I & II
Electromagnetics I & II

Electronics I & II
Electronic Communications I & II
Fluid Mechanics /
   Dynamics I & II
Fourier Analysis
Geometry I & II
Group Theory I & II
Heat Transfer I & II
LaPlace Transforms
Linear Algebra
Math for Computer Applications
Math for Engineers I & II
Math Made Nice-n-Easy Series
Mechanics I, II, & III
Microbiology
Modern Algebra
Molecular Structures of Life

Numerical Analysis I & II
Organic Chemistry I & II
Physical Chemistry I & II
Physics I & II
Pre-Calculus
Probability
Psychology I & II
Real Variables
Set Theory
Sociology
Statistics I & II
Strength of Materials &
   Mechanics of Solids I & II
Thermodynamics I & II
Topology
Transport Phenomena I & II
Vector Analysis

If you would like more information about any of these books,
complete the coupon below and return it to us or visit your local bookstore.

RESEARCH & EDUCATION ASSOCIATION
61 Ethel Road W. • Piscataway, New Jersey 08854
Phone: (732) 819-8880   **website: www.rea.com**

Please send me more information about your Math & Science Essentials books

Name _____

Address _____

City _____ State _____ Zip _____

"The ESSENTIALS" of LANGUAGE

Each book in the **LANGUAGE ESSENTIALS** series offers all the essential information of the grammar and vocabulary of the language it covers. They include conjugations, irregular verb forms, and sentence structure, and are designed to help students in preparing for exams and doing homework. The **LANGUAGE ESSENTIALS** are excellent supplements to any class text or course of study.

The **LANGUAGE ESSENTIALS** are complete and concise, with quick access to needed information. They also provide a handy reference source at all times. The **LANGUAGE ESSENTIALS** are prepared with REA's customary concern for high professional quality and student needs.

Available Titles Include:

French   Italian

German   Spanish

If you would like more information about any of these books,
complete the coupon below and return it to us or visit your local bookstore.

RESEARCH & EDUCATION ASSOCIATION
61 Ethel Road W. • Piscataway, New Jersey 08854
Phone: (732) 819-8880   **website: www.rea.com**
Please send me more information about your LANGUAGE **Essentials books**

Name _____

Address _____

City _____ State _____ Zip _____

MAXnotes®

REA's Literature Study Guides

MAXnotes® are student-friendly. They offer a fresh look at masterpieces of literature, presented in a lively and interesting fashion. **MAXnotes**® offer the essentials of what you should know about the work, including outlines, explanations and discussions of the plot, character lists, analyses, and historical context. **MAXnotes**® are designed to help you think independently about literary works by raising various issues and thought-provoking ideas and questions. Written by literary experts who currently teach the subject, **MAXnotes**® enhance your understanding and enjoyment of the work.

Available **MAXnotes**® include the following:

Absalom, Absalom!	Henry IV, Part I	Othello
The Aeneid of Virgil	Henry V	Paradise
Animal Farm	The House on Mango Street	Paradise Lost
Antony and Cleopatra	Huckleberry Finn	A Passage to India
As I Lay Dying	I Know Why the Caged	Plato's Republic
As You Like It	Bird Sings	Portrait of a Lady
The Autobiography of	The Iliad	A Portrait of the Artist
Malcolm X	Invisible Man	as a Young Man
The Awakening	Jane Eyre	Pride and Prejudice
Beloved	Jazz	A Raisin in the Sun
Beowulf	The Joy Luck Club	Richard II
Billy Budd	Jude the Obscure	Romeo and Juliet
The Bluest Eye, A Novel	Julius Caesar	The Scarlet Letter
Brave New World	King Lear	Sir Gawain and the
The Canterbury Tales	Leaves of Grass	Green Knight
The Catcher in the Rye	Les Misérables	Slaughterhouse-Five
The Color Purple	Lord of the Flies	Song of Solomon
The Crucible	Macbeth	The Sound and the Fury
Death in Venice	The Merchant of Venice	The Stranger
Death of a Salesman	Metamorphoses of Ovid	Sula
The Divine Comedy I: Inferno	Metamorphosis	The Sun Also Rises
Dubliners	Middlemarch	A Tale of Two Cities
The Edible Woman	A Midsummer Night's Dream	The Taming of the Shrew
Emma	Moby-Dick	Tar Baby
Euripides' Medea & Electra	Moll Flanders	The Tempest
Frankenstein	Mrs. Dalloway	Tess of the D'Urbervilles
Gone with the Wind	Much Ado About Nothing	Their Eyes Were Watching God
The Grapes of Wrath	Mules and Men	Things Fall Apart
Great Expectations	My Antonia	To Kill a Mockingbird
The Great Gatsby	Native Son	To the Lighthouse
Gulliver's Travels	1984	Twelfth Night
Handmaid's Tale	The Odyssey	Uncle Tom's Cabin
Hamlet	Oedipus Trilogy	Waiting for Godot
Hard Times	Of Mice and Men	Wuthering Heights
Heart of Darkness	On the Road	Guide to Literary Terms

RESEARCH & EDUCATION ASSOCIATION
61 Ethel Road W. • Piscataway, New Jersey 08854
Phone: (732) 819-8880   **website: www.rea.com**

Please send me more information about MAXnotes®.

Name _____

Address _____

City _____ State _____ Zip _____

REA's Problem Solvers

The "PROBLEM SOLVERS" are comprehensive supplemental text-books designed to save time in finding solutions to problems. Each "PROBLEM SOLVER" is the first of its kind ever produced in its field. It is the product of a massive effort to illustrate almost any imaginable problem in exceptional depth, detail, and clarity. Each problem is worked out in detail with a step-by-step solution, and the problems are arranged in order of complexity from elementary to advanced. Each book is fully indexed for locating problems rapidly.

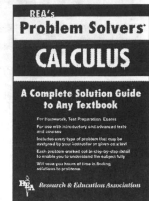

ACCOUNTING
ADVANCED CALCULUS
ALGEBRA & TRIGONOMETRY
AUTOMATIC CONTROL
    SYSTEMS/ROBOTICS
BIOLOGY
BUSINESS, ACCOUNTING, & FINANCE
CALCULUS
CHEMISTRY
COMPLEX VARIABLES
DIFFERENTIAL EQUATIONS
ECONOMICS
ELECTRICAL MACHINES
ELECTRIC CIRCUITS
ELECTROMAGNETICS
ELECTRONIC COMMUNICATIONS
ELECTRONICS
FINITE & DISCRETE MATH
FLUID MECHANICS/DYNAMICS
GENETICS
GEOMETRY
HEAT TRANSFER

LINEAR ALGEBRA
MACHINE DESIGN
MATHEMATICS for ENGINEERS
MECHANICS
NUMERICAL ANALYSIS
OPERATIONS RESEARCH
OPTICS
ORGANIC CHEMISTRY
PHYSICAL CHEMISTRY
PHYSICS
PRE-CALCULUS
PROBABILITY
PSYCHOLOGY
STATISTICS
STRENGTH OF MATERIALS &
    MECHANICS OF SOLIDS
TECHNICAL DESIGN GRAPHICS
THERMODYNAMICS
TOPOLOGY
TRANSPORT PHENOMENA
VECTOR ANALYSIS

*If you would like more information about any of these books,
complete the coupon below and return it to us or visit your local bookstore.*

RESEARCH & EDUCATION ASSOCIATION
61 Ethel Road W. • Piscataway, New Jersey 08854
Phone: (732) 819-8880   **website: www.rea.com**

Please send me more information about your Problem Solver books

Name _____

Address _____

City _____ State _____ Zip _____

REA's Test Preps
The Best in Test Preparation

- REA "Test Preps" are **far more** comprehensive than any other test preparation series
- Each book contains up to **eight** full-length practice tests based on the most recent exams
- **Every** type of question likely to be given on the exams is included
- Answers are accompanied by **full** and **detailed** explanations

REA publishes over 60 Test Preparation volumes in several series. They include:

Advanced Placement Exams(APs)
Biology
Calculus AB & Calculus BC
Chemistry
Computer Science
Economics
English Language & Composition
English Literature & Composition
European History
Government & Politics
Physics B & C
Psychology
Spanish Language
Statistics
United States History

College-Level Examination Program (CLEP)
Analyzing and Interpreting Literature
College Algebra
Freshman College Composition
General Examinations
General Examinations Review
History of the United States I
History of the United States II
Human Growth and Development
Introductory Sociology
Principles of Marketing
Spanish

SAT II: Subject Tests
Biology E/M
Chemistry
English Language Proficiency Test
French
German

SAT II: Subject Tests (cont'd)
Literature
Mathematics Level IC, IIC
Physics
Spanish
United States History
Writing

Graduate Record Exams (GREs)
Biology
Chemistry
Computer Science
General
Literature in English
Mathematics
Physics
Psychology

ACT - ACT Assessment

ASVAB - Armed Services Vocational Aptitude Battery

CBEST - California Basic Educational Skills Test

CDL - Commercial Driver License Exam

CLAST - College Level Academic Skills Test

COOP & HSPT - Catholic High School Admission Tests

ELM - California State University Entry Level Mathematics Exam

FE (EIT) - Fundamentals of Engineering Exams - For both AM & PM Exams

FTCE - Florida Teacher Certification Exam

GED - High School Equivalency Diploma Exam (U.S. & Canadian editions)

GMAT CAT - Graduate Management Admission Test

LSAT - Law School Admission Test

MAT- Miller Analogies Test

MCAT - Medical College Admission Test

MTEL - Massachusetts Tests for Educator Licensure

MSAT- Multiple Subjects Assessment for Teachers

NJ HSPA - New Jersey High School Proficiency Assessment

NYSTCE: LAST & ATS-W - New York State Teacher Certification

PLT - Principles of Learning & Teaching Tests

PPST- Pre-Professional Skills Tests

PSAT - Preliminary Scholastic Assessment Test

SAT I - Reasoning Test

TExES - Texas Examinations of Educator Standards

THEA - Texas Higher Education Assessment

TOEFL - Test of English as a Foreign Language

TOEIC - Test of English for International Communication

USMLE Steps 1,2,3 - U.S. Medical Licensing Exams

U.S. Postal Exams 460 & 470

RESEARCH & EDUCATION ASSOCIATION
61 Ethel Road W. • Piscataway, New Jersey 08854
Phone: (732) 819-8880   **website: www.rea.com**

Please send me more information about your Test Prep books

Name _____

Address _____

City _____ State _____ Zip _____

REA's Test Prep Books Are The Best!

(a sample of the <u>hundreds of letters</u> REA receives each year)

" I did well because of your wonderful prep books... I just wanted to thank you for helping me prepare for these tests. "

Student, San Diego, CA

" My students report your chapters of review as the most valuable single resource they used for review and preparation. "

Teacher, American Fork, UT

" Your book was such a better value and was so much more complete than anything your competition has produced — and I have them all! "

Teacher, Virginia Beach, VA

" Compared to the other books that my fellow students had, your book was the most useful in helping me get a great score. "

Student, North Hollywood, CA

" Your book was responsible for my success on the exam, which helped me get into the college of my choice... I will look for REA the next time I need help. "

Student, Chesterfield, MO

" Just a short note to say thanks for the great support your book gave me in helping me pass the test... I'm on my way to a B.S. degree because of you! "

Student, Orlando, FL

(more on next page)

REA's Test Prep Books Are The Best!

(a sample of the <u>hundreds of letters</u> REA receives each year)

" I am writing to congratulate you on preparing an exceptional study guide. In five years of teaching this course I have never encountered a more thorough, comprehensive, concise, and realistic preparation for this examination. "
Teacher, Davie, FL

" I have found your publications, *The Best Test Preparation...*, to be exactly that. "
Teacher, Aptos, CA

" I used your *CLEP Introductory Sociology* book and rank it 99% — thank you! "
Student, Jerusalem, Israel

" Your *GMAT* book greatly helped me on the test. Thank you. "
Student, Oxford, OH

" I recently got the *French SAT II* Exam book from REA. I congratulate you on first-rate French practice tests. "
Instructor, Los Angeles, CA

" Your *AP English Literature and Composition* book is most impressive. "
Student, Montgomery, AL

" The REA *LSAT* Test Preparation guide is a winner! "
Instructor, Spartanburg, SC

(more on previous page)